EVALUATING RESEARCH IN SOCIAL PSYCHOLOGY
A GUIDE FOR THE CONSUMER

LAWRENCE S. WRIGHTSMAN

Consulting Editor

The Environment and Social Behavior: Privacy, Personal Space, Territory, and Crowding
Irwin Altman, The University of Utah

Contemporary Issues in Social Psychology, 3rd Edition
John C. Brigham, Florida State University
Lawrence S. Wrightsman, University of Kansas

The Behavior of Women and Men
Kay Deaux, Purdue University

Research Projects in Social Psychology: An Introduction to Methods
Michael King, California State University, Chico
Michael Ziegler, York University

Evaluating Research in Social Psychology: A Guide for the Consumer
Clara Mayo, Boston University
Marianne LaFrance, Boston College

Toward Understanding Women
Virginia E. O'Leary, Oakland University

Three Views of Man: Perspectives from Sigmund Freud, B. F. Skinner, and Carl Rogers
Robert D. Nye, State University of New York, College at New Paltz

Theories of Personality
Duane Schultz, The American University

Interpersonal Behavior
Harry C. Triandis, University of Illinois at Urbana-Champaign

Social Psychology, 2nd Edition
Lawrence S. Wrightsman, University of Kansas

EVALUATING RESEARCH IN SOCIAL PSYCHOLOGY

A GUIDE FOR THE CONSUMER

Clara Mayo
Boston University

Marianne LaFrance
Boston College

Brooks/Cole Publishing Company
Monterey, California
A Division of Wadsworth Publishing Company, Inc.

© 1977 by Wadsworth Publishing Company, Inc., Belmont, California 94002. All rights reserved. No part of this book may be reproduced, stored in a retrieval system, or transcribed, in any form or by any means—electronic, mechanical, photocopying, recording, or otherwise—without the prior written permission of the publisher: Brooks/Cole Publishing Company, Monterey, California 93940, a division of Wadsworth Publishing Company, Inc.

Printed in the United States of America

10 9 8 7 6 5 4 3 2 1

Library of Congress Cataloging in Publication Data

Mayo, Clara Alexandra Weiss, 1931–
  Evaluating research in social psychology.

  Bibliography: p. 299
  Includes index.
  1. Social psychology. 2. Social psychology—Methodology. 3. Evaluation research (Social action programs) I. LaFrance, Marianne, 1947– joint author. II. Title.
HM251.M37   301.1'01'8   76-46363
ISBN 0-8185-0214-2

Production Editor: *Fiorella Ljunggren*
Interior and Cover Design: *John Edeen*

*To our fathers,
Joseph and Thomas,
who taught us the value of criticism,
and
our mothers, Maria and Florence,
who helped us to appreciate it*

PREFACE

Social psychology these days is not a calm and settled field, and, in our view, that's not such a bad thing. We find intellectual controversy exhilarating and intrinsic to knowledge building. So we have written a book in social psychology that invites students to share our critic's corner.

We've tried to write a book on research that teaches students to think about social psychology, to appreciate its complexity, and to weigh its strengths and weaknesses alike. We believe that to think critically is to honor by taking seriously. The analogy of consumer guidelines that we have adopted throughout the book is intended to help the reader evaluate research by asking critical questions and making intelligent comparisons. There is agreement that students can benefit from careful reading of primary sources, but there is often doubt that this can be done without guidance. The consumer analogy is used not only because it is relevant and timely, but also because it can strengthen students' confidence in their ability to appraise research. Specific guidelines are offered in each chapter to assist the reader to become a more skillful consumer of research.

The book covers many recognized topics in social psychology as well as several newer ones just beginning to engage the attention of researchers. Each chapter sets two research selections in context by presenting the theories, findings, and methods generally used in research on that topic. In each chapter, one laboratory experiment on the selected topic is paired with a field study—a strategy that highlights both substantive and methodological issues for the student. Specific study questions preceding the two research selections and a comparative analysis following them are intended to help the reader to think about how social psychology works and not merely to incorporate the facts of the field. Given its research orientation, the book is designed to be used as a primary text in courses emphasizing methods and experimentation and as a supplement in other courses in social psychology. The chapters' structure, which distinguishes substantive content and methodological focus, gives instructors flexibility in use.

In the spirit of critique, we gratefully acknowledge the help of our reviewers who pointed to the strengths and weaknesses of our arguments with care and verve. We thank J. William Dorris, then at the University of Massachusetts at Amherst, Robert Love of the American University in Washington, D.C., Charles McClintock of the University of California at Santa Barbara, D. W. Rajecki of the University of Wisconsin at Madison, Joan Sieber of California State University at Hayward, and, most especially, Albert A. Harrison of the University of California at Davis. As consulting editor, Larry Wrightsman was generous with his time and advice. In our view, the relationship of writer to editor is a very special one; we are grateful indeed to Bill Hicks whose gentle prodding included a recipe for salmon sauce as well as reprints of social-psychological lore we might have missed. We were blessed as well with skillful help with our prose from our colleague and typist, Gina Abeles, who suggested that our reference to Michelangelo's Sistine Chapel was inexact, and our production editor, Fiorella Ljunggren, who helped us find a felicitous alternative to that reference. In the end, of course, it is we who are responsible for the contents of this book, and we offer it herewith to students and colleagues for debate and critique.

Clara Mayo
Marianne LaFrance

CONTENTS

Chapter 1

HOW TO BE AN INTELLIGENT RESEARCH CONSUMER   1

    Read carefully   3
    Check guarantees   3
    Look beyond flashy merchandising   4
    Look for durability and long-term benefits   5
    Pay attention to the cost-quality relation   5
    Buy from a reputable person   6
    Know consumer vocabulary   7
    Do comparison shopping   11
    Appreciate the principle of "do it yourself"   13
    Prepare a list   14
    Social psychology and the consumer analogy   16

Chapter 2

ATTRACTION   19

    Theories of attraction   21
    Determinants of attraction   23
    Research methods in the study of attraction   27
    Two research examples   32
        Zick Rubin, Measurement of romantic love   33
        Donn Byrne, Charles R. Ervin, and John Lamberth,
            Continuity between the experimental study of
            attraction and real-life computer dating   42
    The studies compared   51
    Consumer evaluation   55

Chapter 3

INTERPERSONAL DISTANCE 57

Interpersonal space research 58
Explanations of interpersonal distancing 61
Research methods in interpersonal distance 63
Two research examples 67
   Kenneth B. Little, Cultural variations in social schemata 69
   James C. Baxter, Interpersonal spacing in natural settings 76
The studies compared 83
Consumer evaluation 85

Chapter 4

HELPING BEHAVIOR 87

Explanations of prosocial behavior 88
Research on bystander intervention 91
Methods in the study of prosocial behavior 94
Two research examples 98
   John M. Darley and Bibb Latané, Bystander intervention in emergencies: Diffusion of responsibility 100
   Irving M. Piliavin, Judith Rodin, and Jane A. Piliavin, Good samaritanism: An underground phenomenon? 107
The studies compared 118
Consumer evaluation 120

Chapter 5

AGGRESSION 123

Origins of aggression 124
Some situational influences on aggressive behavior 128
Methods used in research on aggression 129
Two research examples 136
   Leonard Berkowitz and Anthony LePage, Weapons as aggression-eliciting stimuli 137

Charles W. Turner, John F. Layton, and Lynn S. Simons, Naturalistic studies of aggressive behavior: Aggressive stimuli, victim visibility, and horn honking   143
The studies compared   153
Consumer evaluation   155

Chapter 6

GROUP DECISION MAKING: EXTREMITY SHIFTS   157

Research on risk in group decisions   159
Methods in the study of group-induced shifts   162
Two research examples   165
  Michael A. Wallach, Nathan Kogan, and Daryl J. Bem, Group influence on individual risk taking   167
  Clark McCauley, Christopher L. Stitt, Kathryn Woods, and Diana Lipton, Group shift to caution at the race track   179
The studies compared   183
Consumer evaluation   186

Chapter 7

ATTRIBUTION   189

Attribution as person perception   191
Models of the attribution process   192
Research on attribution   195
Methods in the study of attribution   198
Two research examples   202
  Michael D. Storms, Videotape and the attribution process: Reversing actors' and observers' points of view   204
  Stephen G. West, Steven P. Gunn, and Paul Chernicky, Ubiquitous Watergate: An attributional analysis   215
The studies compared   226
Consumer evaluation   228

Chapter 8

ATTITUDE CHANGE 231

Cognitive dissonance 233
Research on cognitive dissonance 235
Criticisms of dissonance theory 237
Methods in dissonance research 240
Two research examples 243
   Elliot Aronson and Judson Mills, The effect of severity of initiation on liking for a group 245
   Anthony N. Doob, J. Merrill Carlsmith, Jonathan L. Freedman, Thomas K. Landauer, and Soleng Tom, Jr., Effect of initial selling price on subsequent sales 250
The studies compared 256
Consumer evaluation 259

Chapter 9

ATTITUDE-BEHAVIOR DISCREPANCY: PREJUDICE AND RACISM 261

Explanations of prejudice and racism 262
Research on attitude-behavior consistency in interracial interaction 266
Methods in research on prejudice and racism 269
Two research examples 276
   Shirley Weitz, Attitude, voice, and behavior: A repressed affect model of interracial interaction 277
   Daniel A. Johnson, Richard J. Porter, and Patricia L. Mateljan, Racial discrimination in apartment rentals 285
The studies compared 293
Consumer evaluation 295

Epilog 297

References 299

Index 311

1

HOW TO BE AN INTELLIGENT RESEARCH CONSUMER

CHAPTER OUTLINE

Read Carefully
Check Guarantees
Look beyond Flashy Merchandising
Look for Durability and Long-Term
    Benefits
Pay Attention to the Cost-Quality Relation
Buy from a Reputable Person
Know Consumer Vocabulary
   Laboratory Experiment
   Field Experiment
   Field Study
Do Comparison Shopping
   Refinement of Questions
   Manipulation of Antecedent Conditions
   Subject Awareness
   Comparing Alternative Methods

Appreciate the Principle of "Do It
    Yourself"
Prepare a List
   Statement of the Problem
   Method
   Results
   Discussion and Conclusions
Social Psychology and the Consumer
    Analogy
   The Value of Critique
   Plan of the Book

How many times have you said to yourself when listening to or reading a report of research findings "I just don't buy that"? Yet, when asked to pinpoint specific objections to the research, you don't know where to begin. In contrast, when you go out to buy a stereo component, for example, you can think of some features that you do and do not want. As consumers, we learn the hard way that all products are not alike and that to get what we want we have to become intelligent shoppers. Whether we are aware of it or not, we are just as much consumers of a special product: research. For example, the media bombard us daily with newsworthy vignettes concerning psychological research. Pick up any issue of the weekly newsmagazines, and you'll find regular features on behavioral research. Among the popular monthlies devoted to such research are *Psychology Today, Human Behavior, Society,* and the like.

This book will help you to become as intelligent a consumer of behavioral research as you are of goods and services. When you make a purchase, you take many factors into account. Before buying a car, you check a consumer guide to find out how each make and model is rated on such things as gas mileage, resale value, maintenance history, and design specifications. Buying a car on the basis of a single feature is a decision one often later regrets; a car bought for the fun of quick starts and high speeds may become an annoying burden during gasoline price increases. Depending on your goals, you value different features, but what you know from the start is that you want to avoid getting stuck with a lemon. This applies to research as well; certain gross errors can be identified and avoided, but the choice among desirable features still remains a difficult one. In research, as with cars, your goals as researcher or consumer help determine the priorities. In the chapters to come, you will be reading pairs of representative studies that differ in important ways. The guidelines offered will help you to make comparisons among the sometimes conflicting findings and different methods. These guidelines are adapted from consumer practice to make you more aware of the skills and knowledge you already have. You do not come unequipped for this task, for whether you know it or not, you have been a research consumer for some time.

You are an indirect purchaser and supporter of research through the taxes you pay, which are part of governmental money expended on social psychological research. Through actual consumer purchases, you indirectly support the research funded by private foundations and industry. Through tuition, you partly support the social-psychological research done on campus and so, in many ways, are a distant provider for the kind of research discussed in this book. You are also a consumer of the research product itself whenever research findings are applied in the many social contexts of which you are a part. Dating services operate on principles generated in attraction research; student-union facilities take into account studies of student environmental behavior and preferences; political candidates present themselves to you in keeping with voter attitude surveys; and salesmen apply the findings of conformity research to you. In research, too, there are many opportunities to say "I buy it", and the guidelines below are aimed at making that decision easier.

Read Carefully

Intelligent food buying involves reading the labels on cans and packages and carefully noting the ingredients, quantities, and prices. Consumers are cautioned not to buy by name or appearance alone. One consumer manual even urges buyers to take a magnifying glass to the market so as to read the fine print. In appraising the studies in this book, careful reading is essential. Often researchers and students alike are tempted with the shorthand question "What did the study find?" without noting the essential ingredients of questions asked, procedures applied, people tested, and so forth. The methods used in any study are the "fine print" of the account and should be as carefully noted as the results, for in research, too, a chain is only as strong as its weakest link; the results of a study are only as good as the means that were used to collect them.

The introduction to a study is also important to read, because it is there that the author attempts to place the study in a historical context and to plead a case for its importance. Therein you should find the answer to your question "Why should I buy this at all?" The researcher tries to describe in the introduction where he or she got the idea for the study and whether it is a very new one or derives from ambiguities or controversies in previous work.

Check Guarantees

To check guarantees is a variant of the injunction to read the fine print, but it goes further in suggesting that there are questions to be asked beyond the material presented. In painting, it may be desirable to convey an impression of a landscape in broad strokes, giving the essential feel of the scene, without exact rendering of detail. In research, the account must be a more faithful representation of reality, for, in this sense at least, research (and social-psychological research in particular) is not an art but a science. The selections in this book are taken from the professional journals that social psychologists use to inform themselves of the progress on a particular topic. Of necessity, these articles represent only an abbreviated account of what the research was all about. Often, if students want to do a study similar to the one they are reading, they will not find enough detail about what exactly was done and must write to the author for further information. The selections in this book, drawn from the professional journals, are more complete than other accounts of the same research. These selections were reviewed and recommended for publication by two or three psychologists not known to the authors, and many of them were revised in accordance with editorial suggestions. Many articles were rejected during this process either because they presented major methodological flaws or because they added little to our knowledge of social behavior. Although the articles presented here are not exhaustive accounts of the research, they are dense with detail. The consumer checklist preceding each pair of studies is intended to ease your task in reading.

Other reports of research are usually far sketchier. In textbooks, often only the results are given, and the surrounding qualifications are lost. For example, Berkowitz (1971) has described an experiment whose findings have been systematically distorted in a number of textbooks. In the interest of finding simple generalizations or a coherent body of results, the complexities and ambiguities of specific studies are often omitted. Media accounts of research frequently prune down the complexities even further. Reporters in search of science news are looking for major breakthroughs, and this search often leads to distorting the importance of a given study. The body of research preceding the reported findings is rarely mentioned, and this absence of context increases distortion.

Before you decide to buy or not to buy the outcome of a particular study, you may wish to check the guarantees—that is, to check that what the author says in the introduction is an adequate representation of previous work and that what he or she says in the conclusion does not generalize beyond the actual results.

Look beyond Flashy Merchandising

Behind every product there is a technical production process. Some advertisements tell you at length about how a product is made by showing pictures of factories and machinery or by talking about the ritual of tea-leaf and coffee-bean selection. You end up knowing a lot about the *how* of the product and little about the *what* of it; you are expected to assume that, if so much care is taken in the making of it, then it must be good. Sometimes after seeing a film all you remember are the special effects—such as flashbacks, dissolves, and closeups—and you have trouble saying what the film was about. When that happens, there's something wrong with the film. Techniques are means to an end; the end product must be more than a showpiece for the technology that led up to it.

Similarly, if after reading a social-psychological study you remember only how it was done—for example, a clever manipulation or a cute procedure—there is something wrong, something lacking in the study. We have stressed earlier in the chapter the importance of paying attention to the method, of reading more than just the results of a study. But the method is important precisely in relation to the questions posed and answers found and should not stand out for its own sake, because of ingenuity and gimmickry. This "fun-and-games" approach has been criticized by Ring (1967):

> Clever experimentation on exotic topics with a zany manipulation seems to be the guaranteed formula for success, which, in turn, appears to be defined as being able to effect a *tour de force*. . . . One sometimes gets the impression that an ever-growing coterie of social psychologists is playing (largely for one another's benefit) a game of "can you top this?" Whoever can conduct the most contrived, flamboyant, and mirth-producing experiments receives the highest score [p. 117].

Unnecessary deceptions and procedures dominated more by style than by substance are included in Ring's criticism. Several research selections in the chapters ahead make use of deception—an issue discussed specifically in the chapters on prosocial behavior and on aggression.

A good study is anchored fore and aft; it connects explicitly to some preceding theoretical point or network of ideas, and the practical outcomes of the method employed raise further questions that extend beyond the experiment itself. A science that merely amuses by its ingenuity is not a science. Ring (1967) suggested several remedial questions that investigators might ask themselves:

1. Does this research really deal with a problem of some broad (not necessarily applied) human significance, or does it represent . . . merely an interest . . . [of] one's own?
2. Is this research part of a program of systematic inquiry (or likely to initiate one), or is it really likely to wind up a one-shot affair?
3. Does this research unavoidably entail using a deception-experiment paradigm? [p. 122].

Objection is made not to flamboyant and dramatic experimentation as such but, rather, to the pursuit of such styles for their own sakes. It is when the fun of spectacular doings outweighs their substance that concern arises. (Conversely, as McGuire (1967) noted, it is equally fallacious to assume that the deadly dull is necessarily significant.) Consequently, the good research consumer here is advised to evaluate the study as a whole and not to be dazzled by weird contrivances.

Look for Durability and Long-Term Benefits

In addition to avoiding surface gimmicks and sales features, buy a product with durability in mind. Research should never be content merely with describing events as they occur at a particular time and place. The intent should always be to suggest that these events would reoccur in essentially the same way in any place and at any time sufficiently similar to those of the situation observed. As described by Agnew and Pyke (1969), researchers seek generalization through time and space. Finding that metal expanded when placed in a hot oven at an Eastern university and contracted when placed in a hot oven at a Western research center would be disconcerting indeed and would make it very difficult to predict what would happen to metal so treated in your locale. Science is the search for durable information, information that withstands the variables of time and place. The criterion of durability applies more to the observations than to the explanations of how the observations came about. In research, one may argue about the meaning of observations but should not have to argue about the observations themselves.

A key feature in durability is that the method should have unearthed a cause-effect relation, not created it. The cause-effect relation should withstand such tests of time and place that it can be revealed by methods other than the one originally used to find it. As you read the studies in this book, consider their durability by asking yourself how strong a case you can make that the results would have occurred (1) by the same method at another time and place and (2) by a variety of different methods. The first feature is called *replication* and the second *convergent validity*. Durability requires both. An example can be found in research that tries to evaluate the effect of an appeal to fear on smoking behavior. Replication would involve using the same fear appeal in the same procedure with a group of subjects similar to those originally studied to see if the same change occurred. Convergent validity would involve assessing the effect of a fear appeal through questionnaire responses about the dangers of smoking, daily logs of smoking behavior, neighborhood cigarette sales, and so forth. If the same results are obtained both by replication of the same method in different places and times and by a variety of methods, the research results can be said to have durability. Consequently, as a consumer, you are more justified in buying these results.

Pay Attention to the Cost-Quality Relation

It is often said that in research, as in consumership, you get what you pay for. Some will advise that, given a choice, the higher-priced product is likely to be of higher quality and hence the better buy; others say that the cheaper purchase is likely to be the better one. While in everyday practice most people operate between these extremes, there is a widespread belief that if something costs more it is worth more. Therefore, if you read a report of research involving hundreds of subjects and a large well-funded staff engaged for several years in time-consuming procedures, you may be drawn to the questionable conclusion that that research is better than others because it is bigger. No more warranted is the assumption that smaller is necessarily better. The quality of research is more dependent on clear thinking and good methodology than on dollars spent. To the degree to which thinking and methodology take time (and since time costs money), there is a cost-quality relation.

Having been a consumer all your life, you have learned some means for assessing the quality of a product or service. Making decisions about the quality of a research idea is more difficult because the criteria are less explicit and less generally agreed upon. Moreover, the aura of objectivity with which the scientific enterprise cloaks itself discourages questions about the relative merits of the ideas proposed for study. It is much easier to ask how much something cost than to ask whether it should have been bought at all. Similarly, in the area of research, it is easier to ask how many subjects and how many computer programs were used than to ask whether the idea was worth testing in the first place. Maslow underlined this point when he aptly said that that which is not worth doing is not worth doing well. In other words, the fact that an idea cost considerable time, money, or energy should not be used as the sole standard for buying it. If cost alone were the issue, you would likely choose the cheapest project; if quality were the only salient point, then you would obviously choose the best one. But decisions are usually arrived at after due consideration of both factors simultaneously.

In thinking about cost and quality together, four combinations stand out. First, there are products of high cost and high quality, the kind of projects referred to when we announce "money is no object." The other extreme—low cost and low quality—has no place in research; even a small pilot study must have some quality in order to be useful in planning future work. Low-cost/low-quality research products stand too great a chance of doing harm to be worth the risk. The other two combinations of cost-quality relations—products of high cost and low quality and products of low cost and high quality—are mixed combinations. The former are sometimes cursed as "lemons," and the latter, the "bargains," are quite rare and widely sought both in the marketplace and in research. Obviously, these descriptions characterize extremes, and most consumer and research products represent less clear-cut cost-quality choices. Nonetheless, any research question, small or large, must deal with cost-quality issues and can be evaluated accordingly.

Although most research decisions are thought to be based primarily on the quality of the idea, the fact is that some research is not taken on because it is too costly. The scarcity of longitudinal studies in social psychology can be attributed directly to these studies' cost in time and money; an example is the study of the development of intimate relationships, which is rarely carried out because it is too expensive. Another example is that of cross-cultural studies. Although most social psychologists are vulnerable to the criticism that their findings apply only to the culture of the United States, and although it is critical to know whether research findings have wider applicability, few cross-cultural studies are done because of their prohibitive costs. Costs are relative, though, and must be considered in relation to anticipated benefits. Longitudinal or cross-cultural research is costly in monetary terms, but the results may do more in the long run to explain the nature of social behavior than would numerous short-term or sample-specific (and therefore less expensive) studies.

Buy from a Reputable Person

One of the first recommendations made to novice shoppers either through consumer guides or, more informally, through word-of-mouth is to buy from a reliable dealer and to avoid "fly-by-night" operations. Implicitly, this caution suggests that a firm "in the business" for 25 years is probably more trustworthy than one that has been around for only a few days. Especially when you make a major purchase, you tend to feel more confident if you know the dealer and have heard others speak of his or her reliability and honesty.

When newcomers to psychology first encounter such expressions as "Doe (1934)" or "Smith (1974)" in texts and research articles, they are apt to be somewhat confused as to the intended meaning. In psychology, as in art or music or architecture or philosophy, the creator of a work is usually designated. Thus we speak of Beethoven's Fifth, Michelangelo's *Pietà*, and Kant's *Critique of Pure Reason*. This referencing is done to identify who said or did what in what year; equally important, it points to the person who must in the end receive the praise or criticism for the work. In the behavioral sciences too we have our Picassos and da Vincis, or, at the very least, authors in whose work we trust, people whose findings have proved to be durable in the past and whose explanations have held up under the scrutiny of critical audiences—in other words, investigators who have earned the public trust. A potential, and often real, problem with this approach is that the rush to accept the known, the familiar, and the reputable can blind us to the new, the unfamiliar, and the controversial. Science is replete with stories of investigators who are initially thought by the reputable establishment to be deluded or crazy, only to be recognized much later as correct and innovative.

It may seem strange to compare a scientist with a dealer, because the comparison seems to run counter to our idea of the scientific product as being objective, pure, and autonomous with respect to the person who originated it. Truth is truth—isn't it?—regardless of who says it. But truth is not always so self-evident. Scientists sometimes disagree. Some of the following selections present contradictory findings or contradictory explanations to account for the same findings. One way of choosing among them is to establish which is the more reliable investigator, and reputation is one guide to reliability. But there are better ways to decide whom to believe. Consider these questions:

1. Given that, potentially, the results of a study may have been "caused" by a number of factors, what has the investigator done in order to rule out (that is, control for) the irrelevant factors and elucidate the real ones?
2. Has the investigator presented enough of his or her actual findings (raw data) for you to assess the adequacy of his or her analysis and conclusions? Some publications impose restrictions that preclude the printing of raw data. In all cases, however, this information should be retained by the investigator and be available.
3. What indications of concern for the welfare and privacy of research subjects has the investigator given? Has unnecessary deception of the subjects been avoided?
4. Given that social behavior is a major concern of many other scholarly disciplines, is there any indication that the researcher is aware of how the topic has been explored elsewhere?
5. Given that research is a personal enterprise, how explicit has the investigator made his or her values and biases?

Know Consumer Vocabulary

In order to become a more intelligent consumer, you need to learn the meaning of some new words. When you buy a car on credit, for example, you may have to decide between a dealer-sponsored finance plan and a bank financing arrangement. If so, before you can begin comparing financing plans, you must know what the terminology means. Therefore, you will want to learn not only the general vocabulary of financing arrangements but many specific terms as well. In research, too, there is a special vocabulary pertaining both to the general nature of investigation and to the specifics of a particular approach. Some of you reading this book were first attracted to psychology by a curiosity about people and were baffled to find psychology laden with jargon and special terms. This may have even led you to lose interest in the field because you thought that the important questions were no longer being asked. As a consumer, you are willing to learn some new things to get what you want; in fact, a consumer search often begins with finding out what the "shop talk" is—that is, the terms that people "in the know" use to make good decisions. In research as well, it is worth the effort to learn new terms in order to answer questions worth asking. Intelligent comparisons of methods or procedures require a clear understanding of the terms involved. Although some terms commonly used in research are introduced in this chapter, they will become clearer as they are applied to the research examples in each of the following chapters.

A current conflict among social psychologists centers on the relative merits of experimentation in the laboratory and in the field. Before you can make a sensible evaluation of this debate, you need to know what is meant by *laboratory experiments, field experiments,* and *field studies.* Each of the next eight chapters contains a section in which representative uses of each method are described.

Laboratory Experiment. A *laboratory experiment* seeks to assess the effect of one or more independent (manipulated) variables on one or more dependent (observed) variables, while controlling for other potential influences. The term *laboratory* is used not because the experiment involves test tubes and burners but because it takes place in an environment designed expressly for research. If you want to study group decisions, for example, you might conduct the group meeting in a room with a one-way mirror through which you can observe the process without being seen. The term *to experiment* means to determine whether one or more factors cause one or more effects. At its simplest, this involves comparing two situations that are exactly alike except for the fact that in one situation the causal effect is present and in the other situation the causal effect is absent. Suppose you were interested in the effect of size of student work groups (independent variable) on quality of student projects (dependent variable). In order to determine the effect of your independent variable, you would need to have groups of different sizes, perhaps consisting of two, four, or six students. In order to assess the impact on the dependent variable, you would have to have some way of comparing products, such as having teachers rate the quality of the students' projects. These raters, of course, would be unaware of which group produced what work. Since other factors might also produce differences in quality—such as working time, prior experience in groups of a certain size, or student ability for the task—these would have to be controlled. One way of controlling such variables is to make the subjects' experiences as uniform as possible, save for the manipulation of the independent variable. In our example, this would mean giving all a fixed time in which to complete the assignment. Another control involves random selection and random assignment of subjects in order to assure that the groups do not differ in any systematic way at the beginning of the experiment. The purpose of the laboratory experiment, then, is to discover the relations between an independent and a dependent variable. Relevant questions are: Are the variables related? If so, how are they related? How strong are the relations? The laboratory experiment establishes these relations by control, specificity, and precision. As seen in the example above, controls are intended to either minimize or hold constant other potentially influential variables so as to allow the effects of the designated one to emerge. It takes careful thought to determine what the appropriate controls might be.

Being specific about the independent variable lets you and others interested in repeating your study know exactly how you defined the variable you studied. For example, saying that you studied the differences in the quality of work produced by small, medium, and large groups is less specific than indicating that by small you mean two persons; by medium, four; and by large, six. Being precise about the dependent variable means being definite and unambiguous about the measurements you take. If your raters evaluated the student products by labeling them as good, fair, and poor, you would have less assurance that they would rate these products the same way a day or two later than if you asked them to make ratings on a more precise scale that gave examples of what each rating point means.

Consumers become aware that some products have unanticipated attributes. Beneficial drugs have unpleasant side effects; large classes are considered economically efficient but may produce a sense of alienation in both students and teachers. The laboratory experiment too has been found to have some unanticipated, negative consequences. This discovery has fueled the controversy among social psychologists concerning exclusive reliance on laboratory methods.

Experimental Artifacts. A number of these unanticipated side effects of the laboratory method have been described and grouped together as *experimental artifacts* (Rosenthal & Rosnow, 1969). One of the benefits of the laboratory is freedom from the influences rampant in the real situations in which the behavior of interest is found. The laboratory was assumed to be free of contaminating influences; therefore, it was particularly disconcerting to social psychologists to discover that the laboratory too is an environment with particular influences on behavior. You will become familiar with this issue in some of the laboratory experiments described in the chapters ahead.

Of special concern was the finding that the laboratory experiment is marked by *demand characteristics* (Orne, 1969). Just as many settings convey cues concerning the behavior appropriate to those settings, so too does the laboratory. If elements of architecture, design, and the behavior of other people provide cues in, say, supermarkets, churches, and classrooms, in the laboratory, cues are provided by the equipment, the instructions, and the experimenter's behavior. Often people say at the end of a study that they hope they've helped and not messed up the results. Clearly, energy has gone into figuring out what the experimenter expects and then into producing it.

Related to this artifact is that of *evaluation apprehension* (Rosenberg, 1965), or the research participants' concern with being seen in a good light by the experimenter. Psychologists are assumed to have special insights into human nature, and people who take part in research are often concerned that they may inadvertently reveal negative things about themselves. Subjects fear that the psychologist may judge them to be stupid, weak, sexually inadequate, or any number of other things people would rather not be. In this vein, research participants ask at the conclusion of the procedure whether they "did all right." Like a sensitivity to demand characteristics, this concern with evaluation may lead people to present themselves as they wish to be seen rather than as they really are in the context the experiment seeks to test.

Field Experiment. A *field experiment* is a research study in a natural setting, within which (as much as the setting permits) one or more independent variables are manipulated and their effect on one or more dependent variables is assessed. An experiment is said to take place in the field not because it takes place in a meadow but because it is conducted in a setting where the behavior of interest might occur naturally. Presumably, experimental artifacts are reduced and generalizability of findings is strengthened in the field. For example, doubts about the generalizability of laboratory simulations of intergroup conflict have led some researchers to conduct experiments in natural settings where conflict between groups is likely to arise. As described more fully in Chapter 9, Sherif and his colleagues (1961) operated a boys' summer camp to study intergroup conflict. After selecting campers from different areas (to minimize the chance of previous acquaintance), they conducted sports tournaments to generate conflict through competition. Such competition occurs naturally in summer-camp programs and occasionally leads to conflict. But this being an experiment, the investigators could not leave the occurrence of conflict to chance. The fact that they operated the camp themselves gave them control over assignment of campers to groups and over the scheduling and intensity of competition. This control over competition was necessary because the researchers wanted to be able to say that whatever conflict resulted was the product of the competition and not of personality clashes or other factors. While operating the camp themselves gave the researchers considerable control over scheduled competition, it nonetheless afforded less control than the laboratory; many events occurred in the boys' camp over which the experimenters had little control. This made it more difficult to rule out alternative explanations for the resulting conflict than would have been possible in a more controlled and specific laboratory experiment. On the other hand, the conflict seen in the camp setting was stronger than the kind of conflict that can easily be created in the laboratory and was sustained by real-life features.

In sum, while the laboratory experiment, because of better controls, allows a more accurate assessment of the relation between variables, the field experiment lends itself to greater generalization. Control and generalizability are the key elements in internal validity and external validity, respectively. A good study, wherever conducted, should have both. *Internal validity* requires that the experimenter be able to say that changes in the dependent variable are solely the results of changes in the independent variable. *External validity* refers to the degree to which the investigator can generalize results to other peoples, places, and times. Generalizing from the field experiment is made easier by the similarity between the test situation and other natural settings. A disadvantage of the field experiment lies in the limitations imposed on the researcher by the rules and conventions of the real world. Schools, hospitals, and business establishments may place restrictions on the random assignment of "subjects," whom they regard as students, patients, and clients. They may also place similar constraints on the manipulation of "conditions," which they regard as services rendered. The nonrandomization of subjects and a limited control of experimental conditions necessarily reduce the specificity and precision of field experiments, and hence the confidence in the relations established is weakened.

Field Study. The *field study* involves establishing relations between observed behavior and probable antecedent conditions by using various means, including observation, interviewing, and document search. The field study cannot be delineated as precisely as the laboratory or the field experiments, because the label is a catchall for different studies that do not fit the experimental model. Quite often, field studies are done after natural events have occurred, in an effort to gain understanding of what might have led to the observed behavior. A researcher's attention is drawn to a situation or event and, after observing it carefully, he or she starts asking questions as to its cause. Despite the frequency of this after-the-fact approach, it is not the only possible way to carry out a field study. For example, Newcomb (1943) studied the entire student population of Bennington College for four years to assess the impact of this liberal sociopolitical college environment on students' attitudes. On the basis of questionnaires, interviews, and observations, Newcomb concluded that the longer the students had been at that college, the more liberal they had become in their views.

It is clear that the field study, like the field experiment, derives some advantage from its location in a real setting. In the case of the Bennington study, for example, the cost of creating as rich a fabric of social and political norms in the laboratory would have been prohibitive. That study shared two advantages with field experiments (as described above)—realism and strength of variables. Mere enrollment as a student could have been taken as an indicator of exposure to the variable under study—effect of college environment. Yet Newcomb tried to intensify even this all-encompassing variable by assessing degree of commitment, or involvement with the school, and found more change on the part of those who were most involved. This assessment of involvement illustrates one attempt to compensate for the greatest disadvantage of the field study—its weakness in assigning causality. The positive features of the Bennington study are represented by a large sample (whole student body), the longitudinal focus (over four years), and the use of a variety of assessment techniques. Despite these considerable advantages, there remains the enduring problem of all field studies—that of internal validity. In other words, the question concerning what specifically there is about the "college experience" that changes student attitudes remains unanswered. Even if it were possible by careful comparisons of the information collected to gain some understanding of specific causal relations, it would still be difficult to make generalizations from field studies. Would these causal relations hold for any population other than that which attended Bennington College in the late 1930s? The lack of control over random assignment of subjects to conditions, which is almost invariably true of field studies, limits conclusions about causality.

The distinctions made here among laboratory experiments, field experiments, and field studies provide a general orientation toward the specific studies presented in the chapters that follow. It should be noted that the researcher's choice among these approaches is based on a number of considerations. Each approach has certain advantages and disadvantages. What can be said is that the dictates of the research question should govern as much as possible the choice of method.

Do Comparison Shopping

Faced with the problem of an overgrown front lawn, you might go out to buy a lawnmower. As a good consumer, you would go to several stores and compare the relative merits of various makes and models. In research, this comparison shopping might lead you to consider different methods of studying a particular problem. You select a lawnmower after weighing such factors as quality, price, features, and guarantees. You select a research approach in similar ways. As you compare lawnmowers, however, it may become clear to you that a lawnmower won't do the job you had in mind. Similarly, you may realize that the research method you are considering doesn't address the questions you're asking. Also, you might find that you're getting more than you expected. For instance, you might end up buying a lawnmower that also mulches leaves or blows snow; while you started out only to cut grass on your lawn, you might end up with a device for more general care of your property. But not all extra features are good for your purpose. If you live in a mild climate or want to spend as little as possible, you don't want extra features. Comparison shopping gives access to new possibilities, but whether these are desirable for *you* depends on *your* questions and needs.

Refinement of Questions. In choosing a method, the experimenter faces many difficult decisions that require maximum explicitness as to the questions being asked. One of the first problems faced by the novice experimenter is phrasing a question so that it can be answered. Issues such as "Why does mankind wage war?" or "Why do some people work harder than others?" need considerable refinement before any method can be applied to search for answers. Conversely, one of the pitfalls that entrap experienced researchers is letting familiar methods reshape the questions to be asked. Often the availability of experimental equipment or the familiarity with particular test instruments dictates the pursuit of questions along relatively unproductive lines. One is reminded of the drunkard who, having dropped his house key in the dark, looks for it down the street under a lamppost because the light is better there. It is important to remember that methods are only means; it is the questions that are the ends.

Even when the questions are clear and the method appropriate, no study will answer all the questions it raises. The understanding of social behavior is a cumulative process resting on the comparison and reconciliation of a number of empirical studies. Such comparisons are made more difficult by changes made by successive experimenters at all levels of the research enterprise. Even within the same general topic, hypotheses are never formulated in exactly the same way, nor are similar methods and analyses used. Comparisons are therefore necessarily imperfect. Nonetheless, comparisons must be made to arrive at any cumulative understanding of social behavior. Among the many dimensions that might be used for such comparisons, the two selected here are central. Manipulation of the research situation and subject awareness of being studied are dimensions invoked repeatedly when research is critically appraised.

Manipulation of Antecedent Conditions. Studies can vary according to the extent to which the investigator exercises control over causal factors. The two extremes of this dimension are represented by the laboratory experiment and by the post-hoc field study. In the former, the experimenter exercises maximum control over events preceding measurement of the dependent variable. Manipulation of the test situation by selection of subjects, assignment to independent experimental conditions, and predetermination of response formats is more easily carried out in a situation specially designed for the purpose. Instead, the field study imposes few restrictions on the observed events.

Subject Awareness. Participants in research may or may not be aware of being studied; also, they may or may not know what aspect of their behavior is of interest to the investigators. These two kinds of awareness have different effects. Laboratory experiments are marked by high subject awareness of being under study, and many use deception to conceal the nature of the behavior being measured. Field studies using interviews are high in both kinds of awareness, for the interviewee is clearly conscious of being studied and direct questions often reveal the topic of interest. Field studies using observation and archival document search involve little or no subject awareness of either kind. Most field experiments included in this book also leave subjects unaware of being the object of experimentation.

Comparing Alternative Methods. Just knowing that different methods exist doesn't tell which is best to use; knowing that manipulation of antecedent conditions and subject awareness figure in all research doesn't always dictate a choice. The best method is the method that fits the problem you want to study. To illustrate this point, consider the question of the effects that seeing others give help has on your helping behavior. Does the sight of someone helping make you more likely to help? You might try to measure this modeling effect (that is, the effect of watching the actions of other people) by interview—for example, by asking people whether they would be more likely to donate to a charity if they saw someone doing so than if they did not. The interview clearly involves high subject awareness. One of the disadvantages of such a direct method is that people often don't know how they would behave in a given situation. Also, in trying to please the interviewer, they may give the most socially acceptable response. In the interviews described, many respondents might say that they would help another no matter what the situation, since in our society helping others is considered a good behavior. An advantage of the interview, on the other hand, is that, by asking people directly, you can be more certain that they are taking into account the dimension you are interested in.

Another way of determining whether modeling has an effect is to observe from a distance. Observation of this kind (called *naturalistic observation*) is usually low in both manipulation and subject awareness. In this low-manipulation procedure, you may observe a model and a subsequent helping act by someone else, without knowing whether this other person was aware of the model's behavior and, if so, what effect it had on him or her. This doubt can be reduced by making the observations systematic as to time or distance between model-donor and subject or by specifying cues that indicate that the model has been seen. One advantage of the naturalistic observation is that it leaves the subject unaware of being studied; another is that it includes all the environmental and interpersonal factors that may sustain such charitable giving in a real-life situation.

Note that from some perspectives you may not attend equally to all these issues; namely, you may wish to know how people think they would behave and be unconcerned about their actual behavior, or you may not care about their perceptions of themselves and care only about their actual behavior. Different questions require different methods, and any method has benefits and costs.

Still another method may involve doing a field experiment in which you might retain the realism of the sidewalk situation and exercise some control over variability by sending experimental confederates to donate money at specified intervals. Or the entire enterprise might be moved to the laboratory in order to sort out the different contributions made by the various variables in the situation. For example, if observation in the natural setting suggests that race, sex, or age of model and subject make a difference in giving patterns, the relative importance of these variables can then be assessed by systematically varying them in a laboratory experiment.

In summary, choosing a method after comparison shopping depends on the questions being asked in the investigation, the stage of existing knowledge about the behavior under study, and the stylistic preferences of the researcher. Observation and open-ended inquiry are sometimes seen as more appropriate to the early stages of investigation on a particular topic. Experiments high in manipulation of antecedent conditions are more appropriate to testing specific cause-effect relations. As to stylistic preferences, an investigator's training and experience in a particular research technique may lead him to prefer that technique to others because he is confident of knowing its advantages while also knowing how to minimize its quirks and pitfalls.

Appreciate the Principle of "Do It Yourself"

Increasingly, consumers are making their own products from kits and raw materials; these activities range from mounting a set of shelves to making a high-fidelity amplifier from a manufacturer's kit. Consumers typically engage in such projects for several reasons. Pride of craftsmanship and creative urges, as well as the belief that a better product results, figure largely in the motivation to start such endeavors. Some people are also attracted by the thought of obtaining a product at lower cost. In research, too, investigators must be inventive; in a sense, the entire enterprise of designing a study is a creative act. But the specific emphasis here is on those instances of "do-it-yourself" activity that take place after comparison shopping or other efforts have failed to turn up a suitable method for the question at hand. The investigator must then develop an alternative procedure, a new test, a novel apparatus, or an entirely new approach to the problem. Here are a few examples.

Methods high in subject awareness led to a concern with reactivity—whether subjects might be reacting to the method itself rather than engaging in the behavior under study—and *unobtrusive measures* (measures taken without attracting the subjects' attention) were devised as alternatives (Webb, Campbell, Schwartz, & Sechrest, 1966). For example, a rough indication of the popularity of topical current events might be derived from comparing the frequency with which library books and magazines covering these topics are borrowed or from comparing the evidence of wear (such as creasing, thumbprints, underlinings, and so forth) on different pages of such books and magazines.

As psychologists began to work outside the laboratory in more natural settings, they experienced difficulty in implementing classical experimental designs in the real world.

An innovative alternative was suggested by Campbell and Stanley (1963), who advanced the possibility of quasi-experimental modifications that would maximize the exercise of controls in natural settings. They suggested a time-series approach to study the effects of new treatments over a period of time—for example, the effects of a new therapy on a group of patients. In a time-series design, one makes a series of observations of the prospective patients in order to establish a "baseline." After a baseline has been established, treatment takes place; this, in turn, is followed by yet another series of observations. The efficacy of the treatment is established by comparing the baseline rates before and after treatment. The extended period of measurement gives some assurance that it was indeed the treatment, rather than any other concurrent events, that produced the observed changes. An example of a time-series approach is found in Chapter 5.

These innovations constitute genuine contributions to methodology because they provide means of answering questions that would not be answered with existing methods. The "do-it-yourself" urge, however, has led researchers astray at different times and in different ways. Novices are sometimes moved to devise their own scales, measures, and inventories out of ignorance of what exists and what has been done. They may lack the necessary skills to do a productive search of the literature or the broad knowledge of the field that would make it possible to readily retrieve a wide range of methods that have been used. This problem is compounded by the tendency to rely on very recent work only and to fail to recognize the degree to which basic questions about social behavior recur and reappear. The experienced investigator, on the other hand, may fall victim to the myth noted by Kaplan (1964) that the most serious problems in research lie in methodology. Adherents of that view may spend so much time in perfecting a given scale or measure that they never come to study the question the measure was originally designed to answer. To reiterate, the essential task is posing questions of theoretical or practical importance, and this may at times involve the breaking of new methodological ground.

Prepare a List

These days, when people are watching their budgets carefully, shoppers are advised to make a list before going to the market and then stick to it. Knowing what you're looking for guards you against impulse buying because it enables you to impose your own order and priorities on the store setting and thus be less likely to respond to merchandising gimmicks. Accounts of research differ in the amount of detail they give on the procedure and findings, but, regardless of presentation, you will end up with the most information available if you know what you're looking for. Having a list of what you want to know about any study is a helpful guide to evaluating what's there and to comparing one investigator's offerings with those of another. In reading any description of research, try to get the following information.

Statement of the Problem. All accounts of research published in professional journals begin with an introduction that contains a statement concerning the problem the researcher set out to study. If an experiment is being described, the problem will be stated in terms of independent and dependent variables. In a field study, the problem may not be as specifically stated, but there will also be some indication, sometimes in the form of a question, of the researcher's interest. Consequently, you will want to know not only what has been studied but also why this problem is of interest. To that end, the author must give you some indication of what others have found on the topic and why the work to be presented is of special significance and value. In journal articles, where space is very limited, the literature review is often necessarily compressed. Nonetheless, you should be able to get a clear idea of how others have approached the topic and what has led the researcher to single out the specific problem studied. A common shortcut is for the author to cite only one or two studies immediately preceding the reported work, perhaps in the expectation that the truly interested readers will then go to those articles, check their references, and thereby work their way backward to a broader understanding of the topic. While this assumption is economical with respect to journal space, the better literature reviews give at least some highlights of the topic over time. The goal of the literature review is to provide the rationale behind the author's questions. At the end of the introduction, therefore, you will usually see a succinct statement of what the researcher expects to find.

Method. The guiding principle in evaluating a research report is that the account should permit you to extract all the information you need to repeat the study yourself. Again, given the stringent space restrictions of professional publications or the emphasis on results in popular journalism, this goal can seldom be attained. It nonetheless remains a useful focus for information seeking. Another key feature of the account of method is that it should be descriptive rather than interpretive or persuasive.

In formal research reports, the description of method is often further subdivided into sections on design, subjects, measurement techniques, and procedure. The section on *design* states the number of independent and dependent variables that have been considered in the study and how many levels (for example, high and low; small, medium, and large) of each were involved. The section describing the sample of *subjects* tells how many there were, how they were selected for the study, and what their relevant characteristics of age, sex, or social status were. The terms *random selection* and *random assignment* should not be used as attractive decorations. Randomization procedures should be described specifically, and, if they were not used, reasons should be given for the procedures that were used in selecting the subjects.

The section on *measurement* gives a brief description of how the variables in the experiment were operationalized. To *operationalize* means to make abstract definitions of variables more concrete and specific. For example, in an experiment on group size and productivity, group size would be described as operationalized by indicating the exact size of each group—say, two, four, and six students. The dependent variable of productivity and any control conditions used would be stated in similarly specific terms. The measurement section also describes in detail any tests, scales, stimulus presentations, rating forms, or other assessment techniques employed. If a test has been adapted from other studies, the original source should be given and the changes made should be clearly described. Where new methods have been devised for the measurement of complex social phenomena, the description may necessarily be lengthy and detailed.

Finally, the *procedure* should describe what happens to subjects from the moment they enter the study to the moment they leave it. Instructions given to subjects should be stated exactly as they were given (if space permits) or should be paraphrased accurately. Given the significance of the subject-awareness dimension described above, the importance of accurately reported procedures cannot be overstressed. For the reader to understand how the subject experienced the experiment, there must be an accurate account of what was said and done during the experiment. Laboratory experimenters have become sensitized to the potential artifacts (unanticipated side effects) inherent in their procedures. In field experiments and field studies, the artifacts have not been recognized as clearly, and the accounts of this research are often careless in reporting what was actually said to and done with those under study. Without sufficient detail in the methods section, results cannot be understood or evaluated. Concerns about the internal or external validity of research always center on the specifics of the methods employed.

Results. There is a convention in research reporting that results should be described without interpretation. Although in longer and more formal accounts this convention is followed, an increasing number of authors report and discuss findings concurrently. Without doubt this makes for more pleasant reading, but it also invites overstatement and distortion. When there is some temporal and spatial separation between the findings of an experiment and the discussion of their meaning, readers are freer to come up with their own interpretations of the findings. If they are not told "the" meaning, readers may find alternative explanations for the results. In any case, the results that bear on whether the hypotheses that the experiment was meant to test have or have not been supported must be clearly and accurately stated, and the statistical analysis should be described. Watch for wishful overstatement of marginal results; statements such as "findings approached significance" are less than convincing. Although certain trends revealed by an experiment may be interesting and suggestive, they do not deserve the same attention as findings that meet the author's stated criteria of statistical acceptance. Learn to read tables without fear; they are often more accurate representations of what was found than the words that describe them.

Discussion and Conclusions. Here the researcher tells you what the findings mean and ties this interpretation back to the introduction. He or she tries to fit the findings to the literature in general and indicates what the next steps in research on the topic might be. Look here also for the researcher's assessment of what the limitations of the study might be. The most obvious limitations lie in the factors that remain uncontrolled in the study. In evaluating a study, be sure to consider the likelihood that an uncontrolled factor may have altered the results. A variety of uncontrolled factors that can influence experimental findings are noted in the comparisons of studies in the chapters ahead. Read carefully and critically how the author accounts for findings that do not support predictions. One can choose to blame the method or question the theory. Most often, researchers elect to point out deficits in their own methods, and you must then assess the worth of the proposed corrections. Watch also for the level of conclusion reached. Keep problems of external validity in mind in assessing the credibility of the leap to generalization that the investigator makes.

This shopping list of things to look for in research will not fit equally well all studies presented in this book. Each selection, however, is preceded by a "product description" to give you a preview of the information ahead and by a "consumer checklist" to help you formulate specific questions for that selection. The checklist will at least allow you to see what information you don't have and thus will give substance to your gut feelings of "I buy it" or "It's not for me."

Social Psychology and the Consumer Analogy

At the beginning of this chapter, we said that "this book will help you to become as intelligent a consumer of behavioral research as you are of goods and services." This consumer approach, offered to elicit an active involvement on your part and to make you aware that you already have some tools to work with, was adopted throughout this chapter and will be offered again in the chapters to follow. It is our hope that you will extend this approach much further, much beyond the scope of this book or of the subject matter in your course—even beyond your immediate social environment. Social-psychological information permeates many of the spheres that touch your life, and we hope that the principles discussed here will help you to organize your reaction to and your evaluation of this information.

An advantage of the consumer analogy is that it stresses the value of considered decisions. Unqualified reactions to research have limited value, and impulse buying of research findings is, at the very least, hard to defend against someone who happens to disagree with you. It should be noted, however, that there are aspects of the consumer analogy that don't quite fit the research situation. More specifically, three limitations should be considered here: in research, you can hardly have too much knowledge; research is process more than it is product; and good research depends on more than good methods. First, in most major purchasing decisions, you gradually narrow down the choices until you finally settle on a single purchase; you rarely buy two or three of the same item. In research, instead, several replications of the same idea are welcome. In addition, research findings are expected to be cumulative, and, as a research consumer, you might easily wish to buy them all. What we are saying here is that, as a consumer of research, you don't have to narrow down your choices in order to settle on a single piece of research; as a matter of fact, you don't even have to decide whether one is better than another. When you read the pairs of studies presented in the following chapters, use the consumer analogy to compare the studies in order to judge what is good and bad in each—not in order to decide which is the better one.

This comparison points to the second limitation of the consumer analogy. In most major consumer purchases, after having made a choice, you can relax and assume that the matter is settled for some time. Research, instead, is more a process than an accumulation of products and findings. As a process, research is ongoing and any decision is necessarily a temporary one. Research is continuous change, and part of the excitement lies in the development of ideas. Our own enthusiasm for social psychology comes not from knowing what the score is at any moment but from knowing how the game is played. We hope to share this enthusiasm with you in the chapters to come by helping you discover some of the rules of the game, identify some of the noted players, and find out how you yourself can get into the game.

The third reservation about applying the consumer analogy to the research situation is that criteria for evaluating research are more illusory than those for evaluating market products. In purchasing insurance, for example, it is quite possible to make a complete list of the desirable features and to evaluate various policies on the basis of such a list. In research, this can be done—up to a point—to appraise the methods used in a study. But good research depends on more than good methods, although some social psychologists argue that the only research projects that should be conducted are those for which valid and reliable methods exist. This makes for one kind of good research but certainly restricts what the social psychologist can attempt to know. We would argue that ideas have precedence and that methods are means to the end of discovery. Ideas are much harder to evaluate, however, and the consumer guidelines offered here are of limited help in deciding whether the ideas in the studies to follow are worth studying.

The Value of Critique. As you read this volume, it will become increasingly clear that we place high value on critique as a dynamic force in the research enterprise. Some people approach research in quest of answers or, at the very least, in pursuit of confirmation of their world view. Readers with that goal in mind are likely to be unsettled by this book. Any activity looks less orderly and clear-cut as you get close to it, and social psychology is no exception. To take a critical look at research involves incurring some dangers. To make negative statements is to risk encouraging those who would dismiss it all, those who greet the discovery of an unsurmounted difficulty as an indication that the entire field is worthless. To compliment some aspect of research, on the other hand, is to risk confirming devotees in their views. The task, as we see it, is to shape the critical stance so as to draw both skeptics and true believers into appreciating ambiguity and into using uncertainty to push toward better methods and sharper

18   CHAPTER 1

questions. We believe that to critique is to honor by getting involved, and we invite you to become involved.

Plan of the Book. The next eight chapters examine some major topics in social psychology. Each chapter features two studies reprinted, without editing, as they appeared in the professional literature. The studies were selected so as to permit comparisons of different methods used to study the same content area. In several chapters, the laboratory experiment is a landmark study in the sense that it is invariably cited when the topic is reviewed. Each pair of studies is preceded by three sections. The first one presents the most commonly accepted explanations for the kind of social behavior examined by the two studies. The second section reviews major research findings on the topic under discussion, in order to set the selections in context. The third section gives examples of the use of a variety of research methods. Just before the research selections, you will find a brief summary of the two studies and a consumer checklist, in the form of specific methodological questions, to guide your reading. The selections are followed by critical comparisons and by a consumer evaluation that makes use of some of the guidelines suggested in this chapter. Although from the topical point of view the chapters could be read in any order, they are presented here in a sequence suggested by the increasing complexity of the methods used in the studies. Issues raised in the critical comparisons following the research in the chapters on attraction, distancing, and altruism prepare the ground for more difficult problems in the second half of the book.

22

ATTRACTION

CHAPTER OUTLINE

Theories of Attraction
    Reinforcement Theories
        Reward Explanation
        Exchange Model
        Criticism of Reinforcement
            Explanations
    Arousal and Labeling Theory
Determinants of Attraction
    Proximity
    Personal Attributes
        Physical Attractiveness
        Competence
    Similarity
    Complementarity
Research Methods in the Study
    of Attraction
    Laboratory Experiments
    Field Experiments
    Naturalistic Observation and Archival
        Search
    Surveys and Interviews

Two Research Examples
    Product Description
    Consumer Checklist
    Zick Rubin, *Measurement of romantic love.*
    Donn Byrne, Charles R. Ervin, and John Lamberth, *Continuity between the experimental study of attraction and real-life computer dating.*
The Studies Compared
    Subject Selection
        The Computer-Dating Study
        The Romantic-Love Study
    Measures of Attraction
Consumer Evaluation
    Cost-Quality Relation
    Durability

In 1973 *Time* magazine reported how Gough Whitlam, the then Prime Minister of Australia, met his wife:

> In 1942, 6 ft. 4 in. Whitlam married a fellow student, 6 ft. 2 in. Margaret Dovey, daughter of a Sydney lawyer who later became a Supreme Court Justice in New South Wales. They met at a university party when, as Margaret puts it, their eyes found each other across the heads of their smaller companions.

News items of this kind appeal because they speak directly to our own and our friends' experience. Searching for explanations for that instant attraction, you might say "It's chemistry." You may think that such attraction just happens, such meetings can't be arranged, and that it is a little wrong to try to examine the process too closely. But at the same time, you've probably brought people together yourself, in the hope that they would like each other, that the magic would happen. Sometimes it works; sometimes it doesn't. It would be nice to know what makes the difference. Psychologists too would like to know more about such encounters, because attraction, friendship, and love are among the most basic of human experiences. This chapter presents some explanations of how and why attraction occurs and discusses current research to set the two selections in context.

Most researchers would agree with Newcomb's (1961) definition of attraction as an orientation toward another that is either positive or negative and intense or not. Most research deals with attraction rather than with friendship or passionate love. Intense feelings of love are hard to generate in research subjects, who have come for an hour or two to earn money or course credit and help out the investigator. Thus, the more pragmatic may avoid research on love because it cannot be studied easily in standard experimental ways. In the research that has been done, the questions posed are modest and the methods used are simple. Over 80% of this research involves strangers who have never met prior to the experiment (Huston, 1974). Attraction among strangers pertains to only a small part of the spectrum of positive orientations toward others.

Interpersonal ties can vary from shallow relationships to deep attachments (Levinger & Snoek, 1972). In shallow relationships, a person is aware of another but does not interact much with that person. In the second selection included in this chapter, research participants interact at this minimal level; they are provided with information about a stranger and then meet that person for a short while. At a second level of involvement are those relationships that, although superficial, are characterized by a greater degree of interaction. Many semiformal relationships bounded by the performance of one's occupation fall into this category. Especially in urban life, there are many persons—such as custodians, elevator operators, and fellow workers—with whom we have frequent but relatively shallow encounters. Finally, there are relationships in which partners influence each other and become interdependent. The first research selection (Rubin, 1970) included here describes relationships at this more involved level.

THEORIES OF ATTRACTION

Reinforcement Theories

Dominant among the explanations of why you find one person more attractive than another is that the more attractive person is the one who reinforces you more. You like those who make you feel good. This sounds pretty straightforward. Some theories put the emphasis on how another rewards you by providing good things or good feelings. Other theories put more emphasis on how in a relationship the rewards are negotiated between two people so that a satisfying exchange occurs.

Reward Explanation. A reinforcement theory derived from classical conditioning guides the thinking of the authors of the second research selection (Byrne, Ervin, & Lamberth, 1970). This model has several elements: interpersonal events can be described as either reinforcing or punishing; reinforcing events are experienced positively, and punishing events negatively; stimuli associated with these events also evoke positive or negative feelings; and the stimuli that evoke positive feelings are liked, while those associated with negative feelings are disliked. Therefore, you like those who reward you, because they come to be associated with positive feelings. This formulation led to a tentative law of attraction: attraction is a positive linear function of the proportion of positive reinforcements (Byrne & Clore, 1970; Byrne & Nelson, 1965). Rewards come in several forms. You may find an encounter rewarding simply because the other person is good to be with; he is competent, attractive, or funny. You may also find another attractive because of indirect rewards; she is powerful or rich and thereby provides you with things or experiences you like.

In the particular reward explanation used by Byrne and his colleagues, much emphasis is placed on the reinforcing properties of *similarity.* In their view, persons strive to interpret their surroundings in logical and coherent ways. In trying to make sense of the world, people rely on their own impressions but also on the confirmation of these impressions by other people. Similarity leads to attraction, because people who are similar on a number of attitudes stand a greater chance of confirming each other's views on other things as well. People who are dissimilar are likely to disagree and make each other uncomfortable about what are the realities of the world around them.

Exchange Model. Reward explanations are useful in predicting initial attraction especially when you ignore the interpersonal interaction and concentrate only on what each person is getting out of the relationship. Interest in how rewards are exchanged and negotiated by two people over time led to the formulation of an exchange model to explain the development of attraction (Homans, 1956; Thibaut & Kelley, 1959).

Based on economic analogies, the exchange model comprises four elements: rewards, costs, outcome, and comparison level. Relationships are believed to involve rewards (defined much as in the reinforcement explanations) and costs, or negative aspects. Subtracting negative costs from positive rewards yields the outcome. If the costs are greater than the rewards, there is a negative outcome; if the reverse is true, a positive outcome results. The model also takes other alternative situations into account. Obviously, positive outcomes result in attraction. But negative outcomes as well may result in sustained relationships when all other alternatives appear worse. Thus, people remain in bad relationships because the costs assigned to the alternative of loneliness are experienced as worse than those of the unpleasant relationship. This cognitive appraisal of a given relationship against other available situations yields a minimum expectation called the *comparison level.*

Criticisms of Reinforcement Explanations. The inadequacies of the exchange model point to the need for clear statements about what specifically is rewarding to whom and when. In present formulations, anything and everything can be rewarding. Much after-the-fact reasoning goes into the argument that, if attraction is present, something must have been rewarding. To be truly explanatory, the rewards must be defined *before* attraction is found; good explanations are predictive.

Reinforcement explanations implicitly suggest that the greater the reward, the better the relationship; the more you experience someone as rewarding you, the more you should like that person. This is not always the case, however. Sometimes receiving more praise (and, therefore, reward) than you think you deserve can bring about guilt feelings. These feelings, in turn, may lead you to dislike and reject the person who makes you feel guilty.

It should be noted, however, that reinforcement explanations have most often been used to explain initial attraction, not sustained relationships. What is rewarding clearly changes as a relationship develops over time. No doubt, as the Whitlam's eyes met 6 feet above the floor in 1942, some interest was sparked; but to understand attraction processes in full, we need to know what has happened between them in the next 35 years.

Arousal and Labeling Theory

Some have reacted to the reinforcement theories of attraction by objecting that they seem particularly deficient in accounting for passionate love. The intense emotion that has inspired so many poets and artists seems ill-accounted for by hedonistic theories. Furthermore, passionate love is often associated with negative feelings of fear, pain, and frustration as well as with positively reinforcing experiences (Berscheid & Walster, 1974). Love is thought to be more fragile and of briefer duration than liking. Testimony, both clinical and literary, abounds on the predictable waning of passionate love in marriage, and advice proliferates on what to do in the "afterglow" (Reik, 1944).

Basing their approach on a two-component theory of emotion (Schachter, 1964) that stresses the connection between physiological arousal and cognitive interpretation of the situation, Walster and Berscheid (1971) proposed that individuals experience passionate love when they are intensely aroused physiologically and when situational cues indicate that passionate love is the right label to apply to the state of arousal. The importance we attribute to intense arousal is reflected in the common doubt expressed by the question "Can this be love if I don't feel anything very powerful?" Labeling occurs when we decide whether it is appropriate to label one's arousal as love. A queasy stomach may be love or may be food poisoning; time and place help us to decide which. This two-component theory would suggest that arousal and labeling play an equally important role in explaining passionate love.

This theory found some unusual support in the finding that men physiologically aroused by being threatened with electric shock were more attracted by a woman confederate than men in the control condition, who were not aroused (Brehm, Gatz, Goethals, McCrommon, & Ward, 1970). Apparently, arousal from an irrelevant event was interpreted by these men as attraction, given a situation facilitating such labeling. Perhaps this process helps explain the sudden intensity of wartime romances. The cues that allow you to label arousal as love are not very explicit and lead to much ambiguity and concern. Berscheid and Walster (1974) report that the one thing college students most often ask about love is how to tell it from infatuation. They cite findings showing that the term *infatuation* is used to describe a love relationship that has ended (Ellis & Harper, 1961). It may be that love is an elusive label for arousal, one for which this culture provides few clear-cut cues.

Rubin (1974a) suggests three components of romantic love: attachment, caring, and intimacy. The first two are attributes or states of the individual evinced by a capacity to become attached to and to care for another. Intimacy adds an interpersonal dimension and links the individual state of being "in love" with the dyadic relationship of loving. The first research selection in this chapter reports Rubin's earlier efforts to distinguish liking, which involves attachment and caring, from loving, which requires the third component—intimacy—as well.

DETERMINANTS OF ATTRACTION

The literature on attraction, especially that concerning encounters among strangers, is extensive and varied. The two selections that follow are representative of two questions frequently posed—"How do we distinguish between liking and love?" and "How are attraction and similarity related?"—and of the methods most commonly used to investigate such questions. The second study clearly belongs to the largest category of attraction research, that in which someone is asked to indicate attraction toward a stranger on the basis of information provided by the experimenter. This study addresses the question dealing with the effect of similarity on attraction. Therefore, in setting that experiment in context, we shall devote a certain amount of attention to the role of similarity in attraction. The first selection deals instead with the problem of distinguishing between liking and loving, and the research reviewed below places that problem in a broader context of determinants of attraction.

Since evaluation is such a dominant aspect of our thinking, it is not surprising that evaluation of others should be invoked in the attempt to understand almost any kind of interpersonal behavior, from working with others, teaching and learning from them, and talking with them to dating and marrying them. This section deals with the determinants of attraction per se and as they pertain to the two selections included here. More general reviews can be found in Lott and Lott (1965), Aronson (1969a), Berscheid and Walster (1969), Murstein (1971), Levinger and Snoek (1972), Byrne and Griffitt (1973), and Huston (1974).

Proximity

Taking another look at the Whitlam's meeting described earlier, we might ask how social psychologists would begin to account for their immediate attraction toward each other. Obviously, for two people to become attracted, they must first have access to each other. For the Whitlams, a party served as occasion for their meeting. Many other settings provide such opportunities, but, whatever the setting, two people must be in some proximity for attraction to develop. For example, in a study of friendship among various married couples in student housing, the distance between apartments appeared to have a clear effect on the choice of friends. People in neighboring apartments were more likely to spend time together than people whose apartments, although located on the same corridor, were farther apart. People with apartments on the same stairwell and in other locations where their traffic patterns met were also more likely to be friends (Festinger, Schachter, & Back, 1950). Not only is proximity necessary for an initial meeting to take place, but proximity plays an important role in the development and maintenance of friendship. Long-lasting relationships between pen pals notwithstanding, intimate friends often become estranged when separated by large distance. Many students attending a college distant from home find that the nature of their relationships with friends back home undergoes profound changes. Without the frequent chance meeting, without easy access to the friends' life patterns, one loses touch. It is no accident that we speak of losing "touch," since touch is the sense modality that requires closest distance.

Personal Attributes

Given that the Whitlams had to be in the same place at the same time in order to meet, attraction was more likely to develop if they met often in the same places and if they possessed some qualities generally considered attractive in their society. Consider the answers often given in the advice column of magazines and newspapers to readers who write to find out what they can do to make friends and become more popular. These readers are generally advised to go to places where others congregate (such as churches, volunteer organizations, and activity centers) and to develop traits that will attract others—specifically, physical attractiveness and competence, which are the most-often cited attributes.

Physical Attractiveness. Research supports the advice columns; an improved appearance through better grooming and well-selected attire is more likely to attract others. One study, for example, revealed that males in simulated interaction with videotapes interacted more with and rated more positively a physically attractive woman than an unattractive one (Barocas & Karoly, 1972). Another study, using both male and female subjects in more naturalistic settings, showed that physical attractiveness was the most powerful indicator of liking in randomly matched computer dates (Walster, Aronson, Abrahams, & Rottman, 1966). Part of the explanation for the dominance of physical attractiveness in initial attraction lies in the widespread belief that physical attractiveness goes with a number of other socially desirable traits (Dion, Berscheid, & Walster, 1972).

While these findings seem to do no more than reflect some truisms of our society, their implications have greater import. There are situations in which our cultural values and norms would suggest that appearance does not and should not matter. Research extending the above findings contradicts these values and norms in at least two contexts—courts and counseling centers. Barocas and Vance (1974) obtained ratings of clinical status and predictions of future adjustment from counselors in a college counseling center for male and female clients seeking help with personal adjustment problems. At another time, they also got ratings of attractiveness of these clients from counselors and receptionists. Regardless of sex of counselor or client, attractiveness ratings by counselors were significantly related to their estimates of how well the clients would do after ending treatment. This relation was particularly pronounced for female clients of female counselors, and the male investigators attributed this finding to the personal knowledge female counselors had of the role that appearance plays in women's "interpersonal success." This study, however, does not permit a directional analysis; that is, it is not possible to say whether sicker clients are judged to be uglier or uglier clients to be sicker and what the validity of these ratings is. Another setting in which, strange as it may seem, physical attractiveness was found to have an effect is the courtroom. Using simulated jury procedures in an examination-cheating case, students rated guilt and appropriate punishment of defendants of the opposite sex (Efran, 1974). The evidence presented was identical for all defendants; their files, however, included their photographs, some of which showed attractive people and others unattractive people. Although only 7% of the jurors said that they believed that physical attractiveness should play a role in judicial decisions, clearly demonstrating the presence of a norm against the influence of attractiveness in courtrooms, in fact, physically attractive defendants were judged less guilty, given less punishment, and found more attractive by jurors. There was some indication that this influence was more pronounced for male jurors with female defendants.

Incidentally, it should be noted that physical attractiveness is not an unqualified asset. For example, when college students were asked to determine the appropriate sentence for defendants found guilty of a crime, good-looking defendants got lighter sentences for crimes deemed unrelated to their looks (burglary) but harsher sentences for crimes in which attractiveness played a part. An attractive woman whose crime involved an investment swindle received a severe penalty, presumably because she used her looks in effecting the crime (Sigall & Ostrove, 1975).

Competence. Given our society's emphasis on competence and achievement, it seems almost as obvious a truism as "beautiful is good" to say "competent is good." And within limits, this is certainly true; people who are good at what they do are better liked than inept and incompetent blunderers. But there is an element of paradox in the relation between a high order of competence and attraction. Aronson (1972) has suggested that an occasional lapse on the part of the highly competent may make him or her more attractive than high competence consistently demonstrated. He noted an increase in Kennedy's popularity as president after the abortive attempt to invade Cuba in the Bay of Pigs incident of 1961. Aronson speculated that an acknowledged blunder on the part of a man seen as highly competent made him appear more human and more likeable. In an experiment to test this idea, students heard tape recordings of candidates for a College Bowl program being asked typical quiz-show questions (Aronson, Willerman, & Floyd, 1966). From the tape recordings it appeared that the candidates were either highly competent (92% correct) or mediocre (30% correct); also, some of them committed a blunder (spilled coffee over themselves) and some did not. The highly competent person who committed the blunder was rated as the most attractive, followed by the competent-no blunder, by the mediocre-no blunder, and last (and least attractive) by the mediocre student who spilled the coffee. As intriguing as the notation of the human flaw as a source of attraction might be, it has its limits. The very low rating received by the average blunderer is not to be ignored. The flaw may make only the distant and very superior more lovable. Kiesler and Goldberg (1968) were unable to replicate these findings. And, furthermore, not everyone finds even the highly competent blunderer attractive; subjects with superior ability were found to be negative toward another superior person who blundered (Mettee & Wilkins, 1972). Also, Deaux (1972) found that a blunder increased attractiveness only when males rated males; all other sex combinations failed to yield this effect. These findings seem to support the proposition that, in general, competence is an attribute that makes a person more attractive—but not to everyone under any circumstances.

Similarity

Soon after people meet, the conversation generally turns to exploring possible similarities. Among students, it is often the "Where are you from? Do you know so-and-so?" routine that helps establish common ground. For the Whitlams, it was their height that apparently represented an initial point of similarity. Clearly being the same height as one's friends is not of high priority for most people, but in the case of the Whitlams, who were unusually tall in comparison to the other guests at the party, perhaps being both over 6 feet tall was of special importance. The fact that their heights made them similar to each other and different from the others around them gave height a salience for this couple that it would not have had for other people or for the Whitlams in another setting. The Whitlams could then proceed from this initial eye contact to discover what else they had in common. They were both university students, which, in those days and in their milieu, suggests similarities in social class and family background. Social class often serves as a vehicle for a wide range of attitudes and tastes, so that new friends may discover with great pleasure the seemingly magic sharing of a fondness for chamber music, foreign films, and ethnic foods. In addition to the real similarities thus uncovered, people will enhance the attraction they feel for one another by assuming further similarities that are still to be tested (Levinger & Breedlove, 1966).

Most of the research on attraction has focused on attitude similarity. In the laboratory, studies have examined the amount of attraction expressed toward another person who is described as holding more or less similar attitudes to those of the respondent. The second research selection in this chapter belongs to this group of studies. In general, these laboratory experiments have found that the greater the similarity, the greater the liking (Byrne, 1971). This linear function has been found to hold not only with the college students on whom most of the laboratory studies were done but also with elementary-school children (Byrne & Griffitt, 1966) and older people (Griffitt, Nelson, & Littlepage, 1972).

In field studies such as Newcomb's (1961) study of dormitory acquaintance processes, similarity was found to operate in more complicated ways. Over the course of a semester, male students developed friendships with those who were similar to themselves in attitudes and values, but this actual similarity was a less powerful predictor of initial attraction, presumably because it takes time to discover such similarity. Several recent field studies on college roommates and urban friendship patterns do not support simple notions of similarity. The combined effects of salience and of the relation between actual and perceived similarities serve to complicate the ways in which specified similarities function in real relationships.

Complementarity

Two people who know each other well are usually able to describe the ways in which they are similar and those in which they differ. Friendship and love incorporate differences as well as similarities. Perhaps you know a couple in which a lively talker is matched with a quiet listener or in which the dominance of one complements the submissiveness of the other. The discovery that such major differences exist in stable, enduring relationships seems at first glance to contradict the notion that similarity plays a strong part in attraction. But it may not be an either-or matter. Some have suggested that attraction is enhanced by similarity in the more transient and culture-bound attitudes and by complementarity in the more enduring personality traits (Winch, 1952). There is conflicting research evidence on the latter point; some people have been found to prefer those similar in personality (Banta & Hetherington, 1963) and others to prefer those opposite in personality (Rychlak, 1965). Whether people prefer similarity or difference may depend on which personality trait is considered. For married couples, the most consistent complementary traits have been found on the dominance-submission dimension (Winch, 1958). It may be that, as a relationship develops over time, complementarity gains precedence over similarity (Kerckhoff & Davis, 1962). The important thing, in any case, appears to be that the similarities and complementarities involved be rewarding to both parties.

An interesting variation on this theme stresses the connection between relationships in one's family and one's later social relationships. Friends and partners in love will get along better and longer if their relationships duplicate their family experiences (Toman, 1971). The best matches are that between the older brother of sisters and the younger sister of brothers and that between the younger brother of sisters and the older sister of brothers. Relationships between only children seem to have the least chance of permanence and success. Comparing divorced and intact marriages, Toman (1971) found support for this duplication of sibling-role relationships.

So far, we have discussed some of *what* is known about attraction; in the pages that follow, we shall concentrate on *how* this information was obtained.

RESEARCH METHODS IN THE STUDY OF ATTRACTION

Like many other psychological phenomena, interpersonal attraction is easy to experience but very hard to define. You are drawn to the "good vibes" of one and withdraw from the "bad vibes" of another, but you are at a loss about how to describe exactly what your feelings are. Social psychologists too have these feelings in their daily lives, and at times they too are at a loss about how to describe them; but in their researcher role, they must define attraction in ways specific enough to allow it to be studied. With specific definitions, it becomes possible to test when and why certain notions about attraction hold and when and why they do not.

We have described in some detail how social psychologists might go about explaining how a pair like the Whitlams met and married. Experimental social psychologists, however, do not stop at speculation. They ask for evidence, and they want to know not only that attraction occurred but how it developed. If your primary sources of information are newspaper stories and friendly gossip, you might attend only to those instances of attraction that confirm your expectations and ignore those that do not. On the other hand, you might be so struck with the differences among various situations that you dismiss any common elements. In contrast, if you are a researcher, your task is to find the common principles while, at the same time, preserving the divergent complexity. To understand a phenomenon does not mean to make it simple or to rob it of richness and depth. How, then, do social psychologists study attraction?

Kaplan (1964) illustrates with a little story the methods of the behavioral scientist. A strange object from outer space falls to earth. After repeated unsuccessful attempts by physicists and astronomers to determine its identity, a psychologist is called in to see what he can discover. After a brief pause, the psychologist asks "What is your name?" and the object responds "Ralph." This anecdote highlights an important difference between the methods available to physical scientists and those available to behavioral scientists. The former cannot ask their "subject" what it is, how it is feeling, or what it thinks about its own behavior. Behavioral scientists, on the other hand, can and do ask for self-reports by means of interviews, questionnaires, and scales of various kinds.

One self-report measure widely used in attraction studies is the six-item Interpersonal Judgment Scale developed by Byrne (1966). Four of the items ask for evaluation of another's intelligence, knowledge of current events, morality, and adjustment. They are included primarily to divert attention from the two specific attraction items, which measure general liking for the other person and desirability of the other as a work partner. Subjects are presented with the following alternatives and asked to indicate which of them most closely expresses their feelings. Each response alternative is assigned a numerical scale value. In the Liking group, the first alternative is given a value of 7 and the last (reflecting strong dislike) is given a score of 1. In the Working Together group, the first alternative (strong dislike) is scored 1 and the last (strong liking) is scored 7. The sum of the scores of the two checked items represents the degree of attraction.

The scale items take the following form:

Liking *(check one)*
___ I feel that I would probably like this person very much.

___I feel that I would probably like this person.
___I feel that I would probably like this person to a slight degree.
___I feel that I would probably neither particularly like nor particularly dislike this person.
___I feel that I would probably dislike this person to a slight degree.
___I feel that I would probably dislike this person.
___I feel that I would probably dislike this person very much.

Working Together in an Experiment *(check one)*
___I believe that I would very much dislike working with this person in an experiment.
___I believe that I would dislike working with this person in an experiment.
___I believe that I would dislike working with this person in an experiment to a slight degree.
___I believe that I would neither particularly dislike nor particularly enjoy working with this person in an experiment.
___I believe that I would enjoy working with this person in an experiment to a slight degree.
___I believe that I would enjoy working with this person in an experiment.
___I believe that I would very much enjoy working with this person in an experiment.*

Laboratory Experiments

In literally dozens of studies using the Interpersonal Judgment Scale, Byrne (1969) and his colleagues explored the relation between attitudinal similarity and attraction. In a representative laboratory experiment (Byrne, 1961), college-student subjects, who had been given a 26-item attitude scale earlier in the semester, were recruited for a study of interpersonal judgment. They were given certain information about another individual and then asked to make several judgments concerning that person. The subjects were randomly assigned to two experimental groups—similar-attitude group and dissimilar-attitude group. In the similar-attitude group, subjects were presented with a scale, ostensibly filled out by a stranger, that matched exactly their own responses to the same scale. Subjects in the dissimilar-attitude group received a scale reflecting the direct opposites of their views. Analysis of responses on the Interpersonal Judgment Scale revealed a significant effect for similarity: people like those whom they perceive as similar to themselves more than those whom they perceive as dissimilar. Because no actual interaction takes place between subject and stimulus person, this technique has been referred to as the *simulated-stranger* or *phantom-other method*.

It may have occurred to you while reading the above description that the experimenter took a somewhat indirect route in order to find out whether attitude similarity elicits attraction. "Phantoms" were engaged, and pertinent questions buried amid a host of irrelevant ones. The purpose was to reduce the tendency people have to provide what they think is the "right" answer rather than one that reflects how they really feel. If the typical Byrne procedure seems a trifle indirect (although perhaps necessarily so), the following laboratory experiment conducted by Aronson and Linder (1965) will probably come across as downright circuitous.

The experiment tried to find out whether you prefer someone who changes his view of you from negative to positive or someone who keeps feelings positive toward you all along. Reasoning that a more spontaneous response would be forthcoming if an individual were actually in a certain situation instead of just being asked to imagine it, the experimenters directed a rather complicated script to be enacted in the context of a verbal conditioning experiment. The script went along the following lines: female subject talks with preprogrammed experimental confederate, overhears confederate evaluating her to the experimenter, engages in another conversation with confederate,

*From *An Introduction to Personality: A Research Approach,* by D. Byrne. © 1966. Reprinted by permission of Prentice-Hall, Inc., Englewood Cliffs, New Jersey.

eavesdrops again, converses once more, overhears again, and so on through a number of combinations of interactions and overheard evaluations.

As presented here, this plot description is tightly compressed. The experimenters provided a cover story to make these conversations and eavesdroppings plausible, but the script was nonetheless a complicated experience for the subjects. Female subjects were randomly assigned to four different groups, each characterized by a different sequence of expressed feelings toward the subject. In one group, the confederate reacted positively toward the subject throughout all seven interchanges; in a second group, the confederate responded negatively across all seven sessions; in the third group, the confederate began with negative reactions toward the subject but gradually came around to regard the subject positively by the final session; and the fourth group reversed that sequence by starting positively and ending negatively. Subjects were told that they were helping the experimenter "run" a subject (actually a confederate) in order to make these pairings of conversation and observations seem plausible. Finally, subjects were asked by an interviewer to rate their feelings toward the confederate on a 21-point scale from -10 to $+10$. This occurred only after the experimenters went to great lengths to present a plausible cover story as to why this evaluation was necessary. The hypothesis that the confederate would be liked better in the Negative-Then-Positive condition than in the Positive-Positive condition was confirmed. The hypothesis that the confederate would be liked better in the Negative-Negative condition than in the Positive-Negative condition was not statistically supported.

While in many cases it would seem appropriate and enlightening to ask a person directly what he or she feels toward another, this may not always be the best approach. When you are asked whether you like someone, the direct reply is but one of several that might enter your mind. You may not be totally clear yourself concerning what your feelings are at the moment. You may also wonder about what the interviewer will think of you, who will know your evaluation, whether the other person reciprocates your feelings, and, more generally, how you can best present yourself in the situation. For this reason, questionnaires are often regarded as reactive measures; that is, you react to the process of being questioned as well as to the question itself.

Field Experiments

To have a friend is to have someone we can talk to about day-to-day happenings as well as about more private and intimate aspects of ourselves. One line of investigation into the friendship process has inquired about the role of self-disclosure. Rubin (1974b) conducted a field experiment in an airport departure lounge to assess the effects of varying degrees of self-disclosure and trust on reciprocal disclosures by strangers. The procedure involved having a male or a female college student approach a solitary man or woman in a departure lounge and ask whether the subject would write a sentence or two about himself or herself for a class project on handwriting analysis. The experimenter-student explained that the class would be comparing the handwritings of class members with the handwritings of other people; therefore, the experimenter-student would write a little about himself or herself first. Subjects were asked to look at the experimenter's sample and then to write a sentence or two about themselves. The level of intimacy of the experimenter's sample (low, medium, or high) constituted an independent variable. Handwriting samples from the subjects were then analyzed for the degree of intimacy of their content. In line with the experimenter's intimacy hypothesis, reciprocity was found; subjects responded to varying levels of self-disclosure in like fashion. A second independent variable, involving whether the experimenter mechanically copied the sample from a prepared card or apparently created it on the spot, was also included.

When subjects received highly intimate disclosures ostensibly created on the spot, they reacted with distrust and retreated to lower levels of disclosure.

As social psychologists have entered the real world to do field experimentation, they have found themselves in a wide variety of settings, including zoos, subways, supermarkets, and race tracks, but perhaps none so unusual as that in a study reported by Walster, Walster, Piliavin, and Schmidt (1973). In an effort to test whether the strategy of "playing hard to get" results in greater attraction than the strategy of being "easy," these researchers turned to a prostitute's chambers. The prostitute, serving as experimenter, either played hard to get by indicating that she was busy with other activities and hence selective about her clients or acted in the conventional fashion. The dependent variable was measured in two ways: the prostitute's assessment of the client's attraction to her and the number of times within the next 30 days that the client sought further contact. The hard-to-get hypothesis was not supported. The authors report that "if anything, those clients who were told that the prostitute did not take just anyone were *less* likely to call back and liked the prostitute less than did other clients" (p. 116).

Although the two studies above are relatively comparable with respect to the degree of manipulation of antecedent conditions in a field context, they vary in the amount of subject awareness. Apparently, subjects in the Walster, Walster, Piliavin, and Schmidt (1973) study were totally unaware that their behavior was under experimental scrutiny. Subjects in the Rubin (1974b) study, while aware that something about themselves was being tested, probably were less experimentally aware than subjects in a laboratory setting. The dramatic settings selected for these studies contribute to their interest but may also give rise to questions about flashy merchandising, particularly in the case of the prostitute study.

Naturalistic Observation and Archival Search

Although a great deal of social-psychological research involves high subject awareness and high manipulation of antecedent conditions, other kinds of research methodology, involving a low amount of awareness and manipulation, can also lead to informative results. One such kind is methodology that avails itself of the reservoir of information provided by archival data. With respect to attraction, people unwittingly leave traces and signs of their patterns of attraction in a number of accessible places. For example, Carey (1969) compared romantic song lyrics of the 1950s with those of the 1960s and found that the songs of the 1960s described attraction as more actively controlled by the participants and left less in the hands of fate. The method involved selecting 227 different songs from the summer issues of four magazines—*Hit Parader, Song Hits Magazine, Country Song Round Up,* and *Billboard*—as well as the top 30 listings of a San Francisco radio station. Lyrics were then classified on the basis of two criteria: acceptance of romantic notions about relationships (that is, fatalistic acceptance of demands of others) and open or implied criticism of conventional society. Carey concluded that the comparison revealed a major difference in orientation between the popular songs of the 1950s and those of the 1960s. Autonomy of the sexes, freedom of choice, and the legitimacy of physical attraction without love were all newly sung about in the 1960s.

Another kind of research methodology involving low awareness and manipulation is that in which behavior is unobtrusively observed in natural settings. Sechrest (1969) used the campus of the University of Hawaii as a natural setting for the observation of physical contact in two cultural groups. An earlier study by Church and Insko (1965), using a self-report measure, found different attitudes toward sex among Hawaiian students of various Oriental ancestries. Sechrest chose not to ask students of different cultural backgrounds how much physical contact they had with members of the opposite sex; instead, he systematically observed them in a variety of campus locations. Observers were instructed to sample mixed-sex couples representing four combinations of culture and sex: Caucasian couples, Oriental couples, Caucasian male-Oriental female couples, and Oriental male-Caucasian female couples. Then the couples were coded with regard to the type of physical contact in which they engaged: no contact, holding hands, arm in arm, embracing, and kissing. Results showed that couples of Oriental extraction displayed less physical contact than did Caucasian couples and that mixed-culture couples demonstrated an intermediate amount of contact. These results were found to be consistent with the earlier findings regarding verbal attitudes toward sex.

Unobtrusive methods such as those using archival search and systematic observation require ingenuity both in locating the data and in tracing causality so as to reveal social psychological processes. If care is taken to assure validity, these methods can provide access to a rich store of information otherwise inaccessible.

Surveys and Interviews

Investigators often prefer the more obtrusive methods, like surveys and interviews, because the subject's own point of view is what is being sought. Laumann (1969), for example, was interested in a number of issues concerning friendships of urban men. He randomly selected his subjects from over a thousand native-born, White males that had been chosen for a larger study. Subjects were interviewed in their homes and were asked, among other things, to indicate their own age, occupation, education, political-party preference, and religious preference as well as those of their closest friends. A randomly selected friend was telephoned for a brief interview after his full name and address had been furnished by the original respondent. Comparison of the friend's self-report with the original respondent's views of the friend's characteristics revealed higher accuracy for the relatively objective characteristics (age and occupation) than for the less objective characteristics (political attitudes). Errors, however, were not randomly distributed; when present, they were slanted in the direction of the respondent's own preferences. In addition, the friend was asked the same six questions concerning educational and political values that the respondent had answered. Interestingly enough, there was scant support for the hypothesis that there is high attitude agreement among friends. It would seem then that long-term friends do not show the attitude-similarity effects that laboratory experiments have so consistently found.

Studies concerned with continuing and developing relationships (in which partners are near-strangers at the beginning of the study) are rare. By far, the greatest number of studies in social psychology are one-shot affairs. Longitudinal studies in general are notable in their scarcity. An exception was Newcomb's study of what he called the "acquaintance process" (1961). Newcomb rented a house large enough for about 17 students. He recruited unacquainted male freshmen, offering them free room and board in exchange for their participation in some social-psychological research. Before arrival, the men completed lengthy questionnaires concerning their attitudes and values on a wide variety of issues including the policies that should be followed in the house with regard to eating and cleaning, personal habits, sex, and public affairs. In addition, they were asked to make guesses about their future roommates' attitudes on the same issues. Each subsequent week, subjects were again asked about some subset of their attitudes, the attitudes of the other men, the nature of their friendships with the other subjects, and the amount of contact they had with one another. Newcomb found that knowing how similar the male students were initially made it possible for him to predict who would eventually become whose friend. The acquaintance process took time presumably because in dormitory living it took the men a while to discover those who were actually similar to themselves.

TWO RESEARCH EXAMPLES

Product Description

Both of the following studies are distinctive in the literature dealing with attraction in that they combine obtrusive and unobtrusive measures. Both studies have borrowed from the emerging literature on nonverbal communication, which suggests that people can convey information about their feelings through gaze and interpersonal distance. In the first selection, Rubin relates attraction, as measured by a scale, to gaze; in the second, Byrne, Ervin, and Lamberth assess attraction by means of interpersonal space and self-report scale responses. In this second experiment, although the procedure did begin in the laboratory, the focus is on the way in which the manipulated variable of similarity affects attraction in a relatively naturalistic context. Byrne, Ervin, and Lamberth predicted that (1) the greater the similarity, the greater the attraction, (2) the greater the physical attractiveness, the greater the attraction, and (3) the relation between attraction and similarity is greater when people are led to focus on their similarity. These hypotheses were tested by comparing the simulated-stranger procedure with a "real-life" computer dating condition. Students were selected for attitude similarity or dissimilarity on the basis of a 50-item attitude scale administered to 420 undergraduates. Male-female pairs were selected for having made many or few similar responses; some of the pairs were told about this similarity and others were not. Each couple was sent from the laboratory on a half-hour "Coke date." When the couple returned, the interpersonal distance the subjects maintained while standing in front of the experimenter's desk was noted; then the subjects were asked to evaluate each other on the Interpersonal Judgment Scale (see attraction items on pp. 27–28). Results confirmed the experimenters' first two predictions but not the third one. A follow-up was done at the end of the semester to check on the durability of the findings obtained.

The first selection, by Rubin, presents three progressive steps, only the last of which is aimed at testing specific hypotheses. First, Rubin developed two scales to measure the difference between loving and liking. Second, he had students respond to the scales for target figures of differing intimacy and checked whether in fact the students applied love-scale items more often to dating partners than to friends. Finally, he conducted a laboratory study to assess in some behavioral fashion the construct validity of the love scale. Rubin wanted to show that lovers and "likers" not only check off different scale items but behave differently in other ways as well. He predicted that pairs high on the love scale would gaze into each other's eyes more than pairs low on the scale. Results supported Rubin's prediction.

As indicated in Chapter 1, it pays to know what you're looking for when you go shopping. As you read the two following selections, know what you are looking for by keeping the following questions in mind.

Consumer Checklist

- How specific is the list of ingredients on the product label?
    How were the samples picked?
    How many people took part in each phase of these studies?
- How much was product testing a part of the manufacturing process?
    What kind of measures were used?
    Were the scale items easy to say no to?
    What was the purpose of the followup in the second selection?
    How was scale validity established in the first selection?

MEASUREMENT OF ROMANTIC LOVE[1]

ZICK RUBIN[2]

Department of Social Relations, Harvard University

This study reports the initial results of an attempt to introduce and validate a social-psychological construct of romantic love. Starting with the assumption that love is an interpersonal attitude, an internally consistent paper-and-pencil love scale was developed. The conception of romantic love included three components: affiliative and dependent need, a predisposition to help, and an orientation of exclusiveness and absorption. Love-scale scores were only moderately correlated with scores on a parallel scale of "liking," which reflected a more traditional conception of interpersonal attraction. The validity of the love scale was assessed in a questionnaire study and a laboratory experiment. On the basis of the emerging conception of love, it was predicted that college dating couples who loved each other a great deal (as categorized by their love-scale scores) would spend more time gazing into one another's eyes than would couples who loved each other to a lesser degree. The prediction was confirmed.

Love is generally regarded to be the deepest and most meaningful of sentiments. It has occupied a preeminent position in the art and literature of every age, and it is presumably experienced, at least occasionally, by the vast majority of people. In Western culture, moreover, the association between love and marriage gives it a unique status as a link between the individual and the structure of society.

In view of these considerations, it is surprising to discover that social psychologists have devoted virtually no attention to love. Although interpersonal attraction has been a major focus of social-psychological theory and research, workers in this area have not attempted to conceptualize love as an independent entity. For Heider (1958), for example, "loving" is merely intense liking—there is no discussion of possible qualitative differences between the two. Newcomb (1960) does not include love on his list of the "varieties of interpersonal attraction." Even in experiments directed specifically at "romantic" attraction (e.g., Walster, 1965), the dependent measure is simply a verbal report of "liking."

The present research was predicated on the assumption that love may be independently conceptualized and measured. In keeping with a strategy of construct validation (cf. Cronbach & Meehl, 1955), the attempts to define love, to measure it, and to assess its relationships to other variables are all seen as parts of a single endeavor. An initial assumption in this enterprise is that love is an *attitude* held by a person toward a particular other person, involving predispositions to think, feel, and behave in certain ways toward that other person. This assumption places love in the mainstream of social-psychological approaches to interpersonal attraction, alongside such other varieties of attraction as liking, admiration, and respect (cf. Newcomb, 1960).

The view of love as a multifaceted attitude implies a broader perspective than that held by those theorists who view love as an "emotion," a "need," or a set of behaviors. On the other hand, its linkage to a particular target implies a more restricted view than that held by those who regard love as an aspect of the individual's personality or experience which transcends particular persons and situations (e.g., Fromm, 1956). As Orlinsky (1970) has

---

[1] This report is based on a doctoral dissertation submitted to the University of Michigan. The research was supported by a predoctoral fellowship from the National Institute of Mental Health and by a grant-in-aid from the Society for the Psychological Study of Social Issues. The author is grateful to Theodore M. Newcomb, chairman of the dissertation committee, for his invaluable guidance and support. Mitchell Baris, Cheryl Eisenman, Linda Muller, Judy Newman, Marlyn Rame, Stuart Katz, Edward Krupat, and Phillip Shaver served as observers in the experiment, and Mr. Shaver also helped design and assemble the equipment.

[2] Requests for reprints should be sent to the author, Department of Social Relations, Harvard University, Cambridge, Massachusetts 02138.

From *Journal of Personality and Social Psychology,* 1970, *16*(2), 265–273. Copyright 1970 by American Psychological Association. Reprinted by Permission.

suggested, there may well be important common elements among different varieties of "love" (e.g., filial love, marital love, love of God). The focus of the present research, however, was restricted to *romantic love,* which may be defined simply as love between unmarried opposite-sex peers, of the sort which could possibly lead to marriage.

The research had three major phases. First, a paper-and-pencil love scale was developed. Second, the love scale was employed in a questionnaire study of student dating couples. Third, the predictive validity of the love scale was assessed in a laboratory experiment.

Developing a Love Scale

The development of a love scale was guided by several considerations:

1. Inasmuch as the content of the scale would constitute the initial conceptual definition of romantic love, its items must be grounded in existing theoretical and popular conceptions of love.

2. Responses to these items, if they are tapping a single underlying attitude, must be highly intercorrelated.

3. In order to establish the discriminant validity (cf. Campbell, 1960) of the love scale, it was constructed in conjunction with a parallel scale of liking. The goal was to develop internally consistent scales of love and of liking which would be conceptually distinct from one another and which would, in practice, be only moderately intercorrelated.

The first step in this procedure was the assembling of a large pool of questionnaire items referring to a respondent's attitude toward a particular other person (the "target person"). Half of these items were suggested by a wide range of speculations about the nature of love (e.g., de Rougemont, 1940; Freud, 1955; Fromm, 1956; Goode, 1959; Slater, 1963). These items referred to physical attraction, idealization, a predisposition to help, the desire to share emotions and experiences, feelings of exclusiveness and absorption, felt affiliative and dependent needs, the holding of ambivalent feelings, and the relative unimportance of universalistic norms in the relationship. The other half of the items were suggested by the existing theoretical and empirical literature on interpersonal attraction (or liking; cf. Lindzey & Byrne, 1968). They included references to the desire to affiliate with the target in various settings, evaluation of the target on several dimensions, the salience of norms of responsibility and equity, feelings of respect and trust, and the perception that the target is similar to oneself.

To provide some degree of consensual validation for this initial categorization of items, two successive panels of student and faculty judges sorted the items into love and liking categories, relying simply on their personal understanding of the connotations of the two labels. Following this screening procedure, a revised set of 70 items was administered to 198 introductory psychology students during their regular class sessions. Each respondent completed the items with reference to his girlfriend or boyfriend (if he had one), and also with reference to a nonromantically viewed "platonic friend" of the opposite sex. The scales of love and of liking which were employed in the subsequent phases of the research were arrived at through factor analyses of these responses. Two separate factor analyses were performed—one for responses with reference to boyfriends and girlfriends (or "lovers") and one for responses with reference to platonic friends. In each case, there was a general factor accounting for a large proportion of the total variance. The items loading highest on this general factor, particularly for lovers, were almost exclusively those which had previously been categorized as love items. These high-loading items defined the more circumscribed conception of love adopted. The items forming the liking scale were based on those which loaded highly on the second factor with respect to platonic friends. Details of the scale development procedure are reported in Rubin (1969, Ch. 2).

The items forming the love and liking scales are listed in Table 1. Although it was constructed in such a way as to be factorially unitary, the content of the love scale points to three major components of romantic love:

TABLE 1
Means, Standard Deviations, and Correlations with Total Scale Scores of Love-Scale and Liking-Scale Items

Love-scale items	Women $\bar{X}$	SD	r^a Love	r Like	Men $\bar{X}$	SD	r^a Love	r Like
1. If ___ were feeling badly, my first duty would be to cheer him (her) up.	7.56	1.79	.393	.335	7.28	1.67	.432	.304
2. I feel that I can confide in ___ about virtually everything.	7.77	1.73	.524	.274	7.80	1.65	.425	.408
3. I find it easy to ignore ___'s faults.	5.83	1.90	.184	.436	5.61	2.13	.248	.428
4. I would do almost anything for ___.	7.15	2.03	.630	.341	7.35	1.83	.724	.530
5. I feel very possessive toward ___.	6.26	2.36	.438	−.005	6.24	2.33	.481	.342
6. If I could never be with ___, I would feel miserable.	6.52	2.43	.633	.276	6.58	2.26	.699	.422
7. If I were lonely, my first thought would be to seek ___ out.	7.90	1.72	.555	.204	7.75	1.54	.546	.328
8. One of my primary concerns is ___'s welfare.	7.47	1.62	.606	.218	7.59	1.56	.683	.290
9. I would forgive ___ for practically anything.	6.77	2.03	.551	.185	6.54	2.05	.394	.237
10. I feel responsible for ___'s well-being.	6.35	2.25	.582	.178	6.67	1.88	.548	.307
11. When I am with ___, I spend a good deal of time just looking at him (her).	5.42	2.36	.271	.137	5.94	2.18	.491	.318
12. I would greatly enjoy being confided in by ___.	8.35	1.14	.498	.292	7.88	1.47	.513	.383
13. It would be hard for me to get along without ___.	6.27	2.54	.676	.254	6.19	2.16	.663	.464

Liking-scale items	Women $\bar{X}$	SD	r Love	r^b Like	Men $\bar{X}$	SD	r Love	r^b Like
1. When I am with ___, we are almost always in the same mood.	5.51	1.72	.163	.270	5.30	1.77	.235	.294
2. I think that ___ is unusually well-adjusted.	6.36	2.07	.093	.452	6.04	1.98	.339	.610
3. I would highly recommend ___ for a responsible job.	7.87	1.77	.199	.370	7.90	1.55	.281	.422
4. In my opinion, ___ is an exceptionally mature person.	6.72	1.93	.190	.559	6.40	2.00	.372	.609
5. I have great confidence in ___'s good judgment.	7.37	1.59	.310	.538	6.68	1.80	.381	.562
6. Most people would react very favorably to ___ after a brief acquaintance.	7.08	2.00	.167	.366	7.32	1.73	.202	.287
7. I think that ___ and I are quite similar to each other.	6.12	2.24	.292	.410	5.94	2.14	.407	.417
8. I would vote for ___ in a class or group election.	7.29	2.00	.057	.381	6.28	2.36	.299	.297
9. I think that ___ is one of those people who quickly wins respect.	7.11	1.67	.182	.588	6.71	1.69	.370	.669
10. I feel that ___ is an extremely intelligent person.	8.04	1.42	.193	.155	7.48	1.50	.377	.415
11. ___ is one of the most likable people I know.	6.99	1.98	.346	.402	7.33	1.63	.438	.514
12. ___ is the sort of person whom I myself would like to be.	5.50	2.00	.253	.340	4.71	2.26	.417	.552
13. It seems to me that it is very easy for ___ to gain admiration.	6.71	1.87	.176	.528	6.53	1.64	.345	.519

Note.—Based on responses of 158 couples. Scores on individual items can range from 1 to 9, with 9 always indicating the positive end of the continuum.
a Correlation between item and love scale total *minus that item.*
b Correlation between item and liking scale total *minus that item.*

1. *Affiliative and dependent need*—for example, "If I could never be with _____, I would feel miserable"; "It would be hard for me to get along without _____."

2. *Predisposition to help*—for example, "If _____ were feeling badly, my first duty would be to cheer him (her) up"; "I would do almost anything for _____."

3. *Exclusiveness and absorption*—for example, "I feel very possessive toward _____"; "I feel that I can confide in _____ about virtually everything."

The emerging conception of romantic love, as defined by the content of the scale, has an eclectic flavor. The affiliative and dependent need component evokes both Freud's (1955) view of love as sublimated sexuality and Harlow's (1958) equation of love with attachment behavior. The predisposition to help is congruent with Fromm's (1956) analysis of the components of love, which he identifies as care, responsibility, respect, and knowledge. Absorption in a single other person is the aspect of love which is pointed to most directly by Slater's (1963) analysis of the social-structural implications of dyadic intimacy. The conception of liking, as defined by the liking-scale items, includes components of favorable evaluation and respect for the target person, as well as the perception that the target is similar to oneself. It is in reasonably close accord with measures of "attraction" employed in previous research (cf. Lindzey & Byrne, 1968).

Questionnaire Study

The 13-item love and liking scales, with their component items interspersed, were included in a questionnaire administered in October 1968 to 158 dating (but non-engaged) couples at the University of Michigan, recruited by means of posters and newspaper ads. In addition to the love and liking scales, completed first with respect to one's dating partner and later with respect to a close, same-sex friend, the questionnaire contained several personality scales and requests for background information about the dating relationship. Each partner completed the questionnaire individually and was paid $1 for taking part. The modal couple consisted of a junior man and a sophomore or junior woman who had been dating for about 1 year.

Each item on the love and liking scales was responded to on a continuum ranging from "Not at all true; disagree completely" (scored as 1) to "Definitely true; agree completely" (scored as 9), and total scale scores were computed by summing scores on individual items. Table 1 presents the mean scores and standard deviations for the items, together with the correlations between individual items and total scale scores. In several cases an inappropriate pattern of correlations was obtained, such as a love item correlating more highly with the total liking score than with the total love score (minus that item). These inappropriate patterns suggest specific revisions for future versions of the scales. On the whole, however, the pattern of correlations was appropriate. The love scale had high internal consistency (coefficient alpha was .84 for women and .86 for men)[3] and, as desired, was only moderately correlated with the liking scale ($r = .39$ for women and .60 for men). The finding that love and liking were more highly correlated among men than among women ($z = 2.48$, $p < .02$) was unexpected. It provides at least suggestive support for the notion that women discriminate more sharply between the two sentiments than men do (cf. Banta & Hetherington, 1963).

Table 2 reveals that the love scores of men (for their girlfriends) and women (for their boyfriends) were almost identical. Women *liked* their boyfriends somewhat more than they were liked in return, however ($t = 2.95$, $df = 157$, $p < .01$). Inspection of the item means in Table 1 indicates that this sex difference may be attributed to the higher ratings given by women to their boyfriends on such "task-related" dimensions as intelligence, good judgment, and leadership potential. To the extent that these items accurately represent the construct of liking, men may indeed tend to be more "likable" (but not more "lovable") than women. Table 2 also reveals, however, that there was no such sex

TABLE 2
Love and Liking for Dating Partners and Same-Sex Friends

Index	Women $\bar{X}$	Women SD	Men $\bar{X}$	Men SD
Love for partner	89.46	15.54	89.37	15.16
Liking for partner	88.48	13.40	84.65	13.81
Love for friend	65.27	17.84	55.07	16.08
Liking for friend	80.47	16.47	79.10	18.07

Note.—Based on responses of 158 couples.

[3] Coefficient alpha of the liking scale was .81 for women and .83 for men.

difference with respect to the respondents' liking for their same-sex friends. The mean liking-for-friend scores for the two sexes were virtually identical. Thus, the data do not support the conclusion that men are generally more likable than women, but only that they are liked more in the context of the dating relationship.

Table 2 also indicates that women tended to *love* their same-sex friends more than men did ($t = 5.33$, $df = 314$, $p < .01$). This result is in accord with cultural stereotypes concerning male and female friendships. It is more socially acceptable for female than for male friends to speak of themselves as "loving" one another, and it has been reported that women tend to confide in same-sex friends more than men do (Jourard & Lasakow, 1958). Finally, the means presented in Table 2 show that whereas both women and men *liked* their dating partners only slightly more than they liked their same-sex friends, they *loved* their dating partners much more than their friends.

Further insight into the conceptual distinction between love and liking may be derived from the correlational results presented in Table 3. As expected, love scores were highly correlated both with respondents' reports of whether or not they were "in love" and with their estimates of the likelihood that they would marry their current dating partners. Liking scores were only moderately correlated with these indexes.

Although love scores were highly related to perceived marriage probability, these variables may be distinguished from one another on empirical as well as conceptual grounds. As Table 3 indicates, the length of time that the couple had been dating was unrelated to love scores among men, and only slightly related among women. In contrast, the respondents' perceptions of their closeness to marriage were significantly correlated with length of dating among both men and women. These results are in keeping with the common observations that although love may develop rather quickly, progress toward marriage typically occurs only over a longer period of time.

The construct validity of the love scale was further attested to by the findings that

TABLE 3
INTERCORRELATIONS AMONG INDEXES OF ATTRACTION

Index	1	2	3	4
Women				
1. Love for partner				
2. Liking for partner	.39			
3. "In love"[a]	.59	.28		
4. Marriage probability[b]	.59	.32	.65	
5. Dating length[c]	.16	.01	.27	.46
Men				
1. Love for partner				
2. Liking for partner	.60			
3. "In love"[a]	.52	.35		
4. Marriage probability[b]	.59	.35	.62	
5. Dating length[c]	.04	−.03	.22	.38

Note.—Based on responses of 158 couples. With an N of 158, a correlation of .16 is significant at the .05 level and a correlation of .21 is significant at the .01 level (two-tailed values).

[a] Responses to question, "Would you say that you and ___ are in love?", scored on a 3-point scale ("No" = 0, "Uncertain" = 1, "Yes" = 2).

[b] Responses to question, "What is your best estimate of the likelihood that you and ___ will marry one another?" Scale ranges from 0 (0%–10% probability) to 9 (91%–100% probability).

[c] The correlation across couples between the two partners' reports of the length of time they had been dating (in months) was .967. In this table, "dating length" was arbitrarily equated with the woman's estimates.

love for one's dating partner was only slightly correlated with love for one's same-sex friend ($r = .18$ for women, and $r = .15$ for men) and was uncorrelated with scores on the Marlowe-Crowne Social Desirability Scale ($r = .01$ for both women and men). These findings are consistent with the assumption that the love scale was tapping an attitude toward a specific other person, rather than more general interpersonal orientations or response tendencies. Finally, the love scores of the two partners tended to be moderately symmetrical. The correlation across couples between the woman's and the man's love was .42. The corresponding intracouple correlation with respect to liking was somewhat lower ($r = .28$). With respect to the partners' estimates of the probability of marriage, on the other hand, the intracouple correlation was considerably higher ($r = .68$).

LABORATORY EXPERIMENT: LOVE AND GAZING

Although the questionnaire results provided evidence for the construct validity of the emerging conception of romantic love, it remained to be determined whether love-scale scores could be used to predict behavior outside the realm of questionnaire responses. The notion that romantic love includes a component of exclusiveness and absorption led to the prediction that in an unstructured laboratory situation, dating partners who loved each other a great deal would gaze into one another's eyes more than would partners who loved each other to a lesser degree.

The test of the prediction involved a comparison between "strong-love" and "weak-love" couples, as categorized by their scores on the love scale. To control for the possibility that "strong" and "weak" lovers differ from one another in their more general interpersonal orientations, additional groups were included in which subjects were paired with opposite-sex strangers. The love scores of subjects in these "apart" groups were equated with those of the subjects who were paired with their own dating partners (the "together" groups). In contrast to the prediction for the together groups, no difference in the amount of eye contact engaged in by the strong-apart and weak-apart groups was expected.

Method

Subjects

Two pools of subjects were established from among the couples who completed the questionnaire. Those couples in which both partners scored above the median on the love scale (92 or higher) were designated strong-love couples, and those in which both partners scored below the median were designated weak-love couples. Couples in which one partner scored above and the other below the median were not included in the experiment. Within each of the two pools, the couples were divided into two subgroups with approximately equal love scores. One subgroup in each pool was randomly designated as a together group, the other as an apart group. Subjects in the together group were invited to take part in the experiment together with their boyfriends or girlfriends. Subjects in the apart groups were requested to appear at the experimental session individually, where they would be paired with other people's boyfriends or girlfriends. Pairings in the apart conditions were made on the basis of scheduling convenience, with the additional guideline that women should not be paired with men who were younger than themselves. In this way, four experimental groups were created: strong together (19 pairs), weak together (19 pairs), strong apart (21 pairs), and weak apart (20 pairs). Only 5 of the couples contacted (not included in the above cell sizes) refused to participate—2 who had been preassigned to the strong together group, 2 to the weak together group, and 1 to the strong apart group. No changes in the preassignment of subjects to groups were requested or permitted. As desired, none of the pairs of subjects created in the apart groups were previously acquainted. Each subject was paid $1.25 for his participation.

Sessions

When both members of a scheduled pair had arrived at the laboratory, they were seated across a 52-inch table from one another in an observation room. The experimenter, a male graduate student, explained that the experiment was part of a study of communication among dating and unacquainted couples. The subjects were then asked to read a paragraph about "a couple contemplating marriage" (one of the "choice situations" developed by Wallach & Kogan, 1959). They were told that they would subsequently discuss the case, and that their discussion would be tape recorded. The experimenter told the pair that it would take a few minutes for him to set up the tape recorder, and that meanwhile they could talk about anything except the case to be discussed. He then left the room. After 1 minute had elapsed (to allow the subjects to adapt themselves to the situation), their visual behavior was observed for a 3-minute period.[4]

Measurement

The subjects' visual behavior was recorded by two observers stationed behind a one-way mirror, one facing each subject. Each observer pressed a button, which was connected to a cumulative clock, whenever the subject he was watching was looking across the table at his partner's face. The readings on these clocks provided measures of *individual gazing*. In addition, a third clock was activated whenever the two observers were pressing their buttons simultaneously. The reading on this clock provided a measure of *mutual gazing*. The mean percentage of agreement between pairs of observers in 12 reliability trials, interspersed among the experimental sessions, was 92.8. The observers never knew whether a pair of subjects was in a strong-love or weak-love group. They were sometimes able to infer whether the pair was in the together or the apart condition, however. Each observer's assignment alternated between watching the woman and watching the man in successive sessions.

Results

Table 4 reveals that as predicted, there was a tendency for strong-together couples to engage in more mutual gazing (or "eye con-

[4] Visual behavior was also observed during a subsequent 3-minute discussion period. The results for this period, which differed from those for the prediscussion waiting period, are reported in Rubin (1969, Ch. 5).

TABLE 4

Mutual Gazing (in seconds)

Group	n	$\bar{X}$	SD
Strong together	19	56.2	17.1
Weak together	18[a]	44.7	25.0
Strong apart	21	46.7	29.6
Weak apart	20	40.0	17.5

[a] Because of an equipment failure, the mutual-gazing measure was not obtained for one couple in the weak-together group.

TABLE 5

Mutual Focus

Group	n	$\bar{X}$	SD
Strong together	19	44.0	9.8
Weak together	18	34.7	14.0
Strong apart	21	35.3	14.6
Weak apart	20	32.5	9.4

Note.—Mutual focus = $100 \times \dfrac{\text{mutual gazing}}{\text{woman's nonmutual gazing} + \text{man's nonmutual gazing} + \text{mutual gazing}}$

tact") than weak-together couples ($t = 1.52$, $p < .07$, one-tailed). Although there was also a tendency for strong-apart couples to make more eye contact than weak-apart couples, it was not a reliable one ($t = .92$).

Another approach toward assessing the couples' visual behavior is to consider the percentage of "total gazing" time (i.e., the amount of time during which at least one of the partners was looking at the other) which was occupied by mutual gazing. This measure, to be referred to as *mutual focus*, differs from mutual gazing in that it specifically takes into account the individual gazing tendencies of the two partners. It is possible, for example, that neither member of a particular pair gazed very much at his partner, but that when they did gaze, they did so simultaneously. Such a pair would have a low mutual gazing score, but a high mutual focus score. Within certain limits, the converse of this situation is also possible. Using this measure (see Table 5), the difference between the strong-together and the weak-together groups was more striking than it was in the case of mutual gazing ($t = 2.31$, $p < .02$, one-tailed). The difference between the strong-apart and weak-apart groups was clearly not significant ($t = .72$).

Finally, the individual gazing scores of subjects in the four experimental groups are presented in Table 6. The only significant finding was that in all groups, the women spent much more time looking at the men than the men spent looking at the women ($F = 15.38$, $df = 1/150$, $p < .01$). Although there was a tendency for strong-together subjects of both sexes to look at their partners more than weak-together subjects, these comparisons did not approach significance.

Discussion

The main prediction of the experiment was confirmed. Couples who were strongly in love, as categorized by their scores on the love scale, spent more time gazing into one another's eyes than did couples who were only weakly in love. With respect to the measure of individual gazing, however, the tendency for strong-together subjects to devote more time than the weak-together subjects to looking at their partners was not substantial for either women or men. This finding suggests that the obtained difference in mutual gazing between these two groups must be attributed to differences in the *simultaneousness*, rather than in the sheer quantity, of gazing. This conclusion is bolstered by the fact that the clearest difference between the strong-together and weak-together groups emerged on the percentage measure of mutual focus.

This pattern of results is in accord with the assumption that gazing is a manifestation of the exclusive and absorptive component of romantic love. Freud (1955) maintained that "The more [two people] are in love, the more completely they suffice for each other [p. 140]." More recently, Slater (1963) has

TABLE 6

Individual Gazing (in seconds)

Group	Women			Men		
	n	$\bar{X}$	SD	n	$\bar{X}$	SD
Strong together	19	98.7	23.2	19	83.7	20.2
Weak together	19	87.4	30.4	19	77.7	33.1
Strong apart	21	94.5	39.7	21	75.0	39.3
Weak apart	20	96.8	27.8	20	64.0	25.2

linked Freud's theory of love to the popular concept of "the oblivious lovers, who are 'all wrapped up in each other,' and somewhat careless of their social obligations [p. 349]." One way in which this oblivious absorption may be manifested is through eye contact. As the popular song has it, "Millions of people go by, but they all disappear from view— 'cause I only have eyes for you."

Another possible explanation for the findings is that people who are in love (or who complete attitude scales in such a way as to indicate that they are in love) are also the sort of people who are most predisposed to make eye contact with others, regardless of whether or not those others are the people they are in love with. The inclusion of the apart groups helped to rule out this possibility, however. Although there was a slight tendency for strong-apart couples to engage in more eye contact than weak-apart couples (see Table 5), it fell far short of significance. Moreover, when the percentage measure of mutual focus was employed (see Table 6), this difference virtually disappeared. It should be noted that no predictions were made concerning the comparisons between strong-together and strong-apart couples or between weak-together and weak-apart couples. It seemed plausible that unacquainted couples might make use of a relatively large amount of eye contact as a means of getting acquainted. The results indicate, in fact, that subjects in the apart groups typically engaged in as much eye contact as those in the weak-together group, with the strong-together subjects outgazing the other three groups. Future studies which systematically vary the extent to which partners are acquainted would be useful in specifying the acquaintance-seeking functions of eye contact.

The finding that in all experimental groups, women spent more time looking at men than vice versa may reflect the frequently reported tendency of women to specialize in the "social-emotional" aspects of interaction (e.g., Strodtbeck & Mann, 1956). Gazing may serve as a vehicle of emotional expression for women and, in addition, may allow women to obtain cues from their male partners concerning the appropriateness of their behavior. The present result is in accord with earlier findings that women tend to make more eye contact than men in same-sex groups (Exline, 1963) and in an interview situation, regardless of the sex of the interviewer (Exline, Gray, & Schuette, 1965).

Conclusion

"So far as love or affection is concerned," Harlow wrote in 1958, "psychologists have failed in their mission. The little we know about love does not transcend simple observation, and the little we write about it has been written better by poets and novelists [p. 673]." The research reported in this paper represents an attempt to improve this situation by introducing and validating a preliminary social-psychological conception of romantic love. A distinction was drawn between love and liking, and its reasonableness was attested to by the results of the questionnaire study. It was found, for example, that respondents' estimates of the likelihood that they would marry their partners were more highly related to their love than to their liking for their partners. In light of the culturally prescribed association between love and marriage (but not necessarily between liking and marriage), this pattern of correlations seems appropriate. Other findings of the questionnaire study, to be reported elsewhere, point to the value of a measurable construct of romantic love as a link between the individual and social-structural levels of analysis of social behavior.

Although the present investigation was aimed at developing a unitary conception of romantic love, a promising direction for future research is the attempt to distinguish among patterns of romantic love relationships. One theoretical basis for such distinctions is the nature of the interpersonal rewards exchanged between partners (cf. Wright, 1969). The attitudes and behaviors of romantic love may differ, for example, depending on whether the most salient rewards exchanged are those of security or those of stimulation (cf. Maslow's discussion of "Deficiency Love" and "Being Love," 1955). Some of the behavioral variables which might be focused on in the attempt to distinguish among such patterns are in the areas of sexual behavior, helping, and self-disclosure.

REFERENCES

Banta, T. J., & Hetherington, M. Relations between needs of friends and fiancees. *Journal of Abnormal and Social Psychology,* 1963, **66**, 401–404.

Campbell, D. T. Recommendations for APA test standards regarding construct, trait, and discriminant validity. *American Psychologist,* 1960, **15**, 546–553.

Cronbach, L. J., & Meehl, P. E. Construct validity in psychological tests. *Psychological Bulletin,* 1955, **52**, 281–302.

de Rougemont, D. *Love in the western world.* New York: Harcourt, Brace, 1940.

Exline, R. V. Explorations in the process of person perception: Visual interaction in relation to competition, sex, and need for affiliation. *Journal of Personality,* 1963, **31**, 1–20.

Exline, R., Gray, D., & Schuette, D. Visual behavior in a dyad as affected by interview content and sex of respondent. *Journal of Personality and Social Psychology,* 1965, **1**, 201–209.

Freud, S. Group psychology and the analysis of the ego. In, *The standard edition of the complete psychological works of Sigmund Freud.* Vol. 18. London: Hogarth, 1955.

Fromm, E. *The art of loving.* New York: Harper, 1956.

Goode, W. J. The theoretical importance of love. *American Sociological Review,* 1959, **24**, 38–47.

Harlow, H. F. The nature of love. *American Psychologist,* 1958, **13**, 673–685.

Heider, F. *The psychology of interpersonal relations.* New York: Wiley, 1958.

Jourard, S. M., & Lasakow, P. Some factors in self-disclosure. *Journal of Abnormal and Social Psychology,* 1958, **56**, 91–98.

Lindzey, G., & Byrne, D. Measurement of social choice and interpersonal attractiveness. In G. Lindzey & E. Aronson (Eds.), *Handbook of social psychology.* Vol. 2. (2nd ed.) Reading, Mass.: Addison-Wesley, 1968.

Maslow, A. H. Deficiency motivation and growth motivation. *Nebraska Symposium on Motivation,* 1955, **2**.

Newcomb, T. M. The varieties of interpersonal attraction. In D. Cartwright & A. Zander (Eds.), *Group dynamics.* (2nd ed.) Evanston: Row, Peterson, 1960.

Orlinsky, D. E. Love relationships in the life cycle: A developmental interpersonal perspective. Unpublished manuscript, University of Chicago, 1970.

Rubin, Z. *The social psychology of romantic love.* Ann Arbor, Mich.: University Microfilms, 1969, No. 70–4179.

Slater, P. E. On social regression. *American Sociological Review,* 1963, **28**, 339–364.

Strodtbeck, F. L., & Mann, R. D. Sex role differentiation in jury deliberations. *Sociometry,* 1956, **19**, 3–11.

Wallach, M. A., & Kogan, N. Sex differences and judgment processes. *Journal of Personality,* 1959, **27**, 555–564.

Walster, E. The effect of self-esteem on romantic liking. *Journal of Experimental Social Psychology,* 1965, **1**, 184–197.

Wright, P. H. A model and a technique for studies of friendship. *Journal of Experimental Social Psychology,* 1969, **5**, 295–309.

(Received September 30, 1969)

CONTINUITY BETWEEN THE EXPERIMENTAL STUDY OF ATTRACTION AND REAL-LIFE COMPUTER DATING[1]

DONN BYRNE[2]

Purdue University

CHARLES R. ERVIN

University of Texas

AND JOHN LAMBERTH

Purdue University

> As a test of the nonlaboratory generalizability of attraction research, a computer dating field study was conducted. A 50-item questionnaire of attitudes and personality was administered to a 420-student pool, and 44 male-female pairs were selected on the basis of maximal or minimal similarity of responses. Each couple was introduced, given differential information about the basis for their matching, and asked to spend 30 minutes together at the Student Union on a "coke date." Afterward, they returned to the experimenter and were independently assessed on a series of measures. It was found that attraction was significantly related to similarity and to physical attractiveness. Physical attractiveness was also significantly related to ratings of desirability as a date, as a spouse, and to sexual attractiveness. Both similarity and attractiveness were related to the physical proximity of the two individuals while they were talking to the experimenter after the date. In a follow-up investigation at the end of the semester, similarity and physical attractiveness were found to predict accurate memory of the date's name, incidence of talking to one another in the interim since the coke date, and desire to date the other person in the future.

A familiar but never totally resolved problem with any experimental findings is the extent to which they may be generalized to the nonlaboratory situation. At least three viewpoints about the problem may be discerned. First, and perhaps most familiar, is instant generalization from the specific and often limited conditions of an experiment to any and all settings which are even remotely related. This tendency is most frequently seen at cocktail parties after the third martini and on television talk shows featuring those who popularize psychology. Second, and almost as familiar, is the notion that the laboratory is a necessary evil. It is seen as an adequate substitute for the real world, only to the extent that it reproduces the world. For example, Aronson and Carlsmith (1968) ask, "Why,

[1] This research was supported in part by Research Grant MH-11178-04 from the National Institute of Mental Health and in part by Research Grant GS-2752 from the National Science Foundation. The authors wish to thank James Hilgren, Royal Masset, and Herman Mitchell for their help in conducting this experiment.

[2] Requests for reprints should be sent to Donn Byrne, Department of Psychology, Purdue University, Lafayette, Indiana 47907.

then, do we bother with these pallid and contrived imitations of human interaction when there exist rather sophisticated techniques for studying the real thing [p. 4]?" They enumerate the advantages of experiments over field study, but emphasize that good experiments must be realistic in order to involve the subject and have an "impact" on him. Concern with experimental realism often is expressed in the context of positing qualitative differences between the laboratory and the outside world; it is assumed that in moving from simplicity to complexity, new and different principles are emergent. Third, and least familiar in personality and social psychology, is a view which is quite common in other fields. Laboratory research is seen not as a necessary evil but as an essential procedure which enables us to attain isolation and control of variables and thus makes possible the formulation of basic principles in a setting of reduced complexity. If experiments realistically reproduce the nonlaboratory complexities, they provide little advantage over the field study. Continuity is assumed between the laboratory and the outside world, and complexity is seen as quantitative and not quali-

From *Journal of Personality and Social Psychology*, 1970, *16*(1), 157–165. Copyright 1970 by American Psychological Association. Reprinted by permission.

tative. To move from a simple situation to a complex one requires detailed knowledge about the relevant variables and their interaction. Application and the attainment of a technology depend upon such an approach.

With respect to a specific psychological phenomenon, the problem of nonlaboratory generalization and application may be examined more concretely. The laboratory investigation of interpersonal attraction within a reinforcement paradigm (Byrne, 1969) has followed a strategy in which the effect of a variety of stimulus variables on a single response variable was the primary focus of interest. A model has evolved which treats all relevant stimuli as positive or negative reinforcers of differential magnitude. Attraction toward any stimulus object (including another person) is then found to be a positive linear function of the proportion of weighted positive reinforcements associated with that object. Attitude statements have been the most frequently employed reinforcing stimuli, but other stimulus elements have included personality variables (e.g., Griffitt, 1966), physical attractiveness (e.g., Byrne, London, & Reeves, 1968), economic variables (Byrne, Clore, & Worchel, 1966), race (e.g., Byrne & Ervin, 1969), behavioral preferences (Huffman, 1969), personal evaluations (e.g., Byrne & Rhamey, 1965), room temperature (Griffitt, 1970a), and sexual arousal (Picher, 1966).

Considering just one of those variables, attitude similarity-dissimilarity, why is it not reasonable to propose an immediate and direct parallel between laboratory and nonlaboratory responses? One reason is simple and quite obvious, but it seems often to be overlooked. Laboratory research is based on the isolation of variables so that one or a limited number of independent variables may be manipulated, while, if possible, all other stimulus variables are controlled. In the outside world, multiple uncontrolled stimuli are present. Thus, if all an experimental subject knows about a stranger is that he holds opinions similar to his own on six out of six political issues, the stranger will be liked (Byrne, Bond, & Diamond, 1969). We cannot, however, assume that any two interacting individuals who agree on these six issues will become fast friends because (a) they may never get around to discussing those six topics at all, and (b) even if these topics are discussed, six positive reinforcements may simply become an insignificant portion of a host of other positive and negative reinforcing elements in the interaction. A second barrier to immediate applicability of a laboratory finding lies in the nature of the response. It is good research strategy to limit the dependent variable (in this instance, the sum of two 7-point rating scales), but nonlaboratory responses may be as varied and uncontrolled as the stimuli. The relationship between that paper-and-pencil measure of attraction and other interpersonal responses is only beginning to be explored (e.g., Byrne, Baskett, & Hodges, 1969; Efran, 1969). The third barrier lies in the nature of the relationship investigated. For a number of quite practical reasons, the laboratory study of attraction is limited in its time span and hence might legitimately be labeled the study of first impressions. Whether the determinants of first impressions are precisely the same as the determinants of a prolonged friendship, of love, or of marital happiness is an empirical question and one requiring a great deal of research.

In view of these barriers to extralaboratory application of experimental findings, how may one begin the engineering enterprise? The present research suggests one attempt to seek a solution. Specifically, a limited dating situation is created in which the barriers to application are minimized. Independent variables identified in the laboratory (attitude similarity, personality similarity, and physical attractiveness) are varied in a real-life situation, and an attempt is made to make the variables salient and to minimize the occurrence of other stimulus events. Even though similarity has been the focus of much of the experimental work on attraction, the findings with respect to physical attractiveness have consistently demonstrated the powerful influence of appearance on responses to those of the opposite sex and even of the same sex. Both field studies (Megargee, 1956; Perrin, 1921; Taylor, 1956; Walster, Aronson, Abrahams, & Rottmann, 1966) and laboratory investigations (Byrne et al., 1968; McWhirter, 1969; Moss, 1969) have shown that those who are physically attractive elicit more positive responses than do those who are unattractive. The laboratory response measure was retained so that a common reference point was available, but additional response variables were also used in order to extend the generality and meaning of the attraction construct. Finally, in this experiment, the interaction was deliberately limited in time so that it remained close to a first-impression relationship. Given these deliberately limited conditions, it was proposed that the positive relationship between the proportion of weighted positive reinforcements and attraction is directly applicable to a nonlaboratory interaction. Specifically, it was hypothesized that in a computer dating situation (*a*) attraction is a joint function of similarity and physical attractiveness, and (*b*) the greater the extent to which the specific elements of similarity are made salient, the greater is the relationship between similarity and attraction.

The variety of ways in which similarity and attraction could be investigated in a field situation raises an interesting question of strategy. It should be kept in mind that there is no magic about the similarity effect. Similarity does not exude from the pores; rather, specific attitudes and other characteristics must be expressed overtly. It would be relatively simple to design a computer dating experiment in which no similarity effects would be found. For example, one could lie about the degree of similarity, and in a brief interaction, the subjects would not be likely to discover the deception. Another alternative would be to provide no information about similarity and then to forbid the subjects to talk during their date. Negative results in such studies would be of no importance as a test since they are beyond the boundary conditions of the theory. Another possible study would give no initial similarity information and then require an extended interaction period, but that has already been done. That is, people in the real world do this every day, and numerous correlational studies indicate that under such conditions, similarity is associated with attraction. The strategy of the present research was frankly to maximize the possibility of securing a precise similarity attraction effect in a real-life setting; in subsequent research, the limiting conditions of the effect may be determined.

Method

Attitude-Personality Questionnaire

In order to provide a relatively broad base on which to match couples for the dating process, a 50-item questionnaire was constructed utilizing five variables. In previous research, a significant similarity effect has been found for authoritarianism (Sheffield & Byrne, 1967), repression-sensitization (Byrne & Griffitt, 1969; Byrne, Griffitt, & Stefaniak, 1967), attitudes (Byrne, 1961, 1969), EPPS items,[3] and self-concept (Griffitt, 1966, 1970b). Each variable was represented by 10 items which were chosen to represent the least possible intercorrelations within dimensions; the rationale here was the desire to maximize the number of *independent* scale responses on which matching could be based.

Simulated Stranger Condition

In order to provide a base line for the similarity effect under controlled conditions, a simulated stranger condition was run in which the other person was represented only by his or her purported responses to the attitude-personality questionnaire. The study was described as an investigation of the effectiveness of the matching procedures of computer dating organizations. Subjects were told, "Instead of arranging an actual date, we are providing couples with information about one another and asking for their reactions." The simulated scales were prepared to provide either a .33 or .67 proportion of similar responses between stranger and subject. The subject was asked to read the responses of an opposite-sex stranger and then to make a series of evaluations on an expanded version of the Interpersonal Judgment Scale. This scale consists of ten 7-point scales. The measure of attraction within this experimental paradigm (Byrne, 1969) consists of the sum of two scales: liking and desirability as a work partner. This attraction index ranges from 2 to 14 and has a split-half reliability of .85. In addition, four buffer scales deal with evaluations of the other person's intelligence, knowledge of current events, morality, and adjustment. These variables are found to correlate positively with attraction, but they have somewhat different antecedents and are included in the analysis simply as supplemental information. Three new scales, added for the present study in order to explore various responses to the opposite sex, asked the subject to react to the other person as a potential date, as a marriage partner, and as to sexual attractiveness. Finally, a tenth scale was added in order to assess a stimulus variable, the physical attractiveness of the other person. In addition, the physical attractiveness of each subject was rated by the experimenter on the same 7-point scale on which the subjects rated one another.

[3] Unpublished data collected by Donn Byrne and John Lamberth.

Computer Dating Condition

Selection of dating couples. The attitude-personality questionnaire was administered to a group of 420 introductory psychology students at the University of Texas, and each item was scored in a binary fashion. By means of a specially prepared program, the responses of each male were compared with those of each female; for any given couple, the number of possible matching responses could theoretically range from 0 to 50. The actual range was from 12 to 37. From these distributions of matches, male-female pairs were selected to represent either the greatest or the least number of matching responses. There was a further restriction that the male be as tall as or taller than the female. Of the resulting pairs, a few were eliminated because (a) one of the individuals was married, (b) the resulting pair was racially mixed, or (c) because of a failure to keep the experimental appointment. The remaining 88 subjects formed 24 high-similar pairs, whose proportion of similar responses ranged from .66 to .74, and 20 low-similar pairs, whose proportion of similar responses ranged from .24 to .40.

Levels of information saliency. The experiment was run with one of the selected couples at a time. In the experimental room, they were introduced to one another and told:

In recent years, there has been a considerable amount of interest in the phenomenon of computer dating as a means for college students to meet one another. At the present time, we are attempting to learn as much as possible about the variables which influence the reactions of one individual to another.

In order to create differential levels of saliency with respect to the matching elements, subjects in the salient condition were told:

Earlier this semester, one of the test forms you filled out was very much like those used by some of the computer dating organizations. In order to refresh your memory about this test and the answers you gave, we are going to ask you to spend a few minutes looking over the questions and your answers to them.

The answers of several hundred students were placed on IBM cards and run through the computer to determine the number of matching answers among the 50 questions for all possible pairs of male and female students. According to the computer, the two of you gave the same answers on approximately 67% (33%) of those questions.

In the nonsalient condition, they were told:

Imagine for the purposes of the experiment that you had applied to one of the computer dating organizations and filled out some of their information forms. Then, imagine that the two of you had been notified that, according to the computer, you match on approximately 67% (33%) of the factors considered important.

All subjects were then told:

For our experiment, we would like to create a situation somewhat like that of a computer date. That is, you answered a series of questions, the computer indicated that you two gave the same responses on some of the questions, and now we would like for you to spend a short time together getting acquainted. Specifically, we are asking you to spend the next 30 minutes together on a "coke date" at the Student Union. Here is 50¢ to spend on whatever you would like. We hope that you will learn as much as possible about each other in the next half hour because we will be asking you a number of questions about one another when you return.

Measures of attraction. When they returned from the date to receive their final instructions, an unobtrusive measure of attraction was obtained: the physical distance between the two subjects while standing together in front of the experimenter's desk. The distance was noted on a simple ordinal scale ranging from 0 (touching one another) to 5 (standing at opposite corners of the desk). The subjects were then separated and asked to evaluate their date on the Interpersonal Judgment Scale.

Follow-up measures. At the end of the semester (2–3 months after the date), it was possible to locate 74 of the 88 original subjects who were willing to answer five additional questions. Each was asked to write the name of his or her computer date and to indicate whether or not they had talked to one another since the experiment, dated since the experiment, and whether a date was desired or planned in the future. Finally, each was asked whether the evaluation of the date was influenced more by physical attractiveness or by attitudes.

RESULTS

Simulated Stranger Condition

The mean attraction responses of two simulated stranger conditions [4] which were run

---

[4] Originally, the plan was to run the simulated stranger groups just after the computer dating groups. An unexpected finding was that almost all of the responses were positive and that the subjects were attired more attractively than is usual among undergraduates reporting for experimental sessions. From anecdotal olfactory evidence, even the perfume and shaving lotion level was noticeably elevated. In retrospect, it seemed clear that because the computer dating study was widely discussed and because this experiment was so labeled, the overwhelming majority of the 34 subjects were expecting to go on a date as part of their task. It then became necessary to rerun the simulated stranger groups at the end of the semester when the expectations of dates had diminished. The two levels of similarity were run under two different experimental titles, "Computer Dating" and "Evaluational Processes." The data reported in this paper are from these latter two experiments.

separately from the computer dating experiment are shown in Table 1. Analysis of variance indicated that the similarity variable yielded the only significant effect ($F = 4.00$, $df = 1/46$, $p =$ approximately .05).

On the remaining items of the Interpersonal Judgment Scale, the only other significant similarity effect was on the intelligence rating ($F = 7.30$, $df = 1/46$, $p < .01$). Interestingly enough, there were several differences between the differently labeled experiments on the other Interpersonal Judgment Scale items. More positive responses were given in the "computer dating" experiment than in the "evaluational processes" experiment with respect to knowledge of current events ($F = 8.07$, $df = 1/46$, $p < .01$), adjustment ($F = 6.10$, $df = 1/46$, $p < .02$), and desirability as a marriage partner ($F = 6.57$, $df = 1/46$, $p < .02$). The sexual attractiveness item yielded a significant interaction effect ($F = 4.93$, $df = 1/46$, $p < .03$), with the dissimilar stranger rated as more sexually attractive in the computer dating experiment and the similar stranger as more sexually attractive in the evaluational processes experiment. While these latter findings are gratuitous, they suggest the importance of minor variations in the stimulus context and the sensitivity of the Interpersonal Judgment Scale items to such variations.

Predicting Attraction in the Computer Dating Condition

The mean attraction responses for male and female subjects at two levels of information saliency and two levels of response similarity are shown in Table 2. Analysis of variance indicated the only significant effect to be

TABLE 1

MEAN ATTRACTION RESPONSES TOWARD SIMILAR AND DISSIMILAR SIMULATED STRANGERS WITH TWO DIFFERENT TITLES FOR EXPERIMENT

Title of experiment	Proportion of similar responses	
	.33	.67
Evaluational processes	9.47	10.78
Computer dating	10.21	11.33
M	9.84	11.06

Note.—The mean attraction responses were 10.12 and 10.77 for the evaluational processes and computer dating experiments, respectively.

TABLE 2

MEAN ATTRACTION RESPONSES OF MALES AND FEMALES WITH SIMILAR AND DISSIMILAR DATES AT TWO LEVELS OF SALIENCY CONCERNING MATCHING INFORMATION

Level	Proportion of similar responses	
	Low	High
Male Ss Information		
Salient	10.00	11.91
Nonsalient	10.56	11.38
Female Ss Information		
Salient	10.73	11.82
Nonsalient	10.33	12.15

that of proportion of similar responses ($F = 13.67$, $df = 1/40$, $p < .001$). The attempt to make the matching stimuli differentially salient did not affect attraction, and there were no sex differences.

The other variable which was expected to influence attraction was the physical attractiveness of the date. It is interesting to note in the simulated stranger condition that while the manipulation of similarity influenced attraction, it had no effect on guesses as to the other person's physical attractiveness ($F < 1$). Thus, data in the computer dating condition indicating a relationship between attractiveness and attraction would seem to result from the effect of the former on the latter. Two measures of attractiveness were available: ratings by the experimenter when the subjects first arrived and by each subject of his or her own date following their interaction. The correlation between these two measures was significant; the correlation between the experimenter's ratings of male subjects and the females' ratings of their dates was .59 ($p < .01$) and between the experimenter's ratings of female subjects and the males' ratings of their dates was .39 ($p < .01$). As might be expected, the subject's own ratings proved to be better predictors than did the experimenter's ratings. In Table 3 are shown those correlations between physical attractiveness ratings and Interpersonal Judgment Scale responses which were consistent across sexes.

Thus, the first hypothesis was clearly confirmed, but there was no support for the second hypothesis.

TABLE 3

CORRELATIONS BETWEEN RATINGS OF PHYSICAL ATTRACTIVENESS OF DATE AND EVALUATIONS OF DATE

Variable	Attractiveness of date Rated by Ss		Attractiveness of date Rated by E	
	Male Ss	Female Ss	Male Ss	Female Ss
Attraction	.39**	.60**	.07	.32*
Dating	.66**	.57**	.21	.33*
Marriage	.56**	.55**	.18	.34*
Sex	.77**	.70**	.53**	.44**

* $p < .05$.
** $p < .01$.

With respect to the prediction of attraction, it seems likely that a combination of the similarity and attractiveness variables would provide the optimal information. In Table 4 are shown the mean attraction responses toward attractive (ratings of 5–7) and unattractive (ratings of 1–4) dates at two levels of response similarity. For both sexes, each of the two independent variables was found to affect attraction.[5] The physical attractiveness variable was significant for both males ($F = 3.85$, $df = 1/39$, $p < .05$) and for females ($F = 10.44$, $df = 1/40$, $p < .01$). The most positive response in each instance was toward similar attractive dates, and the least positive response was toward dissimilar unattractive dates. An additional analysis indicated no relationship between an individual's own physical attractiveness (as rated by the date) and response to the other person's physical attractiveness.

Other Effects of Similarity and Attractiveness

On the additional items of the Interpersonal Judgment Scale, similarity was found to have

[5] The use of the term "independent variable" for physical attractiveness may be a source of confusion. In this experiment, there was obviously no manipulation of physical appearance, but attractiveness was conceptualized as one of the stimuli determining attraction. In other experiments, attractiveness has been successfully manipulated as an independent variable (e.g., Byrne et al., 1968; McWhirter, 1969; Moss, 1969). In the absence of any evidence that attraction determines perception of physical attractiveness (and some evidence to the contrary), it seems reasonable to consider attractiveness as an antecedent variable in studies such as the present one and that of Walster et al. (1966).

a significant positive effect on ratings of the date's intelligence ($F = 4.37$, $df = 1/40$, $p < .05$), desirability as a date ($F = 8.92$, $df = 1/40$, $p < .01$), and desirability as a marriage partner ($F = 4.76$, $df = 1/40$, $p < .05$).

The simplest and least obtrusive measure of attraction was the proximity of the two individuals after the date, while receiving their final instructions from the experimenter. If physical distance can be considered as an alternative index of attraction, these two dependent variables should be correlated. For females, the correlation was $-.36$ ($p < .01$) and for males, $-.48$, ($p < .01$); in each instance the greater the liking for the partner, the closer together they stood. Another way of evaluating the proximity variable is to determine whether it is influenced by the same independent variables as is the paper-and-pencil measure. For both sexes, physical separation was found to correlate $-.49$ ($p < .01$) with similarity. Thus, the more similar the couples, the closer they stood. Because similarity and proximity are necessarily identical for each member of a pair, it is not possible to determine whether the males, the females, or both are responsible for the similarity-proximity relationship. When the physical attractiveness measure was examined, however, there was indirect evidence that proximity in this situation was controlled more by the males than by the females. For females, there was no relationship between ratings of the male's appearance and physical separation ($r = -.06$). For males, the correlation was $-.34$ ($p < .05$).

In the follow-up investigation at the end of the semester, 74 of the 88 original subjects

TABLE 4

MEAN ATTRACTION RESPONSES OF MALES AND FEMALES WITH SIMILAR AND DISSIMILAR DATES WHO ARE RELATIVELY ATTRACTIVE AND UNATTRACTIVE

Physical attractiveness of date	Proportion of similar responses	
	Low	High
Male Ss		
Attractive	10.55	12.00
Unattractive	9.89	10.43
Female Ss		
Attractive	11.25	12.71
Unattractive	9.50	11.00

were available and willing to participate. For this analysis, each subject was placed in one of three categories with respect to the two stimulus variables of similarity and attractiveness. On the basis of the same divisions as were used in the analysis in Table 4, subjects were either in a high-similarity condition with a physically attractive date, a low-similarity condition with a physically unattractive date, or in a mixed condition of high-low or low-high. To maximize the possible effect, frequency analysis was used in comparing the two homogeneous groups ($N = 40$).[6] In response to the question about the date's name, the more positive the stimulus conditions at the time of the date, the more likely was the subject to remember correctly the date's name ($\chi^2 = 8.47$, $df = 1$, $p < .01$). With respect to talking to the other individual during the period since the experiment, the relationship was again significant ($\chi^2 = 4.95$, $df = 1$, $p < .05$). The same effect was found with regard to whether the individual would like or not like to date the other person in the future ($\chi^2 = 5.38$, $df = 1$, $p < .05$). The only follow-up question which failed to show a significant effect for the experimental manipulation was that dealing with actual dating; even here, it might be noted that the only dates reported were by subjects in the high-similarity, high-attractiveness condition.

The only other question in the follow-up survey represented an attempt to find out whether the subjects could accurately verbalize the stimuli to which they had been found to respond. Of the 74 respondents, about one-third indicated that both attitudes and physical attractiveness determined their response to the partner, while about one-sixth of the subjects felt they had responded to neither variable. With the remaining half of the sample, an interesting sex difference emerged. Physical attractiveness was identified as the most important stimulus by 14 of the 18 males, while attitudes were seen as the most important stimulus by 16 of the 19 females ($\chi^2 = 14.30$, $df = 1$, $p < .001$). The present subjects seemed to have accepted Bertrand Russell's observation that "On the whole, women tend to love men for their character, while men tend to love women for their appearance." In contrast to these verbal sentiments, it might be noted that the date's physical attractiveness correlated .60 with attraction responses of female subjects and only .39 among male subjects. A further analysis compared the similarity-attraction effect and the attractiveness-attraction effect for those subjects who indicated one or the other stimulus variable as the more important. The similarity-attraction effect did not differ between the two groups ($z < 1$). It has been reported previously that awareness of similarity is not a necessary component of the similarity effect (Byrne & Griffitt, 1969). There was, however, a difference in the attractiveness effect. For the subjects identifying attractiveness as the major determinant, physical attractiveness correlated .63 ($p < .01$) with attraction responses; for the subjects identifying similarity as the major determinant, attractiveness correlated $-.04$ (*ns*) with attraction. The difference was a significant one ($z = 2.16$, $p < .05$).

Conclusions

Perhaps the most important aspect of the present findings is the evidence indicating the continuity between the laboratory study of attraction and its manifestation under field conditions. At least as operationalized in the present investigation, variables such as physical attractiveness and similarity of attitudes and personality characteristics are found to influence attraction in a highly predictable manner.

The findings with respect to the physical distance measure are important in two respects. First, they provide further evidence that voluntary proximity is a useful and unobtrusive measure of interpersonal attraction. Second, the construct validity and generality of the paper-and-pencil measure of attraction provided by the Interpersonal Judgment Scale is greatly enhanced. The significant relationship between two such different response measures is comforting to users of

---

[6] When the 33 individuals who were heterogeneous with respect to similarity and attractiveness were included in the analysis, they fell midway between the similar-attractive and dissimilar-unattractive groups on each item. The probability levels were consequently reduced to the .02 level on remembering the date's name and to the .10 level on the talking and desire to date items.

either one. In addition, the follow-up procedure provided evidence of the lasting effect of the experimental manipulations and of the relation of the attraction measures to such diverse responses as remembering the other person's name and engaging in conversation in the weeks after the termination of the experiment.

The failure to confirm the second hypothesis is somewhat puzzling. It is possible that present procedures, designed to vary the saliency of the elements of similarity, were inadequate and ineffective, that the actual behavioral cues to similarity and dissimilarity were sufficiently powerful to negate the effects of the experimental manipulation, or that the hypothesis was simply incorrect. There is no basis within the present experiment on which to decide among these alternatives.

In conclusion, it must be emphasized that striking continuity has been demonstrated across experiments using paper-and-pencil materials to simulate a stranger and to measure attraction (Byrne, 1961), more realistic audio and audiovisual presentations of the stimulus person (Byrne & Clore, 1966), elaborate dramatic confrontations in which a confederate portrays the stimulus person (Byrne & Griffitt, 1966), and a quasi-realistic experiment such as the present one, in which two genuine strangers interact and in which response measures include nonverbal behaviors. Such findings suggest that attempts to move back and forth between the controlled artificiality of the laboratory and the uncontrolled natural setting are both feasible and indicative of the potential applications of basic attraction research to a variety of interpersonal problems.

REFERENCES

Aronson, E., & Carlsmith, J. M. Experimentation in social psychology. In G. Lindzey & E. Aronson (Eds.), *The handbook of social psychology*. Vol. 2. (2nd ed.) Reading, Mass.: Addison-Wesley, 1968.

Byrne, D. Interpersonal attraction and attitude similarity. *Journal of Abnormal and Social Psychology,* 1961, 62, 713–715.

Byrne, D. Attitudes and attraction. In L. Berkowitz (Ed.), *Advances in experimental social psychology*. Vol. 4. New York: Academic Press, 1969.

Byrne, D., Baskett, G. D., & Hodges, L. Behavioral indicators of interpersonal attraction. Paper presented at meeting of the Psychonomic Society, St. Louis, November 1969.

Byrne, D., Bond, M. H., & Diamond, M. J. Response to political candidates as a function of attitude similarity-dissimilarity. *Human Relations,* 1969, 22, 251–262.

Byrne, D., & Clore, G. L., Jr. Predicting interpersonal attraction toward strangers presented in three different stimulus modes. *Psychonomic Science,* 1966, 4, 239–240.

Byrne, D., Clore, G. L., Jr., & Worchel, P. Effect of economic similarity-dissimilarity on interpersonal attraction. *Journal of Personality and Social Psychology,* 1966, 4, 220–224.

Byrne, D., & Ervin, C. R. Attraction toward a Negro stranger as a function of prejudice, attitude similarity, and the stranger's evaluation of the subject. *Human Relations,* 1969, 22, 397–404.

Byrne, D., & Griffitt, W. Similarity versus liking: A clarification. *Psychonomic Science,* 1966, 6, 295–296.

Byrne, D., & Griffitt, W. Similarity and awareness of similarity of personality characteristics as determinants of attraction. *Journal of Experimental Research in Personality,* 1969, 3, 179–186.

Byrne, D., Griffitt, W., & Stefaniak, D. Attraction and similarity of personality characteristics. *Journal of Personality and Social Psychology,* 1967, 5, 82–90.

Byrne, D., London, O., & Reeves, K. The effects of physical attractiveness, sex, and attitude similarity on interpersonal attraction. *Journal of Personality,* 1968, 36, 259–271.

Byrne, D., & Rhamey, R. Magnitude of positive and negative reinforcements as a determinant of attraction. *Journal of Personality and Social Psychology,* 1965, 2, 884–889.

Efran, M. G. Visual interaction and interpersonal attraction. Unpublished doctoral dissertation, University of Texas, 1969.

Griffitt, W. B. Interpersonal attraction as a function of self-concept and personality similarity-dissimilarity. *Journal of Personality and Social Psychology,* 1966, 4, 581–584.

Griffitt, W. B. Environmental effects of interpersonal affective behavior: Ambient effective temperature and attraction. *Journal of Personality and Social Psychology,* 1970, 15, 240–244. (a)

Griffitt, W. B. Personality similarity and self-concept as determinants of interpersonal attraction. *Journal of Social Psychology,* 1970, in press. (b)

Huffman, D. M. Interpersonal attraction as a function of behavioral similarity. Unpublished doctoral dissertation, University of Texas, 1969.

McWhirter, R. M., Jr. Interpersonal attraction in a dyad as a function of the physical attractiveness of its members. Unpublished doctoral dissertation, Texas Tech University, 1969.

Megargee, E. I. A study of the subjective aspects of group membership at Amherst. Unpublished manuscript, Amherst College, 1956.

Moss, M. K. Social desirability, physical attractiveness, and social choice. Unpublished doctoral dissertation, Kansas State University, 1969.

PERRIN, F. A. C. Physical attractiveness and repulsiveness. *Journal of Experimental Psychology,* 1921, **4**, 203–217.

PICHER, O. L. Attraction toward Negroes as a function of prejudice, emotional arousal, and the sex of the Negro. Unpublished doctoral dissertation, University of Texas, 1966.

SHEFFIELD, J., & BYRNE, D. Attitude similarity-dissimilarity, authoritarianism, and interpersonal attraction. *Journal of Social Psychology,* 1967, **71**, 117–123.

TAYLOR, M. J. Some objective criteria of social class membership. Unpublished manuscript, Amherst College, 1956.

WALSTER, E., ARONSON, V., ABRAHAMS, D., & ROTTMANN, L. Importance of physical attractiveness in dating behavior. *Journal of Personality and Social Psychology,* 1966, **4**, 508–516.

(Received December 11, 1969)

THE STUDIES COMPARED

These two studies pose somewhat different questions. Byrne and his colleagues are interested in how people come to meet in the first place—what attracts them to each other. Rubin addresses the issues of what happens after the initial acquaintance; he looks for differences between the states of attraction that characterize loving and liking. The specific hypotheses of the Byrne et al. study are that more similarity and greater physical attractiveness generate more attraction and that the more "up front" the similarity is the more it influences attraction. Only the first of these expectations has been confirmed. The Rubin article is a report of a series of steps involved in developing a research instrument to assess whether there are differences between loving and liking. The difference between a popular magazine quiz on "Do you really love your mate?" and a research instrument is the series of steps you take to insure that you are really measuring what you think you are measuring. Further, the research instrument should have predictive validity; it should be able to predict actual behavior consistent with the theme addressed in the questionnaire.

In concluding their reports, the investigators in both studies indicate that they now have evidence to support their views about the nature of attraction. Before you can share their confidence, you will want to review their respective evidence in some detail. There are two aspects of evidence to be considered. One aspect addresses the question of whether the investigator can legitimately say that the results found are due to the situation or circumstances produced (Byrne) or examined (Rubin). The second issue is whether the results obtained can generalize to situations and people other than those studied here. Of particular relevance to this point is the excellent discussion in the introduction to the second selection of alternative routes toward establishing the generality of a phenomenon.

Subject Selection

The subjects in both these studies were college students, a population frequently involved in social-psychological research. This is not surprising, given the mutual accessibility of researchers and students and the legitimacy of asking those who are learning about psychology to take an active part in creating it. For many topics of interest to social psychologists, the college student's behavior can be assumed to be like that of many other people. The processes of attraction and acquaintance among students, however, is likely to differ considerably from that of other populations. Close friendships of middle age, the extramarital fling, homosexual pairings, the explorative attractions of the socially mobile, the second pairings of the divorced and the widowed, and the "one-night stand" may all result from and be subject to processes quite different from those accessible to research on dating college students. Not only are age, social class, and stage of development in life likely to make a difference in the way attraction functions, but even among college students there are likely to be relationships that do not follow the same rules as "dating." For a number of topics in psychology, college students can be assumed to behave like other people, but as far as the topic of attraction is concerned, there is some reason to wonder whether the attraction processes in college students who are dating are like those of other people and situations.

The Computer-Dating Study. Further questions can be raised about whether the college students sampled in these studies were representative even of *their* larger group. You need to ask how the subjects were selected in the first place and how they were assigned to the different experimental conditions. With regard to the second selection, this question is difficult to answer. It takes a careful search of the article to collect information about the nature of the sample. You are told that 420 students in the introductory-psychology course filled out an attitude-personality questionnaire. This is presumably the population from which further sampling was done for the various experimental conditions. For the computer-dating condition, the method of subject selection is fairly clear, although not much information is given on the differential effect of various losses from the sample. The first step in selection was to compare the responses of male and female students in the class in order to find combinations of heterosexual pairs with the most or least matching responses. The potential number of matches meeting this criterion is not stated, but after eliminating more pairs for discrepancies in height, race, and marital status, as well as for not showing up for the experiment, 88 pairs were left. There is obviously no objection to reducing sample size in order to fit research objectives, but it is important to know how many pairs were eliminated for which reason. Knowing this enables you to assess more precisely the composition of the final sample and thus to feel more confident about the generalizability of the findings. Hence, it would be good to know the range and extent of possible pairings made by the computer analysis scores. We must avoid the naive error that 420 questionnaire respondents constitute 210 pairs. For example, if the women outnumber the men (a common situation in introductory-psychology courses), the number of possible heterosexual pairs cannot exceed the number of men in the sample. On the other hand, if there are equal numbers of males and females, then the potential pairings far exceed 210 (that is, if there are 420 people in a group made up of 210 males and 210 females, the number of possible pairings is not 210 but 44,100.) Obviously, the criterion of matching scores reduces this number, but, in the absence of such information, you are left in doubt about whether the 24 high-agreement pairs and the 20 low-agreement pairs represent the total possible number of pairs meeting the criterion. In other words, is the occurrence of high and low agreement a rare event, or were these pairs selected from many more pairs who agreed one-third or two-thirds of the time?

In the other main condition described in the second selection, called the simulated-stranger condition, virtually no information was given about the sample. In a footnote on page 45, you learn that 34 people participated initially but that they were not the group on which the reported results were based. When the data for these initial participants were analyzed, attraction ratings for both similar and dissimilar simulated strangers were found to be unexpectedly equivalent and positive. On the basis of much preceding work with the simulated-stranger condition, the investigators judged these findings to be an unintended consequence of the recruitment procedure. Looking back on their procedure, they concluded that many subjects arrived at the experiment expecting to meet an actual date. Apparently, this so heightened (artificially) all attraction responses that the differences between similar and dissimilar pairs could not emerge (assuming them to exist). Byrne and his colleagues reported that they then repeated the simulated-stranger condition, recruiting subjects under two different experimental labels—evaluational-processes experiment and computer-dating experiment. The results of this repetition of the simulated-stranger condition were those reported in the selection above. Regrettably, you are given even less information about the selection, composition, and assignment of subjects for this repetition. The number of subjects recruited under each label is not stated. A reader who is knowledgeable in rules of statistical analysis may be able to guess from the way the results are reported that the data are based on 46 people. There is no clue about the population from which these people were recruited, and you don't know if they were part of the original 420 who answered the attitude-personality questionnaire. Nor do you learn how many were recruited for each experiment label, how they were assigned to these labels, and how many men and women took part overall and by experiment label.

The Romantic-Love Study. The first selection describes the three phases of a research attempting to distinguish loving from liking and including the development and use of a "love scale." Different people participated in the three parts of the research. The first sample consisted of 198 introductory-psychology students who answered a 70-item questionnaire during regular class sessions, with instructions to complete the items with reference to both a girlfriend or boyfriend and a platonic friend of the opposite sex. In the second stage of research, 158 dating but not engaged couples responded to a revised set of 26 items. These couples were recruited by posters and ads specifying actual dating as the criterion for coming to the experiment. This recruitment procedure was necessary in this phase of the research because the experimenter wanted people who were actually dating rather than people who would respond with hypothetical others in mind. Furthermore, the term *dating* has a shared meaning among college students that may exclude from the sample a number of intense relationships in which the distinctions between loving and liking might take different forms. For example, couples who are living together may not consider themselves as dating and thus exclude themselves from the sample. The third stage of the research sampled from these 158 couples to obtain pairs in which both partners scored at the high or low end of the love scale. These pairs then took part in the behavioral study to see whether scale scores did in fact make for differences in behavior. The possible selection bias mentioned with respect to the 158 respondents applies to this subset of them as well. Other people who are in love but do not define themselves as dating might behave differently.

Measures of Attraction

Both of these studies are strong in that they use obtrusive as well as unobtrusive measures; this use of several kinds of measures gives you greater confidence that you are in fact measuring something real rather than something produced by the nature of the measure itself. The Byrne et al. study of computer dating has the advantage of taking place almost entirely outside the laboratory and, therefore, of being quite close to real-life situations. Although the measurement of how close the two individuals in each couple stood did in fact take place in the experimenter's office, the events of which the distance was an indicator occurred during a real date. Furthermore, this study has the rare feature of including a follow-up several months after the study was conducted. Given that the Byrne group wanted to say something about the relation between similarity and attraction, the confidence in the existence of such relation is greater if it persists some time after the experiment is over.

The two studies have a problem in common—the social desirability of their topic. Since in our society attraction is considered a good thing, there may be a strong tendency among the laboratory subjects to present themselves as liking the other research participants. There is some confirmation of this bias in the Rubin study, which reports no mean scores below the midpoint rating for any item. Although at face value the scales appear to have considerable range, subjects used mostly their upper ranges—those indicating a high degree of loving; from a possible range of 9 to 117, the median score was 92 for real dating couples. A related problem is that the items in these scales are so worded that people who unthinkingly answer yes to a question are regarded as liking or loving a lot. In designing such scales, this bias toward "yea-saying" is sometimes controlled by including items in which disagreement contributes to a high score. For example, Item 2 of the love scale might have been worded "I feel that I *cannot* confide in X about virtually anything," thus requiring those who want to make a positive statement to register disagreement with the item.

Self-report measures such as Byrne's Interpersonal Judgment Scale and the Rubin liking and loving scales are subject to general problems of what is called *reactivity*. In reading these studies, you may have wondered why psychologists seem to seek answers to an apparently simple question in such elaborate ways. Why don't they just ask people if they're in love or if they like each other? Most simply, psychologists cannot be sure that the question "Are you in love?" will be understood the same way by all those questioned. Two people who have very different feelings may nonetheless answer yes to the question, thereby erroneously including themselves among those believed to share the feeling the psychologist wants to identify. Conversely, two people who *do* share that feeling may both answer no to the question because they interpret it differently. They would then inadvertently be excluded from those in whom the psychologist is interested. In short, asking more questions on a single theme increases your chances of determining the real attitude, thus compensating for possible fluctuations of interpretation. With regard to this issue, if you compare Rubin's liking scale with the two questions asked by the Byrne group, the Rubin study appears to be the stronger. Asking more questions is not in itself an absolute advantage, for too many questions can tire and bore the respondent; but a carefully constructed questionnaire stands less chance of misinterpretation than do one or two questions.

The fact that researchers must find some way to measure what they're interested in is probably becoming evident to you. This operationalizing of the variables, as it is called, can take various forms. Frequently, the dependent variable (the behavior that emerges in the experimental context) is measured by a scale or questionnaire. In many experiments, the scale that is used has been developed in previous work, and this previous use is taken as some testimony that the scale offers an adequate operational definition. As a consumer of such studies, you aren't given much direct evidence to support the conclusion that the variables have been adequately operationalized, although you may be able to check the earlier work. Thus, in the computer-dating study, the authors make reference to a dozen preceding studies, extending back over a decade. Ten years from now, there may be studies that will use the loving and liking scales with only brief reference to Rubin's article as the source of the measure. At this point, the article is an exemplary description of the careful steps taken in the development of such a measure. It outlines a sequence of steps, from the conception of loving as a distinct and measurable entity to the creation of a scale and the demonstration of its usefulness. The first step involves collecting potential items from a wide variety of sources. Rubin used both preceding research and theorizing as well as suggestions from literary works and popular thought. A good investigator does not rely on his or her own idiosyncratic experiences with the attitude in question.

The items thus collected were submitted to a group of people who responded to them in terms of their understanding of liking and loving. This screening begins to eliminate vague and confusing items that might be judged to belong to either realm. This process taps *consensual validity* and assures that the items selected reflect general agreement about which items measure liking and which items measure loving. The second step proceeds to test the *discriminant validity* of the scales; do items labeled as loving actually apply more to a date than to a friend? Grouping together all the judgments made about friends and all those made about dates, Rubin carried out a factor analysis to see what items were in fact used to make the two kinds of judgments. Factor analysis is a technique for identifying items that share a common underlying theme. Items are grouped as a result of the fact that a person who agrees with any one item is also likely to agree with all others in the cluster more than with items in another group. Rubin's goal here was to check that the items on the liking scale clustered together more than any of them related to any loving item and that the same clustering held true for the loving scale. Furthermore, within each scale, Rubin sought items that were not identical in their relation to the whole scale, so that he could feel reasonably confident that he was measuring a range of liking and loving. At this point, the scales were considerably shorter, and Rubin had some confidence that they measured different entities.

The third step deals with *predictive validity* and the question of whether a high score on the scales can predict behavior in any way. Rubin was primarily interested in loving and therefore concerned himself with whether dating partners who, on the basis of their high scale scores, loved each other very much would behave differently from those who, according to their scale scores, loved each other less. He found that high-scoring couples looked at each other more—a finding that can be taken as an indicator of the scale's predictive validity. The three steps described are part of construct validation, and Rubin, by careful and logical analysis, demonstrated that his scale measured what he says it did.

CONSUMER EVALUATION

Cost-Quality Relation

The two selections you have read are methodologically strong and their quality can be considered high. They combined different kinds of measures—an approach that strengthens confidence in the findings. The second study incorporates a follow-up and a real-life component. Although these careful steps increase the quality of the product, they do so at some cost. Relatively large samples were used in initial assessments that led to later selections of subjects. The follow-up described in the second selection takes more time and effort and thus costs more than initial subject recruitment. In this instance, the results of the follow-up limit the possible generalizations from the main findings because, although the more similar and attractive pairs remembered their partners, even these pairs had had very little real contact with each other after the experiment.

The first selection clearly illustrates the high cost of careful scale construction. Newspapers and magazines contain many rating and self-report forms that are, for the most part, no more costly than the writer's time in jotting them down. Scales that meet validity criteria, however, are the products of slow and costly product testing. The steps in scale construction involve not only many respondents but respondents of known characteristics with respect to the dimension under study.

Durability

The Byrne et al. study offers convincing demonstration of the role of attitude similarity in initial attraction. The use of behavioral as well as self-report measures provides some evidence of durability. The Rubin selection describes some initial steps toward measuring that elusive state called love. The measures devised distinguish liking and loving among college students in our society and provide a hint that these feelings are associated with certain differences in the behaviors of these couples. But, as it stands, the product is a very specialized one, albeit one of high quality. Levinger (1972) captured the problem succinctly by describing attraction research as located in a "little sandbox" rather than in the "big quarry" the phenomenon occupies in the real world. These studies have built exemplary castles in the sandbox, castles whose foundations may or may not support bigger structures.

3

INTERPERSONAL DISTANCE

CHAPTER OUTLINE

Interpersonal Space Research
    Spatial Invasion
    Relationship Variables
    Sex Differences
    Cultural Influences
Explanations of Interpersonal Distancing
    Distancing as Expression of
        Possessiveness
    Distancing as Compensation
    Distancing as Learned Behavior
Research Methods in Interpersonal
    Distance
    Laboratory Experiments
    Field Experiments
    Naturalistic Observations
    Scales and Interviews

Two Research Examples
    Product Description
    Consumer Checklist
    Kenneth B. Little, *Cultural variations in
        social schemata.*
    James C. Baxter, *Interpersonal spacing
        in natural settings.*
    The Studies Compared
    Instructions to Subjects
    Demand Characteristics
    Measurement of Interpersonal Distance
    Consumer Evaluation
    Cost-Quality Relation
    Durability

57

Often, as you walk down the street, you'll see a friend coming toward you. At some point after spotting him or her, you'll smile or wave. Then you'll greet each other and, after that, the two of you may stop near each other to talk before going your separate ways. The distances involved in the various phases of that interaction are what this chapter is about. How do people arrange themselves in space for the various social encounters they have? One problem with studying this topic is that such spatial arrangements lie mostly outside your awareness. It is only when your expectations are violated that you are likely to take account of interpersonal spacing; if someone gets too close, you may feel that he is pushy; if someone stands too far away, you may feel that he is cold and unfriendly. At those times, you do notice the spacing and, in wondering about what's going on, you wonder about the other person.

When people from different cultures meet, the question of spatial arrangements is likely to come up because, in addition to possible obvious differences in language and clothing, you may notice subtle nonverbal differences, including how close together people stand. The anthropologist Edward Hall (1959) noticed these differences while watching United Nations delegates from the balcony above a lounge. In his book *The Silent Language,* he described a "UN waltz," in which an Arab diplomat in conversation with an Englishman would move close to his listener to get within comfortable talking distance. The Englishman, reacting to what he must have felt was too close a distance, would back away. From the balcony, the pair appeared to be engaged in a dance, as the approach by one and the avoidance by the other moved them across the floor.

INTERPERSONAL SPACE RESEARCH

People return from a visit abroad with many such anecdotes, but an understanding of the social processes involved requires more than description. The following are some of the findings and explanations of what interpersonal distance is all about. When social psychologists refer to studies on interpersonal distance, they use several different terms. The term *personal space,* introduced by Sommer (1969), refers to "an area with invisible boundaries surrounding a person's body into which intruders may not come" (p. 26). Goffman's (1971, p. 29) similar definition stresses the negative reactions people express when their personal space is encroached upon. This initial understanding of spatial behavior has broadened to include interpersonal distance, territoriality, density, and crowding. *Interpersonal distance* was introduced to describe the distances *between* interactants in a variety of situations. Although the terms territoriality, density, and crowding are also used, they will not be considered directly in this chapter. *Territoriality* concerns itself with spaces people use consistently over time and that they consider "theirs" (Edney, 1974). *Density* usually refers to the actual available space per person, whereas *crowding* refers to the subjective feelings about the space (Linder, 1974). These terms cannot always be kept neatly separate. For example, the sense of what is comfortable space around one's body varies with respect to situations and relationships. If you were alone in an elevator with one other person and that person stood right next to you, you would be quite uncomfortable. If you were in a crowded elevator, exactly that same interpersonal distance would be accepted by you as perfectly natural.

Spatial Invasion

Studies of spatial invasion take place in settings like the elevator. In work pioneered by Sommer and his students (1969), spatial invasions are carried out in a variety of natural settings, including hospitals and college libraries. Upon finding a student seated alone at a large library table, the typical procedure involves sitting down in the chair next to him or her and recording the reactions of the student whose space has been "invaded." Typical reactions include averting the head, putting an elbow between oneself and the other person, treating the invader as an object, and, as a last resort, leaving the scene (Felipe & Sommer, 1966). Other procedures involve leaving markers like clothing or books and noting how much they protect a space an occupant has left (Sommer & Becker, 1969). Spatial invasions involve both interpersonal distance and territoriality. For instance, when people in conversation are standing less than 4 feet apart, passersby are reluctant to walk between them even when walking around them is made inconvenient (Cheyne & Efran, 1972; Efran & Cheyne, 1973, 1974). Conversational space is like property, and trespassing is not welcome. Rules exist about what are appropriate interpersonal distances, and violation of these rules usually produces a negative reaction.

Relationship Variables

As illustrated in the computer-dating study in the preceding chapter, interpersonal spacing can be taken as an indicator of attraction; people stand closer to people they like. Interpersonal spacing can also be taken as an indication of differences in status and intimacy; those standing close are likely to be friends rather than strangers and of equal rather than unequal status. The first research selection in this chapter illustrates these relations. Other research concerning status shows that the closer the members of a small discussion group sit to the group leader, the more favorably they are perceived by fellow group members (Delong, 1970) and that people of equal status sit closer together than people of unequal status (Lott & Sommer, 1967). With regard to intimacy, Mehrabian (1968) found that people stand closer to people they like and that, when someone stands close, it is interpreted as a sign of liking. Conversely, interpersonal distance is increased when people interact with people they don't like. For example, Kleck (1968) conducted several experiments to determine the effects of "stigmatizing" conditions, such as identifying someone as an epileptic or an amputee. The experiments showed that college students sat further away from an alleged epileptic or amputee than they did from the same person without the stigmatizing condition.

Sex Differences

Both research selections included in this chapter address the issue of sex differences in interpersonal spacing. The generalization is often made that women have smaller personal-space zones than men (Evans & Howard, 1973). In a study in which a male and a female experimenter got closer and closer to students of both sexes until told to stop, women allowed both experimenters to get closer to them than men did (Hartnett, Bailey,

& Gibson, 1970). But it is doubtful whether this can be interpreted to mean that women prefer closer interpersonal distances; in fact, when the subjects in this study were asked to walk toward the experimenters until *they* (the subjects) wanted to stop, women stopped at a greater distance. As to men, it seemed to make no difference whether they were approached or approaching. Such findings have usually been interpreted as reflecting a more submissive emotive quality in women that leads them to welcome interpersonal closeness. An alternative interpretation is that women tolerate more spatial invasion as a result of socialization that inhibits the assertiveness associated with defense of territory. A recent spatial-invasion experiment in libraries found that females responded to invasion with flight more quickly than males (Polit & LaFrance, in press). It should be noted that findings on sex differences may be associated with the procedures used. Women operating within the constraints of an experimental design that requires them to ask someone not to come closer may allow a closer approach than they would in a field study, in which escape from the situation is a viable alternative.

Yet another view of sex differences is suggested by Freedman and his associates (1972), who reported an interaction between sex and spatial density on measures of cooperation and aggression. In a number of studies, they found that, under conditions of high density, females were more cooperative and less aggressive than males. Density was manipulated by having the same number of people interact in smaller or larger rooms. These experimenters' explanation suggests that density intensifies the typical expectation for a given situation. Women expect encounters with other women to be sociable and friendly, while men expect more competitive and possibly aggressive interactions with other men; high density accentuates these expectations. This reasoning is allied to the social-learning explanation for interpersonal distance described in the next section. In summary, sex differences in interpersonal spacing are not well understood, a fact that should be kept in mind in evaluating the findings of the two selections included in this chapter.

Cultural Influences

It was Hall's (1966) work on proxemics that stimulated most of the interest in how cultural differences affect interpersonal spacing, and both studies included in this chapter make cultural variables their central concern. Hall (1966) delineated a number of interaction distances, including intimate distance (0 to 1½ feet), personal distance (1½ to 4 feet), social distance (4 to 10 feet), and public distance (beyond 10 feet). When a lecturer visits your campus, you might hear the talk at a public distance; at the reception following the lecture, you might be separated from the guest by a social distance; finally, if you offer the speaker a ride, you would interact with him or her at a personal distance. This sequence might even end in an encounter involving intimate distance. Hall noted that distance determines the kind of interaction that can take place and that people will seek distances appropriate to the sort of encounter they plan to have. Which distances are considered appropriate to which encounters differs with different cultures. Among the UN delegates described by Hall (1959), people from Arabic cultures seemed to prefer a closer social distance than Anglo-Saxons. In an empirical test of some of Hall's observations, preferred conversational distances of male Arab students were compared with those of American students at the same university in the United States (Watson & Graves, 1966). As predicted, the Arabs faced each other more directly, sat closer, talked louder, touched more, and had more eye contact than the American students. In an expanded study (Watson, 1970), people from contact cultures (Arabs, Latin Americans, and Southern Europeans) showed smaller interpersonal distances than members of noncontact cultures (Asians, Northern Europeans, and Indian-Pakistanis). Another study (Forston & Larson, 1968), involving Latin American foreign students, found no cultural differences in interpersonal conversational distances; this finding, however, may be a function of procedural differences. In contrast to those in the Watson and Graves (1966) study, the foreign students in this study were speaking with strangers rather than with friends, in English rather than in their native language, and on an assigned topic rather than in a free conversation. All these elements might reduce the salience of the rules of the culture of origin. The first research selection presents findings in keeping with results indicating that members of contact cultures prefer closer distances than those of noncontact cultures.

The second selection addresses the operation of subcultural differences within this country and is based on such studies as the one by Willis (1966), who found that Blacks greet each other at further distances than do Whites and that interracial pairs seek larger interaction distances than same-race pairs. An extensive observational field study by Jones (1971) compared dyadic-interaction distances for four subcultures in six New York City neighborhoods. No subcultural differences were found for Black Americans, Puerto Ricans, Italians, and Chinese. Jones advanced the notion that there may be a common culture of poverty that prescribes interaction rules overriding subcultural ones. Supporting this view, Aiello and Jones (1971) found that middle-class White children maintained larger distances in play than did Black or Puerto Rican children. It seems likely that members of subcultures existing within American society have knowledge of their own subcultural rules and of those of the dominant culture. This awareness may lead to variability in observed interaction distances.

The existence of cultural differences in interpersonal distancing may cause difficulties in cross-cultural encounters. When two people from different cultures interact, each uses different cues to interpret the other's behavior and each may easily misinterpret the relationship, the activity, or the emotions involved.

EXPLANATIONS OF INTERPERSONAL DISTANCING

The research on interpersonal distancing is notable for its nontheoretical nature. After years of inattention to spatial behavior, social psychologists have begun to study this behavior prolifically but in a regrettably random way. Absence of theory has led researchers to merely describe what is out there, without much indication of thinking about what it might mean. Theory is an essential device for interpreting and changing the generalizations derived from empirical findings. Theorizing is a symbolic enterprise that guides the discovery of new generalizations; without it, research yields a virtually meaningless array of experiences. Experiments are limited to making modest alterations in the patterns found (for example, spatial invasions) and noting to what extent behavior changes. Not only are there virtually no tests of theory in the literature on personal space, but there are even relatively few explanations for the behavior described. Three of the more common attempts at explaining spatial behavior are considered below.

Distancing as Expression of Possessiveness

Borrowing from ethological studies of animal territoriality, some investigators have regarded interpersonal distances as expressions of human territoriality. As noted in more detail in the chapter on aggression, Lorenz (1966) and Ardrey (1966) are among the proponents of the view that humans, like animals, seek distance among themselves to minimize the destructive impact of aggressive instincts. In Ardrey's (1966) view, humans have an instinctual drive to occupy and defend territories, because territories provide the security, stimulation, and identity essential to survival. Although some evidence of territorial behavior can be noted in humans, critics regard the ethological analogies as oversimplifications. Humans vary widely in their forms of territorial expression (Alland, 1972), and, as the research on spatial invasion shows, defense of territory is a far rarer occurrence in humans than in animals. While cross-species comparisons can be suggestive and useful, literal equivalents are to be avoided. Humans do not refurbish their houses for the same reasons birds build nests, and nations do not fight wars for the same reasons prides of lions defend territories.

A sociological rather than ethological approach to interpersonal distancing is offered by Goffman (1971). He uses the term *claim* to describe an entitlement to possess, control, use, or dispose of something. When the entitlement is complete, Goffman speaks of the claims as *fixed territories*. The right to possess, control, use, and dispose of one's land or house is an example of a fixed territory. *Situational territories,* like park benches and library tables, permit of temporary claims, with the right of use and some control but no possession or disposal. Lastly, *egocentric territories* move with the person and include personal possessions such as clothing, as well as the spatial contours elsewhere termed *personal space.* Goffman suggests that when two individuals are alone in a setting, concern about personal space becomes concern over interpersonal distance (1971, p. 30). In the main, this approach to distance is no more explanatory than the ethological one.

Distancing as Compensation

Argyle and Dean (1965) regard interpersonal distancing as one of a number of nonverbal behaviors that combine to provide a mutually satisfying level of intimacy in social encounters. Intimacy is defined as a joint function of interpersonal distance, eye contact, body orientation, facial expression, and other related variables. The affiliation-conflict theory formulated by Argyle and Dean postulates a state of equilibrium in which the approach forces balance the avoidance forces in any social encounter. Expectation, past experience, and social custom determine what is a comfortable equilibrium for a given encounter; if that equilibrium is disturbed, compensatory change will reestablish it. For example, in the "UN waltz" described above, Anglo-Saxons moved away when approached by Arab delegates. But suppose they were seated or standing in a setting where such movement was not possible; then, the compensatory change to restore a comfortable equilibrium might take place in another nonverbal modality. For example, the Anglo-Saxon could reduce the unwanted intimacy by gaze avoidance, by facing away from the Arab, by making the conversation more casual, or by any number of other compensations.

A given person will have different comfortable equilibrium levels depending on where he or she is and with whom. The physical distance at which most people interact with an intimate in private is much closer than that at which they interact with an acquaintance in public. In any case, the theory suggests that when the equilibrium is disturbed some behavioral compensation takes place. Empirical support for this theory is strongest for relations between eye contact and distance and between body orientation and distance (Patterson, 1973). Closer approaches typically result in less-confronting orientations and reduced eye contact.

Distancing as Learned Behavior

Variations in distances found to be comfortable led to the application of social-learning theory to distancing behavior. Social-learning theory (Rotter, 1972) explains goal-directed behavior as a function of two concepts, expectancy and reinforcement value. Your expectancy that you will actually be reinforced for a behavior is based on your past experience with that situation, and so is the value of the reinforcement. Positive reinforcements in the past strengthen your expectation that positive reinforcements will occur in the present and thereby increase the chance that you will repeat that behavior. The specific expectancy for a particular situation generalizes to similar situations. Much of Rotter's (1966) work was concerned with describing such generalized expectancies, or personality traits. Chief among these is the dimension of locus of control. *Locus of control* refers to a person's general belief that events happen either as a result of his or her own efforts (internal control) or as a consequence of luck, chance, or fate (external control).

The application of social-learning theory to interpersonal distancing holds that those with an external locus of control ("externals") prefer greater interpersonal distances than those with an internal locus of control ("internals") (Duke & Nowicki, 1972). The assumption is made that externals, feeling less in control of events that befall them, find spatial closeness more threatening, and especially so with strangers. With friends and relatives, instead, the theory predicts no differences in spatial distancing based on locus of control expectancies. Confirmation of these predictions by experimental results has led to the hope that the social-learning model can serve to organize spatial research theoretically. To what extent this ambitious promise will be realized remains to be seen, but it does seem to place undue reliance on the personality predisposition expressed by locus of control. Consider to what extent this explanation can encompass situational differences, cultural variations, or animal spatial behavior.

RESEARCH METHODS IN INTERPERSONAL DISTANCE

A general problem in research is the selection of appropriate measures. In social psychology, because of the broad spectrum of social issues, this selection becomes a highly demanding and creative task for the researcher. Phenomena like attraction or prejudice can prove very elusive when attempts are made to assess them directly and unequivocally. Other phenomena, on the other hand, appear to be susceptible of precise and unambiguous assessment, and interpersonal space is one of them. The operational definition of interpersonal space, as measured in centimeters or feet or whatever, appears to be appropriate to the conceptual definition of the variable. It seems then, with this one variable at least, that we do not have to infer its presence—we can measure it directly.

As we shall see in the following chapters, variables like altruism and aggression admit of many operational definitions because the conceptual variables themselves are multifaceted. Altruism encompasses a wide variety of behaviors, from charitable donations to heroic rescues, and so does aggression, which includes everything from physical assault to critical comment. Although interpersonal space appears conceptually simpler, the operational definitions have been varied and numerous. Laboratory strategies have included instructions to subjects to approach an experimenter (Dosey & Meisels, 1969) or a life-sized picture of another person (Argyle & Dean, 1965) or a coatrack (Horowitz, Duff, & Stratton, 1964) until they feel that they are at a comfortable distance. Subjects have also been asked to arrange distances between photographs (Kleck, 1967), silhouettes (Levinger & Gunner, 1967), geometric forms (Kuethe, 1962), or real persons (Little, 1965) in order to represent particular interpersonal events. In addition to unobtrusive measurements of people in naturalistic settings (Jones, 1971), subjects have been given a variety of obtrusive paper-and-pencil measures and asked to indicate their preferred distances (Dosey & Meisels, 1969).

While this variety suggests an implicit recognition of a more complex nature of interpersonal space than was initially thought, little attempt was made until very recently to assess the amount of convergence among these various measures. Knowles &

Johnsen (1974) examined their underlying commonalities and noted two dimensions: level of participation required of the subject—that is, whether he or she was involved directly or was an outside arranger—and obtrusiveness—that is, whether the subject was aware of what was being measured. The two research selections to follow represent the two opposite ends of these dimensions. The laboratory study by Little entails spatial arrangements by aware subjects, whereas Baxter studies active spacing unobtrusively in a natural setting.

Laboratory Experiments

Laboratory experiments on interpersonal distance are concerned mainly with the effect of different contexts on spatial behavior. Several methods are used to vary context, including instructional, social, and environmental manipulation.

In the first methodological approach, subjects are presented with identical instructions, except for the substitution of a few words. In a study of this kind, Rosenfeld (1965) asked half of his subjects to enter a room and seek the approval of the person they found in the room (actually a confederate who had been trained to behave in the same way toward all subjects). Before entering the room, subjects were told to imagine that they were entering a dormitory lounge to win approval from the person they found there. The other half of the subjects were instructed to avoid winning approval from the person in the room. Each subject was then given a chair to take with her. Interpersonal distance was measured by measuring how close to the experimental confederate the subjects placed their chairs. Approval-seeking subjects placed themselves closer to the confederate than did the approval-avoiding subjects.

A laboratory study that combines both social and environmental manipulations is one by White (1975). As in the Rosenfeld procedure described above, subjects were asked to place a chair at a suitable distance to engage in conversation with an experimental confederate. These conversations were part of an ongoing orientation program for college freshmen. Interpersonal distance between the two seated speakers was measured unobtrusively as the sum of two distances: from front-of-chair leg to front-of-chair leg and from bridge of nose to chair front. The social manipulation involved a status variable and consisted of introducing the confederate as either a peer of the subject (a college freshman like the subject) or as a superior (a research professor). The environmental manipulation involved varying the size of the room in which the conversations took place. Previous research had shown that people tend to sit closer in larger rooms than in smaller ones. Results confirmed this environmental prediction but showed no effects of the social manipulation. This was surprising, since prior research had indicated that people sit closer to others of equivalent status than to those of different status.

Field Experiments

In the laboratory experiments described above, interpersonal distance was measured as unobtrusively as possible. Although the subjects were probably aware that some aspect of themselves was under study, considerable care was taken to conceal the measuring process. In both experiments, this was done by measuring the distance between chairs after the end of the conversation.

In an effort to minimize subject awareness even further, a number of investigators have taken their designs into the field. The "field" for Barefoot, Hoople, and McClay (1972) was the area surrounding a drinking fountain in a public building. While most studies of spatial invasion have concentrated on the reactions of the invaded, this study focused on the potential invaders. Reasoning that close personal proximity can be aversive, Barefoot and associates predicted that people seek to avoid situations in which they might come too close to another. To operationalize this situation, an experimenter sat either very close to (1 foot) or far from (10 feet) a drinking fountain. The dependent measures were the percentage of people who drank from the fountain and the time people spent drinking. Fewer subjects drank, and for a shorter time, in the close condition but only with a female experimenter; there were no significant effects for male experimenters. Apparently, this was the result of people avoiding an activity that might violate another's space; but why women should prove to be a greater barrier than men is unclear.

Other favored experimental "fields" are the college library and cafeteria. In a series of short experiments, Sommer and Becker (1969) investigated the conditions under which territorial claims for sharing available space would be made in the presence of another. Reasoning that, if given the option, people tend to seek maximum distance between themselves and others, these investigators predicted that fewer people would enter a small room if someone else was already there. An account was kept of the number of people coming into a room, which contained three tables, when someone sat at the middle table, as opposed to the number of people who entered the room when nobody was there. While people delayed their entry longer if someone else was already in the room, there were no differences in the numbers of people who actually entered the room.

The remaining miniexperiments reported in the Sommer and Becker article were concerned with testing the conditions under which claims for space are made in the absence of a person actively occupying a particular space. Various markers, including a wrapped sandwich, a sweater draped over a chair, and some paperback books, were placed on an unoccupied soda-fountain table. Results indicated that unmarked tables were occupied significantly sooner than tables where some personal marker had been left. Variations were then introduced into a study-hall environment to assess whether a person would defend another's space in the latter's absence. These variations included the selection of a table occupied by one person, the entry and then the apparently temporary exit of a confederate who left some personal possessions behind, and finally the entry of another confederate who signaled his intention to take the seat of the now absent confederate. The dependent measure was the number of times that the subject defended the confederate's space. Only when the subject was asked directly if the seat was taken did he defend his neighbor's territory.

In both field experiments described above, subject awareness of being studied was intentionally kept low, thus reducing the reactivity of the responses. Hence, subjects were reacting fairly spontaneously to the experimental manipulations rather than to the observation process itself. This is for the most part a plus for these field experiments. On the negative side, there is the difficulty of ruling out alternative explanations—an enduring problem in field research. Both experiments included control groups to rule out that people were avoiding tables or drinking fountains even when there were no signs of another's occupancy, but some relevant sources of influence were not controlled. For example, Barefoot, Hoople, and McClay (1972) report that many of the potential subjects worked in the building housing the drinking fountain and hence became aware of the experiment. While these workers were not included in the data analysis, there are still some unexplored questions about familiarity with the setting and the like.

Naturalistic Observations

Researchers who conduct field studies do so on the assumption that validity is enhanced by assessing behavior in the physical and social environment that gives rise to it. Less concerned with introducing experimental manipulations and more concerned with observing behavior as it occurs naturally, these investigators have observed interpersonal distances in a variety of public places.

Aiello and Jones (1971) observed the interpersonal space selected in school playgrounds by interacting pairs of first- and second-grade children from three subcultural groups. Black and Puerto Rican samples were selected from a lower-class elementary school, whereas observations of the White samples were taken at a middle-class elementary school. Praiseworthy care was taken in the preparation of the "teacher-judges"; for example, the judges were kept ignorant of the research hypotheses, and they were trained to collect the data with a high level of accuracy and agreement. The judges were asked to record interaction distances of dyads during recess periods in school playgrounds, as soon as the children were seen conversing and remaining relatively stationary. The study revealed some significant subcultural differences— among them, that White children stand farther apart than either Black or Puerto Rican children. It was also found that White boys stand farther apart than White girls, but no such sex differences were detected for the Puerto Rican or Black samples. Despite considerable strengths in the observational procedures used by Aiello and Jones, one weakness seems to be that observations were made by different observers in the different settings. The subcultural differences recorded may be due as much to these variations as to real differences in subcultural behaviors. Such ambiguity is not uncommon in naturalistic observations, but it can be reduced, as shown in the second selection included in this chapter.

Most studies make measurements at a single point in time. An exception is the observational study by McGrew and McGrew (1975), dealing with the spacing behavior of preschool children during group development. More specifically, these investigators looked at differences in interpersonal distancing both as a function of time spent together and as a function of the children's being either veterans or new recruits of the preschool group. Observations were made of each child minute by minute during play periods, and the observed distances were recorded on the nursery-school floorplan. These distances were later categorized according to an eight-point system ranging from peer contact to solitary play. Despite considerable distancing consistency over time, there was some tendency toward joint occupancy of the same spaces, especially for the nursery-experienced children. Comparisons made with primate spatial behavior indicated provocative similarities in the amount of time children and monkeys spend in proximity to others.

These observational techniques are time consuming and require the sustained presence of trained observers. Subject awareness is kept low, except for the effect of the observers, whose presence may be minimally noticeable and quickly adapted to. Observational procedures allow for little experimenter manipulation of antecedent conditions. Both studies observed play periods, which may be situations freer of the constraints that govern other school settings, thus allowing greater range for the spatial behavior under study. Interpersonal distancing occurs largely outside the person's awareness; since this may be especially true with children, observations are preferable to measures depending on self-report.

Scales and Interviews

There have been few large-scale survey studies of spatial behavior. One such study involved an interesting test of time-territory relations (Edney, 1972). The investigator hypothesized that territorial possessiveness would be strengthened by long-term association with a place. He selected suburban houses defended by fences and No Trespassing signs and comparable houses with no such defenses. Edney's interviews with the occupants confirmed his prediction that those in defended houses had lived there longer and expected to continue to live there longer.

As a rule, since interview studies tend to ask fairly direct questions, they are characterized by high subject awareness both of being studied and of the researchers' intent. The Edney (1972) study is unusual in this regard, for, although subjects were aware of someone at their door asking questions, the investigator's actual purpose was not obvious; questions dealt with the occupants' time perspective and not with the fence/no-fence distinction that was the researcher's concern.

The use of scales and paper-and-pencil measures has had considerable appeal in the study of spatial distancing, in part because the creation and measurement of real spacing are sometimes cumbersome and in part because distance estimates can be inaccurate. The fact that spaces can be represented in maps, floor plans, and spatial layouts makes the development of scales appealing. A recent measure—the Comfortable Interpersonal Distance Scale (Duke & Nowicki, 1972)—is a paper-and-pencil figural layout. It consists of a display resembling an asterisk, with eight lines coming from a central point, each line ending in a randomly numbered point identified as a door to an imaginary room. Typical instructions ask subjects to imagine themselves standing at the central point and to mark on each radius where they would want a person approaching them from each door to stop. The scale developers report satisfactory test-retest reliabilities for a two-week interval. In a validity check, moderate correlations between scale scores and approach distances allowed real persons in an experimental setting were obtained (Duke & Kiebach, 1974). As the scale can be group-administered, it is an efficient measure of personal space. Obviously, it does not take the interactional aspects of interpersonal distancing into account, but it may be useful for measuring a person's preferences in this regard.

In the first study reprinted below, a similar representational measure is used. Representational measures have a common history in the work done by Kuethe (1962, 1964) on "social schemata"—that is, how people think social stimuli should be arranged. Kuethe's measure involved placing yellow-felt outlines of humans or objects on a blue-felt field stretched on a wall of the experimental room. The nap of the felt permitted the felt outlines to cling wherever placed and to leave no marks when moved. The technique was modified by Levinger and Gunner (1967) by use of silhouettes made of sticky black tape placed on ditto paper. For scoring interpersonal distances, the paper can be placed on an illuminated glass box with graph paper superimposed. Scoring of distances is virtually error-free, a permanent record is obtained, and the procedure can be group-administered.

Such scales are high in subject awareness, since respondents know that they are being studied and they also know what particular aspects of their behavior the researcher is concerned about. The Duke and Nowicki (1972) measure is reported to be free of social-desirability effects, presumably reflecting the fact that subjects are not strongly constrained by any rules concerning how closely one should let an unspecified person approach.

TWO RESEARCH EXAMPLES

Product Description

These days, the familiar expression "What a small world this is!" seems to have become increasingly appropriate. This may be due to several reasons. For example, because of crowding, you may now quite literally be bumping into more people; also, people with all varieties of ethnic and cultural backgrounds are finding themselves more and more in the same locales. Consequently, cultural differences are becoming more than an academic concern. Both selections to follow address, with different methods, the issue of cultural differences in interpersonal spacing.

In the first study, Little (1968) used a laboratory setting to determine how people from different cultures spatially arrange social stimuli. He hypothesized that people from "contact" cultures (for example, Italians) would prefer closer interpersonal distances than would people from noncontact cultures (for example, Scots). He made three additional predictions: females would prefer closer distances than males, friends would select closer distances than strangers, and pleasant encounters would result in smaller-space arrangements than unpleasant ones.

College students from five cultures were asked to imagine various situations in which two people might be interacting. They were given two dolls and were instructed to arrange them on a piece of paper as if a real encounter were taking place. Nineteen different situations were described and, consequently, 19 spatial distances were noted. Little found support for his cultural and situational predictions; however, the sex differences were more complex than expected.

In the second selection presented here, Baxter (1970) examined the interpersonal spacing of subject pairs representing three ethnic subgroups within American culture. Regarding his approach as exploratory, Baxter did not state specific hypotheses. However, in view of previous work by Hall (1966) and Little (1968), Baxter did expect to find differences in the pairs' interpersonal spacing according to ethnic-group membership, age, and sex of the participants, as well as indoor or outdoor location of the encounter.

Baxter chose as his research location a zoo visited by large numbers of people of both sexes and of different ages and ethnic backgrounds. The interpersonal distance maintained by the pairs passing between two observation points was unobtrusively coded. Results indicated significant subcultural, sex, and age differences. As you've seen in the chapter on attraction, comparing two studies takes careful reading. The checklist below might be of help when you compare the two selections that follow.

Consumer Checklist

- How was the product developed?
    What information does the study provide about the instructions to subjects?
    Do people of different cultures react the same way to being in an experiment?
- What care was taken to ensure a quality product?
    Are there differences in the ways in which these studies standardize their observations?

CULTURAL VARIATIONS IN SOCIAL SCHEMATA [1]

KENNETH B. LITTLE

University of Denver

Social interaction distances among 5 national groups, United States American, Swedish, Greek, Southern Italian, and Scot, were studied using doll placements to elicit 19 different social schemata. There was considerable agreement among the groups as to the ordering of the distances for the different transactions, but significant differences among nationalities as to the mean distance at which the various interactions were judged as taking place. The hypothesis that the Mediterranean culture Ss would have closer interaction distances as compared to North European Ss was confirmed at a high level of significance; the hypotheses that *all* interaction involving female surrogates would be seen as occurring at closer distances than those involving males was not supported. In general, female-female transactions of an intimate nature, or those involving unpleasant topics, will be judged as occurring at closer distances than male-male interaction. For interactions with authority figures or with superiors, on the other hand, the female-female distances will be judged as occurring at substantially greater than male-male. (Since the Ss in this study were always the same sex as the stimulus figures this conclusion cannot be generalized to cross-sex judgments.) The major single factor determining distances in dyadic schemata appears to be the relationship between the members with the specific content or affective tone of the transaction as the next most important.

Social schemata as defined and elaborated by Kuethe (1962a, 1962b, 1964) and Kuethe and Stricker (1963) refers to the tendency of human subjects to group humanoid stimulus objects together. The grouping generally occurs with high agreement among members of the same culture in both patterns of arrangement and the distances separating the objects. It is asserted that common social experiences determine the modal response and that deviations from it are the result of idiosyncratic factors such as personality dynamics, needs, and the like. The work of Kuethe and Weingartner (1964), Fisher (1967), and Weinstein (1965, 1967) is based on the second assumption.

Lewit and Joy (1967) have argued, however, that the groupings may result from factors independent of the *social* experiences of the subjects. For example, the use of stimulus figures suggesting motion may facilitate or minimize the tendency toward grouping depending upon the direction of the implied movement. Such stimulus factors are learned but not necessarily "social" in nature. Social schemata for Lewit and Joy are thus but one of the determinants of the grouping of social objects with "kinetic" schemata and possibly even broader organizing principles such as "socio-spatial" schemata operating to determine the final arrangement.

The arguments of Lewit and Joy seem somewhat tangential to Kuethe's definition of social schemata since he repeatedly states that they emerge only under "ambiguous" or "minimal information" conditions. It is obviously possible to structure the stimulus characteristics of social objects so that grouping—in the sense of the objects being placed close together—would be highly improbable. An example might be two figures with knives extended toward each other. Similarly, it seems equally likely that little difference would ensue between the placements of inanimate objects or symbols and that of human surrogates if the conditions of manipulation or instructions to the subject insured that the humanoid stimuli were viewed as nonanimate by that subject. The converse is quite certainly true; in free placement of 6-inch doll figures and plain gray cylinders of the same size under identical instructions, correlations have been obtained ranging from .68 to .92

[1] This research was supported in part by Grant MH-08142 from the United States Public Health Service and in part from a grant from the Faculty Research Fund of the University of Denver.

From *Journal of Personality and Social Psychology*, 1968, *10*(1), 1–7. Copyright 1968 by American Psychological Association. Reprinted by permission.

between placements with nondiffering means for distances between dolls and distances between cylinders.

The study reported here stems from a somewhat different research orientation than in those cited above. The approach to measurement is the opposite of that of the investigators cited above in that it assumes, a priori, that social schemata exist—and exist in a highly structured form. The goals of measurement are to describe the schemata (in inches of separation of figures, angle of placement, etc.) and to determine by experimental manipulation or examination of natural variations the specific factors that determine an individual schema.

Social schemata defined in this fashion—as reproduced interaction distances between individuals—and elicited as described above, tend to result in figure placements that fall into the usual personal space zones, that is, intimate, casual-personal, or social-consultative (cf. Hall, 1959, 1966; Sommer, 1959). However, several factors which will modify *specific* distances between figures have already been established: the nature of the interaction, assumed or specified degree of acquaintance of the members, the setting in which the transaction occurs, sex of dyad members, sex of subjects, etc. (Little, 1965; Little, Ulehla, & Henderson, 1968). Based, as the judgments must be, upon experiences of the subjects in observing social interactions, a number of other intra- and extraindividual factors seem reasonable. One of the most likely candidates is the cultural background of the observer. The evidence for cultural variation in distances for "live" transactions is strong (e.g., Hall, 1959), so it is a reasonable assumption that members of different cultural groups should have social schemata differing in interaction distances.

The purpose of the present study was to examine variations in social schemata among five different national groups: United States American, Greek, Southern Italian, Swedish, and Scot. The two Mediterranean groups were selected as examples of contact peoples and the North European as noncontact. (A "contact culture" is one that has a minimum of taboos against physical contact in public social situations, e.g., two men embracing or walking arm in arm—cf. Hall, 1966.) Since the research was primarily to locate such differences as might exist, only a minimal number of hypotheses were advanced. These were: (*a*) Individuals from contact groups (Greek and Italian) will have social schemata characterized by closer distances than those from noncontact groups (Scots and Swedes); (*b*) on the average, schemata involving female surrogates will be characterized by closer distances than those involving males; (*c*) there will be an increase in distance between dyad members as the content of the interaction varies from pleasant through neutral to unpleasant. On the basis of earlier work (Little, 1965; Little et al., 1968), the additional prediction was added that there would be a linear decrease in distance between dyad members as a function of degree of acquaintance imputed to them.

Method

Materials. The materials for determining the social schemata consisted of four gray plastic dolls, two male and two female. The figures were designed to represent men and women of college age in relaxed, neutral standing positions and were highly stylized, that is, faces were rounded off, clothing (casual) barely suggested, etc. Figures of the same sex were approximately the same size and scaled 1 inch to 1 foot, that is, the figures were about 6 inches tall for the males and 5.4 inches for the females.

Instructional sets. Nineteen structured situations were used in addition to one example and one practice item. Table 1 gives the English versions of the instructional sets. Sixteen were identical for men and for women except for pronoun changes; for three, different wordings (in parentheses) were used for female subjects. Nine of the items (Numbers 1 to 9) constituted a balanced set of three levels of acquaintanceship (friend, acquaintance, stranger) and three levels of affective tone of conversational topic (pleasant, neutral, unpleasant); six items (10–15) tapped superior-subordinate relations and interaction with an authority; and the remaining four items (16–19), intimacy versus consultation in the transactions.

All items were translated into Swedish, Italian, and Greek and back-translated by native speakers of the language concerned. The final set for each national group was then further checked for regional or local linguistic variations by a native-speaking psychologist in the locale in which they were to be administered.[2]

[2] The author is deeply grateful for the assistance of the following individuals and institutions: Gustavo Iacono, Maria Sbandi, and Roberto Gentile, Institute of Psychology, University of Naples; George

TABLE 1
Instructional Sets

Degree of acquaintance and affective tone of communication

1. Two good friends talking about a pleasant topic.
2. Two good friends talking about a topic that is neither particularly pleasant nor unpleasant.
3. Two good friends talking about an unpleasant topic.
4. Two acquaintances talking about a pleasant topic.
5. Two acquaintances talking about a topic that is neither particulary pleasant nor unpleasant.
6. Two acquaintances talking about an unpleasant topic.
7. Two strangers talking about a pleasant topic.
8. Two strangers talking about a topic that is neither particularly pleasant nor unpleasant.
9. Two strangers talking about an unpleasant topic.

Superior-subordinate and authority interactions

10. A policeman questioning a person about some burglaries that have occurred in the neighborhood. (A teacher questioning a student about the theft of some important books from the library.)
11. An employer reprimanding an employee for some errors in his work.
12. A manager of a shop being asked by one of the assistants the best way to carry out a task.
13. A person asking a policeman how to get to a certain address. (A new student asking a teacher for directions to a classroom.)
14. A worker and his foreman having an argument over the best way of carrying out a task. (A seamstress and a designer having an argument over the best way of completing a garment.)
15. A shop owner discussing the weather with his assistant.

Intimate versus consultative interactions

16. Two people talking about some business affairs. One of them is consulting with the other about the best way to carry out the deal.
17. Two people talking about the best place to shop.
18. Two people talking very intimately together. They are unhappy since a mutual friend has just been killed in an accident.
19. Two people talking about some intimate matters. They are disagreeing on the best course of action to take.

Subjects. The subjects were native-born undergraduate college students in the Universities of Denver, Naples, Lund, and Edinburgh. For Greek subjects, students at Pierce College and the Athenian Polytechnical Institute were used. Table 2 gives the number of male and female subjects involved.

Procedure. Each subject was tested individually by a native-born research assistant. *The dolls were of the same sex as the subject in every case.* Instructions were to place the pair of dolls on a piece of and Vasso Vassiliou, James Georgas, Mariella Papayannis, and Mania Seferis, Athenian Institute for Anthropos; Martin Johnson and students, Department of Psychology, University of Lund; and Halla Beloff and students, Department of Psychology, University of Edinburgh.

12 × 18-inch newsprint so that they "looked natural" for the specified transaction. Each item had been typed on a 3 × 5-inch card which was handed to the subject with the request that he read it aloud before arranging the dolls. He was informed that the sheet of paper represented a fairly large, quiet room and that there were no other people around. After the subject had placed the dolls to his satisfaction, he was asked how the conversation might go between the two individuals. (The purpose of this request was to minimize for the subject the experimenter's interest in the interaction distance.) The experimenter then drew a line around the base of each figure to mark position and angle of placement, and proceeded to the next item with a new piece of newsprint. Ten different random orders of the 19 experimental items were used; the example item and practice item were always administered first.

The stimulus figures were apparently sufficiently abstract so that subjects had no difficulty "projecting" different roles onto them. The one exception was comments from two Greek females subjects that one of the figures should have been in a more "respectful" attitude for Item 11.

Results

Since different angles of placement of figures for the same situation might affect distances between them, an initial analysis was made of this factor. The responses of each subject were classified into nine categories of directness of confrontation starting with face-to-face placements and ending with back-to-back. The last four categories (side-by-side to back-to-back) were found to account for only 2.3% of the total number of placements and were eliminated from further analysis. Distance scores in such arrangements were treated as missing data. Among the remaining five categories, analysis of variance indicated no significant differences in distance ($F = 1.11$, $df = 4/438$) as a function of angle of placement. Consequently, the distance scores were used without correction.

Table 2 gives the mean distance between dolls (in twelfths of an inch) for instructional set by sex and by national group. Previous work (Little, 1965) indicates that close to a direct scale translation can be made for placement of doll-like figures and placement of actors for the same situation, that is, a distance of $1/12$ inch for the dolls will be about 1 inch for humans.

The first analyses made were to test the hypotheses advanced. For the first (closer average figure placements for contact versus

TABLE 2
Mean Distance between Figures in Twelfths of an Inch for Five National Groups

Item	American M	American F	Swede M	Swede F	Scot M	Scot F	Greek M	Greek F	Italian M	Italian F	Average M	Average F
n^a	53	53	42	43	50	50	35	35	36	35	216	216
1	21.6	19.4	25.7	22.5	23.9	30.5	23.8	18.4	23.5	21.6	23.7	22.5
2	25.6	29.2	29.9	28.8	33.7	38.6	24.7	23.3	28.2	29.7	28.4	29.9
3	28.0	25.8	32.1	21.2	28.6	36.4	25.1	18.4	27.0	24.3	28.2	25.2
4	25.9	26.8	26.8	25.6	25.6	41.6	28.7	20.3	26.9	25.8	26.8	28.0
5	27.5	36.4	32.8	29.8	28.1	39.1	28.2	24.1	29.3	27.6	29.2	31.4
6	27.7	28.8	30.2	28.6	31.5	36.8	23.2	19.8	31.1	26.4	28.7	28.1
7	31.0	33.1	36.4	34.4	32.4	37.1	32.2	25.3	31.2	28.7	32.6	31.7
8	31.4	38.0	34.5	37.5	35.3	40.6	28.7	26.7	34.1	30.1	32.8	34.6
9	31.5	38.1	33.1	36.9	37.6	36.7	37.1	28.4	35.8	32.0	35.0	34.4
10	27.9	34.8	30.3	33.5	38.0	49.0	30.9	28.7	34.0	34.5	32.2	36.1
11	30.3	38.2	39.2	44.7	51.3	48.9	36.2	29.5	38.1	35.3	39.0	39.31
12	31.5	36.6	37.4	39.4	39.7	45.7	32.8	32.7	38.2	31.9	35.9	37.3
13	30.4	39.1	33.8	40.0	29.3	49.3	22.5	28.1	27.7	34.5	28.7	38.2
14	30.6	32.6	33.3	40.9	39.2	42.8	28.0	27.5	35.2	30.6	33.3	34.9
15	34.2	44.6	41.8	48.4	53.2	50.5	40.2	43.9	42.6	39.2	42.4	45.3
16	27.5	31.5	29.8	27.5	33.6	44.7	30.4	23.6	30.6	25.5	30.4	30.6
17	27.7	27.8	31.5	32.2	26.7	36.9	28.0	22.4	31.6	29.0	29.1	29.7
18	20.0	14.1	25.3	18.8	18.4	20.7	22.5	17.3	22.3	21.9	21.7	18.6
19	21.6	22.7	27.3	22.6	31.1	28.7	25.5	19.7	26.8	20.6	26.5	22.9
Av.	28.0	31.5	32.2	32.3	33.5	39.7	28.9	25.2	31.3	28.9	30.8	31.5

[a] The n varies slightly for different items because of missing data.

TABLE 3
Analysis of Variance of Distances between Figures for Three Degrees of Acquaintance and Three Levels of Affective Tone

Source	df	MS	F
Sex (S)	1	2972.6	1.9
Nationality (N)	4	4111.5	2.7*
S × N	4	4311.6	2.8*
Error$_{SN}$	340	1525.5	—
Acquaintance (A)	2	29164.7	77.5***
S × A	2	171.0	—
N × A	8	307.8	—
S × N × A	8	237.5	—
Error$_{ASN}$	680	376.5	—
Affective Tone (T)	2	6186.2	18.7***
T × S	2	1267.3	3.8*
T × N	8	355.4	—
T × S × N	8	237.5	—
Error$_{TSN}$	680	331.2	—
A × T	4	1022.5	3.8**
S × A × T	4	122.2	—
N × A × T	16	218.9	—
S × N × A × T	16	126.8	—
Error$_{ATSN}$	1360	270.6	—

* $p < .05$.
** $p < .01$.
*** $p < .001$.

noncontact cultures), a test was made of the difference between mean placements over all 19 schemata for Greek and Italian subjects combined ($n = 141$) and Scot and Swedish subjects ($n = 185$). The difference was quite significant ($t = 8.8$) and in the direction predicted. The respective mean values were 28.6 and 34.4. A similar test made of the differences in average distance between placements of female figures and that of males (including American subjects in this case) gave mean values of 31.5 and 30.8, respectively. The t was not significant and the direction of the mean difference was opposite that expected.

For hypotheses c and d regarding the effects of degree of acquaintance and affective tones of the interaction, an analysis of variance (Table 3) was made of the response to instructional Sets 1–9. Since the computer program could not handle unequal Ns, a random sample was taken of 35 subjects in each subject group.

Two of the four main effects in the analysis were significant at less than the .001 level: the degree of acquaintance imputed to the figures and affective tone of the interaction. The nationality of the subjects was significant at less than the .05 level and sex differences, as before, were nonsignificant.

Among national groups, Greeks had the closest average schemata, Americans and Italians next (with no significant difference between them), then Swedes, and finally Scots. As for the two attributes of the instuctional sets provided to the subjects (imputed degree of acquaintance and affective tone of the conversation), friends are seen as interacting closer together than acquaintances, and acquaintances closer than strangers. In regard to affect, however, although pleasant topics clearly produced the closest placement of the figures, the neutral and unpleasant topic situations were not significantly different with a trend for the latter-judged interaction distances to be closer. This effect is produced entirely by the transactions between friends and between acquaintances; the judgments of interactions of strangers is as predicted, that is, a linear increase in distance as the topic goes from pleasant to unpleasant.

Of the six two-factor interactions, one was significant at less than the .01 level (Acquaintance × Affective Tone) and two at less than the .05 level (Sex × Nationality and Sex × Affective Tone). The first reflects the pattern differences described above. The other two give some clues as to the lack of any definitive result in the overall test for sex differences. In regard to the first interaction, Italian and Greek women place female figures significantly closer than their male counterparts place *male* figures. On the other hand, Scot and American females place female figures significantly farther apart than male figures are placed by the men of those nationalities. Swedish subjects treat the male and female stimulus objects almost identically. In the Sex × Affective Tone effect, women perceive neutral topics as discussed at greater distances and unpleasant topics at closer distances than do male subjects.

A somewhat similar situation occurs in the comparison of social consultative transactions with intimate ones. The latter clearly takes place at closer distances than the former, with females using significantly closer distances than males.

A separate analysis was made of the responses to authority and superior-subordinate instructional sets. Four items (Numbers 10, 11, 12, and 13) were selected from the six administered. These items appeared with high factor loadings on a single factor in analyses conducted on the 19 items separately for men and women subjects. Sums of the distances for the four items combined were used as factor score estimates, and an analysis of variance was made by sex of subject (confounded with sex of stimulus objects) and national origin. The difference between the means of the two sexes was quite marked ($F = 9.0$; $df = 1/422$) as were differences among nationalities ($F = 5.5$; $df = 4/422$). The interaction effect was not significant.

In the main effects, women see interactions of women with authority figures or superiors taking place at a greater distance than men view similar transactions of male figures. The differences among nationalities paralleled that observed for means over all 19 items (Table 2).

A comparison was also made of the *patterns* of means presented in Table 2. A rank-order correlation of the distances for the 19 items was computed for each possible pairing of the 10 subject groups. The rhos ranged from .59 to .92, with an average of .78. There would thus seem to be a substantial amount of agreement among the several groups as to ordering of the distances appropriate for different transactions.

As a final analysis, reliabilities of the responses to the individual items and reliabilities of the average response to all 19 were estimated using the relationship of within-subjects variation to between-subjects variation. Item reliabilities ranged from .64 to .79 among the 10 groups; reliabilities of average scores (across 19 items), from .97 to .99. In other work, test-retest reliabilities for individual items ranged between .66 and .93 depending upon the particular instructional set and the sex of the judges,

Discussion

The results of the study indicate considerable similarity among the five national groups in overall *ordering* of distances for the schemata used. Since all groups represent the Western European culture in some fashion, this ordering is perhaps to be expected. The conclusion holds, however, only for the instructional sets used here, by no means a random selection of all possible schemata. By judicious selection of topical schemata, one could probably raise or lower the rhos at will.

Within the general agreement on ordering are marked differences in average *distances* at which the various transactions are judged to take place. The most clear-cut is the difference between the two Mediterranean groups and the North European subjects. Insofar as the doll arrangements accurately reflect interaction distances within the society, the stereotypes about the contrasted groups are correct. The surprising observation was the greater similarity of Americans to the Italian subjects than to either Swedes or Scots. No immediate explanation of this phenomenon can be offered.

Since women subjects made placements of female figures only and male subjects of male figures only, conclusions about subject sex differences must be made with caution. While it is rather clear that the two groups of subjects view transactions of their same-sex surrogates as occurring at quite different distances for many situations, no inferences can be made about cross-sex judgments. However, pilot work now in progress suggests very strongly that the schemata of judges of opposite sex from that of the stimulus objects may be quite different from those of judges of the same sex. For example, women see the interactions of men as occurring at a greater distance than do male subjects. (This in itself could be construed as an example of sex-determined distortion of social perception since there is presumably a "true" modal interaction distance regardless of the gender of the observer.)

Within sex groups the instructional sets obviously provide a structure that influence the responses markedly. As with the experimental manipulation of stimulus characteristics made by Lewit and Joy (1967) the perception of the situation is changed with resulting differences in response.

The results of the analyses of the characteristics of the instructional sets have significant implications for studies such as that of Weinstein (1965, 1967) and of Fisher (1967). The stated or assumed degree of acquaintance of dyad members has very powerful effects on the distance at which the transactions are seen as taking place. A similar situation exists with regard to the affective tone of the transaction (pleasant, neutral, unpleasant), and with its formal nature (intimate, casual, or consultative). At a minimum, the variation in the several *subjects'* assumptions add error variance to the estimation of the schemata; at its most invidious, the *experimenter's* assumptions regarding the relationship, topic, or nature of the interaction will be conveyed to the subject unwittingly (cf. Rosenthal, 1967) with a resultant distortion of the schemata in the direction of expectations.

This limitation applies to some extent to any method for eliciting social schemata but mostly to the modifications of Kuethe's technique used by Weinstein and Fisher and the procedure used in the present study. The use of printed instructions minimizes the problem somewhat but does not eliminate it.

This sensitivity of social schemata to the nuances of implied or overt instruction is both a strength and a weakness (described above). The strength lies in the ease with which one may manipulate the experimental conditions or subject expectations. The use of dolls, silhouettes, etc., in free placement, particularly with instructional sets, provides a sensitive and reliable method for assessing not only the schemata themselves but also the marked individual differences that characterize them.

References

Fisher, R. L. Social schema of normal and disturbed school children. *Journal of Educational Psychology,* 1967, **58**, 88–92.

Hall, E. T. *The silent language.* New York: Doubleday, 1959.

Hall, E. T. *The hidden dimension.* New York: Doubleday, 1966.

Kuethe, J. L. Social schemas. *Journal of Abnormal and Social Psychology,* 1962, **64**, 31–38. (a)

KUETHE, J. L. Social schemas and the reconstruction of social object displays from memory. *Journal of Abnormal and Social Psychology,* 1962, **65,** 71–74. (b)

KUETHE, J. L. The pervasive influence of social schemata. *Journal of Abnormal and Social Psychology,* 1964, **68,** 248–254.

KUETHE, J. L., & STRICKER, G. Man and woman: Social schemata of males and females. *Psychological Reports,* 1963, **13,** 655–661.

KUETHE, J. L., & WEINGARTNER, H. Male-female schemata of homosexual and non-homosexual penitentiary inmates. *Journal of Personality,* 1964, **32,** 23–31.

LEWIT, D. W., & JOY, V. D. Kinetic versus social schemas in figure grouping. *Journal of Personality and Social Psychology,* 1967, **7,** 63–72.

LITTLE, K. B. Personal space. *Journal of Experimental Social Psychology,* 1965, **1,** 237–247.

LITTLE, K. B., ULEHLA, Z. J., & HENDERSON, C. L. Value congruence and interaction distances. *Journal of Social Psychology,* 1968, in press.

ROSENTHAL, R., & JACOBSEN, L. *Pygmalion in the classroom: Self-fulfilling prophecies and teacher expectations.* New York: Holt, Rinehart & Winston, 1967.

SOMMER, R. Studies in personal space. *Sociometry,* 1959, **22,** 247–260.

WEINSTEIN, L. Social schemata of emotionally disturbed boys. *Journal of Abnormal Psychology,* 1965, **70,** 457–461.

WEINSTEIN, L. Social experience and social schemata. *Journal of Personality and Social Psychology,* 1967, **6,** 429–434.

(Received March 21, 1968)

INTERPERSONAL SPACING IN NATURAL SETTINGS*

JAMES C. BAXTER
University of Houston

> Observations were made of the interpersonal spacing of 859 subject pairs in several natural settings at various times over a two-month period. Subjects were classified according to Anglo-, Black-, or Mexican-American ethnic group; adult, adolescent, or child age level; male-male, female-female, or male-female sex combination; and indoor or outdoor observation setting. Ratings of interpersonal distance were made from an unobtrusive location in each setting. Results confirmed expectations of ethnic, age, and sex group patterns in spacing and also revealed an interesting location difference. Implications of the findings in areas of interpersonal dynamics and environmental design are discussed.

A principle which has gained recognition in recent years is that people from different cultural backgrounds learn to define and utilize geographic space in different ways. Thus, culturally differentiated groups tend to prefer different spatial arrangements of participants involved in social interactions, and usually prefer to interact with each other at different interpersonal distances—some tightly clustered, others more widely spaced (Little, 1968). While the quality and type of interaction involved affects the spacing adopted (Hall, 1966; Little et al., 1968), a given type of interaction also tends to be conducted at different distances in different cultures. An acceptable distance for a personal conversation between adult males of equivalent status under given conditions in an Arab culture, for example, may be quite unacceptable or even anxiety arousing in a Northern European culture (Hall, 1966).

A number of investigations from a variety of research traditions have tended to confirm these general observations (Patterson, 1968; Sommer, 1966). Groups which have received most attention have been East European, Arabic, and Mediterranean cultures. E. T. Hall (1966) has argued that, in general, these groups tend to interact under much more proximal conditions and frequently can be seen touching each other during encounters. A substantial amount of anecdotal data has supported this contention. Systematic data from Watson and Graves (1966) have demonstrated such differences between Arabs and Americans under standardized real life conditions, and Little (1968) has supported the finding with a variety of cultural groups using symbolic tasks.

The extension of work of this sort would appear to be necessary and quite useful. A number of promising implications from such data can be identified in areas such as interpersonal and social processes and in environmental design. For example, it could be argued that people interacting more proximally expose themselves to a much different "view" of each other, and therefore utilize different cues in the interaction process (Frede et al., 1968). From a design standpoint, considerably different spatial requirements are imposed by people preferring interpersonal closeness and contact (Alexander, 1967).

While the dominant cultural heritage in the United States has been Northern European, significant minorities from other backgrounds exist. To the extent that such subcultures show corresponding or similar differences in space usage, they may prefer different interaction conditions and, therefore, may require certain design alterations for optimal interpersonal function (Carr, 1967). Very little information is available to date regarding preferred interaction distances of subcultural groups in this country. A study by Willis (1966) is an exception, and provides a beginning point for investigation. He used either black or white experimenters of both sexes as observers of the social greet-

---

*This investigation was supported in part by National Institute of Dental Research Grant, DE 138–05, awarded to Richard I. Evans. Appreciation is expressed to Douglas Jackson for serving as the primary rater throughout the study and to Susan J. Fiester and Steven D. Kantor for serving as reliability raters.

From *Sociometry*, 1970, *33*(4), 444–456. Reprinted by permission.

ing distances of either black or white subjects in several types of natural settings. While his results were complex, one finding relevant to the present investigation was that black subjects generally tended to greet others (especially other blacks) at greater distances. He also found that greeting distances involving one or more women were shorter. That is, they apparently delayed greetings and social interaction until the interpersonal distance was much smaller. While not specifically focusing on these issues, an early study by Efron (1941) also reported differences in body contact and spacing patterns. He studied East European Jewish and Southern Italian subcultures as they conversed on New York City streets. In general, he found greater closeness and more physical contact among his Jewish subjects. However, these observations were quite secondary to other emphases of the investigation. They also provide no information on spacing patterns of other subgroupings such as age and sex combinations.

The present investigation was designed to examine the distances at which people interacted with each other in several natural settings. Three subcultural groupings, along with three sex combinations and three age levels were studied in two types of settings. The general location chosen for the observations was the Houston zoo. This setting was selected because it is an attractive location, consistently drawing large numbers of people to fixed observation points. Further, representatives of all the major ethnic and social groupings of the city can be found in large numbers, and they typically are seen interacting spontaneously under pleasant circumstances in natural groupings. The groupings are very often family units, but also reflect social and some fraternal groupings.

Two person groups of Anglo-, Black-, or Mexican-American ethnic composition were divided into three sex combinations: two males, two females, or one male and one female; and into three age levels: adults, adolescents, and children. Finally, observations were made in both indoor and outdoor settings.

While the purpose of the investigation was primarily exploratory, several expectations were formulated on the basis of previous work. In general, the Mexican groups were expected to interact most proximally (Hall, 1966), while the Negro groups were expected to interact at greatest distances (Willis, 1966). Groups composed of one or two females were expected to interact most closely (Sommer, 1962; Willis, 1966), although the absence of sex differences in some previous research (Baxter and Phelps, 1970; Little et al., 1968) made this expectation quite reserved. Differences in spacing in different settings were also expected. In general, subject groups were expected to interact more proximally in indoor settings (Baxter and Phelps, 1970; Little, 1965). Finally, while little research has focused specifically on the issue, observers often agree that young children interact with each other and with adults under more proximal conditions (cf. Argyle and Dean, 1965), especially when excited or threatened. Thus, the children were expected to interact more proximally under present conditions.

Method

After some pilot observations of interaction patterns and traffic flow in the zoo, four locations were chosen for the observations. These locations were two indoor settings: the Toucan bird exhibit in the aviary and the baby gorilla exhibit in the children's zoo; and two outdoor settings: the Diana monkey cage in the primate area and the Kodiak bear enclosure in the heavy mammal area. These locations were selected because the traffic flow was moderately heavy, people usually tended to pause briefly and interact with each other while observing the animals, and each setting had a bench opposite it, on which an observer could position himself. These benches were approximately 10 feet from the observation area in each case and were generally out of view of people passing by.

As people passed each of the settings they were classified for ethnic, sex, and age grouping, and distance ratings were made and inconspicuously recorded on a tabulation sheet. The following procedure was used in classifying subjects and making ratings. Two person groups were identified in terms of how they approached an observation setting from previous exhibits. If they came to the setting in a two person grouping, they were considered for classification. Other types of groupings were ignored. Further, ethnic classification was made on the basis of external appearance and language. Black subjects were identified on the basis of skin color and physiognomic features, while Mexican subjects were identified on the basis of appearance and language, if possible. Most remaining subjects, with the exception of obvious orientals were classified as Anglo. Any cues available were taken into consideration, and doubtful subjects were ignored. Three sex groupings were identified: male-male, male-female, and female-female combinations. The final classification was made on the basis of age. When both members of the pair were 20 years of age or above, they were classified as adult; when both were between 10 and 20, they were classified as adolescent; and when both were between five and 10, they were classified as children. Pairs which crossed age or ethnic groups were ignored.

Thus, several criteria determined whether subjects were included in the present sample. They had to approach an observation area in a pair grouping, and they could not be carrying children or large parcels nor be pushing strollers. Moreover, they had to be classifiable into one of the ethnic and age groupings. Any pairs meeting these conditions were rated, regardless of how they arranged themselves upon stopping at the exhibit. While it cannot be estimated with certainty, perhaps one-tenth to one-fifth of the people passing the settings were classifiable, and therefore became subjects. In all, 859 subject pairs were included in the present observations.

Interpersonal distance judgments were made by one rater as he observed a pair approach an observation setting and stop to look at the exhibit. When the pair passed a previously designated point on their way to the setting, the observer began a fixed timing interval. After 10 seconds had elapsed, he judged the distance between the pair to the nearest one-quarter foot from nose to nose. Typically, this caught subjects standing side-by-side looking at the animal. Of course, the judgment was made at that time, no matter what the actions or positions of the pair were. The 10 second interval was introduced for two reasons. It took the decision of when to judge the interpersonal distance out of the rater's hands. It also allowed the subjects enough time to "settle" into an observation position, but not so long an interval that many potential subjects had passed out of the observation area before it had elapsed.[1]

The observations were made at varying time periods during the months of June and July, 1969. Primary emphasis was placed on weekends, although weekdays were also used. On each observation day, observations were made at all settings.

One adult male judge who was unacquainted with the specific expectations of the investigation served as the rater throughout the period of the study. A considerable amount of discussion with and training of the rater preceded the point at which he began making ratings, and periodic visits and observations by the author throughout the course of the observations helped maintain his concern with accuracy. Two additional raters, one man and one woman, were trained as alternate raters about half-way through the observation period. Their ratings were intended to provide an overall estimate of the primary rater's reliability. The alternate raters judged distances with the primary rater at varying times during the middle period of observation. In all cases, agreement of the judgments regarding the ethnic group, age level, and sex combination of subjects to be rated was quite high. Distance measurements were recorded separately by the two raters. The delay interval was timed by the primary rater in all cases. The timing of each rating was signaled to the comparison rater by the primary rater; although no other communication occurred between raters during rating sessions. Comparisons of rating patterns were not made until the completion of all ratings to be made by each comparison rater. The ratings of the primary judge correlated .94 with his female comparison rater for 38 subject pairs and .88 with his male comparison rater for 68 subject pairs. The means of the raters' judgments were within .55 feet of each other using the female comparison and .11 feet using the male comparison. In general, the level of classification and rating agreement was quite high and appeared to be adequate for present purposes.

Results

The interpersonal distance ratings of the primary rater were entered into a four-way analysis of variance design and analyzed according to an unweighted means solution. Main factors of the design were defined by: the ethnic group of the subject pair (Anglo-, Black-, or Mexican-American), the age level category of the subjects (adult, adolescent, or child), the sex combination of the subjects (male-male, male-female, or female-female), and the location of the observations (indoor or outdoor). Results of this overall analysis are summarized in Table 1. The means of the 54 cells of the design are also presented for examination in Table 2.

Seven of the 15 comparisons attained significance at conventional levels of confidence, and an eighth comparison approached significance ($p < .10$). The most impressive result of the analysis is the difference in spacing attributable to ethnic groupings (F = 126.57; df = 2/805; $p < .001$). This effect is quite sizable, and accounts for approximately 32 percent of the total variability of the sample (Vaughan and Corbollis, 1969). Evaluation of the individual means involved indicates that the Mexican groups stood closest ($\bar{X} = 1.78$; N = 160), Anglos were intermediate ($\bar{X} = 2.29$; N = 427), and Blacks stood most distant ($\bar{X} = 2.66$; N = 272). Analysis of the differences between means by t-tests indicates that each ethnic group differs from the other significantly (t's > 7.40; p's <

---

[1] During the pilot investigation period, observations were made on 120 subject pairs for purposes of refining procedures. A 15 second interval was used during this period. However, it proved to be too long, since a high percentage of the adult Negro males were found to have moved beyond the observation area within this time. The shorter interval corrected this problem in most cases.

TABLE 1

SUMMARY OF THE ANALYSIS OF THE VARIANCE OF INTERPERSONAL DISTANCE RATINGS

Source	d.f.	M.S.	F
Ethnic Group (E)	2	34.53	126.57****
Age (A)	2	10.24	37.53****
Sex (S)	2	3.48	12.77****
Location (L)	1	0.33	1.20
E × A	4	0.53	1.96*
E × S	4	2.08	7.64****
E × L	2	1.54	5.65***
A × S	4	0.77	2.82**
A × L	2	0.04	<1.00
S × L	2	0.39	1.45
E × A × S	8	0.78	2.87***
E × A × L	4	0.12	<1.00
E × S × L	4	0.14	<1.00
A × S × L	4	0.27	1.01
E × A × S × L	8	0.16	<1.00
Error	805	0.27	....

*$p < .10$.   ***$p < .005$.
**$p < .025$.   ****$p < .0010$.

$.001$).[2] It is also of interest to note that the order of the ethnic group means was maintained in each of the three first-order interactions where ethnic groupings were distinguished for age and sex classifications and for observation setting. Thus, the expectation of differential spacing of the three ethnic groups was clearly supported.

The age groupings also differed significantly in the interpersonal distances adopted ($F = 37.53$; $df = 2/805$; $p < .001$). This

[2] The pooled error term derived from the analysis of variance table was used for the comparison of all simple effects.

effect is moderately large, and accounts for approximately 10 percent of the total variance of the sample. Individual means revealed that the children interacted most proximally ($\overline{X} = 1.99$; $N = 257$), adolescents were intermediate ($\overline{X} = 2.28$; $N = 212$), and adults interacted at greatest distances ($\overline{X} = 2.46$; $N = 390$). All three individual comparisons were significant (t's > 3.60; p's $< .001$), and the order of the age groups remained consistent when the groups were distinguished for ethnic and sex classifications and for location of observation. Again, results were consistent with expectations guiding the study.

A final main effect which attained significance is attributable to the sex groupings of the subjects ($F = 12.77$; $df = 2/805$; $p < .001$). However, while the effect is reliable, only about three percent of the total variability of the sample is controlled by the sex groupings of the subjects. Individual comparisons revealed that the male-female groups interacted most proximally ($\overline{X} = 2.11$; $N = 386$), the female-female groups were intermediate ($\overline{X} = 2.23$; $N = 238$), and the male-male groups were most distant ($\overline{X} = 2.39$; $N = 235$). Again, all three groupings differed significantly from each other (t's > 2.40; p's $< .02$). In contrast to the other main effects, however, the order of the sex groupings did not remain constant within the ethnic and age combinations and across observation settings. In any case, the result is in general agreement with prior expectations. The modest level of the effect and its inconsistency

TABLE 2

MEAN INTERPERSONAL DISTANCE RATINGS FOR EACH COMBINATION OF ETHNIC, AGE, SEX, AND LOCATION CONDITIONS

Ethnic group	Sex combination	Indoor Adult	Indoor Adolesc.	Indoor Child.	Outdoor Adult	Outdoor Adolesc.	Outdoor Child.
Anglo	M–M	2.72	2.71	2.07	2.72	2.47	2.05
	M–F	2.33	2.04	1.89	2.59	2.22	1.92
	F–F	2.45	2.03	1.94	2.46	2.41	2.21
Black	M–M	3.15	2.67	1.81	3.16	2.84	2.20
	M–F	2.77	2.01	2.14	2.99	2.63	2.26
	F–F	2.89	2.89	2.64	2.83	2.96	2.99
Mexican	M–M	2.14	2.34	2.09	1.97	2.11	1.75
	M–F	1.65	1.94	1.57	1.83	1.65	1.50
	F–F	2.00	1.56	1.39	1.67	1.54	1.30

across groups is interesting, since previous work has been inconsistent in reporting sex differences in spacing.

Four interactions reached conventional levels of significance. Of these, the ethnic group by sex group comparison (E x S) and the ethnic group by sex group by age group comparison (E x S x A) appear most meaningful. These interactions account for approximately eight and nine percent of the total sample variance, respectively. Examination of the patterns of means involved indicates that the Anglos and Blacks showed sex group differences such that the male-female groups stood closest and the male-male groups stood most distant in relation to each other. The Mexicans showed a different pattern, however. For them, the female-female group interacted most proximally, while the male-male group was most distant. Examination of the second-order interaction of these factors with age (i.e. E x S x A) revealed that the ethnic differences in which of the sex groupings interacted most proximally was clearest for adolescents and adults, but was absent among the children. The Anglo children essentially failed to show sex group effects, while both the Mexican and Black children showed strong, albeit different patterns. The female-female group interacted most proximally within the Mexican groups and at the greatest distance within the Black groups.

Two additional interactions attained significance, each of which accounted for approximately two percent of the total sample variability. The age by sex group comparison (A x S) revealed that the sex combination differences were most pronounced within the adolescent groups, and were minimal within children's groups. However, the most interesting effect is attributable to the ethnic group by location of observation comparison (E x L). Evaluation of group means reveals that while the Anglos interacted at approximately the same distances both in the indoor locations and in the outdoor settings, this is not true of the Blacks and Mexicans. Indeed, their patterns of interaction are reversed ($t = 3.36$; $df = 4.28$; $p < .001$), with the Mexicans interacting more closely in outdoor settings and the Blacks interacting more closely in indoor settings. Thus, the general expectation that subjects would cluster more tightly in indoor settings was not supported. This pattern only occurred in the Black groups.

The final comparison, the ethnic group by age group interaction (E x A), attained significance at a marginal level of confidence and actually accounts for only one percent of the total variance. The means contained in this comparison reveal that the ethnic group differences are most pronounced among adults, and tend to be less noticeable among adolescents and children.

Discussion

The pattern of results reveals striking ethnic, age, and sex group effects in interpersonal spacing. In fact, approximately 67 percent of the total variability of the sample was controlled by these effects and their combinations. The most impressive single finding, however, is attributable to the ethnic group membership of the subject pairs. The tendency for Mexican subjects of all ages and sex groupings to interact most proximally is consistent with Hall's (1966) and Little's (1968) reports that Mediterranean cultures, and presumably American subcultures of this origin, interact at closer distances. Indeed, they not only stood closer together, but informal observation also suggested that they very frequently touched each other and often held each other by the hand or arm or one member stood with his arm around the waist of the other. This was rarely observed in the Anglo and Black groups. The tendency for Blacks to stand at greater distances is consistent with Willis' (1966) findings concerning greeting distances. Thus, the present results reveal rather small but exceedingly consistent subcultural differences between subjects interacting in natural settings in pre-established groupings.

The age group differences also achieved significance and were associated with a meaningful proportion of the total variability. Perhaps most interesting, however, is the fact that the ethnic group differences in spacing were present even in the youngest subject groups. While the size of these differences increased with age, their presence in the children's groups suggests that schemata of appropriate spatial arrangements are learned early in the childhood period and persist into adulthood. These data, while interesting also tend to add support to other studies (cf. Baxter and Phelps, 1970; Fisher, 1967; Weinstein, 1967) of the importance of spatial schemata in young children. The present data corroborate this generalization using unobtrusive ratings of children in natural interactions.

Sex group differences were extremely reliable, although quite minor in the present data. While significant differences were found, they generally controlled rather small proportions of the variance, and were inconsistently maintained across age and ethnic groupings. While it is correct to conclude that groupings with one or two female members interacted more proximally under most conditions, the differences were generally slight. Perhaps a variety of factors contributed to the weak and inconsistent effects. One factor may have been the variability in role relationships among the participants. It may be, for example, that more family units including spouses, siblings, etc., were observed in some ethnic groupings as compared with others, where more nonfamilial groupings may have occurred. It seems reasonable to expect that if greater control could be exerted over the role relationships of subjects observed, more dependable sex differences would emerge.

An especially interesting, although somewhat minor effect, can be seen in the ethnic group by location of observation result. The Anglo groups tended to interact consistently in both interior and exterior settings. However, the Mexican groups clustered more closely when interacting outdoors, while the Black groups clustered more when indoors. The basis for this contrast is entirely unclear. If it can be assumed, however, that clustering is increased with external threat (Feshbach and Feshbach, 1963; Latané, 1969; Schachter, 1959) it may be possible that the groups tend to feel more exposed or threatened in different types of physical settings. Of course, physical factors such as the differing levels of background noise, heat, ambient light, etc. could also influence the differential spacing patterns. Interesting implications for setting design intended for use by different subcultural groups are evident, however. If this result can be shown to be dependable and subject to replication, it would seem reasonable to think in terms of designing fewer open, exposed spaces in areas intended primarily for Mexican-American use. Perhaps the prevalence of wall enclosed spaces in Spanish architecture is a guide to the validity of such an implication.

The present ethnic group by location of observation differences also tend to cast some light on inconsistencies in previous data. Little (1965) expected to find differences in doll placement distances when indoor vs. outdoor settings were involved. He reasoned that tighter clustering would occur in indoor settings since, in general, the degree of interpersonal intimacy expected in indoor locations was greater. His overall results were inconsistent. In some comparisons, he found closer placements in outdoor settings, in others he found a tendency for tighter clustering in indoor settings. Since Little used white adults as subjects, the present Anglo adult groups would seem most comparable. For these groups, the present results are entirely consistent with Little's data. Essentially, they failed to respond differently to different locations. On the other hand, a study by Baxter and Phelps (1970) also sought indoor vs. outdoor differences in spacing. The reasoning involved was the same as that developed by Little. In that study, the result emerged as expected. That is, closer doll placements occurred in indoor settings as contrasted with outdoor locations. The Baxter-Phelps study used Negro preschool children as subjects. Thus, the present data indicating that Black-American subjects show the expected effect of clustering more tightly together when indoors is also consistent with the earlier Baxter-Phelps data. The overall result, then, clearly indicates that differences in interpersonal clustering in indoor vs. outdoor settings depends on the subcultural membership of the subjects. This area would appear to warrant further investigation aimed at determining the basis for the differences.

E. T. Hall (1966) has observed that interacting with people at different distances has the effect of exposing one to differing types and intensities of sensory data. For example, very close contact allows tactile, olfactory and thermal information essentially unavailable to subjects interacting under more distant conditions. The quality and intensity of visual and auditory information can be said to vary similarly. Thus, groups interacting under differing spacing conditions may be relying to varying degrees on different channels of information and may be employing different communication mechanisms. The present data suggest that such differences may be present among ethnic, age, and sex groupings when they interact under spontaneous conditions.

Some final implications of the present results seem worthy of note. Since the various subject groupings tend to adopt consistent, albeit slight, differences in spacing, it would seem reasonable to assume that both participants in the interactions may be contributing to establishing and maintaining their desired spatial arrangement. Indeed, observing the subjects as they interact in these settings leads one very quickly to the impression that the spacing process is an intricate one which is contributed to by both parties. As soon as one member leans too close, the other smoothly compensates. When one member moves too far away, the other quickly closes the gap. Further, it would appear that the process proceeds outside awareness, for the most part, and is usually very smooth and rapid in its operation.

Given the substantial ethnic group and age differences in spacing, it would follow that cross-group interactions would be interesting to examine. That is, given that an adult Mexican male and an adult Black male interacted under specified conditions, it would follow that they would both tend to "work" toward inconsistent spacing arrangements. Since inappropriately close spacing has been shown to be anxiety arousing (Baxter and Deanovich, 1970; Felipe and Sommer, 1966), one of the participants would be expected to be uncomfortable in the situation. Assuming that inappropriately distant spacing may be seen as rejecting or inappropriately formal, the other participant may be expected to view the encounter as equally unsatisfying. No direct data are available on the matter at present. However, the present study suggests that investigations along these lines would prove especially significant in terms of delineating subtle determinants of social encounter processes and their outcomes.

REFERENCES

ALEXANDER, C. The city as a mechanism for sustaining human contact. In W. R. Ewald (Ed.), *Environment for man.* Bloomington: Indiana University Press, 1967.

ARGYLE, M., & DEAN, J. Eye contact, distance and affiliation. *Sociometry,* 1965, **28,** 289–304.

BAXTER, J. C., & DEANOVICH, B. F. Anxiety arousing effects of inappropriate crowding. *Journal of Consulting and Clinical Psychology,* 1970.

BAXTER, J. C., & PHELPS, A. T. Space utilization in pre-school children. Unpublished manuscript, 1970.

CARR, S. The city of the mind. In W. R. Ewald (Ed.), *Environment for man.* Bloomington: Indiana University Press, 1967.

EFRON, D. *Gesture and environment.* New York: King's Crown Press, 1941.

FELIPE, N., & SOMMER, R. Invasions of personal space. *Social Problems,* 1966, **14,** 206–214.

FESHBACH, S., & FESHBACH, N. Influence of the stimulus object upon the complementary and supplementary projection of fear. *Journal of Abnormal and Social Psychology,* 1963, **66,** 498–502.

FISHER, R. L. Social schema of normal and disturbed school children. *Journal of Educational Psychology,* 1967, **58,** 88–92.

FREDE, M. C., GAUTNEY, D. B., & BAXTER, J. C. Relationships between body image boundary and interaction patterns on the MAPS test. *Journal of Consulting and Clinical Psychology,* 1968, **32,** 575–578.

HALL, E. T. *The hidden dimension.* Garden City: Doubleday, 1966.

LATANÉ, B. Gregariousness and fear in laboratory rats. *Journal of Experimental Social Psychology,* 1969, **5,** 61–69.

LITTLE, K. B. Personal space. *Journal of Experimental Social Psychology,* 1965, **1,** 237–247.

LITTLE, K. B. Cultural variations in social schemata. *Journal of Personality and Social Psychology,* 1968, **10,** 1–7.

LITTLE, K. B., ULEHLA, Z. J., & HENDERSON, C. Value congruence and interpersonal distance. *Journal of Social Psychology,* 1968, **75,** 249–253.

PATTERSON, M. Spatial factors in social interactions. *Human Relations,* 1968, **21,** 351–361.

SCHACHTER, S. *The psychology of affiliation.* Stanford: Stanford University Press, 1959.

SOMMER, R. The distance for comfortable conversation: A further study. *Sociometry,* 1962, **25,** 111–116.

SOMMER, R. Man's proximate environment. *Journal of Social Issues,* 1966, **22,** 59–70.

VAUGHAN, G. M., & CORBOLLIS, M. C. Beyond tests of significance: Estimating strength of effects in selected ANOVA designs. *Psychological Bulletin,* 1969, **73,** 204–213.

WATSON, O. M., & GRAVES, T. D. Quantitative research in proxemic behavior. *American Anthropologist,* 1966, **68,** 971–985.

WEINSTEIN, L. Social experience and social schemata. *Journal of Personality and Social Psychology,* 1967, **6,** 429–434.

WILLIS, F. N., Jr. Initial speaking distance as a function of the speakers' relationship. *Psychonomic Science,* 1966, **5,** 221–222.

THE STUDIES COMPARED

It is clear from reading these two studies that the investigators were concerned with essentially the same problem; they were interested in the effects that different cultural backgrounds have on the way people position themselves in interpersonal encounters. However, the methods chosen to pursue this common interest are dramatically different and represent classical distinctions between an experimental laboratory approach and a naturalistic observational one.

Instructions to Subjects

With respect to instructions given to the participants, the differences between the methods emerge clearly. In Baxter's study, the visitors to the zoo were not aware of being subjects in a study; in Little's work, subjects knew that they were participating in a psychological experiment. You are not told how Little's subjects were recruited or whether the procedure was the same in different countries. In addition, you have only a general description of the actual instructions given to the subjects about the task. This is an important methodological point, since different instructions from the experimenters may have elicited different responses from the subjects, thus leaving open the question about whether the differences obtained were purely a function of culture or whether the subjects perceived the task in different terms.

Demand Characteristics. The procedure of any experiment gives rise to the question "How did the participants perceive the experience?" This question is especially salient in cross-cultural work. In everyday life, there are always cues about what to do; architecture, decor, and lighting, for example, tell that you are in a place of worship, and therefore you know that you are expected to be quiet, reverent, and attentive. The experimental setting too provides cues as to appropriate behavior; these were described in Chapter 1 as the demand characteristics of the experiment. Little regarded the demand characteristics of his study as an asset, since they permitted easy manipulation of the acquaintanceship and affective-tone variables. But potentially negative effects of these demand characteristics were overlooked. The use of printed instructions has both advantages and disadvantages. Printed instructions eliminate some of the vocal cues through which an experimenter might communicate the behavior he or she hopes to find; but the very act of handing out printed instructions may send other messages of formality, distance, evaluation, and authority, which may have different impacts on the subject's behavior in different cultures. It is very likely that the relationships between experimenters and subjects take different forms in different cultures and that the demand characteristics are responded to in different ways. In some cultures, courtesy requires that one respond to a questioner as best as one can in terms of the questioner's expectations. Self-report experiments such as Little's are therefore more susceptible to demand characteristics than those measuring the subject's spatial behavior directly. When subjects place dolls on a board, they must imagine how the behavior in question occurs in real life and translate this into placing the dolls. When interpersonal distance is measured unobtrusively in everyday encounters, instead, no such translation is required; the situational cues that shape the natural behavior are present and demand characteristics are reduced.

It is difficult to assess the potential impact of demand characteristics on Little's findings, given the scarcity of information about the instructions to both subjects and research assistants and about the testing situations prevailing in each country. In

Baxter's study, demand characteristics do not play a part, since the pairs observed did not know they were being studied nor were special situations created. Baxter took a further precaution against the chance that experimenter bias might influence the estimates of pair distances by using observers who were not aware of the aims of the study. Little gives no information about the briefing of the research assistants.

Measurement of Interpersonal Distance

Baxter's study also provides an excellent example of precision and control applied to observations in a naturalistic setting. When the rules concerning what is to be recorded are clearly specified, the observations can be readily replicated by other investigators and in other settings. The next time you find yourself in a relatively crowded public place, such as a bus terminal or a theater lobby, try to make observations of interpersonal spacing. Since people are constantly moving about, you might wonder when you should make your observations. This problem of when to make observations in a natural setting is a recurrent one and one to which Baxter found an ingenious solution. In order to make subject selection more objective and consistent, he used a fixed time interval from the moment the couple passed a designated point. Distance estimates to the nearest one-quarter foot are probably adequate enough measures, although such distance estimates differ according to the body orientation of the subject pair. Baxter points out that when most of the observations were made, pairs were standing side by side looking at the animals. This is an important piece of information because, if different arrangements of the pairs had occurred with any frequency, these might have confounded the results. For example, what if pairs of children stood front to back, with the shorter child in front, looking at the exhibits? Or if pairs from one cultural group stood angled more to face each other? These variations in orientation could have contaminated the results.

Another strong asset of this study is the care taken in establishing the reliability of observations. Observational methods are often criticized for not taking into due account the biases of the observers. Baxter took care to have two additional raters—a man and a woman—make their own observations for comparison with those of his principal male rater. All were unaware of the predictions of the study. This procedure safeguarded against errors of judgment caused by the uniqueness of a given observer's style. Also worth noting is the care taken to make observations at different times of day in order to guard against errors introduced by observations that might be specific to a particular time only.

In Little's study, research assistants drew outlines of the bases of each pair of dolls to record the distances at which the dolls had been placed. This provided a visible and permanent record from which measurements could then be made and rechecked at any time. You may have some questions, however, about the procedure followed before these doll outlines were drawn. Little reports that the assistants drew the outlines after each subject "had placed the dolls to his satisfaction" and had recounted a conversation that might have taken place between the two dolls. No time restrictions were placed on the subjects, and no record was kept of either the time it took the subjects to place the dolls or the time it took them to recount the conversation. Nothing is said about the number of changes in doll placement a subject might have made until "satisfaction" was achieved. If students in different cultures spent different amounts of time in selecting the best placements of the dolls, those taking longer may be responding to influences other than those determining schemata.

CONSUMER EVALUATION

Cost-Quality Relation

Many of the differences that have emerged from our comparison of these two studies typify the differences that exist between laboratory and field studies. Both Little and Baxter aim at a high-quality product that will enable them to shed light on cultural variations in spacing behavior. As pointed out in Chapter 1, cross-cultural and longitudinal studies are rare in psychological research because of their high costs. Recall that most of the studies of cultural variations described earlier in this chapter use foreign students in an attempt to assess cultural variations. The use of foreign students is doubtless a less expensive but also a less valid procedure. The cost of doing a study like Little's is high, but there is some confidence that it is worth it. Naturalistic observations are generally moderately expensive, but the sample size of Baxter's study (859 pairs) increased the cost considerably; on the other hand, the large size of the sample allowed numerous comparisons and increased the scope of the findings.

In his discussion, Little pointed out that the advantages of his method included easy manipulation of the experimental conditions, replicability of procedures, and sensitivity of measures. The experimental format allowed Little to specify concrete hypotheses—that is, that there are differences and that these differences take a particular direction. Furthermore, the experimental format also allowed Little to rule out alternative explanations—namely, that observed differences were produced by conditions in which he was *not* interested. Little was also able to raise questions of a causal nature; for example, he was able to ask whether a pleasant situation would effect closer spacing than an unpleasant one. But the precision and control of the experimental format can create certain drawbacks of which Little himself must have been aware when he worried about the effects of the questioning process.

Durability

Both the Little and the Baxter studies are often cited by other researchers in support of the existence of cultural differences in interpersonal distancing. As mentioned in Chapter 1, when you read a study, you should ask yourself to what extent the questions posed have been answered and to what extent the results can be generalized to settings other than that studied. While there are potentially contaminating effects in both of these studies, it can be argued that both are relatively strong in internal validity. In other words, you can have reasonable confidence that their conclusions are justified.

With regard to generalization, there is a difference between Little's laboratory experiment and Baxter's field study. If the focus of the research is on the study of interpersonal distances, the Baxter study is the stronger in that it actually assesses such distances directly. The Little experiment can generalize most appropriately to the domain of social schemata or cognitive representations of interpersonal distances. To speak about cultural differences in distances on the basis of this study, one must accept the assumption that social schemata are accurate reflections of spacing behavior.

4

HELPING BEHAVIOR

CHAPTER OUTLINE

Explanations of Prosocial Behavior
  Norms of Prosocial Behavior
  Cognitive Analysis of Prosocial Behavior
Research on Bystander Intervention
  Victim Characteristics
  Ambiguity of the Situation
  Familiarity with the Situation
  Implicit Rules
  Mood
  Presence of Others
Methods in the Study of Prosocial Behavior
  Laboratory Experiments
  Field Experiments
  Field Studies
  Scales, Surveys, and Interviews
Two Research Examples
  Product Description
  Consumer Checklist
  John M. Darley and Bibb Latané, *Bystander intervention in emergencies: Diffusion of responsibility.*
  Irving M. Piliavin, Judith Rodin, and Jane Allyn Piliavin, *Good Samaritanism: An underground phenomenon?*
The Studies Compared
  Independent Variable Manipulation
  Control of Extraneous Influences
  Minimizing Error
  Deception
  Results Compared
Consumer Evaluation
  Read Carefully
  Check Durability

On March 13, 1964, Kitty Genovese was knifed to death in the parking lot of her apartment building in New York City. In that city, murders are common enough to pass from notice barely remarked upon. Such might have been the case with the Kitty Genovese killing had the police not reported two weeks later that 38 people had witnessed the crime and none had aided the victim or called the police. This widespread failure to help was page-one news, and it set in motion an outcry of public concern expressed in letters to the editor, in commentaries by behavioral scientists, psychiatrists, and public officials, and eventually in a book (Rosenthal, 1964). All accounts of the crime make it hard to understand the passivity of the 38 witnesses. Returning to her home in a middle-class neighborhood, Kitty Genovese was stabbed as she left her car in the parking lot. She cried out for help, and, as lights went on and windows opened, her attacker was frightened off and drove away. He soon returned to stab her again, and again she cried out for help and screamed that she was dying. Again lights went on, and the attacker drove away. Still no one came to Ms. Genovese's help, and no one called the police. She had crawled to the entrance of her building when the murderer returned for his final attack. The murder took 35 minutes, during which 38 witnesses watched, waited, and failed to help. The account of the slaying caught the attention of social psychologists John Darley and Bibb Latané and led to a series of studies on bystander intervention, including the first research selection in this chapter. Questions about what makes people helpful, sharing, charitable, and generous to others have become prominent in research in social psychology since that time, and much has been learned about *prosocial behavior.*

Yet, on December 25, 1974, Sandra Zahler was beaten to death in her apartment in the building that overlooks the parking lot in which Kitty Genovese had been murdered ten years earlier. Her body was found the next day, and a neighbor reported hearing her scream. This neighbor said she did nothing because she thought it was the building superintendent's job to investigate. She did not attempt to alert him to the problem (if she had, she might have discovered that, it being Christmas Day, he was out). Police were quoted as saying that the slaying bore little resemblance to the 1964 murder because, while 38 neighbors heard the Genovese murder, only one neighbor heard the Zahler murder and failed to report it. If 37 others had overheard this attack, would someone have helped?

EXPLANATIONS OF PROSOCIAL BEHAVIOR

The murder of Kitty Genovese captured public attention not so much for the death of the young woman herself but for the behavior of the considerable number of people who might have helped but did not. The dismay you experience at reading the account is widely shared because there seems to be a common understanding that these witnesses should have done something. The existence of such "shoulds" reflects the existence of norms of behavior about helping others.

Norms of Prosocial Behavior

The belief that people should help one another is deeply ingrained into the moral fabric of our culture. Religious teaching contains many references to helping, and parables about the lives of religious figures often dramatize their selfless devotion to others. The Bible reminds you to love your neighbor; children are taught to help and share with others. Gouldner (1960) has suggested that there exists a universal norm in this regard, a *norm of reciprocity,* that prescribes that you should help those who have helped you. This norm, perhaps derived from the Golden Rule of doing unto others as they do unto you, is reflected, for example, in social exchanges like letter writing or gift giving. The norm of reciprocity generalizes beyond the original exchange. If you cannot return a favor, you may help another person instead; your mother sends you a cake and you invite a neighbor to share it. Thus the norm of reciprocity explains a wide range of helpful behavior. Although Gouldner (1960) believed the norm of reciprocity to be universal, he realized that it may be conditional on how the recipient interprets the act of helping. If the recipient sees that the helper receives considerable benefit from the help offered, the recipient experiences less pressure to reciprocate. This applies also to situations in which help can be expected because of the helper's role or competence. For example, you would feel less obligated to return help rendered by a passing nurse who gave you first aid than help rendered by a passerby with no professional qualifications (and obligations) to help.

Gouldner (1960) mentioned that the norm of reciprocity is suspended in situations in which the person helped is too old, too weak, or too sick to reciprocate. In such situations, there is another norm—the *norm of social responsibility*—which prescribes that people should help others who need help (Berkowitz, 1972; Berkowitz & Daniels, 1963). Specifically, this norm applies to those who are dependent on the helper for assistance. As Staub (1972) has pointed out, the difference between these two norms is that the norm of social responsibility applies to the *stimulus* for prosocial behavior, while the norm of reciprocity applies to the *response* to such stimulus. The norm of social responsibility speaks to our everyday sense of what altruistic acts are all about, since the norm prescribes that we should help without any expectation of benefit for ourselves. The norm of reciprocity requires a response only when the helpful act is indeed seen as selfless. A person can be said to be socialized into this culture to the extent to which he or she is implicitly aware of these norms. But knowing that you should do something does not always assure that you will do it. Those who witnessed the Kitty Genovese killing were doubtless aware of the norm of social responsibility; their behavior, therefore, was apparently determined by other considerations. Witnesses interviewed after the incident (Rosenthal, 1964) gave many excuses for not helping; the fact that they felt that excuses were called for gives some indication that they were, at some level, aware of the norm of social responsibility.

Darley and Latané (1970) have criticized explanations based on norms precisely because people do fail to help. If the norms of social responsibility and reciprocity supplied all the explanations needed for prosocial behavior, there would not be considerable variation in when and how people will help. In our culture, there are many more norms of social behavior than norms of social responsibility and reciprocity; in specific situations, different norms often offer contradictory injunctions. When norms about minding one's own business conflict with norms about helping, the result may be that no prosocial behavior occurs in that situation. The fact that norms are often mentioned as after-the-fact reasons for a certain behavior does not mean that norms determined that behavior. Normative explanations are more descriptive than predictive and, as such, are lacking in explanatory power.

Cognitive Analysis of Prosocial Behavior

Occasionally, people rush unthinkingly into an emergency situation and help. Far more often, however, prosocial behavior is based on thought and decision. People ask what's going on, wonder whether help is needed, and decide whether they will intervene or not. This was clearly true in the Kitty Genovese murder. The 38 witnesses who failed to help did not see themselves as indifferent or apathetic as they watched the crime being committed. In public interviews, they described distress and fascination and much thought accompanying their failure to help. Latané and Darley (1970) undertook research (including the study presented here) that led to a model of the cognitive sequence an individual goes through in arriving at a decision to intervene. While this explanation is aimed specifically at reactions to emergencies, it has some applicability to other helping situations as well.

Latané and Darley (1970) began with the assumption that most emergencies are ambiguous situations. Before a bystander takes action, he or she will go through a cognitive process that comprises four steps. The first step is *noticing* the situation. There were doubtless more than 38 people living in the buildings overlooking the parking area in which the attack on Kitty Genovese occurred. Some may have been sound asleep; others may have been drunk, watching the late movie on television, or making love—all conditions of self-absorption that may prevent noticing an event nearby. The second step in the cognitive process is *interpreting* the event as a situation that might require help—that is, defining the event as an emergency. The 38 witnesses to the murder (and perhaps others who did not ever admit to the police that they noticed the crime) all made it to this second step in the cognitive analysis. But, at this point, some decided not to help, because they did not interpret what they heard as an emergency; one called it a lovers' quarrel; others dismissed the cries as part of the usual noise of city nights. The third step in the bystander's cognitive process requires that the person take *responsibility*. It is probably here that most of the 38 witnesses dropped out of the decision process. Each decided that it was not up to him or her to intervene. The reasons for shunning responsibility are (and were on that occasion) many—fear of getting hurt, concern that one's help may be rebuffed, and so on.

One of the most intriguing outcomes of Latané and Darley's work was the discovery that a solitary witness to an emergency is more likely to help than is a group of witnesses. This major finding of the study included in this chapter was explained by the authors in terms of what they called *diffusion of responsibility*. Somehow, the knowledge that others have witnessed an event inhibits to a greater or lesser extent the taking of personal responsibility. If only one person had heard Kitty Genovese's cries, that person might have helped. The 38 witnesses could see one another's lights go on; they could even see their neighbors at the windows; but they could not know whether anyone had summoned help. Each person could assume that it was not his or her own responsibility to act; someone else probably should and would help. The norm of social responsibility may well be operating for each witness at this point, but each individual shares the sense of responsibility with 37 others, and, as a consequence, this sense of responsibility is weakened in each person. As the Zahler crime indicates, even one other presumed witness (the janitor) can inhibit a neighbor's helping.

Finally, having noticed the situation, interpreted it as an emergency, and taken personal responsibility, the potential helpers must *decide what to do* (the fourth step in the cognitive process). In the Kitty Genovese murder, someone might have gone to her aid directly during one of the intervals in which the assailant had left the scene. With even less risk, anyone might have called the police. Someone finally did after 35 minutes. Evidently, cognitive analysis takes time; and for most people it is a troubled decision process. As the two research selections show, situational characteristics help determine how many people stop at which point in the cognitive analysis that can lead to or inhibit prosocial intervention.

RESEARCH ON BYSTANDER INTERVENTION

Victim Characteristics

In thinking about those 38 people who watched the murder, you may have begun to wonder about the victim. Maybe there was something about Kitty Genovese that kept those people from coming to her aid. Her sex should have been an asset, for women tend to be helped more in a variety of situations (Latané & Dabbs, 1972; Morgan, 1973). But assaults on women may be an exception. In a study involving a psychodrama of a family argument, more men than women generally intervened to stop the fight in scenes involving all combinations of male or female aggressors against same or opposite sex. However, there was a startling exception to this pattern of intervention. No male intervened when a female was being physically attacked and beaten by a male (Borofsky, Stollak, & Messé, 1971). Kitty Genovese was perhaps at a special disadvantage in being the victim of a male attacker. Furthermore, the attack was probably witnessed primarily by male tenants or by couples in which the decision to intervene might have been left up to the male. It is not clear in either the experiment or the actual crime why there is this reluctance to aid a woman attacked by a man.

One possible reason for the failure to help may be found in the way the belief in justice affects reactions to situations that seem to call for help. In a series of studies, Lerner (1970) found that the more unjust the victim's suffering appears to be, the more negative are the descriptions of the victim by the witnesses. Lerner interpreted these findings in terms of the observer's desire to believe that this is a just world in which people get what they deserve, in which only good things happen to good people and bad things happen only to bad people. The witnesses of Kitty Genovese's murder may have decided in those crucial 35 minutes that she was getting what she deserved. Especially when feeling powerless to help, observers may devalue the victim to sustain their belief in basic justice. And, contrary to what one may expect, the greater the victim's pain, the less likely the intervention by observers, as demonstrated by an experiment in which subjects watching persons receiving differing amounts of shock responded more slowly when the victim was in greater pain (Baron, 1970).

Another victim characteristic that has been the object of study is his or her dependency condition—how badly the victim needs help. Berkowitz (1972) studied this dependency condition without recourse to situations involving pain or suffering. Using an experimental design in which subjects worked for a supervisor who was more or less dependent on their productivity, Berkowitz and his colleagues consistently found more productivity under high-dependency conditions. This finding did not prove to be particularly robust when tested in other situations of dependency, especially when the effort required of the helper was greater. But dependency is certainly a factor in eliciting help.

Common sense would suggest that help is more likely given to attractive victims than to unattractive ones. In one of the studies referred to above (Berkowitz & Daniels, 1963), subjects worked harder for supervisors they liked than for supervisors they disliked. In another study (Staub & Sherk, 1970), fourth graders shared a crayon longer with a classmate they liked than with one they didn't like. But attractiveness is very much in the eye of the beholder, and a variety of factors such as age, sex, race, and social class may contribute variably to a victim's attractiveness for a potential helper: it is not an attribute a victim can rely upon in expecting help from others.

Ambiguity of the Situation

Two of the steps in the cognitive analysis we have examined are particularly critical in determining intervention: noticing an event and interpreting it as a situation requiring help from the observer. Seemingly minor differences in the situation can drastically increase the number of witnesses who will help. Yakimovich and Saltz (1971) staged an incident in which a workman (actually an experimental confederate) fell from a ladder while washing the windows of a university building in which subjects were filling out questionnaires. The workman screamed and lay on the pavement clutching his ankle. All subjects rushed to the window, but only 29% offered help. This percentage was increased to 81% when the workman cried out for help. The cry for help apparently made it easier for subjects to interpret the situation as one in which help was needed. In a similar study, the workman was heard to fall from a ladder in an adjacent room, either with or without accompanying verbal signs of injury (Clark & Word, 1972). All subjects in the unambiguous situation (that is, the fall accompanied by cries) went to the workman's aid, while only 70% helped when the fall was not accompanied by verbal signs of distress. Furthermore, those in the unambiguous situation responded within 8 seconds on the average, while subjects unsure of the situation took approximately 56 seconds to respond—a delay that, in a real emergency, could be of great importance to the victim. When subjects were asked why they did or did not help, their answers clearly revealed that differences in interpretation of the situation had occurred.

In a field experiment where passersby were asked by someone in distress to make a phone call or mail a package, more helping occurred when the victim emphasized her distress than when she appealed to the responsibility of the helper (Langer & Abelson, 1972). Requests describing the victim's pain or stress elicited much more help than appeals such as "Would you do something for me?"

Familiarity with the Situation

From the above evidence, it is clear that there are things the victim can do to reduce the ambiguity of the situation and thereby increase the chances of getting help. There are also aspects of the helper's situation that make a difference, and familiarity with the surroundings is one of them. Latané and Darley (1970) described field studies conducted at a subway station and at an airport in New York. They made the assumption that, on the average, New Yorkers found on a subway platform are more likely to be familiar with their surroundings than people found in an airport waiting room. A confederate with bandaged leg and crutch fell near a stranger sitting alone in a subway platform or in the airport lounge. Twice as many people in the subway station offered help. A check on the researchers' assumption of familiarity differences confirmed that the subway riders knew more about their surroundings (for example, the location of exits, stairways, and telephones) than the airport patrons and that those who used the subway most frequently were most likely to help. These findings suggest that a victim seeking help ought to address his or her appeals to bystanders who look at home in the situation. But, when we think of the lack of response on the part of Kitty Genovese's neighbors, we may start questioning the value of this suggestion.

Implicit Rules

Part of being familiar with a situation is knowing what is appropriate in that situation; thus, a stranger generally has more trouble picking up subtle cues about the rules of behavior implicit in the situation. Recall the hesitancy you feel in an unfamiliar library or cafeteria and how you watch others to find out how the place works. Becoming familiar with the unwritten rules of various situations is an essential part of the socialization process for both foreigners and children. Parents can often be observed in public places of some formality (such as churches and museums) trying to tell their children what these unwritten rules are. Countless studies show that, as children get older, they tend to conform more and more to such rules (Bryan & London, 1970).

But apparently this conformity serves to restrict helping behavior. Children's helpful responses to sounds of distress from an adjoining room increased from kindergarten to second grade but decreased thereafter (Staub, 1970). Older children said that they did not help because they feared the experimenter's disapproval. In a subsequent similar study (Staub, 1971), some children were given permission to enter an adjoining room, others were forbidden to enter the room, and others were given no information concerning the room. When sounds of distress were heard from the next room, more children who had been given permission to enter helped. For these seventh graders, receiving no instructions was equivalent to a prohibition. When the study was repeated with young adults, most went to the aid of the victim regardless of their having received permission or not. But specific prohibition to enter the next room reduced helping considerably. Apparently, these adults had learned an implicit rule about the priority of giving help, a rule that was inhibited only by express prohibition. For children, instead, the adult's explicit permission was needed. In the Kitty Genovese murder, witnesses may have failed to help in response to some implicit rules of urban life to mind one's own business and leave others alone.

Mood

Among intimates, the refusal to adhere to a request is sometimes accompanied by the statement "I'm just not in the mood." Conversely, expansive good feelings toward others are sometimes the manifestation of an especially happy mood. In other words, "moods" can and do affect prosocial behavior. For example, subjects who were told that they had done extremely well on a series of tasks subsequently donated more money to a fund-raising effort than subjects who were told that they failed (Isen, 1970). Even small kind gestures can have an effect on helping behavior, as indicated by a field experiment in which some students were given cookies while studying in a library and others were not; all students were then asked to volunteer for an experiment involving either a helping role or a nonhelping role (Isen & Levin, 1972). The students who had received cookies were more inclined to volunteer for the helping role, while those who had not received cookies were more inclined to volunteer for the nonhelping role.

Since these results might be explained as easily by imitation of a helpful, cookie-giving model as by a happy mood brought about by the cookies, these same investigators worked with a situation not involving a model. They used the familiar situation of finding a coin in the slot of a pay telephone, with the small sense of euphoria that such finding produces in most people. When subjects left the phone booths, they encountered an experimental confederate who dropped a manila envelope of papers in their paths. The effects of even that small mood change were dramatic. Among women shoppers, all those who found a dime in the booth helped pick up the papers and none of those who did not find a dime helped. It is a bit surprising that, in the absence of other constraints, so small an event as finding a dime should make so clear a difference in helping behavior.

Presence of Others

The first research selection in this chapter makes the vivid point that the presence of others inhibits the individual's prosocial behavior. The reasoning behind the inhibiting effects of others involves, among other things, assumptions about the individual's reluctance to appear foolish or intrusive. Somehow the passive watching of an event by a group of onlookers seems to be governed by the rule that the situation calls for a passive stance and that any violation of that rule lays the person open to derision from the others. Latané and Rodin (1969) proposed that people witnessing an emergency in the presence of friends would feel the inhibiting effects of the presence of others less than those watching among strangers. Indeed, they found that subjects waiting with a friend responded to an accident staged in the next room sooner than subjects waiting with a stranger. However, the response rate for those with a friend was still half of that for people waiting alone. These findings confirm the inhibiting effects of the presence of others but at the same time indicate that these effects are somewhat attenuated by the relationship between the bystanders. Another study (Ross, 1971) sought to test if these inhibiting effects are reduced by the fact that the other bystanders are not very threatening. College male students were exposed either to smoke billowing into the room or to an accident next door; some of the subjects were alone, some were in the company of two other students, and some were with two young children. Again, the presence of others reduced the bystanders' tendency to help. All students alone helped, but very few (16%) of those grouped with other students did so; about half of those who were with children took helping action. These findings led to the conclusion that children as bystanders are perhaps less threatening and at the same time make the adult's sense of responsibility more pronounced.

METHODS IN THE STUDY OF PROSOCIAL BEHAVIOR

A review of the methods used in the study of prosocial behavior reveals a striking preponderance of field experimentation. The surge of interest in helping behavior stimulated by the Genovese murder in 1964 coincided with a dissatisfaction in social psychology with laboratory methods. As indicated in Chapter 1, there was dismay over newly discovered artifacts of laboratory experimentation (Rosenthal & Rosnow, 1969) and concern over the ethics of deception (Kelman, 1967). As a consequence, helping behavior may have been studied so much in field settings not because of any necessary connection between field settings and helping but because of methodological preoccupations among social psychologists at the time. It is also possible that the first attempts at field experimentation by social psychologists concentrated on helping because it was quite unlikely that someone would object to manipulations designed to increase people's helping behavior.

The range of helping behavior assessed in the field is considerable. Operational definitions of prosocial behavior include fixing flat tires (Bryan & Test, 1967), picking up dropped packages (Isen & Levin, 1972; Wispé & Freshley, 1971), returning lost wallets (Hornstein, Fisch, & Holmes, 1968), helping to carry boxes (Rudestam, Richards, & Garrison, 1971), mailing lost letters (Deaux, 1974), donating to charitable causes (Bryan & Test, 1967; Bryan & Walbek, 1970; Wheeler & Wagner, 1968), waiting on distressed customers (Schaps, 1972), as well as the bystander intervention in emergencies investigated by the selections in this chapter. The ingenuity shown by all these researchers is obvious, but you must be careful not to draw sweeping conclusions from a combination of these various findings, since one of the few studies that used several different operational definitions of prosocial behavior (Gergen, Gergen, & Meter, 1972) found that people who help in one situation don't necessarily help in another.

Laboratory Experiments

As indicated earlier, the surge of interest in prosocial behavior is usually credited to the work of Darley and Latané—work done primarily in the laboratory. Before these studies, however, Berkowitz and his colleagues had been investigating the effects of dependency on helping behavior, and their work, too, was done in the laboratory. This group of investigators used a single research design in a decade of laboratory work summarized in Berkowitz (1972). The standard procedure was the following. College students, mostly males, were recruited for an experiment on supervisory ability. A worker (the subject) was then asked to construct paper boxes or envelopes for a supervisor. In high-dependency conditions, the worker subject was told that the supervisor's chances of winning a prize depended on the worker's output; in low-dependency conditions, the subject was told that the quality of the supervisor's own behavior determined the award. The operational measure of helping was the number of boxes constructed under different conditions or the difference in output between a practice session and later experimental conditions. The pattern of results consistently supported the importance of dependency as a determinant of prosocial behavior.

Recent interest has turned to prosocial behavior involving intervention in thefts. A field experiment of this nature is described in the next section, but this question was also first studied in the laboratory. Latané and Darley (1970) staged a theft in the presence of male undergraduates waiting to be interviewed for a study on urban-living conditions. A confederate approached the receptionist's desk when she left the room and stole money from an envelope. Subjects witnessed this act either alone or in the company of another naive subject. Most subjects said nothing about the theft when the receptionist returned; but of the few who did report the thief, most were lone witnesses. Subjects questioned afterward denied seeing the theft or distorted its meaning by saying that the thief was only making change or taking the money by accident. The manipulated condition here was the size of the witnessing group, and subject awareness was controlled by deception.

Field Experiments

A recent field experiment (Moriarty, 1975) increased considerably the rate of intervention in staged thefts by eliciting prior verbal commitment from a witness to watch the victim's belongings. Thefts were staged at a beach and at a public cafeteria. In the first setting, the confederate victim placed a beach blanket within 5 feet of the subject and turned a portable radio to a local rock station. After a few minutes, the victim spoke to the subject and then walked away to wait unseen until the theft was completed. The commitment manipulation consisted in either a request by the victim to "watch my things" or a request for a match. A few minutes later, the confederate thief walked by, picked up the radio, and went off with it in the opposite direction from the victim. An observer nearby recorded whether the subject noticed the theft and whether he or she responded by attempting to stop the thief. About 30% of the subjects later said that they had not noticed the theft, and this was confirmed by the observer. Of those who did notice the theft, 58% pursued and stopped the thief. Commitment accounted for most of these interventions. With a prior commitment request to watch the victim's possessions, 95% of the subjects intervened to stop the theft; without prior commitment, only 20% did so. It should be noted that subjects were told at the earliest possible moment that the theft was not genuine and made aware of the purpose of the study. This debriefing is rare in field experiments, a point to be considered in evaluating the second research selection in this chapter. In a replication of this experiment, the theft of an unattended suitcase was staged in a busy cafeteria at lunchtime. The results were essentially the same. It is interesting to note that this replication could not be completed, because the cafeteria manager, although sympathetic with the aims of the research, came to feel that the procedures were too intrusive to patrons. This kind of concern is a genuine problem with field experiments that introduce manipulations into the natural pattern of events.

A different sort of procedure to assess a different kind of helping has come to be known as the "broken-bag caper" (Wispé & Freshley, 1971)—a jocular designation that invites a criticism of the fondness for dramatic scripts or the staging of "capers" in the conduct of social-psychological research. The original study using this procedure was concerned with interracial helping and was conducted in supermarket parking lots. Six supermarkets in predominantly Black neighborhoods were selected, and six supermarkets in White neighborhoods were then matched to them with regard to size, volume of business, and price of goods. One Black and one White woman, serving as confederates, dropped a bag of groceries about 20 feet from the main door of the market upon a signal from an observer that a subject was approaching. Subjects were male and female unaccompanied and unburdened shoppers. Helping behavior was coded according to whether subjects ignored the incident, reacted but did not help, or gave perfunctory or positive help. One-third gave no help at all, and only 20% gave positive help. No race differences were noticed, and the only sex difference found was in the Black sample, in which men helped both Black and White women more than any other group did. A partial replication of this experiment was conducted by Lerner and Frank (1974), who used all combinations of race and sex for "package droppers" and only White male and female subjects. They found no differences on the basis of either race or sex. In this replication, 44% of the subjects gave some form of help—about the same rate of helping as in the Wispé and Freshley study (1971), in which, if one combined the two categories of perfunctory and positive help, 41% of the subjects helped.

In these field experiments, as in those discussed earlier, every attempt was made to control antecedent conditions and subjects were not aware of being in experiments.

Field Studies

Somewhat surprisingly, while field experiments on prosocial behavior are fairly numerous, field studies using observational or archival methods are rare. Field studies are marked by low subject awareness and low manipulation of antecedent conditions. The following are virtually lone examples rather than representatives of a group of studies.

Severy and Davis (1971) reported an observational study of the helping behavior of normal and retarded children. Fifty-five children aged 3 to 5 and 8 to 10 years, both normal and retarded, were observed in school and day-care settings during one hour of free-play time. The rating was done by two teachers and two observers, and each observation was coded extensively. These observations and the teachers' ratings on eight pairs of positive and negative helping words yielded 55 variables, which were factor analyzed. Contrary to expectations, older normal children were less helpful than younger normal children or retardates. The older retardates attempted to help more than any other group and succeeded in helping as often.

An archival study was reported by Bryan and Davenport (1968), who examined the amount of money given to help various cases described in the annual Christmas appeal of the *New York Times'* "One Hundred Neediest Cases." These researchers found that the greatest numbers of contributions were made to child-abuse cases and to problems requiring medical aid. Cases describing psychological illness or moral transgressions elicited the least help from readers. The researchers attributed these differences in donations to the assumptions the donors made about what caused the victims' distress. More help was given when the victim was in need because of circumstances beyond his or her control, less when the distress could be construed as the victim's fault.

Scales, Surveys, and Interviews

These methods, too, have rarely been used in research on prosocial behavior. One study that did employ these methods high in subject awareness and low in manipulation of antecedent conditions dealt with extremely altruistic acts, as exemplified by Christians in Nazi-occupied Europe who risked their lives to save Jews (London, 1970). Just as the Kitty Genovese murder stimulated the work on bystander intervention, so did the Eichmann trial inspire this study of Christians who helped Jews. A California rabbi wrote a magazine article on the testimony given at the trial about the lone person who helped Jews at a concentration camp. This led to a television documentary featuring interviews with some rescuers and later to the pilot interview study reported by London (1970). A total of 27 rescuers and 42 rescued immigrants were interviewed in the United States and Israel, and standardized interview schedules amenable to quantification were used. Interviewers began by asking the subject to tell what the relevant incidents were, what background events led up to these incidents, and "parenthetically," to state personal values and attitudes. This pattern of questioning was seen as conducive to a friendly, comfortable atmosphere in which sensitive questions could be asked without deception. As the researchers could not obtain funding for their study, the results were never analyzed, nor were more interviews done. The researchers' impression, however, was that it was easier to describe the prosocial behavior in question than the motives leading to it and that the rescuers seemed to have certain characteristics in common—a spirit of adventure, an intense identification with a moral parental model, and a degree of social marginality.

A study done on more accessible populations was that of Walker and Mosher (1970), also dealing with altruistic people. The subjects of this study were sorority women on campus. Sororities were paid nominal sums to have members answer questionnaires and name three women who, in their opinion, exemplified altruistic ideals and three who did not. In interviews, all the women who had been named by their sorority's members described what they would do in five hypothetical situations calling for help and answered questions about their prosocial attitudes and feelings. Correlations were computed among all the measures. In contrast to their expectations, the investigators found that moderate rather than high altruism (as defined by the researchers' emphasis on intrinsic satisfaction) was the predominant motive for helping. The women's prosocial behavior seemed to derive from the norm of reciprocity and to be more directed at friends than at strangers.

TWO RESEARCH EXAMPLES

Product Description

The first selection, by John Darley and Bibb Latané, is generally credited with initiating the current wave of interest in altruistic behavior. In a laboratory setting, Darley and Latané tested the situational prediction that the helping behavior of a lone bystander to an emergency is different from that of a group of bystanders. College students were led to believe either that they were the only ones to hear someone apparently having an epileptic seizure or that others, as well as themselves, were privy to the call for help. The hypothesis that the more bystanders there are to an emergency, the less likely and the more slowly anyone will intervene was strongly supported. Two other manipulations—one varying group composition and the second varying sex of subject—had no significant effects.

A different type of emergency is investigated by Piliavin, Rodin, and Piliavin in the second selection. In an attempt to replicate and extend the Darley and Latané study in a field setting, these researchers used a design with several independent variables. First, it was hypothesized that, if a male victim (Black or White) collapsed in a subway train, he would receive help primarily from members of his own race. Furthermore, the nature of the distress was thought to make a difference in the amount of helping extended; specifically, it was hypothesized that a cane-carrying victim would elicit more assistance than a drunk victim. Third, a modeling condition was introduced to determine whether the presence of helpful others would bring about more aid than the absence of models. Finally, the design also included two other independent variables: size of group and sex of helper. On the basis of previous work by Darley and Latané, it was predicted that the greater the number of bystanders, the less the helping; no prediction was made with regard to the other independent variable, the helper's sex.

In contrast to the findings presented by Darley and Latané, these field investigators recorded a very high incidence of overall helping; in particular, their "cane" victim (who bears the clearest resemblance to the Darley and Latané epileptic) received help *every time* he collapsed. Other points of dissimilarity between this field study and the earlier laboratory study are evident. Piliavin and his associates found no support for the bystander effect; furthermore, they found that males helped significantly more than females, while the laboratory study had demonstrated no sex effects.

With regard to the race and victim manipulations, Piliavin and his colleagues found that, although race had no significant main effects, it did have more influence on helping behavior when the victim was drunk than when the victim was ill. An ill victim was likely to be helped by Blacks and Whites alike, regardless of whether the victim was Black or White. It was also noticed that the drunk victim was helped less quickly and less frequently than the ill victim. Lastly, no clear-cut modeling effects were found, but, as you will see, this seemed to be due more to the model's tardy arrival than to any lack of specific modeling influences.

Consumer Checklist

- How is each product put together?
    Are there differences in the kind or amount of experimental control used in these two studies?
- Are there any "environmental" costs entailed in the manufacture of either or both of these products?

Does the first selection show any evidence of methodological problems attendant upon the use of deception?

What are some of the ethical concerns raised by the use of deception in both settings?

- Considering similarities in product conception, how do you account for differences in product outcome?

Why did the laboratory experiment find that the greater the number of bystanders the less the helping, while the field experiment did not?

BYSTANDER INTERVENTION IN EMERGENCIES:
DIFFUSION OF RESPONSIBILITY [1]

JOHN M. DARLEY AND BIBB LATANÉ
New York University   *Columbia University*

Ss overheard an epileptic seizure. They believed either that they alone heard the emergency, or that 1 or 4 unseen others were also present. As predicted the presence of other bystanders reduced the individual's feelings of personal responsibility and lowered his speed of reporting ($p < .01$). In groups of size 3, males reported no faster than females, and females reported no slower when the 1 other bystander was a male rather than a female. In general, personality and background measures were not predictive of helping. Bystander inaction in real-life emergencies is often explained by "apathy," "alienation," and "anomie." This experiment suggests that the explanation may lie more in the bystander's response to other observers than in his indifference to the victim.

Several years ago, a young woman was stabbed to death in the middle of a street in a residential section of New York City. Although such murders are not entirely routine, the incident received little public attention until several weeks later when the New York Times disclosed another side to the case: at least 38 witnesses had observed the attack—and none had even attempted to intervene. Although the attacker took more than half an hour to kill Kitty Genovese, not one of the 38 people who watched from the safety of their own apartments came out to assist her. Not one even lifted the telephone to call the police (Rosenthal, 1964).

Preachers, professors, and news commentators sought the reasons for such apparently conscienceless and inhumane lack of intervention. Their conclusions ranged from "moral decay," to "dehumanization produced by the urban environment," to "alienation," "anomie," and "existential despair." An analysis of the situation, however, suggests that factors other than apathy and indifference were involved.

A person witnessing an emergency situation, particularly such a frightening and dangerous one as a stabbing, is in conflict. There are obvious humanitarian norms about helping the victim, but there are also rational and irrational fears about what might happen to a person who does intervene (Milgram & Hollander, 1964). "I didn't want to get involved," is a familiar comment, and behind it lies fears of physical harm, public embarrassment, involvement with police procedures, lost work days and jobs, and other unknown dangers.

In certain circumstances, the norms favoring intervention may be weakened, leading bystanders to resolve the conflict in the direction of nonintervention. One of these circumstances may be the presence of other onlookers. For example, in the case above, each observer, by seeing lights and figures in other apartment house windows, knew that others were also watching. However, there was no way to tell how the other observers were reacting. These two facts provide several reasons why any individual may have delayed or failed to help. The responsibility for helping was diffused among the observers; there was also diffusion of any potential blame for not taking action; and finally, it was possible that somebody, unperceived, had already initiated helping action.

When only one bystander is present in an emergency, if help is to come, it must come from him. Although he may choose to ignore it (out of concern for his personal safety, or desires "not to get involved"), any pres-

[1] This research was supported in part by National Science Foundation Grants GS1238 and GS1239. Susan Darley contributed materially to the design of the experiment and ran the subjects, and she and Thomas Moriarty analyzed the data. Richard Nisbett, Susan Millman, Andrew Gordon, and Norma Neiman helped in preparing the tape recordings.

From *Journal of Personality and Social Psychology*, 1968, 8(4), 377–383. Copyright 1968 by American Psychological Association. Reprinted by permission.

sure to intervene focuses uniquely on him. When there are several observers present, however, the pressures to intervene do not focus on any one of the observers; instead the responsibility for intervention is shared among all the onlookers and is not unique to any one. As a result, no one helps.

A second possibility is that potential blame may be diffused. However much we may wish to think that an individual's moral behavior is divorced from considerations of personal punishment or reward, there is both theory and evidence to the contrary (Aronfreed, 1964; Miller & Dollard, 1941, Whiting & Child, 1953). It is perfectly reasonable to assume that, under circumstances of group responsibility for a punishable act, the punishment or blame that accrues to any one individual is often slight or nonexistent.

Finally, if others are known to be present, but their behavior cannot be closely observed, any one bystander can assume that one of the other observers is already taking action to end the emergency. Therefore, his own intervention would be only redundant—perhaps harmfully or confusingly so. Thus, given the presence of other onlookers whose behavior cannot be observed, any given bystander can rationalize his own inaction by convincing himself that "somebody else must be doing something."

These considerations lead to the hypothesis that the more bystanders to an emergency, the less likely, or the more slowly, any one bystander will intervene to provide aid. To test this proposition it would be necessary to create a situation in which a realistic "emergency" could plausibly occur. Each subject should also be blocked from communicating with others to prevent his getting information about their behavior during the emergency. Finally, the experimental situation should allow for the assessment of the speed and frequency of the subjects' reaction to the emergency. The experiment reported below attempted to fulfill these conditions.

Procedure

Overview. A college student arrived in the laboratory and was ushered into an individual room from which a communication system would enable him to talk to the other participants. It was explained to him that he was to take part in a discussion about personal problems associated with college life and that the discussion would be held over the intercom system, rather than face-to-face, in order to avoid embarrassment by preserving the anonymity of the subjects. During the course of the discussion, one of the other subjects underwent what appeared to be a very serious nervous seizure similar to epilepsy. During the fit it was impossible for the subject to talk to the other discussants or to find out what, if anything, they were doing about the emergency. The dependent variable was the speed with which the subjects reported the emergency to the experimenter. The major independent variable was the number of people the subject thought to be in the discussion group.

Subjects. Fifty-nine female and thirteen male students in introductory psychology courses at New York University were contacted to take part in an unspecified experiment as part of a class requirement.

Method. Upon arriving for the experiment, the subject found himself in a long corridor with doors opening off it to several small rooms. An experimental assistant met him, took him to one of the rooms, and seated him at a table. After filling out a background information form, the subject was given a pair of headphones with an attached microphone and was told to listen for instructions.

Over the intercom, the experimenter explained that he was interested in learning about the kinds of personal problems faced by normal college students in a high pressure, urban environment. He said that to avoid possible embarrassment about discussing personal problems with strangers several precautions had been taken. First, subjects would remain anonymous, which was why they had been placed in individual rooms rather than face-to-face. (The actual reason for this was to allow tape recorder simulation of the other subjects and the emergency.) Second, since the discussion might be inhibited by the presence of outside listeners, the experimenter would not listen to the initial discussion, but would get the subject's reactions later, by questionnaire. (The real purpose of this was to remove the obviously responsible experimenter from the scene of the emergency.)

The subjects were told that since the experimenter was not present, it was necessary to impose some organization. Each person would talk in turn, presenting his problems to the group. Next, each person in turn would comment on what the others had said, and finally, there would be a free discussion. A mechanical switching device would regulate this discussion sequence and each subject's microphone would be on for about 2 minutes. While any microphone was on, all other microphones would be off. Only one subject, therefore, could be heard over the network at any given time. The subjects were thus led to realize when they later heard the seizure that only the victim's microphone was on and that there was no way of determining what any of the other witnesses were doing, nor of discussing the event and its possible solution with the others. When these instructions had been given, the discussion began.

In the discussion, the future victim spoke first, saying that he found it difficult to get adjusted to New York City and to his studies. Very hesitantly, and with obvious embarrassment, he mentioned that he was prone to seizures, particularly when studying hard or taking exams. The other people, including the real subject, took their turns and discussed similar problems (minus, of course, the proneness to seizures). The naive subject talked last in the series, after the last prerecorded voice was played.[2]

When it was again the victim's turn to talk, he made a few relatively calm comments, and then, growing increasingly louder and incoherent, he continued:

> I-er-um-I think I-I need-er-if-if could-er-er-somebody er-er-er-er-er-er-er give me a little-er-give me a little help here because-er-I-er-I'm-er-er-h-h-having a-a-a real problem-er-right now and I-er-if somebody could help me out it would-it would-er-er s-s-sure be-sure be good . . . because-er-there-er-er-a cause I-er-I-uh-I've got a-a one of the-er-sei-----er-er-things coming on and-and-and I could really-er-use some help so if somebody would-er-give me a little h-help-uh-er-er-er-er-er c-could somebody-er-er-help-er-uh-uh-uh (choking sounds). . . . I'm gonna die-er-er-I'm . . . gonna die-er-help-er-er-seizure-er-[chokes, then quiet].

The experimenter began timing the speed of the real subject's response at the beginning of the victim's speech. Informed judges listening to the tape have estimated that the victim's increasingly louder and more disconnected ramblings clearly represented a breakdown about 70 seconds after the signal for the victim's second speech. The victim's speech was abruptly cut off 125 seconds after this signal, which could be interpreted by the subject as indicating that the time allotted for that speaker had elapsed and the switching circuits had switched away from him. Times reported in the results are measured from the start of the fit.

Group size variable. The major independent variable of the study was the number of other people that the subject believed also heard the fit. By the assistant's comments before the experiment, and also by the number of voices heard to speak in the first round of the group discussion, the subject was led to believe that the discussion group was one of three sizes: either a two-person group (consisting of a person who would later have a fit and the real subject), a three-person group (consisting of the victim, the real subject, and one confederate voice), or a six-person group (consisting of the victim, the real subject, and four confederate voices). All the confederates' voices were tape-recorded.

Variations in group composition. Varying the kind as well as the number of bystanders present at an emergency should also vary the amount of responsibility felt by any single bystander. To test this, several variations of the three-person group were run. In one three-person condition, the taped bystander voice was that of a female, in another a male, and in the third a male who said that he was a premedical student who occasionally worked in the emergency wards at Bellevue hospital.

In the above conditions, the subjects were female college students. In a final condition males drawn from the same introductory psychology subject pool were tested in a three-person female-bystander condition.

Time to help. The major dependent variable was the time elapsed from the start of the victim's fit until the subject left her experimental cubicle. When the subject left her room, she saw the experimental assistant seated at the end of the hall, and invariably went to the assistant. If 6 minutes elapsed without the subject having emerged from her room, the experiment was terminated.

As soon as the subject reported the emergency, or after 6 minutes had elapsed, the experimental assistant disclosed the true nature of the experiment, and dealt with any emotions aroused in the subject. Finally the subject filled out a questionnaire concerning her thoughts and feelings during the emergency, and completed scales of Machiavellianism, anomie, and authoritarianism (Christie, 1964), a social desirability scale (Crowne & Marlowe, 1964), a social responsibility scale (Daniels & Berkowitz, 1964), and reported vital statistics and socioeconomic data.

RESULTS

Plausibility of Manipulation

Judging by the subjects' nervousness when they reported the fit to the experimenter, by their surprise when they discovered that the fit was simulated, and by comments they made during the fit (when they thought their microphones were off), one can conclude that almost all of the subjects perceived the fit as real. There were two exceptions in different experimental conditions, and the data for these subjects were dropped from the analysis.

Effect of Group Size on Helping

The number of bystanders that the subject perceived to be present had a major effect on the likelihood with which she would report the emergency (Table 1). Eighty-five percent of the subjects who thought they alone knew of the victim's plight reported the seizure before the victim was cut off, only 31% of those who thought four other bystanders were present did so.

---

[2] To test whether the order in which the subjects spoke in the first discussion round significantly affected the subjects' speed of report, the order in which the subjects spoke was varied (in the six-person group). This had no significant or noticeable effect on the speed of the subjects' reports.

TABLE 1

EFFECTS OF GROUPS SIZE ON LIKELIHOOD AND SPEED OF RESPONSE

Group size	N	% responding by end of fit	Time in sec.	Speed score
2 (S & victim)	13	85	52	.87
3 (S, victim, & 1 other)	26	62	93	.72
6 (S, victim, & 4 others)	13	31	166	.51

Note.—p value of differences: $\chi^2 = 7.91$, $p < .02$; $F = 8.09$, $p < .01$, for speed scores.

Every one of the subjects in the two-person groups, but only 62% of the subjects in the six-person groups, ever reported the emergency. The cumulative distributions of response times for groups of different perceived size (Figure 1) indicates that, by any point in time, more subjects from the two-person groups had responded than from the three-person groups, and more from the three-person groups than from the six-person groups.

Ninety-five percent of all the subjects who ever responded did so within the first half of the time available to them. No subject who had not reported within 3 minutes after the fit ever did so. The shape of these distributions suggest that had the experiment been allowed to run for a considerably longer time, few additional subjects would have responded.

Speed of Response

To achieve a more detailed analysis of the results, each subject's time score was transformed into a "speed" score by taking the reciprocal of the response time in seconds and multiplying by 100. The effect of this transformation was to deemphasize differences between longer time scores, thus reducing the contribution to the results of the arbitrary 6-minute limit on scores. A high speed score indicates a fast response.

An analysis of variance indicates that the effect of group size is highly significant ($p < .01$). Duncan multiple-range tests indicate that all but the two- and three-person groups differ significantly from one another ($p < .05$).

Victim's Likelihood of Being Helped

An individual subject is less likely to respond if he thinks that others are present. But what of the victim? Is the inhibition of the response of each individual strong enough to counteract the fact that with five onlookers there are five times as many people available to help? From the data of this experiment, it is possible mathematically to create hypothetical groups with one, two, or five observers.[3] The calculations indicate that the victim is about equally likely to get help from one bystander as from two. The victim is considerably more likely to have gotten help from one or two observers than from five during the first minute of the fit. For instance, by 45 seconds after the start of the fit, the victim's chances of having been helped by the single bystanders were about 50%, compared to none in the five observer condition. After the first minute, the likelihood of getting help from at least one person is high in all three conditions.

Effect of Group Composition on Helping the Victim

Several variations of the three-person group were run. In one pair of variations, the female subject thought the other bystander was either male or female; in another, she thought the other bystander was a premedical student who worked in an emergency ward at Bellevue hospital. As Table 2 shows, the

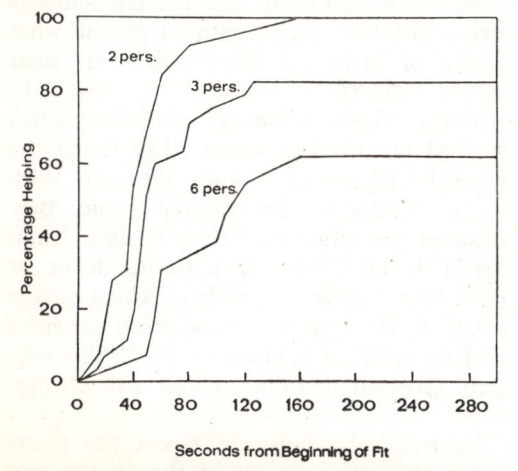

FIG. 1. Cumulative distributions of helping responses.

[3] The formula for the probability that at least one person will help by a given time is $1 - (1 - P)^n$ where n is the number of observers and P is the probability of a single individual (who thinks he is one of n observers) helping by that time.

TABLE 2

EFFECTS OF GROUP COMPOSITION ON LIKELIHOOD
AND SPEED OF RESPONSE[a]

Group composition	N	% responding by end of fit	Time in sec.	Speed score
Female S, male other	13	62	94	74
Female S, female other	13	62	92	71
Female S, male medic other	5	100	60	77
Male S, female other	13	69	110	68

[a] Three-person group, male victim.

variations in sex and medical competence of the other bystander had no important or detectable affect on speed of response. Subjects responded equally frequently and fast whether the other bystander was female, male, or medically experienced.

Sex of the Subject and Speed of Response

Coping with emergencies is often thought to be the duty of males, especially when females are present, but there was no evidence that this was the case in this study. Male subjects responded to the emergency with almost exactly the same speed as did females (Table 2).

Reasons for Intervention or Nonintervention

After the debriefing at the end of the experiment each subject was given a 15-item checklist and asked to check those thoughts which had "crossed your mind when you heard Subject 1 calling for help." Whatever the condition, each subject checked very few thoughts, and there were no significant differences in number or kind of thoughts in the different experimental groups. The only thoughts checked by more than a few subjects were "I didn't know what to do" (18 out of 65 subjects), "I thought it must be some sort of fake" (20 out of 65), and "I didn't know exactly what was happening" (26 out of 65).

It is possible that subjects were ashamed to report socially undesirable rationalizations, or, since the subjects checked the list *after* the true nature of the experiment had been explained to them, their memories might have been blurred. It is our impression, however, that most subjects checked few reasons because they had few coherent thoughts during the fit.

We asked all subjects whether the presence or absence of other bystanders had entered their minds during the time that they were hearing the fit. Subjects in the three- and six-person groups reported that they were aware that other people were present, but they felt that this made no difference to their own behavior.

Individual Difference Correlates of Speed of Report

The correlations between speed of report and various individual differences on the personality and background measures were obtained by normalizing the distribution of report speeds within each experimental condition and pooling these scores across all conditions ($n = 62-65$). Personality measures showed no important or significant correlations with speed of reporting the emergency. In fact, only one of the 16 individual difference measures, the size of the community in which the subject grew up, correlated ($r = -.26$, $p < .05$) with the speed of helping.

DISCUSSION

Subjects, whether or not they intervened, believed the fit to be genuine and serious. "My God, he's having a fit," many subjects said to themselves (and were overheard via their microphones) at the onset of the fit. Others gasped or simply said "Oh." Several of the male subjects swore. One subject said to herself, "It's just my kind of luck, something has to happen to me!" Several subjects spoke aloud of their confusion about what course of action to take, "Oh God, what should I do?"

When those subjects who intervened stepped out of their rooms, they found the experimental assistant down the hall. With some uncertainty, but without panic, they reported the situation. "Hey, I think Number 1 is very sick. He's having a fit or something." After ostensibly checking on the situation, the experimenter returned to report that "everything is under control." The subjects accepted these assurances with obvious relief.

Subjects who failed to report the emergency showed few signs of the apathy and indifference thought to characterize "unresponsive bystanders." When the experimenter entered her room to terminate the situation, the subject often asked if the victim was "all right." "Is he being taken care of?" "He's all right isn't he?" Many of these subjects showed physical signs of nervousness; they often had trembling hands and sweating palms. If anything, they seemed more emotionally aroused than did the subjects who reported the emergency.

Why, then, didn't they respond? It is our impression that nonintervening subjects had not decided *not* to respond. Rather they were still in a state of indecision and conflict concerning whether to respond or not. The emotional behavior of these nonresponding subjects was a sign of their continuing conflict, a conflict that other subjects resolved by responding.

The fit created a conflict situation of the avoidance-avoidance type. On the one hand, subjects worried about the guilt and shame they would feel if they did not help the person in distress. On the other hand, they were concerned not to make fools of themselves by overreacting, not to ruin the ongoing experiment by leaving their intercom, and not to destroy the anonymous nature of the situation which the experimenter had earlier stressed as important. For subjects in the two-person condition, the obvious distress of the victim and his need for help were so important that their conflict was easily resolved. For the subjects who knew there were other bystanders present, the cost of not helping was reduced and the conflict they were in more acute. Caught between the two negative alternatives of letting the victim continue to suffer or the costs of rushing in to help, the nonresponding bystanders vacillated between them rather than choosing not to respond. This distinction may be academic for the victim, since he got no help in either case, but it is an extremely important one for arriving at an understanding of the causes of bystanders' failures to help.

Although the subjects experienced stress and conflict during the experiment, their general reactions to it were highly positive. On a questionnaire administered after the experimenter had discussed the nature and purpose of the experiment, every single subject found the experiment either "interesting" or "very interesting" and was willing to participate in similar experiments in the future. All subjects felt they understood what the experiment was about and indicated that they thought the deceptions were necessary and justified. All but one felt they were better informed about the nature of psychological research in general.

Male subjects reported the emergency no faster than did females. These results (or lack of them) seem to conflict with the Berkowitz, Klanderman, and Harris (1964) finding that males tend to assume more responsibility and take more initiative than females in giving help to dependent others. Also, females reacted equally fast when the other bystander was another female, a male, or even a person practiced in dealing with medical emergencies. The ineffectiveness of these manipulations of group composition cannot be explained by general insensitivity of the speed measure, since the group-size variable had a marked effect on report speed.

It might be helpful in understanding this lack of difference to distinguish two general classes of intervention in emergency situations: direct and reportorial. Direct intervention (breaking up a fight, extinguishing a fire, swimming out to save a drowner) often requires skill, knowledge, or physical power. It may involve danger. American cultural norms and Berkowitz's results seem to suggest that males are more responsible than females for this kind of direct intervention.

A second way of dealing with an emergency is to report it to someone qualified to handle it, such as the police. For this kind of intervention, there seem to be no norms requiring male action. In the present study, subjects clearly intended to report the emergency rather than take direct action. For such indirect intervention, sex or medical competence does not appear to affect one's qualifications or responsibilities. Anybody, male or female, medically trained or not, can find the experimenter.

In this study, no subject was able to tell how the other subjects reacted to the fit. (Indeed, there were no other subjects actually present.) The effects of group size on speed of helping, therefore, are due simply to the perceived presence of others rather than to the influence of their actions. This means that the experimental situation is unlike emergencies, such as a fire, in which bystanders interact with each other. It is, however, similar to emergencies, such as the Genovese murder, in which spectators knew others were also watching but were prevented by walls between them from communication that might have counteracted the diffusion of responsibility.

The present results create serious difficulties for one class of commonly given explanations for the failure of bystanders to intervene in actual emergencies, those involving apathy or indifference. These explanations generally assert that people who fail to intervene are somehow different in kind from the rest of us, that they are "alienated by industrialization," "dehumanized by urbanization," "depersonalized by living in the cold society," or "psychopaths." These explanations serve a dual function for people who adopt them. First, they explain (if only in a nominal way) the puzzling and frightening problem of why people watch others die. Second, they give individuals reason to deny that they too might fail to help in a similar situation.

The results of this experiment seem to indicate that such personality variables may not be as important as these explanations suggest. Alienation, Machiavellianism, acceptance of social responsibility, need for approval, and authoritarianism are often cited in these explanations. Yet they did not predict the speed or likelihood of help. In sharp contrast, the perceived number of bystanders did. The explanation of bystander "apathy" may lie more in the bystander's response to other observers than in presumed personality deficiencies of "apathetic" individuals. Although this realization may force us to face the guilt-provoking possibility that we too might fail to intervene, it also suggests that individuals are not, of necessity, "noninterveners" because of their personalities. If people understand the situational forces that can make them hesitate to intervene, they may better overcome them.

REFERENCES

ARONFREED, J. The origin of self-criticism. *Psychological Review,* 1964, **71**, 193–219.

BERKOWITZ, L., KLANDERMAN, S., & HARRIS, R. Effects of experimenter awareness and sex of subject on reactions to dependency relationships. *Sociometry,* 1964, **27**, 327–329.

CHRISTIE, R. The prevalence of machiavellian orientations. Paper presented at the meeting of the American Psychological Association, Los Angeles, 1964.

CROWNE, D., & MARLOWE, D. *The approval motive.* New York: Wiley, 1964.

DANIELS, L., & BERKOWITZ, L. Liking and response to dependency relationships. *Human Relations,* 1963, **16**, 141–148.

MILGRAM, S., & HOLLANDER, P. Murder they heard. *Nation,* 1964, **198**, 602–604.

MILLER, N., & DOLLARD, J. *Social learning and imitation.* New Haven: Yale University Press, 1941.

ROSENTHAL, A. M. *Thirty-eight witnesses.* New York: McGraw-Hill, 1964.

WHITING, J. W. M., & CHILD, I. *Child training and personality.* New Haven: Yale University Press, 1953.

(Received July 8, 1967)

GOOD SAMARITANISM:

AN UNDERGROUND PHENOMENON?[1]

IRVING M. PILIAVIN
University of Pennsylvania

JUDITH RODIN
Columbia University

AND JANE ALLYN PILIAVIN[2]
University of Pennsylvania

> A field experiment was performed to investigate the effect of several variables on helping behavior, using the express trains of the New York 8th Avenue Independent Subway as a laboratory on wheels. Four teams of students, each one made up of a victim, model, and two observers, staged standard collapses in which type of victim (drunk or ill), race of victim (black or white) and presence or absence of a model were varied. Data recorded by observers included number and race of observers, latency of the helping response and race of helper, number of helpers, movement out of the "critical area," and spontaneous comments. Major findings of the study were that (a) an apparently ill person is more likely to receive aid than is one who appears to be drunk, (b) race of victim has little effect on race of helper except when the victim is drunk, (c) the longer the emergency continues without help being offered, the more likely it is that someone will leave the area of the emergency, and (d) the expected decrease in speed of responding as group size increases—the "diffusion of responsibility effect" found by Darley and Latané—does not occur in this situation. Implications of this difference between laboratory and field results are discussed, and a brief model for the prediction of behavior in emergency situations is presented.

Since the murder of Kitty Genovese in Queens, a rapidly increasing number of social scientists have turned their attentions to the study of the good Samaritan's act and an associated phenomenon, the evaluation of victims by bystanders and agents. Some of the findings of this research have been provocative and nonobvious. For example, there is evidence that agents, and even bystanders, will sometimes derogate the character of the victims of misfortune, instead of feeling compassion (Berscheid & Walster, 1967; Lerner & Simmons, 1966). Furthermore, recent findings indicate that under certain circumstances there is not "safety in numbers," but rather "diffusion of responsibility." Darley and Latané (1968) have reported that among bystanders hearing an epileptic seizure over earphones, those who believed other witnesses were present were less likely to seek assistance for the victim than were bystanders who believed they were alone. Subsequent research by Latané and Rodin (1969) on response to the victim of a fall confirmed this finding and suggested further that assistance from a group of bystanders was less likely to come if the group members were strangers than if they were prior acquaintances. The field experiments of Bryan and Test (1967), on the other hand, provide interesting findings that fit common sense expectations; namely, one is more likely to be a good Samaritan if one has just observed another individual performing a helpful act.

Much of the work on victimization to date has been performed in the laboratory. It is commonly argued that the ideal research strategy over the long haul is to move back and forth between the laboratory, with its

[1] This research was conducted while the first author was at Columbia University as a Special National Institute of Mental Health Research Fellow under Grant 1-F3-MH-36, 328-01. The study was partially supported by funds supplied by this grant and partially by funds from National Science Foundation Grant GS-1901 to the third author. The authors thank Virginia Joy for allowing the experimental teams to be recruited from her class, and Percy Tannenbaum for his reading of the manuscript and his helpful comments.

[2] Requests for reprints should be sent to Jane Allyn Piliavin, Department of Psychology, University of Pennsylvania, 3813-15 Walnut Street, Philadelphia, Pennsylvania 19104.

From *Journal of Personality and Social Psychology,* 1969, *13*(4), 289–299. Copyright 1969 by American Psychological Association. Reprinted by permission.

advantage of greater control, and the field, with its advantage of greater reality. The present study was designed to provide more information from the latter setting.

The primary focus of the study was on the effect of type of victim (drunk or ill) and race of victim (black or white) on speed of responding, frequency of responding, and the race of the helper. On the basis of the large body of research on similarity and liking as well as that on race and social distance, it was assumed that an individual would be more inclined to help someone of his race than a person of another race. The expectation regarding type of victim was that help would be accorded more frequently and rapidly to the apparently ill victim. This expectation was derived from two considerations. First, it was assumed that people who are regarded as partly responsible for their plight would receive less sympathy and consequently less help than people seen as not responsible for their circumstances (Schopler & Matthews, 1965).

Secondly, it was assumed that whatever sympathy individuals may experience when they observe a drunk collapse, their inclination to help him will be dampened by the realization that the victim may become disgusting, embarrassing, and/or violent. This realization may, in fact, not only constrain helping but also lead observers to turn away from the victim—that is, to leave the scene of the emergency.

Aside from examining the effects of race and type of victim, the present research sought to investigate the impact of modeling in emergency situations. Several investigators have found that an individual's actions in a given situation lead others in that situation to engage in similar actions. This modeling phenomenon has been observed in a variety of contexts including those involving good Samaritanism (Bryan & Test, 1967). It was expected that the phenomenon would be observed as well in the present study. A final concern of the study was to examine the relationship between size of group and frequency and latency of the helping response, with a victim who was both seen and heard. In previous laboratory studies (Darley & Latané, 1968; Latané & Rodin, 1969) in-

creases in group size led to decreases in frequency and increases in latency of responding. In these studies, however, the emergency was only heard, not seen. Since visual cues are likely to make an emergency much more arousing for the observer, it is not clear that, given these cues, such considerations as crowd size will be relevant determinants of the observer's response to the emergency. Visual cues also provide clear information as to whether anyone has yet helped the victim or if he has been able to help himself. Thus, in the laboratory studies, observers lacking visual cues could rationalize not helping by assuming assistance was no longer needed when the victim ceased calling for help. Staging emergencies in full view of observers eliminates the possibility of such rationalization.

To conduct a field investigation of the above questions under the desired conditions required a setting which would allow the repeated staging of emergencies in the midst of reasonably large groups which remained fairly similar in composition from incident to incident. It was also desirable that each group retain the same composition over the course of the incident and that a reasonable amount of time be available after the emergency occurred for good Samaritans to act. To meet these requirements, the emergencies were staged during the approximately $7\frac{1}{2}$-minute express run between the 59th Street and 125th Street stations of the Eighth Avenue Independent (IND) branch of the New York subways.

Method

Subjects

About 4,450 men and women who traveled on the 8th Avenue IND in New York City, weekdays between the hours of 11:00 A.M. and 3:00 P.M. during the period from April 15 to June 26, 1968, were the unsolicited participants in this study. The racial composition of a typical train, which travels through Harlem to the Bronx, was about 45% black and 55% white. The mean number of people per car during these hours was 43; the mean number of people in the "critical area," in which the staged incident took place, was 8.5.

Field situation. The A and D trains of the 8th Avenue IND were selected because they make no stops between 59th Street and 125th Street. Thus, for about $7\frac{1}{2}$ minutes there was a captive audience who, after the first 70 seconds of their ride, became

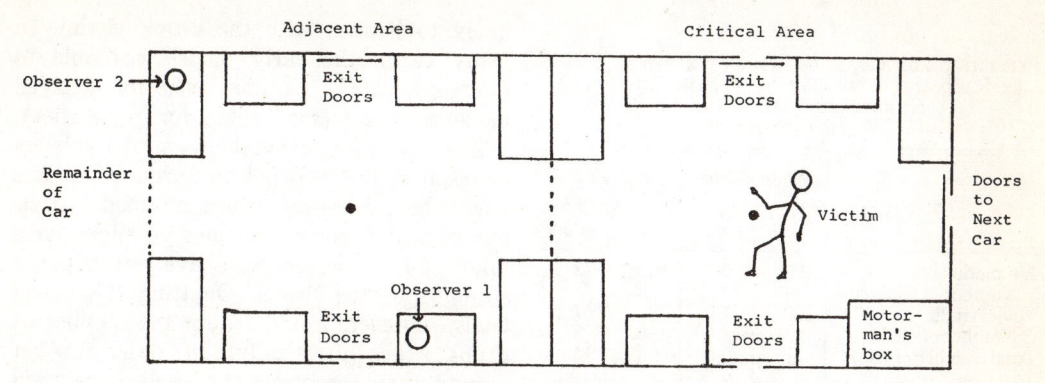

FIG. 1. Layout of adjacent and critical areas of subway car.

bystanders to an emergency situation. A single trial was a nonstop ride between 59th and 125th Streets, going in either direction. All trials were run only on the old New York subway cars which serviced the 8th Avenue line since they had two-person seats in group arrangement rather than extended seats. The designated experimental or critical area was that end section of any car whose doors led to the next car. There are 13 seats and some standing room in this area on all trains (see Figure 1).

Procedure

On each trial a team of four Columbia General Studies students, two males and two females, boarded the train using different doors. Four different teams, whose members always worked together, were used to collect data for 103 trials. Each team varied the location of the experimental car from trial to trial. The female confederates took seats outside the critical area and recorded data as unobtrusively as possible for the duration of the ride, while the male model and victim remained standing. The victim always stood next to a pole in the center of the critical area (see Figure 1). As the train passed the first station (approximately 70 seconds after departing) the victim staggered forward and collapsed. Until receiving help, the victim remained supine on the floor looking at the ceiling. If the victim received no assistance by the time the train slowed to a stop, the model helped him to his feet. At the stop, the team disembarked and waited separately until other riders had left the station. They then proceeded to another platform to board a train going in the opposite direction for the next trial. From 6 to 8 trials were run on a given day. All trials on a given day were in the same "victim condition."

Victim. The four victims (one from each team) were males between the ages of 26 and 35. Three were white and one was black. All were identically dressed in Eisenhower jackets, old slacks, and no tie. On 38 trials the victims smelled of liquor and carried a liquor bottle wrapped tightly in a brown bag (drunk condition), while on the remaining 65 trials they appeared sober and carried a black cane (cane condition). In all other aspects, victims dressed and behaved identically in the two conditions. Each victim participated in drunk and cane trials.[3]

Model. Four white males between the ages of 24 and 29 assumed the roles of model in each team. All models wore informal clothes, although they were not identically attired. There were four different model conditions used across both victim conditions (drunk or cane).

1. *Critical area—early.* Model stood in critical area and waited until passing fourth station to assist victim (approximately 70 seconds after collapse).
2. *Critical area—late.* Model stood in critical area and waited until passing sixth station to assist victim (approximately 150 seconds after collapse).
3. *Adjacent area—early.* Model stood in middle of car in area adjacent to critical area and waited until passing fourth station.
4. *Adjacent area—late.* Model stood in adjacent area and waited until passing sixth station.

When the model provided assistance, he raised the victim to a sitting position and stayed with him for the remainder of the trial. An equal number of trials in the no-model condition and in each of the four model conditions were preprogrammed by a random number table and assigned to each team.

---

[3] It will be noted later that not only were there more cane trials than drunk trials, they were also distributed unevenly across black and white victims. The reason for this is easier to explain than to correct. Teams 1 and 2 (both white victims) started the first day in the cane condition. Teams 3 (black) and 4 (white) began in the drunk condition. Teams were told to alternate the conditions across days. They arranged their running days to fit their schedules. On their fourth day, Team 2 violated the instruction and ran cane trials when they should have run drunk trials; the victim "didn't like" playing the drunk! Then the Columbia student strike occurred, the teams disbanded, and the study of necessity was over. At this point, Teams 1 and 3 had run on only 3 days each, while 2 and 4 had run on 4 days each.

TABLE 1

PERCENTAGE OF TRIALS ON WHICH HELP WAS GIVEN, BY RACE AND CONDITION OF VICTIM, AND TOTAL NUMBER OF TRIALS RUN IN EACH CONDITION

Trials	White victims		Black victim	
	Cane	Drunk	Cane	Drunk
No model	100%	100%	100%	73%
Number of trials run	54	11	8	11
Model trials	100%	77	—	67%
Number of trials run	3	13	0	3
Total number of trials	57	24	8	14

Note.—Distribution of model trials for the drunk was as follows: critical area: early, 4; late, 4; adjacent area: early, 5; late, 3. The three model trials completed for the cane victim were all early, with 2 from the critical area and 1 from the adjacent area.

Measures. On each trial one observer noted the race, sex, and location of every rider seated or standing in the critical area. In addition, she counted the total number of individuals in the car and the total number of individuals who came to the victim's assistance. She also recorded the race, sex, and location of every helper. A second observer coded the race, sex, and location of all persons in the adjacent area. She also recorded the latency of the first helper's arrival after the victim had fallen and on appropriate trials, the latency of the first helper's arrival after the programmed model had arrived. Both observers recorded comments spontaneously made by nearby passengers and attempted to elicit comments from a rider sitting next to them.

RESULTS AND DISCUSSION

As can be seen in Table 1, the frequency of help received by the victims was impressive, at least as compared to earlier laboratory results. The victim with the cane received spontaneous help, that is, before the model acted, on 62 of the 65 trials. Even the drunk received spontaneous help on 19 of 38 trials. The difference is not explicable on the basis of gross differences in the numbers of potential helpers in the cars. (Mean number of passengers in the car on cane trials was 45; on drunk trials, 40. Total range was 15–120.)

On the basis of past research, relatively long latencies of spontaneous helping were expected; thus, it was assumed that models would have time to help, and their effects could be assessed. However, in all but three of the cane trials planned to be model trials, the victim received help before the model was scheduled to offer assistance. This was less likely to happen with the drunk victim. In many cases, the early model was able to intervene, and in a few, even the delayed model could act (see Table 1 for frequencies).

A direct comparison between the latency of response in the drunk and cane conditions might be misleading, since on model trials one does not know how long it might have taken for a helper to arrive without the stimulus of the model. Omitting the model trials, however, would reduce the number of drunk trials drastically. In order to get around these problems the trials have been dichotomized into a group in which someone helped *before* 70 seconds (the time at which the early model was programmed to help) and a group in which no one had helped by this time. The second group includes some trials in which people helped the model and a very few in which no one helped at all.[4] It is quite clear from the first section of Table 2 that there was more immediate, spontaneous helping of the victim with the cane than of the drunk. The effect seems to be essentially the same for the black victim and for the white victims.[5]

What of the total number of people who helped? On 60% of the 81 trials on which the victim received help, he received it not from one good Samaritan but from two, three, or even more.[6] There are no significant differ-

[4] If a comparison of latencies is made between cane and drunk nonmodel trials only, the median latency for cane trials is 5 seconds and the median for drunk trials is 109 seconds (assigning 400 seconds as the latency for nonrespondents). The Mann-Whitney U for this comparison is significant at $p < .0001$.

[5] Among the white victim teams, the data from Team 2 differ to some extent from those for Teams 1 and 4. All of the cane–after 70 seconds trials are accounted for by Team 2, as are 4 of the 5 drunk-before 70 trials. Median latency for cane trials is longer for Team 2 than for the other teams; for drunk trials, shorter. This is the same team that violated the "alternate days" instruction. It would appear that this team is being rather less careful—that the victim may be getting out of his role. The data from this team have been included in the analysis although they tend to reduce the relationships that were found.

[6] The data from the model trials are not included in this analysis because the model was programmed to behave rather differently from the way in which most real helpers behaved. That is, his role was to raise the victim to a sitting position and then appear

TABLE 2

TIME AND RESPONSES TO THE INCIDENT

Trials on which help was offered:	Total number of trials		% of trials on which 1+ persons left critical area[b]		% of trials on which 1+ comments were recorded[b]		Mean number of comments	
	White victims	Black victim	White victims	Black victim	White victims	Black victim	White victims	Black victim
Before 70 sec.								
Cane	52	7	4%	14%	21%	0%	.27	.00
Drunk	5	4	20%	0%	80%	50%	1.00	.50
Total	57	11	5%	9%	26%	18%	.33	.18
After 70 sec.								
Cane	5	1	40%	—	60%	—	.80	—
Drunk	19	10	42%	60%	100%	70%	2.00	.90
Total	24	11	42%	64%	96%	64%	1.75	.82
χ^2	36.83	[a]	$\chi^2_{time} = 23.19$		$\chi^2_{time} = 31.45$			
p	<.001	<.03	$p < .001$		$p < .001$			
			$\chi^2_{cane-drunk} = 11.71$		$\chi^2_{cane-drunk} = 37.95$			
			$p < .001$		$p < .001$			

Note.—Percentage and means not calculated for n's less than 4.
[a] Fisher's exact test, estimate of two-tailed probability.
[b] Black and white victims are combined for the analyses of these data.

ences between black and white victims, or between cane and drunk victims, in the number of helpers subsequent to the first who came to his aid. Seemingly, then, the presence of the first helper has important implications which override whatever cognitive and emotional differences were initially engendered among observers by the characteristics of the victim. It may be that the victim's uniformly passive response to the individual trying to assist him reduced observers' fear about possible unpleasantness in the drunk conditions. Another possibility is that the key factor in the decisions of second and third helpers to offer assistance was the first helper. That is, perhaps assistance was being offered primarily to him rather than to the victim. Unfortunately the data do not permit adequate assessment of these or other possible explanations.

Characteristics of Spontaneous First Helpers

Having discovered that people do, in fact, help with rather high frequency, the next question is, "Who helps?" The effect of two variables, sex and race, can be examined. On

to need assistance. Most real helpers managed to drag the victim to a seat or to a standing position on their own. Thus the programmed model received somewhat more help than did real first helpers.

the average, 60% of the people in the critical area were males. Yet, of the 81 spontaneous first helpers, 90% were males. In this situation, then, men are considerably more likely to help than are women ($\chi^2 = 30.63$; $p < .001$).

Turning now to the race variable, of the 81 first helpers, 64% were white. This percentage does not differ significantly from the expected percentage of 55% based on racial distribution in the cars. Since both black and white victims were used, it is also possible to see whether blacks and whites are more likely to help a member of their own race. On the 65 trials on which spontaneous help was offered to the white victims, 68% of the helpers were white. This proportion differs from the expected 55% at the .05 level ($\chi^2 = 4.23$). On the 16 trials on which spontaneous help was offered to the black victim, half of the first helpers were white. While this proportion does not differ from chance expectation, we again see a slight tendency toward "same-race" helping.

When race of helper is examined separately for cane and drunk victims, an interesting although nonsignificant trend emerges (see Table 3). With both the black and white cane victims, the proportion of helpers of each race was in accord with the expected 55%–45%

TABLE 3

Spontaneous Helping of Cane and Drunk by Race of Helper and Race Victim

Race of helper	White victims			Black victim			All victims		
	Cane	Drunk	Total	Cane	Drunk	Total	Cane	Drunk	Total
Same as victim	34	10	44	2	6	8	36	16	52
Different from victim	20	1	21	6	2	8	26	3	29
Total	54	11	65	8	8	16	62	19	81

Note.—Chi-squares are corrected for continuity. White victims, $\chi^2 = 2.11$, $p. = 16$; black victim, $p = .16$ (two-tailed estimate from Fisher's exact probabilities test); all victims, $\chi^2 = 3.26$, $p = .08$.

split. With the drunk, on the other hand, it was mainly members of his own race who came to his aid.[7]

This interesting tendency toward same-race helping only in the case of the drunk victim may reflect more empathy, sympathy, and trust toward victims of one's own racial group. In the case of an innocent victim (e.g., the cane victim), when sympathy, though differentially experienced, is relatively uncomplicated by other emotions, assistance can readily cut across group lines. In the case of the drunk (and potentially dangerous) victim, complications are present, probably blame, fear, and disgust. When the victim is a member of one's own group—when the conditions for empathy and trust are more favorable—assistance is more likely to be offered. As we have seen, however, this does not happen without the passing of time to think things over.

Recent findings of Black and Reiss (1967) in a study of the behavior of white police officers towards apprehended persons offer an interesting parallel. Observers in this study recorded very little evidence of prejudice toward sober individuals, whether white or black. There was a large increase in prejudice expressed towards drunks of both races, but the increase in prejudice towards blacks was more than twice that towards whites.

Modeling Effects

No extensive analysis of the response to the programmed model could be made, since there were too few cases for analysis. Two analyses were, however, performed on the effects of adjacent area versus critical area models and of early versus late models within the drunk condition. The data are presented in Table 4. While the area variable has no effect, the early model elicited help significantly more than did the late model.

Other Responses to the Incident

What other responses do observers make to the incident? Do the passengers leave the car, move out of the area, make comments about the incident? No one left the car on any of the trials. However, on 21 of the 103 trials, a total of 34 people did leave the critical area. The second section of Table 2 presents the percentage of trials on which someone left the critical area as a function of three variables: type of victim, race of victim, and time to receipt of help (before or after 70 seconds). People left the area on a higher proportion of trials with the drunk than with the cane victim. They also were far more likely to leave on trials on which help was not offered by 70 seconds, as compared to trials on which help was received before that time.[8] The frequencies are too small to

[7] It is unfortunate from a design standpoint that there was only one black victim. He was the only black student in the class from which our crews were recruited. While it is tenuous to generalize from a sample of one, the problems attendant upon attributing results to his race rather than to his individual personality characteristics are vitiated somewhat by the fact that response latencies and frequencies of help to him in the cane condition fall between responses to Teams 1 and 4 on the one hand and Team 2 on the other.

[8] Individuals are also somewhat more likely to leave the area with the black victim than with the white victims ($\chi^2 = 3.24$, $p < .08$). This race effect is most probably an artifact, since the black victim ran more drunk trials than cane trials, the white victims, vice versa.

TABLE 4

Frequency of Help as a Function of Early (70 Seconds) versus Late (150 Seconds) and Adjacent versus Critical Area Programmed Models

Help	Critical area			Adjacent area			Both areas		
	Early	Late	Both	Early	Late	Both	Early	Late	Total
Received	4	2	6	5	1	6	9	3	12
Not received	0	2	2	0	2	2	0	4	4
Total	4	4	8	5	3	8	9	7	16

Note.—Early versus late: $p < .04$ (two-tailed estimate from Fisher's exact test). All three cane-model trials were early model trials; two critical area, one adjacent. Help was received on all. Table includes drunk trials only.

make comparisons with each of the variables held constant.

Each observer spoke to the person seated next to her after the incident took place. She also noted spontaneous comments and actions by those around her. A content analysis of these data was performed, with little in the way of interesting findings. The distribution of number of comments over different sorts of trials, however, did prove interesting (see Section 3 of Table 2). Far more comments were obtained on drunk trials than on cane trials. Similarly, most of the comments were obtained on trials in which no one helped until after 70 seconds. The discomfort observers felt in sitting inactive in the presence of the victim may have led them to talk about the incident, perhaps hoping others would confirm the fact that inaction was appropriate. Many women, for example, made comments such as, "It's for men to help him," or "I wish I could help him—I'm not strong enough," "I never saw this kind of thing before—I don't know where to look," "You feel so bad that you don't know what to do."

A Test of the Diffusion of Responsibility Hypothesis

In the Darley and Latané experiment it was predicted and found that as the number of bystanders increased, the likelihood that any individual would help decreased and the latency of response increased. Their study involved bystanders who could not see each other or the victim. In the Latané and Rodin study, the effect was again found, with bystanders who were face to face, but with the victim still only heard. In the present

TABLE 5

Mean and Median Latencies as a Function of Number of Males in the Critical Area

No. males in critical area	Cane			Drunk		
	White victims	Black victim	Total	White victims	Black victim	Total
1–3						
M	16	12	15	—	309	309
Mdn.	7	12	7	—	312	312
N	17	2	19		4	4
4–6						
M	20	6	18	155	143	149
Mdn.	5	4	5	105	70	73
N	23	4	27	4	4	8
7 and up						
M	3	52	9	107	74	97
Mdn.	1	52	1.5	102	65	84
N	14	2	16	7	3	10
Kruskal-Wallis Test (H)			5.08			6.01
p			.08			.05

Note.—Means and medians in seconds. Model trials omitted; no response assigned 400 seconds.

Legend

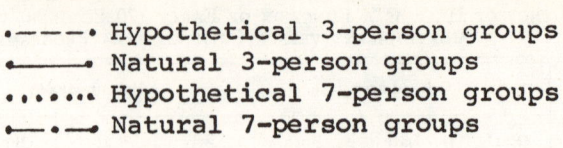

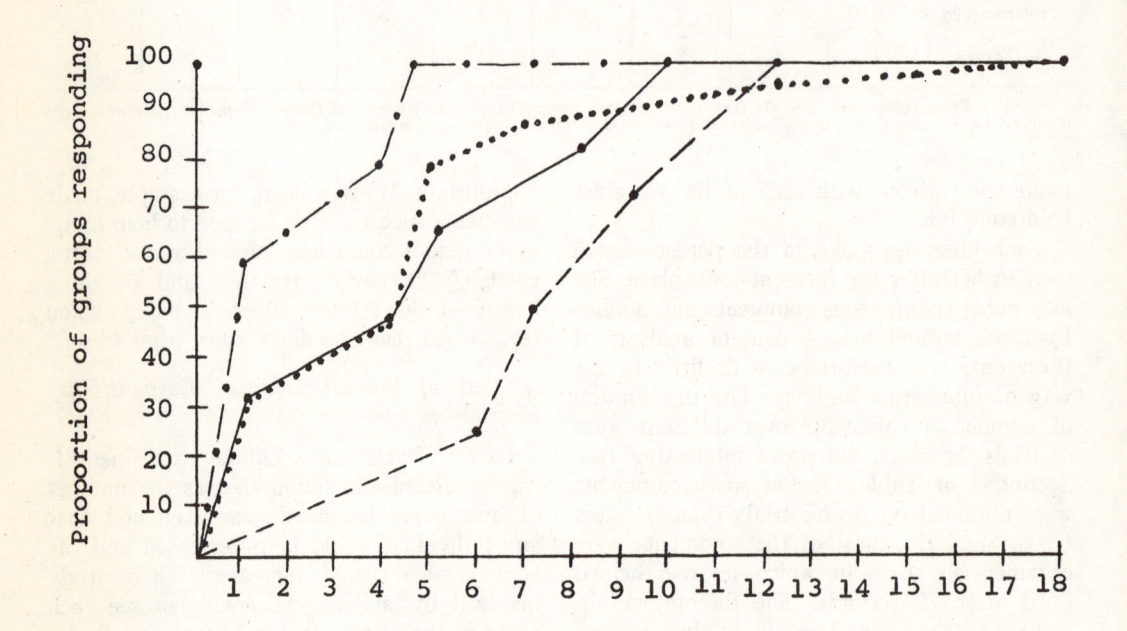

•---• Hypothetical 3-person groups
•—• Natural 3-person groups
•••••• Hypothetical 7-person groups
•—•—• Natural 7-person groups

Seconds from occurence of collapse to helping response from one member of group

FIG. 2. Cumulative proportion of groups producing a helper over time (cane trials, white victims, male helpers from inside critical area).

study, bystanders saw both the victim and each other. Will the diffusion of responsibility finding still occur in this situation?

In order to check this hypothesis, two analyses were performed. First, all nonmodel trials were separated into three groups according to the number of males in the critical area (the assumed reference group for spontaneous first helpers). Mean and median latencies of response were then calculated for each group, separately by type and race of victim. The results are presented in Table 5. There is no evidence in these data for diffusion of responsiiblity; in fact, response times, using either measure, are consistently faster for the 7 or more groups compared to the 1 to 3 groups.[9]

As Darley and Latané pointed out, however, different-size real groups cannot be meaningfully compared to one another, since as group size increases the likelihood that one or more persons will help also increases. A second analysis as similar as possible to that used by those authors was therefore performed, comparing latencies actually obtained

[9] The total number of people in the car was strongly related to the number of males in the critical area. Similar results are obtained if latencies are examined as a function of the total number of people in the car.

for each size group with a base line of hypothetical groups of the same size made up by combining smaller groups. In order to have as much control as possible the analysis was confined to cane trials with white victims and male first helpers coming from the critical area. Within this set of trials, the most frequently occurring natural groups (of males in the critical area) were those of sizes 3 ($n = 6$) and 7 ($n = 5$). Hypothetical groups of 3 ($n = 4$) and 7 ($n = 25$) were composed of all combinations of smaller sized groups. For example, to obtain the hypothetical latencies for groups of 7, combinations were made of (a) all real size 6 groups with all real size 1 groups, plus (b) all real size 5 groups with all real size 2 groups, etc. The latency assigned to each of these hypothetical groups was that recorded for the faster of the two real groups of which it was composed. Cumulative response curves for real and hypothetical groups of 3 and 7 are presented in Figure 2.

As can be seen in the figure, the cumulative helping response curves for the hypothetical groups of both sizes are lower than those for the corresponding real groups. That is, members of real groups responded more rapidly than would be expected on the basis of the faster of the two scores obtained from the combined smaller groups. While these results together with those summarized in Table 5 do not necessarily contradict the diffusion of responsibility hypothesis, they do not follow the pattern of findings obtained by Darley and Latané and are clearly at variance with the tentative conclusion of those investigators that "a victim may be more likely to receive help . . . the fewer people there are to take action [Latané & Darley, 1968, p. 221]."

Two explanations can be suggested to account for the disparity between the findings of Table 5 and Figure 2 and those of Darley and Latané and Latané and Rodin. As indicated earlier in this paper, the conditions of the present study were quite different from those in previous investigations. First, the fact that observers in the present study could see the victim may not only have constrained observers' abilities to conclude there was no emergency, but may also have overwhelmed with other considerations any tendency to diffuse responsibility. Second, the present findings may indicate that even if diffusion of responsibility *is* experienced by people who can actually see an emergency, when groups are larger than two the increment in deterrence to action resulting from increasing the number of observers may be less than the increase in probability that within a given time interval at least one of the observers will take action to assist the victim. Clearly, more work is needed in both natural and laboratory settings before an understanding is reached of the conditions under which diffusion of responsibility will or will not occur.

Conclusions

In this field study, a personal emergency occurred in which escape for the bystander was virtually impossible. It was a public, face-to-face situation, and in this respect differed from previous lab studies. Moreover, since generalizations from field studies to lab research must be made with caution, few comparisons will be drawn. However, several conclusions may be put forth:

1. An individual who appears to be ill is more likely to receive aid than is one who appears to be drunk, even when the immediate help needed is of the same kind.
2. Given mixed groups of men and women, and a male victim, men are more likely to help than are women.
3. Given mixed racial groups, there is some tendency for same-race helping to be more frequent. This tendency is increased when the victim is drunk as compared to apparently ill.
4. There is no strong relationship between number of bystanders and speed of helping; the expected increased "diffusion of responsibility" with a greater number of bystanders was not obtained for groups of these sizes. That is, help is not less frequent or slower in coming from larger as compared to smaller groups of bystanders; what effect there is, is in the opposite direction.
5. The longer the emergency continues without help being offered (a) the less impact a model has on the helping behavior of observers; (b) the more likely it is that individuals will leave the immediate area; that

is, they appear to move purposively to another area in order to avoid the situation; (c) the more likely it is that observers will discuss the incident and its implications for their behavior.

A model of response to emergency situations consistent with the previous findings is currently being developed by the authors. It is briefly presented here as a possible heuristic device. The model includes the following assumptions: Observation of an emergency creates an emotional arousal state in the bystander. This state will be differently interpreted in different situations (Schachter, 1964) as fear, disgust, sympathy, etc., and possibly a combination of these. This state of arousal is higher (a) the more one can empathize with the victim (i.e., the more one can see oneself in his situation—Stotland, 1966), (b) the closer one is to the emergency, and (c) the longer the state of emergency continues without the intervention of a helper. It can be reduced by one of a number of possible responses: (a) helping directly, (b) going to get help, (c) leaving the scene of the emergency, and (d) rejecting the victim as undeserving of help (Lerner & Simmons, 1966). The response that will be chosen is a function of a cost-reward matrix that includes costs associated with helping (e.g., effort, embarrassment, possible disgusting or distasteful experiences, possible physical harm, etc.), costs associated with not helping (mainly self-blame and perceived censure from others), rewards associated with helping (mainly praise from self, victim, and others), and rewards associated with not helping (mainly those stemming from continuation of other activities). Note that the major motivation implied in the model is not a positive "altruistic" one, but rather a selfish desire to rid oneself of an unpleasant emotional state.

In terms of this model, the following after-the-fact interpretations can be made of the findings obtained:

1. The drunk is helped less because costs for helping are higher (greater disgust) and costs for not helping are lower (less self-blame and censure because he is in part responsible for his own victimization).

2. Women help less because costs for helping are higher in this situation (effort, mainly) and costs for not helping are lower (less censure from others; it is not her role).

3. Same-race helping, particularly of the drunk, can be explained by differential costs for not helping (less censure if one is of opposite race) and, with the drunk, differential costs for helping (more fear if of different race).

4. Diffusion of responsibility is not found on cane trials because costs for helping in general are low and costs for not helping are high (more self-blame because of possible severity of problem). That is, the suggestion is made that the diffusion of responsibility effect will increase as costs for helping increase and costs for not helping decrease. This interpretation is consistent with the well-known public incidents, in which possible bodily harm to a helper is almost always involved, and thus costs for helping are very high, and also with previous research done with nonvisible victims in which either (a) it was easy to assume someone had already helped and thus costs for not helping were reduced (Darley & Latané) or (b) it was possible to think that the emergency was minor, which also reduces the costs for not helping (Latané & Rodin).

5. All of the effects of time are also consistent with the model. The longer the emergency continues, the more likely it is that observers will be aroused and therefore will have chosen among the possible responses. Thus, (a) a late model will elicit less helping, since people have already reduced their arousal by one of the other methods; (b) unless arousal is reduced by other methods, people will leave more as time goes on, because arousal is still increasing; and (c) observers will discuss the incident in an attempt to reduce self-blame and arrive at the fourth resolution, namely a justification for not helping based on rejection of the victim.

Quite obviously, the model was derived from these data, along with data of other studies in the area. Needless to say, further work is being planned by the authors to test the implications of the model systematically.

REFERENCES

Berscheid, E., & Walster, E. When does a harm-doer compensate a victim? *Journal of Personality and Social Psychology,* 1967, **6,** 435–441.

Black, D. J., & Reiss, A. J. *Studies in crime and law enforcement in major metropolitan areas.* (Report submitted to the President's Commission on Law Enforcement and Administration of Justice) Washington, D. C.: United States Government Printing Office, 1967.

Bryan, J. H., & Test, M. A. Models and helping: Naturalistic studies in aiding behavior. *Journal of Personality and Social Psychology,* 1967, **6,** 400–407.

Darley, J., & Latané, B. Bystander intervention in emergencies: Diffusion of responsibility. *Journal of Personality and Social Psychology,* 1968, **8,** 377–383.

Latané, B., & Darley, J. Group inhibition of bystander intervention in emergencies. *Journal of Personality and Social Psychology,* 1968, **10,** 215–221.

Latané, B., & Rodin, J. A lady in distress: Inhibiting effects of friends and strangers on bystander intervention. *Journal of Experimental Social Psychology,* 1969, **5,** 189–202.

Lerner, M. J., & Simmons, C. H. Observer's reaction to the "innocent victim": Compassion or rejection? *Journal of Personality and Social Psychology,* 1966, **4,** 203–210.

Schachter, S. The interaction of cognitive and physiological determinants of emotional state. In L. Berkowitz (Ed.), *Advances in experimental social psychology.* Vol. 1. New York: Academic Press, 1964.

Schopler, J., & Matthews, M. W. The influence of the perceived causal locus of partner's dependence on the use of interpersonal power. *Journal of Personality and Social Psychology,* 1965, **4,** 609–612.

Stotland, E. A theory and experiments in empathy. Paper presented at the meeting of the American Psychological Association, New York, September 1966.

(Received October 21, 1968)

THE STUDIES COMPARED

Good research design allows an investigator to answer questions as clearly and validly as possible. To this end, design involves three kinds of control. First, good design permits the investigator to create different levels of the independent variable in order to see whether such differences have a differential impact on the dependent variable. Second, good design rules out other potential influences by holding them constant across all conditions. Third, good design minimizes random error through standardization of procedures.

Independent Variable Manipulation

The first research selection is a classic laboratory experiment and, as such, exemplifies the strengths inherent in that approach. The method permits the investigators to center their interest on the bystander variable. Through instructions and tape-recorded interactions, Darley and Latané were able to create three different levels of the independent variable: subject alone with victim, subject plus one other bystander with victim, subject plus four other bystanders with victim.

Although the field experiment by Piliavin and colleagues shows concern with creating systematic differences in all independent variables, it is marred by some flaws in this regard. Specifically, the modeling variable was not cleanly operationalized. The aim was to create a modeling condition and a no-modeling condition; a closer look at these two conditions, however, shows that they did not differ from each other. The investigators picked a 70-second time interval before the model intervened. As it turned out, this interval was too long, and, as a consequence, it was as though no model intervened at all. This time interval apparently was selected on the basis of past research, but no references are provided. In addition, this problem might have been avoided with more extensive pilot testing of the procedure. As implemented, the design did not allow for the test of the effects of a model.

Control of Extraneous Influences

Another clear asset of laboratory experimentation is the control it affords over the influence of other factors. Specifically, Darley and Latané arranged their experiment so as to rule out effects created by having the experimenter visible to the subjects when the emergency occurred. The field experiment did not control so well for this effect. Observers are clearly needed, since the experiment requires accurate recording of the helping responses, but they may not have been as "unobtrusive" as the investigators intended. In a field setting, observers are harder to disguise than in the laboratory, and hence they become part of the very scene they are attempting to observe. In this specific case, the nonparticipant stance of the observers may have had its own undesirable effects, since presumably their presence was more noticeable under uncrowded (few bystanders) than under crowded (many bystanders) condition. A tentative conclusion with regard to the sex differences found is that, since the observers were women, their inactivity unintentionally modeled nonintervention for other women in the subway. This possibility is strengthened by the fact that no sex differences were found in other helping studies (Lerner & Frank, 1974; Wispé & Freshley, 1971).

Minimizing Error

A crucial aspect of any experimental procedure involves the standardization of conditions, so that all subjects undergo exactly the same experience, except for variations created in the independent variable. For example, attempts are made to avoid error due to boredom, fatigue, or inexperience on the part of the persons conducting the experiment. In the laboratory study, the epileptic fit was tape-recorded, so that, when replayed to successive subjects, the performance was always the same. Standardization difficulties became acute, however, in the study carried out in the subway car. Here, the victim's collapse was enacted live many times. Some control was achieved by randomizing the order of the conditions, but, as indicated in a footnote, one team neglected the prescribed randomization of performances because the victim in that team didn't like playing the drunk. If this preference did emerge in one team, it may well have emerged in other teams in the form of qualitatively different performances.

Casting matters as well. Since there was only one Black student in the class from which the confederates for the study were recruited, only one Black played the victim role. Strict control is achieved by having more than one performer in a role, lest the effects be attributable to that individual rather than to the experimental role conditions. The investigators also report that a university student strike cut short the study. These factors, some only partially avoidable by the experimenters, were in fact only partially controlled in the experiment. The care expended on randomization of conditions and subjects illustrates ingenuity and concern with maximizing the control of antecedent conditions. No experiment is flawless in this regard, and field experiments are usually more susceptible to the influence of uncontrolled extraneous variance. Although laboratory experiments are intrinsically stronger in matters of control, they suffer from other shortcomings, among them the problems associated with deceiving subjects. The manipulation of antecedent conditions, which is so central a feature of the laboratory experiment, often entails deception in the attempt to make the conditions seem real.

Deception

When obtrusive self-report measures are used in research, two kinds of problems emerge. First, if the measure is transparent, subjects may report less undesirable behavior than they would actually show if unaware. In the case of prosocial behavior, aware subjects may exaggerate the amount of helping they would normally give. Second, subjects responding to direct questions may not know what governs their behavior. In fact, witnesses to emergencies often claim that they are not influenced by the presence of others.

To counteract these two problems, researchers sometimes create the semblance of a real situation through deception and thereby seek to elicit spontaneous behavior. Whenever deception is used, ask yourself whether the simulation worked; that is, did subjects believe that an emergency was indeed occurring? In the first selection, a question about the deception was asked as part of a 15-item checklist of thoughts that crossed the subject's mind as he heard the seizure tape. The item, which read "I thought it must be some sort of fake," was endorsed by 30% of the subjects—a high percentage of people to report suspicion. Darley and Latané do not comment on the degree to which this suspicion may have undermined the success of the deception manipulation, nor do they indicate how these particular subjects behaved or how many were in the alone condition or in the with-others condition in the experiment. A replication by Horowitz (1971) found that subjects' comments indicating doubt about what was happening (or what to do) may be further indications of suspicion rather than decisional conflict, as Darley and Latané suggest. It seems fair to say that, in the laboratory studies, the deception worked only partially.

Deception is generally considered a problem peculiar to the laboratory. The assumption is made that being the object of study places people on guard and makes them suspicious. Deception is more likely to arouse suspicion in the laboratory than in field situations, in which people have no indication that they are being studied. In field experiments, deception is more an ethical than a methodological problem. People are exposed to potentially stressful events without their consent, and, in the absence of debriefing, no information is given or received about how these events occurred. As information about field experimentation becomes more widely known, people may come to question whether any unusual event they witness is an experiment, and the effects of this assumption are hard to predict (Staub, 1974).

Results Compared

The results of the two studies included in this chapter seem to be in conflict, but, on closer examination, one realizes that it is difficult to make precise direct comparisons. The critical conceptual argument made by Darley and Latané here and elsewhere postulates a sharp difference between the reaction of an individual who knows that he or she alone is witness to an emergency and the reaction of an individual who is one of many witnesses. The Piliavin, Rodin, and Piliavin study had no condition comparable to that of the subject as lone witness—the condition that produced the highest level of help in the laboratory study. The mean number of people in the critical area in which the staged incident occurred was 8.5, and the reported breakdowns into 3- and 7-person groups do not indicate any alone condition. It may be, therefore, that the bystander effect is not a simple linear function of the number of bystanders. This more complex structure of the bystander effect may account for the seeming contradiction in findings.

CONSUMER EVALUATION

Read Carefully

A casual reading of either or both of these studies can make the results seem contradictory, whereas attentive reading and thinking reveals considerable consensus between the findings. Careful comparisons reveal methodological and substantive issues that even the most careful reading of one article alone would not disclose. For example, the idea of bystander apathy has a simple appeal and makes possible a facile condemnation of people who fail to help. The laboratory study was stimulated by the failure of Kitty Genovese's neighbors to come to her aid, and the experiment found that the presence of others was an apparently critical deterrent to intervention. The fact that cane-carrying victims received so much help in the subway was therefore a surprise and should provide an incentive to attempts at finding ways of reconciling the results.

Check Durability

One of the complaints often directed at laboratory research is that the behavior found there cannot be generalized to natural settings. The concern is that behavior observed in the laboratory may be as much a function of this special setting as of the variables under the experiment's control. If this is so, then the independent variable (the number of bystanders) may need the same conditions (instructions, an experimenter, and so forth) to produce helping behavior in the real world.

As we mentioned earlier, these special characteristics of the setting (demand characteristics) are not confined to the laboratory. Every environment contains a variety of elements that suggest the appropriate behavior for that setting, and this is especially true of helping—an aspect of behavior very much governed by norms. Currently, there is a misplaced faith in social-psychological research that credits field experimentation with freedom from problems of demand characteristics. The field experiment we have been discussing ostensibly failed to find a bystander effect—a result perhaps explained in part by the fact that the witnesses represented a captive audience for the $7\frac{1}{2}$-minute train run. That nonstop run may have demand characteristics due to the fact that it prevents escape from the situation. Staub (1974), in staging accidents on city streets, found that pedestrians crossed to the other sidewalk to avoid having to deal with a situation that might require helping. The bystander effect may not be missing from the real world as much as from the world of captive audiences.

5

AGGRESSION

CHAPTER OUTLINE

Origins of Aggression
   Ethological Explanations of Aggression
      Criticisms of the Ethological Position
      Problems of Cross-Species Generalization
   Explanations Linking Frustration to Aggression
   Social Learning Explanations of Aggression
Some Situational Influences on Aggressive Behavior
   Effects of Models on Adult Aggressive Behavior
   Exposure to Aggressive Cues
Methods Used in Research on Aggression
   Methods Used in the Laboratory
      The Aggression Machine
      The Berkowitz Paradigm
   Examples of Field Experiments
   Use of Archives
   Naturalistic Observation
   Field Studies Involving Surveys and Interviews

Two Research Examples
   Product Description
   Consumer Checklist
   Leonard Berkowitz and Anthony LePage, Weapons as aggression-eliciting stimuli.
   Charles W. Turner, John F. Layton, and Lynn S. Simons, Naturalistic studies of aggressive behavior: Aggressive stimuli, victim visibility, and horn honking.
The Studies Compared
   Deception
      Suspicion
   Confounding Variables in the Field Experiment
   Sex Differences
Consumer Evaluation
   Product Durability
   Flashy Merchandising

If we think, even casually, of some social-psychological behaviors, we will not hesitate to say that they are inherently complicated. The functioning of groups, the development of attraction, and the changing of attitudes—just to mention a few— are examples of issues that, even at first glance, appear to be complex and hard to figure out. Aggression, on the other hand, is usually assumed to be a simpler behavior. When you see someone intentionally harming another, you probably think you are witnessing a simple act. If the attacker tries to explain his actions, you're likely to think or say "There's nothing to explain; I saw you do it." Aggressive acts have a vivid presence, a seeming directness, and a surface explicitness that invites simple explanations; people are believed to be either aggressive or not. Aggression is action and taps strong emotion, and it is easily equated with simply being human. This chapter focuses on the function of aggressive cues in creating, stimulating, and guiding the expression of aggression. In reading the chapter, you may come to share our view that aggression is anything but simple. We are concerned that perpetuating the myth that aggression is simple and basic to human nature may inhibit attempts to reduce, alter, or eradicate violence.

ORIGINS OF AGGRESSION

Ethological Explanations of Aggression

Ethologists have produced a wide range of studies of animal behavior; mating, food gathering, and dominance hierarchies are only a few of the topics that have attracted the ethologists' attention. Applications of these findings to humans have been few and modest. But in one area—aggression—popular ethologists (Ardrey, 1966; Lorenz, 1966; Morris, 1968; Tiger, 1969) have speculated freely about the similarities between animal and human behavior. These ethologists regard aggression as instinctive and as adaptive in assuring the survival of the fittest. Aggression in animals is kept in check by inhibitory rituals and appeasement modes, also instinctive in origin. Lorenz (1966) suggests that humans lack these instinctive inhibitions to offset aggression and posits that these inhibitions and restraints failed to evolve in humans because they were not needed. Lorenz argues that humans possess few natural attack features like sharp teeth and claws and thus are biologically ill equipped to inflict mortal damage on one another. Lorenz further claims that it was only the development of technological weapons (from clubs to bombs) that upset the natural ecological balance by making it possible for humans to be more destructive than nature "intended." This argument seems to overlook the human capacity to strangle, push someone off a high place, or smash the human body against hard objects—direct destructive acts that are carried out without tools. The core of the ethological position is two-fold: humans in the roles of aggressors develop very destructive tools, and humans in the roles of victims engage in few and weak restraining acts. The interplay of these two factors results in a high degree of aggression in humans.

Criticisms of the Ethological Position. The argument that aggression is instinctual rather than learned needs physiological evidence (Moyer, 1971). It has been found that particular brain areas, when stimulated, produce aggressive behavior and others, when stimulated, inhibit aggressive behavior (Delgado, 1969). But even such discoveries are less than conclusive evidence for ethological explanations of human aggression. Two limitations must be considered. First, the fact that stimulation of a particular brain area produces aggression does not mean that the reaction is innately determined. Learned response patterns are also stored in the brain and are presumably responsive to stimulation. Second, stimulation of certain brain areas does not always produce aggression. Even when it does, the aggressive expression is shaped by environmental factors. Monkeys remain sensitive to long-standing social patterns even under electrical stimulation by an experimenter.

These limitations make an unqualified instinct theory hard to support. It is more likely that even in laboratory animals there are environmental determinants for aggressive behavior. Such behavior is then intensified by the internal state of the organism. Environmental determinants are even more important for humans, whose complexity and capacity for symbolization are bound to affect expressions of aggressive behavior. In warfare, for example, dehumanizing the victim makes it possible to kill with little felt aggression; dehumanizing is a symbolic process.

Problems with Cross-Species Generalization. Although popularizations of ethological views have been widely read, their acclaim in scientific circles has been more limited. Questions are raised about the validity of generalizations about aggression from one animal species to another. The observations of popular ethologists are based on few animals in few species (often in captivity); their conclusions, therefore, may be applicable only to limited populations in selected settings (Nelson, 1974). Ethologists who work in the field have noted that in most animal species confrontations rarely result in aggression; the far more frequent reaction is flight. Fromm (1973) has questioned why instinctivists don't talk more about the innate impulse for flight. If intraspecies aggression is such an uncommon reaction, then the amount of behavior that any instinct notion of aggression is left to explain is much more limited than the popularizers suggest.

More pertinent to this chapter are the criticisms directed at extending these ethological speculations to humans. For a more extensive review of these objections, see Nelson's (1974) excellent summary, which points out the danger of confusing developmental and hereditary patterns when generalizing to human behavior. Uniformity of aggressive behavior observed within a species is no guarantee of innateness. The "fixed action patterns" described by ethologists are often molded and shaped by environmental forces—to some extent in animals and most certainly so in humans. Human rituals are clearly not genetically transmitted; they are learned through imitation and direct experience and mediated by the environmental context. Despite this important difference, Lorenz and others continue to draw direct analogies from observations of animal behavior.

The arena in which human learning about aggression takes place is broad and diversified. Cultural variations in both amounts and modes of aggression are striking, with some cultures clearly more peaceful and less combative than others. Instinct explanations tend to deal with cultural differences by postulating the existence of benign outlets that dissipate aggressive energy. As you will see later in the chapter, there is strong evidence that exposure to aggression actually strengthens, rather than weakens, aggressive behavior in humans. The important role that learning plays in human behavior makes this possibility quite likely. For instance, Lorenz's suggestion that sports are suitable outlets for aggression is not well founded. Nations committed to competitive sports are not especially noted for peaceful policies. A study of sports fans (Goldstein &

Arms, 1971) found more hostility among those who attended a football game than among those who watched a gymnastics match. Riots and violence at major sports events are not uncommon. In summary, the direct application of relatively simpleminded ethological observations of restricted animal populations to human behavior offers limited insights into human aggression. What instinctual basis there may be is widely modifiable by the biological and social environment as it is individually experienced.

Explanations Linking Frustration to Aggression

In contrast to popular notions, if you ask psychologists what causes aggression, most of them are likely to mention frustration. The frustration-aggression hypothesis was first offered as absolute (Dollard, Doob, Miller, Mowrer, & Sears, 1939); that is, it postulated that all frustration leads to aggression and that all aggression is the result of frustration. This original formulation was soon modified (Miller, 1941) to indicate that frustration is an "instigation to aggression," thus allowing for outcomes other than aggression. Still later versions of the frustration-aggression hypothesis have taken human cognitive processes and value systems more into account. For a clear presentation of the evolution of this explanation of aggression, see Berkowitz (1962, 1969).

In the original proposition, frustration was defined as interference with goal-directed activity. Two problems have been associated with this definition (Tedeschi, Smith, & Brown, 1974). First, research has shown that goal-interference defined (operationalized) as failure, especially at experimental tasks, does not result in aggression. Second, manipulations of frustration can produce increases in behaviors other than aggression. Frustrated people don't always aggress; they may withdraw, find something else to do, or try again. Such findings led to new questions about when frustration does and does not lead to aggression. Once again, we can see the familiar pattern of a course of research leading to the realization that the implications of an initially simple idea are not so simple and that the idea requires modification. Greater subtlety is needed to account for the varieties of human behavior.

There is also a more basic logical problem with the frustration-aggression theory, even in its modified form. This problem was underlined by Kaufmann (1970), who pointed to an inherent circularity in the frustration-aggression hypothesis, a circularity based largely on the unobservable character of one or the other element. If people are observed aggressing, the inference is made that they must have been blocked or frustrated *because* they are now seen behaving aggressively. Conversely, if persons are observed to be frustrated, they are assumed to feel some aggression even when none is exhibited. The problem with circular reasoning is that you can't win. Good theory lets you be specific about the elements in the behavior and about the manner in which these elements are linked.

This circular reasoning can be straightened by defining the behavioral elements clearly; frustration must be redefined to include internal as well as external referents. For example, in order to define an internal referent, "goal interference" must be shown to have had some psychological impact on the individual *before* the aggressive act took place. Also, both the inner and the outer frustration must be amenable to independent observation or measurement. In the absence of tangible aggression, effective measures of inner frustrations are tremendously difficult to achieve. As a result, the predictive power of explanations linking frustration and aggression has been severely hampered. The section on methods below presents some attempts at operationalizing independently both frustration and aggression, and you can decide how effective you find them to be.

Social-Learning Explanations of Aggression

As you have seen so far, inferences based on a theory that assumes that aggression is instinctual in origin and inferences linking aggression to frustration offer only partial explanations for aggressive behavior. When you consider the complexity of any human social behavior, it seems obvious that much of it is learned. Take so basic a survival behavior as eating. You need to eat and, by and large, you eat what you like (at least in this culture). But what you like to eat is determined by learning, not by instinct. You select the foods you prefer in markets, restaurants, refrigerators, and at the dinner table. So, too, with other behavioral patterns. With regard to aggression, Bandura (1973) has described three elements that any learning explanation must take into account—how aggression is developed or acquired, what factors instigate its occurrence, and what conditions maintain its performance.

Bandura explained the acquisition of aggressive behavior patterns by two distinct processes: direct experience and observation of others engaged in aggressive acts. Direct experience teaches aggression in that it helps the person who behaves aggressively to get good things or avoid bad things. For instance, a child's aggressive behavior may get him or her (more often him) good intangibles like adult attention and approval and good tangibles like desirable toys or food wrested away from another child. Adults too can be taught to add new aggressive behaviors to their repertoires by reward, as seen in the training of combat soldiers. Similarly, you may learn through direct experience that aggression prevents bad consequences. Acts of self-defense may be seen in this light, as might aggressive actions aimed at convincing either victim or audience that one is not a pushover. The second acquisition process is one in which aggression is learned through observation of another's aggressive actions. Learning by direct experience and learning by observation are not competitive explanations of how aggression is learned. Both processes occur in everyone. When the relative strengths of learning by imitation and by direct experience were examined experimentally in children, observation produced more learning than direct rewarded experience (Bandura & McDonald, 1963). Clearly, both children and adults acquire much of their new behavior through observation and imitation of others. In a recent review of developmental psychology, Hetherington and McIntyre (1975) were moved to comment

> A well known behavior modifier once said it was time research on the application of operant methods passed beyond atheoretical "Whoopee!" studies where with each new behavior conditioned the investigator yelled, "Whoopee! We can condition ____!" It now seems clear that under the right circumstances children will imitate almost anything. Whoopee! [p. 113].

All of us are exposed to a much larger number of people and actions than we imitate; we don't imitate and learn everything others do. It then becomes important to know under what conditions observational learning does and does not take place. The simplest application of social-learning theory would suggest that behavior observed to be rewarding is imitated and behavior observed to bring about punishment is not. An experiment testing children's imitation of filmed aggression confirmed this expectation (Bandura, Ross, & Ross, 1963). Of even greater interest was the observation that, when children were promised rewards for reproducing the behavior seen in the film, all children behaved more aggressively. This indicated that even the children who had watched the model being punished for the aggressive acts had learned the behavior, although they did not behave aggressively in the play session following the film viewing (when they were not promised rewards for imitating the aggressive behavior). The distinction between performing and learning an action is important (Bandura & Walters,

1963). All the children learned the aggressive acts through observation of the filmed model, but whether they performed these acts was determined by the conditions of punishment or reward in which the model's actions took place. In the second research selection in this chapter, sounding a car horn at an annoying driver is used as a measure of aggressive behavior. Such actions are within every driver's repertoire. Learning to honk is probably learned along with learning to drive, but whether the act is performed depends on the other cues in the situation.

SOME SITUATIONAL INFLUENCES ON AGGRESSIVE BEHAVIOR

While initially Bandura and his associates were concerned with the learning of aggressive behavior, they soon acknowledged the important distinction between behavior learned and behavior performed. You often hear of real crimes modeled step by step after a television play and carried out soon after the showing of the play. The form and substance of the plot are probably learned by observation, but there also have to be cues present in the real environment of the criminals to instigate the actual aggressive actions. Not much is known about the situational influences that elicit aggression and sustain its performance. Summarized here are some experimental studies on modeling and on the role of aggressive cues. This material sets a context for the two research selections in this chapter.

Effects of Models on Adult Aggressive Behavior

The effects of an aggressive model on the behavior of adults (Baron, 1971; 1972) have been examined in several studies. In one of them (Baron & Kepner, 1970), subjects gave longer and stronger shocks to an experimental confederate who insulted them when they had just seen someone else give high levels of shock. The presence of another person who acts aggressively seems to either reduce inhibitions against aggression or suggest an acceptable level of aggressive performance to subjects who later find themselves in the same situation. But there are limits to the power of an aggressive model. Adults are at least as sensitive as children to other situational factors. For instance, if a nonaggressive model is also present in the situation or if the aggressor is criticized, there is less aggressive behavior on the part of those who observed the aggressive model. What may be going on in this situation is that the presence of a nonaggressive model suggests to the observer that behavior other than aggression is possible in the situation. The expression of criticism, while not offering an explicit alternative, may at least suggest that aggression is not the best possible behavior in that context.

Exposure to Aggressive Cues

There are other conditions that elicit or maintain aggressive actions, and these have been explored experimentally by investigators who have worked with Leonard Berkowitz, using the basic research design developed by him (see section on methods below). Their research is based on the theory of frustration-aggression, with the important modification that frustration is seen as leading to arousal, which is then guided by aggression cues. For instance, Turner and Berkowitz (1972) found that how much a person aggressed after seeing violent movie scenes depended on how much the viewer identified with the person shown aggressing in the film. Similarly, Berkowitz

(1965) varied the cue value of a confederate who received shocks in the context of a learning task by describing the confederate as either a physical-education major interested in boxing or a speech major. The labels served as subtle messages to aggress to a greater or lesser degree. Subjects who had been angered and who had seen a prizefight scene from the movie *Champion* gave more shocks to the confederate when he was introduced as a boxer than when he was described as a speech major. Presumably, in this situation it is the similarity of the real victim to the filmed victim that acts as an aggressive cue.

The effect of similarity suggests yet another condition that governs what does or does not become an aggressive cue—how the viewers interpret the violence they are shown (Geen & Stonner, 1974). Subjects who were angered by a confederate and who saw a movie scene of a gunfight that they were told was motivated by revenge subsequently aggressed more than unangered subjects who were told that the gunfight involved other motives. In summary, what seems to be happening with respect to situational factors is that adults are influenced by aggressive (and other) models but only to the extent to which they identify with the aggressor, perceive the victim as similar to the aggressive model's victim, and interpret the behavior as harmfully aggressive.

If live models can influence others to act aggressively, can the presence of physical aggressive stimuli do likewise? In the two studies included in this chapter, the presence of guns as aggressive cues is investigated directly.

METHODS USED IN RESEARCH ON AGGRESSION

From the preceding review, you may have sensed that, since aggression is a topic of commanding interest not only to psychologists, researchers from many disciplines have studied this subject. With a diversity of professionals all with different training, this means that a wide range of methods have been used—more specifically, methods other than laboratory experiments. Different methods imply different definitions of aggression. Consider, for example, archival research, which examines records of various sorts, or interview approaches, which inquire of participants and observers how an aggressive act came about. These methods make possible certain definitions of the aggression variable. Field methods, on the other hand, can be used to study real actions intended to harm another. When you hear reports of assaults, murders, or riots, you may wonder why the people did it but you don't question that aggression was involved.

Laboratory research, instead, is a more limited method of research on aggression because of the limited kinds of aggression it can study. What is generally a strength of the laboratory method—that events can be staged under the experimenter's control and the reactions of naive subjects assessed—does not work well when studying aggression. The scope of the dependent variable (aggressive behavior) is obviously a function of the extent to which the independent variable(s) can be manipulated by the investigator. This very specificity, which is ordinarily an asset of laboratory methods, proves restrictive in the study of aggression. There are real ethical and practical limits on experimentally produced behavior that is intentionally harmful; murders and assaults (and many other aggressive acts) cannot be staged in the laboratory. As a result, the laboratory experiments usually involve deception and generate a wide range of operational definitions of aggression. This range of definitions includes behavior that, on the face of it, would not be easily classified as aggression. Choosing to play with a ball rather than a doll (Lovaas, 1961) and negatively evaluating another's intelligence (Berkowitz & Rawlings, 1963) are not very devastating acts of aggression. Even if you grant these actions some aggressive component, when they are enacted in a laboratory experiment it is not clear that the subject intends to harm another. Often the experimenter has produced a context in which the "aggressive" act is legitimized by the procedure or, at the very least, in which the subject's intent is not assessed—a point further developed in the discussion of the first research selection in this chapter.

Methods Used in the Laboratory

The Aggression Machine. The problems associated with actually harming another person in the laboratory have led to the development of methods that combine face validity (apparent harmful aggression) with ethical constraints (actually harmless). An apparatus developed by Buss (1961), called the Aggression Machine, has been widely used in laboratory research. The machine is a shock generator housed in a cabinet garnished with elaborate lights, levers, and buttons and with caution signs indicating shock levels. This device is used to provide a subject with an instrument to aggress against another person, usually a confederate of the experimenter. In order to convince the subject of the painful nature of the shocks, he is given low-level, albeit painful, sample shocks at the beginning of the experiment. This is in fact the only shock experienced by anyone in the study. In actuality, the levers on the machine are wired not into the shock generator but into an event recorder that registers both the level and the duration of the shock applied by the subject. The machine is not then a method for aggressing against another but a means of recording a subject's response to the experimental condition. While ostensibly a tool for the subject, it is in fact a tool for the experimenter.

Most commonly, this apparatus has been used in the context of a learning experiment. Subjects are deceived into believing that they are paired with another subject (actually the experimenter's confederate) and that they randomly select roles (actually rigged so the subject is always a teacher). The "learner" is programmed to make a prescribed number of mistakes, and the subject is invited to administer shocks to signal these mistakes. The level and duration of shock applied represent the measure of aggression. Since the subject could use the lowest shock level briefly to signal errors, any increase in level or duration of shock is interpreted as an intention to harm the "learner." In an experiment of this kind, subjects who had been frustrated delivered slightly stronger shocks to an experimental confederate than subjects who had not been frustrated (Buss, 1963).

The machine has been used not only in conjunction with learning experiments but also as an adjunct to various other deceptions. For instance, subjects who receive shocks from an experimental confederate to indicate a poor evaluation of an essay they've written can use the machine to retaliate. What has been found is that subjects match the levels of shock they've received; they meet the provocation with equivalent retaliation (Berkowitz & Green, 1962). Another use of the machine has been in the context of a reaction-time task in which subjects are led to think that they are competing with another player. The slower player loses and receives a shock whose level has been preset and made known by the opponent. In fact, the subject is playing against a predetermined program of losses and increasing shock levels. Here, too, subjects respond by raising their retaliatory shock levels to match those they receive (Taylor & Epstein, 1967).

The Berkowitz Paradigm. The Aggression Machine has been used by Berkowitz and associates in a series of studies involving a complex and consistent research design. The design is complicated both in the operational definitions of the factors and in the elaborate experience the subjects undergo. Typically, three factors are involved, and two levels of each variable are introduced; the psychologist's shorthand for this is a 2 × 2 × 2 factorial design. In the Berkowitz paradigm, this means that the first variable, degree of aggression readiness, is produced at two levels—a high level created by angering the subject through insults and a low level created by treating him in a neutral manner. The second variable consists of showing or not showing an aggressive film scene to half the angered and unangered subjects, and the third variable is represented by making the confederate whom the subject will shock similar to or different from the characters portrayed in the film. The design is called a 2 × 2 × 2 factorial design because the three numbers represent the three independent factors, and the numerical value 2 represents the levels of each variable that is presented. Thus, a 3 × 4 design would have two independent variables, one with three levels (perhaps high, medium, and low something) and the other with four. Both research selections in this chapter employ factorial designs—techniques preferred by social psychologists because they make possible the study of multiple causes and effects and their interactions.

The Berkowitz paradigm, too, involves deceiving subjects with regard to the purpose of the experiment. This deception, coupled with the need to make the experimental factors impactful and strong, results in a complicated experience for the subjects, as the Berkowitz and LePage selection that follows clearly illustrates. In general, these studies show that angered subjects who have seen a violent film will aggress against a confederate who resembles a character in that film (Berkowitz, 1965; Berkowitz & Geen, 1966).

All laboratory studies of this kind involve a high degree of awareness on the part of the subjects that they are being studied. The deception is obviously intended to reduce subject awareness of what specifically is being studied and of what the subject's responses mean. But successful deception cannot be taken for granted, and each investigator should offer evidence as to the efficacy of the deceptions employed. You should consider this issue when you read the first selection. Laboratory studies such as the ones described above are high in manipulation of antecedent conditions. A variation in the laboratory approach are studies of aggression that include some physiological measures. These studies are as high in manipulation as other laboratory studies but are considered lower in subject awareness on the assumption that even subjects aware of the experimenter's intent could not control their blood pressure. A summary of this approach is presented by Hokanson (1970).

Examples of Field Experiments

Field experiments are gaining some popularity in social psychology because they seem to represent optimal combinations of the dimensions of subject awareness and experimenter control. It is possible to manipulate the antecedent conditions so that the subjects' awareness of being part of an experiment and of what the experiment entails is reduced to a minimum. Not all field experiments, however, are successful in eliminating these and other kinds of problems, as the following two examples make clear. Harris (1974) had experimental confederates crowd into lines in stores, banks, restaurants, and airport check-in and ticket windows and had them note the reactions of persons thus intruded upon. She controlled the sex of the confederate, whether he or she said "excuse me" or not, where the intrusion took place (in front of the third or twelfth person in line), the sex of the subject, and the social status of the subject as indicated by clothing and general appearance. The behavior of the subjects was rated, both on verbal and on nonverbal dimensions, from polite to threatening and from smiles to shoves. Harris found that men of low status near the front of the line responded most aggressively; same-sex pairs were more aggressive than mixed-sex pairs, and female experimenters received more nonverbal than verbal aggression from subjects. While this study allowed considerable control of experimental conditions and capitalized on a natural event that is unlikely to arouse subject awareness, it did not (and by its very nature perhaps could not) elicit a very powerful form of aggression.

A truer measure of what most people would consider aggressive behavior was obtained in a field experiment on television violence and aggression (Feshbach & Singer, 1971). Experimenters were able to control the kind of television programs that boys in private schools and institutions watched by randomly assigning viewers to either violent or nonviolent programs for six weeks. The boys took a number of tests to measure their aggressive tendencies, and staff members recorded the number of aggressive incidents in which the boys were involved. In contrast to most of the research on effects of media violence, this field experiment found no increase in aggressive behavior for boys who had watched an unlimited amount of violent television programs. In fact, boys of lower social status and boys with aggressive tendencies as measured in the questionnaires seemed to show less aggression after watching the violent television programs. This single instance of nonsupport for a modeling explanation of the effects of media violence has been subjected to considerable methodological critique from those who favor social-learning explanations. Bandura (1973) has pointed out that the subjects were forced to take part in the experiment and some were angry at being deprived of their favorite violent programs. Since, in order to minimize anger and keep the experiment going, the researchers allowed some subjects in the nonviolent group to watch a few of their favorite violent programs, the requisite experimental control was thus contaminated. Also, although the supervisors who reported the aggressive behavior were supposed to be unaware of the nature of the study, it is hard to believe that such secrecy could be maintained in a closed institutional setting in which the restrictions concerning the programs that the students were allowed to watch were the subject of constant controversy among the boys. If the supervisors guessed the purpose of the study, their awareness further contaminated the experimental controls. Despite these and other major shortcomings, this field experiment did assess more long-term (six weeks) effects of media violence on aggressive behavior than is possible in the laboratory.

A more recent investigation, however, has documented again the deleterious effects of viewing filmed violence (Leyens, Camino, Parke, & Berkowitz, 1975). Like the Feshbach and Singer experimental study, this investigation studied boys in a field setting and over a period of time, but, unlike Feshbach and Singer, these researchers effected considerable experimental control, which enabled them to rule out the kind of alternative explanations that plagued the earlier study. The results clearly pointed to an impressive increase in aggressive behavior following exposure to violent movies.

Use of Archives

Public documents record some of the more severe manifestations of human aggression. While archival research constitutes the extreme in low subject awareness, it also gives the investigator relatively little control over the reactions being assessed. The events in question are generally long past, and the researcher is somewhat at the mercy of what people chose to record at the time. Investigators can bring ingenuity to the ways in which they combine and compare the available information, and therein lies the power of archival research.

Using the *New York Times* Index for the period between 1913 and 1963, Lieberson and Silverman (1965) found 72 events that they classified as race riots. Content analysis of the newspaper accounts of these events, supplemented by other written reports, yielded the conclusion that race riots are precipitated by incidents involving interracial violation of social norms concerning bodily injury and segregation taboos. Using census data to compare cities that did and did not have race riots during the study period, the authors found more riots in cities where Blacks had begun to enter White occupations and neighborhoods and where their representation in government was inadequate, as evidenced by few Black police and larger populations per city councilman.

Although archival materials give access to information about more serious forms of aggression than it is possible to generate in the laboratory, they give researchers less scope in determining what information is needed to understand the processes involved. Census figures, public documents, newspaper accounts, and the like are all subject to selective bias. The time, place, and circumstances under which the events were recorded and the audience for which they were intended are less available to scrutiny than the procedures used in the laboratory.

Naturalistic Observation

Naturalistic observations, if systematic, do make some circumstances of data collection known to the research consumer. The rules by which the observations were made are generally clearly set forth in the account of the study. One example of such a naturalistic field study was done in two nursery schools. Patterson, Littman, and Bricker (1967) observed the interaction of 3- and 4-year-old middle-class children over a period of 26 weeks. The observers recorded aggressive acts initiated by children and the responses of the victims to these attacks. These investigators found that if aggression in nursery school is rewarded, more aggressive acts occur—a finding they interpreted according to a social-learning approach. They concluded that nursery school served as a training ground for aggression, particularly for active children who interact a lot with other children.

Naturalistic observations generally entail low awareness on the part of the subjects of being under study. In contrast to the Feshbach and Singer (1971) field experiment, in which the children filled out questionnaires and were restricted in their television viewing, the children in the Patterson, Littman, and Bricker study were simply observed pursuing their regular nursery-school routine. If the observers were introduced to the setting in a skillful way, there should have been little awareness of them by the subjects. On the other hand, the naturalistic observation does not give the researchers any control over what happens; they cannot stage situations that would provoke aggressive behavior but must wait until such acts occur.

Field Studies Involving Surveys and Interviews

Similarly low in manipulation of antecedent conditions are the studies that inquire through surveys and interviews what happened and how a participant or observer felt about a particular aggressive event. These procedures involve high awareness on the part of the subjects, since direct inquiry is made of them. Questions such as "What did you see?" "How did you feel?" "What do you think?" make a respondent very aware that he or she is the focus of the researcher's interest. Here, too, researchers have no control over the events being investigated, but they do control the kind of questions being asked. For example, in one survey (Blumenthal, Kahn, Andrews, & Head, 1972), 1400 males were interviewed about the extent to which they perceived social protest as violence. Responses to such questions as "Do you think of looting as violence?" and "Do you think of police beating students as violence?" varied according to the general value system of the men who were questioned. Most did think of social protest as violent and of police action as nonviolent.

A more theoretically derived interview study was conducted by Bandura and Walters (1959), who asked 52 adolescent boys and their parents about their family relationships and their attitudes toward antisocial behavior. Half of the boys had a history of aggressive behavior. Bandura and Walters asked 43 questions, each with a set of probes to assure a complete discussion of the themes raised. Independent raters then coded the answers to the questions according to a predetermined set of criteria derived from the social-learning assumptions that guided the study. The family relationships of the aggressive boys were marked by less warmth and particularly by less-affectionate interaction with the father. The more aggressive boys also described themselves as less guilty about their antisocial behavior.

Surveys and interviews have a face validity that is appealing. To approach city residents after a riot and ask "What happened?" seems to get at what is wanted. But there are problems. Interviewees may not know and, if they do know, they may not be willing to tell the interviewer. Even if they both know and tell the interviewer, systematic differences may emerge among groups of interviewees that are hard to interpret. Suppose boys with aggressive histories all described relationships with their fathers differently from boys who did not have such histories. These patterns of answers would tell you that there was some connection between the father-son relationship and aggressive behavior. But the question concerning which is cause and which is effect is hard to answer. Did something in the father-son relationship cause the son's aggressive behavior, or did the aggressive behavior cause the parental relationship to be different from that of boys who do not aggress? Disentangling cause-effect relations in human affairs is difficult but very important. Consider the following complex and ingenious attempt to do so.

In 1960, Eron studied the television-viewing habits of 875 third-grade children in a semirural county in New York State. The children's preferences for violent or nonviolent television were assessed by asking each mother to name her child's three favorite television programs. These programs were then categorized as being violent or nonviolent by two independent raters. A second measure of the children involved asking their peers to rate them on a ten-item aggressive-behavior scale. Classmates were asked questions such as "Who pushes and shoves other children?" and "Who starts a fight over nothing?" Eron computed a correlation of these two measures and found a significant relation between 8- and 9-year-old boys' preferences for violent television programs and measures of their aggressive behavior as assessed by their peers. Boys who preferred violent television programs were rated as significantly more aggressive than boys who preferred nonviolent television programs (Eron, 1963). A field study of this kind can provide us with a great deal of information about the extent of the relation in the everyday environment between two variables such as television preferences and aggressive behavior. By itself, however, the field study cannot specify the nature or direction of the operating causality. Perhaps aggressive boys are drawn to violent television because it fits their view of the world, or, alternatively, perhaps television watching elicits and/or models aggressive responses from those who were not initially so disposed.

As we have discussed earlier, the experimental approach within a laboratory setting is particularly suited to answering questions of causality. Antecedent conditions (independent variables) can be varied, and their effects on consequent conditions (dependent variables) assessed. However, a number of research questions can and should be asked in other than the laboratory environment and with other than experimental methodologies. Long-term effects are one case in point. It can be argued, for example, that many social-psychological phenomena are quietly but persistently cumulative and either may not be in evidence within the confines of a one-hour laboratory experiment or, if observed there, may bear little resemblance to real-life behavior. Exposure to film-mediated aggression may be such a phenomenon. To answer this question, Eron and his associates (1972) conducted a ten-year follow-up on 427 teenagers—half of those studied in 1960. Preference for violent television was assessed by asking the individual himself to indicate his four current favorite television programs. These were categorized again as violent or nonviolent by independent raters. Peer ratings were again used to measure aggressive behavior, although the instrument was slightly revised in order for it to be suitable for the now older sample.

The primary purpose of this second testing ten years later was not just to compute another correlation between preference for violent television and aggressive behavior. Rather, it was an attempt to look at the "before" and "after" in order to say something more definitive about the direction of the causality in this nonexperimental field study. Eron and his colleagues applied a sophisticated statistical method called the *cross-lagged panel correlation technique* to the data in order to estimate which was the predominant influence—aggressive behavior or viewing violence on television. We will not go into all the mechanics involved in this technique, but we refer you instead to the relevant primary sources (Campbell, 1963; Eron, Huesman, Lefkowitz, & Walder, 1972; Rozelle & Campbell, 1969) for greater detail. It is sufficient for the present to indicate some of the reasoning involved and how it was applied to Eron's data. As you will recall, four measures were involved: preference for violent programming at age 8 (3rd grade) and at age 18 (13th grade) and measurement of aggressive behavior at age 8 and at age 18. Figure 1 represents these data points.

The correlations of interest to us now are the two cross-lag ones—the first, assessing the relation existing between preference for violent television at time 1 and aggression at time 2, and the second, documenting the relation between aggression at time 1 and preference at time 2. These relations are crossed and lagged in that the two variables in question are correlated with each other (crossed) and over a ten-year period (lagged). Using the cross-lagged technique, one can infer that preferences for violent television influence (cause) aggressive behavior and not the reverse. This inference is correct if the correlation between preference in the 3rd grade and aggression in the 13th grade is greater than the correlation between aggression in the 3rd grade and preference in the 13th grade. As seen in Figure 1, the former correlation was significantly high and positive (.31) and greater than the latter correlation, which was very low and nonsignificant (.01).

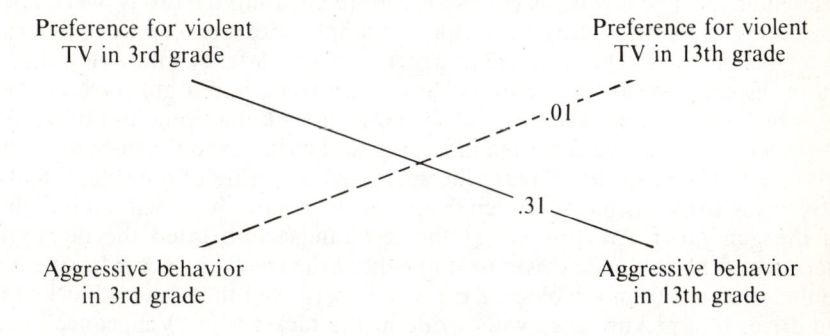

Figure 1. Cross-lag correlations between preference for violent television and aggression over a ten-year period. (Adapted from "Does Television Violence Cause Aggression?" by R. V. Eron, L. R. Huesman, M. M. Lefkowitz, and L. O. Walder, *American Psychologist,* 1972, *27,* 253–263. Copyright 1972 by American Psychological Association. Reprinted by permission.)

The comparison then supports the hypothesis that preference for violent television programs is a cause of aggressive behavior.

This complex study represents a serious attempt to grapple with important problems of causality in a field setting. It also presents a technique adapted from other social sciences that may prove to have far-reaching implications for social psychologists if the present trend toward more field research continues.

TWO RESEARCH EXAMPLES

Product Description

Both of the following studies are concerned with the impact of aggressive cues on behavior. The first, by Berkowitz and LePage, is a laboratory experiment designed to test the hypothesis that the presence of aggressive objects leads to more attack on an available target than would occur in the presence of a neutral object. Volunteer male college students participated in the study. The design corresponded generally to the paradigm presented in the preceding section and used in much of Berkowitz's research on aggression. In this case, there was a 2 × 3 factorial design with an added control group, making a total of seven conditions. There were two levels of arousal (angered or unangered subjects) and three stimulus conditions (guns belonging to confederate, guns left by previous experimenter, and no guns). Subjects participated in the standard bogus learning task, in which they could ostensibly shock another person for committing errors. In two of the stimulus conditions, a revolver and a shotgun were lying next to the shock machine while the subject carried out the learning task. An additional control condition was added, in which the subject conducted his teaching with a badminton racket lying near the shock machine. Subjects who had previously been angered by the confederate gave him more shocks when the teaching took place with guns lying on the table than when there were no guns around or when there was a badminton racket. The authors contend that the mere presence of weapons, even when they are not the tools of aggression themselves, may facilitate or strengthen aggressive behavior.

The second selection, by Turner, Layton, and Simons, presents three components: a survey and two field experiments on aggressive aspects of driving behavior. The first part involved a survey based on a lengthy questionnaire about driving. Twelve of the questions, dealing with irritation directed at other drivers, were selected for analysis. Responses indicated that hostile reactions were frequent, although rarely overt. The field experiments involved obstructing a driver at a stoplight with a pickup truck that carried varying aggressive cues. The measure of aggression was latency and amount of horn honking in response to the obstruction. The pickup truck had a gun rack in the rear window, which was either empty or had a rifle in it (one manipulation of aggressive cues). Another manipulation consisted in adding to the rifle condition a bumper sticker designed to either increase or decrease the aggressive meaning of the rifle. Finally, the truck driver was either visible or hidden from view by a curtain (which did not obstruct view of the gun rack). An observer at the test intersection rated the demographic characteristics of the first male driver to stop behind the truck and recorded the latency and number of honks from the blocked car. It was predicted that drivers blocked by an invisible driver of a pickup truck with a rifle in the rack and a "Vengeance" bumper sticker would honk sooner and more than those in other conditions. The design permitted some assessment of the relative contributions of these factors and of their interaction. The results apparently supported the prediction. Some refinements introduced in the second field experiment shed further light on the importance of individual differences and the merits of alternative explanations.

Consumer Checklist

- How is the product developed?
  First Selection:
    Who's deceiving whom about what?
    What did the subjects think they were supposed to do?
  Second Selection:
    Could the horn honking have been due to other causes than the rifle?
- For whom is the product designed?
    What do these studies say about sex differences?

WEAPONS AS AGGRESSION-ELICITING STIMULI[1]

LEONARD BERKOWITZ and ANTHONY LePAGE[2]

University of Wisconsin

> An experiment was conducted to test the hypothesis that stimuli commonly associated with aggression can elicit aggressive responses from people ready to act aggressively. 100 male university students received either 1 or 7 shocks, supposedly from a peer, and were then given an opportunity to shock this person. In some cases a rifle and revolver were on the table near the shock key. These weapons were said to belong, or not to belong, to the available target person. In other instances there was nothing on the table near the shock key, while for a control group 2 badminton racquets were on the table near the key. The greatest number of shocks was given by the strongly aroused Ss (who had received 7 shocks) when they were in the presence of the weapons. The guns had evidently elicited strong aggressive responses from the aroused men.

Human behavior is often goal directed, guided by strategies and influenced by ego defenses and strivings for cognitive consistency. There clearly are situations, however, in which these purposive considerations are relatively unimportant regulators of action. Habitual behavior patterns become dominant on these occasions, and the person responds relatively automatically to the stimuli impinging upon him. Any really complete psychological system must deal with these stimulus-elicited, impulsive reactions as well as with more complex behavior patterns. More than this, we should also be able to specify the conditions under which the various behavior determinants increase or decrease in importance.

The senior author has long contended that many aggressive actions are controlled by the stimulus properties of the available targets rather than by anticipations of ends that might be served (Berkowitz, 1962, 1964, 1965). Perhaps because strong emotion results in an increased utilization of only the central cues in the immediate situation (Easterbrook, 1959; Walters & Parke, 1964), anger arousal can lead to impulsive aggressive responses which, for a short time at least, may be relatively free of cognitively mediated inhi-

[1] The present experiment was conducted by Anthony LePage under Leonard Berkowitz' supervision as part of a research program sponsored by Grant G-23988 from the National Science Foundation to the senior author.

[2] Now at the University of Portland.

From *Journal of Personality and Social Psychology,* 1967, 7(2), 202–207. Copyright 1967 by American Psychological Association. Reprinted by permission.

bitions against aggression or, for that matter, purposes and strategic considerations.[3] This impulsive action is not necessarily pushed out by the anger, however. Berkowitz has suggested that appropriate cues must be present in the situation if aggressive responses are actually to occur. While there is still considerable uncertainty as to just what characteristics define aggressive cue properties, the association of a stimulus with aggression evidently can enhance the aggressive cue value of this stimulus. But whatever its exact genesis, the cue (which may be either in the external environment or represented internally) presumably elicits the aggressive response. Anger (or any other conjectured aggressive "drive") increases the person's reactivity to the cue, possibly energizes the response, and may lower the likelihood of competing reactions, but is not necessary for the production of aggressive behavior.[4]

A variety of observations can be cited in support of this reasoning (cf. Berkowitz, 1965). Thus, the senior author has proposed that some of the effects of observed violence can readily be understood in terms of stimulus-elicited aggression. According to several Wisconsin experiments, observed aggression is particularly likely to produce strong attacks against anger instigators who are associated with the victim of the witnessed violence (Berkowitz & Geen, 1966, 1967; Geen & Berkowitz, 1966). The frustrater's association with the observed victim presumably enhances his cue value for aggression, causing him to evoke stronger attacks from the person who is ready to act aggressively.

More direct evidence for the present formulation can be found in a study conducted by Loew (1965). His subjects, in being required to learn a concept, either aggressive or nature words, spoke either 20 aggressive or 20 neutral words aloud. Following this "learning task," each subject was to give a peer in an adjacent room an electric shock whenever this person made a mistake in his learning problem. Allowed to vary the intensity of the shocks they administered over a 10-point continuum, the subjects who had uttered the aggressive words gave shocks of significantly greater intensity than did the subjects who had spoken the neutral words. The aggressive words had evidently evoked implicit aggressive responses from the subjects, even though they had not been angered beforehand, which then led to the stronger attacks upon the target person in the next room when he supposedly made errors.

Cultural learning shared by many members of a society can also associate external objects with aggression and thus affect the objects' aggressive cue value. Weapons are a prime example. For many men (and probably women as well) in our society, these objects are closely associated with aggression. Assuming that the weapons do not produce inhibitions that are stronger than the evoked aggressive reactions (as would be the case, e.g., if the weapons were labeled as morally "bad"), the presence of the aggressive objects should generally lead to more intense attacks upon an available target than would occur in the presence of a neutral object.

The present experiment was designed to test this latter hypothesis. At one level, of course, the findings contribute to the current debate as to the desirability of restricting sales of firearms. Many arguments have been raised for such a restriction. Thus, according to recent statistics, Texas communities having virtually no prohibitions against firearms have a much higher homicide rate than other American cities possessing stringent firearm regulations, and J. Edgar Hoover has maintained in *Time* magazine that the availability of firearms is an important factor in murders (Anonymous, 1966). The experiment reported here seeks to determine how this influence may come about. The availability of weapons obviously makes it easier for a person who wants to commit murder to do so. But, in addition, we ask whether weapons can serve as aggression-eliciting stimuli, causing an angered individual to display stronger violence than he would have shown in the absence of such weapons. Social significance aside, and at a more general theoretical level, this research also attempts to demonstrate that situational stimuli can exert "automatic" control over socially relevant human actions.

METHOD

Subjects

The subjects were 100 male undergraduates enrolled in the introductory psychology course at the University of Wisconsin who volunteered for the experiment (without knowing its nature) in order to earn points counting toward their final grade. Thirty-nine other subjects had also been run, but were discarded because they suspected the experi-

---

[3] Cognitive processes can play a part even in impulsive behavior, most notably by influencing the stimulus qualities (or meaning) of the objects in the situation. As only one illustration, in several experiments by the senior author (cf. Berkowitz, 1965) the name applied to the available target person affected the magnitude of the attacks directed against this individual by angered subjects.

[4] Buss (1961) has advanced a somewhat similar conception of the functioning of anger.

menter's confederate (21), reported receiving fewer electric shocks than was actually given them (7), had not attended to information given them about the procedure (9), or were run while there was equipment malfunctioning (2).

Procedure

General design. Seven experimental conditions were established, six organized in a 2 × 3 factorial design, with the seventh group serving essentially as a control. Of the men in the factorial design, half were made to be angry with the confederate, while the other subjects received a friendlier treatment from him. All of the subjects were then given an opportunity to administer electric shocks to the confederate, but for two-thirds of the men there were weapons lying on the table near the shock apparatus. Half of these people were informed the weapons belonged to the confederate in order to test the hypothesis that aggressive stimuli which also were associated with the anger instigator would evoke the strongest aggressive reaction from the subjects. The other people seeing the weapons were told the weapons had been left there by a previous experimenter. There was nothing on the table except the shock key when the last third of the subjects in both the angered and nonangered conditions gave the shocks. Finally, the seventh group consisted of angered men who gave shocks with two badminton racquets and shuttlecocks lying near the shock key. This condition sought to determine whether the presence of *any* object near the shock apparatus would reduce inhibitions against aggression, even if the object were not connected with aggressive behavior.

Experimental manipulations. When each subject arrived in the laboratory, he was informed that two men were required for the experiment and that they would have to wait for the second subject to appear. After a 5-minute wait, the experimenter, acting annoyed, indicated that they had to begin because of his other commitments. He said he would have to look around outside to see if he could find another person who might serve as a substitute for the missing subject. In a few minutes the experimenter returned with the confederate. Depending upon the condition, this person was introduced as either a psychology student who had been about to sign up for another experiment or as a student who had been running another study.

The subject and confederate were told the experiment was a study of physiological reactions to stress. The stress would be created by mild electric shocks, and the subjects could withdraw, the experimenter said, if they objected to these shocks. (No subjects left.) Each person would have to solve a problem knowing that his performance would be evaluated by his partner. The "evaluations" would be in the form of electric shocks, with one shock signifying a very good rating and 10 shocks meaning the performance was judged as very bad. The men were then told what their problems were. The subject's task was to list ideas a publicity agent might employ in order to better a popular singer's record sales and public image. The other person (the confederate) had to think of things a used-car dealer might do in order to increase sales. The two were given 5 minutes to write their answers, and the papers were then collected by the experimenter who supposedly would exchange them.

Following this, the two were placed in separate rooms, supposedly so that they would not influence each other's galvanic skin response (GSR) reactions. The shock electrodes were placed on the subject's right forearm, and GSR electrodes were attached to fingers on his left hand, with wires trailing from the electrodes to the next room. The subject was told he would be the first to receive electric shocks as the evaluation of his problem solution. The experimenter left the subject's room saying he was going to turn on the GSR apparatus, went to the room containing the shock machine and the waiting confederate, and only then looked at the schedule indicating whether the subject was to be angered or not. He informed the confederate how many shocks the subject was to receive, and 30 seconds later the subject was given seven shocks (angered condition) or one shock (nonangered group). The experimenter then went back to the subject, while the confederate quickly arranged the table holding the shock key in the manner appropriate for the subject's condition. Upon entering the subject's room, the experimenter asked him how many shocks he had received and provided the subject with a brief questionnaire on which he was to rate his mood. As soon as this was completed, the subject was taken to the room holding the shock machine. Here the experimenter told the subject it was his turn to evaluate his partner's work. For one group in both the angered and nonangered conditions the shock key was alone on the table (no-object groups). For two other groups in each of these angered and nonangered conditions, however, a 12-gauge shotgun and a .38-caliber revolver were lying on the table near the key (aggressive-weapon conditions). One group in both the angered and nonangered conditions was informed the weapons belonged to the subject's partner. The subjects given this treatment had been told earlier that their partner was a student who had been conducting an experiment.[5] They now were reminded of this, and the experimenter said the weapons were being used in some way by this person in his research (associated-weapons condition); the guns were to be disregarded. The other men were told simply the wea-

---

[5] This information evidently was the major source of suspicion; some of the subjects doubted that a student running an experiment would be used as a subject in another study, even if he were only an undergraduate. This information was provided only in the associated-weapons conditions, in order to connect the guns with the partner, and, consequently, this ground for suspicion was not present in the unassociated-weapons groups.

pons "belong to someone else" who "must have been doing an experiment in here" (unassociated-weapons group), and they too were asked to disregard the guns. For the last treatment, one group of angered men found two badminton racquets and shuttlecocks lying on the table near the shock key, and these people were also told the equipment belonged to someone else (badminton-racquets group).

Immediately after this information was provided, the experimenter showed the subject what was supposedly his partner's answer to his assigned problem. The subject was reminded that he was to give the partner shocks as his evaluation and was informed that this was the last time shocks would be administered in the study. A second copy of the mood questionnaire was then completed by the subject after he had delivered the shocks. Following this, the subject was asked a number of oral questions about the experiment, including what, if any, suspicions he had. (No doubts were voiced about the presence of the weapons.) At the conclusion of this interview the experiment was explained, and the subject was asked not to talk about the study.

Dependent Variables

As in nearly all the experiments conducted in the senior author's program, the number of shocks given by the subjects serves as the primary aggression measure. However, we also report here findings obtained with the total duration of each subject's shocks, recorded in thousandths of a minute. Attention is also given to each subject's rating of his mood, first immediately after receiving the partner's evaluation, and again immediately after administering shocks to the partner. These ratings were made on a series of 10 13-point bipolar scales with an adjective at each end, such as "calm-tense" and "angry-not angry."

Results

Effectiveness of Arousal Treatment

Analyses of variance of the responses to each of the mood scales following the receipt of the partner's evaluation indicate the prior-shock treatment succeeded in creating differences in anger arousal. The subjects getting seven shocks rated themselves as being significantly angrier

TABLE 1

ANALYSIS OF VARIANCE RESULTS FOR NUMBER OF SHOCKS GIVEN BY SUBJECTS IN FACTORIAL DESIGN

Source	df	MS	F
No. shocks received (A)	1	182.04	104.62*
Weapons association (B)	2	1.90	1.09
A × B	2	8.73	5.02*
Error	84	1.74	

* $p < .01$.

TABLE 2

MEAN NUMBER OF SHOCKS GIVEN IN EACH CONDITION

Condition	Shocks received 1	Shocks received 7
Associated weapons	2.60$_a$	6.07$_d$
Unassociated weapons	2.20$_a$	5.67$_{cd}$
No object	3.07$_a$	4.67$_{bc}$
Badminton racquets	—	4.60$_b$

Note.—Cells having a common subscript are not significantly different at the .05 level by Duncan multiple-range test. There were 10 subjects in the seven-shocks-received–badminton-racquets group and 15 subjects in each of the other conditions.

than the subjects receiving only one shock ($F = 20.65$, $p < .01$). There were no reliable differences among the groups within any one arousal level. Interestingly enough, the only other mood scale to yield a significant effect was the scale "sad-happy." The aroused–seven-shocks men reported a significantly stronger felt sadness than the men getting one shock ($F = 4.63$, $p > .05$).

Aggression toward Partner

A preliminary analysis of variance of the shock data for the six groups in the 3 × 2 factorial design yielded the findings shown in Table 1. As is indicated by the significant interaction, the presence of the weapons significantly affected the number of shocks given by the subject when the subject had received seven shocks. A Duncan multiple-range test was then made of the differences among the seven conditions means, using the error variance from a seven-group one-way analysis of variance in the error term. The mean number of shocks administered in each experimental condition and the Duncan test results are given in Table 2. The hypothesis guiding the present study receives good support. The strongly provoked men delivered more frequent electrical attacks upon their tormentor in the presence of a weapon than when nonaggressive objects (the badminton racquets and shuttlecocks) were present or when only the shock key was on the table. The angered subjects gave the greatest number of shocks in the presence of the weapons associated with the anger instigator, as predicted, but this group was not reliably different from the angered–unassociated-weapons conditions. Both of these groups expressing aggression in the presence of weapons were significantly more aggressive than the angered–neutral-object condition, but only the associated-weapons con-

TABLE 3

Mean Total Duration of Shocks Given in Each Condition

Condition	Shocks received 1	Shocks received 7
Associated weapons	17.93c	46.93a
Unassociated weapons	17.33c	39.47ab
No object	24.47bc	34.80ab
Badminton racquets	—	34.90ab

Note.—The duration scores are in thousandths of a minute. Cells having a common subscript are not significantly different at the .05 level by Duncan multiple-range test. There were 10 subjects in the seven-shocks-received–badminton-racquet group and 15 subjects in each of the other conditions.

dition differed significantly from the angered–no-object group.

Some support for the present reasoning is also provided by the shock-duration data summarized in Table 3. (We might note here, before beginning, that the results with duration scores—and this has been a consistent finding in the present research program—are less clear-cut than the findings with number of shocks given.) The results indicate that the presence of weapons resulted in a decreased number of attacks upon the partner, although not significantly so, when the subjects had received only one shock beforehand. The condition differences are in the opposite direction, however, for the men given the stronger provocation. Consequently, even though there are no reliable differences among the groups in this angered condition, the angered men administering shocks in the presence of weapons gave significantly longer shocks than the nonangered men also giving shocks with guns lying on the table. The angered–neutral-object and angered–no-object groups, on the other hand, did not differ from the nonangered–no-object condition.

Mood Changes

Analyses of covariance were conducted on each of the mood scales, with the mood ratings made immediately after the subjects received their partners' evaluation held constant in order to determine if there were condition differences in mood changes following the giving of shocks to the partner. Duncan range tests of the adjusted condition means yielded negative results, suggesting that the attacks on the partner did not produce any systematic condition differences. In the case of the felt anger ratings, there were very high correlations between the ratings given before and after the shock administration, with the Pearson rs ranging from .89 in the angered–unassociated-weapons group to .99 in each of the three unangered conditions. The subjects could have felt constrained to repeat their initial responses.

Discussion

Common sense, as well as a good deal of personality theorizing, both influenced to some extent by an egocentric view of human behavior as being caused almost exclusively by motives within the individual, generally neglect the type of weapons effect demonstrated in the present study. If a person holding a gun fires it, we are told either that he wanted to do so (consciously or unconsciously) or that he pulled the trigger "accidentally." The findings summarized here suggest yet another possibility: The presence of the weapon might have elicited an intense aggressive reaction from the person with the gun, assuming his inhibitions against aggression were relatively weak at the moment. Indeed, it is altogether conceivable that many hostile acts which supposedly stem from unconscious motivation really arise because of the operation of aggressive cues. Not realizing how these situational stimuli might elicit aggressive behavior, and not detecting the presence of these cues, the observer tends to locate the source of the action in some conjectured underlying, perhaps repressed, motive. Similarly, if he is a Skinnerian rather than a dynamically oriented clinician, he might also neglect the operation of aggression-eliciting stimuli by invoking the concept of operant behavior, and thus sidestep the issue altogether. The sources of the hostile action, for him, too, rest within the individual, with the behavior only steered or permitted by discriminative stimuli.

Alternative explanations must be ruled out, however, before the present thesis can be regarded as confirmed. One obvious possibility is that the subjects in the weapons condition reacted to the demand characteristics of the situation as they saw them and exhibited the kind of behavior they thought was required of them. ("These guns on the table mean I'm supposed to be aggressive, so I'll give many shocks.") Several considerations appear to negate this explanation. First, there are the subjects' own verbal reports. None of the subjects voiced any suspicions of the weapons and, furthermore, when they were queried generally denied that the weapons had any effect on them. But even those subjects who did express any doubts about the experiment typically acted like the other subjects. Thus, the eight nonangered-weapons subjects who had been rejected gave only 2.50 shocks on the average, while the 18 angered–no-object or neutral-object men who had been discarded had a mean of 4.50 shocks. The 12 angered-weapons subjects who had been rejected, by contrast, delivered an average of 5.83 shocks to their partner. These latter people were evidently also influenced by the presence of weapons.

Setting all this aside, moreover, it is not altogether certain from the notion of demand characteristics that only the angered subjects would be inclined to act in conformity with the experimenter's supposed demands. The nonangered men in the weapons group did not display a heightened number of attacks on their partner. Would this have been predicted beforehand by researchers interested in demand characteristics? The last finding raises one final observation. Recent unpublished research by Allen and Bragg indicates that awareness of the experimenter's purpose does not necessarily result in an increased display of the behavior the experimenter supposedly desires. Dealing with one kind of socially disapproved action (conformity), Allen and Bragg demonstrated that high levels of experimentally induced awareness of the experimenter's interests generally produced a decreased level of the relevant behavior. Thus, if the subjects in our study had known the experimenter was interested in observing their *aggressive* behavior, they might well have given less, rather than more, shocks, since giving shocks is also socially disapproved. This type of phenomenon was also not observed in the weapons conditions.

Nevertheless, any one experiment cannot possibly definitely exclude all of the alternative explanations. Scientific hypotheses are only probability statements, and further research is needed to heighten the likelihood that the present reasoning is correct.

REFERENCES

ANONYMOUS. A gun-toting nation. *Time,* August 12, 1966.

BERKOWITZ, L. *Aggression: A social psychological analysis.* New York: McGraw-Hill, 1962.

BERKOWITZ, L. Aggressive cues in aggressive behavior and hostility catharsis. *Psychological Review,* 1964, **71,** 104–122.

BERKOWITZ, L. The concept of aggressive drive: Some additional considerations. In L. Berkowitz (Ed.), *Advances in experimental social psychology.* Vol. 2. New York: Academic Press, 1965. Pp. 301–329.

BERKOWITZ, L., & GEEN, R. G. Film violence and the cue properties of available targets. *Journal of Personality and Social Psychology,* 1966, **3,** 525–530.

BERKOWITZ, L., & GEEN, R. G. Stimulus qualities of the target of aggression: A further study. *Journal of Personality and Social Psychology,* 1967, **5,** 364–368.

BUSS, A. *The psychology of aggression.* New York: Wiley, 1961.

EASTERBROOK, J. A. The effect of emotion on cue utilization and the organization of behavior. *Psychological Review,* 1959, **66,** 183–201.

GEEN, R. G., & BERKOWITZ, L. Name-mediated aggressive cue properties. *Journal of Personality,* 1966, **34,** 456–465.

LOEW, C. A. Acquisition of a hostile attitude and its relationship to aggressive behavior. Unpublished doctoral dissertation, State University of Iowa, 1965.

WALTERS, R. H., & PARKE, R. D. Social motivation, dependency, and susceptibility to social influence. In L. Berkowitz (Ed.), *Advances in experimental social psychology.* Vol. 1. New York: Academic Press, 1964. Pp. 231–276.

(Received October 5, 1966)

Naturalistic Studies of Aggressive Behavior: Aggressive Stimuli, Victim Visibility, and Horn Honking

Charles W. Turner, John F. Layton, and Lynn Stanley Simons
University of Utah

> Three studies extended laboratory research on aggression to a naturalistic setting which involved horn honking from drivers as a measure of aggression; the studies were adapted from Doob and Gross. The results from a survey (Study 1) of 59 drivers suggested that they were frequently irritated by and aggressive toward other drivers. A second study (using a 3 × 2 factorial design with 92 male drivers) indicated that manipulations of a rifle in an aggressive context and victim visibility (dehumanization) both significantly influenced horn honking rates subsequent to obstruction at a signal light. A third study with 137 male drivers and 63 female drivers examined the interactive effects of a rifle, an aggressively connotated bumper sticker, and individual subject characteristics (sex and an exploratory index of self-perceived status) on horn honking. The results for three studies in naturalistic settings offer possible extensions of laboratory based findings on aggression. The role of inhibitions in modifying the pattern of results was also discussed.

There has been considerable recent controversy about the validity of laboratory studies of aggression (Buss, Booker, & Buss, 1972; Feshback & Singer, 1971; U.S. Surgeon General's . . . Committee on Television, 1972). For example, some researchers have suggested that the commonly used measures of aggression may not have external validity. Thus, variables which affect laboratory-based responses may not influence naturally occurring aggressive responses.

One possible limitation of the laboratory setting is that subjects may sharply modify their behavior if they believe that someone is carefully monitoring and evaluating their reactions. According to Turner and Simons (1974), when subjects were led to believe that the experimenter was monitoring their responses to weapons, they were less likely than nonaware subjects to shock their partners. Awareness of the experimenter's purpose apparently caused subjects to inhibit aggressive behavior. In order to reduce the subject's inhibitions, researchers have introduced a variety of deceptions to minimize beliefs that the experiment was designed to evaluate aggressive behavior. However, many subjects today may be too sophisticated for the deceptions commonly used in the laboratory. Thus, some laboratory findings could be artifactual for two reasons. First, subjects may be responding primarily to awareness of deceptions rather than the experimental treatments (Page & Scheidt, 1971; Stricker, Messick, & Jackson, 1969). Second, their primary motivation may often be to portray themselves in a favorable light to the experimenter (Rosenberg, 1969).

Since some laboratory results may be produced by experimental artifacts such as evaluation apprehension, suspicion, negativism, and sophistication, it is important that attempts be made to investigate aggressive behavior in subjects who are not aware that they are being studied. The primary purpose of the present research was to assess whether naturalistic manipulations conceptually similar to laboratory procedures can affect human aggressive responses. Laboratory researchers have attempted to manipulate arousal, aggressive stimulation (Berkowitz, 1974; Geen & O'Neal, 1969), and dehumanization (Milgram, 1965;

Numerous individuals assisted in the completion of the present research and manuscript. We are especially indebted to Irwin Altman, Martin Chemers, Don Hartmann, Alex and Rhonda Klistoff, Ken Murray, Robert Van Wyngarden, and Jack White for their advice and assistance. The research was partly supported by University of Utah Research Committee Funds 1745 to Charles W. Turner.

Requests for reprints should be sent to Charles W. Turner, Department of Psychology, University of Utah, Salt Lake City, Utah 84112.

From *Journal of Personality and Social Psychology*, 1975, *31*(6), 1098–1107. Copyright 1975 by American Psychological Association. Reprinted by permission.

Zimbardo, 1969). In an exploratory attempt to extend laboratory research to a naturalistic setting, a rifle in an aggressive context (aggressive stimuli) and victim visibility (dehumanization) were manipulated in the present study for obstructed (and possibly aroused) drivers at a signal light.

In order to develop an appropriate naturalistic setting to measure aggressive responses, guidelines were adapted from Webb, Campbell, Schwartz, and Sechrest's (1966) analysis of unobtrusive measures. The following criteria were adopted to reduce subjects' perceptions that they were being studied and to develop adequately sensitive and independent measures of aggression: (a) There should be relatively low inhibitions about the behavior so that the base level responding would be considerably above zero probability, (b) the response should not be likely to produce contagion effects on other's aggression, (c) the subject's anonymity should be preserved, (d) the experimental setting should be reasonably naturalistic so that the procedures would not be an unusual imposition on the subjects or endanger them in any way, (e) the subjects should remain in the experimental setting for short periods of time such that they would not be exposed to more than one experimental treatment, and (f) the experimental treatments could be randomly assigned to subjects.

Study 1

Doob and Gross (1968) have offered one possible procedure for a naturalistic study of aggression. Their findings suggest that horn honking might be an aggressive reaction toward low-status drivers who prevent the flow of traffic at a signal light. Anecdotal evidence suggests that many drivers become aggressive when "frustrated" by the behavior of other drivers. Parry (1968) surveyed English drivers concerning their aggressive reactions while driving. His findings suggest that hostile reactions while driving included facial expressions, verbalizations such as swearing, hand gestures, tailgating, light flashing (high beams), and horn honking. Some drivers also reported actual fist fights or attempts to chase other drivers off the road. Parry's findings suggest that many drivers may become angry and aggressive while driving. In order to determine whether similar hostile reactions occur in Salt Lake City, a survey was conducted based on Parry's questionnaire. Thus, Study 1 was designed to determine whether there was a sufficiently high base rate of anger and aggressive responses from drivers so that experimental treatments might be expected to produce reliable results.

Method

Subjects and Procedure

The subjects were sampled from the population of frequent drivers in Salt Lake City. One hundred homes were randomly selected from the city address directory. When an investigator located a residence, the most frequent male or the most frequent female driver (randomly determined) was asked to complete Parry's (1968) driving survey. Acceptable subjects were located in 93 homes. The subjects were given a stamped envelope to return the questionnaire. If they did not respond within 2 weeks, they were again encouraged to complete the questionnaire. The subjects were assured of the complete confidentiality of their responses. Fifty-nine (63%) of the delivered questionnaires were returned.

Results and Discussion

Twelve questions (of 77) from Parry's (1968) questionnaire were selected for analysis, and the results (see Table 1) are reported separately for males and females. The findings suggest that a high proportion of "frequent" drivers sometimes become angry or are irritated by the driving behaviors of other drivers. For example, 77% of males and 56% of females reported "swearing under their breaths" at other drivers, while 50% of males and 15% of female drivers reported "flashing their lights in anger" at other drivers. While overt hostile responses were not reported by a majority of drivers on every question (e.g., Questions 1, 2, 10, and 12), there does appear to be evidence that hostile reactions to other drivers are a frequent occurrence. If the verbal reports are accurate reflections of actual driving situations, then a large number of drivers might be frequently irritated by the behavior of other drivers. This anger or irritation could sometimes lead to an overt aggressive response if such a response is readily available

TABLE 1

PERCENTAGES OF FEMALE AND MALE RESPONDENTS REPORTING HOSTILE REACTIONS TO QUESTIONNAIRE ITEMS

Questionnaire item	Male respondents (%)	Female respondents (%)
I am easily provoked when driving.	23	18
I lose my temper when another driver does something silly.	40[a]	41
I have been known to flash my lights at others in anger.	50	15
I get annoyed if the traffic lights changed to red as I approached them.	23	23
I make rude signs at other motorists when I am provoked.	15	11
At times, I've felt that I could gladly kill another driver.	12	18
If someone suddenly turns without signaling, I get annoyed.	58	92
I swear out loud at other drivers.	23	41
I swear under my breath at other drivers.	77	56
I have given chase to a driver who has annoyed me.	12	4
If the driver behind has his lights shining in my mirror, I pay him back in some way.	23	12
I am usually impatient at traffic lights.	19	7

Note. The samples are based on the responses of 26 men and 27 women.
[a] One subject did not complete the item.

(e.g., horn honking following an obstruction at a signal light).

STUDY 2

The present research was primarily designed to extend laboratory-based procedures for investigating possible determinants of aggressive reactions in a naturalistic setting. Hence, the procedure of Doob and Gross (1968) was adapted in order to manipulate exposure to aggressive stimuli and to attempt manipulations of inhibitions by dehumanization of the subject's "victim." The alleged victim (an experimental confederate) would potentially frustrate all subjects by obstructing them at a signal light.

Berkowitz and LePage (1967) manipulated aggressive stimulation by exposing some subjects to a pistol and a shotgun. One possible analogous field manipulation of aggressive stimuli would be to present a rifle in the gun rack of a pickup truck, especially since rifles are often carried that way in Utah. However,

a high proportion (perhaps 50%) of Utah males have used rifles frequently in a "sporting" context. It is possible that weapons (a rifle or a pistol) are not always perceived as aggressive stimuli when they have been observed frequently in a nonaggressive context; for example, the rifles may be perceived as sporting equipment somewhat like a fishing pole or skis. In the present experiment, an attempt was made to vary the salience of an aggressive meaning for a rifle by pairing it with an ostensible bumper sticker having an aggressive or a nonaggressive label. This manipulation is somewhat analogous to one employed by Berkowitz and Alioto (1973). They led some subjects to believe that a filmed football game was a "grudge" match, while other subjects were encouraged to think of the game simply as a sporting event. Subjects watching an apparent grudge match were more likely to see an aggressive meaning to the players' actions and were more likely to shock a partner who had previously angered them. Berkowitz and Alioto's (1973) findings suggest that the *context* of stimulus materials may play an important role in determining whether the material is viewed with an aggressive meaning.

In an attempt to vary the subject's inhibitions about being aggressive, the mutual visibility of the victim and subject was varied. According to findings by Milgram (1965), subjects appeared to be more willing to administer shock to an ostensible fellow subject when they were both less likely to see and to be seen by the victim. In addition, Zimbardo (1969) has proposed that deindividuation of both the subject and victim (dehumanization) can increase the probability of aggressive behavior.

Method

Subjects

Experimental treatments were randomly assigned to 92 male drivers who served as subjects. Nine additional subjects were dropped from the sample, since they were females ($n=4$) or male drivers of older vehicles ($n=5$). These subjects were approximately evenly distributed across conditions. The subjects were an arbitrarily selected sample of drivers of late-model vehicles (less than 6 years of age) in a 20 × 20 block region of a mixed business–residential district of Salt Lake City. Only newer car drivers were employed because high-status victims seem to lead to inhibitions in honking (Doob & Goss, 1968). It is possible that older car drivers would perceive themselves as having low status relative to the victim, which could lead to inhibitions masking the effects of independent variables. The experimental treatments were run on Saturdays from 9 a.m. to 5 p.m. It was assumed that Saturdays would produce a broader based sample of drivers from the potential population of all drivers, since fewer would be working. Moreover, the influence of "rush hour" traffic conditions could be minimized by testing on Saturdays.

Experimental Design

A 3 × 2 between-subjects factorial design was employed to manipulate aggressive stimulation and victim visibility (dehumanization). The subject was obstructed at a signal light for 12 sec. by an older model (1964) pickup truck with a gun rack in the rear window. The aggressive stimulation variable had three levels: (a) The gun rack was left empty (control), (b) a .303-calibre military rifle was placed in the gun rack and a bumper sticker was attached to the truck in order to reduce the perceived aggressiveness of the rifle (Rifle & "Friend" bumper sticker), or (c) the rifle was paired with a bumper sticker designed to increase the perceived aggressiveness of the rifle (Rifle & "Vengeance" bumper sticker). The bumper stickers were attached to the tailgate of the truck directly in line with the subject's vision, and they could be easily removed and reattached after each trial. The bumper stickers measured approximately 4 × 15 inches (102 × 381 mm), and the words (3 inches, or 76 mm, high) were printed with broad lettering (⅜ inch, or 9.5 mm, thick), so that they could be easily read at 50 feet (15 m). The words *friend* and *vengeance* were selected from the aggressive or altruistic lists of Parke, Ewall, and Slaby (1972). Ratings by 30 college students indicated that the word *vengeance* was highest (without also being rated high in anxiety) and *friend* was lowest on an aggressive–nonaggressive dimension from the words in Parke et al.'s lists.

Victim visibility (dehumanization) was manipulated by closing a curtain across the rear window of the pickup (without obstructing the view of the gun rack) in half of the conditions (low visibility) and leaving the curtain open in the other conditions (high visibility). The experimental conditions were run in blocks of six such that each condition was completed before any condition was replicated.

Procedure

The procedure was modeled closely after Doob and Gross (1968). An experimental confederate driving a pickup truck timed his arrival at an intersection at approximately the same time that the light turned red. If a male driver of a late-model apparently privately-owned vehicle came to a complete stop behind the confederate before the light changed to green, the driver confederate started the trial (if the conditions were not satisfied, the trial was aborted). When the light turned green, the driver-confederate started a stopwatch, faced straight ahead, and kept his brake lights on to avoid any indication that he might be having trouble with the pickup. At the end of 12 sec., the confederate moved forward with the traffic. Thus, the subjects were obstructed at the light for 12 sec. The first driver in line behind the confederate was always considered to be the subject. An observer was placed in an inconspicuous spot at the intersection so that the subject would be unlikely to see him. The observer rated demographic characteristics of the subject before the trial began (e.g., age and sex of subject; age of car, make of car, number of occupants, and general traffic density). Based on the observer's ratings, nine subjects were dropped from the sample, since they were either females or male drivers of older vehicles. The deleted subjects were inadvertently exposed to treatments when the driver-confederate could not see them clearly in his mirror. The driver's side-view mirror was partly obstructed with tape so that his reflection would not be visible to the subjects behind him when the curtain was closed. The tape also prevented the confederate from clearly seeing the subject's vehicle, and he misjudged the sex or vehicle age of some subjects. The observer's judgments were employed to establish the vehicle age or sex of subjects. The observers started a stopwatch when the light turned green and recorded the latency and frequency of honks from the subject. The observers received at least 1 hour of pretraining in the rating procedures.

RESULTS AND DISCUSSION

Subject's honking responses were dichotomized into those honking (scored as 1) and those not honking (scored as 0). According to Lunney (1970) and D'Agostino (1971), analysis of variance procedures may be applied to dichotomous data when sample sizes are reasonably large (for error, $df = 20$) and the sample proportions (means) fall between .20 and .80. Typically, hypotheses about proportions are tested with the binomial distribution, but the binomial is closely approximated by the normal distribution for n greater than 10, especially when the "population proportion" or null hypothesis is approximately .50. Since these conditions were satisfied with the present data ($\bar{n} = 15.2$; $\bar{p} = .42$), the analysis of variance procedures were employed.

The rates of honking are reported in Table 2. Five independent planned contrasts (Kirk, 1968, pp. 73–76; 178–182) were computed on the six cell means using

TABLE 2

PERCENTAGE OF HORN HONKING IN THE EXPERIMENTAL CONDITIONS OF STUDY 2

	Aggressive stimulation			
Victim visibility	Control	Rifle present		Mean %
		Friend bumper sticker	Vengeance bumper sticker	
Low visibility (curtain closed)	33.3$_I$ ($n = 15$)	46.7$_{II}$ ($n = 15$)	76.5$_{III}$ ($n = 17$)	52.2
High visibility (curtain open)	21.4$_{IV}$ ($n = 14$)	29.4$_V$ ($n = 17$)	42.9$_{VI}$ ($n = 14$)	31.2
Mean %	27.4	38.0	59.7	

Note. Cell entries refer to the percentages of subjects producing at least one honk. Numbers in parentheses refer to cell sizes. The Roman numerals specify the order of the contrast weights which were applied to means. For example in Contrast B ($-\frac{1}{2}, -\frac{1}{2}, +1, 0, 0, 0$), the contrast weight $+1$ was applied to Condition III (rifle present/vengeance bumper sticker).

an unweighted-means solution for the unequal sample sizes. The contrast weights for each mean are presented in order according to the cell subscripts (I–VI) which are reported in Table 2: Contrast A = $-\frac{1}{3}, -\frac{1}{3}, -\frac{1}{3}, +\frac{1}{3}, +\frac{1}{3}, +\frac{1}{3}$; Contrast B = $-\frac{1}{2}, -\frac{1}{2}, +1, 0, 0, 0$; Contrast C = $-1, +1, 0, 0, 0, 0$; Contrast D = $0, 0, 0, -\frac{1}{2}, -\frac{1}{2}, +1$; Contrast E = $0, 0, 0, -1, +1, 0$. The results of the planned contrast analysis indicated that the closed curtain significantly increased the rate of honking compared with the open curtain treatment, for Contrast A: $F(1, 86) = 4.43$, $p < .05$. In addition, the honking rate for the rifle/vengeance condition ($\bar{X} = .765$) was significantly higher than the average ($\bar{X} = .400$) of the other two conditions ([rifle/friend + control] $\times \frac{1}{2}$) when the curtain was closed, for Contrast B: $F(1, 86) = 5.98$, $p < .02$, but the effect was not significant when the curtain was open, for Contrast D: $F(1, 86) = 1.37$, $p > .20$. The two remaining contrasts (C and E) which compared the rifle/friend condition to the control condition were also nonsignificant ($F < 1.0$).

The results of the present study are generally consistent with the reasoning that led to the procedures, since both victim visibility and the rifle/vengeance condition increased horn honking. Thus, the present findings tentatively suggest that dehumanization and the presence of a rifle which is perceived as an aggressive stimuli can increase the probability of aggressive responding in a naturalistic setting. The rifle did not significantly influence the rate of honking when it was in a friendly or "prosocial" context (Contrasts C and E), nor did the rifle/vengeance condition significantly influence honking when the victim was visible (Contrast D). The fact that the rifle/vengeance condition honking rate was significantly higher only when the victim was not visible may be consistent with laboratory procedures used to study aggressive behavior. That is, most researchers in the laboratory typically isolate the victim from the subject in order to lower inhibitions about giving shocks. Similarly, in the present study, reduced visibility of the victim (when the curtain was closed) might have increased the rate by reducing inhibitions.

STUDY 3

One limitation of the procedure in Study 2 was that the rifle and the vengeance bumper sticker were not independently manipulated. Thus, the findings for the rifle/vengeance condition might have been due to either object alone or to the interactive effects of both objects. In Study 3, the rifle and the vengeance bumper sticker were independently manipulated so that their hypothesized interactive effects on horn honking could be tested. The vengeance bumper sticker was designed to increase the likelihood that subjects would perceive an aggressive connotation to the rifle. Previous laboratory findings suggest that uninhibited subjects would be more aggressive when they viewed stimuli with an aggressive meaning (Berkowitz & Alioto, 1973). Since it was possible that inhibitions might mask any effects of the rifle and the vengeance bumper sticker, the dehumanization (curtain) manipulation of Study 2 was employed for all conditions in an attempt to lower inhibitions.

The work of Doob and Gross (1968) suggests that there may be strong individual differences (e.g., status and sex differences) in driver's reactions to obstruction at a stoplight. Based, in part, on Doob and Gross's findings, male drivers of older vehicles and female drivers were not used as subjects in Study 2 because it was assumed that they would inhibit horn honking. Doob and Gross found that male subjects honked less at higher than lower status victims, possibly because high-status victims produced inhibitions about honking. Presumably, the lower the *subject's* self-perceived status, the higher the *victim's* status (relatively) is likely to appear. Thus, self-perceived status relative to the victim may influence willingness to honk as an aggressive response.

In the present investigation, the subjects were divided into two groups based on the age of the vehicle they were driving. This procedure was employed in an attempt to derive an exploratory measure of subject's self-perceived status. It is possible that the older a person's car, the less likely he would be to perceive himself as higher in status than the confederate in the pickup truck. Since the vehicle age variable could reflect other differences than self-perceived status (e.g., differential likelihoods of being frustrated due to different experiences with stalled automobiles), the variable was included only as an exploratory assessment of possible status differences.[1]

Several researchers (summarized by Bardwick, 1971, chap. 7) have found different patterns of male and female aggressive behavior. Further, Doob and Gross (1968) found different horn honking reactions in men and women, since women had longer latencies for their first honks. Based on these findings, it was assumed that males and females might not respond with horn honking in the same way to the manipulations of the present study if horn honking reactions to obstruction at a signal light reflect aggressive responses. Hence, the subject's sex was recorded to permit separate comparisons of the experimental manipulations for males and females. It is possible that the effects of the rifle or the vengeance bumper sticker would be significant only with male subjects driving new vehicles, since other subjects might inhibit horn honking responses.

---

[1] Status was varied by vehicle age rather than model for several reasons. It was assumed that different models might not be consistently perceived as representing high or low status by all drivers (e.g., sports cars vs. luxury sedans). Moreover, it was difficult to determine how subjects would judge older model, expensive vehicles relative to newer model, less expensive vehicles. There might be considerable inconsistency in perceptions of status for model-cost and model-age variations.

Method

Subjects

Male ($n = 137$) and female ($n = 63$) drivers of apparently privately owned vehicles served as subjects. Subjects were selected by the same procedures used in Study 2 except that no restrictions were placed on the age of drivers' vehicles or sex of subjects. Four additional subjects were dropped from the sample due to recording errors (i.e., not recording age of vehicle or sex of subject).

Experimental Design

Each subject was exposed to one level of a weapon (rifle vs. no rifle) manipulation and one level of the bumper sticker (vengeance bumper sticker vs. no bumper sticker) manipulation in an attempt to independently manipulate perceived aggressiveness of the rifle. The status of the subjects was also classified according to a median split (approximately) on the age of the subjects' vehicle (new vehicle: less than or equal to 4 years old; old vehicle: more than 4 years old).

Procedure

The procedure was identical to Study 2 except for the independent manipulation of the bumper sticker and the rifle. In addition, both male and female drivers were exposed to the treatments. Two pickup trucks (1969 models) were used to introduce the experimental conditions. These trucks were 5–6 years newer than the truck used in Study 2. Hence, the victims' perceived status in Study 3 might have been higher than that of the victim in Study 2.

Hidden observers started a stopwatch when the light turned green and recorded the latency and frequency of honks. The raters also recorded information about subject's age, sex, and age of vehicle. The raters received at least 1 hour of pretraining in the rating procedures. In order to assess the reliability of observer ratings, two raters were employed for two separate samples of subjects (Sample A = 62 subjects from Study 3; Sample B = 46 subjects from an unpublished study testing other hypotheses about the effects of a rifle). The percentage agreement between the raters for presence or absence of a honk was 100% in Sample A and 96% in Sample B. The reliability (r_{xx}) for rated age of subject's auto was .83 for Sample A and .78 for Sample B; most of the disagreements occurred for older age autos. Reliabilities for frequency of honking were .94 in Sample A and .87 in Sample B; reliability for latency of honking was .90 for both Samples A and B. No attempt was made to record or rate duration of honks, since reliabilities of ratings would have been too low, and adequately sensitive, portable tape recorders were not available to record the honks.

RESULTS AND DISCUSSION

As in Study 2, subject's horn honking responses were dichotomized into those honking (scored as 1) and those not honking (scored as 0). According to the reasoning advanced above, it was assumed that the effects of the rifle would be most pronounced when it appeared in an aggressive context (i.e., the bumper sticker). Predictions about the interactive effect of the rifle and the bumper sticker can be tested most directly by a planned comparison procedure. The primary interaction hypothesis was tested by a contrast that compared the rifle/vengeance condition to the average of the other three rifle and vengeance combinations (Contrast A: $-\frac{1}{3}$, $-\frac{1}{3}$, $-\frac{1}{3}$, +1). Two additional independent contrasts were selected: The second contrast compared the rifle/no bumper sticker condition to the two no rifle conditions (Contrast B: $-\frac{1}{2}$, $-\frac{1}{2}$, +1, 0); the third contrast compared the two no rifle conditions (Contrast C: −1, +1, 0, 0). The pooled results for Contrasts B and C represent deviations from the main hypothesis. The mean rates (proportions) of subject honking which are reported separately for new- and old-vehicle male drivers and for female drivers are presented

TABLE 3
PERCENTAGE OF HORN HONKING IN THE EXPERIMENTAL CONDITIONS OF STUDY 3

Experimental conditions			
No rifle present		Rifle present	
No bumper sticker (I)	Vengeance bumper sticker (II)	No bumper sticker (III)	Vengeance bumper sticker (IV)
Male drivers of new vehicles			
50.0 ($n = 18$)	33.3 ($n = 12$)	30.4 ($n = 23$)	65.0 ($n = 20$)
Male drivers of old vehicles			
56.2 ($n = 16$)	38.1 ($n = 21$)	46.2 ($n = 13$)	14.3 ($n = 14$)
Female drivers			
80.0 ($n = 15$)	50.0 ($n = 16$)	50.0 ($n = 16$)	50.0 ($n = 16$)

Note. Cell entries refer to the percentages of subjects producing at least one honk. Numbers in parentheses refer to cell sizes. The Roman numerals specify the order of the contrast weights which were applied to means. For example, in Contrast A ($-\frac{1}{3}$, $-\frac{1}{3}$, $-\frac{1}{3}$, and +1), the contrast weight +1 was applied to Condition IV (rifle present–vengeance bumper sticker).

TABLE 4
SUMMARY OF THE CONTRAST ANALYSIS FOR HORN HONKING RATES IN STUDY 3

Source	df	MS	F
Males drivers of new vehicles			
Hypothesis (Contrast A)	1	.948	4.03*
Deviation from hypothesis (Contrast B + C)	2	.193	<1
Male drivers of old vehicles			
Hypothesis	1	1.228	5.23*
Deviation from hypothesis (Contrast B + C)	2	.128	<1
Error for males	129	.235	
Female drivers			
Hypothesis	1	.117	<1
Deviation from hypothesis (Contrast B + C)	2	.471	1.92
Error for females	59	.244	

Note. The harmonic mean ($\bar{n}$) for new-vehicle males was 17.21, for old-vehicle males, $\bar{n} = 15.48$, and for females, $\bar{n} = 15.72$.
* $p < .05$.

in Table 3. The results for the contrast analysis are summarized in Table 4.

New-Vehicle Male Drivers

The results for the planned comparisons indicated that the rate of honking in the rifle/vengeance condition with new-vehicle male drivers was significantly higher than the average of the other three rifle/bumper sticker conditions, for Contrast A: $F(1, 129) = 4.03$, $p < .05$. The other three conditions did not differ significantly from each other, for Contrast B + C: $F < 1.0$. It should also be noted that there is no single alternative contrast to A for new-vehicle male drivers which could be significant, maximum alternative contrast $F(1, 129) = 1.6$, $p > .20$. Hence, the results tentatively support the predictions leading to the present procedures. Although the rifle/vengeance condition was significantly different from the average of the other three conditions, a careful inspection of the means reported in Table 3 indicates that it was not significantly different from the control condition. One possible explanation for the somewhat weaker results obtained in Study 3 is based on the fact that the confederate-victims drove newer vehicles (3–4 years old) in Study 3 as compared to an 8–9-year-old vehicle in Study 2. Perhaps some subjects inhibited honking to victims in the newer trucks in Study 3 because the victims were perceived to be of relatively high status. Since Doob and Gross (1968) found evidence of inhibitory reactions toward high-status victims, perhaps the weaker findings in the present study were partly accounted for by inhibitory processes.[2]

Old-Vehicle Male Drivers

The three planned contrasts (A, B, C) were employed to assess the effects of treatments for old-vehicle male drivers. The results for Contrast A indicated that the rifle/vengeance condition produced significantly lower rates of honking than the other three conditions, $F(1, 129) = 5.23$, $p < .05$. The other three conditions did not differ significantly (Contrast B + C: $F < 1.0$). One possible explanation can be offered for these findings: When the old-vehicle drivers were exposed to the rifle in an aggressive context (the bumper sticker), they were more likely to perceive an aggressive meaning to the rifle and hence to their own honking responses. If they perceived their honks as potentially aggressive, they might have inhibited reactions in the presence of a higher status victim. These interpretations are somewhat similar to those offered by Ellis, Weinir, and Miller (1972), who found that subjects produced lower levels of shock giving in the presence of a rifle and a pistol. Apparently for their subjects, the weapons produced inhibitions about being aggressive. The present findings tentatively suggest that the presence of a rifle in an aggressive context (like the bumper sticker) for some male subjects may produce inhibitions rather than stimulate more aggression.

Female Drivers

The planned contrasts (A, B, C) were also applied to the cell means for female subjects. Neither Contrast A $(F < 1.0)$ nor the deviation Contrasts B + C, $F(2, 59) = 1.92$, $p < .20$, were significant. The differences between conditions also were not significant when female subjects were divided by the age of their vehicles (new and old). However, the results for the females must be interpreted cautiously, since there were fewer subjects in any condition; thus, the condition differences might be significant with sample sizes as large as those obtained for the male subjects. The lower frequency of female subjects resulted from the fact that most drivers were males, at least on Saturdays.

GENERAL DISCUSSION

The primary reason for employing a naturalistic paradigm in the present research was to explore the possibility that laboratory procedures could be extended to a setting where subjects were unaware that they were being studied. While there are many advantages to naturalistic studies, one disadvantage results from the fact that it is difficult to obtain validity or manipulation checks from subjects to determine their perceptions of the experimental treatments. For example, it was not possible in the present research to assess directly any effects of the vengeance bumper sticker on subject's perception of the rifle or to measure independently possible differences in inhibitions produced by the victim visibility or vehicle age variables. As a consequence, any inferences about possible mediating principles can be offered only very tentatively, since alternative interpretations can be offered for the present results. Additional research is required before any firm conclusions are warranted about the present manipulations and the dependent measures.

The results of a survey and two naturalistic experiments in the present research tentatively suggest that findings somewhat analo-

---

[2] In order to assess the robustness of the aggressive stimulation manipulation which was reflected in the comparison of the rifle/vengeance condition to the control (no rifle/no bumper sticker) condition, the results for Study 2 and Study 3 were reanalyzed. A 2 × 2 factorial analysis of variance was computed using Study 2–Study 3 as one factor and the aggressive stimulation manipulation as the second factor. The results indicated that the aggressive stimulation factor was significant, $F(1, 56) = 5.78$, $p < .02$, while neither the other factor (study replication) nor the interaction was significant ($F < 1.0$). The absence of a significant interaction suggests that the pattern of results was similar in the two studies for the effect of the rifle/vengeance condition versus the control condition.

gous to laboratory research on aggression can be produced in a naturalistic setting. For example, male subjects in Study 2 were more likely to honk at a victim when he was not visible. Similarly, Milgram (1965) found in a laboratory setting that subjects were more likely to harm a victim who was not visible. Zimbardo's (1969) construct of dehumanization provides one possible explanation for the effects of victim visibility. According to the construct, inhibitions against harming a victim are lowered in the absence of cues which "humanize" a victim. The present curtain manipulations might have "dehumanized" the victim by removing visual cues from him which might have reduced possible inhibitions against horn honking as an aggressive response.

However, there is another interpretation possible for effects of the curtain manipulation. For example, the horn honking subsequent to obstruction at the light might be interpreted better as a "signal" response rather than as aggression. Since the subjects could not see the driver-confederate when the curtain was closed, they might have thought that he was being inattentive at the light. Thus, they might have used their horns to signal that the light had changed. Anecdotal evidence suggests that drivers often honk at others to attract their attention or to warn them about some danger. This alternative interpretation of the horn honking measure cannot be dismissed. Nevertheless, the pattern of findings (including the results of the survey in Study 1) suggests that drivers may become frustrated and angry at other drivers, and this anger or frustration can lead to various hostile reactions such as light flashing, swearing, or hand gestures. Presumably, horn honking might also be perceived as an aggressive response by subjects, especially in the presence of aggressive stimuli.

Male drivers of new vehicles in Study 2 gave more honks when they were exposed to the rifle/vengeance bumper sticker condition but only if they could not see the confederate. In one sense, the findings of Study 3 replicate the results for Study 2, since the honking rate in the rifle/vengeance condition was significantly higher (Contrast A) only for male drivers of new vehicles (the confederate was not visible for any subjects in Study 3).

In the present research, the vengeance bumper sticker condition was added to the rifle manipulation in an attempt to extend laboratory studies of an aggressive context for stimuli (Berkowitz & Alioto, 1973) in a naturalistic setting. The vengeance bumper sticker context was selected in an attempt to increase the salience of the aggresive connotation for the rifle. Otherwise, it was possible that an aggressive meaning of the rifle would not be salient in the gun rack of a pickup truck (e.g., it might be viewed as sporting equipment such as a fishing pole or skis). The present results are somewhat analogous to the results of Berkowitz and Alioto (1973), who found that the context in which a football game was presented played an important role in determining what aggressive reactions followed the game. When the filmed game was characterized as a "grudge match" as opposed to a sporting event, subjects were more likely to perceive an aggressive meaning to the football player's actions, and they were more likely to shock a partner who had previously insulted them. Similarly, the vengeance bumper sticker might have modified horn honking responses in the presence of the rifle because its aggressive meaning was more salient.

One important finding in Study 3 was the strong individual differences in subjects' reactions. Although male drivers of new vehicles with nonvisible victims honked more when exposed to both the rifle and the vengeance bumper sticker, the higher rates did not occur for all subjects. When male drivers of new vehicles *could* see their victim, or when male drivers of old vehicles and female drivers were exposed to the rifle/vengeance condition, they did not honk more. One possible explanation for the lower honking rates is that these subjects might have inhibited horn honking responses, especially in the presence of the rifle/vengeance condition. For example, if male drivers of old vehicles perceived themselves to be of lower status than the confederate, they might have inhibited horn honking as an aggressive response due to fears of retaliation from the high status driver in front of them. The results suggest the possibility that the presence of aggressive stimuli might lead to lower levels of aggression from many individuals due to inhibitions about engaging in aggressive behavior. Hence, there might be important limitations on the generalizability for the effects of aggressive stimuli on horn honking responses and, possibly, on other aggressive and antisocial responses.

As with the victim visibility manipulations, there are several possible explanations for the present aggressive stimulus manipulations. For example, the rifle/bumper sticker combination might have served as a classically conditioned aggressive stimulus which elicited aggression (Berkowitz & LePage, 1967); it might have served as a retrieval cue (Tulving & Thomson, 1973) to remind subjects of previous experiences with aggressive stimuli (e.g., violent portrayals in the mass media), or it might have served as a cue which changed the subject's perceptions of the aggressive meaning of their responses (Berkowitz & Alioto, 1973; Berkowitz & Turner, 1974).

Since there are alternative explanations for the present findings which cannot be dismissed, no firm conclusions can be offered about which principles best explain the results until additional research is completed. Still, the present research provides procedures which might be used to extend laboratory research to naturalistic settings where subjects do not know that they are being studied.

REFERENCES

Bardwick, J. M. *Psychology of women: A study of bio-cultural conflicts.* New York: Harper & Row, 1971.

Berkowitz, L. Some determinants of impulsive aggression: Role of mediated associations with reinforcements for aggression. *Psychological Review,* 1974, *84*, 165–176.

Berkowitz, L., & Alioto, J. T. The meaning of an observed event as a determinant of its aggressive consequences. *Journal of Personality and Social Psychology,* 1973, *28*, 206–217.

Berkowitz, L., & LePage, A. Weapons as aggression-eliciting stimuli. *Journal of Personality and Social Psychology,* 1967, *7*, 202–207.

Berkowitz, L., & Turner, C. W. Perceived anger level, instigating agent, and aggression. In H. London & R. E. Nisbett (Eds.), *Thought and feeling: Cognitive alteration of feeling states.* Chicago: Aldine, 1974.

Buss, A. H., Booker, A., & Buss, E. Firing a weapon and aggression. *Journal of Personality and Social Psychology,* 1972, *22*, 296–302.

D'Agostino, R. B. A second look at analysis of variance on dichotomous data. *Journal of Educational Measurement,* 1971, *8*, 327–333.

Doob, A. N., & Gross, A. E. Status of frustrator as an inhibitor of horn-honking responses. *Journal of Social Psychology,* 1968, *76*, 213–218.

Ellis, D. P., Weinir, P., & Miller, L. Does the trigger pull the finger? An experimental test of weapons as aggression eliciting stimuli. *Sociometry,* 1971, *34*, 453–465.

Feshback, S., & Singer, R. D. *Television and aggression: An experimental field study.* San Francisco: Jossey-Bass, 1971.

Geen, R. C., & O'Neal, E. C. Activation of cue-elicited aggression by general arousal. *Journal of Personality and Social Psychology,* 1969, *11*, 289–292.

Kirk, R. E. *Experimental design: Procedures for the behavioral sciences.* Belmont, Calif.: Brooks/Cole, 1968.

Lunney, G. H. Using analysis of variance with a dichotomous dependent variable: An empirical study. *Journal of Educational Measurement,* 1970, *7*, 263–269.

Milgram, S. Some conditions of obedience and disobedience to authority. *Human Relations,* 1965, *18*, 57–76.

Page, M. M., & Scheidt, R. J. The elusive weapons effect: Demand awareness, evaluation apprehension, and slightly sophisticated subjects. *Journal of Personality and Social Psychology,* 1971, *20*, 304–318.

Parke, R. D., Ewall, W., & Slaby, R. G. Hostile and helpful verbalizations as regulators of nonverbal aggression. *Journal of Personality and Social Psychology,* 1972, *23*, 243–248.

Parry, M. *Aggression on the road.* London: Tavistock, 1968.

Rosenberg, M. The conditions and consequences of evaluation. In R. Rosenthal & R. Rosnow (Eds.), *Artifact in behavioral research.* New York: Academic Press, 1969.

Stricker, L. J., Messick, S., & Jackson, D. N. Evaluating deception in psychological research. *Psychological Bulletin,* 1969, *77*, 273–295.

Tulving, E., & Thomson, D. M. Encoding specificity and retrieval processes in episodic memory. *Psychological Review,* 1973, *80*, 352–373.

Turner, C. W., & Simons, L. S. Effects of subject sophistication and evaluation apprehension on aggressive responses to weapons. *Journal of Personality and Social Psychology,* 1974, *30*, 341–348.

United States Surgeon General's Scientific Advisory Committee on Television and Social Behavior. *Television and growing up: The impact of television violence.* Washington, D.C.: U.S. Government Printing Office, 1972.

Webb, E. J., Campbell, D. T., Schwartz, R. D., & Sechrest, L. *Unobtrusive measures: Nonreactive research in the social sciences.* Chicago: Rand McNally, 1966.

Zimbardo, P. G. The human choice: Individuation, reason, and order versus deindividuation, impulse and chaos. In W. J. Arnold & D. Levine (Eds.), *Nebraska Symposium on Motivation* (Vol. 17). Lincoln: University of Nebraska Press, 1969.

(Received January 17, 1974)

THE STUDIES COMPARED

Deception

People are complicated creatures. Sometimes they think and then act; other times they act and then think; most often they do both simultaneously. Research aimed at understanding social behavior is beset with the task of producing a situation that is real enough to the subjects for them to take it seriously and then act in a natural fashion. If you were interested, as Berkowitz and LePage were, in determining how people react rather spontaneously to the sight of weapons, you would want to create a situation in which subjects acted without thinking. In particular, given the dictates of laboratory experimentation and its demand characteristics, you would want your subjects *not* to think about what they should do.

In their search for natural, spontaneous behavior from subjects, experimenters often create a situation designed to divert subjects' attention from the behavior under study. These diversions can take a variety of forms. One tack consists in simply not telling the subjects the true purpose of the experiment. Another strategy involves detailed staging of a whole scene supposed to lead the subjects to believe that one thing is taking place, while quite another is actually occurring. Although both forms are diversionary, the term deception is usually reserved for the latter case.

Many experimenters have elected to use deception in the study of aggression, because direct probing might evoke very qualified responses from subjects. Aggression has all kinds of negative connotations; therefore, most experimental researchers have elected to come in the back way in the hope of seeing aggression as it really is. A good case, then, can be made for the use of deception. But deception is not an unqualified asset, and the counterarguments are numerous. For example, the very attempts to divert subjects' attentions may inadvertently create suspicion.

Suspicion. Stricker, Messick, and Jackson (1969) have described a number of ways in which subjects learn about deception procedures and become suspicious of them. Deception may be increasingly ineffective with student populations such as that used by Berkowitz and LePage, because students may have been told about deception experiments by friends, may have been in such experiments themselves, or may have heard them described in mass media, lectures, or texts such as this one.

A general suspicion of research leads subjects to search for clues in the experimental procedure that will tell them what is going on. Needless to say, subjects are not too eager to admit that they saw through the deception, since such admission violates the unspoken contract between researcher and subject in which the latter agrees to do what is asked. The experimenter hopes to circumvent this reluctance by use of postexperimental questionnaires or interviews designed to discover subjects who were not deceived. In the Berkowitz and LePage study, 21 subjects were dropped for admitting suspicion. According to the report, most of these subjects were suspicious of the confederate and expressed doubts that he was in fact a real subject like themselves. There was however more to the cover story than the confederate. Why were the weapons there? Berkowitz and LePage report no suspicion concerning the weapons manipulation. Page and Scheidt (1971) have suggested, however, that the subjects of that study reported no suspicion not necessarily because they felt none but because the postexperimental questions were too vague to elicit answers indicating suspicion. In several attempts to replicate the Berkowitz and LePage findings, Page and Scheidt (1971) interviewed subjects with a detailed postexperimental questionnaire. In response to these more direct questions, subjects reported substantially more suspicion than those in the original study did. Page and Scheidt found that half the subjects were aware of the purpose of the weapons, 82% were suspicious of the stooge, and 89% were aware of the revenge hypothesis. These investigators thus distinguished between two forms of suspicion: subjects can experience general suspicion of the experiment as well as more specific demand awareness; that is, they guess what specific hypothesis is being tested. Demand awareness is a more severe research problem than general suspicion, because it suggests systematic rather than idiosyncratic responses to something the experimenter does not control. Both kinds of suspicion were expressed by subjects in the LePage and Scheidt replications.

This finding is troublesome enough with regard to the laboratory experiment by Berkowitz and LePage, but it raises further questions when the "weapons effect" is pursued in a field setting. As the investigators in the second selection point out, it is not possible in field experiments to check what the subjects made of the experimental situation, since they are not aware at all of being in an experiment. The postexperimental questionnaire gives valuable information which it is difficult to do without, as clearly indicated by the Turner, Layton, and Simons speculations about the effects of age of vehicle, driver characteristics, interpretations of bumper stickers, and the like.

Confounding Variables in the Field Experiment

The aim of experimental design is to keep variables in tight enough control so that findings can be attributed to the variables under study in a clear-cut and unambiguous way. Variables are said to be confounded when the results could be attributed to a factor unspecified or uncontrolled by the experimenter. Consider this example. Suppose you decide to see whether Whites score higher than Blacks in intellectual achievement. You find two samples, administer your test, and indeed find that the Whites score higher. Then it occurs to you that maybe your White sample had more education than your Black sample; you check and find that this is so. It is now equally plausible that your difference is due to race or to years of schooling. In your study, the variables of race and education are confounded.

In the second study, by Turner, Layton, and Simons, three groups participated in each visibility condition. One group was the control group, and they were blocked by a pickup truck that had neither rifle nor bumper sticker. The second group saw a rifle and "Friend" bumper sticker, and the third group saw the rifle paired with a "Vengeance" bumper sticker. The crucial question here is whether the presence of an aggressively loaded stimulus (the rifle) would elicit more aggressive behavior (horn honking). We need, therefore, to examine differences in horn honking when the rifle was present and when it was absent. But there is a problem here due to the fact that the effect was found only when the rifle was present but paired with the "Vengeance" bumper sticker. In the absence of an experimental condition with the bumper sticker only, these results are hard to interpret. Was the horn honking produced by the rifle, by the bumper sticker, or by both? The proper controls would call for six conditions: rifle with no bumper sticker, rifle with "Friend" sticker, rifle with "Vengeance" sticker, no rifle and no sticker, "Friend" sticker with no rifle, and "Vengeance" sticker with no rifle. Study 3 in the second selection meets these design requirements by focusing particularly on the rifle-"Vengeance" condition in which the horn-honking effect was noted. This latter procedure reduced the confounding by separating the rifle condition from the bumper-sticker condition. The apparent simple effect disappears under these conditions. This emphasizes once again the need for and the importance of controlled designs whether in the laboratory or in the field.

Sex Differences

Much laboratory research in social psychology uses only male subjects or only female subjects. But often it is very important to employ both males and females. The laboratory study here tested only male responses. As is also common practice, no indication is given in the discussion that this sample selection may limit the generalization of the results. Data from the field experiments and survey, however, show that such limitations do indeed exist. Women drivers generally reported fewer hostile reactions to other drivers on the questionnaire and, when included in the experiment, showed none of the effects noted for male drivers. The investigators attributed these findings to small sample sizes, although 15 subjects per cell should be sufficient for the statistical procedures applied. Indeed, the fact that 15 subjects per cell is sufficient seems to be indicated by the researchers' analyses of male drivers in old and new vehicles. In this latter comparison, there were fewer than 15 subjects in several cells of the analysis.

It would probably be more appropriate to seek some substantive explanation of the (non)results for female subjects. Aggression studies generally use male subjects because results with male samples are more clear-cut. Given the sizeable influence of learning in the acquisition, eliciting, and maintenance of aggressive behavior, it should not be surprising that the conditions and effects differ for men and women. But this is seldom if ever tested, and any explanation that seeks to relate aggressive cues to the display of aggressive behavior must take these factors into account.

CONSUMER EVALUATION

In a more popularized account of the Berkowitz and LePage study, Berkowitz (1968) interpreted their results in the following way: "Guns not only permit violence, they can stimulate it as well. The finger pulls the trigger, but the trigger may also be pulling the finger" (p. 22).

If such were indeed the case, then we would have a very powerful effect. Perhaps it is not only the availability of weapons but the mere sight of them that produces aggression. The implication for gun control seems profound.

Product Durability

Do we have a finding that will withstand the test of time? Berkowitz and LePage found a solid weapons effect: angered subjects gave significantly more shocks to the anger instigator in the presence of weapons than did other angered subjects in the neutral-object condition. In its relatively short history, the study has been reprinted a number of times, and its results have been reported in a variety of media including textbooks and the popular press. The failures to replicate (what, in our consumer analogy, we would call the consumer complaints) have yet to find quite that wide a readership. Page and Scheidt (1971) failed to find a consistent weapons effect, and a study by Buss, Booker, and Buss (1972) even pointed to the *inhibitory* effect of the presence of weapons. In a still later replication of the Berkowitz and LePage study, Turner and Simons (1974) also found a reversal of the weapons effect; the subjects in this experiment were less aggressive when exposed to the presence of weapons than when they were not. In the second selection here, the findings indicated that the weapons effect is not as simple or as enduring as first thought. It seems fair to say at present that the test model of the product as initially marketed has little durability. Given the large role of learning in aggressive behavior, there is probably something to the weapons effect. But the weapons effect as generated under laboratory conditions may not take the form it takes in other contexts, or it may not exist at all. At present you need to be willing to consider both alternatives.

Flashy Merchandising

The discussion above was concerned with the practical methodological problems attendant on elaborate experimental deceptions. But there are ethical considerations as well. You may wish to consider the validity of the means-ends reasoning used to justify deceiving subjects in order to get at their "real" behavior. If deception is the only way in which experimenters can study a given behavior with appropriate experimental control, does this end justify the deceptive means? At another level, is there a justification for eliciting aggression in people who were unangered and presumably unaggressive before volunteering their assistance to the experimenter? There is a pressing social need to understand more about aggression. Is the experimental creation of aggression by deception the best or only way to do it? Both studies included here involved deceptions of sorts and created angered states in subjects in the hope that aggressive behavior would be elicited. Laboratory studies are invariably exposed to more criticism on these grounds because student subjects are less free to escape the situation than the unaware subject drivers at the street light. The latter do not have an experimenter urging them to press their horns.

6

GROUP DECISION MAKING: EXTREMITY SHIFTS

CHAPTER OUTLINE

Research on Risk in Group Decisions
   The Typical Experiment
   Findings and Explanations
      Will It Happen Again?
      How Do You Explain It?
Methods in the Study of Group-Induced Shifts
   Laboratory Experiments
   Field Experiments
   Observational and Archival Studies
Two Research Examples
   Product Description
   Consumer Checklist
   Michael A. Wallach, Nathan Kogan, and Daryl J. Bem, *Group influence on individual risk taking.*
   Clark McCauley, Christopher L. Stitt, Kathryn Woods, and Diana Lipton, *Group shift to caution at the race track.*
The Studies Compared
   The Measurement of Risk
      Instructional Set
      Response Alternatives
   Research Design
   Analyses and Interpretation of Results
Consumer Evaluation
   Flashy Merchandising
   Durability

Recent years have seen the emergence of countless groups whose purpose is to help you change something about yourself that you haven't been able to change by yourself. There are groups to help you stop smoking or drinking, lose weight, exercise, raise your consciousness of sex, race, or culture, and be a better parent, lover, and friend—and many more. These groups proliferate because they seem to succeed where people by themselves have failed.

Why are these groups effective? Persons trying to change something about themselves are often at a loss about how they can possibly do it. A group provides a forum for the sharing of solutions. You find yourself saying things, doing things, thinking things that you had never said, done, thought before. The presence of others and your interactions with them clearly have important effects. Social psychologists have devoted considerable research to trying to find out the systematic nature of these effects: when you are with others in a group, are you different from the way you are when you are alone?

Many of the decisions of daily living are hard to make alone. In group discussions, you learn what others think and what they plan to do. You can offer your own ideas and tentative plans and gauge the others' reactions to them. Often, this process lessens your ambiguity and doubts and makes a decision possible. We all have had the experience of being at a loss about what to do for an evening. We call some friends, and suddenly alternatives we hadn't thought of become available. What this very familiar example suggests is that others provide not only information but also an impetus to make a choice that often differs from the choice we would have made alone. This difference in decision processes has caught the attention of researchers, and many studies have been devoted to decision making in groups and to the question of how the decisions made by individuals differ from those made in a group.

The research has been guided by two divergent assumptions. One view derives from observations of mob and crowd behavior and suggests that group decisions tend to be more extreme than individual decisions; in the presence of others, an individual is bolder and more daring than he or she alone would be. A group in the aftermath of a party will follow someone's suggestion to go for a midnight swim, when the individual members of the group would not do this alone. The other view of groups takes the opposite position, based on research showing that groups act to bring deviants into line (Schachter, 1951) and that groups are more cautious and deliberate in their decisions than individuals (Barnlund, 1959). In this vein, it has been said that a camel is a horse put together by a committee. These two views of how groups affect decisions have been called the *decision-convergence* view and the *decision-polarization* view. Research in keeping with a convergence position has focused on conformity and on the degree to which group decisions represent a compromise of individual views. Research on polarization has centered on those group decisions that reflect the more extreme of the individual views represented in the group. Most of the work on polarization has concentrated on a phenomenon first termed the *risky shift* when it was discovered in 1961. The risky shift was so called because the decisions people made after group discussion were found to be riskier than those that the individual members of the group had made by themselves before the discussion.

The risky shift has attracted a large volume of social-psychological research. Myers and Lamm (1975) noted the existence of more than 300 articles on risky shift by researchers in 12 countries. The two research selections in this chapter capture some of the research issues concerning risk taking in group decisions. The reasons underlying the popularity of the topic will be discussed in detail later on in the chapter, but a few points should be mentioned here. The initial findings on the risky shift were surprising in that they ran counter to the then prevailing view of groups as leading to the convergence of individual views. Results that challenge prevalent findings often attract more attention than those that confirm the known. After a research question has been posed and research has been conducted, the efforts immediately following are usually directed at simple replications to verify if the findings are correct or not. Replications are often followed by extensions that test the generality of the phenomenon and then by "crucial experiments" that seek to rule out competing explanations.

Another reason why the risky-shift phenomenon has attracted considerable attention is its seeming broad practical implications. If groups make riskier decisions than individuals, what decisions should or should not be entrusted to committees? And who should decide on expansive ventures in a corporation, on risky procedures in surgery, on negotiation strategies in diplomacy—groups or individuals? It suddenly seemed as if social psychologists were on to a direct and fairly simple effect of group discussion on decision making, and the risky shift appeared to be a phenomenon that might have far-reaching implications.

RESEARCH ON RISK IN GROUP DECISIONS

The Typical Experiment

Most of the studies on this topic closely parallel the original design, and more than 80% of them even use the same task (Dion, Baron, & Miller, 1970). If you were a subject in one of these experiments, you would be given a questionnaire, (the Choice-Dilemmas Questionnaire) describing various hypothetical situations calling for a choice between two courses of action—one riskier but potentially more rewarding and one less risky but also less promising. Here is an example of one such situation.

> Mr. A, an electrical engineer, who is married and has one child, has been working for a large electronics corporation since graduating from college 5 years ago. He is assured of a lifetime job with a modest, though adequate, salary, and liberal pension benefits upon retirement. On the other hand, it is very unlikely that his salary will increase much before he retires. While attending a convention, Mr. A is offered a job with a small, newly founded company which has a highly uncertain future. The new job would pay more to start and would offer the possibility of a share in the ownership if the company survived the competition of the larger firms.
>
> Imagine that you are advising Mr. A. Listed below are several probabilities or odds of the new company's proving financially sound.
>
> Please check the *lowest* probability that you would consider acceptable to make it worthwhile for Mr. A. to take the new job.
>
> ___The chances are 1 in 10 that the company will prove financially sound.
>
> ___The chances are 3 in 10 that the company will prove financially sound.

___The chances are 5 in 10 that the company will prove financially sound.

___The chances are 7 in 10 that the company will prove financially sound.

___The chances are 9 in 10 that the company will prove financially sound.

___Place a check here if you think Mr. A should *not* take the new job no matter what the probabilities.*

Usually the questionnaire contains 12 situations, similar to those described in the first research selection. You are asked to respond to each one by indicating the *lowest* probability of success that you would consider acceptable in order to recommend that the person in the dilemma adopt the riskier course of action. After this initial pretest of the levels of risk you would find acceptable, you take part in the experimental treatment. In most cases, this means joining with about four subjects (who have also filled out the questionnaires), discussing each situation with the group, and arriving at a joint decision about the level of risk all of you would now consider acceptable. Finally, you are asked to consider once again the situations by yourself and to make another set of recommendations. This constitutes a third measure of the level of risk you find acceptable.

Findings and Explanations

Will It Happen Again? The first wave of studies was concerned with replication of the shift to risk. Replication can take the form of quite literal repetition of what was done by the original investigator, or it may be a conceptual replication in which elements of the original study are systematically varied to test the limits of the finding. No one study is ever thought to settle all questions about a phenomenon, and researchers are more willing to accept something that can be shown to occur and reoccur. Since, before the unexpected findings of the first experiment (Stoner, 1961) on the risky-shift phenomenon, the prevailing opinion was that groups are more conservative and cautious than individuals, these findings were greeted with a certain degree of skepticism. It simply did not seem likely that group decisions could in fact be riskier than the individual decisions made before the group discussion. Therefore, studies were undertaken to discover when, where, and with whom the risky shift could be made to occur.

The phenomenon at first appeared to be remarkably stable. The risky shift was found to take place with men and women, students and professionals, children and adults, and citizens of over a dozen different countries. While some investigators were testing the generality of the risky shift with diverse populations, others were exploring the experimental situation used by Stoner. Taking Stoner's findings as valid, these researchers sought to find out what parts of the procedure made the shift occur. How much could be pared away without losing the risky shift? Clearly something happens to an individual between the initial private judgment and the following joint decision, and researchers concerned themselves with determining more specifically what that something might be. The shift in choices began to appear as a subtler effect than had been supposed at first, and, in the search for explanations, other variations were explored.

How Do You Explain It? In his pioneering experiment, Stoner found the opposite of what he had predicted. He had assumed that group discussion would result in decisions marked by caution, because those with extreme judgments would be pressured by fellow group members to moderate their views. But, in fact, he found that group discussions seemed to produce a movement toward more extreme positions, and the search for an

---

*From *Risk Taking: A Study in Cognition and Personality,* by N. Kogan and M. A. Wallach. Copyright © 1964 by Holt, Rinehart and Winston, Inc. Reprinted by permission.

explanation was on. What could be causing people to advocate riskier solutions after discussing the situations with others?

The familiarization hypothesis. Some thought that the risk-shift phenomenon might have nothing to do with the group discussion. A *familiarization* explanation was suggested, which held that time spent in discussion merely made participants more familiar with the options and that it was this increased understanding that made higher odds more acceptable on rerating. Several studies compared the reratings given by subjects who had put more individual time into studying the options (by making lists of pros and cons and writing out arguments) with the ratings that had resulted from traditional group discussions. These studies (Bateson, 1966; Flanders & Thistlethwaite, 1967) found that a risky shift followed this familiarization procedure, but the results proved hard to replicate. Consequently, the present view is that a familiarization explanation is not enough to account for the choice shifts found.

The leadership hypothesis. Other researchers thought that the decision shifts might have something to do with group-influence processes after all. Instead of the original conformity explanation, which assumed that the pressures were in the direction of conforming to the average view, these psychologists proposed that the explanation might lie in undue influence wielded by high-risk takers. This *leadership* explanation held that individuals who advocate higher risks on the Choice-Dilemmas Questionnaire have more dominant personalities and make their influence especially felt in a group of which they are a part. Doubt was cast on the leadership explanation (Vidmar, 1970) by the finding that in groups made up only of low-risk takers there was a shift to risk despite the absence of high-risk-taking leaders. It appears, therefore, that the influence of powerful people is not enough and that there may be something in the group process itself that produces the shift.

The hypothesis of diffusion of responsibility. If the influence process is not in the hands of dominant leaders, perhaps there is something about group membership and association with others that may yield an explanation of the risky shift. The motto "United we stand; divided we fall" may reflect a folk wisdom also shared by people who meet to discuss the advice they would give someone facing certain decisions in life. An explanation based on *diffusion of responsibility* was offered, which argued that decision making gives rise to anxiety and that anxiety is alleviated by sharing the responsibility with others. To make a risky decision alone is to invoke the fear of failure; to share such a decision with others tends to reduce that fear. A decision shaped by others and shared with others does not leave you quite so alone with the responsibility for it. The diffusion explanation is favored by the authors of the first research selection in this chapter.

The hypothesis of diffusion of responsibility is undermined by findings that indicate that discussion is not absolutely essential to the shift. Some shift to risk occurs just from knowing what ratings others have given or merely from listening to a tape of another group discussing the choice dilemmas. In both cases, to argue that diffusion occurs by some vicarious identification with a group of which one is not a part is to stretch the theory rather thin. Another finding also undermines this explanation. Two items on the Choice-Dilemmas Questionnaire reliably produce shifts to greater caution (more of this later); items written by other investigators also produce shifts to caution. Since diffusion of responsibility assumes the potency of risk-induced fears, it cannot explain shifts to caution. This latter finding seems to indicate that groups polarize around extreme choices of either risk or caution.

The culture-value hypothesis. Maybe there is something particularly valuable about extreme choices (Brown, 1965). A *culture-value* explanation rests on the two assumptions that (1) risk is a value and (2) most people think of themselves as riskier than others. The theory accounts for the risky shift by assuming that the group enhances a tendency already present in the individual. In our society, it is argued, moderate risk taking is a social value. A number of studies (for example, Levinger & Schneider, 1969; Madaras &

Bem, 1968) have shown that people admire high-risk takers and think of themselves as more willing to take risks than the average person; they like to regard themselves as daring venturesome people. Given this self-perception, the group discussion produces a "'risky shift" in several ways. Those who discover that their ratings are the riskiest for the group in question are likely to draw some satisfaction from the realization that they in fact embody their own (and others') ideal and thus hold to their position. Those who hold views that, by social comparison, turn out to be more cautious are discomfited and change their ratings to fit their self-image. The result is an intensification of the attitudes present before the discussion. The dilemmas that elicit risk taking from the very beginning reflect the greatest shifts after discussion; those that involve little initial risk taking (or even a tendency toward caution) show little shift. The culture-value notion is stronger in this respect than other explanations, since it can be used to explain both risk and caution shifts, and, what's more, it can be used predictively to identify the direction of change induced by group discussion. The initial levels of risk advocated for a given situation give an indication of whether the situation taps a general value of risk.

Despite the strength of the culture-value explanation, it too is not in itself sufficient to account for extremity shifts. If the process were entirely one of adjustments to repair damaged self-images, mere knowledge that others hold riskier views should be enough to produce a shift to risk. While such an effect occurs, it is of smaller magnitude than the combined effect of knowledge of others' risk choices and discussion. At this point, the explanations diverge along two paths to account for how group discussion produces the shift. Some investigators put more emphasis on cognitive processes and the level and quality of information provided in the group discussion (Vinokur, 1971); others note the importance of affective processes whereby people are motivated to be perceived favorably by others (Jellison & Riskind, 1970).

The former view takes a cognitive approach: the role of group discussion is to change people's minds about how valuable the outcome is. In each choice situation, the person changes the level of acceptable risk *not* because he or she is riskier after discussion but because he or she wants the outcome more. The subjective evaluation of the outcome changes because better use is made of the information shared in the discussion; to survive after dangerous heart surgery, to prosper in one's own store, or to win the crucial football game is recognized as worth more risk. A test of this explanation was provided by Kahan (1975), who constructed a scale that permitted subjects to advocate different odds without changing the level of risk found acceptable. In the explanations stressing social comparison during group discussion, two elements stand out: (1) people want to make a good impression on others, and (2) people taking high risks are seen as more able than those taking low risks. In situations in which ability matters (like most risk items of the Choice-Dilemmas Questionnaire), shift toward greater risk occurs after discussion, because low-risk takers want to be more like the high-risk takers, whom they see as more able.

Current thinking is moving toward a reconciliation of these views (Myers & Lamm, 1975; Pruitt, 1971). The two ideas taken together incorporate the social and cognitive aspects of group interaction and can be used to explain a range of attitude shifts wider than risk. In particular, taking both the social and the cognitive elements into account may equip us better to deal with the diversity of group-induced attitude shifts found with methods other than the Choice-Dilemmas Questionnaire.

METHODS IN THE STUDY OF GROUP-INDUCED SHIFTS

Throughout this book, we have considered methods along two dimensions: degree of subjects' awareness of being studied and degree of manipulation of antecedent conditions. Most methods used to study group influence on individual risk taking are high in subject awareness. Subjects, generally aware of being studied and faced with tasks that require choice decisions involving risk probabilities, can probably detect that risk and caution are the focus of the experimenter's interest. The degree of manipulation of antecedent conditions is moderately high in virtually all studies. The Choice-Dilemmas Questionnaire is used in all but a handful of studies. It is an instrument in which the developers have predetermined the kind of risks to be considered, the sort of information provided about the situations, and the six levels of probability from which the subject must choose. The instrument was developed over some years by Kogan and Wallach (1964), used by Stoner (1961) in studying group decisions, and employed in the same form by most researchers since. There are a number of methodological concerns that have arisen about this instrument. Since it is the one used in the first research selection in this chapter, these issues are considered in the discussion of that article. Here we examine some methods other than the Choice-Dilemmas Questionnaire that have been used in the study of group influence on decision making.

Laboratory Experiments

Quite similar to the Choice-Dilemmas Questionnaire from the points of view of subject awareness and manipulation of antecedent conditions are the gambling situations that have been used to study risk taking. These situations are typically used in the laboratory; therefore, the subjects know that they are under study, and the experimenters determine the structure and payoffs of the tasks and the conditions under which they are presented. An example of such a betting situation is a task in which subjects gamble on which of the two lights will go on (Wolosin, Wolosin, & Zajonc, 1968, 1969). One light has a high probability of occurrence but a small payoff; the other light has a lower probability but a slightly larger payoff. This task can be described as presenting individuals with uncertain outcomes of fixed probabilities and expected values. Tasks involving betting on dice (Blank, 1968) or a roulette wheel (Pruitt & Teger, 1969) also show these characteristics. Results with gambling tasks have been equivocal.

Proponents of gambling methods favor them over such instruments as the Choice-Dilemmas Questionnaire on the grounds that they are simpler and more quantifiable and thereby permit more uncontaminated examination of risk-related decision processes. They argue that the subjective values in hypothetical decisions involving career choices and surgical procedures vary more unpredictably among subjects and over time than the more stable elements of gambling tasks. A possible drawback of the typical gambling task is that, as used in the laboratory, it contains no threat of loss to the subject. In several of Zajonc's studies, the subjects were guaranteed a minimum payment and could keep their winnings above that amount, but they did not incur the possibility of loss. Subjects responding to the Choice-Dilemmas Questionnaire, instead, are faced with the possibility of a bad outcome for the hypothetical person in the dilemma, who faces risks involving loss of life, income, and prestige. This may be one reason why the dilemmas instruments have appealed to researchers more; they seem to tap life risks that are and can be debated by groups and thus seem more appropriate to studies on how groups (presumably family, friends, colleagues) influence individual risk taking.

Some investigators, perhaps doubting the familiarity of college students with gambling, have constructed situations closely resembling the gambling format but without direct reference to wagers and stakes. These tasks, too, involve fixed probabilities and expected values but are couched in different terms. Wallach, Kogan, and Bem (1964) asked subjects to choose ten questions, varying in difficulty, from the College Board Entrance Examination; more money could be won by answering more difficult questions. A risky shift was found for group consensus decisions.

A different analog to gambling situations was developed by Malamuth and Feshbach (1972). They gave subjects $10 to make eight telephone calls to persons who were identified as being in one of two places. The charge for a person-to-person call was $1.20, so the subject picking the most cautious strategy could call all eight people and be left with 40¢. The riskier strategy involved making one or more station-to-station calls at 75¢ each. This design, too, employs the basic gambling paradigm of uncertain outcomes based on fixed probabilities and known values. A risky shift was indicated by the fact that subjects in groups decided to make station-to-station calls more often than individuals did.

Field Experiments

Low in subject awareness but similar to the preceding methods on the dimension of manipulation of antecedent conditions are efforts to involve student subjects in situations with real risks to the participants. These differ from gambling situations in that an effort is made to escape the playfulness of gambling and to produce risk conditions of personal consequence. Obviously, ethical considerations limit the range of risk situations one would impose on subjects. The situation that has been used is that of the examination process common to most courses. Clement and Sullivan (1970) asked 85 students in an introductory-psychology course to choose one of eight examination schedules preselected to reflect different levels of risk. Risk was defined as the possibility of receiving a final grade higher than deserved but at the risk of receiving a grade lower than deserved. It was then announced that, because of the diverse individual selections made, discussion sections would be allowed to permit groups to select their preferred examination schedules. Discussions were held and group decisions reached and implemented. The private choices made before discussion were all from the conservative half of the choices available, and group discussion produced a conservative shift. This finding is in keeping with polarization explanations, which suggest that discussion enhances the choice tendency already present in the group, and contradicts the simpler view that group decisions are riskier.

A similar study was conducted in Israel by Yinon, Shoham, and Lewis (1974), and a similar shift to caution was found. In addition, this study included a role-playing condition in which students who were not in the course affected by the decision simply indicated their preference for the grading methods identified by risk level. In the role-playing condition, a shift to risk was found after group discussion. This latter finding suggests that some of the stability of risky shifts found with the Choice-Dilemmas Questionnaire may be a function of its hypothetical role-playing nature. When the decision makers must bear the consequences, more cautious decisions follow group discussion.

Similarly, varying the costs of decisions affects the nature of the shift following discussion. Reingen (1973) asked business students to respond individually and in groups to three purchasing situations involving industrial goods. These hypothetical situations differed in the severity of the negative consequences involved. A risky shift was found with low-risk situations, none with moderate risk, and a shift to caution with high-risk decisions. Using the standard risky-shift design, Johnson and Andrews (1971) asked women college students to rate the lowest probability of success that would lead them to try new consumer products. The results were the same as those of Reingen's, with risky shift after group discussion found only for low-risk products. The Choice-Dilemmas Questionnaire consistently reveals shifts with a variety of populations. It is clear from these attempts to vary the situations that some of this consistency may be attributable to the method as well as to the group decision-making process.

Observational and Archival Studies

Methods reviewing the choices made by people as they carry out their regular life routines are obviously low on both dimensions of subject awareness and manipulation of antecedent conditions. People are usually not aware that any research is in progress, and the experimenters do not intervene in the antecedent conditions. One example is a longitudinal study by Semin and Glendon (1973) of the staff-evaluation committee of a medium-sized English commercial firm. The six-member committee was studied for a year, and their evaluations of secretarial and clerical jobs were reviewed. In the course of making evaluations, each committee member allotted points in individual ratings on five job dimensions; the point total determined job level. After group discussion in which all individual ratings were disclosed, a joint decision was made and implemented through channels. The investigators collected all ratings and did analyses like those in the standard Choice-Dilemmas Questionnaire experiments. In this study, no shifts were found. The authors suggest that an established group has a common body of information and a shared frame of reference, factors that reduce the differences between individual and group decisions.

Another approach was taken by Walker and Main (1973) in an archival study that compared court decisions in civil-liberties cases made by individual federal district court judges to decisions in similar cases made by three-judge panels. Group decisions yielded more libertarian outcomes than decisions by individual judges. Both these studies lend themselves more to a polarization explanation than to narrower interpretations of risk shift.

TWO RESEARCH EXAMPLES

Product Description

The two following studies are examples of a laboratory and of a field approach to the study of risk decisions under group influence. The Wallach, Kogan, and Bem study is the first published work by the originators of the Choice-Dilemmas Questionnaire after its use by Stoner in a master's thesis done under the direction of Wallach and Kogan. It is the forerunner of the massive body of research generated by the Choice-Dilemmas Questionnaire and the theoretical questions it aroused. Comprehensive reviews of this work have been published by Clark (1971), Vinokur (1971), Pruitt (1971), and Dion, Baron, and Miller (1970). The second research selection, by McCauley and his associates, is one of the rare field experiments in the risky-shift literature.

The Wallach, Kogan, and Bem study is directed at three questions: (1) whether the Stoner finding could be generalized to a population of other than male business students, (2) whether the risky shift would persist in time beyond the end of the group discussion, and (3) whether the effect might be related to perceived group influence. Individual decisions by male and female students on the Choice-Dilemmas Questionnaire were followed by group discussion and decision and then by individual postdiscussion decisions. In addition, the students rated fellow group members on degree of influence and popularity. In a follow-up two to six weeks later, the students were individually asked to reconsider their Choice-Dilemmas Questionnaire responses. The researchers found a risky shift that endured some weeks after the experiment. Group members showed high agreement on who was most influential in the group discussion, and these highly influential members turned out to be those with higher initial individual risk scores.

McCauley and his associates sought to test the generality of risky shift in the world beyond the laboratory. Male racetrack bettors were offered two dollars to bet on another horse in the same race. All were asked to name the horse just wagered on. Half the subjects were then asked to join with two others in reaching a group consensus to select another horse to bet on, while the other half made the next bet on the basis of individual decisions. Experimenters noted the odds on all bets. Unlike previous laboratory research on the risky shift, they found a shift to caution among racetrack bettors in the group-decision-making condition.

Consumer Checklist

- What technical machinery is used in the manufacturing process?
    Does the wording of instructions make any difference?
    Is the range of choices the same in both studies?
- Does the product meet design specifications?
    What particular question is answered by a design
        that compares subjects' later performance with their earlier performance?
- Does it matter how the product is assembled?
    How is risk calculated in the second selection?

GROUP INFLUENCE ON INDIVIDUAL RISK TAKING[1]

MICHAEL A. WALLACH[2]
Massachusetts Institute of Technology
NATHAN KOGAN
Educational Testing Service
AND DARYL J. BEM
University of Michigan

What are the effects of group interaction on risk and conservatism in decision making? By risk and conservatism we mean the extent to which the decision maker is willing to expose himself to possible failure in the pursuit of a desirable goal. Consider the situation in which several individuals working separately arrive at a series of decisions, and then are brought together to arrive at a group consensus regarding those decisions. What relationship should one expect to find between the individual decisions and the group consensus?

On the basis of prior experimental studies of individual and group judgment (e.g., Schachter, 1951; see also the section on group pressures and group standards in Cartwright & Zander, 1960, pp. 165–341), we should predict an averaging effect, i.e., group decisions randomly distributed around the average of the prediscussion individual decisions. Such an effect would seem to imply a process of minimizing individual losses, or minimizing the maximum individual concession. The cited studies report that inducements toward compromise and concession seem to be exerted most strongly toward group members whose initial individual views are most deviant from the central tendency.

An equally, if not more, compelling alternative hypothesis is that the group discussion will lead to increased conservatism, relative to the average of the prior individual decisions. One may cite the observations of Whyte (1956), among others, concerning the outcomes of conferences and meetings in bureaucratic organizations. Whyte argues that the use of committees and teams in the management of business and other kinds of enterprises leads inexorably to an inhibition of boldness and risk taking, a concentration on the conservative course when a choice must be made between more and less risky courses of action. How are such effects to be explained? First, it may be that the very nature of the group process or atmosphere encourages such a trend: there may be a fear, for example, of appearing foolhardy to others. Alternatively, or in addition, it is possible that the mechanism underlying an increase in conservatism is one of greater influence being exerted within the group by members whose individual conservatism tendencies are stronger. These two interpretations are not incompatible, of course, since the group process, if encouraging of conservatism, will enhance the influence of the initially more conservative members.

Finally, consideration should be given to the remaining and least likely possibility—that group interaction will eventuate in increased risk taking relative to the average of the prior decisions of the group members working separately. In this regard, Osborn (1957) has reported that group interaction may lead to quite radical, bold, problem solutions. While Osborn claims that special conditions must exist if such effects are to be observed, attempts to produce such conditions experimentally (Taylor, Berry, & Block, 1958) have yielded no evidence whatever for the so-called "brainstorming" phenom-

[1] This research was supported by a grant (G-17818) from the National Science Foundation. A master's thesis by J. A. F. Stoner at MIT's School of Industrial Management, with D. G. Marquis and M. A. Wallach as faculty advisers, was instrumental in inspiring the present investigation. We are greatly indebted to J. A. F. Stoner and D. G. Marquis for their aid and advice, and to V. Raimy and M. Wertheimer for facilities at the University of Colorado in Boulder. Thanks also are due S. Messick and A. Myers for comments.
[2] Now at Duke University.

From *Journal of Abnormal and Social Psychology*, 1962, 65(2), 75–86. Copyright 1962 by American Psychological Association. Reprinted by permission.

enon. Thibaut and Kelley (1959, pp. 267–268) discuss the conflicting evidence on this issue. We might, in passing, also mention mass or crowd phenomena, in which extreme actions taken by groups are well beyond the capacities of the members of such groups considered individually (Brown, 1954; Turner & Killian, 1957). The relevance of such mass phenomena to group decision making in a laboratory context, however, is probably quite remote. In sum, increased risk taking as a consequence of group interaction appeared to us to be the least feasible of the three possibilities discussed above.

An examination of the literature reveals little experimental research which addresses itself explicitly to the problem of the present investigation. Lonergan and McClintock (1961) report that membership in an interdependent group led to no significant move toward greater conservatism or risk taking in a betting situation involving monetary gain or loss. Since the group situation was so structured that a consensus was not required, however, this experiment is not directly relevant to the aims of the present study. Hunt and Rowe (1960) report no difference between three-person groups and individuals in riskiness of investment decisions. However, the brevity of the group interaction (15 minutes) and the disruptive influence of having the various groups meet within sight of each other in a large room render their results inconclusive. Atthowe (1961), comparing individual and dyadic decisions in the choice of the better of two alternative wagers, found greater conservatism in the dyadic decisions. But the relevance of this result to the problem at hand is called into question when we learn that the alternative wagers were presented to the subjects as "problems taken from the mathematical reasoning section of an advanced intelligence test and arranged as wagers" (p. 115). This could well contribute to a conservative strategy.

We turn, finally, to a study by Stoner (1961), which provides the starting point for the research to be reported. Using male graduate students of industrial management as subjects, Stoner observed that a group consensus regarding degree of risk to be taken in resolving a "life dilemma" situation deviated from the average of prediscussion decisions in the direction of greater risk taking. These results took us by surprise. We wondered whether the finding could be generalized to other subject populations, whether it was an enduring effect, and whether it might have anything to do with relationships between risk taking and perceived group influence.

One issue that arises in interpreting Stoner's (1961) study concerns the effect that expectations about one's role might have on the results. Thus, a group of male graduate students of industrial management might make more risky decisions qua group than would each such student individually—the result obtained by Stoner—because the presence of their peers reminds each that one of the positively sanctioned attributes of the business manager role which they occupy or aspire to occupy is a willingness to take risks in their decision making. Stoner's use of a male business school sample, therefore, leaves open the possibility that his results may be a function of this particular group's self-assigned professional role alone. It also is possible that a group of males, regardless of their professional role, might make more risky decisions when gathered together because the presence of other males serves as a reminder that one of the expected indications of manliness in our society is a willingness to be bold and daring in decision making. Conversely, a group of females might make more conservative decisions when gathered together, or at least might fail to shift in a risky direction, since risk taking tendencies are not likely to be mutually reinforced in groups for whom risk is not a positive social value (see, e.g., Komarovsky, 1950; Milner, 1949; Wallach & Caron, 1959).

In the present experiment, we shall employ samples of male and female undergraduates enrolled in a liberal arts curriculum at a large state university. If the effects observed by Stoner (1961) are found to hold for both of the above samples, this would constitute strong evidence for the generality of the phenomenon and its independence of occupational and sex role considerations. Furthermore, the use of previously unacquainted subjects whose ascribed status is initially equal will insure that whatever effects are obtained cannot be attributed to an association between initially high or low status, on the one hand, and risk or conservatism, on the other. If initial status levels were unequal, low status individuals might simply adopt the standards of those whose status is high—an outcome which would tell us nothing about the effect of group interactional processes as such on individual risk taking.

One should distinguish initially ascribed status from status indices (e.g., perceived influence and popularity) derived from the group experience. Since such indices may bear some relation to initial risk taking level, the necessary sociometric-type judgments will be obtained.

Finally, evidence will be presented with regard to the following two questions: Is the group induced effect on risk taking limited only to the group member's overt compliance in the group setting or does it also extend to his covert acceptance when he makes postgroup decisions as an individual (see Festinger, 1953; Kelley & Thibaut, 1954)? To what extent are group effects on individual decision making relatively enduring or short-lived?

METHOD

Assessment of Level of Conservatism or Risk Taking

The instrument used for assessing level of conservatism or risk taking, as developed in some of our prior research (Kogan & Wallach, 1961; Wallach & Kogan, 1959, 1961), is called an "opinion questionnaire" and contains descriptions of 12 hypothetical situations. The central person in each situation must choose between two courses of action, one of which is more risky than the other but also more rewarding if successful. For each situation the subject must indicate the lowest probability of success he would accept before recommending that the potentially more rewarding alternative be chosen. The probabilities listed are 1, 3, 5, 7, and 9 chances of success in 10, plus a final category (scored as 10) in which the subject can refuse to recommend the risky alternative no matter how high its likelihood of success.

The situations were so designed as to cover a wide range of content, and may be summarized as follows:

1. An electrical engineer may stick with his present job at a modest but adequate salary, or may take a new job offering considerably more money but no long-term security.

2. A man with a severe heart ailment must seriously curtail his customary way of life if he does not undergo a delicate medical operation which might cure him completely or might prove fatal.

3. A man of moderate means may invest some money he recently inherited in secure "blue chip" low return securities or in more risky securities that offer the possibility of large gains.

4. A captain of a college football team, in the final seconds of a game with the college's traditional rival, may choose a play that is almost certain to produce a tie score, or a more risky play that would lead to sure victory if successful, sure defeat if not.

5. The president of an American corporation which is about to expand may build a new plant in the United States where returns on the investment would be moderate, or may decide to build in a foreign country with an unstable political history where, however, returns on the investment would be very high.

6. A college senior planning graduate work in chemistry may enter university X where, because of rigorous standards, only a fraction of the graduate students manage to receive the PhD, or may enter university Y which has a poorer reputation but where almost every graduate student receives the PhD.

7. A low ranked participant in a national chess tournament, playing an early match with the top-favored man, has the choice of attempting or not trying a deceptive but risky maneuver which might lead to quick victory if successful or almost certain defeat if it fails.

8. A college senior with considerable musical talent must choose between the secure course of going on to medical school and becoming a physician, or the risky course of embarking on the career of a concert pianist.

9. An American prisoner-of-war in World War II must choose between possible escape with the risk of execution if caught, or remaining in the camp where privations are severe.

10. A successful businessman with strong feelings of civic responsibility must decide whether or not to run for Congress on the ticket of a minority party whose campaign funds are limited.

11. A research physicist, just beginning a 5-year appointment at a university, may spend the time working on a series of short-term problems which he would be sure to solve but which would be of lesser importance, or on a very important but very difficult problem with the risk of nothing to show for his 5 years of effort.

12. An engaged couple must decide, in the face of recent arguments suggesting some sharp differences of opinion, whether or not to get married. Discussions with a marriage counselor indicate that a happy marriage, while possible, would not be assured.

The response categories are arrayed from chances of 1 in 10 upward for the odd items and in the reverse order for the even items, thus, counterbalancing for any possible order preference effect in choice of probability levels. An overall conservatism-risk taking score is derived by adding the scores for the separate items. The larger this score, the greater the subject's conservatism.

Our prior research, cited above, yielded split-half Spearman-Brown reliability coefficients ranging from .53 to .80 for various age and sex samples, suggesting that the instrument possesses satisfactory internal consistency. The results of the present experiment will provide evidence, furthermore, of high test-retest reliability.

Regarding the instrument's construct validity as a risk taking measure, our earlier studies, cited above, have yielded findings consistent with a risk taking interpretation. For example, degree of conservatism as measured with the present instrument increases with age from young adulthood to old age for both males and females, and increases with degree of subjective probability of personal failure in a motor skill game with actual motor skill controlled.

Experimental Condition

Subjects. The subjects were invited to participate in an experiment which would take no longer than 2 hours and for which remuneration would be provided. Six subjects were scheduled for any one time, with every effort being made to insure that previously acquainted persons were not signed up for the same session. A total of 167 subjects participated in the experimental condition—14 all-male groups and 14 all-female groups.[3] The subjects were liberal arts students enrolled in summer session courses at the University of Colorado in Boulder.

Prediscussion individual decisions. The experiment was run in a seminar room around a very long table. For the initial administration of the questionnaire, subjects took alternate seats with the experimenter at one end. The six subjects were requested to read the instructions to the questionnaire and to look over the first item. The experimenter then emphasized two points in further standard instructions: that the more risky alternative is always assumed to be more desirable than the safer course, if the former should prove successful; that the odds which the subject marks indicate the lowest odds the subject would be willing to take and still advise the central figure to give the risky alternative a try. The subjects were told there was no time limit, that they should consider

---

[3] Of the 14 male groups, 13 contained six subjects each, and one contained five subjects. A subject in one of the six-person male groups misunderstood instructions for the prediscussion individual decisions, so that his decision scores were removed prior to analysis. All 14 of the female groups contained six subjects each. A subject in each of 2 female groups misunderstood instructions for the prediscussion individual decisions, so that the decision scores of these two females were removed prior to analysis.

each of the 12 situations carefully, and that they could return to an earlier question if they wished to. The conservatism-risk instrument then was filled out individually by each of the six subjects in a group administration session that took about 20 minutes. To avoid giving any of the subjects the feeling that they were being rushed, the questionnaires were not collected until all had finished.

Group discussion and consensual group decisions. Without having had any prior expectation that they would be requested to discuss their decisions, the six subjects were then asked to move together into a discussion group at one end of the table. They now each were given another copy of the questionnaire, and a stand-up cardboard placard with the identification letter K, L, M, N, O, or P on it was placed before each subject. The experimenter then told them that the questionnaire now before them was the same one they just finished taking. They had taken it, he continued, to familiarize them with all the situations and to give them some idea where they might stand on each. Now he wanted the group to discuss each question in turn and arrive at a unanimous decision on each. This time they could not return to a question, but rather had to discuss each one until the group decision was reached before going on to the next. When the group reached its decision on a question, all subjects were to mark it on their questionnaires in order to have a record. The group would be completely on its own, the experimenter not participating in the discussion at all.

The experimenter then retired to the other end of the table in order to be as far from the group as possible. A question that often arose before discussion had started was what to do if a deadlock occurs. The experimenter's standard reply was:

> Most groups are able to come to some decision if those who disagree will restate their reasons, and if the problem is reread carefully.

Most groups succeeded in reaching a unanimous decision on most items, although an occasional deadlock did occur on one or another item. The group discussions were of such a nature as to indicate that the participants were highly involved in the decision tasks.

Postdiscussion individual decisions. After the discussion was over, the experimenter proceeded to ask the group members to spread apart for some further individual work and to take their questionnaires and identification placards with them. In standard instructions, he requested them to go back over the situations and indicate their own present personal decisions with a "P." He noted that while in some cases the subjects may have agreed with the group decision, in other cases they may have disagreed with it. In the former cases the P would be placed on the same line as the check mark; in the latter cases, on a different line.

While the consensual decisions by the group would indicate the public effect of the discussion process, the private postdiscussion decisions made once again on an individual basis would indicate whether the discussion process had influenced covert acceptance as well as public compliance.

Rankings for influence and popularity. After the postdiscussion individual decisions had been made, a ranking sheet was passed out to each subject requesting that he rank everyone in the group (identified by their letter placards), including himself, in terms of how much each influenced the final group decision. Then each subject was requested to rank everyone in the group (except, of course, himself) in terms of how much he would like to become better acquainted with each.

The rankings for influence provided the information needed for examining possible relationships between strength of individual risk taking or conservatism tendencies, on the one hand, and degree of influence in the group, on the other. If such relationships existed, it seemed to be of interest to determine whether they were specific to perceived influence or would prove to be dependent upon the subject's popularity; hence the second set of rankings.

Secrecy instructions. After the ranking sheets were collected, the experimenter told the group that the research would be carried out in coming weeks, and that they could now appreciate why it would be important for the content of the experiment to be kept secret, since a person who even knew that the group would be discussing the same questions which he had filled out individually would have a tendency to mark logically defensible answers instead of his true opinion, etc. The subjects therefore all were sworn to secrecy. Various indications suggest that this pledge was faithfully kept.

Post-postdiscussion individual decisions. A further session of individual decision making took place approximately 2–6 weeks later for some subjects. These subjects individually were given the conservatism-risk questionnaire a third time and were asked to reconsider the situations. The standard instructions emphasized that the experimenter was not interested in testing the subject's memory, but rather wanted the subject truly to *reconsider* each situation. The instructions thus oriented the subjects away from simply trying to recall their prior decisions. Each subject was paid for this further work.

Control Condition

Subjects. Control subjects were obtained in the same way as the experimental subjects, and likewise received remuneration for their work. The controls were signed up to participate in two sessions: the first to last about 20 minutes; the second, exactly 1 week later, to last about 15 minutes. A total of 51 subjects participated in the control condition—24 males and 27 females. Like the experimental subjects, the controls were liberal arts students enrolled in summer session courses at the University of Colorado in Boulder.

First individual decision session. The first session was identical to the prediscussion individual decision part of the experimental condition. From six to eight subjects of the same sex, scheduled for the same time, filled out the conservatism-risk instrument while sitting together in physical conditions identical to those of the experimental subjects and at approximately the same time of day as the experimental subjects had worked. Exactly the same instructions were provided as had been given the experimental subjects.

After the first session, the control subjects were sworn to secrecy. They also were told that they would be taking a similar questionnaire the next week, and that it was extremely important that they not discuss it with one another nor with anyone else, since such discussion might affect the way they filled out next week's questionnaire.

Second individual decision session. The same control subjects who had participated in a particular first individual decision session came back exactly 1 week later. After checking that no discussion had taken place in the intervening week among the controls, the experimenter handed out new copies of the questionnaire and explained that this questionnaire was identical to the one taken last week. Each subject was requested to go back over the situations and reconsider them, the experimenter emphasizing that he was not interested in testing the subject's memory but rather wanted the subject truly to *reconsider* each situation. The instructions were so designed, therefore, as to dissuade the subject from assuming that the most socially acceptable thing to do would be to try to make the same decisions that he had made a week ago. Change was encouraged rather than discouraged. Control subjects were sworn to secrecy again at the end of the second session.

RESULTS

Consensual Group Decisions Compared with Prediscussion Individual Decisions

Tables 1 and 2 examine, for male and female groups, respectively, the significance of the conservatism difference between the mean of the prediscussion individual decisions made by the members of each group and that group's consensual decisions. The basic test is carried out using the total conservatism score, which consists of all 12 item scores combined. Tests also are carried out for each item separately.

In the case of the total score, a group's difference score is the sum of the 12 unanimous group decision scores minus the average of the prediscussion total individual decision scores for the six members.[4] Since larger scores indicate greater conservatism, a negative difference (or score decrease) indicates a

[4] Any deadlocked item is, of course, not included in either term for the group in question.

TABLE 1

SIGNIFICANCE OF CONSERVATISM DIFFERENCE BETWEEN MEAN OF PREDISCUSSION INDIVIDUAL DECISIONS FOR A GROUP'S MEMBERS AND GROUP'S CONSENSUAL DECISION:
MALES

Item	Mean difference[a]	Number of groups[b]	t
All combined	−9.4	14	6.46****
1	−1.0	14	4.34****
2	−0.2	14	<1.00
3	−1.1	13	2.19*
4	−1.8	13	6.18****
5	+0.1	13	<1.00
6	−1.2	13	3.35**
7	−2.0	14	9.64****
8	−1.1	14	1.97
9	−1.0	10	3.67**
10	−0.4	13	<1.00
11	−1.1	12	4.37***
12	+0.8	11	2.34*

[a] In Tables 1, 2, 3, 4, 6, and 7, a negative difference signifies a risky shift, a positive difference signifies a conservative shift.
[b] In Tables 1 and 2, number of groups for an item is less than 14 when one or more groups deadlocked on that item. Any deadlocked item is, of course, not included when calculating scores for all items combined.
* $p < .05$.
** $p < .01$.
*** $p < .005$.
**** $p < .001$.

shift in the risky direction. A t test is used to determine whether the 14 difference scores for the groups of each sex are significantly different from zero (McNemar, 1955, pp. 108–109).[5] These total score data indicate a move in the risky direction significant beyond the .001 level for the 14 male groups, and a move in the risky direction significant beyond the .005 level for the 14 female groups. Furthermore, the degree of shift is not significantly different for the two sexes.

In the case of the scores for a single item, a group's difference score consists of the unanimous group decision on that item minus the average of the prediscussion individual decision scores on that item for the six members. Once again a negative difference or score decrease indicates a shift in the risky direction, and a t test is applied to determine whether the difference scores for all groups that reached a unanimous decision on the item in question are significantly different from zero. For both the male and female groups, we find that 10 of the 12 items show shifts in the risky direction, 7 of them significant in

[5] All significance levels cited in this study are based on two-tailed tests.

each case. Five of those 7 are the same for both sexes. Only 2 items show any indication for either sex of not sharing in the general shift toward greater risk taking: Items 5 and 12. It should be noted that these two items exhibited, in our previous research, the lowest correlations with the overall risk-conservatism score, suggesting that they are relatively impure measures of the psychological dimension being tapped by the other 10 items.

In sum, the evidence from Tables 1 and 2 indicates a strong move toward greater risk taking when groups arrive at unanimous decisions, compared with the risk levels ventured by the same persons in prediscussion individual decisions. Furthermore, this move toward greater risk taking obtains for females as well as for males.

A further question concerns the extent to which the risky shift is consistent from one group to another. Consider one example of several consistency tests that have been conducted, all of which yield highly similar results. Suppose we define a group as showing a risky shift from prediscussion individual decisions to consensual group decisions if the difference score for its total score, as defined above, is a negative one. Fourteen out of 14 male groups and 12 out of 14 female

TABLE 2

SIGNIFICANCE OF CONSERVATISM DIFFERENCE BETWEEN MEAN OF PREDISCUSSION INDIVIDUAL DECISIONS FOR A GROUP'S MEMBERS AND GROUP'S CONSENSUAL DECISION:
FEMALES

Item	Mean difference	Number of groups	t
All combined	−9.4	14	3.91***
1	−1.0	13	4.17***
2	−0.6	14	1.65
3	−0.4	14	1.12
4	−1.4	14	2.60****
5	+0.7	14	1.90
6	−0.8	13	2.63****
7	−2.0	12	3.21**
8	−1.7	14	5.26*****
9	−0.8	12	1.19
10	−1.5	13	3.18**
11	−0.9	13	2.28*
12	+0.6	6	2.00

* $p < .05$.
** $p < .01$.
*** $p < .005$.
**** $p < .025$.
***** $p < .001$.

TABLE 3

SIGNIFICANCE OF CONSERVATISM DIFFERENCE BETWEEN MEAN OF PREDISCUSSION INDIVIDUAL DECISIONS FOR A GROUP'S MEMBERS AND MEAN OF POSTDISCUSSION INDIVIDUAL DECISIONS FOR A GROUP'S MEMBERS: MALES

Item	Mean difference	Number of groups	t
All combined	−10.4	14	9.12****
1	− 1.0	14	4.32****
2	− 0.6	14	2.87*
3	− 1.1	14	3.04**
4	− 1.7	14	8.14****
5	+ 0.1	14	<1.00
6	− 1.1	14	3.79***
7	− 1.8	14	7.80****
8	− 1.1	14	3.54***
9	− 1.1	14	3.99***
10	− 0.3	14	<1.00
11	− 0.8	14	4.36****
12	+ 0.1	14	<1.00

* $p < .02$.
** $p < .01$.
*** $p < .005$.
**** $p < .001$.

groups are found to move in the risky direction, both results being very significant by a sign test. Such a finding demonstrates, therefore, that the risky shift phenomenon is quite consistent across groups.

Postdiscussion Individual Decisions Compared with Prediscussion Individual Decisions

In Tables 3 and 4 we present, once again for male and female groups, respectively, the significance of the difference between the mean of the prediscussion individual decisions and the mean of the postdiscussion individual decisions made by the members of each group. The basic test once again is provided by the total conservatism score, but tests also are presented for each item separately.

For the total score, a group's difference score consists of the average of the postdiscussion total individual decision scores for the members minus the average of the prediscussion total individual decision scores for the same members. Negative difference scores again indicate risky shifts, and a t test is applied to determine whether the 14 difference scores for the groups of each sex are significantly different from zero. We find, once again, a shift in the risky direction significant beyond the .001 level for the 14 male groups,

and a risky shift significant beyond the .005 level for the 14 female groups. As before, the degree of shift is not significantly different for the two sexes.

Turning to the scores for each separate item, a group's difference score consists of the average of the postdiscussion individual decision scores on that item minus the average of the prediscussion individual decision scores on that item. With a negative difference score indicating a risky shift and a t test applied to indicate whether the 14 difference scores for each sex on an item are significantly different from zero, we find that 9 of the 12 items show separate significant shifts in the risky direction for the male groups (with one additional item shifting nonsignificantly in the same direction), and that 8 of the 12 items show separate significant shifts toward greater risk taking for the female groups (with two additional items shifting nonsignificantly in that direction). The 8 items showing significant risky shifts for the females are among the 9 showing significant risky shifts for the males. Items 5 and 12 once again are the only ones for either sex showing any indication of not sharing in the general shift toward greater risk taking found in both sexes.

There is clear evidence, therefore, that

TABLE 4

SIGNIFICANCE OF CONSERVATISM DIFFERENCE BETWEEN MEAN OF PREDISCUSSION INDIVIDUAL DECISIONS FOR A GROUP'S MEMBERS AND MEAN OF POSTDISCUSSION INDIVIDUAL DECISIONS FOR A GROUP'S MEMBERS: FEMALES

Item	Mean difference	Number of groups	t
All combined	−8.2	14	3.67**
1	−0.9	14	5.09****
2	−0.7	14	2.67*
3	−0.6	14	2.58***
4	−1.4	14	3.40**
5	+0.6	14	1.85
6	−0.8	14	2.90*
7	−1.7	14	3.56**
8	−1.2	14	4.44****
9	−0.5	14	<1.00
10	−0.7	14	1.95
11	−0.9	14	2.89*
12	+0.7	14	3.66**

* $p < .02$.
** $p < .005$.
*** $p < .025$.
**** $p < .001$.

TABLE 5

COMPARABILITY OF EXPERIMENTAL AND CONTROL
SUBJECTS IN INITIAL CONSERVATISM AND AGE

	Males		Females	
	M	N	M	N
Subject	Mean Initial Overall Conservatism			
Experimental	66.9	82[a]	65.6	82[a]
Control	68.3	24	64.6	27
t	0.41		0.34	
	Mean Age			
Experimental	20.7	82[b]	20.3	84
Control	21.0	24	20.7	27
t	0.41		0.67	

[a] Initial overall conservatism scores were available for 164 of the experimental subjects. See Footnote 2 in text.
[b] One subject forgot to list his age, and one group contained five rather than six subjects.

postdiscussion individual decisions exhibit a strong move toward greater risk taking when compared with prediscussion individual decisions arrived at by the same persons, and do so for both sexes. The group discussion process, in other words, seems to have an effect on private attitudes (postdiscussion individual decisions) that is just as significant as its effect on publicly expressed views (unanimous group decisions).

Once again we may inquire about the extent to which the risky shift is consistent from group to group. Several consistency tests have been carried out, all yielding highly similar results. As an example, suppose we define a group as exhibiting a shift in the risky direction from prediscussion to postdiscussion individual decisions if the difference score for its total score, as defined in this section, is a negative one. Fourteen out of 14 male groups and 12 out of 14 female groups are found to shift in the risky direction, both results being quite significant by a sign test. Such a finding demonstrates, therefore, that the risky shift pheomenon is quite consistent across groups in regard to covert acceptance as well as overt compliance.

Control Subjects

To insure that the move toward greater risk taking just described actually is a result of the group discussion process, we must turn to the findings for the control subjects. The comparability of control and experimental subjects is indicated in Table 5. We note that, in the case both of males and females, the experimental and control subjects have approximately the same initial total conservatism scores, and also are approximately the same in age.[6] Item-by-item comparisons of experimental and control subjects of each sex on initial conservatism scores also were carried out and show that controls and experimentals within sex obtain highly similar scores.

In Tables 6 and 7 we present, for male and female control subjects, respectively, the significance of the difference between decisions made during the first and the second sessions. It will be recalled that one week intervened between these two sessions, and that instructions for the second session requested the subjects not to try simply to remember what they had marked before, but to reconsider their decisions. It is evident that the total conservatism score shows no shift from first to second session for either sex. Turning to the separate tests carried out on each item, we find that none of the 12 items shows a significant shift for the males, and only 1 of the 12 items shows a significant shift for the females. When no group discussion and

[6] It might also be mentioned that, in confirmation of earlier findings (Wallach & Kogan, 1959, 1961), there is no sex difference in initial total conservatism scores for either the experimental or the control subjects.

TABLE 6

SIGNIFICANCE OF CONSERVATISM DIFFERENCE BETWEEN
FIRST AND SECOND DECISIONS BY MALE
CONTROL SUBJECTS

Item	Mean difference	Number of subjects	t[a]
All combined	+1.5	24	<1.00
1	+0.4	24	<1.00
2	−0.3	24	<1.00
3	+0.3	24	<1.00
4	+0.8	24	2.00
5	−0.4	24	1.06
6	0.0	24	<1.00
7	+0.4	24	1.03
8	+0.5	24	1.63
9	−0.1	24	<1.00
10	+0.1	24	<1.00
11	+0.1	24	<1.00
12	−0.4	24	1.42

[a] All t values *ns*.

TABLE 7

SIGNIFICANCE OF CONSERVATISM DIFFERENCE BETWEEN FIRST AND SECOND DECISIONS BY FEMALE CONTROL SUBJECTS

Item	Mean difference	Number of subjects	t
All combined	−2.2	27	1.26
1	−0.4	27	<1.00
2	−0.2	27	<1.00
3	−1.0	27	2.61*
4	−0.4	27	1.12
5	−0.3	27	<1.00
6	−0.2	27	<1.00
7	0.0	27	<1.00
8	0.0	27	<1.00
9	+0.2	27	<1.00
10	+0.3	27	1.03
11	−0.3	27	<1.00
12	+0.1	27	<1.00

* $p < .02$.

achievement of group consensus intervenes, then, there is no systematic shift toward to the findings for the control subjects. The greater risk taking or greater conservatism, and this despite instructions that encourage shifts by emphasizing that we are not interested in the subjects' memories.

The data for the control subjects also provide us with an opportunity for determining the test-retest reliability of the conservatism-risk instrument, with one week intervening and under instructions that encourage change rather than constancy. For the 24 male subjects, the product-moment correlation coefficient between total conservatism scores in the first and second sessions is .78. For the 27 female subjects, the same correlation coefficient is .82. Test-retest reliability of the instrument, therefore, is quite high.

Prediscussion Risk Taking and Influence in the Group

Our data concerning perceived influence within the group consisted in each individual's ranking of all group members, including himself, in terms of how much each influenced the group's decisions. A first question to ask of these influence rankings is: How consistent are they from member to member within a group? To determine the degree of agreement among a group's members in their rankings of one another for influence, Kendall's coefficient of concordance (Siegel, 1956, pp. 229–238) was applied to each group's influence rankings. If the members of a group agree

TABLE 8

DEGREE OF AGREEMENT AMONG GROUP MEMBERS IN RANKINGS OF ONE ANOTHER FOR INFLUENCE[a]

Males Group	N	W	Females Group	N	W
1	6	.64**	1	6	.85**
2	6	.55**	2	6	.61**
3	6	.74**	3	6	.31
4	6	.72**	4	6	.79**
5	6	.70**	5	6	.47**
6	6	.50**	6	6	.67**
7	5	.56*	7	6	.13
8	6	.50**	8	6	.59**
9	6	.62**	9	6	.59**
10	6	.66**	10	6	.69**
11	6	.66**	11	6	.83**
12	6	.55**	12	6	.80**
13	6	.54**	13	6	.70**
14	6	.73**	14	6	.30

[a] Kendall's coefficient of concordance.
* $p < .05$.
** $p < .01$.

regarding who among themselves are more influential and who less so, then W will be significantly large. Table 8 presents the results of these tests for all 28 groups. It is evident that agreement in influence rankings is quite high: the degree of agreement is significant for all 14 of the male groups, and for 11 of the 14 female groups.

Given this high agreement among group members in their rankings of one another for influence, an approximate overall estimate

TABLE 9

PRODUCT-MOMENT CORRELATIONS AMONG INITIAL CONSERVATISM, INFLUENCE, AND POPULARITY[a]

	Males ($N = 82$)[b] r	Females ($N = 82$)[b] r
Initial overall risk taking and influence	.32****	.22*
Initial overall risk taking and popularity	.15	−.04
Influence and popularity	.72*****	.54*****
Initial overall risk taking and influence, popularity held constant[c]	.30***	.28**

[a] Small score values signify greater risk taking, greater influence, and greater popularity.
[b] While all influence and popularity scores are based on the 167 subjects in the experimental condition, the correlations are based on the 164 of those subjects for whom initial overall risk taking scores were available.
[c] Partial correlation coefficients.
* $p < .05$.
** $p < .02$.
*** $p < .01$.
**** $p < .005$.
***** $p < .001$.

of degree of influence for a given group member was obtained by averaging the influence ranks that had been assigned to that person by all members of the group (including that person). The lower the average, the greater that subject's perceived influence (i.e., the higher the assigned influence ranks for that person). These average influence scores for the subjects of each sex were correlated with the initial total conservatism scores obtained by the same subjects. The resulting product-moment correlation coefficients are shown in Table 9. They are significant beyond the .005 and .05 levels for the 82 males and the 82 females, respectively: persons higher in initial risk taking are rated as having more influence on the group decisions.

Average popularity scores for each group member were constructed by averaging the popularity rankings assigned by all the other members of the group. We note in Table 9 that there emerges a very strong relationship between this average popularity score and the average influence score for both the male and the female group members: persons rated high in influence also tend to be rated high in popularity. This general relationship has, of course, been known for some time (see, e.g., Back, 1951; Horowitz, Lyons, & Perlmutter, 1951; Tagiuri & Kogan, 1960), so that our obtaining it here increases our confidence in the respective measures being used to assess influence and popularity. It is further evident in Table 9, however, that degree of initial risk taking is *not* related to degree of popularity within the group for either sex.

Finally, we also find from Table 9 that risk taking and influence are significantly related for each sex when popularity ratings are held constant. The partial correlation coefficients are significant beyond the .01 and .02 levels for the males and females, respectively. It is evident, therefore, that the relationships obtained for both sexes between degree of initial risk taking and degree of influence on group decisions are not dependent upon members' popularity.

Maintenance of the Risky Shift over a Subsequent Period of Time

An interesting further question concerns the extent to which the shift toward greater risk taking, which we have found to result from group discussion, is maintained over a subsequent period of time. We were able to gather evidence on this point for males but not for females. In the case of the former, but not in the case of the latter, a random sample of subjects from the original groups could be obtained for further study. The 22 males who were available for further work were approximately evenly distributed among the 14 original male groups. After a time interval of roughly 2–6 weeks had elapsed since the group session, these subjects individually were given the conservatism-risk questionnaire a third time, as described in the section on procedure.

The comparability of the random male subsample of 22 to the original male experimental condition sample of 82 is evident from the following data on total conservatism scores. The mean prediscussion total conservatism score was 66.9 for the sample of 82, and also was 66.9 for the subsample of 22. The mean postdiscussion total conservatism score, in turn, was 56.6 for the whole sample and 56.2 for the subsample. The t test of the difference scores had yielded a t significant beyond the .001 level ($t = 9.12$) for the whole sample, and it also yielded a t significant beyond the .001 level ($t = 4.70$) for the subsample.

Turning now to the total conservatism scores obtained by this subsample when they took the questionnaire again 2–6 weeks after the group discussion (call these scores the "post-postdiscussion" individual decisions), the mean score is 54.6. The mean of the difference scores obtained by subtracting each subject's prediscussion total conservatism score from his post-postdiscussion total conservatism score is -12.3, with a t test of these difference scores yielding a t value of 4.92 ($p < .001$), hence indicating a risky shift from the prediscussion individual decisions to the post-postdiscussion individual decisions. The mean of the difference scores obtained, in turn, by subtracting each subject's postdiscussion total conservatism score from his post-postdiscussion total conservatism score is only -1.6, and a t test of these difference scores is not significant, hence indicating no further change from the postdiscussion individual decisions to the post-

postdiscussion individual decisions. Item-by-item analyses tell the same story: the only significant item shifts are risky ones, and they are as strong from prediscussion to post-postdiscussion sessions as they are from prediscussion to postdiscussion sessions.

In sum, the data available on the point indicate that the shift in the risky direction found to occur as a result of the group discussion process is maintained over a subsequent period of time.

Discussion and Conclusions

The following conclusions may be drawn from the preceding evidence:

1. Unanimous group decisions concerning matters of risk show a shift toward greater risk taking when compared with prediscussion individual decisions made by the same persons and concerning the same matters. This holds for both sexes.

2. Postdiscussion individual decisions that follow unanimous group decisions exhibit the same kind of shift toward greater risk taking as appears in the group decisions. This is the case for both sexes. Covert acceptance as well as overt compliance, thus, are affected in the same manner by the discussion process.

3. This shift toward greater risk taking as a result of the discussion process is still maintained when 2–6 weeks have elapsed since the discussion occurred. Evidence on this point was available only for males.

4. No shift in risk taking level of individual decisions occurs over time in the absence of the discussion process. This holds for both sexes.

5. There is a positive relationship between degree of risk taking in prediscussion individual decisions and the extent to which group members are perceived by one another as influencing group decisions. This relationship is specific to judgments of influence, in that it obtains when judgments of popularity are held constant, and also no relationship is found between prediscussion individual risk taking and the extent to which group members are judged to be popular. These statements all hold for both sexes.

The present study indicates, then, that group interaction and achievement of consensus concerning decisions on matters of risk eventuate in a willingness to make decisions that are more risky than those that would be made in the absence of such interaction. Furthermore, although initial ascribed status levels of the group members are equal, it is found that persons with stronger individual risk taking proclivities tend to become more influential in the group than persons who are more conservative. Two alternative interpretations of these findings can be suggested; one more group centered, the other more person centered: It is possible that there is at work in these groups a process of diffusion or spreading of responsibility as a result of knowing that one's decisions are being made jointly with others rather than alone. Increased willingness to take risk would eventuate from this decreased feeling of personal responsibility. That initial risk taking and judged influence within the group are positively related could well occur as a consequence of this process, since one of its effects would be for the views of high risk takers to be given more weight by the rest of the group. Alternatively, the fact that high risk takers exert more influence may be a cause of the group's movement toward greater risk taking. It is possible that high risk takers are also more likely to take the initiative in social situations. Of course, these two interpretations are not necessarily mutually exclusive. Both of them may contribute to the group effect.

That females as well as males show the same change toward greater risk taking as a result of the group interaction condition, and that the samples of both sexes were liberal arts university students, renders it unlikely that the results can be explained on the basis of reinforcement by others of one's expectation as to whether one's appropriate role is to be more or less of a risk taker. We noted earlier that Stoner (1961) found a move toward greater risk taking in group as compared to individual decision making by male graduate students of industrial management, and we pointed out that this result might be accounted for in terms of the professional role that they had assigned themselves by becoming graduate students in a business school. Presence of peers might be expected to increase the salience of their business manager role, and a greater willingness to take risks in decision making might well be perceived as one of the attributes of that role. Such a role expectation interpretation is ruled out for the present study, however, through our use of liberal arts students as subjects. In addition, the possibility of explaining the results in terms of males' perceiving their appropriate role as one of willingness to be bold and daring, and being reinforced in this view by interaction with other like-minded males, is ruled out by the present study's obtaining the same results for females as for males. This outcome would not be expected if the findings depended on sex linked role expectations as to whether one should be more risky or more conservative. This outcome also, of course, rules out interpretation in terms of any possible sex linked differences in major fields of study.

That the group induced move toward greater risk taking in individual decisions is still maintained 2–6 weeks after the discussion, provides evidence, incidentally, which supports Lewin's (1947) view that "group carried" attitudinal changes maintain themselves (see also Pelz, 1958).

REFERENCES

ATTHOWE, J. M., JR. Interpersonal decision making: The resolution of a dyadic conflict. *J. abnorm. soc. Psychol.,* 1961, 62, 114–119.

BACK, K. W. Influence through social communication. *J. abnorm. soc. Psychol.,* 1951, 46, 9–23.

BROWN, R. W. Mass phenomena. In G. Lindzey (Ed.), *Handbook of social psychology.* Vol. 2. *Special fields and applications.* Cambridge, Mass.: Addison-Wesley, 1954. Pp. 833–876.

CARTWRIGHT, D., & ZANDER, A. (Eds.) *Group dynamics.* (2nd ed.) Evanston, Ill.: Row, Peterson, 1960.

FESTINGER, L. An analysis of compliant behavior. In M. Sherif & M. O. Wilson (Eds.), *Group relations at the crossroads.* New York: Harper, 1953. Pp. 232–255.

HOROWITZ, M. W., LYONS, J., & PERLMUTTER, H. V. Induction of forces in discussion groups. *Hum. Relat.,* 1951, 4, 57–76.

HUNT, E. B., & ROWE, R. R. Group and individual economic decision making in risk conditions. In D. W. Taylor (Ed.), *Experiments on decision making and other studies.* Arlington, Va.: Armed Services Technical Information Agency, 1960. Pp. 21–25. (Technical Report No. 6, AD 253952)

KELLEY, H. H., & THIBAUT, J. W. Experimental studies of group problem solving and process. In G. Lindzey (Ed.), *Handbook of social psychology.* Vol. 2. *Special fields and applications.* Cambridge, Mass.: Addison-Wesley, 1954. Pp. 735–785.

KOGAN, N., & WALLACH, M. A. The effect of anxiety on relations between subjective age and caution in an older sample. In P. H. Hoch & J. Zubin (Eds.), *Psychopathology of aging.* New York: Grune & Stratton, 1961. Pp. 123–135.

KOMAROVSKY, MIRRA. Functional analysis of sex roles. *Amer. sociol. Rev.,* 1950, 15, 508–516.

LEWIN, K. Frontiers in group dynamics. *Hum. Relat.,* 1947, 1, 2–38.

LONERGAN, B. G., & MCCLINTOCK, C. G. Effects of group membership on risk-taking behavior. *Psychol. Rep.,* 1961, 8, 447–455.

MCNEMAR, Q. *Psychological statistics.* (Rev. ed.) New York: Wiley, 1955.

MILNER, ESTHER. Effects of sex role and social status on the early adolescent personality. *Genet. psychol. Monogr.,* 1949, 40, 231–325.

OSBORN, A. F. *Applied imagination.* New York: Scribner, 1957.

PELZ, EDITH B. Some factors in "group decision." In Eleanor E. Maccoby, T. M. Newcomb, & E. L. Hartley (Eds.), *Readings in social psychology.* (3rd ed.) New York: Holt, 1958. Pp. 212–219.

SCHACHTER, S. Deviation, rejection, and communication. *J. abnorm. soc. Psychol.,* 1951, 46, 190–207.

SIEGEL, S. *Nonparametric statistics for the behavioral sciences.* New York: McGraw-Hill, 1956.

STONER, J. A. F. A comparison of individual and group decisions involving risk. Unpublished master's thesis, Massachusetts Institute of Technology, School of Industrial Management, 1961.

TAGIURI, R., & KOGAN, N. Personal preference and the attribution of influence in small groups. *J. Pers.,* 1960, 28, 257–265.

TAYLOR, D. W., BERRY, P. C., & BLOCK, C. H. Does group participation when using brainstorming facilitate or inhibit creative thinking? *Admin. sci. Quart.,* 1958, 3, 23–47.

THIBAUT, J. W., & KELLEY, H. H. *The social psychology of groups.* New York: Wiley, 1959.

TURNER, R. H., & KILLIAN, L. M. (Eds.) *Collective behavior.* Englewood Cliffs, N. J.: Prentice-Hall, 1957.

WALLACH, M. A., & CARON, A. J. Attribute criteriality and sex-linked conservatism as determinants of psychological similarity. *J. abnorm. soc. Psychol.,* 1959, 59, 43–50.

WALLACH, M. A., & KOGAN, N. Sex differences and judgment processes. *J. Pers.,* 1959, 27, 555–564.

WALLACH, M .A., & KOGAN, N. Aspects of judgment and decision making: Interrelationships and changes with age. *Behav. Sci.,* 1961, 6, 23–36.

WHYTE, W. H., JR. *The organization man.* New York: Simon & Schuster, 1956.

(Received October 17, 1961)

GROUP SHIFT TO CAUTION AT THE RACE TRACK[1]

CLARK McCAULEY, CHRISTOPHER L. STITT

KATHRYN WOODS, AND DIANA LIPTON

Bryn Mawr College

> Group and individual riskiness were compared on $2 "win" bets at the race track. Using the standard pretest-posttest risk-shift design, group discussion to unanimous decision was found to produce a cautious shift in group bets.

The "risky shift" phenomenon was originally reported by Stoner (1961). Using a set of 12 hypothetical choice-dilemma problems devised by Kogan and Wallach, Stoner showed that the riskiness of group decisions was greater than the riskiness of individual decisions made by group members before discussion. The risky shift attracted immediate attention, and a great deal of research in social psychology was directed at extending and understanding Stoner's result.

It is reasonable to suppose that early interest in the risky shift was heightened by the assumption that a consistent difference between group and individual decisions would have important *practical* implications (Pruitt, 1971). After all, ours is a society in which committees and groups frequently make decisions by concensus or vote after group discussion. Unfortunately for hope of practical significance, groups were not consistently more risky than individuals. Groups were found to shift toward risk on some problems and toward caution on other problems (Stoner, 1968). The effects of group discussion are therefore better described as group "risk shifts" rather than as a group "risky shift." Without a simple and consistent difference between group and individual riskiness, hopes for practical application faded.

For no necessary reason, interest in the generality of risk shifts appears to have diminished along with the prospect of practical implications. There had been early efforts to demonstrate the generality of risk shifts with problems other than choice-dilemma problems (Wallach *et al.,* 1964; Bem *et al.,* 1965; Pruitt & Teger, 1969). However, most recent research has concentrated on explaining the risk shifts, especially choice-dilemma shifts, already reliably demonstrated. With reduced hope of practical implications, researchers focused on a *theoretical* understanding of laboratory risk shifts (Pruitt, 1971).

Recently, Cartwright (1971) has noted a number of difficulties in generalizing risk shift results beyond the laboratory: The laboratory setting does not simulate any natural setting; the choice-dilemma problems are hypothetical and projective; and the laboratory groups are *ad hoc.* Cartwright believes the answer to these problems is success in the theoretical emphasis already remarked upon. "If the findings can be given theoretical meaning, then they can be applied to any empirical situation that satisfied the requirements specified by the theory" (Cartwright, 1971).

More successful theory is one possible approach to the problems of generalizability. We believe, however, that the generalizability of group risk shifts can and should be investigated more directly, by experimental studies in field settings. Moreover, the most interesting and basic question concerns the relative riskiness of group and individual decisions in the world outside the laboratory. Theoretical understanding of laboratory risk shifts can hardly provide—by itself—more than a part of the answer to this question.

In an effort to extend the comparison of group and individual risk taking to a more natural setting, we designed an experiment to test for group risk shifts with race track bets. To our knowledge, this is the first field experiment in the risk shift literature; the over-

---

[1] This study was supported by a small Grant made by Bryn Mawr College from NSF Institutional Grant Funds.

whelming majority of risk shift studies have used the original Kogan and Wallach problems or additional problems of the same format. Both risky and cautious group shifts have been obtained on these problems. Risky shifts have been obtained with choices among aptitude test items (Wallach et al., 1964) and with choices among tasks with—supposedly—different probabilities of noxious physical effects (Bem et al., 1965). Both risky shifts (Pruitt & Teger, 1969) and cautious shifts (Zajonc et al., 1968) have been found with explicit gambling choices. It is obvious from these disparate laboratory results that we can have no very clear prediction of the direction of group shift with race track bets.

Still, the choices in the Pruitt and Teger (1969) study were probably most like choices with race track bets. The Pruitt and Teger study required choice among alternative bets where increasing probability of success was associated with decreasing amount to win so as to make Expected Value of all alternatives equal to zero. Choice among such alternatives is close to the situation at the race track, where long shots pay more and favorites pay less such that Expected Value of bets is close to zero, being less than zero by the margin of the track's percentage cut. On the basis of similarities with the Teger and Pruitt problems, our best prediction was for a group risky shift on race track bets.

METHOD

The experiment assessed the effect of group discussion on riskiness of $2 win bets at the racetrack. Riskiness of a bet was measured as the pari-mutuel odds for that bet, with small odds indicating caution and large odds indicating risk. The experimental design was the standard risk-shift paradigm, where shift between pretest riskiness and posttest riskiness is calculated for both groups and individuals. Groups were required to reach unanimous decision on the posttest; individuals could bet the Experimenter's money on any horse, without restriction.

Subjects. The subjects were 88 male bettors at Philadelphia's Liberty Bell Park during the winter, thoroughbred season. The subjects were obtained on two consecutive Saturday afternoons from both levels of the General Admission or grandstand area.

No formal random sampling procedure was followed, but instead every male leaving a $2 Win window within the vicinity of the experimenters at a time when the experimenters were not already engaged in an interview was contacted. It is the authors' impression that this procedure produced a sample in which four types of bettor were underrepresented: (1) "professional" horse players who did not want to discuss their bets; (2) people with hearing deficiencies who could not converse under the noisy conditions; (3) foreigners with whom there was a language problem; and (4) people who refused to participate in a psychological experiment. With the above exceptions the final sample was felt to be reasonably representative of the General Admission crowd at Liberty Bell Park.

Measure of risk. The measure of risk employed in this study was the odds on the pari-mutuel "tote" board at the time a decision was made. The pari-mutuel system employed at the race track requires explanation. All the money bet on the horses of a given race is pooled and a percentage known as the "take" is deducted as revenue for the track and for state and local government. The holders of the winning tickets receive the remainder.

The odds on any horse shown on the totalizator at the track are computed by subtracting the sum bet on the horse from the pool after take and dividing the remainder by the sum bet on the horse. Therefore, for each dollar bet the amount actually returned is the odds plus one, the one being the dollar bet. For instance, "tote" board odds of 5-1 means that five times as much money was bet on all other horses as was bet on the horse concerned. If this particular horse should win, the payoff on a $2 Win ticket would be $12 ($10 plus the original $2 bet).

When betting is begun on a race, experts' opinions of the true odds on each horse are shown and the totalizator keeps the bettors informed, at about 90-sec intervals, until the race starts, as to the correct odds calculated approximately from the actual money bet.

The pari-mutuel odds were used as the measure of risk because these odds are, on the average, correct reflections of a horse's chances of winning (Griffith, 1949).

Procedure. Four experimenters (*Es*) were stationed in the vicinity of the "Sellers" windows during the 25-min betting interval between races. Each *E* approached men leaving a $2 window with the following introduction:

"Excuse me, sir. This is a psychology experiment. Did you just bet on more than one horse?"

It is interesting to note that the four general classes of people discussed above refused to answer this introductory question. The *Es* proceeded with those bettors who acknowledged wagering on only one horse by saying:

"We will buy you a $2 Win ticket on the horse of your choice if you will be in our experiment. OK?"

If the bettor agreed to participate or asked for more information, the *E* explained:

"Here's how the experiment works. We will give you a $2 Win ticket if: First, you will tell us what horse you just bet on with your own money; and second, if you will get together with two other men and decide on one horse for all of you to bet on. All three of you have to agree to bet on the same horse. Will you be in the experiment?"

After obtaining the bettor's final willingness to participate, the *E* recorded the number of the horse the subject had just wagered on and the pari-mutuel odds for that horse (pretest riskiness). Then the E escorted the subject to a predetermined area of the grandstand and waited until four subjects had been obtained.

By blindly pulling one of four numbered cards from his pocket, an E (CM) randomly selected one of the four subjects for the individual treatment condition. The three remaining subjects were placed in the group treatment condition.

Individual treatment. E (CS) told the individual:

"We can only have three men in each group. So you can decide what horse to bet on all by yourself. Remember, you have to pick a horse to win. You have about three minutes to decide and tell me your choice."

Upon receiving the subject's choice the E recorded the horse's number and the pari-mutuel odds for that horse (individual posttest riskiness) while another E purchased the $2 Win ticket for the subject.

Group treatment. E (CM) told the group:

"Remember you all have to agree to bet on the same horse. Remember you have to pick a horse to win. You have about three minutes to decide and tell me your choice."

After the group reached a unanimous decision, the E recorded the number of the horse on which the group had decided and the pari-mutuel odds for that horse (group posttest riskiness) while another E purchased a $2 Win ticket for each of the three subjects.

The above procedure was followed twice before races two through six and once before race seven on each of two consecutive Saturday afternoons (January 15 and 22, 1972).

Results

Initial risk in Group and Individual conditions. Pretest riskiness for each individual was taken to be the odds for the horse bet on by the individual with his own money. Initial riskiness of each group was taken to be the average of the odds for the three horses bet on by group members with their own money.

Pretest odds of both groups and individuals were skewed toward larger odds, as might be expected at a pari-mutuel track where small odds reflect a popular bet and large odds reflect an unpopular bet. Therefore the median odds is most representative of the riskiness of groups and individuals in the experiment. The median pretest odds for 22 groups was 5.4; for 22 individuals it was 5.0. These two medians do not differ significantly or even appreciably. Random assignment of Ss to conditions succeeded in producing comparable levels of initial riskiness for groups and individuals in the experiment.

Risk shifts. Risk shifts were measured as change from pretest odds to posttest odds. For a group, risk shift was group pretest odds (group average) *minus* group unanimous decision odds. For an individual, risk shift was simply pretest odds *minus* posttest odds. Thus, positive shift scores are shifts to smaller odds (cautious shifts) and negative shift scores are shifts to larger odds (risky shifts). Shift scores for Group and Individual conditions are presented in Table 1, in terms of the number of cautious shifts, zero shifts, and risky shifts in each condition. The χ^2 associated with Table 1 is 12.4 ($p < .01$), indicating that group and individual shifts differed in this experiment. By inspection of Table 1, it is clear that most individuals (13 of 22) did not shift in riskiness; in general they bet no differently with the Experimenter's money than with their own. On the other hand, most groups (16 of 22) shifted toward caution. Comparison of the Group and Individual conditions indicates that group discussion and unanimous decision produced a group shift toward caution.

Discussion

The literature of the group risk-shift phenomenon is a literature of laboratory experiments. We argue that further laboratory studies aimed at understanding laboratory risk shifts can and should be complemented by field studies of group-individual differences in risk taking. The present experiment demonstrates the possibility of field studies at the race track. It also demonstrates the necessity of field studies: The laboratory betting study (Pruitt and Teger, 1969) most like the present study found a group risk shift, whereas the present study found a group

TABLE 1
GROUP AND INDIVIDUAL SHIFTS IN RISKINESS OF RACETRACK BETS

Condition	Cautious shifts	Zero shifts	Risky shifts
Group	16	1	5
Individual	6	13	3

cautious shift. Clearly, the generalizability of laboratory risk-shift studies requires further examination.

The group cautious shift at the race track is difficult to interpret without replication and additional study; it raises questions rather than answering any. Is group discussion alone sufficient to produce the race track shift, as is the case with laboratory group shifts (Wallach and Kogan, 1965)? Or might not individuals shift cautious in the same proportion as groups if only individuals were required to change from their pretest bets? After all, the requirement for unanimity is not only the occasion for group discussion; it is also a requirement for change. Is this shift an extremity shift (Moscovici and Zavalloni, 1969), from mild caution to stronger caution? This last question amounts to asking whether the median odds of pretest bets (5.4 to 1 for groups in this experiment) were subjectively risky or cautious. If these pretest odds were seen as cautious, then it is fair to conceptualize the group cautious shift as a shift to increased extremity. Which among the many differences (e.g., subjects, setting, bet choices) between this race track study and the Pruitt and Teger laboratory betting study are responsible for the difference in direction of group shift?

These are a sample of the questions that can be raised in connection with the shift that is, to our knowledge, the first group shift measured in a field experiment. At a purely empirical level, the cautious shift at the track is inconsistent with the risky shift obtained in a similar experiment (Pruitt and Teger, 1969) in the laboratory. This inconsistency suggests that results of laboratory risk experiments are not generalizable outside the laboratory. And at the theoretical level, the cautious shift is inconsistent with the whole set of value theories described by Pruitt (1971) as frontrunners in the race to explain group risk shifts. All versions of value theory share the assumption that "groups shift in a direction toward which most members of the group are already attracted as individuals" (Pruitt, 1971). When the individuals are race track bettors, who have even paid an entrance fee for the opportunity to take risks, it is reasonable to assume that risk is valued more than caution. In which case, all of the value theories predict a risky shift, rather than the cautious shift actually found. This inconsistency between theory and result suggests that theories of laboratory risk shifts are not generalizable outside the laboratory either.

The risk-shift literature is ingrown and laboratory-bound, with elaborate theories competing to explain group shifts of unknown importance outside the laboratory. Group cautious shift at the track represents a first indication that significant group risk shifts occur outside the laboratory. Unfortunately, it appears that shifts outside the laboratory may not be consistent with results and theory from laboratory experiments.

REFERENCES

BEM, D. J., WALLACH, M. A., & KOGAN, N. Group decision making under risk of aversive consequences. *Journal of Personality and Social Psychology,* 1965, **1,** 453–460.

CARTWRIGHT, D. Risk taking by individuals and groups: An assessment of research employing choice dilemmas. *Journal of Personality and Social Psychology,* 1971, **20,** 361–378.

GRIFFITH, R. M. Odds adjustments by American horse-race bettors. *American Journal of Psychology,* 1949, **62,** 290–294.

MOSCOVICI, S., & ZAVALLONI, M. The group as a polarizer of attitudes. *Journal of Personality and Social Psychology,* 1969, **12,** 125–135.

PRUITT, D. G. Choice shifts in group discussion: An introductory review. *Journal of Personality and Social Psychology,* 1971, **20,** 339–360.

PRUITT, D. G., & TEGER, A. I. The risky shift in group betting. *Journal of Experimental Social Psychology,* 1969, **5,** 115–126.

STONER, J. A. F. A comparison of individual and group decisions involving risk. Unpublished master's thesis, Massachusetts Institute of Technology, Sloan School of Management, 1961.

STONER, J. A. F. Risky and cautious shifts in group decisions: The influence of widely held values. *Journal of Experimental Social Psychology,* 1968, **4,** 442–459.

WALLACH, M. A., & KOGAN, N. The roles of information, discussion, and consensus in group risk taking. *Journal of Experimental Social Psychology,* 1965, **1,** 1–19.

WALLACH, M. A., KOGAN, N., & BEM, D. J. Diffusion of responsibility and level of risk taking in groups. *Journal of Abnormal and Social Psychology,* 1964, **68,** 263–274.

ZAJONC, R. B., WOLOSIN, R. J., WOLOSIN, R. A., & SHERMAN, S. J. Individual and group risk taking in a two-choice situation. *Journal of Experimental Social Psychology,* 1968, **4,** 89–106.

(Received July 17, 1972)

THE STUDIES COMPARED

The Measurement of Risk

The Choice-Dilemmas Questionnaire used in the first study has been the stimulus for much of the work in this research area since its introduction in the article reproduced here and in the Kogan and Wallach book (1964). It is an easily administered paper-and-pencil measure, simple to score and apparently readily interpreted. As cited in the article, it has high test-retest reliability, and its use permits comparison between studies. Researchers often set out to replicate an intriguing (or questionable) finding, but in the process of "replication," they are tempted to make various modifications in procedure. These changes sometimes restrict the comparisons that can be made, especially in the event of "failure to replicate." The consistent use of a clearly structured instrument is therefore a strong asset in such comparisons. But allegiance to a single instrument can be overdone. As was pointed out in Chapter 1, a given finding is considerably strengthened by demonstration in a variety of settings by a variety of methods. It has been argued with regard to the risky shift that rigid acceptance of the Choice-Dilemmas Questionnaire led investigators into theoretical controversies concerning the risky shift before its dependency on the measurement instrument was fully explored.

Instructional Set. A number of problems have emerged through closer scrutiny of the instrument. As we review these problems here, keep in mind that they are the products of hindsight—a fact that should be taken into account in applying them to the original use of the Choice-Dilemmas Questionnaire in the Wallach, Kogan, and Bem study. For example, the instructions for expressing both individual and group decisions on the Choice-Dilemmas Questionnaire take quite specific form. The subject is asked to pick the *lowest* probability of success that he or she would consider acceptable for the hypothetical person to choose the potentially more rewarding alternative. The stated focus on the *lowest* probability of success may cue the respondent to the risk dimension under study and may invoke the cultural value of risk that some suggest is the mechanism underlying the risky shift. Some confirmation of this suggestion is gained from a study by Clark and Willems (1969), in which changing the instructions by omitting the word *lowest* from the probability choice failed to produce a risky shift after group discussion. This seemingly minor change had major effects on the subjects, indicating their considerable sensitivity to instructional wording and the potentially systematic effect of such changes. Your reaction to this finding may be a feeling that any effect depending on such minor variations in wording can't be important. It should be noted that the use of the word *lowest* was not just any change in wording; in an effort to make the task clearer, the instructions apparently suggested the direction of the shift rather than allowing subjects more freedom to change from their individual decisions if indeed they chose to change at all. In the second research selection, the instructions give no indication that risk per se is the research focus. Both individuals and groups are instructed merely to pick a horse for the next race.

Response Alternatives. The response formats of the Choice-Dilemmas Questionnaire and of racetrack betting differ in an important way. The Choice-Dilemmas Questionnaire, as might be expected from an instrument designed for research use, presents the subjects with success odds spaced at equal intervals—1, 3, 5, 7, and 9 out of 10 probabilities that the more desirable alternative will succeed. A subject who wishes to change his views can do so along an evenly ordered dimension. In contrast, the racetrack bettor is faced with odds that are not nearly so evenly spaced. In most races, there are a number of horses with low odds of 2:1, 3:2, and the like—in other words, spaced close together—and others with long odds spaced further apart, such as 7:1, 12:1, 20:1. Altering one's bet in a riskier direction may take, therefore, a much greater quantitative leap than is presented in the more orderly Choice-Dilemmas Questionnaire response format.

This issue is of importance, given the information in the racetrack study that the original odds averaged 5:1. Suppose the group discusses two horses that seem equally attractive (subjective probability) and whose odds are 5:3 (more cautious choice) and 8:1 (riskier choice). If something about group discussion suggests a need to change from the individual bets, the apparent shifts to caution may be as much a product of avoiding the greater quantitative leap to the 8:1 odds as seeking the conservative 5:3 choice. The fact that most individual bettors made second bets alone at the same 5:1 average odds supports the idea that something in the discussion stimulated change. The distribution of available bets may be what dictated the direction of the change.

Research Design

The basic research question underlying both studies is "Will groups make more risky decisions than individuals?" Both adhere to the standard within-subjects design, and this approach, strictly interpreted, addresses a slightly different question than the one posed above. The question addressed most directly by the within-subjects design is "Will individuals who have made a particular risk decision be moved to change it to a riskier one after group discussion?" The within-subjects design refers to the fact that the same subjects are asked about their reactions to the Choice-Dilemmas Questionnaire or about their bets twice, first individually and then as a collective choice after group discussion. The within-subjects design favored in most of the risky-shift research allows us to conclude only that shifts in choices have occurred, not necessarily that there are differences between individual and group decisions. The design does not permit us to conclude that discussion itself produced a risky shift but, rather, that discussion produced this shift in association with a pretest. To remedy this problem, the design needs a different kind of control group, one in which group discussion is not preceded by any individual decision making. The members of the control group used in most within-subject designs make two decisions without any intervening discussion; this kind of control group, therefore, does not remedy the problem. An alternative may be a between-subjects design, in which one set of people reach decisions alone and these decisions are compared with consensus decisions of a different group of subjects. In such a design, subjects are tested only once. In fact, two of the investigators involved in the research presented in this chapter combined to make a comparison of a between-subjects and a within-subjects design in a risky-shift study. McCauley, Kogan, and Teger (1971) found that without a pretest, group decisions were not significantly different from individual decisions. Whereas the usual control group in the within-subjects design showed that a pretest alone was not enough to produce the risky shift, this study revealed that group discussion alone was also not enough to produce the risky shift. Therefore, it may be concluded that indeed both pretest and discussion are necessary to produce the risky shift.

Analyses and Interpretation of Results

The results of the Wallach, Kogan, and Bem study proved to be reliable forerunners of ensuing research on the risky shift in that the shift found, although consistent across groups, was small in magnitude. The mean initial total Choice-Dilemmas Questionnaire score found in this study was 66.9, and the mean shift resulting from the group discussion was 10.3. Since the Choice-Dilemmas Questionnaire contains 12 items, the average shift per item expressed in odds was approximately from 6 in 10 to 5 in 10. The riskiness of the shift, while statistically significant, must then be interpreted in light of its being a shift of only 1 in 10 and a shift that takes place in the exact middle of the available range of odds. As Cartwright (1971) pointed out, an overall review of the literature of the shift to risk bears out this finding exactly. It is rare in social-psychological research that such a voluminous area of research should yield such quantitatively similar results. It is most likely the nature and stability of the Choice-Dilemmas Questionnaire that account for these results. That the shift is small and hardly at extremes of high risk casts doubt upon simple assertions that groups tend toward extremes.

Since the findings of this early study have been so faithfully reproduced in subsequent work with the Choice-Dilemmas Questionnaire, the characteristics of the instrument itself are of particular interest. The Wallach, Kogan, and Bem study also provided the first evidence with regard to differences among the Choice-Dilemmas Questionnaire items—differences that have also been found in subsequent studies. As shown in tables 1 and 2 of that article, the largest shifts to risk are found for items 1, 4, and 7. In subsequent studies, items 2 and 10 have been found to show little or no shift to risk; in this study, this same result was obtained, except that a shift was found for females and only in item 10. In other studies, items 5 and 12 show changes in the opposite direction—toward caution. In the Wallach et al. study, this was true only on item 12 and then only for males. In other work, these two items have turned out to show consistent shifts to caution. Note that the authors here saw these items as "impure" measures of the risk dimension and cited the items' low correlations with the overall scores. This is legitimate in a scale-construction procedure in which items that fail to correlate highly with total score are weeded out. Giving the benefits of hindsight due weight, one might reasonably question the wisdom of treating items that shift in the *opposite direction* as potential discards. It would seem that these are not poorly written or poorly conceptualized items that measure nothing relevant to risk; in fact, they are items that measure caution, a characteristic that most would place on what Wallach, Kogan, and Bem call the "conservatism-risk" dimension. Early recognition of this issue might have led more readily to a focus on the polarization effects of group discussion rather than to the persistent adherence to a shift-to-risk interpretation.

In tackling the problem of group-influenced decision shifts in a field setting, McCauley and his associates were confronted with a very different set of data-analysis problems. Instead of using an instrument like the Choice-Dilemmas Questionnaire, which is easily scored and analyzed, these researchers faced new issues in assessing risk levels. They elected to compare the mean of the odds on the horses that each group of three bettors had picked before being recruited into the study with the odds on the horse they jointly selected to bet on after discussion. If the odds on the second horse were higher than the mean of the odds picked earlier, then the group decision could have been said to have resulted in a shift to risk. Your main question in reading this study may well have been whether or not these researchers did obtain the shift to risk that had been found in the laboratory with the Choice-Dilemmas Questionnaire. Alternatively, you may have asked *how* McCauley and his associates got their outcome and wondered about other ways of looking at racetrack betting in terms of risk and caution. The careful consumer of research needs to ask these questions.

This latter question gave rise to a published exchange of views (Abelson, 1973; McCauley & Stitt, 1973). Some of you might wish to look up this debate for yourselves, since such exchanges make interesting reading and constitute tangible evidence of the workings of a cumulative social psychology. In essence, Abelson's questions about alternative ways of considering riskiness of racetrack bets rest on the description of the pretest odds as being "skewed toward larger odds." In such a skewed distribution of scores, the mean of the scores is always higher than the median, or middle, score. He argued that the use of group *means* rather than group *medians* to assess risks produced a seeming shift, where perhaps none had in fact occurred.

Abelson gave a numerical example of the effects of a skewed distribution on means and medians of a typical three-bettor group. For example, you may have three bettors who have chosen to bet on horses at odds of 2, 4, and 10 to 1, respectively. This is a skewed distribution because the odds of 2 and 4 are grouped close together and are far from the 10:1 odds of one of the bettors. The mean for this skewed distribution is 5.3, and the median is 4. In contrast, if the three bettors had picked horses at 2, 4, and 6 to 1 odds, there would not be a skewed distribution (the odds are evenly spaced), and the mean and median would both be 4. Back to the skewed distribution. In the course of discussing their initial bets and considering a joint bet for the next race, these three bettors may have decided to compromise on the middle bet among them and agreed to pick a horse at 4:1 odds. Using the data-analysis procedure of McCauley and associates, this postdiscussion choice would be compared with the 5.3 average odds of these three bettors' initial decision, and the researchers would conclude that a shift to caution had occurred. If there had not been a skewed distribution of bets among the three, the same convergence toward the middle bet analyzed the same way would have appeared to yield no shift at all (that is, the 4:1 joint bet compared to the average pretest odds of 4). Therefore, Abelson argued, it is an artifact of the nature of parimutuel bet distributions analyzed by group means instead of medians that may have produced the apparent shift to caution.

This issue is no mere statistical quibble, because it carries important implications for interpretation. If indeed the decision process in the group was to pick the middle odds, this reflects convergence rather than polarization on the risk dimension. McCauley and Stitt (1973), in their response to Abelson's criticism, indicated that they chose group means in order to make their results comparable to the major body of the risk-decision literature. They presented data to show that, by an analysis of group medians, the shift to caution, although smaller, was still significant. The issue of skewed distributions of odds has been noted as troublesome by other reviewers of the literature (Cartwright, 1971; Vinokur, 1969).

CONSUMER EVALUATION

Flashy Merchandising

The studies presented here and the research area of which they are a part are open to some of the accusations of flashy merchandising that were discussed in Chapter 1. Cartwright (1973) suggested that the label *risky shift* was part of the problem. Had Stoner said that his finding was concerned with group influence on decision making, the research might have taken a different path. The label *risky shift* is still in widespread use (and we have used it here with certain reservations). It serves as a handy label for research long since recognized as dealing with much more than risk. If indeed it is the polarization effects of group influence that are of interest, the evidence of these two studies will likely be of more enduring interest. As Abelson pointed out, the racetrack study is likely to engage interest because of the colorful character of racetracks. The absence of any theoretical explanation by McCauley and his associates contributes to the study's evanescence. Recall that one of the criteria suggested in Chapter 1 for assessing the contribution of a given study was to examine the degree to which the study is anchored in a body of research (both studies in this chapter belong to a research tradition) and the degree to which it suggests new lines of research (this aspect is lacking in the racetrack study).

Durability

The Wallach, Kogan, and Bem study has shown considerable durability over a 15-year period. Its finding of an enduring risky shift for both men and women on the Choice-Dilemmas Questionnaire has been sustained over time. Furthermore, it has proved durable as a stimulator of a large body of research, of which the racetrack study is a small extension. The broader assertion that a risky shift exists in the sense that groups always make riskier decisions than individuals has proven less durable.

The future of this research topic is uncertain. Two possibilities emerge. One is reflected in recent work by Myers and Lamm (1975), suggesting the reinterpretation of the risky shift as a phenomenon of group polarization of individual attitudes. The other possibility was suggested by Brown (1973), who speculated that just as there are situations in which people are moved to conform, so too there are others in which people are motivated to move away from the norm because they seek to be more than average on a desirable dimension (altruism) or less than average on an undesirable one (dishonesty).

7 ATTRIBUTION

CHAPTER OUTLINE

Attribution as Person Perception
Models of the Attribution Process
    Attribution as Naive Psychology
    Attribution as Information Processing
        Actor-Observer Differences
    Attribution as Social Science
Research on Attribution
    Attributions of Success and Failure
        Ability
        Effort
        Task Difficulty
        Luck
        Combined Factors
    Attribution of Responsibility
    Attribution in Actor and Observer Roles
Methods in the Study of Attribution
    Laboratory Experiments
    Surveys and Interviews
    Field Experiments
    Other Methods

Two Research Examples
    Product Description
    Consumer Checklist
    Michael D. Storms, *Videotape and the attribution process: Reversing actors' and observers' points of view.*
    Stephen G. West, Steven P. Gunn, and Paul Chernicky, *Ubiquitous Watergate: An attributional analysis.*
The Studies Compared
    Design Problems
    Standardization of Conditions
    Measurement Differences
Consumer Evaluation
    Cost-Quality Relation
    Flashy Merchandising

The following scene probably has some recognizable features for many of us. Your school has a big weekend coming up, and you've invited a special friend to visit. You've made plans, bought tickets, and are looking forward to the weekend. When, on Friday evening, you return to the dorm to get ready, you get word that your friend is not coming. The message reads, rather cryptically, "Sorry. Not coming. Many pressures. Will write." Naturally, you're upset. Why would your friend do such a thing? Why would a friend act this way?

Human beings spend a lot of time trying to understand one another's behavior. They try to know what caused it (what came before) and to predict what the other is likely to do in the future (what comes after). Social psychologists call this process of analyzing the behavior of others the *attribution process,* and its investigation is today an active frontier in research. So, as you sit in your room and try to figure out why your friend's not coming for the weekend, you make attributions about the causes and meaning of his or her behavior. Your conclusions may or may not be correct, but the attribution process itself is systematic and predictable, as the considerable evidence collected by social psychologists indicates.

This chapter presents current thinking on attribution theory. The two research selections focus on the differences in attributions made by participants and observers in the same situation. You and your friend are likely to attribute the behavior of canceling the weekend plans to quite different causes. As an observer, you are likely to attribute your friend's actions to his or her personal *disposition;* you assume that there is something about the person and his or her tendencies that causes the action to occur. Thinking about the change of plans, you may well decide that your friend is selfish, cold, and uninterested in you. Your friend, on the other hand, is likely to explain his or her actions in *environmental* terms—an unexpected assignment, a job-schedule change, or a parent's brief visit during a business trip.

You might think that the most important question in this situation is "Who's right?" But, as you may have found out yourself in discussing any action in the context of a relationship, that's not an easy question to answer. Furthermore, accuracy (determining who is right) often becomes less important as you examine the process whereby each of you makes attributions about the other and the consequences that these attributions have for future behavior. If you decide that the reasons for your date's actions are internal, you are also likely to think that these same reasons will apply in future situations; therefore, you may also decide not to invite such a cold, uncaring person to visit you again. But, since your friend sees these actions as situationally determined, he or she will probably find your behavior hard to understand. Your next action (a curt note? a nasty phone call?) poses an attributional problem for the other person. "Why did he (or she) do it? Why did he (or she) say that, write that?" your friend wonders. And the same process starts all over again. But this time you, now the actor, interpret your behavior situationally: your friend treated you badly. Your friend, now the observer, makes personal attributions: you are insensitive, demanding, and not ready for a "real" relationship. Before this scene becomes a two-act tragedy, let us consider what the social psychology of attribution has to offer to explain these circumstances.

ATTRIBUTION AS PERSON PERCEPTION

Attribution, insofar as it is concerned with inferences about the causes of behavior, can be applied in any sphere of psychology, and questions of causality are rooted in a long philosophical tradition. As Kelley (1973) says,

> attribution theory is related to a more general field that might be called psychological epistemology. This has to do with the processes by which man "knows" his world, and, more importantly, knows that he knows, that is, has a sense that his beliefs and judgments are veridical [p. 107].

Most social psychologists use the term *attribution* more restrictively to refer to attributions made about the meaning of other people's behavior. As such, attribution theory is rooted in research concerned with person perception. Person-perception research has established that your perceptions of other people have structure, stability, and meaning (Hastorf, Schneider, & Polefka, 1970). Instead of perceiving each event as separate, you structure your perceptions by combining cues into an overall impression. Furthermore, you assume stability by predicting that the behavior will occur again. Finally, to give meaning to these perceptions, you assume intent. Behaviors don't just happen by chance; people make them happen.

Clearly, this thinking process is a very complex and rapid one. An appreciation of its complexity may have been a factor in directing early research efforts to the products of person perception rather than to the process. This early direction was manifested in a concern with *accuracy*. What conditions make it possible for people to be accurate perceivers of others? Why are some people more accurate than others? Despite a persistent popular belief in the individual "who is accurate about people," there is little evidence that such an individual exists—that general judgment ability is a characteristic of some people (Cline, 1964). Furthermore, the research has been plagued by the problem of establishing an appropriate criterion of accuracy (Cronbach, 1955). If you want to know if someone has correctly estimated another's height, you can measure the person. What do you measure if you want to know whether someone has correctly perceived another as nervous, angry, or witty? As you might guess, researchers have tried many different ways to establish accuracy—from personality tests to expert judgment by clinicians and agreement among several judges. None of these criteria proved satisfactory. Thus, research activity shifted from the product of person perception (and therefore accuracy) to the process through which impression formation takes place. Attribution theory is a result of the effort to learn more about *how* people make their interpretation of the behavior of others meaningful.

The attribution process can be seen as involving three necessary steps (Shaver, 1975). First, there must be *observation* of an action. This perception provides the raw material on which attributions are based. If you are present to witness the act, you have the most direct information (but often you must rely on others to provide information). The second step in attribution involves a judgment of *intention*. Actions that are judged to be involuntary or trivial do not provide good material for attribution. Someone eating breakfast is engaged in relatively uninformative behavior, because it is difficult, without additional information, to give meaning to a single instance of habitual behavior. Actions judged to be intentional are rich in attributional potential. But judgment of intention is not sufficient to satisfy the observer's goal of understanding and predicting behavior. The final step involves making a *causal attribution* that provides a satisfying answer to the question "Why?" In our example of the canceled weekend plans, you do take note of the action (your friend's not coming), although the act is not directly observed by you but is relayed through a message. Next, you clearly regard the act as intentional. Finally, your attribution can take two forms: personal and environmental. You might decide that the decision not to come was a product of the situation, or you might attribute it to personal characteristics.

The attribution may come quickly or take hours of deliberation. Whatever amount of time the attribution process takes, the steps remain the same. At each stage, there is a binary choice that may terminate the process. For example, an action unobserved does not require further thought; similarly, an observed action judged unintentional calls for little explanation, and so does an intentional act clearly caused by circumstances. If the situation can be eliminated as a cause, then a personal disposition is made.

MODELS OF THE ATTRIBUTION PROCESS

The study of the attribution process has become within the last few years one of the most popular topics in social psychology. Notable in this development is the fact that theoretical propositions have preceded much of the empirical work. Hence, some of the current enthusiasm may stem from the appeal of testing orderly, theory-derived hypotheses. Social psychology at its best tries to account for both the individual's internal process and the external aspects of a situation, or circumstances. This task is inordinately difficult. Thus, the history of research in social psychology reflects pendulum swings between an interest in the influence of the individual and an interest in the influence of the situation. The interest in attribution processes represents a swing of the pendulum back toward concern with the internal states of the person and an alliance of social psychology with philosophy and cognitive psychology rather than with sociology and behaviorism. Three principal models of the attribution process have been presented, and an excellent summary and critique of them appears in Shaver (1975).

Attribution as Naive Psychology

The first model of the attribution process was proposed by Heider (1958) in his analysis of how the average (naive) person decides what causes a particular behavior. He postulated that two kinds of force, *personal* and *environmental,* are perceived to produce action. He saw personal force as composed of elements of *ability* and *trying;* in order to be seen as responsible for an action, an individual not only must have ability and knowledge but must be perceived as trying to effect action. In arriving at an attribution, the observer follows a logical analysis in which his or her assessment of the other's ability and effort are measured against the environmental factors that hinder or facilitate the action. In thinking about your ruined weekend, you may have decided that your friend could have come (ability) but didn't try (effort). Principal among the environmental forces is *task difficulty.* Many sports (diving, for example) are comprised of events of graduated difficulty. Opportunity and luck are environmental elements that can affect task difficulty. Heider's model of attribution suggests that the more influence is attributed to environmental factors, the less personal responsibility is attributed to the actor.

Applying Heider's framework to the example of the canceled visit, you are likely to arrive at a dispositional attribution by the following analysis: you see your date as having the skill and knowledge necessary for the visit and probably conclude that your friend did not try hard enough. Even when you learn of the environmental constraints, you are likely to feel that he or she has the ability to get the assignment done, could have changed work schedules, and might have postponed the parental casual visit. On the other hand, you may arrive at an environmental attribution upon learning that a storm had closed airports and blocked roads on the route between the two of you.

Attribution as Information Processing

Jones and Davis (1965) expanded upon Heider's theory by concentrating on the dispositions that are based on the *effects* of actions. Their formulation rests on the assumption that behavior results from choices made among a number of alternative actions. In making attributions about a behavior, you mentally review what choices the actor might have had and why he or she did not make those choices. Gradually, you narrow down the inferences and alternatives until one seems most plausible. Consider, for example, the following situation. You hear that a college classmate whom you hardly know has chosen a graduate school with an outstanding national reputation, which offers a generous fellowship and the opportunity to structure a special interdisciplinary program of studies. What does this tell you about this classmate's personal characteristics? Not much, since it is hard to know from the choice he or she made what the person values most—reputation, money, or program flexibility. But if you hear of a classmate who has chosen a school you've never heard of and with a program that is not quite what the candidate wanted, but which offered a large fellowship, you'd probably infer that the classmate valued the money. In other words, you would conclude something about the person from one unique element among the choices. The Jones and Davis model reasons backward from the effects of an action to the disposition. The model follows the Heider formulation in assuming that the actor has the ability and knowledge of effects requisite for carrying out the act.

Another element of the Jones and Davis proposal addresses the relationship between you and the person whose actions you're trying to understand. In the example above, you were making inferences about someone you hardly knew. When you make inferences about someone you do know, the inference process takes on two additional elements. The first, called *hedonic relevance,* has to do with the effect of the action on you. If the action has harmed or offended you, you are more likely to make a dispositional inference than an environmental one; because your weekend plans are spoiled, you are more likely to think that your friend is cold and selfish than he or she couldn't make it. The second element, *personalism,* refers to the extent to which you think the action is aimed at you and you alone. If you suspect that your date may have come if invited by someone else (say, your roommate), you are again more likely to make a dispositional than an environmental inference. One shortcoming of this model is that, despite some concern with the interactional bases of attributions, it applies best to initial encounters. It takes little account of the observer's prior knowledge of the actor and his or her past actions. Obviously, such considerations do enter into your attributions about your date's actions.

Actor-Observer Differences. In an extension of these views, Jones and Nisbett (1971) argued that there is a "pervasive tendency for actors to attribute their actions to situational requirements, whereas observers tend to attribute the same actions to stable personal dispositions" (p. 2). They based this argument on the view that actors and observers differ with regard to the information available to them and to the way in which they use the information they have. The actor has more information than the observer about his or her own emotional state and intention. The actor also has more knowledge about his or her own history and behavior in past situations of the kind the observer is trying to explain. Less obvious are the differences in the ways actor and observer make use of the available information. The major difference resides in what each considers most important. The actor's attention is focused on the situation, and he or she looks outward at the environmental cues in trying to explain behavior. For the observer, the most vivid aspect of the scene is the actor, and other cues retreat into the background.

According to Jones and Nisbett, these attributional differences are increased when the observer is also an actor—that is, when both actor and observer engage in both attributional roles. The observer who is also caught up in interaction, and therefore becomes also actor, is not free to evaluate the other person and the environmental cues dispassionately; rather, the observer-actor is tuned to process those cues that are most salient for his or her own actor responses. The observer-actor's inclination under these circumstances is to seek the simplest possible explanation, such as assuming that the other person will continue to act in the same way in this and other situations. Furthermore, the observer-actor tends to be inattentive to his or her own effect on the other and to attribute the other's actions to personal rather than environmental dispositions.

The different attributions made by actors and observers are the concern of both research selections included in this chapter. The first experiment is an attempt to alter the attributional pattern described here by changing the information available. The second is a demonstration of the pattern in a socially relevant context.

Attribution as Social Science

Other important contributions to the theory of attribution are now being made by Kelley (1967, 1971, 1973). Based also on Heider, Kelley's work is focused on detailing the process through which attributions are made. In looking at attribution as a social-science process, Kelley offers an attributional-data table that can be used to compare one's own attributions with those of others. According to Kelley, the observer considers three classes of data in making an attribution: entities, persons, and time/modality. *Entities* refers to the class of situations to which the one to be explained belongs. The *persons* dimension includes the observer and others among whom relevant comparisons might be made. The *time/modality* dimension takes into account the context in which the attribution is made.

Thus, in evaluating the cancellation of your weekend plans, you compare the situation with similar situations you have experienced with other people you know; on the time/modality dimension, you consider your friend's behavior in other situations with you; and on the persons dimension, you consider your views and those of your friends. Your attributional question is "Was the visit canceled because of me, because of the timing and circumstances of the visit, or because of my friend's personal characteristics?" First, on the entities dimension, you decide whether your friend honors commitments with other people, and finding that your friend does not makes the cancellation nondistinctive, and *distinctiveness,* according to Kelley, is one of three important factors in making attributions. Second, you review other dates with your friend to see if cancellation characterizes them; in other words, you try to see if this weekend's behavior is consistent with past behavior in similar or other situations. *Consistency* is the second factor in making attributions. Third, you note others' actions to see if there is *consensus*. Having ruled out alternative attributions, you make the dispositional attribution that the canceled visit was caused by selfishness and coldness.

For Kelley, the attribution process is also a process of elimination until only one plausible explanation is left. Dispositional attributions are made when consistency is high (your friend has done it to you before) and consensus and distinctiveness are low (other friends don't cancel on you, and your friend does it to others). Situational attributions are made when all three factors—consistency, consensus, and distinctiveness—are high. In recent contributions, Kelley (1971, 1973; Cunningham & Kelley, 1975) has addressed himself to extensions of this model to more complex attributional problems, in which multiple plausible causes are known to the perceiver.

RESEARCH ON ATTRIBUTION

Investigators who have put these models to the test have concentrated mainly on two topics, in addition to the actor-observer differences reflected in the two research selections included here. These topics are attributions of success and failure and attributions of responsibility.

Attributions of Success and Failure

Recall the dual purpose of attribution: to understand the present and to predict the future behavior of another (or oneself). Somewhat related to this dual purpose is the use one can make of attribution to understand why good or bad things happen to people. Observers attribute success or failure to four sources: the actor's ability, the amount of effort expended, the task difficulty, and luck. Note that ability and trying are personal forces and task difficulty and luck are environmental ones.

Ability. The strongest factor leading to ability attributions—that is, the conclusion that it was the actor's ability that resulted in success or the actor's inability that led to failure—is the person's past performance on this or similar tasks. The fact that the person always does well on this task *(consistency)* and the fact that the person does well in similar situations *(generality)* are important determinants of ability attributions. Most experiments (reviewed in Weiner, Frieze, Kukla, Reed, Rest, & Rosenbaum, 1971) find a strong primacy effect for ability attribution; that is, the actor's first performance determines the observers' judgments of his or her overall performance. This consistent finding in laboratory experiments has led to concern about its implications for real-life achievement situations. If you get a low grade on the first examination in a course and the instructor attributes it to your lack of ability rather than to the difficulty of the test, how will your future in the course be affected? And what if the first grade is high? An experiment by Medway and Lowe (1975), described later on in the chapter in the section on methods, suggests that the ability attribution is made more often for positive outcomes than for negative ones.

Ability attributions appear to be sensitive also to cultural norms. For example, sex-role stereotypes affect attributions about success or failure. In assessing reactions to male and female success and failure in sex-linked occupations, Feather and Simon (1975) found that the sex of the actor was a powerful determinant of whether an actor who succeeded (or failed) was described in favorable or unfavorable terms and whether his or her success or failure was seen as having good or bad consequences. Female subjects in particular tended to upgrade successful males and downgrade successful females.

Effort. In deciding the cause of success or failure, it is important to know how hard the person tried. The professional athlete who makes his or her performance look easy is likely to have success credited to ability, whereas the amateur who is seen straining for the same effect may be judged to have reached the goal through effort. Lanzetta and Hannah (1969) have shown that teachers react more negatively to students who fail because of low effort than to students who fail because of low ability or high task difficulty. Students who failed a midterm examination and attributed their failure to low effort had a high estimate of success on future examinations (Bailey, Helm, & Gladstone, 1975).

Task Difficulty. Knowledge of average performance is critical for the attribution of success or failure to task difficulty. In other words, before a given actor's success or failure can be attributed to the degree of difficulty of the task, the average performance must be taken into account. If many people undertake the task and many fail, observers judge it to be a difficult one, and, if the task is difficult, the person is not held responsible for failing it. A performance consistent with average performance leads to an attribution of success or failure based on task difficulty. A performance that is very much above or below average performance leads to a dispositional attribution based on ability or effort (Weiner, 1970).

Luck. In the attribution process, luck is regarded as an unstable element. Whether or not success or failure is attributed to it depends on the previous pattern of outcomes. An apparently random pattern of past performance is attributed more to chance than a systematic one. A person whose pattern of success and failure is a variable one is likely to be considered lucky the next time he or she wins, unlucky if he or she loses.

Combined Factors. From the preceding discussion it appears clear that the attribution of success or failure involves the complex processing of information available along several lines—among them, the person's performance history in this and other situations, and how most others perform in the situation. Although some general patterns have been identified, which indicate when ability, effort, task difficulty, and luck are singled out as agents, performance attribution is complex. In a study using all four dimensions, Feldman-Summers and Kiesler (1974) found that the performances of women and men were attributed to different causes—a finding they explain by suggesting that different attributional patterns come into play for expected and unexpected outcomes. High ability and task ease were used to explain expected success (namely, success by males); motivation and sometimes luck were used to explain unexpected (female) success.

Attribution of Responsibility

An obvious area of concern in looking at the causes of behavior is the attribution of blame and responsibility. From childhood on, you come to know that the question "Who did it and why?" contains a further, implicit question about responsibility and blame. The attribution process in judicial proceedings is concerned with fixing legal responsibility for events. In so doing, the law makes certain exceptions to the general rule that people are responsible for events they cause to happen—for example, in the case of the insane and in that of minors. But often a legal extenuation does not protect the actor from the moral judgments of observers that he or she was to blame. Causality, responsibility, and blame, although conceptually distinct, are often used interchangeably in research, thus giving rise to contradictory results (Fishbein & Ajzen, 1973; Shaver, 1975).

Interest in the topic was stimulated by an experiment by Walster (1966), which examined the degree to which a car owner is responsible for damage done by his parked car rolling downhill. Walster found that subjects held the owner more responsible when the damage was serious than when it was slight. She suggested that observers make this attribution to protect themselves from the unpleasant thought that such an accident could happen to them. Despite the failure to replicate this finding (Phares & Wilson, 1972; Shaw & Skolnick, 1971; Walster, 1967), Shaver (1970) saw some merit in the explanation. He argued that you can reduce the personal threat of certain attributional situations by attributing personal responsibility to the actor only when you can deny the similarity between yourself and the actor. If you can believe that you would never find yourself in similar circumstances, or if your estimate of your ability and knowledge is such that you are convinced you could avoid the bad outcome, you make the blaming attribution about the actor. If you do see yourself as similar to the actor, you attribute the outcome to chance. This attribution protects you from the thought that in the future you might be harshly judged yourself for similar behavior in similar circumstances.

A direct test of this reasoning provided support for the proposition that the more serious the consequences of an accident, the less the accident was attributed to chance, except by subjects who thought they might cause such an accident themselves (Chaikin & Darley, 1973). Such subjects also tended to blame the victim of a severe accident more than subjects who thought that they themselves might be victims. Although defensive attribution does affect responsibility judgments, responsibility attributions are too complex to be explained solely on the basis of the individual's self-protective strategies (Vidmar & Crinklaw, 1974). Cultural norms and sex differences are but two additional factors to be taken into account.

Attribution in Actor and Observer Roles

Most of the research reviewed thus far has dealt with the attributions made by persons when they are in the role of observer. These attributions are of the sort you make while "people watching." But what if the person you're watching is you? The two research selections in this chapter belong to the smaller body of research concerned with the tendency for actors to attribute their own behavior to situational requirements, whereas, as observers, they tend to attribute the same actions to person dispositions (Jones & Nisbett, 1971).

Nisbett and Caputo (1971) asked male college students to describe why they had chosen their major fields of concentration and why they liked their most frequent date. They also asked them the same questions with regard to their best friends. Coding the responses according to dispositional or situational attributions, they found that the students made more dispositional attributions about their friends than about themselves. Nisbett, Caputo, Legant, and Marecek (1973) asked subjects to choose from a number of adjectives the one that best described themselves and the ones that best described four other people differing in age and degree of acquaintanceship with the subjects. Rating themselves, their best friend, an admired acquaintance, their father, and Walter Cronkite, subjects selected fewer adjectives that described personal traits (dispositional attributions) for themselves; the degree of acquaintance, instead, did not make a difference in attribution. A recent extension of this thinking (Taylor & Koivumaki, 1976) found little support for the actor-observer difference. Instead, Taylor and Koivumaki found considerable evidence that dispositional attributions are made for positive behaviors and situational attributions are made for negative behavior, regardless of actor-observer stance.

A distinction of some importance for the second research selection in this chapter is the one made by Miller and Norman (1975) between active and passive observers. Active observers were women students who engaged in actual interaction with another student in a bargaining game. Passive observers watched the two players in the game. Active observers made more dispositional attributions and fewer situational ones than passive observers. Contrary to previous research, actors attributed more personal responsibility to themselves than passive observers did. The investigators linked these findings to the need of the actor to see himself or herself as being in control. Since, in many respects, another person is easier to control than a situation, the active observer attributes more personal responsibility to the other interactant than to the situation.

Differences in attribution between actors and observers quite likely exist. The specific nature of these differences is less clear; actors probably do not invariably make situational attributions about the behavior for which observers make dispositional ones. It is likely that attribution processes are more complex than present research methods reveal; the widespread reliance on quite specific questions in which a respondent must choose between two, and only two, alternatives may obscure more of the complexity of the attribution process than it reveals (Taylor, 1976).

METHODS IN THE STUDY OF ATTRIBUTION

In Chapter 1, we argued that a good research tool is one that is not only objectively good but also appropriate to the question under study. Sometimes you want to know what a person will actually do in a particular situation and not necessarily what he thinks he would do; at other times, it is how a person thinks or feels about himself or others that is of interest to you. Clearly, attribution researchers are more interested in how people think or feel than in what they do. Therefore, they follow the dictum that, if you want to know how a person's mind works, you should ask the person. At present, with a very few exceptions, the dependent measure preferred by attribution researchers is the verbal response. In reviewing samples of methods used in this area, note there are no examples of observational or archival approaches. This is partly due to the aforementioned concentration on subjects' verbal responses, usually expressed as answers to scales or questionnaires. But it may also be due to the social psychologists' inclination to begin their investigations in the laboratory. Field research, when it occurs, is usually carried out only after a line of work has emerged from initial laboratory experimentation. We shall return to this issue later in this section.

Laboratory Experiments

Many questions in social psychology in general and in attribution theory in particular start by asking whether people respond differently to different things going on around them. The obvious way of answering questions of this type is to expose people to different things and ask for their reactions. Research design refines this process by presenting stimuli that are the same in every respect except for the critical variable being studied. For example, if you wanted to know whether people studied better in soft-colored rooms than in bright-colored ones, you would not make the soft-colored room small, cozy, and warm and the bright-colored one large, barren, and cold. If you did that, you would be unable to find out what specifically (color, size, temperature, or atmosphere) made the difference.

Information booklets represent an apparently simple way of giving people a certain amount of information about others, while keeping everything else constant. An example of this approach is a study by Medway and Lowe (1975), investigating attribution of responsibility when the outcome is a severe one and when it is not. More specifically, these researchers were testing the hypothesis that subjects would assign more responsibility to a person for his or her actions when the outcome of those actions was severe and when it was positive than when the outcome was mild or negative.

The method involved giving male and female student subjects experimental booklets and requesting their impressions of the person described in them. All subjects read the same neutral description of a student who had to study selectively for questions likely to be asked in an upcoming exam. The two independent variables were outcome and severity. The outcome variable was manipulated by presenting good or bad outcomes. The student described in the booklets was said either to have chosen the questions well and gotten an A− or to have chosen badly and gotten a D−. The severity variable involved certain consequences of the grade attained. Subjects were told that the student described in the booklets would be required, depending on his grade, to give more or less of his time to participation in research projects. The dependent measure asked subjects to rate the student on six 11-point scales, including their perception of the student's responsibility. As hypothesized, the more serious the consequences attendant upon a negative outcome, the more responsibility attributed to the student by the subjects.

Following similar thinking, another group of investigators (Harvey, Harris, & Barnes, 1975) took a further step to ascertain not only the observer's attributions of an actor's responsibility but the actor's assessment of his own responsibility under conditions differing in severity of outcome. They reasoned that an actor's assessment of his own behavior would not correspond with an observer's attributions of the same action, because the actor has a need to protect his self-esteem; that is, the actor needs to see himself as less responsible for a happening with serious consequences.

Instead of providing male college student subjects with a written account of an event, Harvey, Harris, and Barnes created a more involving situation for both actor and observer. Pairs of subjects were randomly assigned to "teacher" and "observer" roles in a study ostensibly involving shock to a "pupil" (actually an experimental confederate) for incorrect responses on a learning task. The experimental manipulation involved providing both the teacher-actor, who was apparently administering shock for incorrect responses, and the observer with feedback from the pupil. The pupil indicated that he was experiencing either moderate or severe stress as the result of being shocked. Actually, the number of incorrect responses, and hence the number of shocks delivered, was the same in all conditions. Afterward, both teacher and observer were given a form posing seven questions to be answered on 11-point scales. Included were questions concerning how much responsibility the subjects attributed to the teacher for the pupil's distress and how much freedom they thought the teacher had to refuse the request to shock the pupil. As predicted, observers attributed more responsibility to the actors than the actors attributed to themselves. Furthermore, observers saw the actor-teacher as having a considerable degree of freedom to refuse giving the shock, while actors saw themselves in the role of teacher as having very little freedom.

Subjects in both these laboratory studies were obviously highly aware of being in a study, although the potential for reactivity is probably decreased by the lack of a clear-cut socially desirable response for both observers and actors. Although both studies engage in a substantial amount of experimental manipulation, they nevertheless represent two different strategies for effecting differences in the independent variable. The "booklet" procedure is neat and uncomplicated; the "shock" experiment is involved and complex.

Surveys and Interviews

In sharp contrast to laboratory experiments, surveys and interviews involve little or no manipulation of antecedent conditions, except for the selection of a particular population to be sampled. One purpose of using this kind of approach is to extend findings established in the laboratory to other populations or situations. Calhoun, Peirce, and Dawes (1973) selected their population from the adult outpatients in a community mental-health center. On their first interview, the sample of 53 males and 64 females, ranging in age from 18 to 60, were given a five-item questionnaire to complete. They were asked to rate the following aspects of their problem on six-point scales: severity, duration, uniqueness, and internal or external causation. Correlations between attribution to internal and external cause and the other rated aspects indicated that long-standing and more severe psychological problems were seen as being more internally caused. Although the findings are clearly in line with Kelley's (1967) prediction that recurrent behavior tends to be attributed to internal factors, the correlational nature of the data cannot provide information about the direction of causality. Perhaps long-lasting behavior is seen as internally caused or, when behavior is perceived as internally caused, it is also perceived as long lasting.

An unusual sample for an attributional study was the group of 51 Houston police officers interviewed by Rozelle and Baxter (1975). Whereas Calhoun and his associates elected to use a brief, highly structured question format involving rating scales, Rozelle and Baxter chose a longer, open-ended interview approach. Novice and veteran officers were asked to describe what citizen characteristics, traits, or features they focused on when they dealt with someone in their official capacity. Follow-up questions probed more deeply into the behaviors and causal attributions included in these descriptions. Officers were also asked to answer a number of other questions concerning their occupation. The answers to the first question were coded for the number of dispositional (overt or covert) and situational characteristics they used in forming impressions. All policemen focused primarily on person-centered characteristics, with the senior officers indicating more durable features such as "resentment of authority," and the junior officers focusing on more temporary features such as "has something to hide." In order to discern patterns across a number of free-form answers, Rozelle and Baxter categorized the data. It is worth noting, however, that these investigators also reported that the respondents' interpretive processes tended to be multidimensional and with a complex structure. Rating scales, while quantitatively simpler, cannot yield the type of complexity and variability permitted in an open-ended format.

As pointed out several times before, there are problems with self-report measures. The more face-valid the questions are to the inquirer, the more transparent they may be to the subject. Interviewees then may tailor their responses to their perceptions of what is expected rather than provide accurate self-descriptions. But a study by McGee and Snyder (1975) using a questionnaire format found a way around this problem.

The study involved two steps. First, restaurant patrons were observed to see whether they put salt on their food before or after tasting it. Second, these same subjects were approached and asked to fill out the Nisbett et al. (1973) trait-ascription questionnaire, ostensibly for a "course project." This questionnaire consists of 20 polar adjectives (for example, realistic-idealistic), each with the additional alternative of "depends on the situation"; respondents are to check which of the three options for each trait best describes themselves. McGee and Snyder predicted that the more likely individuals were to ascribe personality traits to themselves, the more likely they were to put salt in their food before tasting it. The reasoning was that the individual who does so is presumably doing it in response to dispositional cues related to a particular need or desire ("I like salt"). Results confirmed the prediction. The solution to the problem of the interviewees seeing through the questionnaire consisted simply in the fact that the measure made no mention of seasoning or eating food.

Field Experiments

Impressions people have about themselves are stuff of a particularly private sort; they cannot be observed directly. These impressions can be and usually are sought by questions, but sometimes self-attributions are not very accessible to direct query. Researchers investigating attribution have very rarely sought more indirect and unobtrusive ways of tapping self-attribution. An exception is a study by Uranowitz (1975). He was interested in exploring the notion that people attribute dispositions to themselves under certain circumstances. Specifically, he proposed that, if people do something in the absence of strong external reasons for so doing, they are likely to see themselves as being the kind of person "who does such things." Using helping behavior as his dependent measure, Uranowitz staged a situation in the field in which female subjects were first asked to watch someone else's groceries under either high-justification or low-justification conditions. That is, the experimenter-confederate indicated either that he had lost his wallet inside the supermarket (high justification) or that he was going back to retrieve a dollar (low justification). Next, the staging entailed exposing the subject to a second experimenter who, apparently quite unawares, dropped a small package in front of the subject. The dependent measure was the number of subjects who helped this second person. Results were in the predicted direction: more people helped under the low-justification than under the high-justification condition. Uranowitz reasoned that subjects who respond to a request under minimal justification show more helping behavior in a subsequent situation because they have now made self-attributions of helpfulness. Self-attributions were not, however, measured directly in Uranowitz's experiment. Thus, the investigator's inference process here has made several leaps to arrive at a causal link to self-attribution. The greater the distance between stimulus and response, the greater the likelihood that other factors have become influential.

Other Methods

It is no doubt evident now that the most common attribution-research paradigm involves a sequence that consists of presenting a set of stimulus conditions to subject-judges and then measuring their reactions on a set of scale responses. The stimulus or input goes in and the response or output comes out, and inferences are made about what mental processes must have taken place in between. Attributional processes clearly lie in this twilight region.

To keep inferential error concerning this internal state to a minimum, researchers have sought maximum control over what goes in and over the form the output takes. This concern is no doubt another contributing factor to the current neglect of alternative methods, such as archival search, naturalistic observation, and longitudinal exploration, in the study of attribution. This is not to say that these kinds of methods should be employed to fill the gap merely because they exist; the nature of the question must always dictate tool selection. So, too, we must be wary of phrasing questions in such a way that only research paradigms of the S-R sort are able to accommodate. But if you want to know how attribution processes work naturally or check the ecological validity of laboratory findings, you may want to seek other records such as (auto)biographical material, news reports, and the like. Similarly, as attributional researchers venture into the tricky mechanics of ongoing relationships, whether between warring nations or collaborating colleagues, a longitudinal approach may become the method of choice.

TWO RESEARCH EXAMPLES

Product Description

Both selections in this chapter deal with the question of whether how you interpret your own behavior differs from how others would interpret it or, alternatively, whether how you interpret someone else's behavior differs from how you interpret your own, even when the same behavior is involved. As the above review indicates, one of the most consistently observed attributional phenomena is the tendency for individuals to arrive at relatively more-situational and less-dispositional attributions for their own behavior.

The first selection, by Storms, is a laboratory investigation aimed not only at replicating these findings with regard to actor-observer differences but, more importantly, at reversing them. Storms reasoned that perhaps actor-observer differences are due to the fact that actors and observers have, quite literally, different *visual* perspectives of the behavior in question, since actors cannot visually observe their own behavior. In his experiment, pairs of naive subjects (actors) engaged in a 5-minute get-acquainted conversation while two matched observers watched them. After the conversation, the experimental manipulation was introduced. First, actors were shown either a videotape replay of their conversational partner (a repetition of their original visual perspective as actors) or a videotape replay of themselves in the original conversation (thus seeing themselves from the observer's perspective). Second, the two observers saw either a replay of the same actor they had observed or a videotape of the other participant with whom their matched actor had been talking. Third, a control group was included, which was involved only in the initial conversation, with no replay of it. Storms found that the usual actor-observer attributions were reversed when perspective was reversed; actors saw their behavior as more dispositionally based, whereas observers saw their matched-actor's behavior as more situationally caused. The usual actor-observer differences were replicated when the visual perspective provided by video replay repeated the ordinary visual orientation.

The second selection, by West, Gunn, and Chernicky, employed both laboratory and field elements to bring the testing of actor-observer differences into an unusual and interesting arena—the world of a would-be burglar. The study had two stages: the first of which involved creating a situation that required some subjects to *do* something. These subjects were the actors, and their attributions about their own behavior were obtained. In the second stage, another group of subjects were asked to comment on the behavior of the actors. These were the observers. The primary research question thus became "Will an observer who is merely told about another's behavior interpret it the same way as the person who actually did it?"

As in the Storms approach, West and his colleagues wanted a situation in which the actors would actually engage in some spontaneous behavior. For these investigators, that meant involving actors in an event of more consequence than a get-acquainted conversation. Male and female undergraduate criminology majors were asked to participate in a burglary whose alleged purpose was that of microfilming some important records. In order to maximize the probability that the students would agree to participate, the experimenters made use of all the paraphernalia connected with a professional burglary, such as aerial photographs, blueprints, and the like. Subjects were assigned to four groups, each of which was given a different reason for the crime. In the first two groups, the burglary was to be committed for a governmental agency; but one group was promised immunity from prosecution and the other was not. The third group was told that the enterprise was sponsored by an advertising firm and that the subjects would be rewarded for their efforts. The fourth group was a control group, and the subjects were told that the burglary was an attempt to test whether the burglary plans would work and that nothing would be stolen. After the description of the burglary plans, subjects were asked whether they would participate and what the rationale for their decision was.

In the second part of the study, undergraduate psychology students were given a booklet describing in detail the conditions of the above procedure. These observer subjects were then asked for three things: whether they themselves would have agreed to participate under those circumstances, what reasons a hypothetical person might have given for participating or refusing to participate, and their impressions of this hypothetical person and of the person who requested his services.

Results replicated those of earlier research showing actor-observer differences. The authors argue that such results have implications for an understanding of the different perceptions of a criminal act by observers (including the press) and participants in the crime—for example, in the case of the Watergate crimes.

Consumer Checklist

- How close are the plans to the final products?
    - In the first selection, do the two experimental groups show any other difference than that relating to visual perspective?
    - In the second selection, what information is given concerning the number of subjects who, when first asked, refused to participate? Was the information concerning the persuasion efforts supplied to the observer?
- How are the product components (actor-observer differences) seen by the two manufacturers?
    - How does each study measure the dependent variable?
    - Are differences in measurement and concept important?

VIDEOTAPE AND THE ATTRIBUTION PROCESS: REVERSING ACTORS' AND OBSERVERS' POINTS OF VIEW [1]

MICHAEL D. STORMS [2]

Yale University

Two actor subjects at a time engaged in a brief, unstructured conversation while two observer subjects looked on. Later a questionnaire measured the actors' attributions of their own behavior in the conversation either to dispositional, internal causes or to situational, external causes. Similarly, each observer attributed his matched actor's behavior. Videotapes of the conversation, replayed to subjects before the attribution questionnaire, provided an experimental manipulation of visual orientation. Some actors and observers saw no videotape replay, while other subjects saw a tape that merely repeated their original visual orientations. As predicted for both of these conditions, the actors attributed relatively more to the situation than the observers. A third set of subjects saw a videotape taken from a new perspective—some actors saw a tape of themselves, while some observers saw the other participant with whom their matched actor had been conversing. With this reorientation, self-viewing actors attributed relatively more to their own dispositions than observers. The results indicated the importance of visual orientation in determining attributional differences between actors and observers. Pragmatically, the theoretical framework and results of the study had relevance to the use of videotape self-observation in therapy and T groups.

When an individual observes a behavior and attempts to understand its causes, he is concerned with the relative importance of personal dispositions of the actor and the surrounding social and environmental context. Both an observer who wishes to explain another's behavior and an actor who tries to understand his own behavior attempt to make the appropriate causal attributions. There is reason to believe, however, that actors and observers do not always arrive at the same explanation of the actor's behavior. Jones and Nisbett (1971) have argued that when actors seek to explain their own behavior, they are inclined to give considerable weight to external, environmental (i.e., situational) causes. Observers, on the other hand, place considerably more emphasis on internal, personal (i.e., dispositional) causes of the actor's behavior.

Several studies (Jones & Harris, 1967; Jones, Rock, Shaver, Goethals, & Ward, 1968; McArthur, 1970, 1972; Nisbett, Caputo, Legant, & Marecek, 1973) have been cited in support of this general proposition, and Jones and Nisbett have discussed a variety of factors which might lead to such attributional differences between actors and observers. These factors include (a) differences in information about the event, behavior, and context which is *available* to actors and observers and (b) differences in how information is *processed* by actors and observers. Actors may have private information about some aspects of the event, including their own feelings and the historical context in which the event transpires, while observers may have more complete information about the behavior itself. Furthermore, in the interests of controlling events and predicting the future, actors may attend more to situational variables in an event, and observers may attend more to variations in the actor's behavior.

The present study examines a fundamental difference between actors and observers which may lead, in turn, to some of the information differences postulated by Jones and Nisbett (1971). Perhaps the most obvious difference

---

[1] The research for this article was performed as part of the author's PhD dissertation submitted to the Department of Psychology, Yale University. The author wishes to express his appreciation to Richard E. Nisbett, who served as advisor for the thesis and who has contributed many helpful criticisms of the present article.

[2] Requests for reprints should be sent to the author, who is now at the Department of Psychology, University of Kansas, Lawrence, Kansas 66044.

between actors and observers is that they have, quite literally, different points of view. Actors cannot see themselves act; physically they cannot observe much of their own behavior. They may watch the antecedents of their own behavior, or its consequences, or both. But they do not normally view the behavior itself. In addition to the physical difficulty of watching oneself, there are temporal restrictions which contribute to a lack of self-observation. There may not be enough time or mental capacity to contemplate past behavior, monitor present behavior, and plan future behavior all at once. Finally, there are motivational reasons for avoiding an excess of self-observation. In the interest of acting unself-consciously and maintaining control over the immediate events taking place, the actor may learn that it is dysfunctional to be overly concerned with his own present and past behavior. Instead, it is reasonable to assume that most actors focus on the situation in which they find themselves. They look at, attend to, and think about various changing aspects of the environment in which and to which they must respond.

While the actor is watching the situation in which he finds himself, the observer is probably watching the actor. It is usually interesting and often important to watch the behavior of other people. Consequently, observers are often visually oriented toward the actor. Although an observer can take his eyes off the actor and view other aspects of the situation, he probably sees less of the situation than the actor does. As with actors, the observer's scope is also limited by time. Observers cannot simultaneously watch the actor and observe as much of the situation as the actor can. Moreover, observers may find it more efficient in terms of controlling and predicting the ongoing event to concentrate on the actor's behavior rather than on the actor's situation. Finally, the actor is, after all, part of the observer's situation. For the same reasons that an actor focuses on his own situation, the observer focuses on the behavior of the actor, which is part of his (the observer's) situation.

Thus, we postulate that there is a simple difference between actors and observers. Actors watch their environment (which includes the behavior of other people) more than they watch their own behavior. Observers watch the behavior of the actor more than they watch the actor's situation.

If it is true that attributions are largely influenced by point of view, it should be possible to change the way actors and observers interpret a behavior by changing their visual orientations.

A test of this hypothesis requires some means of changing actors' and observers' orientations. Fortunately, modern technology provides a simple and interesting means to accomplish this change—namely, the use of videotape. Videotapes of an event, taken from various camera angles, can be replayed to actors and observers to redirect their attention to other aspects of the event. Of particular interest is the case in which videotape presents a new visual orientation, that is, when actors are shown a tape of their own behavior from the observer's perspective and when observers are shown a tape of some key aspect of the actor's situation from the actor's perspective. Such reorientation should affect actors and observers so as to weaken (or even reverse) their original attributional biases. Actors who see themselves should make more dispositional attributions about their own behavior. Observers who see another aspect of the actor's situation should become more situational in attributing the actor's behavior.

Thus, the question to be answered by this study is whether actors' and observers' attributions can be significantly influenced, perhaps even reversed, by changing their visual orientation toward an event. The implications of such a question may go beyond immediate theoretical concerns. Discrepancies between actors' and observers' perceptions and interpretations of behavior are of paramount concern to therapists, group relations consultants, and T group trainers. Often such practitioners must attempt to bridge the interpretational gap between actor and observer, patient and therapist, and individual and group.

METHOD

Overview

The hypothesis was tested in an experiment that featured a simple interpersonal event, namely a brief getting-acquainted conversation between two strangers (actors). In addition, two other subjects (observers) were told to watch the conversation but not to participate in it.

Videotape replays of the conversation provided the experimental manipulation. The design made it possible to compare the effects of three orientation conditions: (*a*) one in which no visual reorientation was attempted (no videotape), (*b*) one in which videotape was used simply to repeat the subject's original orientations (same orientation), and (*c*) one in which videotape reversed the orientation of actor and observer (new orientation). In one set of conditions, actors and observers saw a videotape from essentially the same orientation as they had had in "real life." Actors saw a videotape replay of the other participant with whom they were conversing (actor—same orientation), and observers saw a videotape of the same actor they had been observing and about whom they would later answer questions (observer—same orientation). In another set of conditions, actors and observers received an entirely new orientation on videotape. Actors saw a videotape of themselves in the conversation (actor—new orientation), and observers saw a videotape of the other participant with whom their target actor had been conversing (observer—new orientation). In addition, a set of actors and observers were run with no videotape replay.

Subjects

One hundred and twenty Yale undergraduate male volunteers participated in 30 groups of 4. Subjects were solicited by sign-up sheets which specified that people who volunteered for the same session should not be previously acquainted.

Procedure

When each group of four subjects arrived at the experiment, they were told,

> This is a study in an area of social psychology called "interpersonal dynamics." More specifically, I'm interested in what I call "getting acquainted" —that is, what happens when two strangers meet for the first time and initiate their first conversation. Two of you in this study will be having a short, first conversation with each other. In addition, this study calls for two observers.

Subjects were randomly assigned to the role of actor (actually referred to as participant in the script) or observer. Two subjects were assigned to be actors and to have a getting-acquainted conversation together. Each of the remaining two observer subjects was assigned to observe his matched actor during the conversation.

The experimenter then mentioned,

> There is one thing I would like to add to the procedure today. I've gotten hold of some videotape equipment and I will be taping your con-

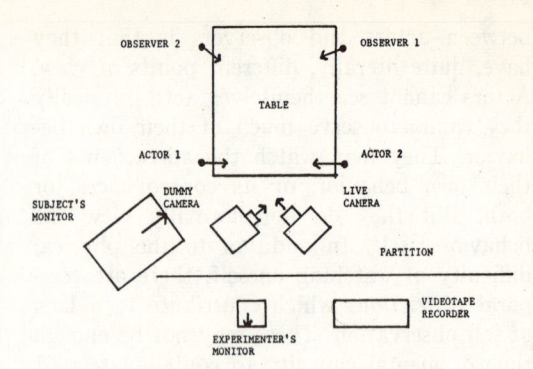

Fig. 1. Setup of the experimental room.

versation. My thought was that it might be useful to you in answering the questionnaires to see the conversation replayed on tape.

Subjects were then seated in the experimental room as shown in Figure 1. Actors sat at one end of the table, across from each other, with one camera focused on each. Observers sat at the other end of the table, diagonally across from and facing their matched actors. The experimenter reiterated that the conversation would last about 5 minutes, that the actors could talk about anything they wished, perhaps starting with their names and where they lived, and that observers should silently watch their matched actors.

After adjusting the equipment, the experimenter signaled to the participants to begin their conversation. Five minutes later, he asked them to stop and wait silently while the tapes were rewound. At this point, the experimental manipulation was performed. A random number table was consulted to determine whether the session would be a control session, in which case the subject would not see any tape, or an experimental session. If an experimental session was indicated, the experimenter continued, "I'm afraid only one camera was working very well and the other one is just too poor to see anything. So we'll only be able to see one of you on the videotape." Experimental subjects were always shown the tape of Actor 1.

Thus one actor, Actor 2, saw a tape of the same participant he had just seen in real life (Actor 1) and was the actor–same orientation subject. The other actor, Actor 1, viewed the tape of himself and was the actor–new orientation subject. Similarly, one observer, Observer 1, saw a tape of the same actor he had been observing in the conversation (Actor 1) and was the observer–same orientation subject. The other observer, Observer 2, saw a tape of the participant whom he had not been observing previously (Actor 1) and was the observer–new orientation subject. Thus each experimental session yielded one subject in each of the four experimental cells.

If a control session was indicated, the experimenter said the following instead: "I'm afraid this is lousy equipment. It just didn't take a good enough picture to be worth our while looking at it. So we'll just have to skip the tapes and go on to the questionnaire." These no-videotape control sessions produced two actor–no-videotape subjects and two observer–no-videotape subjects.

At this point, for control subjects, and after the videotape replay for experimental subjects, the experimenter introduced the questionnaire, stressing that it was confidential and that the subjects would not see each other's responses. When the subjects completed the questions, they were debriefed. At this time, the experimenter raised the issue of experimental deception, but no subject indicated suspicion that the videotape had been a deliberate manipulation or even an essential part of the experiment.

Measures

On the postexperimental questionnaire, actor subjects answered mostly questions about themselves, and observer subjects answered questions about their matched actor. After a few introductory filler items, a page of instructions and the key dependent measures of attribution were presented. The instructions informed subjects that in the next part of the questionnaire they would be asked to describe their own (their matched actor's) behavior along four standard dimensions: friendliness, talkativeness, nervousness, and dominance. Then, for each of the four behaviors, subjects were to indicate how much influence they thought the following two factors had in causing that behavior:

(A) Personal characteristics about yourself (your matched participant): How important were your (his) personality, traits, character, personal style, attitudes, mood, and so on in causing you (him) to behave the way you (he) did?

(B) Characteristics of the situation: How important were such factors as being in an experiment, the "getting acquainted" situation, the topic of conversation, the way the other participant behaved and so on in causing you (him) to behave the way you (he) did?

Thus, on each of the next four pages, three questions were presented. The first asked about the perceived level of behavior on one of the four dimensions, for example, "To what extent did you (your matched participant) behave in a friendly, warm manner?" The question was followed by a 9-point scale labeled extremely friendly (9) to extremely unfriendly (1). Presented next were the two attribution questions: "How important were personal characteristics about you (your matched participant) in causing you (him) to behave that way?" and "How important were characteristics of the situation in causing you (him) to behave that way?" Each of these questions was followed by a 9-point scale labeled extremely important (9) to extremely unimportant (1).

These last two questions, repeated over the four behavioral dimensions, provided the principal and most direct measure of subjects' attributions. These four dimensions were not selected on the basis of any particular theoretical or empirical considerations, but simply because it was anticipated that subjects would manifest behaviors along each of these dimensions and that subjects would be able to make judgments about them. Since the hypothesis was concerned with the relative strength of dispositional versus situational attributions and made no distinctions among the four behavioral dimensions, the appropriate measure was the difference between perceived importance of personal characteristics and perceived importance of situational characteristics in causing the actor's behavior, summed over all four behaviors. This difference score was referred to as the dispositional–situational index. A higher value on this index indicated that a subjects' attributions were relatively more dispositional and less situational. It is important to note this dual meaning of the dispositional–situational index. When an effect is described as "relatively more dispositional," it is equally valid to say "relatively less situational."

A second, less direct measure of the subjects' attributions appeared later in the questionnaire. The subjects were asked to report their estimates of the actor's level of behavior in *general* on each of the four behavioral dimensions, for example, "How friendly a person are you (is your matched participant) in general?" Responses were made on a scale from very friendly (9) to very unfriendly (1). It was then possible to compare these answers to the subjects' previous answers about the actor's level of behavior in the conversation. If a subject had perceived that the actor's behavior in the conversation was due to a stable personal disposition, then the subject would likely have predicted that the actor behaved the same way in general. Thus, dispositional attributions would lead to a low discrepancy between the subject's perception of the actor's behavior in the conversation and his behavior in general. On the other hand, if the subject had thought that the actor's behavior was caused by the situation, he would more likely have reported that the actor behaved differently in general. Thus, situational attributions would lead to greater discrepancy between the subjects' perceptions of the actor's present and general levels of behavior. The simplest measure of this discrepancy was the absolute value of the difference between the present level-of-behavior scores and the general level-of-behavior scores, summed over all four behaviors. This measure was referred to as the present-behavior–general-behavior index. The higher the value of this discrepancy index, the more a subject made situational (or the less he made dispositional) attributions.

The remainder of the questionnaire contained items not directly related to present concerns.

RESULTS

Dispositional versus Situational Attributions for Behavior

The main hypothesis of the present study concerns the effects of videotape reorientation on actors' and observers' causal attributions of the actor's behavior. Before considering the effects of reorientation, however, it is helpful to examine the evidence pertinent to the original Jones and Nisbett (1971) hypothesis that actors are characteristically inclined to attribute causality to aspects of the situation, while observers tend to attribute causality to the actor's disposition. Evidence for this proposition is found in two conditions of the present experiment: the no-videotape cells in which the subjects did not receive any videotape replay, and the same-orientation cells in which the videotape merely repeated the subjects' original visual perspectives.

The relevant data are presented in Table 1. The key dependent measure, the total dispositional–situational index, reflects the relative strength of dispositional and situational attributions; a higher value on this index indicates relatively more dispositional (less situational) attributing. A comparison of the dispositional–situational means for actors and observers in the no-videotape and same-orientation cells reveals that, in both of these conditions, actors attributed relatively more to situational causes than did observers ($p < .12$, $p < .05$, respectively).[3] It is further noted from these data that a videotape which merely repeated the subjects' original orientation had little effect on either actors or observers. Dispositional–situational scores for actors in the same-orientation condition did not differ from those for actors in the no-videotape condition ($q = 1.79$, ns), and scores for observers in the two conditions were also similar ($q = 1$, ns). Thus, under conditions of no videotape and under conditions of repeated videotape orientation, the subject's role as actor or observer was an important determinant of attributions. Actors attributed their own behavior relatively more to situational causes, and observers attributed the behavior relatively more to dispositional causes.

---

[3] These comparisons, and all two cell comparisons in the present study, are based on the q statistic from the Newman-Keuls procedure for testing differences among several means (see Winer, 1962). The degrees of freedom, taken from the overall analysis of variance, equal 114; n equals 20 per cell. The Newman-Keuls is a more stringent test than the usual two-tailed t test.

TABLE 1

DISPOSITIONAL, SITUATIONAL, AND DISPOSITIONAL MINUS SITUATIONAL ATTRIBUTION SCORES TOTALED OVER ALL FOUR BEHAVIORS

Attribution	Same orientation	No videotape	New orientation
Actors' attributions of own behavior			
Dispositional	26.10	27.35	27.50
Situational	25.95	25.10	20.70
Dispositional–situational	.15[a]	2.25[ab]	6.80[c]
Observers' attributions of matched actor's behavior			
Dispositional	27.10	27.30	25.75
Situational	22.20	22.50	24.15
Dispositional–situational	4.90[bc]	4.80[bc]	1.60[ab]

Note. Dispositional–situational means not sharing the same superscript are significantly different at the .05 level or beyond by Newman-Keuls tests.

The main hypothesis of the present study can be examined with the data presented in the last column of Table 1. It was anticipated that actors who saw themselves on videotape would become relatively less situational (more dispositional) in attributions of their own behavior, while observers who saw a videotape of the other participant with whom the actor had been conversing would become relatively more situational (less dispositional) in their attributions of the actor's behavior. Since opposite effects of videotape reorientation were predicted for actors and observers, the hypothesis was properly tested by the interaction between subjects' roles (actor or observer) and videotape orientation. The predicted Role × Videotape Orientation interaction was obtained at beyond the .001 level of confidence ($F = 9.72$, $df = 2/114$, $p < .001$). Neither the main effect for role, nor the main effect for videotape orientation was significant. The interaction reflected a complete reversal of the relative perspectives of actor and observer in the new-orientation condition. In the same-orientation and no-videotape conditions, the actors' attributions were more situational than the observers'. In the new-orientation condition, in contrast, the actors were relatively more dispositional than the observers. This reversed effect was significant in itself ($p < .05$).

Examining the simple dispositional and situational scores also presented in Table 1, it is apparent that reorientation had a stronger influence on the subjects' evaluation of situational factors than on their evaluation of dispositional factors. The array of means for attributions to dispositional causes was in the direction of the predicted interaction, but the effect did not reach significance ($F=1.38$, $df = 2/114$, ns). The situational attribution scores showed the expected reverse pattern, and the interaction was significant ($F = 5.78$, $df = 2/114$, $p < .005$).

The hypothesis is thus strongly supported. Visual orientation has a powerful influence on the attributions of actors and observers. Indeed, the data in Table 1 suggest the strongest possible conclusion: Under some circumstances actual role as actor or observer is unimportant, and visual orientation is totally determinative of attributions.

Two other aspects of the dispositional-situational data are noteworthy. (*a*) Repetition on videotape of essentially the same information which had been presented in real life had little effect on either the actors or the observers. Actors in the same-orientation condition were only slightly and nonsignificantly more situational than no-videotape actors, and same-orientation observers were only slightly and nonsignificantly more dispositional than no-videotape observers. (*b*) The predicted experimental effects were not obtained with equal strength for all four of the behaviors on which the total dispositional-situational index was based.

The fact that videotape in the same-orientation cells had little effect on the subject's attributions suggests that mere repetition of information and the addition of time to review the event did not affect the subject's perceptions of the event. The subjects appear to have absorbed all relevant data about the event during its real-life occurrence. Of course, one would not necessarily expect this to be true of all events. If the episode were more complex or of longer duration, subjects could easily miss important information in vivo. A videotape replay would fill in these informational gaps and could, quite possibly, produce different attributions.

The most noteworthy difference among the four behavioral dimensions was the failure of the dominance dimension to contribute to the experimental effects. Considering each behavioral dimension separately, the Role × Videotape Orientation interaction was significant for friendliness, talkativeness, and nervousness, each at the .025 level of confidence, but was trivial for dominance ($F < 1$). Comments by subjects during the debriefing suggest a possible reason for the failure of dominance to contribute to the experimental effects. Subjects complained that dominance was a difficult dimension on which to judge people in the context of a simple, 5-minute getting-acquainted conversation. While friendliness, talkativeness, and nervousness are dimensions with concrete behavioral counterparts (such as smiling, talking, and fidgeting), apparently dominance is a more abstract dimension and requires a higher order of inference.

When the dominance question was excluded from the analysis, each of the experimental effects was strengthened. Across the remaining three dimensions, the interaction test of videotape reorientation was strengthened from an F of 9.72 to an F of 13.89 ($df = 2/114$, $p < .001$). Tests for the Jones and Nisbett (1971) hypothesis were also strengthened; the contrast between actors and observers in the no-videotape condition was significant at the .05 level, and the contrast between actors and observers in the same-orientation conditions was significant at the .01 level.

Perceived Level of Behavior and Perceived Discrepancy from General Behavior

In addition to the two attribution questions, the subjects also answered questions about the perceived level of behavior on each dimension. Past experiments in this area have typically created a specific, standardized behavior for subjects to attribute. The present experiment, with its unstructured conversations, did not furnish all subjects with the same behavior. This flexibility was desirable, in that it provided a more general test of the attribution hypotheses over several, naturally occurring behaviors. But it also created the possibility that perceptions of the perceived level or intensity of behavior could differ among experimental conditions and thus account for the different attributions. This does not appear to have been the case, however.

There were two ways of calculating perceived level of behavior: (a) by taking the direct value from the 9-point scale for each level-of-behavior response and (b) since the scales were bipolar (for example, 9 = very friendly to 1 = very unfriendly), by taking the deviation of the subject's response from the midpoint of the scale (5). Neither of these measures yielded significant comparisons between any cells in the experiment, either for each behavior considered separately or for all four behaviors totaled. Furthermore, the overall correlations between the total dispositional–situational measure of attributions and the two measures of perceived level of behavior were trivial and nonsignificant ($r = -.049$, for the direct score; $r = -.021$, for the score of deviation from midpoint). Thus, it is apparent that differences in perceived level of behavior could not account for the attribution differences.

Since there were no significant differences in perceived level of behavior, it is meaningful to examine the second measure of subjects' attributions, the present-behavior–general-behavior discrepancy scores. This index reflected the absolute difference between the subjects' perceptions of the actor's *present behavior* (in the conversation) and the actor's *general behavior*, summed over all four behaviors. A small discrepancy would indicate that a subject expected the actor's present behavior to generalize and was thus making a dispositional attribution. A greater discrepancy would indicate less generalization of the actor's behavior and thus a situational attribution.

The results of the present-behavior–general-behavior discrepancy measure, presented in Table 2, corroborated the findings on the dispositional–situational measure of attributions. The effects of videotape reorientation, as tested in the Role × Videotape Orientation interaction, reached significance at $p < .05$, ($F = 3.38$, $df = 2/114$). Again, neither the main effect for role nor the main effect for orientation was significant. Although the direction of differences between the actors and observers in the various conditions was as expected, none of the individual comparisons between cells reached significance on the present-behavior–general-behavior mea-sure, even with the exclusion of the dominance dimension. It appears that the results for the present-behavior–general behavior measure followed the same pattern as, but were generally weaker than, the results for the dispositional–situational measure. The two measures were, incidentally, significantly correlated (overall $r = .361$, $p < .01$).

TABLE 2

PRESENT BEHAVIOR MINUS GENERAL BEHAVIOR DISCREPANCY SCORES SUMMED OVER ALL FOUR BEHAVIORS

Subjects	Same orientation	No videotape	New orientation
Actors	7.15	5.00	4.25
Observers	5.45	4.90	5.90

Discussion

The present study demonstrates that visual orientation has a powerful influence on the inferences made by actors and observers about the causes of the actor's behavior. When videotape was not presented and subjects were left to assume their own orientations, or when videotape reproduced subjects' original orientations, actors attributed their behavior relatively more to situational causes than did observers. This finding supports the Jones and Nisbett (1971) hypothesis that actors' attributions are typically more situational than observers'. But under conditions of reorientation, when subjects saw a new point of view on videotape, the attributional differences between actors and observers were exactly reversed. Reoriented, self-viewing actors attributed their behaviors relatively less to situational causes than did observers. This effect was obtained on two very different measures of attribution across a variety of behavioral dimensions in an unstructured situation.

Mechanisms of Videotape Reorientation

Two important issues arise concerning the possible mechanisms by which video orientation affected attributions. The first issue, one crucial to any laboratory social psychology experiment, concerns experimenter demand characteristics. Demand characteristics could have influenced the results of the present study if the hypotheses had been communicated to subjects either by the experimenter's behavior or by the fact the subjects viewed only one videotape. Both of these possibilities depend on subjects' developing the expectation that videotape had importance for how they should respond. The possibility of communicating the hypotheses was avoided by leading subjects to believe that videotape was not an essential part of the experiment and that the experimenter had wanted to show both tapes but could not, due to circumstances beyond his control. During debriefing, subjects were questioned on their reactions to this hoax; they reported no suspicion that the videotape breakdown had been intentional or important. Moreover, if subjects had been responding to the attribution questions out of desire to support the experimenter's hypotheses, it is unlikely they could have produced the results of the indirect present-behavior–general-behavior measure. This index was derived from the absolute value of the difference between the four level-of-behavior questions and the four general-behavior questions. These questions were widely separated in the questionnaire, and subjects would have had to perform a rather elaborate calculus to produce these results deliberately. Thus, it does not seem likely that the reorientation effects can be accounted for by experimenter demand characteristics.

The second issue involves the possible mechanisms by which videotape caused the predicted attributions. This study was designed to demonstrate that a global manipulation (visual orientation) affects actors' and observers' attributions of the actor's behavior. The study was not designed to separate out the many possible mechanisms by which this might occur. However, some informed speculation is possible.

Jones and Nisbett (1971) proposed several factors that contribute to attributional differences between actors and observers, including differences in the information available about an event and differences in how that information is processed. These two categories are not mutually exclusive, and videotape orientation may have affected aspects of both information availability and information processing. When actors or observers saw a videotape of an event from a different point of view, they may have received some totally new information. The actor may have realized, for the first time, some new aspects of his own behavior; the observer may have seen new aspects of the situation or of the other participant. These new facts could have contributed to changes in subjects' inferences about the cause of behavior. Second, the salience of already available information may have changed for reoriented subjects. Changes in the salience of information have been shown to affect people's perceptions of the reasons for their behavior. For example, Kiesler, Nisbett, and Zanna (1969) found that subjects tended to adopt as explanations of their own behavior motives that were made salient by a confederate. Similarly, subjects in the present study might have formulated their attributions about the actor's behavior on the basis of potential causes which had just been made salient by the videotape. Finally, videotape reorientation may have produced new response sets for subjects. Actors who viewed themselves on tape may have been put into a "self-discovery" frame of mind and thus led to think about their own personality as revealed in their behavior. Similarly, observers who saw a videotape from the actor's point of view may have developed an "empathic" set, imagining themselves to be in the actor's shoes.

It is also of interest to consider the exact nature of the attributional changes evoked by videotape. Changes on the key dependent variable, the dispositional–situational index, were accounted for mostly by changed evaluations of situational causes. Actors assigned a great deal of causality to the situation unless videotape forced them to look away from the situation and toward their own behavior. Observers originally assigned less causality to the situation unless videotape impressed situational factors on them. Differences in attribution to dispositional causes, although in the expected direction, were much weaker than these differences in attribution to situational causes. It may be that the relatively greater amount of change on the situational dimension reflects people's general way of viewing the role of dispositions in causing behavior.

People may characteristically assign fixed and fairly high importance to personal responsibility for behavior. Consequently, they may be left with only one means of modifying their relative assignment of causality and responsibility, namely by varying their evaluations of the situation. In line with this possibility, there may have been a ceiling effect for dispositional attributions in the present study; the overall mean importance assigned to dispositional causes equaled nearly 7 out of a possible 9 scale points. Subjects were thus left with little room to express enhanced dispositional influences.

Up to this point, discussion has been limited to information-related variables which may be modified by video exposure and may in turn affect attributions. Undoubtedly, motivational variables, such as the need to maintain self-esteem and particular self-concepts, could also be affected by videotape observations. One might expect the self-viewing actors in particular to be influenced by such motivations. It is important to note, however, that the present findings were obtained in a situation which was, in many respects, low-key. The behaviors elicited in the getting-acquainted conversations were routine and probably not highly relevant to actors' self-concepts, the interaction between subjects was fairly unemotional, and actors and observers did not have the opportunity to discuss their potentially opposing views of the actor's behavior. It is therefore important to consider whether the present findings would generalize to situations where actors and observers are more emotionally involved, such as in psychotherapy and T groups. There is reason to believe that the present findings have some applicability to the use of videotape even in such emotionally charged settings.

Videotape in Therapy and T Groups

There has been a recent and dramatic increase in the application of videotape feedback in therapy and human relations training. Alger and Hogan (1966a) asserted that "videotape recording represents a technological breakthrough with the kind of significance for psychiatry that the microscope has had for biology [p. 1]." In clinical practice, videotape is frequently used to increase a patient's knowledge of his own behavior (cf. Bailey & Sowder, 1970; Holzman, 1969), and this apparently leads to therapeutic gain. Reivich and Geertsma (1968) reported increased accuracy in patients' knowledge of their own behavior after videotape self-observation. They measured the disparity between a patient's self-ratings on clinical scales and the ratings given him by psychiatric nurses. After videotape self-observation, the ratings of the actor patient came to agree more with the ratings of the observer nurses. Alderfer and Lodahl (1971) found that videotape playback in T groups increased subjects' "openness." Openness was defined as willingness to explore the internal meaning of and accept personal responsibility for an attitude or behavior. Finally, case studies in marital therapy (Alger & Hogan, 1966a; Kagan, Krathwohl, & Miller, 1963) have reported that one or both marriage partners are more willing to assume the blame for a poor relationship after seeing themselves on videotape.

On the other hand, some negative consequences of self-observation have also been reported. For instance, Carrere (1954) used videotape to show alcoholics how they behaved when intoxicated, but he found it necessary to edit the more shocking scenes. The full presentation of their behavior when drunk was too stressful for many of his patients. Parades, Ludwig, Hassenfeld, and Cornelison (1969) similarly reported the lowering of alcoholic patients' self-esteem after viewing their own drunken behavior on tape. Leitenberg, Agras, Thompson, and Wright (1968) gave behavioral feedback (although not video) to phobic patients undergoing behavior modification. These authors found that feedback to patients about successful progress speeds their cure, but information about temporary setbacks interferes with the therapy. Finally, Geertsma and Reivich (1965) reported that some self-viewing depressive patients become more depressed, some schizophrenic patients engage in more bizarre behavior, and some neurotics show an increase in the symptoms characteristic of their particular disorder.

Research to date on the use of videotape in therapy is insufficient to indicate how and with whom it is a beneficial therapy adjunct. It may be possible, however, to apply the findings and the theoretical framework of the present study to the issue of videotape use in therapy. The present study demonstrates that self-observation can change the causal interpretation a person gives to his own behavior. The self-viewing actor (and possibly the self-viewing patient) is more likely to accept personal, dispositional responsibility for his behavior and is less likely to deflect responsibility to the situation.

This attributional consequence of self-observation may help to account for some of the effects of videotape in therapy. For example, the increased openness of T group participants after self-observation may reflect a tendency for each group member to assume more personal, dispositional responsibility for his behavior in the group. Similarly, in marital therapy, the husband or wife who sees himself or herself on videotape may realize for the first time his or her own behavioral contribution to the marital conflict and may be more willing to place a dispositional blame on himself or herself. Finally, the reported increase in agreement between a patient's clinical self-ratings after videotape self-observation and the ratings of observing psychiatric nurses closely parallels the present findings. Self-observation increases an individual's dispositional attributions, thus bringing him more in agreement with the observer's built-in bias for dispositional attributions.

It seems likely that this increase in dispositionality of a patient's attributions would prove to be sometimes therapeutic and sometimes distherapeutic. Successful therapy no doubt usually involves making a patient aware of his own behavior and convincing him to accept personal responsibility for that behavior. Self-observation apparently aids this process and, to that extent, should be therapeutic. However, two potentially negative outcomes of this process might be suggested. First, in becoming more dispositional about their own behavior, individuals who see themselves on videotape may actually underestimate real and viable situational explanations for their behavior. Actors in the present study who saw their own behavior on videotape had a higher mean for dispositional attributions and a lower mean for situational attributions than any other group of subjects. This suggests the possibility that self-viewing actors may have been "undersituational" in attributing their own behavior. That is, videotape may have reoriented these actors so much that they perceived situational causes for their behavior to be even less important than did others who viewed them. And if, as Jones and Nisbett (1971) have suggested, observers are themselves inclined to under-attribute to the situation, this poses a disturbing possibility for therapy. Ironically, the therapist and the self-viewing patient could reach complete agreement about the patient's behavior, yet this agreement could result from a mutual underestimation of the importance of the patient's situation in causing his behavior. This collaborative illusion between patient and therapist could be especially harmful if the patient blames himself for behavior that is in fact due to some aspect of his environment.

Past research on attribution processes has uncovered another area where attributions to the self can have distherapeutic results. Storms and Nisbett (1970) and Valins and Nisbett (1971) have suggested that negative self-labeling which results from attributing uncomplimentary behaviors to dispositions within oneself often lead to a loss of self-esteem and an actual increase in the pathological behavior. For example, insomniacs who attribute their sleeplessness to some negative state within themselves may increase their anxiety and thus aggravate their original condition. Storms and Nisbett proposed that such exacerbation may result whenever self-attributions of a negative disposition increase the individual's anxiety and when anxiety is an irritant to the pathology, such as in impotence, stuttering, and other neurotic conditions. This exacerbation phenomenon may be occurring in some of the therapy cases where negative results have followed the use of videotapes. The finding that self-observation lowers the self-esteem of alcoholic patients might be an instance of this. An alcoholic patient who sees a tape of his own drunken behavior may become quite upset and depressed about himself. Such a traumatic experience may only increase the likelihood that the patient will drink to excess. Whenever a pathology is caused or influenced by a poor self-concept, self-observation of extremely uncomplimentary behavior may serve to retard therapeutic progress.

Research on attribution processes may help to create a theoretical framework for the area of videotape self-observation in therapy settings. The present study suggests that self-observation increases an individual's dispositional attributions of his own behavior and that this brings interpretation of his behavior more in line with an observer's interpretation. In most cases, this should be advantageous to the therapy process, but in certain cases self-attributions could lead to an exacerbation of the original pathology. Therapists would therefore be well advised to look critically at the potential consequences of self-observation. It seems especially important to consider whether a personal, dispositional attribution of the pathological behavior aids the patient to become aware of his problem and to deal with it, or whether self-attribution increases the patient's anxiety to the point of exacerbating his problem.

REFERENCES

ALDERFER, C. P., & LODAHL, T. M. A quasi experiment on the use of experiential methods in the classroom. *Journal of Applied Behavioral Science,* 1971, **7,** 43–69.

ALGER, I., & HOGAN, P. The use of videotape recordings in conjoint marital therapy. Paper presented at the meeting of the American Psychoanalytic Association, Atlantic City, N.J., May 1966. (a)

ALGER, I., & HOGAN, P. Videotape: Its use and significance in psychotherapy. Paper presented at the meeting of the Society of Medical Psychoanalysts, New York Academy of Medicine, New York, September 1966. (b)

BAILEY, K. G., & SOWDER, W. T. Audiotape and videotape self-confrontation in psychotherapy. *Psychological Bulletin,* 1970, **74,** 127–137.

CARRERE, M. J. Le psychochoc cinématographique. *Annales Médico-Psychologiques,* 1954, **112,** 240–245.

GEERTSMA, R. H., & REIVICH, R. S. Repetitive self-observation by videotape playback. *Journal of Nervous and Mental Disease,* 1965, **141,** 29–41.

HOLZMAN, P. S. On hearing and seeing oneself. *Journal of Nervous and Mental Disease,* 1969, **148,** 198–209.

JONES, E. E., & HARRIS, V. A. The attribution of attitudes. *Journal of Experimental Social Psychology,* 1967, **3,** 1–24.

JONES, E. E., & NISBETT, R. E. *The actor and the observer: Divergent perceptions of the causes of behavior.* Morristown, N.J.: General Learning Press, 1971.

JONES, E. E., ROCK, L., SHAVER, K. G., GOETHALS, G. R., & WARD, L. M. Pattern of performance and ability attribution: An unexpected primacy effect. *Journal of Personality and Social Psychology,* 1968, **10,** 317–340.

KAGAN, N., KRATHWOHL, D. R., & MILLER, R. Stimulated recall in therapy using videotape: A case study. *Journal of Counseling Psychology,* 1963, **10,** 237–243.

KIESLER, C. A., NISBETT, R. E., & ZANNA, M. P. On inferring one's beliefs from one's behavior. *Journal of Personality and Social Psychology,* 1969, **11,** 321–327.

LEITENBERG, H., AGRAS, W. S., THOMPSON, L. E., & WRIGHT, D. E. Feedback in behavior modification: An experimental analysis of two cases. *Journal of Applied Behavioral Analysis,* 1968, **1,** 131–137.

MCARTHUR, L. Appropriateness of the behavior and consensus and distinctiveness information as determinants of actors' and observers' attributions. Unpublished manuscript, Yale University, 1970.

MCARTHUR, L. A. The how and what of why: Some determinants and consequences of causal attribution. *Journal of Personality and Social Psychology,* 1972, **22,** 171–193.

NISBETT, R. E., CAPUTO, G. C., LEGANT, P., & MARECEK, J. Behavior as seen by the actor and as seen by the observer. *Journal of Personality and Social Psychology,* 1973, **27,** 154–164.

PARADES, A., LUDWIG, K. D., HASSENFELD, I. N., & CORNELISON, F. S. A clinical study of alcoholics using audio-visual self-image feedback. *Journal of Nervous and Mental Disease,* 1969, **148,** 449–456.

REIVICH, R. S., & GEERTSMA, R. H. Experiences with videotape self-observation by psychiatric inpatients. *Journal of Kansas Medical Society,* 1968, **69,** 39–44.

STORMS, M. D., & NISBETT, R. E. Insomnia and the attribution process. *Journal of Personality and Social Psychology,* 1970, **16,** 319–328.

VALINS, S., & NISBETT, R. E. *Some implications of attribution process for the development and treatment of emotional disorders.* Morristown, N.J.: General Learning Press, 1971.

WINER, B. J. *Statistical principles in experimental design.* New York: McGraw-Hill, 1962.

(Received February 24, 1972)

Ubiquitous Watergate: An Attributional Analysis

Stephen G. West, Steven P. Gunn, and Paul Chernicky
Florida State University

Actor–observer differences in causal attribution were investigated in an experiment involving two separate studies. Study 1 was a field experiment in which 80 subjects (actors) were presented with elaborate plans for burglarizing a local advertising firm under one of four experimental conditions: (a) a control condition, (b) $2,000 (reward), (c) government sponsorship but no immunity from prosecution, and (d) government sponsorship plus immunity. In Study 2, 238 subjects (observers) read a description of a student agreeing or refusing to participate in the burglary under one of the four experimental conditions. Consistent with Jones and Nisbett's 1971 theory, actors made more environmental attributions, while observers made more dispositional attributions. Further, observers made more dispositional attributions when the actor agreed than when he refused, except in the reward condition, where this relationship was reversed. The results are interpreted with reference to the disparate explanations of Watergate offered by the Nixon administration and the press.

During the past 2 years, the news media have spent a large amount of time and effort investigating the series of political crimes that have been termed Watergate. The media have been very troubled by these crimes, which do not fit the usual explanations (e.g., greed) for political crimes. Consequently, they have been forced to search for new explanations of the Watergate crimes. The press has proposed such explanations as the paranoid style of the Nixon administration, the recruitment of an amoral staff of nonpolitical administrators, and even such fanciful explanations as that members of the Nixon administration had been injected with "moral penicillin." On the other hand, several members of the Nixon administration have proposed a very different set of explanations for the Watergate burglary and cover-up. They have suggested that these activities were a natural result of the potentially violent plans of the radical left and that given the available alternative courses of action, such activities were demanded by circumstances. These divergent explanations of the same event by the press and those who were involved may strike one as unusual, defensive, or possibly even reflecting psychodynamic thought disturbances on the part of one group or the other, but such a result is consistent with recent research and theorizing in social psychology.

Jones and Nisbett (1971) have argued that actors (i.e., those actively involved) and observers often have very different perceptions of the causes of the behavior of the actor in a given situation. They point out that while the actor and observer may have identical information concerning the action and its environmental outcomes, the actor generally has more information about his intentions, his emotional state, and the events leading up to the action. Furthermore, the actor's attention is also focused on the environment from which he selects cues to guide his behavior, while the observer's attention is focused on the actor and his behavior. According to Jones and Nisbett, the result of these differences is a tendency for the actor to attribute the cause of his behavior to the environment, while the observer tends to attribute the actor's behavior to dispositional characteristics of the actor.

Supporting Jones and Nisbett's (1971) position are two notable cases in which the press, society's professional observers,

---

We thank Russell D. Clark, III, William Haythorn, Michael Nash, and Lee Sechrest for their comments on the manuscript and Judi Black for her secretarial assistance.

Steven P. Gunn is now at Connecticut College, New London.

Requests for reprints should be sent to Stephen G. West, Department of Psychology, Florida State University, Tallahassee, Florida 32306.

From *Journal of Personality and Social Psychology*, 1975, 32(1), 55–65. Copyright 1975 by American Psychological Association. Reprinted by permission.

have inferred that an extreme action was due to the dispositional characteristics of the people involved, only to discover later through social-psychological research that the behavior in question is, under similar conditions, controlled primarily by a variety of situational factors. These two cases are the blind obedience to authority observed in the German army during World War II and the failure of bystanders to help in dramatic emergency situations.

The first case, blind obedience to authority, provides a good example of the disparity between the conclusions of the press and research. Authors such as Shirer (1960) have suggested that the specialized obedience training of the German army, particularly the officer corps, or some aspect of "German national character" was responsible for the horrible actions carried out on the orders of authorities during World War II. However, in a series of experiments, Milgram (1963, 1964a, 1965, 1974) has demonstrated that situational factors such as the proximity of the subject to the victim, the proximity of the experimenter to the subject, the setting in which the experiment takes place, and group pressure are important determinants of obedience. Thus, consistent with the Jones and Nisbett formulation, observers have ignored the possibility of strong situational pressures within the Germany army that may have been in large part responsible for the actions perpetrated in World War II.

A second case that led to similar public outrage and press coverage was the murder of Kitty Genovese in Queens, New York, in front of 38 witnesses who did not attempt to intervene. The press and other observers pointed to personal factors such as feelings of apathy, dehumanization, and alienation from one's fellow man. However, research by Latané and Darley and their co-workers (Darley & Latané, 1968; Latané & Darley, 1968, 1969; Latané & Rodin, 1969) has shown that groups of bystanders frequently do not help in a wide variety of experimental situations and that the amount of helping is determined by such situational factors as the number of other bystanders (Latané & Darley, 1968, 1969), the others' ability to help (Bickman, 1971; Korte, 1969), the similarity of prior acquaintanceship of the others (Latané & Rodin, 1969; Smith, Smythe, & Lien, 1972), and the ambiguity of the emergency situation (Clark & Word, 1972, 1974). Thus, once again, situational factors are a major determinant of a phenomenon that initially seemed to outside observers to be due to dispositional factors of the actors involved.

Given the possibility of situational determinants of behavior, a very different set of causes for Watergate crimes may be proposed. It may be the case that the Watergate crimes were due to enormous situational pressures on those involved, such as normative expectations within the Nixon administration, the payoff matrix for engaging versus not engaging in these illegal activities, and other pressures that may not have been known or salient to outside observers. If situational factors were important in the Watergate case, then several implications may be drawn from Jones and Nisbett's (1971) theory and recent research on compliance (Allen, 1965; Kiesler & Kiesler, 1969). First, under similar high situational pressures, a significant percentage of a sample of subjects (actors) should agree to engage in similar illegal activities. Second, the percentage of subjects who agree to engage in illegal activities should be a function of situational factors related to compliance. And finally, the subjects, whether they agree or do not agree to engage in illegal activities, should attribute their decision primarily to situational factors, such as potential costs or rewards. However, outside observers should perceive dispositional characteristics rather than situational factors as the cause of the actor's decision.

The derivations were tested in two studies: an experiment and a subsequent interpersonal simulation with observers (Bem, 1967). In the experiment (Study 1), conducted in a field setting, actor subjects were led to believe that they had an opportunity to participate in an illegal burglary. The rationale for the burglary was varied so that some possible situational determinants of compliance in this setting, suggested by the Watergate investigations (Gold, 1973), could be investigated. Three factors considered to be possible determinants of agreement in this situation were studied: (a) sponsorship of the crime by a United States government agency, (b) an offer of a relatively large amount of money for committing the crime, and (c) an offer of immunity from prosecution when the crime is supposedly sponsored by a United States government agency. A control group in which the crime was not sponsored by any agency and the subject could not expect any reward or immunity from prosecution was also included in the design to provide a baseline compliance rate. Since the primary focus of the present experiment was not compliance, it should be sufficient merely to demonstrate differences between experimental conditions. However, based on the testimony during the Watergate hearings and the conformity literature (Allen, 1965; Endler, 1966; Kiesler & Kiesler, 1969), it was predicted that the control condition should have the lowest compliance rate, the government-sponsorship plus immunity-from-prosecution condition should have the highest compliance rate, and the other groups should be intermediate in compliance.

The second study involved comparing the reasons given for participating in the crime by the subjects (actors) in the field experiment and the observers in the interpersonal simulation. Based on Jones and Nisbett's (1971) theory, it was predicted that subjects would tend to attribute their actions to situational factors, while observers would tend to attribute their actions to dispositional characteristics of the subjects.

Method

Field Experiment: Study 1

Subjects (actors). The subjects were 80 students (56 males and 24 females) selected at random from a list of undergraduate majors in criminology. Two restrictions were placed on random sampling: Subjects who were close friends of either the experimenter or the confederate were eliminated, and the percentage of males and females was held constant across conditions.

Procedure. Each subject was initially approached by the experimenter, who was known to most of the subjects as a local private investigator. The experimenter told the subject that he had "a project you might be interested in" and suggested to the subject that they meet at the experimenter's home or at a local restaurant. If the subject asked about the reason for the meeting, he (she) was assured that it would be fully discussed at the later time. Every person approached did make an appointment to meet with the experimenter.

At the later meeting, the experimenter was accompanied by the confederate. The experimenter carried a briefcase that contained elaborate plans for the commission of a burglary of a local advertising firm. Except for the changes in the rationale for the crime, the procedure was constant across experimental conditions.

Subjects were randomly assigned to one of four experimental conditions. In the first two conditions, in which the burglary was to be committed for a government agency (the Internal Revenue Service), the subjects were told that the burglary was for the purposes of microfilming an allegedly illegal set of accounting records maintained by the firm to defraud the United States Government out of 6.8 million tax dollars per year. It was further explained that the company was in reality a front for a Miami investment corporation and that a dual set of records was being kept. The microfilmed records were described as being necessary to get a search warrant and subpoena so that the original records could be seized. In the first condition, the subjects were told that the government had guaranteed them immunity from prosecution if apprehended, while in the second condition, the subjects were warned that there would be no immunity from prosecution if apprehended.

In the third condition, the subjects were told that another local advertising firm had offered $8,000 for a copy of a set of designs prepared by the first firm. The subjects were told that they would be paid $2,000 for their participation in the crime.

In the fourth condition (control) the subjects were told that the crime was being committed merely to determine whether the burglary plans designed by the experimenter would work. The subjects were further told that while an illegal act of burglary would be committed, absolutely nothing would be stolen from the office.

Upon meeting the subject, the experimenter introduced him (her) to the confederate, who played the role of a member of the burglary team. The experimenter gave the rationale for the commission of the crime and revealed the details of the plan in a standard order. If the subject protested that he did not want to discuss the crime, he was asked to listen to the plans on their full detail prior to making a final decision. No subject attempted to leave the situation, nor did any ask that the experimenter leave.

The subjects in all conditions were told that the burglary of an advertising firm located in a local office building had been carefully planned and that a four-person team was necessary to carry it out. This team was to consist of (a) the experimenter, who would monitor police calls in an office inside the building; (b) the confederate, who would serve as an outside lookout; (c) a lock-and-safe expert (not present in the experimental situation), who was described as having an extensive background in military intelligence; and (d) the subject, who was to serve as an inside lookout and who was also to microfilm the advertising agency records. The crime was presented to the subject in elaborate detail, including aerial photographs of the building and the surrounding area, lists of city and state patrol cars, their routes and times, and blueprints of the advertising office. The total effect of the situation was to create as great an impact as possible and to convince the subject that it was a well-planned, professional job with only a minimal chance of being caught.

The subjects were then encouraged to ask questions; these questions were answered by the experimenter. Virtually all of the questions concerned technical details of the plan. The subjects were then asked to come to the final planning meeting, which would take place at the experimenter's office. If the subject refused, the experimenter reemphasized that the plan was foolproof and asked the subject to reconsider his decision. If the subject refused a second time, the experiment was terminated. The confederate, who was blind to the hypotheses, recorded the subject's decision to agree or refuse to participate and summarized the subject's rationale for his decision. The subject's agreement or refusal to participate in the burglary and his reasons for the decision were the major dependent variables. At the conclusion of the experiment, subjects were extensively debriefed, and the nature and the reasons for the deceptions were explained in detail.

Interpersonal Simulation: Study 2

Subjects (observers). The subjects were 238 students from the introductory psychology classes (92 males and 146 females) who volunteered to participate in partial fulfillment of their course requirements. Subjects were run in groups of 30–50 subjects per session; all experimental conditions were represented within each session.

Procedure. Each subject received a mimeographed booklet describing in great detail one of the four conditions used in the field experiment. The subject then answered three sets of dependent measures. The first set (estimations) asked the subject, "If 100 students were presented with this proposal, how many [number] would you guess would agree to participate?" The subject was also asked, "Would you do it?" and was given the opportunity to respond yes, maybe, or no and to write comments.

The second set (attributions) consisted of a free-response measure and a forced-choice measure. For the free-response measure, the following question was used: "Suppose John, an undergraduate student at FSU [Florida State University], after listening to the proposal described above, agreed [refused] to participate. In two or three sentences, briefly describe why John made this decision." For half of the subjects, John was described as agreeing to participate, while for the other half, John was described as refusing to participate in the burglary.[1]

The above two sets of dependent measures constituted the primary dependent measures for the present experiment. In order to eliminate any effects of the order of presentation of the measures, the order in which these two sets of measures were presented was counterbalanced across subjects.

Finally, a third set of measures (personality impressions) was given to the subjects to provide supplemental information as to their perceptions of the personalities of John and the private investigator. Each subject rated both John and the private investigator on the same fifteen 5-point scales, which were anchored with an adjective at each end (e.g., intelligent–unintelligent). For eight of the pairs, the left side of the scale was anchored with the more socially desirable adjective; while for six of the pairs, the left side of the scale was anchored with the less socially desirable adjective.[2]

In summary, a 4 × 2 × 2 design was used with the factors being the four experimental treatments (government sponsorship, reward, immunity, and control), the order in which the estimation measures and attribution measures were presented, and whether John agreed or refused to participate in the burglary.

Results

Compliance Rates

Field experiment: Study 1. The percentage of subjects in each condition agreeing and refusing to participate in the proposed burglary is presented in Table 1. The data were first analyzed using an overall chi-square test,[3] which showed an overall difference in the agreement rates as a function of the four experimental conditions, $\chi^2(3) = 11.8$, $p < .01$. Male and female subjects did not differ in their compliance rates, with Yates's correction, $\chi^2(1) = .63$, *ns*.

---

[1] The forced-choice measure adapted from McArthur (1972) was unaffected by the experimental manipulations and is therefore not discussed.

[2] The social desirability of the adjective pairs had been previously assessed in a pilot study by the first author. One pair, liberal–conservative, did not have a clear-cut socially desirable end.

[3] The expected frequencies in the present chi-square analysis are equal to 4 in four cells (agree to participate). While early writers (e.g., Cochran, 1954; Siegel, 1956) suggested that the use of chi-square was questionable when more than 20% of the cells had expected values between 1 and 5, recent work (Good, Gover, & Mitchell, 1970; Yarnold, 1970; Zahn & Roberts, 1971) has shown that the chi-square test is robust so long as the critical cells have equal expected frequencies that are greater than 1.

The data were further analyzed to investigate the compliance rates of the four experimental groups. Neither the sponsorship by a U.S. government agency nor the offer of a large amount of money for participation led to an appreciable increase in compliance over that in the control condition (Fisher's exact test, both nonsignificant). However, given sponsorship by a U.S. government agency, the offer of immunity from prosecution significantly increased compliance over the rate obtained when no immunity from prosecution was offered, with Yates' correction, $\chi^2(1) = 6.53, p < .02$.

Interpersonal simulation: Study 2. The observer subjects' estimations of the number of college students who would participate in the burglary were subjected to a $4 \times 2 \times 2$ (Conditions $\times$ Decision $\times$ Order) analysis of variance. Of most interest, none of the effects of conditions, namely, the Conditions $\times$ Order, Conditions $\times$ Decision, and Conditions $\times$ Order $\times$ Decision interactions were significant ($p > .20$). Female observers did estimate that a larger number of students (out of a possible 100) would agree to participate than did male observers (for females, $\bar{X} = 27.3$; for males, $\bar{X} = 20.3$), $F(1, 194) = 4.81, p < .03$.

The observer subjects' reports of their personal decisions to agree or refuse to participate are also presented in Table 1. These data were subjected to an overall chi-square analysis paralleling that computed for the actor subjects. Due to the small number of observer subjects who reported that they would agree to participate, those subjects who responded "maybe" were included in the agreement category for the purposes of the analysis. The analysis showed a slight tendency for an overall difference in the compliance rates as a function of the four experimental conditions, $\chi^2(3) = 5.75, p < .20$.

To determine whether the obtained pattern of results differed for the actor and observer subjects, the data were subjected to a $4 \times 2 \times 2$ multidimensional chi-square analysis (Winer, 1971, pp. 855–859). The appropriate test for actor–observer differences is the Conditions $\times$ Actor–Observer $\times$ Decision interaction, which failed to reach significance,

TABLE 1

COMPLIANCE RATES OF ACTORS AND SELF-ESTIMATED COMPLIANCE RATES OF OBSERVERS

Decision	Government sponsorship		Reward	Control
	Immunity	No immunity		
Actor[a]				
Agree	45	5	20	10
Refuse	55	95	80	90
Observer[b]				
Agree	28.1	14.0	12.2	18.2
Refuse	71.9	76.0	87.8	82.8

Note. Data are given in percentages.
[a] For all experimental conditions, $n = 20$.
[b] For experimental conditions $n = 57$, except for the control condition, where $n = 55$.

$\chi^2(3) = 4.70, p < .20$. Once again the Conditions $\times$ Decision (Agree to Participate vs. Refuse to Participate) interaction was significant, $\chi^2(3) = 13.48, p < .005$. These effects taken together indicate that the observer subjects are generally able to produce the same pattern of compliance data as the actor subjects but that the effect of the conditions for the observer subjects is much weaker than for the actor subjects.

Contrary to subjects' estimation for other students, fewer females than males said that they would agree to participate in the proposed burglary (13% of females agreed vs. 27.5% of males), with Yates's correction, $\chi^2(1) = 6.37, p < .025$. This finding contrasts with the results of the field study in which there was actually no difference in compliance between males and females.

Attribution Data

The free-response answers of the actor and observer subjects to the question "Why did you [John] make this decision?" were first reworded into the third person (e.g., "He made his decision because . . .") by a secretary who was blind to the experimental hypothesis. The answers were then typed on slips of paper and coded by two raters who were blind as to the subject's condition, the subject's sex, and whether the subject was an actor or observer. The raters coded each response into one of three mutually exclusive categories: (a) A *disposition* of the actor (attitude or personality trait) caused the

TABLE 2
ATTRIBUTIONS OF ACTORS AND OBSERVERS

Decision	Actor	Observer
Agree	2.25	1.76
Refuse	2.39	2.05

Note. Responses were coded according to the following scale: 1 = a dispositional factor caused the decision, 2 = a combination of dispositional and environmental factors caused the decision, and 3 = an environmental factor caused the decision.

decision, (b) a dispositional factor in *combination* with an environmental factor caused the decision, or (c) an *environmental factor* caused the decision.[4] The intercorrelation of the ratings of the two raters indicated a satisfactory level of reliability ($r = .95$).

The attributions of the actors and observers as to the cause of the decision (i.e., dispositional, environmental, or combination) as a function of the actor's decision to participate in the proposed burglary are presented in Table 2. The analysis of variance showed that as predicted, the actors made more environmental attributions than the observers, $F(1, 304) = 12.05$, $p < .001$. A tendency was also noted for both actors and observers to make more dispositional attributions when the actor agreed than when he refused to participate, $F(1, 304) = 3.54$, $p < .10$.

The observer attribution data were further analyzed taking into account the four experimental conditions. The mean attributions made by the observers as a function of the four experimental conditions and the actor's decision to participate or not to participate in the burglary are presented in Figure 1. A 2 × 4 (Decision × Conditions) analysis of variance showed an effect of the actor's decision, $F(1, 220) = 6.41$, $p < .01$, modified, however, by a Condition × Decision interaction, $F(3, 220) = 4.43$, $p < .01$. In the control, government sponsorship, and immunity conditions, the mean attribution was more dispositional if the actor agreed to participate; whereas in the reward condition, the mean attribution was less dispositional if the actor agreed to participate.

A subsequent analysis that examined possible sex differences in attributions showed one effect of interest, a significant Sex × Agreement interaction, $F(1, 196) = 7.02$, $p < .01$. While the attributions of male observers were strongly affected by whether John agreed or refused to participate (for agree, $\bar{X} = 1.54$; for refuse, $\bar{X} = 2.24$), female observers were affected to a lesser degree by this factor (for agree, $\bar{X} = 1.85$; for refuse, $\bar{X} = 2.00$).

Although analyses paralleling those for the observer data were originally planned for the actor data, the small number of subjects who agreed to participate in two of the conditions precluded a finer statistical breakdown of the actor data.

Personality Impressions

The observer subjects' data for each of the 15 personality impression adjective pairs for both the student and private investigator were subjected to a 4 × 2 × 2 (Conditions × Decision × Order) analysis of variance. The results for the student showed a significant effect for decision in nearly every case. When John was described as agreeing to participate in the burglary, he was rated by the observers as more outgoing, less intelligent, less wealthy, more insecure, less happy, less trustworthy, less generous, more liberal, lower in status, possessing less social poise, less sophisticated, more thrill seeking, and more impulsive than when he was described as refusing to participate in the burglary.[5]

A different pattern of results emerged for the observer's impression of the personality of the private investigator. When the student agreed to participate in the burglary, the private investigator was described as more intelligent, higher in status, more socially poised, and less impulsive.[6] In addition, several effects of the experimental conditions emerged. When the burglary was described as being committed for the government agency (immunity and government sponsorship conditions), the private investigator was rated by the observers as being happier, more generous, and more conservative.

---

[4] For example, "He is the type of person who likes adventure and taking risks" was coded as dispositional, while "The amount of money involved and that the plan was foolproof are why he made his decision" was coded as environmental. For further details on the coding system, contact the first author.

[5] $p < .001$ in each case.

[6] $p < .05$ in each case.

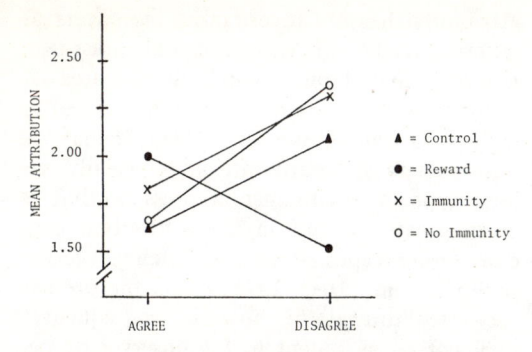

FIGURE 1. Mean attributions of observers on free-response measure ("Suppose John . . ."). The scale of responses is as follows: 1 refers to a personal (dispositional) factor, 2 refers to a combination of dispositional and environmental factors, and 3 refers to an environmental factor.

In summary, based on the present results and previous pilot research on the social desirability of these adjective pairs, it would seem that when the student is described as agreeing to participate in the burglary, he is perceived by the observers as a less socially desirable and more easily persuaded person than when he refuses to participate. In addition, when the student is described as agreeing to participate, the results suggest that the private investigator is perceived as a more effective persuader than when the student is described as refusing to participate.

DISCUSSION

Compliance Rates

In general, the results of the field experiment tended to support the compliance predictions. Subjects offered immunity from prosecution showed the highest rate of compliance, subjects in the control condition showed a low rate of compliance, and subjects in the reward condition showed an intermediate compliance rate. The low rate of compliance in the government sponsorship condition was unexpected but may have been due to the particular agency chosen, the Internal Revenue Service. Several subjects indicated during the debriefing session that they had ambivalent attitudes toward this agency. While on the one hand, they admired the agency's work in the enforcement of laws pertaining to crime and big business, on the other hand, they expressed hostility toward the agency's role in collecting personal income tax. Thus, several of the students indicated that they would not take any risk to help this particular agency. Whether students would take such risks for a more esteemed government agency is an empirical question.

It should be emphasized that the high compliance rates obtained in two of the conditions are a reflection of the strong situational pressures in the experiment. Several techniques were used in the present experiment that have been shown in previous research to increase compliance rates. For example, subjects made an initial commitment to come to a meeting (Freedman & Fraser, 1966) where they faced a unanimous majority (Asch, 1956) with a high level of expertise (Freedman, Carlsmith, & Sears, 1974). While no personality measures were obtained on the subjects in the present experiment, based on the failures of personality measures to predict behavior in other situations in which strong situational pressures were placed on the subject, for example, Milgram's obedience research (Elms & Milgram, 1966) and Latané and Darley's bystander intervention research (Darley & Batson, 1973; Darley & Latané, 1968), it seems unlikely that personality variables would predict a significant portion of the variance in the present experimental situation (also see Mischel, 1973).

The limited success of the observer subjects in reproducing the results of the field experiment is consistent with recent research that directly compares actual subjects with role-playing subjects (Darroch & Steiner, 1970; Horowitz & Rothschild, 1970; West & Brown, 1975; Willis & Willis, 1970). Contrary to the optimism of some earlier writers (Brown, 1965; Greenberg, 1967; Kelman, 1967), in general, role playing has not been entirely successful in replicating the results of laboratory or field experiments with involved subjects. In the present experiment, the observer data taken by themselves, even with a much larger number of subjects than in the field experiment, do not show significant condition differences. In addition, if the maybe category had not been fortuitously included along with the yes and no categories as a possible response to the self-estimation question, the weak condition difference trends observed in the data probably would not have been obtained. The failure of the observers to show even similar condition difference trends when estimating how many subjects would participate further demonstrates the fragile nature of the role-playing data. In conclusion, the failure of role playing in the present research and the other failures of role playing to reproduce the results of experiments in a variety of areas, together with the epistemological questions raised by Freedman (1969), lead us to conclude with Freedman (1969, p. 207) that "role playing is not a substitute for experimental research."

Attribution Data

The results of the experiment supported the prediction derived from Jones and Nisbett's (1971) theory. Actors attributed their behavior to environmental factors, while observers attributed the actor's behavior to dispositions of the actor. This finding is consistent with other recent research comparing the attributions of actors and observers (Nisbett, Caputo, Legant, & Marecek, 1973) and other experimental evidence that attributions follow the focus of attention (Duval & Wicklund, 1973; Storms, 1973).

The effect on the observer's attributions of the actor's decision to agree or refuse to participate in the burglary is consistent with Jones and Davis's (1965) theory of correspondent inferences. According to this theory, if an action is out of role or socially undesirable, the observer is more likely to attribute the action to a disposition of the actor than if the action is in role or socially desirable. Since the observers' impression ratings of a student who agreed to participate were less socially desirable than their ratings of a student who refused to participate, most of the observers probably viewed the burglary as being rather socially undesirable. In support of the above interpretation, previous research (Jones, Davis, & Gergen, 1961; Messick & Reeder, 1972) has demonstrated that observers' attributions become more dispositional as an actor's behavior is perceived as more socially undesirable or out of role.

The Condition × Decision interaction obtained for observer subjects was not predicted, since previous research on other-attribution has not investigated the effects of different types of environmental pressures. However, based on research in the area of self-attribution (Bem, 1967; Deci, 1971; Lepper, Greene, & Nisbett, 1973), it may be that monetary rewards are an especially salient type of environmental pressure that is given greater weight in the attribution process. Other types of rewards such as verbal reinforcement (Deci, 1971) or, in the present case, withdrawal of possible consequences may not be as salient to the observer of behavior, thus leading to dispositional attributions. Those classes of environmental pressure that are salient to observers and, more important, differentially salient to actors and observers can only be determined through future research.

Implications

The present research suggests that when outside observers, including the press, view an action, they tend to give too much weight to dispositional factors as the cause of behavior. In addition, observers seem to be relatively poor role players, so that in some cases, even attempting to put themselves in the role of the actor may not completely eliminate the attributional biases of the observer. Consequently, if an observer is to understand the causes of an actor's behavior, he should try to ascertain the precise situational pressures operating on the actor. In addition, following Jones and Nisbett (1971), the observer should try to understand the past history of the events leading up to the action, the actor's emotional state, and the actor's intentions in choosing to pursue the particular course of action. To the extent that the observer can do these things, he should be able to increase his understanding of the causes of the actor's behavior.

A final point should be made concerning the relative accuracy of the attributions made by actors and observers. It may be argued that the subjects in the field experiment and the members of the Nixon administration did not accurately perceive the "true" causes of their own behavior. This may or may not be the case (see Jones & Nisbett, 1971). However, it is more important, in terms of understanding the causes of the events and in predicting future behaviors, to attempt to understand the situational pressures that the actor perceives to be bearing upon him. For it is the actor's and not the observer's perception of reality that determines the actor's behavior.

Ubiquitous Watergate: Ethical Issues

The field experimental portion of the present study involved elaborate deceptions in which some subjects indicated an implicit agreement to become involved in a potentially illegal and possibly immoral activity. During the experiment and following disclosure of the experimental deceptions, it is possible that some subjects may have experienced some temporary loss of self-esteem: They may have felt embarrassed, guilty, or anxious when confronted with the full meaning of their implied agreement to participate in the alleged break-in. It is precisely this kind of experiment that has raised prior controversy concerning ethics in psychological research (e.g., Baumrind, 1964; Kelman, 1967; Milgram, 1964b). Therefore, we feel that it is important to address the ethical issues posed by the present experiment and to state our position on these issues (see also Cook, 1975).

A number of procedural aspects of the field experiment reported here reflect our concern with ethical considerations. First, the actual experimental manipulations were carried out in a controlled setting so that the subjects could not leave the situation feeling that they had, in fact, become involved in an illegal activity. Second, the experimental manipulations were not forced on any of the subjects. Following an initial information contact by the experimenter, all of the subjects agreed to and attended the experimental "meeting" by their own choice. Third, the present procedure was selected only after alternative procedures such as role playing had been carefully considered. Various alternative research methodologies were discussed with colleagues from several different areas of psychology and were ultimately rejected. The failure of the interpersonal simulation in the present case supports the decision not to rely on role-playing methodology. Fourth, a lawyer-psychologist served as a legal consultant during the planning and implementation of the field experiment in order to protect the legal status of the subjects and experimenters. A review of the field experiment by the State Attorney's Office (in Florida) also found the procedures employed to be legally acceptable.[7] Finally, all subjects were thoroughly debriefed *immediately* after the collection of the dependent variables.

The debriefing procedure closely followed the recommendations of Aronson and Carlsmith (1968, pp. 29–36; 70–73). These involve the gradual revelation of the true purpose of the experiment and a discussion with the subject of the necessity for, and the experimenter's regret in having to use, deception in studying problems of this nature. The subject was encouraged to express his (her) feelings, whether positive or negative, about both the importance of the study and the deceptions employed. Finally, the discussion was conducted in a manner that facilitated the restoration of equality to the experimenter–subject relationship.

While post hoc declarations of experimenter innocence are less noteworthy than the experimental precautions discussed above, none of the subjects appeared to suffer any form of psychological trauma as a result of their participation in the field experiment. On the contrary, during debriefing, many subjects spontaneously commented that they found the experiment to be an interesting and even enlightening experience.

We agree, in principle, with Cook (1975) concerning the desirability of long-term postexperimental follow-ups. In that part of our more recent research involving possible mental, physical, or emotional stress to the subjects, such follow-up data have been routinely collected. As Cook has noted, such a procedure will assist in identifying and ameliorating the long-term effects, if any, of the experimental manipulations. In addition, such results, if published, will provide some *empirical* information upon which to base future ethical codes. Follow-ups of previous research have uniformly failed to demonstrate long-term negative consequences of the experimental manipulations (Clark & Word, 1974; Milgram, 1974; Ring, Walston, & Corey, 1970; Zimbardo, 1974), even though

---

[7] Copies of the legal statement of the State Attorney's Office are available from the first author.

the manipulations may have led to greater potential stress on the part of the subjects than the procedures used in the present experiment. In addition, Resnick and Schwartz (1973) have demonstrated that strict adherence to current (American Psychological Association, 1973) ethical standards in a verbal conditioning experiment led to results that were *opposite* to those usually obtained in such studies and resulted in an increase in the negativity of the subjects' attitudes toward the experiment. We argue, as did Gergen (1973), that "what is needed is factual advice about the possible harmful consequences of various research strategies" (p. 912), both to the subject and to the quality of the research results.

In designing and conducting social-psychological research, experimenters are faced with the task of balancing the value of the information gained from their research against concern for the rights and dignity of their subjects (Aronson & Carlsmith, 1968; American Psychological Association, 1973). From our viewpoint, the present experiment addresses questions of vital importance in contemporary American society: What are some of the situational factors which significantly increase the probability that normally law-abiding citizens will agree to involvement in illegal activities that may violate the civil rights of others? To what extent can the press be considered a veridical source of information concerning the causes of certain actions by governmental leaders? The preceding paragraphs delineate our attention to the rights and dignity of the subjects in this experiment. We have attempted to make every effort to achieve the appropriate balance.

REFERENCES

Allen, V. L. Situational factors in conformity. In L. Berkowitz (Ed.), *Advances in experimental social psychology* (Vol. 2). New York: Academic Press, 1965.

American Psychological Association. *Ethical principles in the conduct of research with human participants.* Washington, D.C.: Author, 1973.

Aronson, E., & Carlsmith, J. M. Experimentation in social psychology. In G. Lindzey & E. Aronson, *Handbook of social psychology* (Vol. 2). Reading, Mass.: Addison-Wesley, 1968.

Asch, S. E. Studies of independence and conformity. A minority of one against a unanimous majority. *Psychological Monographs,* 1956, *70*(9, Whole No. 416).

Baumrind, D. Some thoughts on ethics of research: After reading Milgram's "Behavioral study of obedience." *American Psychologist,* 1964, *19,* 421–423.

Bem, D. J. Self-perception. An alternative interpretation of dissonance phenomena. *Psychological Review,* 1967, *74,* 183–200.

Bickman, L. The effect of another bystander's ability to help on bystander intervention in an emergency. *Journal of Experimental Social Psychology,* 1971, *7,* 367–379.

Brown, R. *Social psychology.* New York: Free Press, 1965.

Clark, R. D., III, & Word, L. E. Why don't bystanders help? Because of ambiguity? *Journal of Personality and Social Psychology,* 1972, *24,* 392–400.

Clark, R. D., III, & Word, L. E. Where is the apathetic bystander? Situational characteristics of the emergency. *Journal of Personality and Social Psychology,* 1974, *29,* 279–287.

Cochran, W. G. Some methods for strengthening common χ^2 tests. *Biometrics,* 1954, *10,* 417–451.

Cook, S. W. A comment on the ethical issues involved in West, Gunn, and Chernicky's "Ubiquitous Watergate: An attributional analysis." *Journal of Personality and Social Psychology,* 1975, *32,* 66–68.

Darley, J. M., & Batson, C. D. "From Jerusalem to Jericho": A study of situational and dispositional variables in helping behavior. *Journal of Personality and Social Psychology,* 1973, *27,* 100–108.

Darley, J. M., & Latané, B. Bystander intervention in emergencies: Diffusion of responsibility. *Journal of Personality and Social Psychology,* 1968, *8,* 377–383.

Darroch, R. K., & Steiner, I. D. Role playing: An alternative to laboratory research? *Journal of Personality,* 1970, *38,* 302–311.

Deci, E. L. Effects of externally mediated rewards on intrinsic motivation. *Journal of Personality and Social Psychology,* 1971, *18,* 105–115.

Duval, S., & Wicklund, R. A. Effects of objective self awareness on the attribution of causality. *Journal of Experimental Social Psychology,* 1973, *9,* 17–31.

Elms, A. C., & Milgram, S. Personality characteristics associated with obedience and defiance towards authoritative command. *Journal of Experimental Research in Personality,* 1966, *1,* 282–289.

Endler, N. S. Conformity as a function of different reinforcement schedules. *Journal of Personality and Social Psychology,* 1966, *4,* 175–180.

Freedman, J. L. Role playing: Psychology by consensus. *Journal of Personality and Social Psychology,* 1969, *13,* 107–114.

Freedman, J. L., Carlsmith, J. M., & Sears, D. O. *Social psychology* (2nd ed.). Englewood Cliffs, N.J.: Prentice-Hall, 1974.

Freedman, J. L., & Fraser, S. C. Compliance without pressure: The foot-in-the-door technique. *Journal of Personality and Social Psychology,* 1966, *4,* 195–202.

Gergen, K. J. The codification of research ethics:

Views of a doubting Thomas. *American Psychologist,* 1973, *28,* 907–912.

Gold, G. (Ed.) *The Watergate hearings: Break-in and cover-up.* New York: Bantam, 1973.

Good, I. J., Gover, T. N., & Mitchell, G. J. Exact distributions for χ^2 and for the likelihood-ratio statistic for the equiprobable multinomial distribution. *Journal of the American Statistical Association,* 1970, *65,* 267–283.

Greenberg, M. S. Role playing: An alternative to deception? *Journal of Personality and Social Psychology,* 1967, *7,* 152–157.

Horowitz, I. A., & Rothschild, B. H. Conformity as a function of deception and role playing. *Journal of Personality and Social Psychology,* 1970, *14,* 224–226.

Jones, E. E., & Davis, K. B. From acts to dispositions: The attribution process in person perception. In L. Berkowitz (Ed.), *Advances in experimental social psychology* (Vol. 2). New York: Academic Press, 1965.

Jones, E. E., Davis, K. B., & Gergen, K. J. Role playing variations and their informational value for person perception. *Journal of Abnormal and Social Psychology,* 1961, *63,* 302–310.

Jones, E. E., & Nisbett, R. E. *The actor and the observer: Divergent perceptions of the causes of behavior.* Morristown, N.J.: General Learning Press, 1971.

Kelman, H. C. Human use of human subjects: The problem of deception in social psychological experiments. *Psychological Bulletin,* 1967, *67,* 1–11.

Korte, C. Group effects on help giving in an emergency. *Proceedings of the 77th Annual Convention of the American Psychological Association,* 1969, *4,* 383–384. (Summary)

Kiesler, C. A., & Kiesler, S. B. *Conformity.* Reading, Mass.: Addison-Wesley, 1969.

Latané, B., & Darley, J. M. Group inhibition of bystander intervention in emergencies. *Journal of Personality and Social Psychology,* 1968, *10,* 215–221.

Latané, B., & Darley, J. M. Bystander apathy. *American Scientist,* 1969, *57,* 244–268.

Latané, B., & Rodin, J. A lady in distress: Inhibiting effects of friends and strangers on bystander intervention. *Journal of Experimental Social Psychology,* 1969, *5,* 189–207.

Lepper, M. R., Greene, D., & Nisbett, R. E. Undermining children's intrinsic interest with extrinsic reward: A test of the "overjustification" hypothesis. *Journal of Personality and Social Psychology,* 1973, *28,* 129–137.

McArthur, L. A. The how and what of why? Some determinants and consequences of causal attribution. *Journal of Personality and Social Psychology,* 1972, *22,* 171–193.

Messick, D. M., & Reeder, G. Perceived motivation, role variations, and the attribution of personal characteristics. *Journal of Experimental Social Psychology,* 1972, *8,* 482–491.

Milgram, S. Behavioral study of obedience. *Journal of Abnormal and Social Psychology,* 1963, *67,* 371–378.

Milgram, S. Group pressure and action against a person. *Journal of Abnormal and Social Psychology,* 1964, *69,* 137–143. (a)

Milgram, S. Issues in the study of obedience: A reply to Baumrind. *American Psychologist,* 1964, *19,* 848–852. (b)

Milgram, S. Some conditions of obedience and disobedience to authority. *Human Relations,* 1965, *18,* 57–76.

Milgram, S. *Obedience to authority.* New York: Harper & Row, 1974.

Mischel, W. Towards a cognitive social learning reconceptualization of personality. *Psychological Review,* 1973, *80,* 252–283.

Nisbett, R. E., Caputo, C., Legant, P., & Marecek, J. Behavior as seen by the actor and as seen by the observer. *Journal of Personality and Social Psychology,* 1973, *27,* 154–164.

Resnick, J. H., & Schwartz, T. Ethical standards as an independent variable in psychological research. *American Psychologist,* 1973, *28,* 134–139.

Ring, K., Walston, K., & Corey, M. Mode of debriefing as a factor affecting subjective reaction to a Milgram-type obedience experiment: An ethical enquiry. *Representative Research in Social Psychology,* 1970, *1,* 67–88.

Shirer, W. *The rise and fall of the Third Reich.* New York: Simon & Schuster, 1960.

Siegel, S. *Non-parametric statistics.* New York: McGraw-Hill, 1956.

Smith, R. E., Smythe, L., & Lien, D. Inhibition of helping behavior by a similar or dissimilar nonreactive fellow bystander. *Journal of Personality and Social Psychology,* 1972, *23,* 414–419.

Storms, M. D. Videotape and the attribution process: Reversing actors' and observers' points of view. *Journal of Personality and Social Psychology,* 1973, *27,* 165–175.

West, S. G., & Brown, T. J. Physical attractiveness, the severity of the emergency and helping: A field experiment and interpersonal simulation. *Journal of Experimental Social Psychology,* 1975, in press.

Willis, R. H., & Willis, Y. A. Role playing versus deception: An experimental comparison. *Journal of Personality and Social Psychology,* 1970, *16,* 472–477.

Winer, B. J. *Statistical principles in experimental design* (2nd ed.). New York: McGraw-Hill, 1971.

Yarnold, J. K. The minimum expectation in χ^2 goodness of fit tests and the accuracy of approximations to the null distribution. *Journal of the American Statistical Association,* 1970, *65,* 864–886.

Zahn, D. A., & Roberts, G. C. Exact χ^2 criterion tables with cell expectancies one: An application to Coleman's measure of consensus. *Journal of the American Statistical Association,* 1971, *66,* 145–148.

Zimbardo, P. G. On the ethics of intervention in human psychological research: With special reference to the Stanford prison experiment. *Cognition,* 1974, *2,* 243–256.

(Received February 28, 1974)

THE STUDIES COMPARED

The first selection you have read is a laboratory experiment, classic in form, with high subject awareness and high manipulation of antecedent conditions. The second study combines laboratory and field experimental components, as did the study by Byrne, Ervin, and Lamberth (1970) presented in Chapter 2. The observers in the study by West, Gunn, and Chernicky were taking part in a laboratory experiment. Recruited from an introductory-psychology course, subjects responded to written material designed to reflect different experimental conditions. Arrangements in the field component of the study minimized subject awareness both of being in an experiment and of the aspects of behavior under study. The cover story presented to the actors by the private investigator was varied so that it would convey the different conditions being manipulated in the study.

Design Problems

The main goal of the Storms study was to test whether a different visual perspective would alter the attributions actors and observers typically make. Would actors, shown their own behavior, come to make more dispositional (rather than situational) attributions about their behavior than they typically offer? The most direct way to answer this question would seem to be to examine a situation from a different visual point of view—for example, have pairs of subjects converse and then show the participants a replay of their conversation, thus providing them with a visual perspective they wouldn't usually encounter. The question would then be whether attributions would turn out to be different from those described by the Jones and Nisbett (1971) model. Why not follow this apparently simple procedure? Sometimes, because of their desire to rule out alternative explanations, investigators arrive at designs that appear unduly complex. A goal of experimental design is to assure that the results obtained can indeed be attributed with confidence to the experimental conditions. Therefore, experimenters struggle to make their own attribution process as explicit and error-free as possible.

Comparison groups are needed in order to collect information ruling out other causal factors. In the Storms study, two such groups were used. The first is a standard control group—standard in the sense that the subjects were not exposed to video replay but simply held a conversation and were asked to make attributions. This control group helps to rule out the possibility that actors and observers would have arrived at dispositional and situational attributions, respectively, even without change in visual perspectives. In this study, the control group was used to demonstrate that actors and observers do in fact make situational and dispositional attributions, respectively. The first experimental group was included to rule out the possibility that the differences found in the second experimental group resulted from the participants' exposure to more information rather than to different information. Therefore, this first experimental group saw the same person twice to rule out the possibility that replay of the conversation itself (rather than a different visual perspective) might account for the effect. Storms argued that he had successfully ruled out alternative explanations by showing that there were no statistical differences in attribution between the control and the first experimental group.

There is, however, another possibility not accounted for by this design. In the design, the second experimental group (which experienced the shift in visual perspective) and the first experimental group (which received the same perspective twice) differed in at least one other way that may be quite important. In addition to a different visual perspective, the second experimental group differed from the first in that it experienced a *shift* in perspective. Couldn't it be that the attributional shift found in the Storms study was due to a sequence effect? Consider a perceptual example. Sometimes your judgment of the color of an object is influenced by the color you have been looking at immediately before; that is, there is an afterimage of the first color that affects your judgment of the second. Sequence effects have long been noted as important in person perception, and they may be important here.

The resolution of this question would seem to call for another comparison group, one in which the subject would see himself before seeing the other. Creating such a comparison group, however, poses technical and conceptual problems. How do you manage to have a subject engaged in conversation with another see only himself so engaged? Use of a television monitor showing the subject and blocking visual access to the other might begin to address these technical problems. But conceptual problems remain. If a person engages in interaction while seeing himself doing so, how do you prevent him from making attributions about the other person before he observes himself? In thinking about this problem, the following possibility occurred to us. Consider a design in which persons are shown themselves engaged in some behavior requiring little thought (for example, mixing a drink), and then they are shown another person performing the same action. This design would provide some information about the extent to which the shift in visual perspective, rather than the visual perspective itself, may account for the results.

The second study is a more straightforward design, being essentially comparable to the control group in the Storms study. Actors engaged in real behavior and reported their attributions; observers read about the actors' behavior and in turn, made attributions.

Standardization of Conditions

In order to establish the differences between the attributions that actors and observers make about the same behavior, it is essential that actors and observers in fact respond to the same behavior; every element must be the same except for the roles of actor and observer. The second research selection encountered procedural problems in making the actor and observer conditions equivalent. In order to be able to examine attributional differences at all, it was necessary to get a number of people to agree to participate in the burglary—that is, a sample of actors whose views could be compared to those of the observers. The investigators' report indicates that persuasion efforts were made. There appear to be several points at which such pressure was exerted. You read that everyone who was approached agreed to come to the first meeting. Given the usual subject-refusal rates, this unanimous consent suggests that recruitment efforts very likely contained some highly persuasive elements. The report of the procedure says nothing about this point. For the experimental session, some refusal opportunities are described. For example, the investigators report that when the reasons for the crime were presented (experimental manipulation of conditions), an unstated number of subjects protested that they didn't even want to discuss the plan further and that these subjects were asked to hear the entire presentation before making up their minds. Another refusal opportunity came after the details of the burglary had been fully described. Presumably all remaining subjects were asked to come to the "second meeting" to make final plans. An unknown number who refused at this point were asked to reconsider. If they refused again, the procedure was terminated for them.

Observers received a booklet describing "in great detail" one of the conditions. No information is given about what, if anything, was written in these descriptions about the persuasion efforts. This point is critical to the attribution differences found. Some actors may have made situational attributions because they were in fact pressured to agree to participate. If this information had been given to the observers, they too might have made more situational attributions. Such attributions are typically found when observers believe the actor to have been coerced into action.

Measurement Differences

These two studies measure the dependent variable in quite different ways, both in regard to method and in regard to conceptualization. The major methodological difference resides in the form of the ratings. In the Storms study, actors and observers themselves rate the degree to which they attribute the actions to dispositional or situational causes. In the second study, the experimental confederate "summarized" the actors' verbal free responses in giving their reasons for agreeing or refusing to take part in the burglary. Observers, instead, wrote "two or three sentences" to make their attributions of why an actor either did or did not participate. In commendably careful fashion, the investigators had all these responses retyped to a standard wording that concealed their actor or observer origins. Coders then classified these statements into three mutually exclusive categories: dispositional, dispositional plus situational, and situational.

The conceptual differences between the measurements used in the two studies are more profound. By using the above three-way classification, the researchers in the second study treated the dispositional-situational distinction as a unitary continuum. This means that the more your view is dispositional, the less it is situational. In contrast, the Storms experiment permitted subjects to make attributions for each causality separately. The use of a nine-point rating for both dispositional and situational inferences allows subjects more latitude and gives the experimenter more information. With this procedure, an action might be viewed as dispositional or situational or both, as well as a combination of the two dimensions.

CONSUMER EVALUATION

Cost-Quality Relation

Considerations of the cost of a study can be raised on several levels. How much time did the study take? How many subjects were obtained and at what cost? Were the procedures or equipment unusually expensive? But cost can also refer to the psychological and social cost represented by harm to subjects. Ethical questions can be raised with regard to the second study, and the authors devote considerable space to a defense of their position. When the study was first published, it was followed by an article on ethical issues in social-psychological research (Cook, 1975), essentially supporting the position taken by the investigators in the study. Many social psychologists, however, would find these arguments inadequate. An additional point raised by Cook is that psychological costs cannot be adequately assessed by a debriefing immediately after the experimental session, since damaging effects may not emerge for some subjects until much later. Researchers incur an obligation to look for long-term effects of their manipulations and to take on the additional costs of counseling or other interventions that may be required to alleviate the damage suffered by their subjects.

Both studies were concerned to keep subjects unaware. Storms accomplished this by omission; he simply didn't tell his subjects why they were asked to converse. He used deception only in so far as he told all subjects that they would be videotaped and lied about equipment failure in explaining one experimental condition. Deception was much more pervasive in the second study; here not only were subjects led to believe that they would take part in a real burglary, but all conditions required elaborate lies about sponsors, plans, and expected outcomes. If you regard withholding of information and deliberate lying as ethically different, then the second study might be judged more harshly than the first.

Flashy Merchandising

Social psychologists are sometimes a trifle indifferent to the uses made of their findings; too often their vision stops at the laboratory door. The "Ubiquitous Watergate" is the kind of study likely to receive considerable media dissemination. It is timely, provocative, and deals with figures of power. Cook (1975) wondered why the journal editors had sought him out to comment on the ethics when deception was such a common practice in research. He speculated that the concern was due to the potential newsworthiness of the study. But it may also be that social psychology is benefiting from its past. When Milgram (1963) reported that an unexpectedly high proportion of subjects could be induced to give painful shocks to a protesting victim, he was accused of inflicting damage to subjects in excess of the benefits derived from the research (Baumrind, 1964).

Studies can be novel and timely without giving rise to questions of flashy merchandising. These questions often arise when the investigators' conclusions extend too far beyond the realm of the study. Interpretive concerns of the authors of the second study center on the social applications of the established actor-observer differences. In particular, their comments on the role of the press and other professional observers are debatable. They argue that if such observers could attend more to an actor's past history, emotional state, or intention, they would make fewer erroneous dispositional inferences. These observers, West and his associates say, would "increase their understanding of the causes of the actor's behavior." This interpretation loses sight of the phenomenological character of attribution processes. The suggested perspective might increase the observer's understanding of the actor's *perception* of the causes of his or her behavior. It does not necessarily speak to the objective causes sought by an investigative reporter, a political analyst, or a behavioral scientist.

Furthermore, you might wonder whether the findings reported in the second study justify extensions to the complex scenario of the Watergate scandal. The press and the Nixon administration differed in their interpretation of many events, only one element of which may reside in actor-observer differences.

8

ATTITUDE CHANGE

CHAPTER OUTLINE

Cognitive Dissonance
   Dissonance Defined
   Dissonance Reduction
Research on Cognitive Dissonance
   Forced Compliance
      Theoretical Explanation of Forced Compliance
      A Major Experiment
      Critiques of the Study
   Effort Expended
Criticisms of Dissonance Theory
   Modifications of Dissonance Theory
   Reinterpretations of the Evidence
   Attempts to Refute Dissonance Theory
      Critique of the Theory
      Critique of Design and Data Analysis
Methods in Dissonance Research
   Laboratory Experiments
   Field Experiments
   Field Studies
      Participant Observation
      Interviews and Surveys
Two Research Examples
   Product Description
   Consumer Checklist
   Elliot Aronson and Judson Mills. *The effect of severity of initiation on liking for a group.*
   Anthony N. Doob, J. Merrill Carlsmith, Jonathan L. Freedman, Thomas K. Landauer, and Soleng Tom, Jr., *The effect of initial selling price on subsequent sales.*
The Studies Compared
   Operational Definitions of Dissonance Arousal
      Operational Definition in the Aronson and Mills Study
      Operational Definition in the Study by Doob and Associates
   Design and Procedures
   Data Analysis
   Interpretive Problems
Consumer Evaluation
   Durability
   Careful Reading

232   CHAPTER 8

Posters and ads appear announcing the coming of a new performing group; the publicity stresses that the event is sure to be a sellout and announces the time when tickets go on sale. You've heard about the group but have never seen them in person. You decide to go, even though you don't know much about their music, and, to be sure to get tickets, you arrive well ahead of the announced time and find a good-sized line waiting. After you've been in line for some time, it starts to rain. You consider going home but decide to stick it out. After a while, the rumor spreads in the waiting line that the performance may be cancelled by civic officials concerned about crowd safety; the sale of tickets is suspended. You wait, but the sale time is postponed again. By now you've put so much effort into waiting that it seems a shame to quit. Finally, the line starts to move, and after many hours you get your ticket and go home, wet, tired, and hungry. The next night you attend the concert and enjoy the group tremendously. Asked about it, you praise the group and declare the evening an unqualified success. A friend who also had not heard the group before and who won the ticket in a music-store giveaway didn't like the concert. You're baffled by your friend's response, because you have similar tastes in music. An argument develops when your friend suggests that your critical judgment must have been warped by the long wait for a ticket. You insist that the only reason you waited in line so long was that you liked the group. You get angrier when your friend tells you that, since you'd never heard the group before, it is unlikely that you waited because you liked the group. The argument gets nowhere, and you both come to the conclusion that maybe you just don't agree on music as much as you thought.

But a social psychologist would look at this situation a little differently. Your impression that you must have waited in line so long for a ticket *because* you liked the group is a natural one. Most of the time you think that your preferences, tastes, and opinions are what cause you to behave as you do. The tendencies to evaluate objects in positive or negative ways are called attitudes. In general, we believe that attitudes lead to behavior; and to a certain degree this is true. But the reverse may also be true; that is, there are times when behavior leads to attitudes, when you like something because of something you have done. Because the study of attitudes has long been a prolific one in social psychology, there is a massive amount of research on attitude formation, measurement, and change. For reviews of this research, you are referred to McGuire (1968) and to the works by Kiesler and Munson (1975), Fishbein and Ajzen (1972), Sears and Abeles (1969), and McGuire (1966).

Within the domain of attitude change, for a long time the prevailing view was that attitudes influence behavior—the point noted above. You are subjected everyday to appeals and information aimed at changing your attitudes toward products, politics, and people, on the assumption that a change in attitude will result in a change in behavior. This assumption continues to be influential and is well represented in recent works on attitude change by Triandis (1971), Suedfeld (1971), Kiesler, Collins, and Miller (1969), and Insko (1967). This approach is not discussed in this chapter, which deals instead with instances in which attitude change is brought about by changes in behavior. The body of research taking this approach, and particularly the theory from which the research derives, would argue that, in the example given at the beginning of this chapter, you did not stand long in line because you liked the musical group but, rather, as your friend intimated, you liked the group because you stood so long in line. Having put in considerable effort and endured a certain amount of discomfort, you justified both by liking the group very much, more than your friend, who won her ticket without effort. The two research selections in this chapter deal with the effects that effort expended have on attitudes toward an object—more specifically, toward a group or a product. The first selection deals with a psychological effort—the initiation ritual undergone to become a member of a group; the second selection deals, instead, with the effort represented by paying a higher price for a product. In each case, an action that is inconsistent with existing attitudes produces discomfort; in turn, the discomfort motivates you to change your attitudes in order to achieve consistency between what you do and what you think.

COGNITIVE DISSONANCE

General interest in social psychology about those situations in which behavior leads to attitudes can be traced to Leon Festinger (1957) and his theory of *cognitive dissonance*. Inspired by widespread observations that persons strive for consistency within themselves, Festinger attempted to explain the cognitive process by which such consistency is achieved. He posited the existence of cognitive "elements" that the individual strives to bring into internal consistency and into correspondence with experienced reality. The definition of elements is relatively broad and imprecise; they can be any idea or set of ideas a person has about his or her own processes or the workings of the world. In the example above, any thoughts, feelings, or information you might have about the group, music, your tastes, waiting in line, fellow ticket seekers, or in fact any thoughts passing through your head could be such cognitive elements.

Dissonance Defined

Festinger was interested in the relations between pairs of these elements, and he described three possible relations: consonance, irrelevance, and dissonance. If, on the way to the concert, you had the thoughts "I go to hear good music" and "I hope to attend this musical performance," these two elements would be said to be consonant. One follows from the other; they fit together without logical and, more importantly, without psychological contradiction. If you had the thoughts "I go to hear good music" and "I wonder if my roommate has picked up my laundry," the two elements might be said to be irrelevant to each other. Paired together, they have no mutual implications. Festinger was most interested in the third set of relations, which he termed *dissonance*. If you thought "I'm the person who chooses concerts carefully so that I go to good ones" and "The performance I went to was lousy," these thoughts would be dissonant. Cognitive dissonance is an uncomfortable state of tension that results when you believe two things that are psychologically inconsistent. In the example above, the opposite of one thought follows from the other.

Festinger says that cognitive dissonance can arise from four sources: (1) logical inconsistency, (2) inconsistency with cultural mores, (3) inconsistency between one view and a more general view, and (4) past experience. An example of dissonance arising from logical inconsistency would be represented by your believing at the same time that you would go to the concert and that no tickets were available. One of these ideas cannot "follow from" the other. If, as you go to the concert, you entertain the two thoughts "I go to hear good music" and "I will listen to the ball game on my transistor radio during the concert" you are faced with dissonance created by cultural mores, since your knowledge of how in our culture audiences are supposed to behave at a concert would run against your plans. In some other culture, these two ideas might not conflict. An example of the third source of dissonance—a specific opinion being in conflict with a more general opinion—can be found in the pairing of "Nothing's worth standing in line for" and "I'm standing in line for this concert." The fourth source of dissonance arises from past experience. If, while you stand in line, it starts to rain and, although you realize that it is raining, you think that you are not going to get wet, dissonance would result, since your past experience suggests that getting wet follows from standing in the rain. Someone who has had no experience with rain would not experience this dissonance.

To know whether dissonance exists requires knowledge of the person's psychological makeup. In order to know whether two thoughts are dissonant because of cultural norms or past experience, it is necessary to know the person's cultural values and experiences. The same thoughts paired together may give rise to dissonance in one person and not in another. Someone standing in line with you and having the same thoughts you had might not have felt any dissonance. Festinger's definition of dissonance has both strengths and weaknesses; it gives the concept of dissonance great generality but makes it hard to say whether dissonance is present in a given situation.

Dissonant relations between cognitive elements were singled out by Festinger because he believed them to be unstable relations. He postulated that, since dissonance is psychologically uncomfortable, people attempt to reduce it by avoiding situations and information that would increase the dissonance or by changing the attitudes involved in the dissonance. Dissonance is thus conceived of as a force for attitude change. The greater the dissonance, the greater the pressure toward consistency. But the magnitude of dissonance is hard to measure. The theory holds that dissonance is greater when the elements brought together are of greater importance to the person, but the theory does not really tell us how one determines the importance of any given element.

Dissonance Reduction

Let's assume that dissonance is unsettling. How may it be reduced? Dissonance reduction is accomplished by changing one of the cognitive elements involved. Festinger suggested three ways in which such changes could be made. In the concert example, it is dissonant for you to have waited so long in line for a concert you later conclude to be bad. Your friend who got her ticket without effort had no such dissonance to resolve. According to Festinger's first means of dissonance reduction, you could reestablish consistency between the effort expended and your presence at a poor concert by leaving early (changing the behavior) or by distorting or denying the fact of your presence, by thinking, for example, that you went as a favor to a friend (changing the perception of the behavior).

The second method is to actually change the environment. Finding yourself present at a poor performance, you could change the environment itself by singing along with the group or by making friends with people seated near you, thereby reducing dissonance by turning a bad musical experience into a good social one. When it is too difficult to change the environment, you may distort the nature of the experience by rationalizing that the performance is good or that waiting in line for the ticket wasn't so bad after all.

Finally, the third means of reducing dissonance is to add new information to the two dissonant elements in order to bring them into greater consistency. Seeking out more information about the performing group or about the setting in which the performance was given might yield some new cognitions that, depending on their importance, might help to reduce the dissonance.

RESEARCH ON COGNITIVE DISSONANCE

Part of the appeal of dissonance theory is its apparent simplicity. As we said earlier, the theory holds that, when dissonant relations exist between cognitive elements, discomfort gives rise to pressures to reduce dissonance. Dissonance reduction may be accomplished through changes in behavior, through changes in cognition, and through exposure to new information.

Dissonance theory has stimulated a prodigious amount of research in the last two decades. This may be attributed in part to the rarity of any theoretical propositions in social psychology. When any general postulates are offered, they are bound to attract attention and especially so when they pertain to that most active area of interest, attitude change. Aronson (1969b) credits the personal creativity of Leon Festinger for the amount of research the theory has generated, in that Festinger had a unique capacity to derive testable hypotheses and research designs from the theory. Deutsch and Krauss (1965) see the appeal of dissonance theory in its capacity to make predictions that are not obvious and to suggest intriguing research manipulations and designs. This section describes how dissonance works in two classes of behavior: forced compliance and the expenditure of effort.

Forced Compliance

Theoretical Explanation of Forced Compliance. Festinger's (1957) theoretical explanation of the forced-compliance situation is in line with the rest of the theory and represents the crux of the view that behavior can lead to attitude change. A person performs an act; the act runs counter to one of the person's beliefs; the person's cognition of having performed the act is dissonant with the person's cognition of holding the belief. If the act can't be undone or denied, the dissonance may be reduced by a change in the belief that will render the belief consistent with the act. *Forced compliance* (a term Festinger takes to mean public compliance without private acceptance) suggests that the situation contains some consonant cognitive elements as well that prevent or reduce dissonance—namely, the knowledge that a reward will be obtained or a punishment avoided. The expected reward or punishment is the force that produces the compliant behavior. It is with regard to the effects of the size of that reward or punishment that dissonance theory makes its distinctive contribution. A very large reward or punishment will result in little dissonance and hence in little change in the privately held attitude. If the reward for the behavior is very large, it constitutes a strong cognitive element consonant with the behavior and makes the dissonance of knowing that one behaved at variance with a personal belief negligible in comparison. Public figures who are well paid to endorse a commercial product do not feel much pressure to like that product, since the reward given justifies the endorsement made. The maximum dissonance results from a reward or punishment just barely sufficient to elicit the desired behavior. As summarized by Aronson (1972), "if an individual makes a statement of belief that is difficult to justify *externally,* he will attempt to justify it *internally* by making his attitudes more consistent with the statement" (p. 111).

A major experiment. Festinger and Carlsmith (1959) tested the forced-compliance paradigm in a much-cited laboratory study in which undergraduates taking part in the experiment spent an hour performing a series of dull and senseless tasks like putting spools on trays and turning pegs, without being told what the purpose of the experiment was. After completing these boring tasks, the subjects were told that another group of subjects would perform those same dull tasks but that, unlike themselves, these other subjects would participate under the impression that the tasks were interesting and enjoyable. The experimenter went on to explain that such information was usually given to subjects by an assistant who was not present at the moment and asked each experimental subject to tell the next "subject" (actually the research assistant) that the experiment was enjoyable and lots of fun. This elaborate deception set the stage for the counterattitudinal behavior; the subject, knowing that the tasks were dull (private belief), would tell another person that they were enjoyable (counterattitudinal behavior).

Two levels of justification were tested. In one condition, subjects were paid one dollar to lie; in the other condition, they were paid 20 dollars. A control group simply performed the tasks, without being asked to talk to subjects afterward. Finally, subjects were interviewed by a different experimenter somewhere else in the psychology department, ostensibly to check up on how psychology experiments were being run. In this interview, subjects were asked if the tasks had been enjoyable and told to rate them on a ten-point scale. As predicted by dissonance theory, subjects who had been paid one dollar rated the tasks more favorably than either controls or subjects who had been paid 20 dollars. The subjects who had been paid only one dollar reduced the dissonance by convincing themselves that the tasks were actually interesting and enjoyable. It is interesting to note that an experiment by Kelman had yielded essentially the same results in 1953 but that these findings were little noted in the absence of a theoretical explanation with the breadth of dissonance theory.

Critiques of the Study. Rosenberg (1965) criticized this study on the grounds that there was not enough separation between the subjects' experience and counterattitudinal act and the interview in which dissonance reduction was measured. He argued that this lack of separation evoked an experimental artifact, which he called *evaluation apprehension,* in which subjects worry about making a good impression on the investigator. Rosenberg felt that subjects in the Festinger and Carlsmith experiment must have suspected that the interview had something to do with the lie they had told and that the high-reward subjects must have felt a need to demonstrate that they had not been influenced by the experimenter's 20-dollar bribe. In an experiment that clearly separated the counterattitudinal-act and reward conditions from the interview, Rosenberg (1965) got the opposite results; subjects who had been paid the most showed the greatest attitude change. In view of the fact that these findings might be better explained by an incentive theory, they cast doubt on dissonance theory.

The experimental manipulations effected by Rosenberg were sufficiently different from the Festinger and Carlsmith procedure to require further investigation. Carlsmith, Collins, and Helmreich (1966) designed a study to show that both a dissonance reduction and an incentive effect could be obtained in the same experiment, depending on operating factors. They noted that Rosenberg's procedure involved anonymous essay writing, while Festinger and Carlsmith asked subjects to lie in a face-to-face encounter with another person. They characterized this difference in terms of commitment, suggesting that dissonance is aroused by the higher commitment inherent in a public lie; college students regard essay writing on virtually any topic as a test of skill rather than as a dissonance-producing act. This analysis is a good example of the rewards of careful reading and thinking, for, without such scrutiny, the salient differences in procedures might have been easily overlooked and the conflict dismissed as irreconcilable. Replicating both dissonance and incentive conditions, Carlsmith, Collins, and Helmreich (1966) found predicted results along both lines. High commitment (the Festinger and Carlsmith replication) produced a dissonance-reduction effect, with low reward yielding the greatest change; low commitment produced incentive results, with high reward showing the greatest attitude change. How dissonance works in forced-compliance situations continues to be the most active area of research on dissonance theory (Kiesler & Munson, 1975).

Effort Expended

Our example of concert-ticket buying as well as the two following selections are concerned with dissonance that results from the investment of effort. As suggested in our example, dissonance theory leads to the prediction that, if a person puts a lot of effort into achieving a goal, that goal is more valuable to that person than to someone who achieves it with little effort. This idea is derived from dissonance conceptualizations about the effects of insufficient rewards; in Festinger's words, "rats and people come to love things for which they have suffered" (1961, p. 11). While Festinger articulated this notion to describe the outcome of a conditioning experiment with rats, this same notion had been proposed earlier by Aronson and Mills (1959) and it appears in the first selection presented in this chapter. They reasoned that women who undergo a difficult initiation procedure to become members of a group will value that group more than those who experience an easy entry. Similarly, the second research selection seeks to demonstrate that paying a higher price enhances the value of a product. Since you will be reading these studies in their entirety, only the general themes are presented here.

The most convincing evidence for dissonance hypotheses concerning effort comes from Zimbardo's (1965) study of effort in counterattitudinal advocacy. Some students were asked to read and others to improvise a speech advocating admission of mainland China to the United Nations. Their task was made more difficult by interfering with their reading and speaking by playing back their own speeches through delayed auditory feedback. Some had to exert a high degree of effort to overcome this interference, whereas for others the delay was shorter and required less effort to overcome. More attitude change was found with high effort. No difference was noted between the reading and improvisation conditions, a finding that not only failed to replicate an earlier study interpreted in dissonance terms (King & Janis, 1956) but left unanswered the somewhat puzzling question concerning why an improvised speech from an experimenter-supplied outline does not require more effort than a speech read from a script. Once again, you can see the importance of noting carefully how an experimenter operationalizes the variable she or he studies. Effort people expend in some activity is obviously open to many interpretations. In Zimbardo's (1965) study, differences in concentration required to overcome auditory feedback produced findings consistent with a dissonance interpretation, while potentially analogous effort required in formulating an improvised speech did not. This sort of empirical muddle, both within and among studies purporting to test dissonance theory, has given rise to extensive criticism and revisions of the theory.

CRITICISMS OF DISSONANCE THEORY

Dissonance theory, almost from the time of its promulgation by Festinger (1957), has evoked more research and more opposition than any other theory of attitude change. In the past two decades, it has consistently attracted strong adherents who are active researchers and critics who denounce the theory as vague and contradictory and the research as methodologically careless. In the initial presentation of the theory, Festinger (1957) indicated that he had considered delaying publication for a few years until more relevant studies had been made and "unclarities" eliminated, but that he had opted for publication in the hope that others would be drawn to the tasks of verification and clarification. These hopes were realized in the energy with which his colleagues and students addressed the theory. Critics and revisionists range from those who buy the theory and seek to improve it, to those who buy the empirical findings and seek to reinterpret them, all the way to those who reject both and seek to refute the approach.

Modifications of Dissonance Theory

In a substantial volume summarizing the research activity that followed Festinger's initial publication, Brehm and Cohen (1962) postulated that commitment is critical to dissonance arousal. Dissonance can apply to any pair of inconsistent cognitive elements; most of the research, however, has dealt with dissonance between a belief and a commitment to action, because such pairing seemed the surest route to dissonance arousal. In our example, the elements "I waited a long time for a ticket, but the concert was no good" constitute such a discrepant pairing of action and belief. Not all contradictions will arouse dissonance; the importance of the belief to the individual plays an essential part in creating dissonance, and commitment to the discrepant action sharpens the dissonance experienced.

Festinger (1964) agreed with this modification of the theory. The coauthor of the first research selection here not only was involved in a number of the critical studies relating to dissonance theory but also provided several integrative suggestions (Aronson, 1968; 1969b). In particular, Aronson (1968) suggested that dissonance arousal resides in the contradiction between cognitive elements and the person's self-concept rather than in the contradiction between any two elements. Of late, Aronson (1972) sees the dissonance phenomenon as one of self-justification. In the absence of external justification, a person will seek internal justification and will reduce dissonance in order to maintain a favorable self-image. In his words, "dissonance theory makes its clearest and strongest predictions in those situations in which the dissonance is a function of a person's behavior that violates his own self-concept" (p. 138).

Reinterpretations of the Evidence

Just as there are those who use the sometimes ambiguous findings from dissonance experiments to revise the theory, there are those who, accepting the findings as they stand, advance alternative explanations. In itself, the existence of alternative explanations for the findings of one or another study is not necessarily damaging to the overall theory, since the power of a theory lies in its capacity to handle a body of evidence better than any other explanation. Kiesler, Collins, and Miller (1969) argue that, if a critic of dissonance theory offers an alternative explanation of a given experiment, that critic "should be prepared to offer the same or a similar explanation for other data accumulated by the theorist" (p. 229).

An alternative explanation for dissonance arising between self-concept and behavior has been suggested by Elms (1972). He posits that guilt rather than dissonance can account for the findings of dissonance experiments. The loss of self-esteem engendered by having lied to prospective subjects gives rise to guilt. The concept of cognitive dissonance is not needed.

A more general reinterpretation of dissonance theory has been advanced from a behaviorist perspective. Rejecting dissonance as a hypothetical construct, Bem (1965; 1967) argued that the findings of the major dissonance-theory experiments could be accounted for more simply in terms of self-perception processes. Bem sought to make the explanation simpler by eliminating any need to refer to an internal state of discomfort. People are seen as observers of their own behavior, reasoning about themselves as they have learned to do from past experience. Bem believed that a person's thinking in a discrepant situation would be like that of any observer—that is, noticing behavior and trying to make sense of it. This analysis led Bem to test the self-perception explanation in an ingenious way. He replicated forced-compliance studies by simply describing the experimental procedure to subjects and asking them what they thought the original subjects had done. In such a replication of the Festinger and Carlsmith study, Bem (1967) found that observers correctly predicted that subjects paid one dollar would have more favorable attitudes toward the experiment than those paid 20 dollars. People as observers of their own behavior presumably say to themselves, "I couldn't have told that lie for only a dollar, so I must have really liked turning those knobs." No state of internal discomfort or dissonance need be invoked to arrive at that conclusion.

Attempts to Refute Dissonance Theory

One of the most damaging attacks on the theory of cognitive dissonance and the body of work deriving from it has come from without—from psychologists not associated with attitude research or even with social psychology. Chapanis and Chapanis (1964) directed their criticisms both at the theoretical concept of dissonance and at the specifics of design of many well-known dissonance experiments.

Critique of the Theory. Chapanis and Chapanis (1964) highlighted the ambiguities surrounding the notion of dissonance. According to the theory, cognitive elements can be brought together in such a way that they result in an uncomfortable state called dissonance. In experimental practice, such dissonance is inferred; it is a hypothetical construct that the experimenter *presumes* exists when behavioral differences are found between "high" and "low" dissonance conditions. But this inference introduces some circular reasoning. When differences are found, they are explained by dissonance reduction; when they are not found, they are dismissed as indications of a failure to arouse dissonance. This reasoning has been used by dissonance researchers to justify discarding subjects when they do not show predicted effects. This questionable practice is defended on the grounds that failure to show dissonance-reduction behavior is a sign that dissonance has not been aroused. An equally plausible explanation for the lack of dissonance effects is that dissonance was induced but failed to affect behavior as predicted.

The remedy to the problems highlighted by Chapanis and Chapanis is to specify more precisely what does and does not produce dissonance and to use a direct independent measure of dissonance arousal. Such a measure would show just how much dissonance is or is not experienced by subjects in the "high" or "low" dissonance conditions. Although much research has been done since this criticism was made, no direct quantitative measure of dissonance has been developed.

Critique of Design and Data Analysis. The Chapanis and Chapanis (1964) commentary is best known for its attack on the way dissonance theory has been tested. These critics make three major points about dissonance experiments: designs are often confounded, selective dropping of subjects is common, and reports of research minimize these problems and overstate limited findings. (Some of these objections are detailed later in this chapter, since they are relevant to the research selections.) Dissonance researchers have responded to the critique (see, for example, Silverman, 1964), and the research has shown increasing methodological rigor, although this is probably less a result of the direct impact of the critique and more a function of increasingly demanding standards for journal publication, once a topic is no longer considered novel or pioneering (Watkins & Johnson, 1972).

In sum, the Chapanis and Chapanis article rendered a "verdict of not proven" for dissonance theory, to which Aronson (1969b, p. 31) objected that theories are not proven, they just generate research. Unfortunately, the research associated with dissonance theory has yielded conflicting findings. Effort has gone more into the exploration of procedural problems of previous experiments than into the basic dimensions of dissonance-induced attitude change itself (Fishbein & Ajzen, 1975).

METHODS IN DISSONANCE RESEARCH

Laboratory Experiments

As indicated by the review of research findings, most studies on dissonance were done in laboratory settings and with college students. Dissonance theory emerged at a time when experimentation in social psychology was equated with laboratory settings, although it should be noted that Festinger himself undertook one field study (as described below) in test of the theory. The laboratory experiments on dissonance involve, as is typical of that approach, high manipulation of antecedent conditions and fairly high subject awareness. Subjects are volunteers who know they are being studied, but, because deception is so widely used, they are presumed to be in ignorance of what aspect of their behavior is under study. A similar condition prevails in the laboratory experiments using physiological measurements. In a forced-compliance study, Buckhout (1966) showed that heart-rate changes accompanied attitude change. Since attitude change signifies the end of dissonance, the slowing heart rates were taken as an indicator of reduced arousal.

As to the manipulation of antecedent conditions, dissonance experiments are noted for elaborate arrangements. This concern with the mechanics of manipulation has led critics (Fishbein & Ajzen, 1975) to liken the dissonance researcher to a theatrical director concerned with "moving and manipulating actors, settings, and props until he is intuitively satisfied with the effects of these manipulations" (p. 515). Experiments like the one by Festinger and Carlsmith (1959) certainly use elaborate scenarios between the pre- and postmeasures of the attitude. The dull tasks, the cover story about the tasks, the mysteriously absent research assistant, the offhand recruitment of the subject to help out, the offer of payment, the convenient presence of the "next" subject, the subject's persuasive lies, and the final interview by a supposed representative of the psychology department— all suggest intricacies of plot and subplot to rival Restoration drama. It is perhaps not surprising, given these complexities, that, when such elaborate experiments produced conflicting results, much subsequent effort went into revising and perfecting the scripts. The procedures were scrutinized to figure out what could have gone wrong, and new manipulations were devised. As a result, a series of dissonance studies often leave the reader marveling at their complexity but wondering a little at whatever happened to the underlying question.

Field Experiments

The best-known of the field experiments on dissonance deals with a phenomenon called *postdecisional dissonance* in context with racetrack betting (Knox & Inkster, 1968). The phenomenon refers to the discomfort that may follow a difficult choice. Dissonance theory holds that choices are made difficult by the fact that neither alternative is ever perfect. Having committed themselves to one alternative, persons are motivated to exaggerate the good aspects of the chosen alternative and the bad aspects of the rejected one. Knox and Inkster conducted two studies. In the first study, bettors were asked to make ratings on a seven-point scale of the likelihood that the horse they had chosen would win the race. Bettors who rated the horse's chances *before* placing their bets gave lower confidence ratings than bettors who rated the horse's chances *after* placing their bets. A second study using the same procedure at a harness track, but with a different rating scale and a different statistical analysis, replicated the findings. The authors concluded that both studies supported the operations of dissonance reduction following commitment to a decision.

A recent failure to replicate, however, places Knox and Inkster's conclusion in doubt (Kusyszyn & Bettridge, 1973). Using the same procedures, Kusyszyn and Bettridge found the opposite of the predicted effects. Bettors who rated the horse's chances before placing their bets reported greater confidence that the horse would win than did bettors who rated the chances after placing their bets. These researchers concluded that the contradictory results may be the product of *experimenter-expectancy effects* (Rosenthal, 1966). An important difference between the study by Kusyszyn and Bettridge and that by Knox and Inkster (1968) was that, in the former, the undergraduate assistants who asked bettors to make ratings were not familiar with the predicted outcomes and had never met the investigators. In the Knox and Inkster study, interviewers were psychology students who knew what the predictions were. These experiments involve moderate manipulation of antecedent conditions (that is, picking bettors before and after they have placed bets) and some subject awareness engendered by the interviewing procedure. No deception was involved in either experiment.

A different approach to the field experiment is exemplified by Bartlett, Drew, Fahle, and Watts (1974). They sent a mailing to registered Democratic and Republican voters that was enclosed in envelopes with the heading "Voters for Nixon" or "Voters for McGovern." The mailing asked the voters' views on the effectiveness of direct mail distribution of political material, ostensibly to evaluate the considerable amounts of money spent on such material in political campaigns. To make responding easy, the enclosed return postcard asked only two questions. The investigators reasoned that voters in dissonant conditions would not return the postcards, since doing so would increase the dissonance they experienced. From a return rate of 18%, twice as many cards came from people in the consonant condition than from people in the dissonant condition. (Republicans receiving the "Voters for Nixon" envelope and Democrats receiving the "Voters for McGovern" were considered to be in the consonant conditions.) It should be noted that the researchers expressed some doubt whether Democrats who received McGovern envelopes could indeed be considered to be in a consonant condition. From the voting patterns in that presidential election, it was clear that many Democratic voters in fact had voted for Nixon. These voters presumably experienced some dissonance when they received the mailing coming from a "Voters for McGovern" source. Like the racetrack studies, this experiment too is moderate in manipulation of conditions and low in subject awareness. Recipients of the mailings were misled about their purpose and were not told that their behavior was under study. Nonetheless, recipients of such solicitations may experience in different degrees a need to make their views known, as evidenced by the finding that more Republicans than Democrats returned postcards. This effect might also have resulted from the misclassification of Democrats in the consonant condition that we mentioned earlier.

Field Studies

Participant Observation. An intriguing assessment of the concept of dissonance in a natural setting actually preceded Festinger's publication of the theory (Festinger, Riecken, & Schachter, 1956). A newspaper account of the forecast by a religious group that, on a certain date, a great flood would end the world came to the attention of Festinger and his collaborators. They saw the situation as an ideal opportunity to test dissonance theory by noting what would happen when the prediction was not confirmed—an outcome they didn't doubt. They infiltrated the group and became more or less participant observers. Their report gives some interesting information on the problems of balancing scientific observation and participation in a highly committed messianic group. On the basis of alleged interplanetary messages, the group's leader forecast the flood for December 21, a time when some student members of the group would be away on vacation. The researchers predicted that those who met refutation of the forecast in a milieu that did not provide social support would lose faith in the group, while those gathered together in mutual social support would reduce dissonance by more active proselytizing. When the flood did not come, the leader explained that it was the group's faith that had saved the world, and her disciples became more energetic in recruiting new members. The student members who awaited the flood alone gave up their religious beliefs and lost confidence in the leader. Both dissonance-theory predictions were confirmed.

In a similar situation, Hardyck and Braden (1962), instead, found no support for the prediction that refutation of belief would lead to proselytizing. They studied members of a Pentecostal church who had spent 42 days and nights in underground fallout shelters awaiting a prophesized nuclear disaster. When the disaster failed to materialize, members of the church concluded that they had misinterpreted the circumstances and that their faith was being tested. In contrast to the dissonance prediction, they made no efforts to proselytize. The investigators attributed their failure to replicate to the possibility that the group they studied, being larger than the group studied by Festinger and his colleagues, provided all the social support needed to reduce dissonance without adding other believers. They also noted that the church members were not ridiculed for their beliefs as was the original group. Whatever the reasons, this failure to replicate also suggests that some revision of the role of social support in dissonance reduction may be in order.

These studies involve little experimenter manipulation of antecedent conditions, since the researchers served as observers of events occurring naturally. But, as we indicated earlier, observation can be problematic under these circumstances. At best, it yields rather subjective data collected by investigators familiar with the dissonance predictions made. Also, the two groups studied represent very special populations; members of doomsday groups may evince dissonance-reduction processes that are very different from those of the general population. The studies are low with regard to subject awareness, since the investigators acted as group members and did not disclose their research purpose. But group membership by participant observers raises a problem. In the original study, the eight observers constituted almost one-fourth of the core membership of the group, and it is hard to believe that their presence did not exert some influence on the group (Elms, 1972).

A recent study by Batson (1975) attempted to test the generality of refuting a religious belief. He assessed intensity of orthodox Christian beliefs in young women in a religious youth program. Leaders of that program then distributed questionnaires on religious beliefs. The materials included an article purporting to prove, on the basis of scholarly findings like the Dead Sea Scrolls, that the New Testament was fraudulent. Based on a posttest of religious beliefs, Batson found that, consistent with dissonance interpretations, believers who accepted the truth of the published report intensified their religious beliefs, while neither those with less-intense beliefs nor those who discredited the article experienced increases in faith. If these findings prove durable, they have pessimistic implications for any attempts to change attitudes. If the believer does not accept the facts, the facts have no impact; if the believer does accept the facts, he or she may reduce dissonance by even stronger adherence to the belief.

Interviews and Surveys. Bell (1974) interviewed men before and after their retirement from work. The interviews dealt with satisfaction in various spheres of life. The dissonance predictions were that disconfirmation of preretirement expectations would lead to reduced satisfaction. This was found to be the case in only one sphere—that of family life, in which men who found themselves spending more time than usual with their families reported less satisfaction with their lives. Failure to find strong support for dissonance predictions in this older population led Bell to wonder whether dissonance processes might be limited to college students or to the laboratory setting.

Another approach, which has been extended into consumer research, involves information processing to reduce postdecisional dissonance. In one study (Ehrlich, Guttman, Schonbach, & Mills, 1957), men who had purchased new cars were interviewed four to six weeks after the purchase to see what advertisements they had read. The prediction was that the postdecisional dissonance would be reduced by reading ads pertaining to the purchased car and ignoring those concerning other cars. Interviewers brought with them magazines and newspapers that the car buyer said he read regularly and showed him all the automobile ads contained in the magazines and newspapers. As predicted, the researchers found that new-car owners had noticed and read more ads for the car they had bought than for other makes.

As we mentioned earlier, interview procedures involve low manipulation of antecedent conditions; they create these conditions through subject selection. It is regrettable that there have been no direct attempts to measure dissonance arousal through interviews, since the nature of this approach would seem to make such assessment possible. Subject awareness in interviews and surveys is high because interviewees know that they are being studied and can often glean the researcher's intent from the nature of the questions. This transparency is less characteristic of interviews like those conducted by Ehrlich and her associates, who disguised their purpose by presenting the interviews as readership surveys.

TWO RESEARCH EXAMPLES

Product Description

One of the characteristics of any good theory is that testable propositions can be derived from it. These propositions can be simply expressed as "If this is so, then this must also be so," and Festinger's theory of cognitive dissonance is a case in point. The two selections below not only share a common theoretical parentage in dissonance theory but also constitute similar tests of a derived hypothesis seeking to relate effort expended in the attainment of a goal and subsequent liking for that goal. More specifically, both studies hypothesize that the greater the effort exerted to obtain a goal, the greater the value assigned to the goal.

Let's return for a moment to the example of your attending the concert after enduring considerable discomfort in order to get a ticket for the performance. An initial assumption is made that *any* experience has positive and negative aspects. Given this, on the one hand, you have the knowledge (cognitive element) that you have gone to considerable trouble to get to the concert; on the other hand, you have attended a concert that you know (cognitive element) is a mixed bag of good and bad, perhaps more bad than good. According to the theory, this is an uncomfortable state of affairs. You can handle the dissonance by either denying the difficulty you experienced in getting the ticket or denying that the concert was pretty bad. If it was particularly difficult to attain the goal (you now have a cold from standing out in the rain), the former option is not feasible; consequently, you deny the drawbacks of the goal and enhance its positive aspects (the concert was great!).

In the first selection, Aronson and Mills hypothesized that the more severe the initiation a person experiences to get into a group, the greater the person's subsequent liking for the group. Using a laboratory study, these researchers varied the effort element by imposing different kinds of initiation rites for group entry. The first group, undergoing severe initiation, was required to go through a test designed to cause a great deal of embarrassment; the second group was required to engage in a mildly embarrassing task; and the third group (the control) underwent no initiation. All three groups were then asked to evaluate an apparently ongoing discussion by the group they were about to enter. Results were as predicted. The discussion group was rated significantly more positively by the subjects who had undergone the severe initiation than by those who had undergone either the mild initiation or no initiation at all.

In the second selection, Doob, Carlsmith, Freedman, Landauer, and Tom designed a field replication of the effort-liking relation. On the basis of Aronson and Mills' work, they reasoned that paying more for a product would lead to valuing it more. Specifically, they hypothesized that "when the initial price is high, a higher *proportion* of buyers should continue to purchase the product than when the initial price is low" (p. 345, italics in the original). Results were reported to be in the predicted direction: products whose initial price was higher outsold products whose initial price was lower. Just what may have produced such differences is the subject of some speculation, however, and we shall return to this in our consumer evaluation.

Consumer Checklist

- What are the raw materials used in the manufacture of this product?
    How adequate is the operational definition of the independent variable in each selection?
    Do we know whether dissonance has been aroused?
- How well is the product put together?
    Does each selection have an appropriate control group?
- Do the products meet performance criteria?
    What are the significance levels for the replications in the study by Doob and his associates?
    Are alternative explanations other than dissonance possible for the results obtained in each selection?

THE EFFECT OF SEVERITY OF INITIATION ON LIKING FOR A GROUP[1]

ELLIOT ARONSON
Stanford University
AND JUDSON MILLS
U. S. Army Leadership Human Research Unit, HumRRO

It is a frequent observation that persons who go through a great deal of trouble or pain to attain something tend to value it more highly than persons who attain the same thing with a minimum of effort. For example, one would expect persons who travel a great distance to see a motion picture to be more impressed with it than those who see the same picture at a neighborhood theater. By the same token, individuals who go through a severe initiation to gain admission to a club or organization should tend to think more highly of that organization than those who do not go through the severe initiation to gain admission.

Two questions are relevant here: 1. Is this "common observation" valid, that is, does it hold true when tested under cotrolled conditions? 2. If the observation is valid, how can it be accounted for? The relationship might be simply a result of differences in initial motivation. To take the case of initiations, persons who initially have a strong desire to join a particular club should be more willing to undergo unpleasantness to gain admission to it than persons who are low in initial interest. Therefore, a club that requires a severe initiation for admission should be joined only by those people with a strong desire to become members. On the other hand, a club that does not require a severe initiation should be joined by some individuals who like it very much, and by others who are relatively uninterested. Because of this self-selection, one would expect persons who are members of clubs with severe initiations to think more highly of their club, on the average, than members of clubs without severe initiations.

But is there something in the initiation itself that might account for this relationship? Is severity of initiation positively related to group preference when motivation for admission is held constant? Such a relationship is strongly implied by Festinger's (1957) theory of cognitive dissonance. The theory of cognitive dissonance predicts this relationship in the following manner. No matter how attractive a group is to a person it is rarely completely positive, i.e., usually there are some aspects of the group that the individual does not like. If he has undergone an unpleasant initiation to gain admission to the group, his cognition that he has gone through an unpleasant experience for the sake of membership is dissonant with his cognition that there are things about the group that he does not like. He can reduce this dissonance in two ways. He can convince himself that the initiation was not very unpleasant, or he can exaggerate the positive characteristics of the group and minimize its negative aspects. With increasing severity of initiation it becomes more and more difficult to believe that the initiation was not very bad. Thus, a person who has gone through a painful initiation to become a member of a group should tend to reduce his dissonance by over estimating the attractiveness of the group. The specific hypothesis tested in the present study is that individuals who undergo an unpleasant initiation to become members of a group increase their liking for the group; that is, they find the group more attractive than do persons who become members without going through a severe initiation.

Method

In designing the experiment it was necessary to have people join groups that were similar in every respect except for the severity of the initiation required for admission—and then to measure each individual's evaluation of the group. It was also necessary to randomize the initial motivation of subjects (Ss) to gain admission to the various groups in order to eliminate

[1] This research was partially supported by a grant from the National Science Foundation, administered by Leon Festinger. The authors are grateful to Leon Festinger for his help and encouragement during the planning and execution of the study.

From *Journal of Abnormal and Social Psychology*, 1959, 59(2), 177–181. Copyright 1959 by American Psychological Association. Reprinted by permission.

systematic effects of differences in motivation. These requirements were met in the following manner: Volunteers were obtained to participate in group discussions. They were assigned randomly to one of three experimental conditions: A *Severe* initiation condition, a *Mild* initiation condition, and a *Control* condition. In the Severe condition, *S*s were required to read some embarrassing material before joining the group; in the Mild condition the material they read in order to join the group was not very embarrassing; in the Control condition, *S*s were not required to read any material before becoming group members. Each *S* listened to the same tape recording which was ostensibly an ongoing discussion by the members of the group that he had just joined. *S*s then evaluated the discussion.

The *S*s were 63 college women. Thirty-three of them volunteered to participate in a series of group discussions on the psychology of sex. The remaining 30, tested at a somewhat later date, were "captive volunteers" from a psychology course who elected to participate in the group discussions on the psychology of sex in preference to several other experiments. Since the results obtained from these two samples were very similar, they were combined in the analysis presented here.

Each *S* was individually scheduled to "meet with a group." When she arrived at the experimental room, she was told by the experimenter (*E*) that he was conducting several group discussions on the psychology of sex. *E* informed her that she was joining a group that had been meeting for several weeks and that she was taking the place of a girl who had to leave the group because of scheduling difficulties. *E* stated that the discussion had just begun and that she would join the other members of the group after he had explained the nature of the experiment to her. The purpose of the foregoing instructions was to confront *S* with an ongoing group and thus make plausible the recorded discussion to which she was to be exposed.

E then "explained" the purpose of the experiment. He said that he was interested in investigating the "dynamics of the group discussion process." Sex was chosen as the topic for the groups to discuss in order to provide interesting subject matter so that volunteers for the discussion groups could be obtained without much difficulty. *E* continued as follows:

> But the fact that the discussions are concerned with sex has one major drawback. Although most people are interested in sex, they tend to be a little shy when it comes to discussing it. This is very bad from the point of view of the experiment; if one or two people in a group do not participate as much as they usually do in group discussions because they are embarrassed about sex, the picture we get of the group discussion process is distorted. Therefore, it is extremely important to arrange things so that the members of the discussion group can talk as freely and frankly as possible. We found that the major inhibiting factor in the discussions was the presence of the other people in the room. Somehow, it's easier to talk about embarrassing things if other people aren't staring at you. To get around this, we hit upon an idea which has proved very successful. Each member of the group is placed in a separate room, and the participants communicate through an intercom system using headphones and a microphone. In this way, we've helped people relax, and have succeeded in bringing about an increase in individual participation.

The foregoing explanation set the stage for the tape recording, which could now be presented to the *S* as a live discussion conducted by three people in separate rooms.

E then mentioned that, in spite of this precaution, occasionally some persons were still too embarrassed to engage in the discussions and had to be asked to withdraw from the discussion group. *S* was asked if she thought she could discuss sex freely. She invariably answered affirmatively. In the Control condition *S* was told, at this point, that she would be a member of the group.

In the other two conditions, *E* went on to say that it was difficult for him to ask people to leave the group once they had become members. Therefore, he had recently decided to screen new people before admitting them to the discussion groups. The screening device was described as an "embarrassment test" which consists of reading aloud some sexually oriented material in the presence of *E*. *S* was told that *E* would make a clinical judgment of her degree of embarrassment, based upon hesitation, blushing, etc. and would determine whether or not she would be capable of participating in the discussion group. He stressed that she was not obligated to take this test, but that she could not become a member unless she did. Only one *S* declined to take the test. She was excluded from the experiment. It was also emphasized, at this point, that the "embarrassment test" was a recent innovation and that the other members had joined the group before it was required for admission. These instructions were included in order to counteract any tendency to identify more strongly with the group as a result of feelings of having shared a common unpleasant experience. Such a process could conceivably bring about a greater preference for the discussion group on the part of *S*s in the Severe condition, introducing ambiguity in the interpretation of the results.

In the Severe condition, the "embarrassment test" consisted of having *S*s read aloud, from 3 × 5 cards, 12 obscene words, e.g., fuck, cock, and screw. *S*s also read aloud two vivid descriptions of sexual activity from contemporary novels. In the Mild condition, *S*s read aloud five words that were related to sex but not obscene, e.g., prostitute, virgin, and petting. In both the Severe and the Mild conditions, after each *S* finished reading the material, she was told that she had performed satisfactorily and was, therefore, a member of the group and could join the meeting that was now in progress.

It was of the utmost importance to prevent the *S* from attempting to participate in the discussion, for if she did, she would soon find that no one was responding to her statements and she would probably infer that the discussion was recorded. To insure their silence, all *S*s were told that, in preparation for each meeting, the group reads an assignment which serves as the focal point of the discussion; for this meeting, the group read parts of the book, *Sexual Behavior in Animals*. After the S had indicated that she had never read this book, E told her that she would be at a disadvantage and would, consequently, not be able to participate as fully in this discussion as she would had she done the reading. He continued, "Because the presence of a participant who isn't contributing optimally would result in an inaccurate picture of the dynamics of the group discussion process, it would be best if you wouldn't participate at all today, so that we may get an undistorted picture of the dynamics of the other three members of this group. Meanwhile, you can simply listen to the discussion, and get an idea of how the group operates. For the next meeting, you can do the reading and join in the discussion." Ss were invariably more than willing to comply with this suggestion. The above instructions not only prevented S from attempting to participate in the discussion but also served to orient her toward the actual content of discussion.

Under the guise of connecting the S's headphones and microphone, E went into the next room and turned on the tape recorder. He then returned to the experimental room, put on the headphones, picked up the microphone, and pretended to break into the discussion which supposedly was in progress. After holding a brief conversation with the "members of the group," he introduced the S to them. Then he handed the headphones to her. The tape was timed so that at the precise moment that S donned her headphones, the "group members" introduced themselves and then continued their discussion.

The use of a tape recording presented all Ss with an identical group experience. The recording was a discussion by three female undergraduates. It was deliberately designed to be as dull and banal as possible in order to maximize the dissonance of the Ss in the Severe condition. The participants spoke dryly and haltingly on secondary sex behavior in the lower animals, "inadvertently" contradicted themselves and one another, mumbled several *non sequiturs*, started sentences that they never finished, hemmed, hawed, and in general conducted one of the most worthless and uninteresting discussions imaginable.

At the conclusion of the recording, E returned and explained that after each meeting every member of the group fills out a questionnaire expressing her reactions to the discussion. The questionnaire asked the S to rate the discussion and the group members of 14 different evaluative scales, e.g., dull–interesting, intelligent–unintelligent, by circling a number from 0 to 15. After completing the questionnaire, S made three additional ratings, orally, in response to questions from E. Nine of the scales concerned the S's reactions to the discussion, while the other eight concerned her reactions to the participants.

At the close of the experiment, E engaged each S in conversation to determine whether or not she was suspicious of the procedure. Only one S entertained definite suspicions; her results were discarded.

Finally, the true nature of the experiment was explained in detail. None of the Ss expressed any resentment or annoyance at having been misled. In fact, the majority were intrigued by the experiment and several returned at the end of the academic quarter to ascertain the results.

Results and Discussion

The sum of the ratings for the 17 different scales provides an index of each S's liking for the discussion group. The means and SDs for the three experimental conditions for this measure are presented in Table 1. Means and SDs are also presented in Table 1 separately for the eight scales which tapped the Ss' attitudes toward the discussion and the seven scales which tapped their attitudes toward the participants. The significance of the differences between the means for the different conditions were determined by t tests. The t values and significance levels are presented in Table 2.

Examination of Table 1 shows that Ss in the Severe condition rated both the discussion and the participants higher than did those in the Control and Mild conditions. The over-all difference between the ratings by Ss in the

TABLE 1

Means of the Sum of Ratings for the Different Experimental Conditions

Rating Scales	Control ($N=21$)	Mild ($N=21$)	Severe ($N=21$)
Discussion [9]			
M	80.2	81.8	97.6
SD	13.2	21.0	16.6
Participants [8]			
M	89.9	89.3	97.7
SD	10.9	14.1	13.2
Total [17]			
M	166.7	171.1	195.3
SD	21.6	34.0	31.9

TABLE 2

Significance Levels of the Differences Between Experimental Conditions

Rating Scales	Control–Severe	Mild–Severe	Control–Mild
Discussion [9]	$t = 3.66$ $P < .001$*	$t = 2.62$ $P < .02$	$t = .29$ N.S.
Participants [8]	$t = 2.03$ $P < .05$	$t = 1.97$ $P < .10$	$t = .15$ N.S.
Total [17]	$t = 3.32$ $P < .01$	$t = 2.33$ $P < .05$	$t = .49$ N.S.

* The P values given are based on both tails of the t distribution.

Severe condition and Ss in the Control condition reaches the .01% level of significance. The over-all difference between the ratings by Ss in the Severe initiation condition and Ss in the Mild initiation condition reaches the .05 level.

These differences cannot be explained by differences in initial motivation to become members of the group, since Ss (with varying degrees of motivation) were randomly assigned to the three experimental conditions. The differences in liking for the group must be considered a consequence of the unpleasant experience. The results clearly substantiate the hypothesis: persons who undergo a severe initiation to attain membership in a group increase their liking for the group. This hypothesis follows directly from Festinger's theory of cognitive dissonance. According to the theory, Ss in the Severe initiation condition held the cognition that they had undergone a painful experience to become members of the discussion group. Then they listened to a dull, banal discussion. Negative cognitions about the discussion which they formed from listening to it were dissonant with the cognition that they had undergone a painful experience to gain membership in this group. The presence of dissonance leads to pressures to reduce it. Ss in this condition could reduce their dissonance either by denying the severity of the initiation or by distorting their cognitions concerning the group discussion in a positive direction. The initiation of the Ss in the Severe condition was apparently too painful for them to deny — hence, they reduced their dissonance by overestimating the attractiveness of the group.

There was no appreciable difference between the ratings made by Ss in the Control condition and those made by Ss in the Mild condition. It would seem that the Mild condition was so devoid of unpleasantness as to constitute little investment in the group. Hence, little dissonance was created. If any dissonance did occur in this situation it would be more realistic for the S to reduce it by minimizing the pain of the initiation, than by distorting her cognitions concerning the discussion. Thus, it is not an initiation per se that leads to increase in liking for a group. The initiation must be severe enough to constitute a genuine investment and to render it difficult to reduce dissonance by playing down the extent of the pain involved.

An examination of Table 1 shows that the rating scales concerning the discussion show greater differences between the conditions than the scales dealing with the evaluations of the participants in the discussion. There are at least two possible explanations for this result: (a) It may be easier for people to express negative criticism about an impersonal discussion than about the people involved. Thus, Ss in the Control and Mild conditions may have inflated their ratings of the participants to avoid making negative statements about fellow college students. (b) It is possible that Ss in the Severe condition had less need to distort their perception of the participants than of the discussion itself. The dissonance of the Ss in the Severe condition resulted from the actual discussion: they experienced dissonance between going through an unpleasant experience and taking part in worthless uninteresting discussions. The most direct way for them to reduce this dissonance would be to change their perceptions of the discussion in a positive direction. The participants in the discussion were peripheral to the cause of dissonance. If Ss in the Severe condition had less need to distort their perceptions of the participants than their perception of the discussion, their evaluations of the participants could be expected to be closer to the evaluations of the participants made by Ss in the Control and Mild conditions.

Summary and Conclusions

An experiment was conducted to test the hypothesis that persons who undergo an unpleasant initiation to become members of a group increase their liking for the group; that is, they find the group more attractive than do persons who become members without going through a severe initiation. This hypothesis was derived from Festinger's theory of cognitive dissonance.

College women who volunteered to participate in discussion groups were randomly assigned to one of three experimental conditions: A *Severe* initiation condition, a *Mild* initiation condition, and a *Control* condition. In the Severe condition, subjects were required to read some embarrassing material before joining the group; in the Mild condition the material they read in order to join the group was not very embarrassing; in the Control condition, subjects were not required to read any material before becoming group members. Each subject listened to a recording that appeared to be an ongoing discussion being conducted by the group which she had just joined. Afterwards, subjects filled out a questionnaire evaluating the discussion and the participants. The results clearly verified the hypothesis. Subjects who underwent a severe initiation perceived the group as being significantly more attractive than did those who underwent a mild initiation or no initiation. There was no appreciable difference between ratings by subjects who underwent a Mild initiation and those by subjects who underwent no initiation.

REFERENCE

FESTINGER, L. *A theory of cognitive dissonance.* Evanston: Row, Peterson, 1957.

Received June 9, 1958.

EFFECT OF INITIAL SELLING PRICE ON SUBSEQUENT SALES [1]

ANTHONY N. DOOB,[2] J. MERRILL CARLSMITH,[3] JONATHAN L. FREEDMAN
THOMAS K. LANDAUER,[4] AND SOLENG TOM, JR.

Stanford University

> Five field experiments investigated the effect of initial selling price on subsequent sales of common household products. Matched pairs of discount houses sold the same product at either a discounted price or the regular price for a short period of time. The prices were then made the same for all stores. The results were consistent with the prediction from dissonance theory that subsequent sales would be higher where the initial price was high.

The "introductory low price offer" is a common technique used by marketers. A new product is offered at a low price for a short period of time, and the price is subsequently raised to its normal level. Since the goal naturally is to maximize final sales of the product, the assumption behind this technique is that it will accomplish this goal. An economic model based entirely on supply and demand would of course predict that the eventual sales would not be affected by the initial price. The lower price would be expected to attract many marginal buyers and produce greater sales; but as soon as the price is raised, these buyers should drop out of the market. The hope of the marketer, however, is that some of these marginal buyers will learn to like the product enough so that they will continue to purchase it even at the higher price.

Unfortunately for the marketer, this may be a vain hope. There are various psychological reasons why we might expect the introductory low price to have an opposite effect from that which the marketers intend, such that the introductory low price would reduce rather than increase eventual sales. Since this technique is so widespread, it provides an unusual opportunity to investigate the applicability of social psychology in a natural setting, and to compare the marketer's predictions with that of social psychology.

The most interesting analysis of this situation is based on the theory of cognitive dissonance (Festinger, 1957). One of the clearest deductions from the theory is that the more effort in any form a person exerts to attain a goal, the more dissonance is aroused if the goal is less valuable than expected. The individual reduces this dissonance by increasing his liking for the goal, and therefore the greater the effort, the more he should like the goal. This prediction has received some substantiation in laboratory experimentation (e.g., Aronson & Mills, 1959; Gerard & Mathewson, 1966). Its applicability to the marketing situation is straightforward: the theory predicts that the higher the price a person initially pays for a product, the more he will come to like it. Presumably this greater liking will produce "brand loyalty" in the form of repeat purchases. Thus, when the initial price is high, a higher *proportion* of buyers should continue to purchase the product than when the initial price is low. Accordingly, although the introductory price will initially attract more customers, we may expect the sales curves for the two conditions to cross at some later point, and the higher brand loyalty induced by the dissonance involved in paying a high price to manifest itself in higher final sales in that condition.

Five experiments were performed to demonstrate that introducing a new brand of a product at a low price for a short time and

---

[1] This study was supported in part by National Science Foundation grants to Carlsmith and to Freedman. The authors are grateful to management and personnel of the discount chain for their cooperation in this research.

[2] Now at University of Toronto.

[3] Requests for reprints should be addressed to J. Merrill Carlsmith, Department of Psychology, Stanford University, Stanford, California 94305.

[4] Now at Bell Telephone Laboratories, Murray Hill, New Jersey.

From *Journal of Personality and Social Psychology*, 1969, 11(4), 345–350. Copyright 1969 by American Psychological Association. Reprinted by permission.

then raising it to the normal selling price leads to lower sales in the long run than introducing the product at its normal selling price. The general design of all the experiments was to introduce the new brand at a low price in one set of stores and, after the price is raised to the normal selling price, compare sales with matched stores where the product was introduced at the normal selling price and held there throughout the course of the experiment.

All of the experiments that are to be reported here were done in a chain of discount houses. All sales figures have been multiplied by a constant in order to maintain confidentiality.

This chain of discount houses differs from most others in a number of important ways. They do not advertise much, and what advertising they do does not include prices on specific items. Price changes occur very seldom in these stores and are usually not advertised. In most cases, prices are lowered because an item is overstocked, and unless the customer remembers the regular selling price, he has no way of knowing that the price is lower than usual. Management in most of these stores is under direct control of the central office. When the manager receives orders from the central office, he has little or no power to change them.

The chain sells a large number of "house brands" at prices lower than the equivalent name brands. These house brands have the same registered trademark, and constitute a brand which customers can easily identify with the store. Generally, the quality of the house brand item is as high as the equivalent name brand, the differences usually being in characteristics which do not directly affect the usefulness of the item (e.g., mouthwash bottles are not as attractive as those of the name brand; the average grain size of powdered detergent is larger than that of the name brand which is chemically equivalent).

The products used in the studies reported here were house brands. All were being introduced into the stores at the time when the study was being run. The particular products used and the price differential were both determined by management.

Experiment I

Method

Twelve pairs of discount houses, matched on gross sales, were randomly assigned to one of two experi-

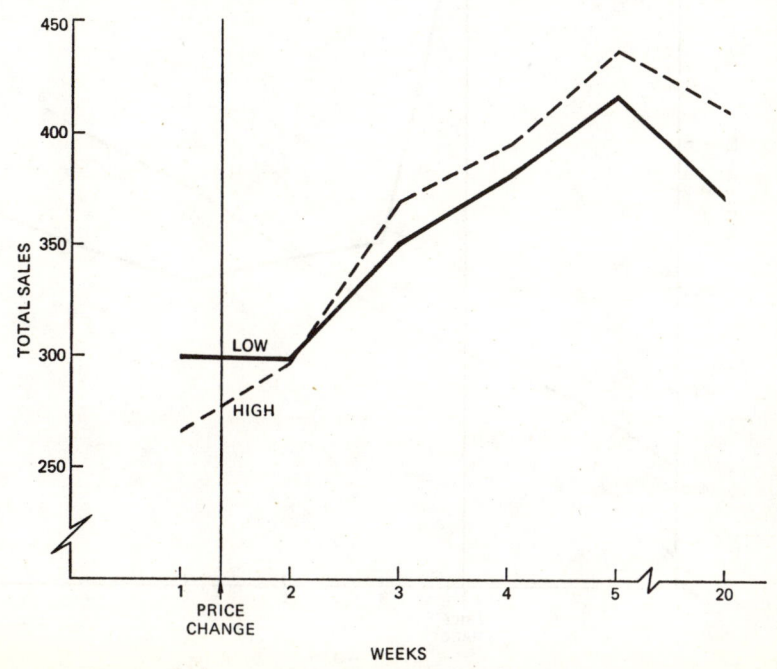

Fig. 1. Mouthwash sales.

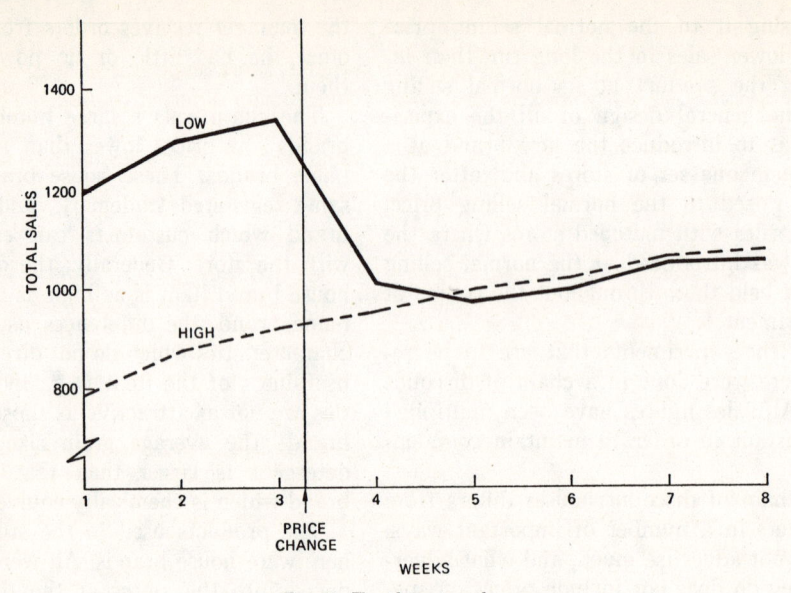

FIG. 2. Toothpaste sales.

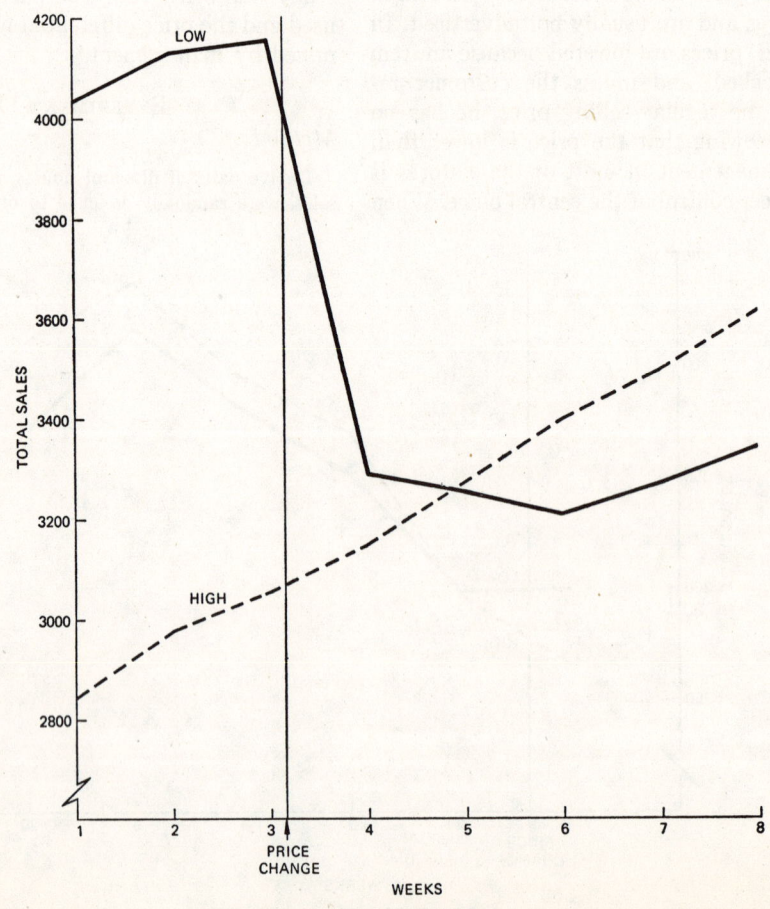

FIG. 3. Aluminum foil sales.

mental conditions. In one store of each pair, the house brand of mouthwash was introduced at $.25 per quart bottle. The price was held at this level for 9 days (two weekends and the intervening days), and then the price was brought up to $.39 for all stores. In the other store, it was introduced at its normal selling price of $.39.

None of the managers had any reason to believe that the price of mouthwash at his store was not the same as in all other stores in the chain. No one was given any special instructions beyond the place in the store where the item was to be sold and its selling price. The location was essentially identical for all stores. In stores where mouthwash was introduced at the low price, the manager received a memo at the end of the first week instructing him to change the price to $.39 after that weekend.

Results

Sales were recorded by the sundries buyer as he replenished stock. At the end of each week these figures were sent to the central office and then relayed to the experimenters. Average sales for the 12 matched stores in each condition are shown in Figure 1. It is estimated that at least 2 weeks had to pass before customers would return to buy more mouthwash, and, therefore, one would not expect there to be any difference between the height of the curves until the third week. In fact, the curves cross at this point, and after this point, it is clear that the stores where the initial selling price was high were selling more mouthwash than stores where the initial price was low. This is true in spite of the fact that more mouthwash was sold the first week in stores where the price was low. Unfortunately, for a variety of reasons, the authors were not able to collect continuous data. They were able, however, to check sales 19 weeks after the price change, and clearly the difference still existed. When sales for Weeks 3, 4, 5, and 20 are combined, sales of mouthwash were higher in the store where the initial selling price was high in 10 of the 12 pairs of stores ($p = .02$).

Sales in the two sets of stores during Weeks 3, 4, 5, and 20 (pooled) were also compared by use of a t test, resulting in a t of 2.11 ($df = 11$, $p < .10$). Thus, stores where the initial selling price was low sold less mouthwash than did stores where the initial selling price was the same as the final selling price.

REPLICATIONS

The same experiment was repeated four times, using different products. The procedures were very similar in all cases. In each experiment, the stores were rematched and randomly assigned independent of all other replications.

Experiment II: Toothpaste

Six pairs of stores were matched on the basis of sundries sales and randomly assigned to conditions in which the selling price for the first 3 weeks was either $.41 or $.49 for a "family size" tube of toothpaste. After 3 weeks, the price in all stores was set at $.49. The results are presented in Figure 2. When the sales for the last 4 weeks are combined as in the previous experiment, four of the six pairs show differences in the predicted direction ($p = .34$). When the more sensitive t test is done on the data from these 4 weeks, the t is 2.26 ($df = 5$, $p < .10$).

Experiment III: Aluminum Foil

Seven pairs of stores were matched on the basis of grocery sales and randomly assigned to conditions in which the selling price for the first 3 weeks was either $.59 or $.64 for a 75-foot roll of foil. After 3 weeks, the price in all stores was set at $.64. The results are presented in Figure 3. For Weeks 5–8

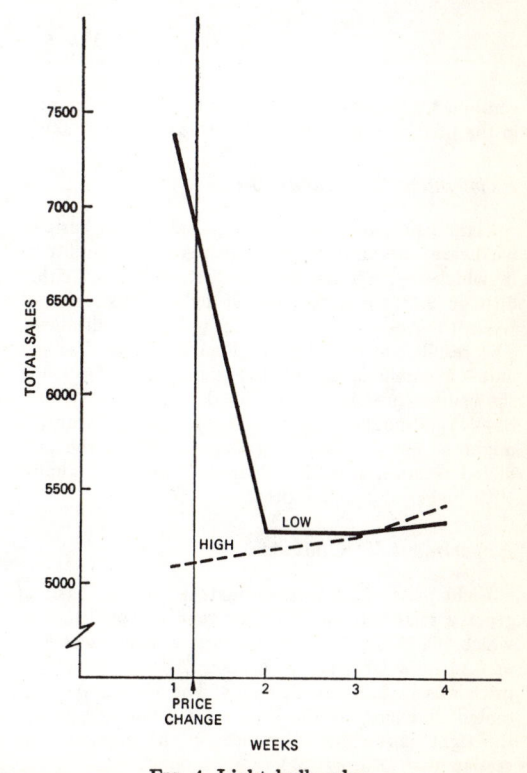

FIG. 4. Light bulb sales.

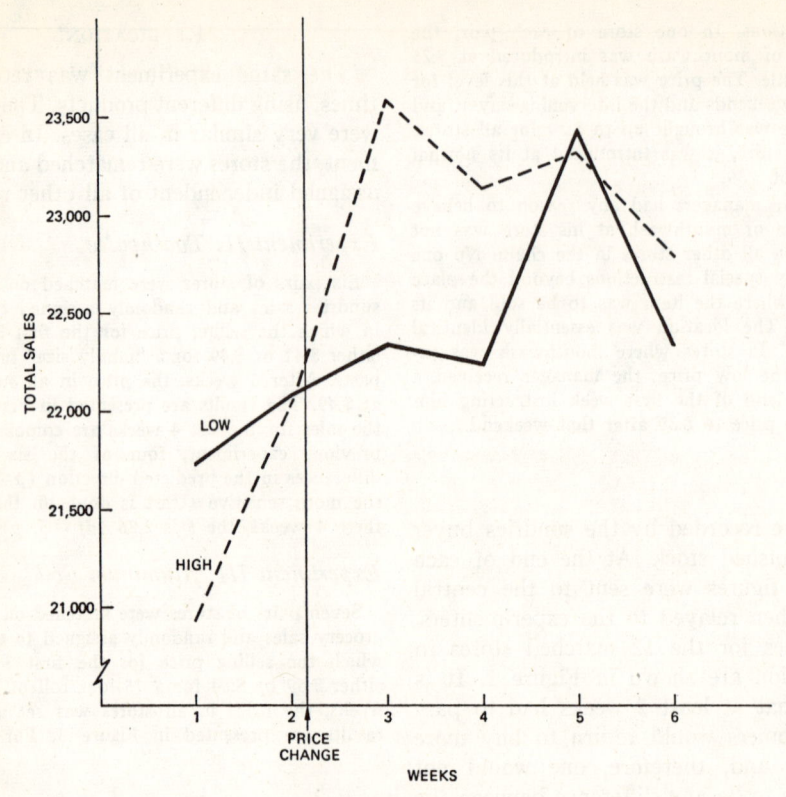

FIG. 5. Cookie sales.

combined, all seven pairs ($p = .01$) show differences in the predicted direction ($t = 5.09$, $df = 6$, $p < .005$).

Experiment IV: Light Bulbs

Eight pairs of stores were matched on the basis of hardware sales and randomly assigned to conditions in which selling price for the first week was either $.26 or $.32 for a package of light bulbs. After 1 week, the price was brought up to $.32 in all stores. The results are presented in Figure 4. For Weeks 3 and 4 combined, six of the eight pairs ($p = .15$) show differences in the predicted direction ($t = .837$, $df = 7$). Although this difference is not significant, it might be noted in Figure 4 that there was the predicted reversal, even though initial sales were almost 50% higher at the low price.

Experiment V: Cookies

Eight pairs of stores were matched on the basis of grocery sales and randomly assigned to conditions in which the selling price for the first 2 weeks was $.24 or $.29 for a large bag of cookies. After 2 weeks, the price was at $.29 for all stores. The results are presented in Figure 5. For Weeks 4–6 combined, six of the eight pairs show differences in the predicted direction ($t = .625$, $df = 7$).

RESULTS

When the results of all five experiments are combined into one test of the hypothesis, a z of 3.63 ($p < .0002$) is obtained. Clearly, so far as this has been tested, the practice of introducing a product at a low price is not a good strategy for this chain of stores to use.

DISCUSSION

These studies indicate that introducing products at a lower than usual price is harmful to final sales. It was earlier argued that one possible reason for this is the lower proportion of buyers who return to a product when the initial price is lower than the normal price. Whether or not this causes eventual sales actually to be lower when the initial price is low is not critical to the argument. If, for example, there is an extremely large difference in initial sales, even a lower proportion of returning buyers may produce an advantage for the initial low price. Similarly, if the product has some special feature which would be expected to produce loyalty merely from exposure, it would be beneficial to maximize initial sales by the use of low introductory offers. In the experiments reported here, neither of these possibilities seems to have been present. For the range of prices studied, even a 50% increase in sales due to the lower price was not enough to overcome the increased consumer loyalty engendered by the higher price. Because of the presence of other identical brands, differing only in price, exposure alone was not enough to produce loyalty.

Whether or not eventual sales are actually lower when the initial price is low is not critical to the argument. From a theoretical point of view, the only essential comparison is the relative proportion of repurchases in the two conditions. A stringent method of showing that this proportion is higher when the initial price is high is to demonstrate that the absolute volume of eventual sales is greater for the high-price condition, even though initial sales are lower. For the products and prices studied here, this was true.

There are at least two alternative explanations of this result. The first is that in the low-initial-price stores the market is glutted after the first few weeks, and it takes a long time for there to be any need to repurchase the product. This might be a partial explanation of the difference between the conditions, but seems implausible as a total explanation. For all the products except light bulbs the length of time that the sales curves were followed exceeded by a goodly margin the marketer's estimate of the normal time until repurchase. Indeed, with mouthwash, for which the repurchase period is about 2 weeks, the difference between conditions is still present 19 weeks after the price switch. Customers might have stocked up by buying more than their usual supply of a product, but pricing practices of this chain of stores makes this unlikely. These stores have rarely used low introductory price offers and they were not advertised as such for the products studied. Buyers therefore had no reason to believe that the "low price" was a special price and accordingly had little reason to stock up on the product. Thus, although one cannot entirely rule out this "glutting the market" explanation, it is not convincing.

A second and more interesting alternative is in terms of what might be called the customers' adaptation level regarding the particular product. When mouthwash is put on sale at $.25, customers who buy it at that price or notice what the price is may tend to think of the product in terms of $.25. They say to themselves that this is a $.25 bottle of mouthwash. When, in subsequent weeks, the price increases to $.39, these customers will tend to see it as overpriced, and are not inclined to buy it at this much higher price. Therefore, sales drop off considerably. In the $.39 steady condition, initial sales are lower, but there is no reason for them to drop off due to this effect. Therefore, introducing it at the ultimate price results in greater sales in the long run than does introducing it at the low price. This explanation fits the data as nicely as does the one in terms of cognitive dissonance. In many ways, they are quite similar and are difficult to distinguish experimentally.

It should be noted that the adaptation level and dissonance explanations are by no means mutually exclusive. It is entirely possible that both mechanisms are operating to some extent. In any case, the basic result stands—the introduction of a product at a low price tended to decrease subsequent sales, and this effect lasted for at least 20 weeks.

REFERENCES

Aronson, E., & Mills, J. The effect of severity of initiation on liking for a group. *Journal of Abnormal and Social Psychology,* 1959, 59, 177–181.

Festinger, L. *A theory of cognitive dissonance.* Stanford, Calif.: Stanford University Press, 1957.

Gerard, H. B., & Mathewson, G. C. The effects of severity of initiation on liking for a group: A replication. *Journal of Experimental Social Psychology,* 1966, 2, 278–287.

(Received August 2, 1968)

THE STUDIES COMPARED

Operational Definitions of Dissonance Arousal

You've been studying hard all evening for an upcoming exam. And then it strikes—you're starved and have a raging attack of the "munchies." You call to your roommate in the kitchen and ask whether there are any munchies in the house. She says "What kind of munchies?" You think for a second and say something definitive like "Well, I don't know—you know, munchies—something good." The dialogue continues back and forth, with you getting a little frustrated because you hadn't intended to make a big deal of it; you just want some simple munchies. And your roommate is getting nowhere with her suggestions. You are at an impasse. A scientist might call it a problem in definition. "Munchies" may or may not have a specific meaning for you, but clearly the definition is not generally agreed upon, since your roommate didn't know what you wanted. You storm into the kitchen, opening refrigerator and cupboards, banging around until you spot a recipe for peanut fudge on the peanut-butter jar. That's it! And with that you've made a leap from a privately-held definition (munchies) to a shared one (peanut fudge). Your roommate now knows what you mean. The next leap in definition is from the shared meaning to the specific operations needed to produce the fudge—what in scientific parlance would be called the fudge's operational definition and in everyday parlance the recipe for the fudge. The operational definition (or the recipe) provides not only the ingredients but directions for putting the ingredients together—that is, a concrete, unambiguous description of what anyone would need to do to produce that particular study (or that particular kind of fudge).

Operational Definition in the Aronson and Mills Study. With behavioral research, operational definitions are an absolute must. The investigator must provide you with a description of the operations used to produce the relevant independent variables. This is done not only to aid replication (will others also get the same result?) but to enable producers and consumers alike to determine what caused what. Had Aronson and Mills provided no details but said only that one group experienced a severe initiation and a second group underwent a mild initiation, there would be no way to check the explanation they give for their results. Instead, Aronson and Mills' study contains a clear description of how the independent variable of severity is operationally defined—reading varying amounts and kinds of embarrassing material. The group in the severe condition read 12 obscene words and 2 sexually oriented passages, whereas the group in the mild condition read only 5 nonobscene sex-related words and no passages. The control group read no material.

Concerning operational definitions, one must ask whether the definition is a good translation of the conceptual variable—in this case, severity. Perhaps the sex material produced a pleasurable experience rather than a severe one. Since a dissonance explanation requires the latter, it is important to check whether in fact the task was experienced as severe by the subjects. It is ironic that in the experimental instructions for the Aronson and Mills study, the subjects were led to believe that they would be observed during the reading for signs of blushing or hesitating—ironic, because the opportunity to check on the severity by physiological or self-report measures was not utilized. The meaning of the experience is crucial, but here, as in many other dissonance studies, no separate assessments to detect the presence of dissonance were made. It is noteworthy that a laboratory replication of the study by Gerard and Mathewson (1966), using differential shock levels to produce different degrees of severity, did query subjects on the "unpleasantness" of the shocks that were administered. Ratings by subjects in that study confirmed differences in discomfort between those who were in the severe-condition group and those who were in the mild-condition group. Such ratings were not done by Aronson and Mills. Since inducing a state of dissonance is critical to the interpretation of differences, the absence of such an independent assessment is a serious shortcoming.

Operational Definition in the Study by Doob and Associates. In the second research selection, the independent variable involves differential pricing of identical items at comparable stores. In each replication, a newly marketed item was offered at one store at the regular price and at another store at a lower introductory price and then at the normal price. The operational definition of effort thus appears to be cost difference for the same item, with the higher price constituting the dissonance condition.

According to strict interpretation of dissonance theory, the independent variable should be the differential pricing of the objects. However, this is not the operational definition that the researchers developed. Instead, their independent variable appears to be the effect of *changing* the price from low to high as compared with the effect of *maintaining* the price at the same high level. This is problematic because a different hypothesis is then being tested and the results have to be understood in a way that is different from the way they would have to be interpreted if the effects of permanently low and of permanently high prices for the same articles were compared. We shall return to this problem in definition later in our discussion of alternatives to dissonance explanations for the data presented. Suffice it to say at the moment that change in price may have had a peculiar influence of its own on buying behavior. Perhaps changing a low price to a high price makes that high price comparatively much more severe than a consistently high price. In terms of dissonance theory, then, it is hard to say which of the two groups experienced the more severe condition.

With this operational definition of the independent variable, the researchers can still investigate the specific hypothesis that introductory lower pricing does not lead to long-term increase in sales. They are not testing a specific proposition from dissonance theory.

Design and Procedures

For an unusually full description of the procedural details of the first selection, see the account given by Aronson and Carlsmith (1968) in the chapter called "Experimentation in Social Psychology." Although the investigators missed a good opportunity to make an independent assessment of dissonance arousal, the study included appropriate checks and controls.

The authors of the second selection have also taken great care in standardizing procedures and guarding against data contamination. Such precautions as initial matching of stores on the basis of sales volume and random assigning of experimental treatments rule out the possibility that the resulting differences were due to initial differences. Replications with different products enhance generalizability. Such particulars as introducing new products with no advertising and keeping store personnel blind to the research enterprise add to the rigor of the procedures.

The problems mentioned above with respect to the operational definition in the first selection become even more acute, however, when you look at the design of the second selection. The results are based on a comparison of the sales of the same product in two groups of stores—one group offering the product at an introductory low price and then raising the price to its normal level, and the other group offering the product at the normal selling price throughout the course of the experiment. The reasoning is that the *higher* price effects the greater liking for the product. But there is another possibility: any change in price may result in eventual lower sales. To rule out such possibility, at least one other control group would have to be included—one that changed price from high to low. This would allow you to determine which of the two explanations is the more viable—the change explanation or the dissonance explanation offered in the second selection.

Data Analysis

For the uninitiated, a statement such as "the results were significant at $p < .05$" is not likely to be very meaningful, although hearing that results were significant seems straightforward enough; no doubt it means that the data are important. But *significance* for the behavioral scientist has a different meaning. It refers not to psychological import, but to statistical difference. It addresses itself to whether the results obtained are due to specifiable causes or only to chance happenings. Where the former is desirable, the latter is not. The expression $p < .05$ is a generally agreed upon, although arbitrary, standard. It means that the chances are only five in a hundred that the obtained results are due to chance.

Analysis of support for dissonance theory based on reported data has been generally criticized (Chapanis & Chapanis, 1964) on the grounds that results are reported as significant when, in fact, the probability of their being due to chance is greater than the usually accepted standard of .05. A close look at the data presented by Doob and his colleagues reveals this same problem. The significance levels for the five products using t tests of total sales were .10, .10, .005, nonsignificant, and nonsignificant, respectively. The first two are somewhat below acceptable limits, and the last two are far below them. Thus only one sales record is actually statistically significant at agreed-upon levels. The analyses of data in the first research selection, instead, yield probability levels within accepted boundaries.

Interpretive Problems

Both studies have interpretive problems, problems they share with much dissonance research. In the first selection, it is not entirely clear that the results obtained are in fact due to dissonance and to dissonance only. Chapanis and Chapanis (1964) suggested three plausible alternatives for the positive ratings given the dull discussion after undergoing the severe initiation. One alternative explanation was that the women became sexually aroused by the procedure, with the result that their positive ratings were associated with pleasure or expectations of pleasure. However, an experiment (Gerard & Mathewson, 1966) using shock rather than embarrassment as an initiation procedure ruled out the sexual-arousal explanation. A second possibility was that the initiation procedure gave the women who survived it a feeling of accomplishment and pride that generalized to their more favorable ratings of the group discussion. Aronson (1969b) argued that the Gerard and Mathewson (1966) study could be used to rule out this alternative as well. He cited the experience of a control group in that study who underwent shock without being told that it was an initiation ritual and who then also rated the group discussion. Since these subjects had experienced the shock, if feelings of success and pride at undergoing an ordeal were at stake, then they too should have rated the discussion favorably. As this was not the case, Aronson maintained that the success interpretation was not tenable. The final alternative suggested by Chapanis and Chapanis (1964) was that the women might have experienced feelings of relief at finding that the group discussion was not as difficult or embarrassing as the initiation ritual led them to expect. This alternative has not been explored directly in further research.

An additional alternative was suggested by Elms (1972). He pointed out that neither the Aronson and Mills study nor the later study by Gerard and Mathewson dealt effectively with the possibility that initiations either by reading sexually loaded words or by receiving shock led prospective group members to expect more from the group discussion than the sample tape recording seemed to offer. He reasoned that a mild initiation followed by a dull discussion tape led to low ratings on consistency grounds. On the other hand, a severe initiation followed by a dull discussion led to high ratings because the women assumed that the group discussion just had to get better.

With regard to the second selection, a different interpretive problem arises. Doob and his associates refer to studies dealing with severity of initiation in discussing their own application of dissonance theory to the marketing situation. They say that the theory predicts that the higher the price paid, the greater the liking for the product. This reasoning would seem to call for the specific prediction that initial high price leads to higher sales than initial low price. In fact, inspection of the figures indicates that sales *drop* for the products introduced at a lower price, not that sales rise for those introduced at a higher price. There is no doubt a clear quantitative difference between the sales volumes under the two conditions; but it is inappropriate to compare sales volumes at low-initial-price and high-price *stores* rather than initial and later *sales* at either price level. Doob and his associates argue that this point is not critical to the roots of the theory. But the fact that so many critics have objected to the imprecision of dissonance theory in specifying the nature of cognitive elements (for example, Kiesler, Collins, & Miller, 1969) would indicate that the point is not so trivial. It makes considerable difference for experimental prediction whether the two elements are "I have expended great effort" and "I see that the product is not so good" or whether they are "I expended little effort" and "I see that the product is not so bad."

CONSUMER EVALUATION

Durability

The Aronson and Mills study has weathered well. Done almost 20 years ago, it has been reprinted many times, is mentioned in virtually every social-psychology textbook, and continues to be integrated into new research on attitude change. Both its findings and method are well regarded. The shortcomings noted by early critics were specific and testable.

There are fewer grounds for confidence in the second selection. To begin with, the study attempts less of a theoretical contribution, since it is conceived of as an extension of the Aronson and Mills findings to the marketplace. Second, it should be noted that other attempts to extend dissonance theory to consumer behavior have failed (Oshikawa, 1969; 1971). Recall that in Chapter 1 we stressed the need for a study to be anchored in a body of work and to offer the opportunity for further study. The failure of the attempts just mentioned indicate that the second study may lack durability both because it doesn't seem to allow for generalization through time and space and because it is difficult to say what further predictions might be made from it.

Borrowing from Mark Twain, we can say that reports of the death of dissonance theory are vastly exaggerated. Reformulations continue to appear (for example, Gerard, Conolley, & Wilhelmy, 1974) as attempts are made to define more precisely the conditions under which dissonance will and will not be aroused.

Careful Reading

The first study describes procedures and statistical analyses clearly; the results are simple and unqualified. Consequently, the study has seldom been misquoted or distorted. The same cannot be said of the second selection. For example, in reporting the results of the experiment on cookie sales, the statement reads "Six of the eight pairs show differences in the predicted direction," but the t test cited is not significant. Only careful reading is likely to reveal this discrepancy, and the assertive verbal statement of findings is the one likely to be quoted.

9

ATTITUDE-BEHAVIOR DISCREPANCY: PREJUDICE AND RACISM

CHAPTER OUTLINE

Explanations of Prejudice and Racism
    Personality and Societal Explanations
    Social Psychological Explanations
        Socialization
        Conformity
        Belief Congruence
    Summary of Explanations
Research on Attitude-Behavior
        Consistency in Interracial
        Interaction
    Negative Attitude, Positive Behavior
    Positive Attitude, Negative Behavior
Methods in Research on Prejudice and
        Racism
    Surveys and Interviews
    Observations and Archival Search
    Field Experiments
    Laboratory Experiments

Two Research Examples
    Product Description
    Consumer Checklist
    Shirley Weitz, Attitude, voice, and
        behavior: A repressed affect
        model of interracial interaction.
    Daniel A. Johnson, Richard J. Porter,
        and Patricia L. Mateljan, Racial
        discrimination in apartment
        rentals.
The Studies Compared
    Measurement of Attitudes and Behavior
    Confounding Variables
    Presentation of Results
    Simulations and Real Encounters
Consumer Evaluation
    Careful Reading
    Durability

Two friends are sitting together, when one points to a man walking by. The following conversation takes place:

"See that man?"

"Yeah."

"I don't like him."

"How come you don't like him? You don't even know him."

"That's how come I don't like him."

In that man's mind, not knowing is synonymous with not liking. When something is strange or different, people often react with caution or even fear. One way of handling the fear is to reject the strange person; the act of rejecting may make the person performing the act more comfortable, since it reduces the fear of the unknown by putting the object of fear at a distance. But every such act involves more than one person. The hostility and rejection that protect the one are offensive and painful to the other. The victim is prejudged and misjudged. Social psychologists identify *prejudice* as negative attitudes toward people who share a group identity perceived as different. When those negative attitudes are expressed in behavior, the act is called *discrimination*. The social interaction that results is one in which the targets of the dislike are sure to get hurt and for which, in subtler ways, everyone pays a price.

Racial prejudice is the most intense form of prejudice in this country. Expressions of racial prejudice that systematically limit and oppress minority-group members are called *racism*. Specifically, racism is "the transformation of race prejudice and/or ethnocentrism through the exercise of power against a racial group defined as inferior by individuals and institutions with the intentional or unintentional support of the entire culture" (Jones, 1972, p. 116). Similarly, Carmichael and Hamilton define racism as decisions and policies that use race as a criterion "for the purpose of subordinating a racial group and maintaining control over that group" (1967, p. 3). The core of the distinction between racism and prejudice is power. Even the most prejudiced person will be less able to express his or her prejudice in ways that harm others if that person is without power.

EXPLANATIONS OF PREJUDICE AND RACISM

Personality and Societal Explanations

When you hear someone utter a racial slur, you are apt to think there's something wrong with a person who thinks and feels like that. Some psychologists think so too, and their explanations of how and why one person is more or less prejudiced than another see prejudice as a sign of abnormal thinking or as a symptom of personality disturbance. Based on Freudian psychoanalytic theory, these explanations attribute prejudice to intrapsychic conflict and see in *scapegoating* one way of dealing with this underlying conflict. For example, sometimes you experience feelings of hostility not directed toward a particular individual. Your job seems constricting, promotion is blocked, the pay is low, and the future uncertain; without a specific person to blame, you turn your hostility against a group of people who have little to do with your problems—you scapegoat them. According to Freudian theory, another way of dealing with intrapsychic conflict is *projection*. The concept of projection depends on the assumption that certain thoughts and feelings are alien and repugnant, and therefore unacceptable. Being unacceptable to the self, these feelings are projected outward onto others. Some Black writers (Cleaver, 1968; Fanon, 1967; Hernton, 1965) have argued that conflictual sexual feelings unacceptable to Whites have been projected by Whites onto Blacks in order to exaggerate Black sexuality and justify race prejudice.

In general, the Freudian explanations that regard prejudice as a form of pathology tell us more about extremes of individual prejudice than about how large numbers of people come to share the same prejudices and tell us very little about how particular groups become the targets of prejudice. Also, there is something incomplete about an explanation of a widespread phenomenon that relies on labeling that phenomenon as pathologic. Furthermore, research support for such theorizing has been less than persuasive.

In contrast to these individualistic views of prejudice are the explanations attempting to account for racist patterns and practices in society overall. In these explanations, prejudice is seen as an attitude supported by a dominating class in order to justify the economic exploitation of a group identified as inferior (Cox, 1948). This analysis, characterized by social-class conflict, is based on Marxist theory. Another kind of conflict analysis centers on conflicts arising between interdependent groups. When there is direct competition for territory or goods, the resulting conflict may find expression in racism. Conflict in desegregating housing projects or neighborhoods may acquire a racist focus when the resources are scarce. If apartments at low rents are hard to come by, White residents may sharpen their opposition to Blacks moving in.

Some of the support for group-conflict explanations comes from field experiments conducted by Sherif and his coworkers (Sherif, Harvey, White, Hood, & Sherif, 1961). After assigning boys who were attending summer camp to two subgroups, these researchers created feelings of competition through win-lose athletic contests between the subgroups. As predicted by group-conflict theory, prejudice resulted and was expressed in name calling, stereotyping, and avoidance between the groups. The prejudice and hostility were then reduced experimentally. The investigators introduced goals that had value for both groups and that could not be achieved by the efforts or resources of either group alone. While this simulation is a convincing demonstration of the theory, it is not clear that the conflict-resolution methods would work with adults not organized in teams and operating under conditions in which long-standing realistic competition exists.

An important difference between personality and societal explanations lies with the kind of change called for in the two levels of explanation. An understanding of why racism exists leads to strategies for change that are different from those suggested by an understanding of the individual dynamics that sustain a greater or lesser degree of individual prejudice. In the first instance, social change is called for; in the latter case, individual change. Typically, these different explanations complement each other. Both levels of explanation are needed to understand the complex machinations of prejudice and racism.

Social-Psychological Explanations

Some explanations of racism and prejudice take the view that prejudice is learned and racist behavior is adopted from other people. The amount of racism and prejudice varies among countries and among geographical regions within countries. Some American Blacks, for example, have chosen to live as expatriates in France or in one of the Scandinavian countries because there they are confronted with less prejudice and fewer racist policies.

Socialization. National differences are often explained in terms of the processes by which a person learns to be part of his or her culture. The term *socialization* refers to the ways in which children learn to believe and to act like other members of their culture. Although usually referred to in context with children, socialization processes apply equally to newcomers to a culture, because they too have to learn the ways of doing and being necessary to be accepted as full-fledged members of the group. The socialization explanation of prejudice holds that children and newcomers learn prejudice just as they learn other customs and practices. Recall the discussion of the role of modeling in the learning of aggressive behavior in Chapter 5. For children, parents are the major socializing agents; it is therefore no surprise that studies consistently find a high correlation between a child's prejudice and that of his or her parents (Mosher & Scodel, 1960). Prejudice is rarely taught directly, but it is implicated in a wide spectrum of parental attitudes that children absorb with the family's atmosphere and lifestyle. Other socialization agents such as playmates, school, and the mass media are also influential in the acquisition of prejudice.

The existence of institutional racism (that is, those routine workings of the social institutions of a culture that have racial discrimination as a by-product) shapes the messages that schools and media send. Many newspapers, magazines, films, and television programs tend to portray minorities in stereotypic ways, perhaps because they aim for easy recognition of characters and events. The consequence of this practice, however, is the perpetuation of the existing stereotypes with successive generations of readers and viewers (Bogel, 1973; Leab, 1975).

Institutional racism is translated into individual prejudice by the child's attempt to make sense of his or her world—an attempt that invariably seeks causality. As discussed in Chapter 7, attributions are made about why things happen as they do. In observing the poor housing and street disrepair in neighborhoods where mostly Blacks live, the child reasons that the conditions observed are caused by the people who live there. The observer makes inferences from evidence at hand and is thus disposed to rationalize the conditions that exist. Another version of this thinking, called "blaming the victim" (Ryan, 1971), holds that the victim of social problems is responsible for his or her fate.

Conformity. Closely related to the socialization explanations of prejudice and racism are those based on the concept of conformity. According to this view, behaviors are adopted in order to conform to social pressure. In fact, conformity may be thought of as the process through which socialization is accomplished; you conform to the rules that others have set for you, and you try to fulfill the expectations that others have with regard to your behavior. But conformity obviously occurs in other than children and newcomers. In a study done in South Africa, Pettigrew (1958) found a strong association between social conformity and prejudice. As racism is the official government policy in South Africa, to conform is to be prejudiced; those most inclined to conform will and do show the most prejudice and racism. Extending this line of reasoning to the United States, Pettigrew (1959) compared Northerners and Southerners on measures of conformity and prejudice. Only in the Southern sample was a strong association found between conformity and prejudice. The explanation offered was that there was more agreement in the South concerning the legitimacy of racism. Thus, those who were most conformist to norms were also most prejudiced. In the North, such agreement was less clear-cut and the tendency to conform less implicated in prejudice and racism. Pettigrew (1958) observed "The problem is clear! Conformity is associated with racial intolerance, while deviance from these norms is associated with racial tolerance" (p. 40).

Belief Congruence. Yet another explanation that relates prejudice to a person's attempt to make sense of the world around emphasizes the power of belief similarity as a basis for interpersonal attraction. Essentially, this view holds that race prejudice works through mechanisms of interpersonal inference. It argues that you tend to think that people who are visibly different from you along racial lines are also likely to be different from you with regard to beliefs you hold dear. If you learn of a belief similarity between yourself and someone of another race, you are more likely to select that person for a friend than someone of your own race who disagrees with you about something in which you strongly believe (Rokeach, Smith, & Evans, 1960).

A number of studies have supported this explanation. Students were asked to express a friendship choice between paired target persons who were either similar or different in race or belief. Specifically, if you were religious, you might be asked to say whether you'd rather befriend a White person who believed in God or a Black person who was an atheist. Predictably, students preferred people who agreed with them and people of the same race. But in the key choices that pitted belief similarity against racial difference, students chose those who agreed with their views even if they were of another race. Studies testing the belief-congruence explanation have been done with a variety of populations in different settings, both in this country and elsewhere. There is therefore reasonable confidence that the effect exists.

Most of the criticism of this explanation of prejudice has been directed at its lack of generality. Prejudice, and more specifically racism, is a far-reaching phenomenon. Belief congruence seems too narrow an explanation to account for the pervasiveness of the phenomenon. Triandis (1961) objected particularly to the narrow focus on friendship. Using a wider range of social-distance choices, he found that race accounted for the ratings more than belief. Rokeach (1961) countered that Triandis had used too vague a statement to indicate whether the target person was similar or different in "philosophy." He argued that belief congruence is activated only when the belief is specific and important to the individual. Stein (1966) suggested that the underlying question that belief-congruence researchers ask White subjects is "If Negroes were more like you than you think they are and believed in the same things you do, could you then like them?" (p. 27). Stein found that race played a larger role than belief similarity in more-intimate relationships and in those perceived as more open to social pressure. In a study that will be described later in the methods section, Mezei (1971) confirmed that it was anticipated parental and peer disapproval that accounted for race-based rejection in more-intimate relationships. When the social-pressure effect was statistically controlled, belief similarity accounted more for choices than race.

The power of social pressure was assessed in a study of roommate choices along race or belief-congruence lines (Silverman, 1974). White subjects were asked to select roommates from brief descriptions of prospective roommates. Some of the subjects were told that their choices were binding, and others were told that their choices were hypothetical. Those who believed they would actually be rooming with the roommate of their choice showed more racial discrimination than those who were making hypothetical choices; the latter selected according to belief congruence. These findings suggest that the conformity and the socialization views of racism have more generality than the belief-congruence explanation. The latter, however, clearly influences friendship choices in situations relatively free from social pressure. Belief congruence may be a powerful explanation of individual differences in race prejudice, especially in individuals who are relatively independent in their behavior.

Summary of Explanations

As we have seen, explanations of racism locate causality at either the societal or the individual level (Ashmore, 1970; Katz, 1975). Social psychologists, instead, focus on some intervening processes rooted in interpersonal interaction. This interactional approach holds somewhat more promise as a basis for planning effective ways to reduce racism. It is most likely that no single "true" explanation exists for so pervasive a problem. Doubtless, there are systemwide causes, just as there are individual causes—intrapsychic conflicts that predispose individuals to extremes of race prejudice. But neither of these explanations suggests what can be done to reduce the everyday workings of race prejudice and its expression in racist policies and actions. Since prejudice manifests itself in interpersonal encounters, it would seem that attempts to change the content of socialization, to reduce unmindful yielding to conformity pressures, and to make similar beliefs more important than race stereotypes has some promise for change. For many years, efforts to reduce prejudice concentrated on changing attitudes and beliefs primarily through education. These efforts met with limited success. Political strategy then shifted to the strengthening and enforcement of civil rights. Social scientists responded by shifting their interest to the discrepancy between verbal attitudes and behavior, as we shall see in the next section.

RESEARCH ON ATTITUDE-BEHAVIOR CONSISTENCY IN INTERRACIAL INTERACTION

The two research selections included in this chapter belong in a context of work reflecting a current controversy in social psychology—the so-called discrepancy between attitudes and behavior. Reviews of this controversy can be found in Calder and Ross (1973), Wicker (1969), and Kelman (1974). In the short history of social psychology, attitudes have consistently been seen as predispositions to respond to social objects (Allport, 1935; 1954). Furthermore, verbal measures of people's beliefs and feelings were presumed to form a good basis for predicting what people would do. Yet, almost from the beginning there has been some evidence that verbal statements—particularly of racial attitudes—do not always correspond to behavior.

Negative Attitude, Positive Behavior

In the early 1930s, LaPiere (1934) and a Chinese couple traveled together and visited about 250 tourist establishments. They were refused service at only one. When LaPiere later wrote to the facilities that had in fact served them asking if they would accommodate Orientals, most replied that they would not. Fifteen years later, essentially the same situation was encountered by a group of three women, including one Black, who ate at 11 suburban restaurants (Kutner, Wilkins, & Yarrow, 1952). Two weeks later, a letter was sent to each place requesting reservations for such an interracial party. When no replies were received, phone calls were made to the restaurant managers, and all evaded the reservation request; although none of them actually refused the request, all avoided an affirmative response by various excuses.

These studies are often cited as evidence for the discrepancy between attitudes and behavior. The studies, however, have been criticized because, for one, the person who expressed the restaurant policy was probably not the same person who served the patrons (Dillehay, 1973). Serving the interracial groups of patrons is a behavior performed by service personnel, while expressing the policy of the restaurant by refusing to accommodate (or evading a request to accommodate) interracial parties is an attitude usually conveyed by the manager. Furthermore, in both studies the behavior preceded the attitude measurement, which might indicate that the fact of having served an interracial group affected the management's attitude. In other words, there might have been negative reactions by either White patrons or staff, or both, as a consequence of serving Blacks, and these reactions might have been reflected in later policy statements. Some indications of these effects can be found in a study by Dutton (1971), which identified some restaurants in Vancouver that had a dress code requiring male patrons to wear ties. Black and White couples were sent to the restaurants; the man in each couple was wearing jacket and turtleneck, in violation of the restaurant's dress code. The fact that Black couples were admitted more often than White couples was interpreted as a sign that a process of reverse discrimination might be operating. A more complex finding of the study was that, if a Black couple violating the dress code was admitted to the restaurant, a following White couple (also violating the code) was admitted more often. It would seem that once an exception had been made along racial lines, rules were more easily relaxed for others coming later.

In all these studies of attitude-behavior discrepancy, the attitude expressed was more negative than the behavior observed. These findings run counter to the conventional expectation that, in a condition of racism, White people want to represent themselves as less prejudiced than their actions would indicate. The attitude-behavior discrepancy one would expect when racism exists is that of expressions of positive attitude in conjunction with negative behavior—not the reverse.

Positive Attitude, Negative Behavior

Several studies have compared White students' expressed racial attitudes with their willingness to be photographed with Black persons of the opposite sex. After responding to a racial-attitude scale, students with high and low prejudice scores were invited to an interview, shown slides of well-dressed interracial couples, and asked if they would be willing to pose for similar photographs. White students signed a "photograph-release statement" contemplating seven degrees of public exposure that the interracial photographs might receive. The least public exposure was the use of the photograph in laboratory research by psychologists; the most public, the use of the photograph in a nationwide publicity campaign advocating racial integration. Although less-prejudiced students were generally more willing to be photographed, nearly one-third of the students showed attitude-behavior discrepancy (DeFleur & Westie, 1958).

In a more methodologically stringent replication, Linn (1965) found greater discrepancy in the direction of attitudes more favorable than behaviors. Methodological changes included a specific attitude measure of willingness to pose for interracial photographs, deception to reduce subject awareness of being in an experiment, and photograph-release forms administered by Black interviewers. Under these conditions, many women students who had verbally agreed to pose for interracial photographs (32 of 34 had so agreed) expressed reluctance to sign the release (12 refused outright and

59% signed fewer releases than they had agreed to). Furthermore, of those who agreed to pose for photographs, 18% failed to appear or later refused to have their pictures taken.

Commitments to interracial interaction seem to show a similar pattern. Fendrich (1967) compared verbal racial attitudes to actual participation in interracial discussion groups. He found some consistency between expressed attitudes and actual attendance at NAACP discussion groups. Only 18% agreed to attend such meetings, and only 10% actually attended. Warner and DeFleur (1969) suggested that social constraint (how public the behavior is going to be) and social distance (how intimate the encounter is going to be) are dimensions determining attitude-behavior consistency. To test their hypothesis, they conducted a field experiment at a university community that was hostile to integration. Students earlier identified on a verbal measure as anti- or pro-Black were sent letters asking for a commitment to engage in interracial encounters. Letters varied with regard to social constraints and social distances marking the activities described. Some letters indicated that the activity would be publicized in the campus paper, and others said that the activity would be held confidential; also, some letters suggested more-intimate and others less-intimate encounters. The response rate was low (only 23% sent back pledges or refusals), and the results were complex. In general, attitude-behavior consistency was found. The least verbally prejudiced were most willing to engage in interracial contacts, especially when their behaviors would not be publicized. When behaviors were public, low-prejudice subjects behaved consistently—that is, showed low prejudice—in activities that maintained status differences. High-prejudice students tended to refuse to engage in public interracial interaction, especially for behaviors that reduced status differences.

Several studies (including that reported in the second selection) have examined racial discrimination in housing as an example of attitude-behavior discrepancy. McGrew (1967) found that landlords who advertised apartments for rent and also said they would rent to Blacks when questioned by phone in fact refused to do so when approached by a Black couple. These apartments were available for rent to White couples both before and after a Black couple was denied the apartment. Similarly, Silverman and Cochrane (1971) asked White homeowners to sign a pledge sponsored by the Urban League not to discriminate in the selling or renting of their homes. Two months later, the homeowners were sent letters asking participation in an attitude study they believed to be unrelated to the pledge solicitation. Respondents were assessed on willingness to sign an open-housing petition and willingness to sell their homes to any financially qualified buyer regardless of race. Some attitude-behavior consistency was found in that, of the 22 who originally signed the petition, 18 endorsed the attitude item favoring petition signing. However, some discrepancy was also found, since only 8 of the 21 pledge refusers indicated on the attitude measure their unwillingness to sign a petition. The attitude item relating to willingness to sell to any qualified buyer was unrelated to petition signing.

These studies serve to emphasize the fact that where attitude-behavior inconsistencies are found, they tend to be complex. The assessment of these discrepancies seems to be very sensitive to the methods used, specifically with regard to two points. First, outcome appears to depend on whether the behavior is assessed before or after the verbal attitude measure, indicating that one may affect the other. This can be understood in terms of the discussion in Chapter 8 on the effect that perceiving one's behavior can have on attitude. Second, attitudes and behaviors are often assessed at different levels of specificity. Attitude will predict behavior if attitude and behavior are measured at equivalent levels of generality (Ajzen & Fishbein, 1970; Liska, 1974). As the attitude measure becomes less specific in what it asks, it is more and more difficult to know just what behavior will be consistent with that attitude. These issues are clearly reflected in the selections to follow.

METHODS IN RESEARCH ON PREJUDICE AND RACISM

Recall the time when you signed up for your first course in psychology. Isn't the feeling you have today of what psychology is all about a good deal different from the expectations you had then? A substantial part of that change is likely to lie in your present awareness of the important role that research plays. Psychologists seem to spend their whole lives measuring things; so much so that they may give the impression that, if something can't be measured, it probably doesn't exist. Also, it may have occurred to you more than once that measurement can lead to the squeezing of round people into square holes or vice versa.

Well, perhaps both impressions are well founded, but the issue of measurement is a complicated one. To get back to the study of prejudice (which is obviously much more than a purely academic concern), on the one hand, there are those who advocate more investment in efforts designed to reduce the incidence of racial discrimination; on the other, there are those who argue that estimates about the presence of racial prejudice are grossly exaggerated and therefore we should turn our attention to matters of more pressing concern. Measurement can be a valuable tool in addressing and assessing these points of view. First of all, it can help us determine the scope of the problem. Also, it can allow us to monitor the effectiveness of change efforts—that is, in what respects these efforts are inadequate, in what ways (if any) they are producing change, what kinds of discrimination they are affecting, and which groups of people they are influencing. The phenomenon of prejudice is far ranging and subtle. We need all the help we can get in understanding its causes and effects, and measurement techniques can give us valuable help in our search for understanding.

There are many measures of prejudice. In looking at any one in particular, you may be tempted to gauge its effectiveness by how completely it captures what prejudice is all about. But you should keep in mind that no single measurement technique is designed to tell the whole story; the objectives of a measure are more modest than that. On the other hand, while designed to stake out only part of the territory, each measure must nevertheless be specific and precise about a number of issues. In the area of prejudice, a measure must tell you what aspect of prejudice it is attempting to assess, convey information about how accurately it is doing what it purports to do, and suggest qualifications regarding its use.

Any reading of the literature on prejudice and racism reveals an enormous variety of measurements in use. What is not always quite so clear is the researchers' rationale for choosing any one particular means. But before we can get to the specific tools of measurement, we need to know what those measures are trying to find out.

Most workers in this area agree that there are many kinds of prejudice and racism. Allport (1954), for example, distinguishes five degrees of antagonism toward out-groups: verbal attack, avoidance, discrimination, physical attack, and extermination. While not intended to be quantitative in construction, this formulation nevertheless points to the variety of racist behaviors possible, ranging from individual verbal expression to mass violence and destruction. A similar typology is offered by Kovel (1970). At the individual level, Kovel distinguished between the "dominative" racist and the "aversive" racist. The former is "the type who acts out of bigoted beliefs—he represents the open flame of race hatred—he openly seeks to keep the Black man down and he is willing to use force to further his ends" (p. 54). The aversive racist is "the type who believes in White race superiority and is more or less aware of it but does nothing about it" (p. 54). Thus, the aversive racist tries to avoid contact with Blacks, and, when contact is unavoidable, his manner is polite, correct, but cool.

The existence of typologies such as the two mentioned above testifies to the multifaceted nature of prejudice. It is not *one* thing, and hence no single measure can aim at assessing it all. One route out of this quandary has been to choose the method that is the best in terms of sound test construction. Surely there must be some measures that are objectively better than others, but the question still is "Better for what?" A given measurement tool must be solid on technical grounds but, more importantly, be appropriate to the kind of prejudice that is being probed. Thus, a psychological interview geared to underlying personality dynamics is not the best on which to gauge the amount of discriminatory behavior existing in housing and employment.

Stated another way, the existence of different types of prejudice and racism poses special problems for researchers interested in assessing racial attitudes. Those persons tending toward the more dominative kind of prejudice may be willing to express negative attitudes toward Blacks on standard questionnaire measures. Those tending toward aversive racism, however, do not admit racial antagonism inwardly or otherwise, and therefore traditional questionnaire measures of their racial attitudes would usually be ineffective. In this latter case then, nonreactive behavioral situations and subtle, unobtrusive measures may be the methods of choice. Furthermore, there are those who argue (Katz, 1970) that the racial attitudes of most Whites are neither all positive nor all negative but primarily ambivalent. The nature of their varied responses and of the methods used to obtain them is likely to depend upon the immediate situational context in addition to the available response alternatives contained in the measurement. Thus, trying to fit the most appropriate measure, or combination of measures, to the phenomenon of racial prejudice is one of the most demanding tasks that a researcher in this area has to face.

Typologies like the ones noted above also make the distinction between attitudes and behavior—a necessary point of departure for anyone doing research in this area. Such a distinction is relatively comparable to the definitional distinction between prejudice and racism. As we mentioned earlier, the frequent lack of correspondence between racial attitudes and behavior—between what people say and what they do—is widely documented. This means that we have to decide not only what specific racial attitudes we are going to open but also how these attitudes are likely to be made manifest—verbal statements? overt action? physiological responsivity? The choices are manifold.

An account of some of these methods follows. Because of the need to measure different aspects of racial relations, to attempt to quantify their various forms, and to seek to delineate their various causes, a variety of strategies have been employed. We organize them, as we have done before, along two dimensions: degree of subject awareness and degree of manipulation of antecedent conditions by the investigator.

Surveys and Interviews

Since, by definition, most investigators regard prejudice as a negative attitude, fairly consistent over time, that people carry around with them and about which they possess self-knowledge, the research strategy most often employed has been the questionnaire or survey format. In its simplest form, this type of attitude measurement consists of asking a series of questions of a representative group of respondents and tabulating the answers. Its goal is to assess the presence and distribution of particular attitudes, although the questionnaire usually does not address the intensity of feeling behind the expression. As such, it is usually high in subject awareness and low in prior experimental management. We present below a few examples of different kinds of self-report measures; as you read about them, keep in mind that elaborate methodological and mathematical procedures are required in order to develop each of these scales.

The Likert method of *summated rating* (1932) involves presenting a series of generalizations or opinions about a relevant group and asking respondents to indicate the extent of their agreement or disagreement with the statements, usually on a five- or six-point scale. Here is a sample item from Likert's (1932) scale.

9. All Negroes belong to one class and should be treated in about the same way.

Strongly Approve	Approve	Undecided	Disapprove	Strongly Disapprove
(1)	(2)	(3)	(4)	(5)

A person's score is the sum of the alternatives endorsed. In the example, high scores indicate positive attitudes toward Blacks.

A second type of self-report scale is the *social distance scale* developed by Bogardus (1933). Respondents are asked to indicate whether they would engage in the following general activities with a specific ethnic group (Negroes, Italians, and so forth).

1. Would marry
2. Would have as regular friends
3. Would work beside in an office
4. Would have several families in my neighborhood
5. Would have merely as speaking acquaintances
6. Would have live outside my neighborhood
7. Would have live outside my country.*

The scale is based on a "successive-hurdles" notion of attitudes; this means that, beginning with Statement 7 and working toward Statement 1, each succeeding statement is seen as a stronger endorsement. It is assumed that a person will move up the scale to a certain point, beyond which he or she will refuse to subscribe further. The person's attitude is characterized by the most extreme statement he or she is willing to endorse.

An important contribution to attitude-scale construction was made by Thurstone (1931) in an *equal interval scale*. As in the Likert format described above, respondents are presented with statements. They are asked to check the statements with which they agree and cross out the statements with which they disagree. The primary difference between the two formats is that, before administration, all the statements of the Thurstone scale are prerated by a group of judges with respect to the degree of favorableness or unfavorableness of each item regardless of the judges' own personal attitudes. Thus, each statement is given a quantitative value. A respondent's score is the average scale value of all the items he or she endorsed.

Two sample items from Thurstone's own scale follow:

Scale Values
- 9.6   9. Give a Negro a high position in society and he will show himself equal to it.
- 0.9   22. The Negro should be considered in the lowest class among human beings.

The higher the median score, the more favorable the attitudes are considered to be.

*From "A Social Distance Scale," by E. Bogardus, *Sociology and Social Research*, 1933, *17*, 256–271. Reprinted by permission.

A current self-report scale to measure White attitudes toward Blacks is the Multifactor Racial Attitude Inventory (MRAI) developed by Woodmansee and Cook (1967). The MRAI is composed of ten ten-item subscales: Integration-Segregation Policy, Black Inferiority, Subtle Derogatory Beliefs, Local Autonomy, Private Rights, Gradualism, Black Superiority, Acceptance in Close Personal Relationships, Ease in Interracial Contacts, and Acceptance in Status-Superior Relationships. A sample item from the "Ease in Interracial Contacts" factor asks the respondent to agree or disagree with the following statement:

I would probably feel somewhat self-conscious dancing with a Negro in a public place.

It is important to note that a good scale is not one that merely appears to measure prejudice but one that can be shown to have good reliability (consistency across repeated administrations) and good validity (it does measure what it purports to measure).

The advantages of attitude scales are probably apparent to you now. Although time consuming in their construction, they are easily administered (either individually or to large numbers of people at a single seating) and easily scored and summarized in quantitative terms. But there are disadvantages as well. Respondents, feeling the lack of personal rapport with a questioner, may not take the test seriously or may be unable to express fully their unique views on a preselected group of statements.

To offset these difficulties, investigators have sometimes turned to a more open-ended format. Open-ended items are usually questions that the respondent is free to answer any way he or she wishes. A well-known study using this method was conducted by Deutsch and Collins (1951) in order to assess whether integrated housing effected more positive attitude change for Whites toward Blacks than segregated housing did. Internally integrated housing projects were matched with internally segregated ones on the proportion of Black and White residents. The procedure involved conducting intensive and long (from 75 minutes to 120 minutes) interviews with homemakers in their own apartments in the projects. General open-ended questions centering on the incidence, location, type, and affective tone of interracial contacts were put to the respondents in a relaxed interview. The responses were coded and summarized after the actual encounter. Results indicated that the attitudes of White homemakers toward Blacks became more positive in the integrated projects and changed little, if at all, in the segregated projects. While these results project an optimistic note, their generality may be limited by unknown selective factors. One such factor has to do with the comparability of attitudes of the White samples toward Blacks *before* contact in the various housing projects. If the White homemakers in the integrated projects had from the beginning more favorable attitudes toward Blacks than those in the segregated projects, then the differences obtained after equal amounts of time in the projects may not have been due at all to increased contact. They may have been there from the beginning. Since investigators using this kind of study cannot always know or arrange for initial comparability of samples, they then cannot always know what caused what.

Observations and Archival Search

We began our description of measures of prejudice and racism with surveys and interviews for a number of reasons. Not only are these strategies abundant and available through measurement catalogs and handbooks, but they are appealing on other grounds as well. They have high face validity; that is, they appear to be asking what one wants to know. They lure with promises of precision; that is, responses can be quantified and individual differences unambiguously revealed. And they appeal to a widespread conviction that "underlying" attitudes are more real and basic than our everyday actions and reactions. But a case can be made for the use of indices other than self-reports in the assessment of racial attitudes. In the first place, there are probably numerous occasions when the targets of racial prejudice are not interested in underlying feelings of racists; what counts is that they be "treated" in a nondiscriminatory fashion. Second, there are arguments against self-reports on methodological grounds, such as that a given respondent may not know or may not care to disclose what his or her real feelings are. A more valid index might then be not what is said but what is done.

A subtle kind of interracial behavior has been studied by Campbell, Kruskal, and Wallace (1966). Reasoning that students do not choose their seats in classrooms at random but on the basis of their wanting to sit next to some students and not next to others, they developed an "aggregation" index. Specifically, they argued that, if race is not a factor in seating preferences, then the number of Blacks and Whites sitting next to each other should be the same when the students choose their seats and when they are randomly assigned to seats. But if Blacks and Whites are attempting to avoid contact with each other, that attempt should be reflected in the degree to which each group sits by itself.

The procedure involved sending an observer into a sample of classes in a few selected colleges and noting seating arrangements by race for each class. These seating charts were then coded according to an aggregation index. The index measured the number of Black-White pairs who occupied lateral adjacent seats against a baseline of number of adjacencies expected by chance, given the number of Black and White students present in a given classroom. The data of major interest came from classrooms observed in two colleges in the fall of two consecutive years. In another measure, these two colleges had been noted as representing the two extremes of the most prejudiced and least prejudiced White students. Application of the index to both schools revealed a negative mean aggregation index indicating significantly fewer Black-White seating adjacencies than would be expected by chance. A comparison of the indices for the two colleges indicated that there were significant school differences. The college that had been previously described as less prejudiced had a significantly lower negative aggregation index than the more-prejudiced college. In other words, although in both schools the number of Black-White seating adjacencies was less than would be expected by chance, more adjacencies were found in the less-prejudiced college than in the more-prejudiced college. Such checks on the validity of the aggregation index against another measure of prejudice not only raises our faith in the value of the index but also suggests that multiple measures of the same thing give more strength to any assessment.

Observations such as the one discussed above are low both in subject awareness and in manipulation of antecedent conditions. Also low on these two dimensions is archival search. An example of archival search is the analysis of magazine ads across a period of almost 20 years with respect to their inclusion and portrayal of Blacks. Cox (1971) examined five magazines *(Life, Saturday Evening Post, New Yorker, Ladies Home Journal,* and *Time)* for all their issues in 1967 and the first half of 1968 and compared them with the issues of these same magazines during 1949 and 1950. More specifically, a tally was made of all ads that contained an identifiable adult and of the proportion of the Blacks appearing in these ads. Next, the Black adults portrayed in the ads were classified as to their probable occupation—specifically, above or below skilled labor. Sample occupations for the former category were business people, entertainers, students, and professionals; maids, cooks, waiters, and laborers comprised illustrations for the latter category. Results indicated that only one-half of 1% of the ads in 1949–1950 included Blacks, a portion that in 1967–1968 had increased to slightly over 2%. But the significant change was noticed with respect to level of occupation. In 1949–1950, 95.5% of Blacks in advertising were represented as having occupations below skilled labor, whereas the proportion had dropped to 30.9% in 1967–1968.

While such results apparently document a movement away from stereotyping Blacks as predominantly lower- or second-class citizens, they may nevertheless lead to a number of unwarranted inferences. Advertising practices may or may not mirror attitudes of the magazine-reading population. These representations may indeed be the result or the cause of changes in racial attitudes, but, on the other hand, they may have nothing to do with such changes. Furthermore, since this study contains only two data points (1949–1950 and 1967–1968), you really have no firm basis for arguing a linear trend. At the very least, you may need additional information—that is, whether and in what ways the investigator was selective in choosing the data-base points.

The two research studies described above are unusual in the social sciences on two counts. First, the "subjects" do not know that they are serving as subjects. Presumably, then, reactivity is kept to a minimum. Second, the research is directed toward events that happened naturally without experimental manipulation. Despite these assets, however, alternative explanations for the results are perhaps more likely than with studies performed under stricter experimental control.

Field Experiments

A compromise between the need for experimental rigor and the avoidance of artificial settings has been proposed in the form of a field experiment. Labeling their method as the "Wrong Number Technique," Gaertner and Bickman (1971) tested the hypothesis that Whites would discriminate against Blacks by helping them less than they would help fellow Whites. A total of 540 Black subjects and 569 White subjects sampled from the Brooklyn telephone directory received what supposedly was a wrong-number telephone call but that quickly developed into a request for assistance. These wrong-number calls were made by either a Black or a White male caller. The messages were grammatically identical, but the pronunciation of the words was varied in order to present the caller as either Black or White. A check made with college student judges on the perceived differences in the callers' voices revealed correct discriminations over 90% of the time. The caller said that his car had broken down and that he had used his last change to make the present call. The dependent measure was the number of subjects (the people receiving the call) who made a call to a service-station number provided by the caller. Results supported the hypothesis. White subjects helped White callers significantly more often than they helped Black callers. Black subjects, on the other hand, accorded about equal help to White and Black callers.

This particular experiment exercised considerable control in a field context. Subjects were randomly selected, and precautions were taken to assess race of subject unobtrusively by noting area of residence. A potential problem arises from the fact that the results may be attributed more to class differences than to race differences. Specifically, the judges who correctly identified the caller as Black or White also perceived the Black caller to be of lower social class and possessing less education. Therefore, race and class are perhaps potentially confounded.

In another example of a field experiment assessing the dynamics of Black-White interaction, the dependent measure was the difficulty experienced by Black and White individuals attempting to cash a personal check drawn on an out-of-town bank (Clark, 1975). Bank policies with respect to personal checks were determined before the actual field experiment by telephone calls to the bank requesting such information. The 16 banks included in the experiment were then grouped into three categories of flexibility with respect to check-cashing policy. A Black or a White individual looking like a hippie or like a conservative type, approached designated tellers with a five-dollar check. Contrary to expectation, results revealed no differences for the three independent variables of race, type of requestor, and type of bank. One significant interaction effect of race with type of bank was represented by the fact that highly inflexible banks had a significantly lower "institutional acceptability" rating for Blacks than for Whites. In other words, these particular banks either refused to cash the check for Blacks or took longer to do so than they did for Whites. This interaction effect did not appear for either moderate- or low-inflexibility banks.

Laboratory Experiments

Investigators who turn to the laboratory do so in an effort to exercise more control than is possible in the field. On occasion, aspects of both laboratory and field experimentation are used in a single study. Such was the case with a study conducted by Dutton and Lake (1973). These investigators tested the hypothesis that "reverse discrimination"—that is, a tendency by Whites in some situations to favor Blacks over Whites—would occur more readily when a person's egalitarian self-concept had been threatened. Subjects who in earlier pretesting had rated themselves as highly egalitarian were recruited for a study ostensibly dealing with voluntary control of autonomic behavior. In an elaborate scenario, they were told that persons evidencing high physiological arousal in response to various situations were revealing significant negative attitude toward those situations. Subjects were then presented with a variety of stimuli that included scenes of interracial interaction, and their physiological responses were apparently recorded. The subjects in the high-threat group were given false high-arousal feedback (apparently reflecting negative attitudes), and the subjects in the low-threat group were given feedback indicating that they were unaroused.

After collecting a two-dollar payment in quarters for participating in the study, the subjects left the laboratory. On their way out, subjects were greeted by a Black or White panhandler asking for spare change. Analysis of amounts given provided the dependent measure. As predicted, subjects in the high-threat group gave significantly more to the Black panhandler than subjects in the low-threat group. The White panhandler received average contributions that didn't show differences between the high- and the low-threat groups. Since the investigators were able to make the groups comparable initially and to control for all subsequent events, their conclusion seems justified. It appears then that threatening someone who sees himself as egalitarian results in amplification of trivial positive responses by the threatened person in order to reaffirm his prejudice-free self-image.

A relatively straightforward laboratory experiment by Mezei (1971) was concerned with sorting out the relative influence of race and belief congruence, perceived social pressure, and type of social interactions on the acceptance and rejection of people. The experiment consisted of four parts: (1) measuring the attitudes of introductory-psychology White and Black students toward communism and civil-rights legislation; (2) presenting four stimulus persons to each subject—a White person and a Black person holding attitudes similar to those of the subject and a White person and a Black person with attitudes dissimilar from those of the subject; (3) evaluation of these four stimulus persons by the subjects on a ten-item social-distance scale measuring the subject's attitudes toward items that ranged from "would marry" through "would eat with" to "would exclude"; and (4) subjects' ratings of the degree of approval or disapproval they expected from parents and friends if they engaged in each of these social interactions with each stimulus person.

Results that did not take into account social pressure indicated that six of the ten interactions were significantly more influenced by belief prejudice than by race prejudice. In other words, subjects rejected stimulus persons more often when they perceived them as holding different beliefs than when they perceived them as being of a different race. When social pressure was taken into account by statistically eliminating it from the prejudice score, belief prejudice became even stronger than race prejudice, now accounting for even intimate social interactions. Apparently, belief differences are more influential than race differences in the evaluation of Blacks by Whites. When race prejudice *per se* seemed more influential, particularly with respect to close encounters, it was due to perceived social pressure against such interracial contact.

TWO RESEARCH EXAMPLES

Product Description

Both studies in this chapter concentrate on the behavioral side of racial prejudice and discrimination. The first, by Weitz, is a laboratory experiment designed to test the relation between what one says one's attitudes toward Blacks are and how one might actually behave in an interracial encounter. White male college students, paid for their participation, were recruited for a study of environmental influences. Each subject was told that he would be working with another subject, described as a Black or a White garage attendant or law student, who (supposedly) was waiting in an adjoining room. Under the guise of facilitating selection of pairs of subjects, the subject was asked for his impression of the person he would be working with, after he read a biographical sketch of that person. In addition to this verbal indicator, overt behavioral measures of subjects' attitudes prior to the interaction were obtained from performance on a series of tasks. Correlational analyses between these latter behavioral measures, particularly voice tone, and the former verbal declaration indicated that there was a positive relation between the verbal measure of friendliness and warmth of voice tone when the other participant was described as White. When the other participant was described as Black, however, a negative relation was obtained between these measures.

The second selection, by Johnson, Porter, and Mateljan, reports a field experiment on racial discrimination in apartment rentals. The measure of discrimination involved three components: apartment availability, cost of rental, and miscellaneous fees. After ascertaining from newspaper ads whether an apartment was available for rental, two teams, each comprising a Caucasian, a Mexican-American, and a Black couple, were directed to a total of 25 apartment-building managers. All couples were instructed to find out whether there was an apartment available for rent, the amount of rent, and the amount of miscellaneous fees required.

Results revealed significant racial discrimination. Blacks found fewer available apartments and were quoted rents and miscellaneous fees higher than those quoted to White couples. Mexican-Americans were discriminated against significantly more often than Caucasians but less often than Blacks. Apparently, here too a discrepancy between what is said (newspaper ads) and what is done (discriminatory behavior) exists.

Consumer Checklist

- How complicated was the process required to manufacture these products?
  In each selection, how many measures were taken and how many produced results?
- Did the manufacturing process result in the product the overall plans called for, or was the product imperfectly rendered?
  In the second selection, what differences were there among observer pairs?
  In the second selection, were observers unaware of the purpose of the study?
- Will the products drive only on the test track?
  Are simulated racial encounters like real racial encounters?
  In each selection, how carefully are results presented?

ATTITUDE, VOICE, AND BEHAVIOR:
A REPRESSED AFFECT MODEL OF INTERRACIAL INTERACTION [1]

SHIRLEY WEITZ [2]

Department of Social Relations, Harvard University

> An experiment was conducted to determine the relationship between verbal attitudes, voice tone, and behavior toward blacks among a "liberal" sample of 80 white college males in the North. A simulated interracial encounter in which subjects expected to interact with a black (or white) stimulus person was used. A general pattern of overt friendliness and covert rejection was found. Friendliness of attitude toward blacks was negatively related to friendliness of (*a*) voice tone and (*b*) behavior directed toward them, while voice tone was positively related to behavior. A repressed affect model, leading to conflicting cues in interracial interaction, was suggested.

The question of the validity of the attitude–behavior link has been an enduring one in social psychology. Numerous studies, especially in race relations, have been devoted to this issue, ending almost invariably in negative or ambiguous results. Wicker (1969) recently reviewed the literature and found

little evidence to support the postulated existence of stable, underlying attitudes within the individual which influence both his verbal expressions and his actions [p. 75].

Despite this unclear picture, the importance of determining the nature of the attitude–behavior relationship remains a critical issue for attitude researchers. This area is of special concern to race relations researchers, and many of the studies have involved black–white contact situations and racial attitude measures. A review of the relevant literature reveals three major problems: (*a*) In many cases, "situationless" attitude toward a general stimulus group was measured, whereas behavior was always measured toward a specific member of that group in a specific situation; (*b*) unusual or molar behavioral indexes were employed, which might be especially prone to situational pressures; (*c*) situational determinants of responses to the attitude measure itself were not considered (e.g., the pencil-and-paper tolerance of white college students in a "liberal" environment).

Reative to Point *a*, it does not seem that we can assume a relationship between a general attitude and a specific behavior before establishing the reality of the subcase—that of a relationship between a specific attitude and a specific behavior. As for Point *b*, it is possible that situational constraints may have a greater part in shaping an overall molar behavioral response, whereas attitude may emerge only through subtle alterations of this molar, situationally determined behavior. We see some evidence for this idea in the Katz and Benjamin (1960) study. In biracial work groups with authoritarian whites, blacks worked harder under conditions of individual rather than group reward (whereas they worked equally hard under both conditions with nonauthoritarian whites). Katz and Benjamin conjectured that blacks were somehow able to sense the hostility of authoritarian whites (although the behavioral measures did not pick up this hostility) and consequently withdrew from interdependent work with them for group reward. It seems possi-

---

[1] This study is based on a doctoral dissertation submitted to the Department of Social Relations of Harvard University. The author wishes to express her special thanks to her advisor, Robert Rosenthal, and to Thomas Pettigrew and Leon Mann for their support and advice.

This research was supported by National Science Foundation Doctoral Dissertation Grant GS 2625 and by supplementary grants from the National Science Foundation fellowship funds of the Department of Social Relations at Harvard.

An abbreviated version of this study was presented at the meeting of the Eastern Psychological Association, New York, April 1971.

[2] Requests for reprints should be sent to Shirley Weitz, who is now at the Department of Psychology, Graduate Faculty, New School for Social Research, 66 West 12th Street, New York, New York 10011.

From *Journal of Personality and Social Psychology*, 1972, 24(1), 14–21. Copyright 1972 by American Psychological Association. Reprinted by permission.

ble, then, that the blacks were responding to behavioral cues of hostility which the authoritarian whites were emitting, but which were too subtle to be picked up by molar behavioral indexes. Such cues might include vocal tone and the use of space—measures that were included in the present study. Thus, although the situation may sometimes be more important than the attitude in determining the molar response, the attitude toward the stimulus object may emerge in subtle colorings of that response—colorings to which the members of the attitude-object group may be especially sensitive, and which, therefore, have important implications for interracial interaction.

Point c, concerning situational determinants of response to the attitude measure, is particularly salient in any society that inculcates a tolerance value that is likely to be evoked by an attitude questionnaire. Thus, Myrdal's (1944) "American dilemma" is largely the societal disjunction between attitudes and behavior, with a tolerant value system conflicting with discriminatory normative patterns. Therefore, especially in a college population where verbal adherence to the value of tolerance is likely to be very high, little information about individual orientations to minority group members is secured by asking questions that elicit strong associations to that tolerance value.

The present study was designed to avoid the three major problems mentioned above by (a) measuring both attitudes and behavior toward the same, specific stimulus person in the same, specific situation, as well as using a general, subtle measure of racial attitude; (b) using several, noncontrived, molecular behavioral indexes which related meaningfully to actual interracial interaction and which were subject to a minimum of outside situational pressures (e.g., voice tone and chair placement); and (c) using an unobtrusive, specific attitude measure which did not make race unduly salient so as not to evoke automatically the societal value of tolerance rather than individual orientations to minority group members. To do this, specific attitude was conceived of as a type of evaluative impression formation based on minimal information. A general attitude measure, administered in an entirely separate setting, was used as well to test its relationship to specific attitude and behavior. The general attitude measure used was subtle and two dimensional, measuring "love prejudice"—the characteristic of white liberals—as well as the more traditional "hate prejudice."

The present study tested the nature of the attitude–behavior link in a simulated interracial encounter. White subjects whose general racial attitudes had been previously measured were told to expect another subject to arrive in the experimental situation. This second subject was supposedly waiting in an adjoining room, and his presence was simulated by tapes of "another research assistant" (fictitious) speaking to him. The subject was given a description of the stimulus person (the other subject) as a prelude to meeting him. The description contained two experimental manipulations: race and social class. The subject was then asked to react in several attitudinal and behavioral ways to the simulated stimulus person.

METHOD

Subjects

The subjects were 80 male paid volunteers drawn from a pool of 200 subjects who had taken the Schuman and Harding (1964) Irrational Pro and Anti scales as paid volunteers from the Harvard Summer School. Thirty of the 80 subjects volunteered spontaneously for the experiment after an ad was posted; the other 50 were solicited by letter. Letters were sent to all subjects in the pool stating that they had been randomly selected for an experiment on "environmental effects on skilled behavior" and inviting them to participate. Only 1 subject in the letter condition expressed any suspicion of a link between the racial attitude measure and the experimental situation. The subjects were probed on this issue during debriefing.

Procedure

Alleged Purpose of the Study

Each subject was told that he would be working with another subject who was expected shortly and would go to an adjoining room before coming in to meet him. While waiting for the "other subject" (who did not exist and was actually the stimulus person), the subject was given several measures of attitude and behavior toward the stimulus person. The rationale given for the measures was that of aiding in the choice of tasks for the subjects to do later on, and, in the case of voice, the performance of a single task by the other subject.

Measures

Voice. The subject was asked to rehearse reading instructions on a paired-associate task as soon as he came in. He was told that he would be reading the instructions to the other subject at a later time (which he did). Both the control and experimental (after receiving the description of the other subject) readings were recorded. A standard selection from each reading for each subject was put on a composite tape, and both readings were rated by a panel of female raters on five dimensions. Thus, a voice score was obtained by subtracting the control rating from the experimental rating for each subject. Effective interrater reliabilities (Rosenthal, 1970) on the five voice dimensions, taking into account the number of raters, were .95 for loud–soft; .72 for warm–cold; .65 for admiring–condescending; .80 for pleasant–unpleasant; and .62 for personal–business-like.

Attitude. The subject was told that he and the other subject would be working on several tasks together, and that we wanted to choose the right tasks for them to do together. The experimenter explained that a test had been devised to predict which tasks would be best for given subject pairs to do. This test involved having one of the subjects indicate his first impressions of the other subject (the specific attitude measure described below). The subject was assured that the other subject would not see his answers. He was also told that the other subject was participating in the selection procedure, but not in the same way (to prevent evaluation apprehension). The subject was then given the written description of the other subject, which contained the experimental manipulations of race and class. Also included in the description was standard filler information for all conditions, such as name (Thomas Rogers), age (28), height (5 feet 11 inches), weight (175 pounds), marital status (married), etc. The variables that were manipulated were occupation and educational status and race. These manipulations created four conditions: black gas station attendant, black law student, white gas station attendant, and white law student. The descriptions were given to the subject in a sealed envelope; hence, the experimenter was not aware of the subject's condition. The subjects were told that a campaign to recruit some subjects from outside of the university was under way in order to allay suspicions about the appearance of a gas station attendant in such a setting.

The specific attitude measure consisted of 18 adjective dimensions, each on a 7-point scale (e.g., trustworthy–untrustworthy, clean–dirty), and a series of related questions (e.g., "How friendly would you feel toward this person in a year's time?" "How much do you like him?"). The form was filled out after the subject had seen the description of the stimulus person described above.

Behavior. The five behavioral measures studied were as follows:

1. Task selection—The experimenter asked the subject to express his own preferences for tasks. He was asked for three choices out of a field of seven tasks. The tasks differed in the closeness of interaction required: physical, social, joint spectatorship.

2. Waiting together—The subject was asked whether he wished to wait together or apart from the other subject (i.e., alone) during a short intermission before beginning the tasks. Responses were scored as together, hesitates, apart.

3. Number of returns—The experimenter said that further sessions for the subject pair might be needed, at the same rate of pay. The subject indicated all of the hours he had free in the following calendar week (Monday through Friday, 9 A.M.–5 P.M., for a total field of 40 possible hours). The number of hours listed as available for returns was taken as the measure here.

4. Chair placement—Two molded plastic chairs were set in a standard position against a wall before the subject came in. At the end of the session, the subject was asked to arrange these chairs for himself and the other subject to sit in for the next part of the experiment (which, of course, never occurred). Photos of the chair placements were taken after the subject left, and these photos were rated on the dimension of friendliness of the interactants (as deduced from chair placement) by 30 female raters. Effective interrater reliability was .96 for this measure.

5. Order—Half of the subjects were given the specific attitude measure at the beginning of the experiment and half at the end. No main effect of order was found, and few interactions were found, so in most cases the results for both orders were combined.

Results

Attitude, Voice, Behavior Correlations

Within the black condition, there was a pattern of significant *negative* correlations between friendliness of verbal attitude (How friendly would you feel toward this person in a year's time?), and (*a*) voice tone, and (*b*) behavior. Significant positive correlations between friendliness of voice tone and behavior were also found (see Table 1). This pattern was not found in the white conditions, which tended to show trends in the direction of attitude–voice–behavior consistency.

The black pattern shown can be seen in the framework of a repressed affect model. Verbal attitudes toward blacks ranged from moderately favorable to extremely favorable in the sample tested. Those with the *most* extreme favorable attitudes had the least friendly voice tone and behavior toward

TABLE 1

PATTERN OF CORRELATIONS BETWEEN VOICE, ATTITUDE, AND BEHAVIOR IN THE BLACK CONDITION

Behavior	Voice		Attitude
	Warmth	Admiring	Friendship
Task selection	−.323[a]*	−.348[a]*	—
	+.316*	+.151	−.319*
Waiting together	−.090	−.103	−.451**
No. returns	+.433**	+.323*	−.315*

Note.—The correlations between behavioral measures were as follows: task choice and waiting (.133); task choice and number of returns (.380); and number of returns and waiting (.140). $N = 40$.
[a] Correlation of voice with attitude measure of friendship.
* $p < .05$.
** $p < .01$.

blacks. It appears that these subjects were repressing negative or conflicted affect toward blacks by overreacting in the positive direction on the verbal measure (the "doth protest too much" syndrome). In other words, they were overreacting to the norm of tolerance prevalent in the college environment. However, on measures for which the norms or means of control were not known (such as voice tone or contact on tasks, number of returns, waiting), the subjects' true (negative) feelings were expressed. Behavior which appeared to offer the fewest demand characteristics worked the best (e.g., waiting together did *not* work; all of the subjects in the black gas station attendant condition chose to wait together, perhaps suggesting the operation of strong demand characteristics).

For the black in real interracial interaction, the above pattern leads to a situation of conflicting cues: positive verbal approach coupled with negative voice tone and behavior. For the white, this conflicted situation doubtlessly leads to anxiety and discomfort, and perhaps even to a tendency to avoid interracial contact.

The subjects who had moderately favorable attitudes toward blacks (and thus had negative attitudes relative to the overreactors) showed the most favorable voice tone and behavior toward them. These subjects were not conflicted and did not overreact to the norm of tolerance; their positive affect was expressed in moderately favorable attitudes and in favorable voice tone and behavior (compared to the negative affect revealed by the overreactors on these measures).

Specific Attitude Measure

Race. Blacks were rated as more intelligent ($p < .004$) and more important ($p < .044$) than whites. Otherwise, there were no significant racial differences in the analysis of variance of ratings on the specific attitude measure. These two variables were probably the most morally tinged of all the adjective dimensions, and were certainly related most directly to the two "hot" issues in race—the dignity and innate ability of blacks—so that in some respects they represent an obtrusive measure of racial attitude (although no subject was asked to rate both blacks and whites, so in that respect it was unobtrusive). The responses of the subjects can be understood as evidence of a "leaning over backward" effect. Another possibility exists—namely, that the subjects were aware at some level of the race manipulation and were responding in a consciously "liberal" way. This effect would not vitiate the results much, since it is the present author's contention that the white liberal response in real interracial encounter is similar to this, in that the subject feels he is responding to a race manipulation rather than to a real person, even outside of the laboratory. One might also view the racial differences in rating intelligence and importance as responses to guilt over being in the position of overtly evaluating a black, since many subjects offered some resistance to the idea of rating another person on the basis of so little information, especially in the case of the black.

TABLE 2

NUMBER OF SIGNIFICANT ($p < .05$) CORRELATIONS AMONG 18 ADJECTIVE DIMENSIONS (OUT OF A POSSIBLE MAXIMUM OF 153 PER CELL)

Race	Class		Total[a]
	Gas	Law	Race
Black	69	47	95
White	53	21	51

[a] Total refers to the correlation matrix collapsed across class.

Although the other adjectives had no significant race effects, another way of looking at the data shows revealing results. Within all cells (Race × Class), the correlations between adjectives are almost universally positive and moderately high. Using statistical significance (at the .05 confidence level) as a point of comparison, one can count the number of significant adjective correlations within each cell and compare them as a rough index of stereotyping (or nonindependence of dimension ratings). Table 2 illustrates the results. Within each class condition, especially in the law student condition, the black is subject to more stereotyping than the white. Between social classes, the gas station attendant is more stereotyped than the law student. Thus, even though adjective ratings of blacks may be just as high or even higher than those of whites, the more hidden and subtle relationships among the dimensions themselves reveal a more stereotyped view toward blacks than whites in terms of relative nonindependence of rating their personal qualities (signifying a categorical, nondifferentiated perception which could serve to hinder interracial interaction).

Class. There were quite a few striking class effects on the specific attitude measure. Ten of the 18 adjective dimensions showed class effects (see Table 3). A combined adjective scale (excluding "wealthy," which was really

TABLE 3
CLASS EFFECTS FOR ADJECTIVE DIMENSIONS ON SPECIFIC ATTITUDE MEASURE

Adjective dimension[a]	$\bar{X}$ Gas station attendant	$\bar{X}$ Law student	F[b]	MS	$p <$
Careful	4.9	5.6	9.360	8.450	.003
Serious	4.4	5.6	34.676	28.800	.001
Persistent	4.8	5.7	15.078	14.450	.001
Wealthy	2.9	3.9	15.044	17.113	.001
Quiet	3.7	4.5	16.308	13.613	.001
Polite	4.6	5.1	4.834	5.513	.031
Intelligent	4.0	6.0	90.159	78.013	.001
Clean	4.8	5.9	24.425	22.050	.001
Reliable	5.0	5.6	8.611	7.200	.004
Strong	5.4	4.9	7.117	6.612	.009

[a] Adjective dimensions are all listed by their positive end, and means are adjusted to run from negative (low) to positive (high).
[b] $df = 1/72$.

TABLE 4
RACE × CLASS INTERACTION ON "STRONG"

Race	Class Gas station attendant	Class Law student
Black	5.3	5.3
White	5.6	4.4

Note.—$F = 7.117$, $df = 1/72$, $MS = 6.613$, $p < .009$.

a validity check for class) was significant for class at the .001 level of probability (for gas station attendant, $\bar{X} = 4.7$; for law student, $\bar{X} = 5.2$). Law students were rated more positively than gas station attendants on all dimensions except strong–weak, where gas station attendants were perceived as stronger than law students. It seems that "strength" was taken in its physical connotation, which would make this exception understandable.

Race × Class interactions. The effect on strong–weak is quite revealing in terms of the maintenance of hidden stereotypes (see Table 4). In short, black law students are just as strong as black gas station attendants, but white law students are not as strong as white gas station attendants. Although the adjective dimension strong–weak is ambiguous as to whether it refers to a moral (i.e., character) or physical quality, it seems as if most subjects interpreted it in its physical sense. One can deduce this from the fact that "strong" showed a class effect opposite to that of the other personality dimensions, in that gas station attendants were seen as stronger than law students, whereas on all of the other significant class effects, law students got the better break in terms of being rated more positively (strong is assumed to be positive relative to weak). Greater physical strength is part of the black and lower-class stereotype, and the belief of the subjects in this stereotype is revealed in the identical ratings of both the black gas station attendant and law student, whereas for whites the gas station attendant was perceived as stronger than the law student. The big difference in this interaction is between the black and the white law student (the race difference for the gas station attendant appears minimal and nonsignificant). The upper-status black represents a status inconsistency to which the subjects responded by assigning an attribute (physical strength) which they associated with lower status.

The combined adjective rating scale (excluding wealthy–poor) shows a trend toward a Race × Class interaction ($p < .063$; see Table 5). While there is little change in positive evaluation between the two classes for whites, there is a sharp increase for blacks—with the black law student getting the most favorable evaluation of all. Thus, the rise in status gives the black a very definite "boost," whereas this is not true for whites. There seems to be a larger cognitive separation between the classes for blacks than for whites (except for strong–weak, as shown above) in the eyes of white liberal subjects. Therefore, while a white law student is only a little more favorably evaluated than a white gas station attendant, a black law student is in a totally different league cognitively than a black gas station attendant. Another way of expressing this is to say that there is more class prejudice shown toward blacks than toward whites, even though this prejudice results in highly favorable evaluations of the black high-status individual.

Chair Placement

No significant race, class or order effects, or interactions were found.

In the black condition, scores on the black pro scale correlated .322 ($p < .05$) with the chair ratings of friendliness (compared to a correlation of .007 in the white condition), which means that the more problack the subjects were, the friendlier their chair placement was rated when those subjects anticipated interaction with a black subject. Likewise, the more antiblack the subjects were, on the basis of the black anti scale, the more *un*friendly their chair placement was likely to be rated ($r = .342$, $p < .05$, compared to $r = -.174$ for the white condition).

An interesting negative relationship was found between admiring (versus condescending) voice ratings and chair ratings in the black gas station attendant condition ($r = -.535$, $p < .05$). All other conditions showed the correlation of these variables to be non significant (black law student, $-.011$; white

TABLE 5
RACE × CLASS INTERACTION ON COMBINED ADJECTIVE SCALE

Race	Class	
	Gas station attendant	Law student
Black	4.7	5.4
White	4.8	5.0

Note.—$F = 3.558$, $df = 1/72$, $MS = 1.225$, $p < .063$.

gas station attendant, $-.373$; white law student, .165). Thus, the more condescending the subjects were in their voices, the friendlier their chair placement was to the black gas station attendant.

General Attitude Measure

The mean scores for the 80 subjects on the Schuman-Harding (1964) scales indicated lower hate prejudice and higher love prejudice than among subjects in Schuman and Harding's (cited in Schuman & Harding, 1964) earlier study. While the irrational pro scores were fairly similar in the present study ($\bar{X} = 50$, $SD = 13$) and in Schuman and Harding's college sample ($\bar{X} = 53$, $SD = 13$), there was considerably less hate prejudice (irrational anti) in the present sample ($\bar{X} = 30$, $SD = 6$) than in the earlier study ($\bar{X} = 47$, $SD = 14$), and also less variation in the population.

The general attitude measure did not correlate with the experimental measures of specific attitude, voice, or behavior, except as indicated above.

A short personal data form administered after the general attitude measure revealed that the subjects came from middle-class parental backgrounds, and by and large envisioned similar life styles (in terms of career and income) for themselves. Most had little contact with blacks and had lived in all-white areas and attended all-white high schools. The majority were attending private colleges and universities with small black enrollments.

DISCUSSION

What happens in a society in which prejudice is no longer socially respectable, but where tradition and many current social structural supports still favor such attitudes? Psychological conflict is the inevitable result. The present study revealed some of the aspects of this conflict model through experimental means. Extremely favorable verbal attitudes were coupled with subtle signs of rejection of blacks across the experimental conditions. In the most dramatic demonstration of the conflict model, verbal racial attitudes were found to be significantly *negatively* related to indexes of actual interracial behavior (the more friendly the attitude, the less friendly the behavior, and vice versa). Thus, attitudes *did* predict behavior, but not in the direction expected. All this occurred among an extremely nonprejudiced sample (as measured by the Schuman-Harding, 1964, scale) of upper-middle-class white college students.

Several earlier studies presaged these findings. Linn (1965) found attitude–behavior prediction to be worse among attitudinal liberals (on race) than conservatives in a study of willingness to pose for interracial photographs. Thus, conservatives generally did not agree to pose, but liberals sometimes did and sometimes did not; their verbal statements bore no relationship to their actions. Verbal overcompensation for negative affect was found by Katz and Benjamin (1960) among authoritarian whites (in biracial work groups), who rated blacks higher on intelligence, maturity, and dominance than did nonauthoritarian whites. Interestingly enough, the blacks were not fooled, as they refused to cooperate with them as much as with the nonauthoritarian whites. Thus, the blacks may have picked up subtle signs of negativity through nonverbal or paralinguistic channels, such as in the voice results in the present study. In another biracial work group study, Mann (1959) found that whites who were ranked as *low* on prejudice by other group members tended to prefer other whites as friends more than whites who were ranked as high on prejudice by other group members.

Katz's (1970) ambivalence hypothesis gives us some insight into this conflict. He maintains that ambivalence (a combination of positive and negative feelings toward the same attitude object) leads to an amplification of both positive and negative feelings toward the group in question. Thus, verbal attitudes seem to be amplified in a positive direction, and behavior aspects seem to be amplified in a negative direction. This may be an exaggeration on an individual level of the society's high verbal sentiments on race and its racist behavioral practices (i.e., Myrdal's, 1944, American dilemma).

The verbal overfriendliness, coupled with vocal and behavioral cues of affective retreat may well lead to unpleasant and uncomfortable interaction for blacks and whites alike. The conflicting signals of the white leave the black in a quandary as to what his expectations should be. But, since vocal and behavioral cues are usually more trustworthy than verbal statements (being less under situational control), the black probably responds with reservations and some hostility (as in Katz & Benjamin, 1960), thus contributing to the white's uneasiness, and beginning the cycle of racial misunderstanding all over again. Increased equal status interracial contact is likely to be the best way to short circuit this cycle by removing the source of the conflict.

The positive relationship between friendliness of voice tone and of behavior is noteworthy, and indicates a channel through which behavioral intentions might be assessed in interracial interaction. Two previous studies have shown similar relationships between voice and behavior. Milmoe, Rosenthal, Blane, Chafetz, and Wolf (1967) found the rated degree of anger in the content-filtered speech of physicians to be a good postdictor of success in referring alcoholics for further treatment (those with the lowest degree of anger had the most success, and vice versa). A year later, Milmoe, Novey, Kagan, and Rosenthal (1968) found a similar relationship between ratings of anxiety, anger, warmth, and pleasantness in content-filtered speech of mothers and their children's behavior over a 23-month period in associated areas (e.g., fretting, crying, attentiveness to voices). The present study differs from the two discussed above in that non-content-filtered samples of real speech were used (the subjects all said exactly the same thing—recital of a set of instructions).

What, then, of the original question of the reality of the attitude–behavior link in race relations? It seems that this relationship takes on a special aura in the case of race relations, in which social norms of what constitutes the "proper" verbal attitude are widely known throughout the population studied. However, instead of wishing away this social desirability aspect, we can use it to detect those individuals who appear to overreact to the norm, possibly due to repression of (negative) affect, and hence are likely to be hesitant about actual interracial interaction. These reservations will be clearly revealed through other channels, however, such as the vocal one, which are less subject to conscious control and thus to the social desirability requirements of the situation. In general, the population studied exhibited conflicting responses toward blacks—a pattern of overt acceptance and covert rejection—so that attitude may prove to be a far more complex entity than previously thought, especially in an area such as race, which is so tied in with every aspect of the social structure. The use of new indexes of attitude, such as voice and proxemic measures, is suggested, especially since they probably serve as valuable cues to blacks as to the likely course of an interaction. Further research should reveal the nature of the nonverbal and paralinguistic channels that transmit complex racial attitudes (on the part of both blacks and whites) in actual interracial interaction.

REFERENCES

Katz, I. *Experimental studies of Negro-white relationships.* (Research Memo RM-70-4) Princeton, N.J.: Educational Testing Service, March 1970.

Katz, I., & Benjamin, L. Effects of white authoritarianism in biracial work groups. *Journal of Abnormal and Social Psychology,* 1960, **61**, 448–456.

Linn, L. S. Verbal attitudes and overt behavior: A study of racial discrimination. *Social Forces,* 1965, **43**, 353–364.

Mann, J. H. The relationship between cognitive, affective and behavioral aspects of racial prejudice. *Journal of Social Psychology,* 1959, **49**, 223–228.

Milmoe, S., Novey, M., Kagan, J., & Rosenthal, R. The mother's voice: Postdictor of aspects of her baby's behavior. *Proceedings of the 76th Annual Convention of the American Psychological Association,* 1968, **3**, 463–464. (Summary)

Milmoe, S., Rosenthal, R., Blane, H. J., Chafetz, M. E., & Wolf, I. The doctor's voice: Postdictor of successful referral of alcoholic patients. *Journal of Abnormal Psychology,* 1967, **72**, 78–84.

Myrdal, G. *An American dilemma.* New York: Harper & Row, 1944. 2 vols.

Rosenthal, R. Estimating effective reliabilities in studies employing judges' ratings. Harvard University: Author, 1970. (Mimeo)

Schuman, H., & Harding, J. Prejudice and the norm of rationality. *Sociometry,* 1964, **27**, 353–371.

Wicker, A. W. Attitudes versus actions: The relationship of verbal and overt behavioral responses to attitude objects. *Journal of Social Issues,* 1969, **25**, 41–78.

(Received July 8, 1971)

RACIAL DISCRIMINATION IN APARTMENT RENTALS[1]

DANIEL A. JOHNSON[2], RICHARD J. PORTER,
AND PATRICIA L. MATELJAN

Claremont Graduate School

> A lack of adequate housing in the Southern California city studied was perceived by minority groups to be the result of racial discrimination. To verify this, 25 apartment houses were visited by male-female couples from three ethnic groups: Mexican-American, Negro, and Caucasian. The couples asked about apartment availability, amount of rent, and miscellaneous fees. Fewer apartments were available to the minority groups than to Caucasians ($p < .02$). Negroes were quoted rents and miscellaneous fees which were higher than those quoted to Caucasians. Overall, Negroes were discriminated against more often than Mexican-Americans, who in turn were more discriminated against than Caucasians. Seventy-six percent of the apartment house managers displayed some overt indication of racial discrimination.

The case has been made by others that segregation in housing is a serious problem. Myrdal (1944) writes that housing segregation and prejudice form a vicious circle in that housing segregation results in less interracial activities, such as school, recreation, shopping, etc. Thus prejudiced whites have little opportunity to see Negroes and other minorities as having the same problem and experiences as themselves (Deutsch & Collins, 1951). Segregation in housing results in increased competition for a limited number of dwelling units, which results in higher rent. Since minority's incomes are usually limited, severe overcrowding occurs due to several families attempting to save money by living together in a unit that is designed for a single family. This results in rapid deterioration of the units. In addition, the economic and psychological burdens contribute, according to Myrdal, to increased delinquency, broken homes, emotional instability, and a general brutalization of life. This supports the rationale for the prejudice that probably contributed to the housing segregation initially.

Racial segregation in cities results when the "gatekeepers" of housing accommodations block access to certain ethnic groups to living accommodations in some geographical locations but not to accommodations in other locations. In some instances certain ethnic groups may not even be allowed to reside in a city. The gatekeeper may be the individual homeowner who has direct control over to whom he sells, rents, or leases his home. A more influential gatekeeper is the professional engaged in the selling, leasing, or renting of living accommodations. When racial segregation results because the gatekeepers' sole criterion for blocking access to living accommodations is ethnic background of the applicant, then racial discrimination is said to occur.

Racial segregation can also occur in areas where: (a) the cost of living accommodation is high, and (b) when the majority or all of the members of certain ethnic groups cannot afford such accommodations. This is usually referred to as economic discrimination.

While racial segregation for Negroes is common throughout the United States, regardless of region or city size (Taeuber & Taeuber, 1965), segregation due to racial discrimination is illegal according to federal and many state laws.

Though racial discrimination is illegal, economic discrimination is not. Consequently in the situation where a minority group is in an economically disadvantaged position, it is not obvious whether a resulting segregation in housing is the result of racial or economic discrimination, or a combination of the two. (It is of course obvious that racial discrimination in other areas, such as in job

---

[1]This study was supported in part by the Psychology Department, Claremont Graduate School, Claremont, California. Arthur Brayfield and Stuart Oskamp supplied valuable assistance in this study.

[2]Requests for reprints should be sent to Daniel A. Johnson, Department of Psychology, Claremont Graduate School, Claremont, California 91711.

From *Journal of Applied Social Psychology,* 1971, *1*(4), 364–377. Reprinted by permission of Scripta Publishing Company.

hiring practices, schooling, and in business financing, can result in the minority groups descending to, or staying in, an economically disadvantaged position. When this occurs housing segregation can ultimately be traced back to racial discrimination, regardless of whether it is or is not practiced by the gatekeepers of housing accommodations.)

So a problem that emerges is how one may ascertain, in a racially segregated city, if the segregation is due to economic or to racial discrimination. One method might be to determine the attitudes of the professional gatekeepers toward renting, leasing, or selling living accommodations to minority groups. However, inconsistencies between behavior and ethnic attitude have been found by a number of researchers (La Piere, 1934; Kutner, Wilkins, & Yarrow, 1952; Minard, 1952; Saenger & Gilbert, 1950).

Therefore, in a study aimed at determining the incidence of racial discrimination, it would probably be less accurate to attempt to measure interracial attitudes, with a subsequent speculation about interracial behavior, than to directly measure the amount and type of racial discrimination. The direct measurement of racial discrimination was the method decided upon for the present study.

The selection of the target city of this study was based on reports of racial segregation existing in the city. Many contacts were made with groups concerned with racial discrimination over a period of several months in early 1970. These groups included the Black Studies Center and Mexican-American Studies Center, both at the Claremont Colleges in Claremont, California, the local Fair Housing Council, local real estate brokers, as well as various minority groups.

The consensus of opinion among these groups was that one of the major problems in the local communities was the lack of adequate housing for members of racial minority groups. The apparent lack of adequate housing was perceived by most minority group members to be the result of racial discrimination by those involved in the selling and renting of houses and apartments. Such perceptions may have been partially influenced by reports in the mass media of suspected or proven housing discrimination in surrounding communities (Anonymous, 1970, Bryant, 1970). Only anecdotal evidence, however, could be found to support the allegation of discrimination in the target city of the present study.

At the time of this study no census data were available that showed the ethnic background of the over 80,000 city residents and where they resided. However, a map, constructed by the local Fair Housing Council, indicated that certain specific areas were occupied predominantly by Caucasians, while residents of other specific areas were indicated to be predominantly Negro, or Negro and Mexican-Americans. The evidence of the map, supported by the personal experience of driving through the city, as well as by testimony of long-time residents, was the basis for the conclusion that the target city was racially segregated.

This target city had been the focus of recent racial disturbances, and it was felt that interracial tensions might be reduced by determining the extent of racial housing discrimination. That is, if minority perceptions were incorrect and the lack of housing was a problem for all persons regardless of ethnic background, then making this information generally known could have an ameliorating effect on racial tension. On the other hand, if racial discrimination in housing did exist, then perhaps some actions could be taken to reduce such inequities, which could also reduce racial tension.

No experimental investigations into this specific area of research were found in the literature. Consequently it was necessary to devise techniques which: (a) could accurately determine the incidence and type of racial housing discrimination in any large community; and (b) would yield results credible to minority group members as well as to the concerned community officials.

The purposes of this study were threefold: (a) to evaluate the extent of racial housing discrimination in a large Southern California city, (b) to provide information for possible use in remedying the problem, and (c) to demonstrate the applicability of behavioral science techniques for detection and measurement of racial segregation due to racial discrimination.

Method

Subjects

The subject population consisted of managers of 25 apartment houses. Twenty-four of the apartments were managed by Caucasians, and one apartment was managed by a Negro. Approximately 70% of the subjects were females. There was no reason to believe that the subjects became aware of their participation in the study.

Observers

The observers were comprised of six couples, with two male-female couples representing each ethnic group—Negro, Mexican-American, and Caucasian. The age range of the Negroes was 20 to 23 years, and that of the Mexican-Americans was 18 to 21. All were college students, articulate, spoke English fluently, and lived in nearby communities. Each minority individual was paid for the approximately 6 hours spent in the study. Gasoline mileage was also paid to each of the drivers. The two male-female couples representing the Caucasian ethnic group consisted of the three experimenters plus an additional white female volunteer; their age range was 25 to 33.

All observers were well dressed in an informal manner; that is, all wore cleaned and pressed dress clothes, although no ties or jackets were worn. Males wore dress slacks, shirts, and shoes, while females wore dresses, or skirts and blouses, and shoes. Wedding rings were supplied to those females having none.

Each observer couple supplied their own automobile, which ranged in age from a 13 year old sedan (used by one of the Caucasian couples) to late model sedans.

Selection of Apartments

Twenty-four apartment buildings were initially selected for observation using the following criteria:
1. The apartment building was in the boundaries of the target city.
2. An advertisement in the previous day's newspaper indicated the availability of an apartment for rent.
3. Each apartment facility contained more than two individual apartments, as evidenced by indication of multiple apartments in the advertisement itself, or by telephone conversations with the manager on the day before the investigation.

Apparatus

Twelve numbered dots, each indicating the location of a selected apartment building, were placed onto each of six street maps. Attached to each map was a list of the addresses of these apartments in the order that they were to be visited by the observer couple. Numbers by the dots also indicated this order.

Each couple was supplied with a street map, record sheets, a clipboard, and printed instructions.

Procedure

During a briefing session just before the observation period, each couple was instructed to assume the roles of a man and wife with no children or pets. If asked by a subject, the male observer was told to say that he worked in the general locale at a middle economic level (e.g., engineer employed at a particular company, assistant manager in a specific department store, etc.).

Each observer couple was told to obtain the following information from every subject: (a) whether or not there was an apartment available for rent, (b) if none was now available, when a vacancy could be expected, (c) the amount of rent for a two-bedroom, unfurnished apartment, and (d) the amount of any miscellaneous fees (e.g., cleaning deposit, key charges, etc.). The observers were also told not to fill out any form that could be construed as a promise to rent.

Each couple was randomly assigned to one of two teams; each team, made up of a couple from each of the three ethnic groups was assigned to visit 12 of the selected apartment buildings. The other team was assigned to the remaining 12 apartments.

A basic assumption underlying the order in which the observers visited the apartment houses was that for those apartments which advertised vacancies, there would be more apartments available for rent in the morning following the advertisement than in the afternoon. The rationale for this assumption was that: (a) managers would not advertise a vacancy unless one was available; and (b) during the course of the day following the advertisement, there would be a smaller number of current renters giving notice of vacating any one apartment building than the number of prospective renters applying for a vacancy at the same apartment. Therefore, there should have been at least as many, and perhaps more, apartments available for rent in the early part of the day, than in the latter part.

A prospective renter would be told that no apartment was available to him for at least two reasons: (a) there was in reality no vacancy at that particular apartment, or (b) the manager did not care to have that particular applicant as a renter. The latter reason would indicate racial discrimination if it was only given to the minority applicants. Then in order to reduce, or eliminate, the former reason (no vacancy) for minority groups being told no apartments were available, the minority couples visited the apartments only in the morning hours, when a maximum number of apartments should have been available. In addition, the Caucasians visited the apartments only in the afternoon of the same day. In this way, if the reason, "no vacancy", was the sole determinate of whether an observer couple was told an apartment was or was not available, the minority couples should have had as many, or more, apartments available to them than the Caucasian couples. Conversely, if more apartments were available to Caucasian couples than to the minority couples, racial discrimination may have been the prime cause. This particular order in apartment visiting produced a conservative test for racial discrimination.

The minority observers started visiting their assigned apartment buildings at the same time (approximately 9:30 AM) on a Saturday. The schedule for visiting apartments was established in such a way that each apartment was visited by a Mexican-American couple and a Negro couple, with a 2 hour separation between visits. Half of the apartments were visited in the order,

Mexican-American, Negro; the remaining apartments in the reverse order. Observers were allowed 20 minutes to visit the apartment building, return to their cars, record the data, and travel to the next assigned apartment.

In the case when a "no vacancy" sign was displayed, or when the manager was not on the premises, the observers called the coordination office, reported this fact, and received the location of a nearby apartment building, the address of which was drawn from the advertising section of the local phone book. The standby address was relayed to the second observer couple when they called in at a prearranged time.

After completing the route, each minority couple was debriefed. Debriefing consisted of an experimenter reviewing each record sheet entry with the observer couple in order to eliminate any ambiguities.

In the afternoon of the same day, a Caucasian observer couple visited every apartment at which a subject had been interviewed by a minority couple. The Caucasian couple asked for the same information asked for by the minority couples.

In every case, the subject interviewed was found in the "office" building or in an apartment indicated as the "manager's apartment." The subject questioned was the person who was at the office desk or who answered the door to the manager's apartment. Married couples many times manage an apartment complex; in the present study all three observer couples interviewed the same subject at 68% of the apartment buildings. In some instances both the man and wife manager team were interviewed by an observer couple, while a follow-up couple interviewed only one spouse of the team.

The situation arose where one minority couple interviewed a couple at a scheduled apartment and the second minority couple failed to find the manager on the premises. This latter couple was then given the address of, and visited, a standby apartment. Later the Caucasian couple interviewed subjects at both apartments, thus resulting in 25 (rather than the scheduled 24) total number of apartments visited in this study. One team visited 13 apartments, the other team 12.

Because of "no vacancy" signs and managers not on the premises, subjects at only 15 apartment houses were interviewed by all three observer couples. Ten other apartment houses were visited by two couples only. The number of apartments visited by a Negro couple and Mexican-American couple only was two; three apartments were visited by only Negro and Caucasian observer couples; and the number visited by Mexican-American and Caucasian couples only was five. Thus, Negro observers interviewed subjects at 20 apartments; Mexican-Americans successfully visited 22 apartments; while Caucasians interviewed subjects at 23 apartments.

Criteria of Discrimination

Racial discrimination could be evidenced by differential treatment according to race in terms of apartment availability, rental costs, or amount of miscellaneous fees.

Availability discrimination. This was judged to occur if either of the two following criteria were met:

1. A subject told one or two observers that an apartment was available, but denied such availability to the remaining couple(s).

2. A subject gave one or two couples a date of apartment availability more than one-half week later than he gave to the other couple(s).

Rental costs. Discrimination was judged to occur if one or two couples were quoted rents higher than those quoted at the same apartment to the other observer couple(s) for an apartment of the same size.

Miscellaneous fees. If the cumulative fees (other than rent) quoted to an observer couple were higher than those quoted to the other couple(s), the former couple was judged to have been discriminated against.

RESULTS

Availability discrimination

At the 15 apartments visited by all three observer couples of a team, there were more apartments available to the Caucasians than to the minority couples combined ($p < .05$) (see Table 1).

Examination of the 20 apartments visited by both Mexican-Americans and Caucasians revealed that there were fewer apartments available to the Mexican-American couples than to the Caucasian couples ($p = .05$) (see Table 2). Similar results were found at the 18

TABLE 1

COMPARISON OF NUMBER OF APARTMENTS AVAILABLE TO CAUCASIAN AND MINORITY OBSERVER COUPLES AT 15 APARTMENTS VISITED BY THREE OBSERVER COUPLES

Number of apartments	Caucasians	Minority couples (combined)
Available	12	13
Not available	3	17

Note. $-\chi^2 = 4.06$; $p < .05$.

TABLE 2

COMPARISON OF NUMBER OF APARTMENTS AVAILABLE TO CAUCASIAN AND MEXICAN-AMERICAN OBSERVER COUPLES AT 20 APARTMENTS VISITED BY BOTH

Number of apartments	Caucasians	Mexican-Americans
Available	16	9
Not available	4	11

Note. $-\chi^2 = 3.84$; $p = .05$.

TABLE 3

COMPARISON OF NUMBER OF APARTMENTS AVAILABLE TO CAUCASIAN AND NEGRO OBSERVER COUPLES AT 18 APARTMENTS VISITED BY BOTH

Number of apartments	Caucasian	Negro
Available	14	6
Not available	4	12

Note. $-\chi^2 = 5.51$; $p < .02$.

TABLE 4

COMPARISON OF NUMBER OF APARTMENTS AVAILABLE TO NEGRO AND MEXICAN-AMERICAN OBSERVER COUPLES AT 17 APARTMENTS VISITED BY BOTH

Number of apartments	Negro	Mexican-American
Available	7	8
Not available	10	9

apartments visited by both Negro and Caucasian couples ($p < .02$) (see Table 3). However, there was no reliable difference between Negroes and Mexican-Americans in terms of availability at the 17 apartments visited by both (see Table 4).

Of the 25 apartments visited, four managers made no apartments available to any of the observers who visited them, presumably because no vacancies existed. One additional manager made an apartment available to the first visiting minority couple, but not to the second minority couple or to the follow-up Caucasian couple; while the vacancy was probably filled between the first and second observers' visits, this was conjecture, and the latter two couples were judged to have been discriminated against according to the established criteria.

Negroes were discriminated against 9 times out of the 20 apartments visited (45%); for Mexican-Americans and Caucasians the percentage of times discriminated against were 36% and 4% respectively (see Table 5). In comparing the two teams, it is apparent that no significant differences existed between like ethnic groups. This suggests that there probably was no large difference between couples of the same race in terms of demeanor when interviewing the subjects (see Table 5).

Apartment Rental Costs

Negroes were quoted rents higher than one or both of the other groups five times. Mexican-Americans and Caucasians were each quoted rents higher than one or both of the other groups twice. No Caucasian couple was ever given a rent quotation higher than that given a Negro, although Negroes were given quotations higher than Caucasians four times (binomial test, 1 tail, $p = .0625$). No other comparisons approached significance. The five high quotes given to Negroes ranged from $5 to $35 with a mean of $12 for each

TABLE 5

COMPARISON OF OBSERVER TEAMS IN TERMS OF APARTMENT AVAILABILITY

	Team A			Team B		
	Negro	Mexican-American	Caucasian	Negro	Mexican-American	Caucasian
Number of apartments available	4	5	9	3	5	9
Total not available	7	6	2	6	6	3
Not available due to discrimination	5	3	0	4	5	1
Total visited	11	11	11	9	11	12

high quote. The Mexican-Americans were given two high quotes of $5 and $10, while Caucasians were given two high quotes of $3 and $5.

Miscellaneous Fees

Negroes were quoted five miscellaneous fees higher than those quoted to Caucasians, though no Caucasian couple was quoted a miscellaneous fee higher than the fee quoted to the Negro couple (binomial test, 1 tail, $p = .031$). No other comparisons were significant. Negroes were quoted high fees ranging from $5 to $50, with a mean of $20.83, over the fees quoted to one or both of the other ethnic groups. Mexican-Americans were quoted five high fees, ranging from $5 to $110, with a mean of $58, over those quoted to the other groups. Caucasians were quoted two fees that were $5 and $20 higher than quoted to one or both of the minority groups. The differences within ethnic groups across teams were not significant (see Table 6).

Combined Discrimination

In some instances, subjects used more than one of the three forms of discrimination described above. Nine subjects used two forms against some observer couples, while one subject used all three forms against one Negro couple. Of the 15 comparisons where all three observers were successful in interviewing a single subject only two subjects showed no discrimination. Of the 10 remaining comparisons, four of the subjects showed no discrimination. That is, of the 25 apartment managers visited 19 (76%) showed some discrimination. When all three forms of discrimination were considered, it was found that Negroes were discriminated against by 15 of the 20 subjects that they visited, Mexican-Americans were discriminated against by 11 of the 22 subjects visited, while Caucasians were discriminated against by 4 of the 23 subjects that they visited.

DISCUSSION

The results of this study indicate that the complaint, registered by many minority group members, of considerable racial discrimination in obtaining living accommodations, is not without basis. Judging from the present study, a Negro couple can expect to be discriminated against in a majority of apartment houses visited, while a Mexican-American may expect some type of discrimination in perhaps as high as 50% of the apartments visited.

The Justice Department of the U.S. government has been successful in prosecuting housing discrimination suits under the 1968 Fair Housing Act. In one recent suit, covering 8000 apartment units in the Los Angeles area, some novel steps against racial bias were taken (Anonymous, 1970).

These steps required that the operators: (a) include nonwhites as well as whites in advertising that depicts persons; and (b) place at least one-third of their advertising for apartments with less than 10% Negro occupancy in a predominately Negro newspaper. Since

TABLE 6
COMPARISON OF OBSERVER TEAMS IN TERMS OF NUMBER OF HIGH VS NORMAL RENT AND FEE QUOTATIONS

	Team A			Team B		
	Negro	Mexican-American	Caucasian	Negro	Mexican-American	Caucasian
Number of high quotes	4	2	1	5	4	1
Number of normal quotes	4	8	10	1	4	9

Note.—Comparison of Negroes, team A vs team B: Fisher test = 0.24. Comparison of Mexican-Americans: Fisher test = 0.20.

most apartment house owners are probably aware that racial discrimination is illegal this could be a possible reason why the minority observer couples in this study had less success in interviewing managers, as indicated by the smaller number of apartments visited by those groups. It is possible that some managers refused to open the door to a minority couple, thereby eliminating the possibility of any legal repercussions that could occur from not renting available apartments to minority groups.

Since the observers were instructed to return to their car before writing down the required information, some errors in recording rent and miscellaneous fees may have occurred. While this is only supposition, since no checks on recording accuracy were taken, it could explain some of the apparent economic discrimination against the Caucasian couples and also perhaps against the minority couples. In future studies, the probability of recording errors could be reduced by instructing the observers to jot down the relevant information on a piece of scratch paper while the manager relates it. This information could then be transcribed to a permanent record sheet after the observers returned to their car.

A separate check of the accuracy of information recording by the observers should perhaps be carried out in the future by having the observers interview a confederate of the experimenters, who would be acting as an apartment manager. Then the accuracy of the observer could be determined and, in addition, a posttest interview with the manager could reveal any possible differences between the observers in terms of behavior during the interview.

The probability of experimenter bias in future studies should be decreased by insuring that the Caucasian and minority couples are not aware of the true purpose of the study. The use of separate facilities for the pretest briefing, and adequate cover stories, could keep the observers unaware of their part in a racial discrimination study.

Managers may have lowered the rental and/or miscellaneous fees during the course of the day, accounting for some apparent economic discrimination. To control for this possibility in the future, Caucasian couples should visit each apartment both before and after the minority couples. This will allow a check on the stability of economic costs.

The difference in ages between the minority couples (mean = 21.9 years) and Caucasians (mean = 28.2 years) may have contributed in part to the discrimination found in this study. If one makes the assumption that some apartment managers would discourage prospective renters in their early 20's but not those in their late 20's, then the relationship between race and discrimination could be spurious. It is not believed, however, that this factor alone could account for the magnitude of discrimination found. It definitely would not account for the apparently greater discrimination practiced against Negroes than against Mexican-Americans, since the Negroes were 2 years older on the average than the Mexican-Americans.

The age factor was uncontrolled in the present study mainly because of the general difficulty in obtaining minority-group confederates which, in itself, is interesting. There was an apparent hostility and/or apathy concerning the study expressed by many members of the minority groups who were contacted. One argument given for not participating in the study was that since racial discrimination was known to exist by all members of the minority communities, why then should they take the trouble of helping the white community prove this fact? Other feelings that may have produced a reluctance to participate were: (a) a suspicion that since the experimenters were white, the minorities could be taking part in a study to "whitewash" the problem by deliberately not finding any discrimination, and (b) a fear that the minorities once again were being used as guinea pigs in another "white man's" experiment, which would produce no benefit for the groups being discriminated against.

Several arguments were used to try to overcome these objections: (a) if indeed racial discrimination in housing is widespread, then it is necessary to prove it to the white community, for only then can steps be taken to overcome the problem, (b) the objectivity of the experimenters was stressed, and it was made explicit that whatever results were found would be faithfully reported, and (c) it was promised that, whatever the findings, the experimenters would actively disseminate the results to concerned groups and to the public communication media.

A review of the study was prominently placed in a widely read newspaper in the Southern California area (Turpin, 1971). Interest in the results of this study was expressed by, among others, the California State Attorney General's Office, the U.S. Justice Department, and the Federal Bureau of Investigation. These organizations have indicated that, since both California and federal civil rights laws may have been broken, more intensive legal investigations should be carried out. An additional effect has been the interest expressed by the local Apartment House Owners Association. This group has initiated recent meetings dealing with discrimination, the purpose of which was to help the local owners and managers overcome their reluctance to renting apartments to minority groups. While no follow-up study has yet been initiated, it is possible that publicizing in the mass media the results of a study such as the present one, which attempted only to measure discriminatory behavior, may act as an agent of change of that very behavior.

That is, if an apartment manager was made aware that several apartments in the community had been evaluated and were found to be discriminating along racial lines, then he or she may infer that this same event could reoccur. If the manager had engaged in racial discrimination, it is possible that the threat of legal repercussions, made possible following detection, might act to inhibit further racial discrimination. Future research should attempt to determine if the mere act of measuring discrimination, and publishing the results, can cause a significant reduction in racial discrimination, or whether more positive steps on the part of social scientists and public officials are needed to gain that result.

SUMMARY

It has been demonstrated that racial discrimination in apartment rentals exists in the city studied. Discrimination was most commonly evidenced by a professed apartment unavailability to minority group members when apartments were made available to Caucasian couples. Racial discrimination was also in evidence when minority group members were quoted higher fees than whites. Negroes were more discriminated against than were Mexican-Americans. Discrimination was displayed by a large majority of apartment house managers visited.

REFERENCES

ANONYMOUS. Consent decree reached in L.A. rental bias suit. *Los Angeles Times,* Los Angeles, Calif., Part 2, July 30, 1970.

BRYANT, PAT. Renter faces greatest bias—Housing council. *Los Angeles Times,* Los Angeles, Calif., San Fernando Valley Section, Part 2, Dec. 27, 1970.

DEUTSCH, M., & COLLINS, MARY E. *Interracial housing: A psychological evaluation of a social experiment.* Minneapolis: Univ. Minnesota Press, 1951.

KUTNER, B., WILKINS, CAROL, & YARROW, PENNY R. Verbal attitudes and overt behavior involving racial prejudice. *Journal of Abnormal and Social Psychology,* 1952, **47**, 649–652.

LA PIERE, R. T. Attitudes vs. actions. *Social Forces,* 1934, **13**, 230–237.

MINARD, R. D. Race relations in the Pocahontas coal field. *Journal of Social Issues,* 1952, **8**, 29–44.

MYRDAL, G. *An American dilemma: The Negro problem and modern democracy.* New York: Harper, 1944.

SAENGER, G., & GILBERT, EMILY. Customer reactions to the integration of Negro sales personnel. *International Journal of Opinion and Attitude Research,* 1950, **4**, 57–76.

TAEUBER, K. E., & TAEUBER, A. F. *Negroes in cities.* Chicago: Aldine, 1965.

TURPIN, D. 19 of 25 apartment managers display overt bias. *Los Angeles Times,* Los Angeles, Calif., Section J, April 4, 1971.

THE STUDIES COMPARED

Measurement of Attitudes and Behavior

Careful reading of the Weitz article indicates that a sizeable number of measures were taken. Attitude assessment included the multi-item Schuman and Harding Irrational Pro and Anti scales, 18 bipolar-adjective pairs, and an unspecified number of "related questions." The specific attitude measure used in establishing the attitude-behavior discrepancy was a single item from this sizeable array of measures. Responses to the one question "How friendly would you feel toward this person in a year's time?" were compared with the voice ratings. No rationale is given for choosing this one item as the most valid measure of attitude—a rationale that would enable readers to evaluate the reasoning on its own terms.

Considerable thought and planning go into the operational definition of the variables in a study. The experimenter's conceptual skills are directed toward getting the best possible measurement of the dimension in question. The use of a single item, chosen from an array of measures, to assess the results raises some methodological issues. In Chapter 2, we discussed the problems involved in using a single item to measure attraction. Scales are comprised of a number of items that share some underlying property. The scale is said to have *convergent validity* to the extent to which different items are tapping the same underlying dimension. Presumably, such is the case with the Schuman and Harding scales, the adjective pairs, and possibly the "related questions." If only one item of this array shows a unique effect, there may be something unusual about the item itself that leads to the differential responses, and the item may not be a measure of the underlying attitude that it is being used to represent. In the present case, the self-referent quality of the item (how friendly are *you?*) and its future orientation (a year from now) may differentiate this item from the other attitude items. Similar questions arise with respect to the measures of behavior. Five voice ratings were made, of which two were used in establishing the attitude-behavior discrepancy. Those with the highest interrater reliability were not used, and no reason is offered concerning why warm-cold and admiring-condescending are voice characteristics more suited to the experimenter's purpose than the others taken into account.

In the second selection, several measures of discrimination were taken, and all were used in a combined index to reflect an overall pattern of discrimination in apartment rentals. This is a strength of this field experiment. In addition, the particular measures selected (availability, rental price, and miscellaneous fees) have great face validity in the sense that you would recognize them readily as legitimate manifestations of housing discrimination. Unlike some operationalizations, these experimental measures have identical counterparts in actual manifestations of discrimination as practiced in everyday life.

Confounding Variables

In the second research selection, good care was exercised in timing the visits by members of minority and majority groups in order to minimize the possibility that the time of the visit could account for an alternative explanation of the findings. The couples from minority groups always went to the housing managers in the morning to reduce the possibility that afternoon refusals to minority applicants could be based on actual morning rentals. Afternoon availability to a White couple *after* a morning refusal to a minority couple increases confidence in the discrimination explanation. Unfortunately, similar care was not exercised with regard to age differences. The White couples were older than the minority couples. The authors acknowledge (but minimize) the possible effects of this confounding variable. As students know, age discrimination in housing exists, with landlords sometimes refusing rentals to younger couples. In order to be sure that discrimination was due to race, all other observer characteristics should have been comparable; that is, the couples should have been of the same age.

Another design problem involves a variant of experimenter bias. The couples were not blind with regard to the investigator's hypotheses, and the effects of this awareness are unknown. But it is possible that anticipation of outcome might have led the different couples to behave differently in their interaction with the housing managers; that is, the minority couples may have elicited more negative responses not because (or not only because) of racial discrimination on the part of the manager but because of the nature of the interpersonal encounter with the housing manager. This is not a serious validity problem, because this kind of self-fulfilling prophecy may in fact govern interracial interactions in real-life housing negotiations.

Presentation of Results

Consider the reasoning in the first selection. The assumption is made that White liberals make positive verbal statements but, since they harbor deep-seated feelings of hostility toward Blacks (repressed affect), these feelings emerge in less controllable behaviors. A number of verbal assessments of attitudes were made, and a number of less obtrusive behavioral measures were taken. The reasoning calls for the existence of negative statistical correlations; that is, positive verbal attitudes are found to coexist with hostile behaviors. This certainly reflects the intuitive assumptions many would make about the workings of prejudice and racism in this country. The anticipated discrepancy was found between attitude and voice characteristics. Task selection and the willingness to return also reflected a more negative stance toward Blacks than verbal expressions of friendliness would have indicated. But what of the willingness to wait with the Black partner? Weitz rejected this measure as a "true" expression of negative feelings on the grounds that it had unanticipated demand characteristics. In support of this reasoning, Weitz cited the fact that everyone elected to wait with the Black gas-station attendant. A close look at Table 1 reveals that the willingness to wait with a partner is negatively correlated with the expressed verbal-attitude item. Such a negative correlation can be interpreted in two ways. In the present case, it can reflect either the situation in which those who said they would be very friendly a year from now refused to wait with the proposed partner *or* the situation in which those who elected to wait with the partner were less friendly. Given the report that all elected to wait in one of the two conditions under consideration in Table 1, it is reasonable to suppose that the negative correlation reflects the latter situation described above. Since most men elected to wait with a Black partner (positive behavior), a negative correlation with expressed attitude can be achieved only if these people expressed less friendliness toward Blacks (negative attitude). This finding runs counter to the conclusion that hostile feelings masked by friendly verbal statements are revealed in hostile behavior.

Simulations and Real Encounters

The second selection used real encounters, thereby incurring the problems of achieving observer comparability as described above. Real people differ and act differently at different times and in interaction with different others. A Black couple who expect rejection may ask questions in an abrupt and hostile way, thus bringing about rejection from landlords; what looks like race discrimination may then be a consequence of interpersonal dynamics. Couples who were refused housing on previous occasions may approach housing managers differently from couples who were not discriminated against. It is, therefore, a real strength of the laboratory study that a high degree of control was made possible by the simulation technique. Identical information was presented to the students in identical ways. The only variation allowed was that of race and class—variables that were the experimenter's central concern. Raters of voice quality and chair placement were blind with regard to the hypotheses of the study. All students read the same standard instructions twice, thus assuring comparable voice samples. These considerable assets of the simulation technique are somewhat attenuated by doubts about the degree to which simulations reflect the essence of real encounters. This is important because a goal of research is to say something about real encounters, not merely simulated ones. It is critical to know whether the simulation in this study did give access to the essential elements of interracial encounters. Also, even if the discrepancy as stated is present in real encounters between White liberal males and Black males, one would have to ask whether Blacks do perceive a discrepancy and, if they do, what effect this may have. How are White-male voices that are rated by (White?) women as condescending and cold perceived by Black males? While not critical to the study itself, this question is important once generalization is attempted.

CONSUMER EVALUATION

Careful Reading

The first selection presents a challenge to the injunction that, as a consumer, you should read the fine print in contracts and on labels, since the study is a large and complex one. But obeying this advice is especially worthwhile in the case of this selection, because it is the fine print that reveals two problems with this study. First, the author speaks of a "most dramatic demonstration" of a repressed-affect model on the basis of her finding that verbal racial attitudes were negatively correlated to behavior. In fact, responses to only one verbal-attitude item showed a negative correlation with two of five aspects of voice quality. Second, a careful reading of the tables suggests that the most powerful negative correlation between attitude and behavior is found between the friendliness item and choosing to wait with partner. But this correlation is not fully discussed, and a careful reading leads to the surmise that it reflects a reversal of other negative correlations reported; specifically, it appears to be a product of hostile attitudes and friendly behavior. As indicated in the literature review, attitude-behavior discrepancies in interracial relationships show no simple directional patterns. As Weitz suggests, prejudice and racism are indeed sources of psychological conflict in our society, but the discrepancies they engender are more complex than this selection would indicate.

Careful reading of the second selection reveals the presence of the confounding variables we described earlier. In their discussion, the authors mention age as a confounding factor but argue that, if landlords had been discriminating on the basis of age, there should have been more refusals of the Mexican-American couples, who were two years younger than the Blacks. Their discussion refers to the greater discrimination apparently practiced against the Black couples, who were two years older, as evidence for minimizing age differences as an alternative explanation for the findings. But a careful perusal of Table 4 shows no difference in discrimination toward Black and Mexican-American couples, thereby weakening the arguments offered. In any case, a two-year age difference probably does not effectively elicit landlord age-related stereotypes, which may instead become operant when the age difference becomes greater, as in the case with the White couples.

Durability

The durability of applied research is more endangered by social change than is the durability of theoretically derived work. It is likely that few changes have occurred in our society as far as racism itself is concerned; but changes in the manifestations of racism have certainly occurred. Changes in social and political climate affect how racism is expressed. A study like that discussed in the second selection is thus more temporally bound to its context. A different time and place might well produce different results. A partial replication of this study in a small Midwestern town found discrimination with regard to availability but none with respect to rents or fees (Donnerstein, Donnerstein, & Koch, 1975). The authors of the second selection are modest in their claims for generalization, but the problem of durability is of concern to the consumer, who wishes to know what use to make of this study. The study in the first selection is less subject to the eroding of time because of its attempt to test a more general notion of attitude-behavior discrepancy, of which racial prejudice is but an example.

EPILOG

The book is almost over, and, like the students to whom we have taught research methods, you may have had different reactions along the way. Learning to interpret research in social psychology is sometimes overwhelming at the beginning. You are confronted with a lot of elements, with many details, and sometimes even with what may seem like strange ways of putting things together. Probably you did expect some difficulty with the material; after all, research is said to be a complicated business carried on by specialists. But you may not have been prepared to find that reading the studies carefully would reveal problems in the studies themselves. Here were studies selected to represent the field of social psychology—studies, one would expect, that are above criticism—and yet they turned out to present problems—indeed, to have flaws. But, hopefully, you also realized that flaws were not the whole picture and that each study had assets as well.

And perhaps, after that initial "rude shock," what was unfathomable began to be accessible. It may seem curious that knowledge of flaws highlights strengths and makes complex ideas more accessible and that there is more to be learned from disarray than from order. As Kaplan (1964) put it, "it may even be that what we see as disarray is to more perceptive eyes a style of dress both useful and elegant" (p. 27).

Our own enthusiasm for social psychology comes from seeing the research enterprise as it is—with its strengths and its limitations, with its achievements and its failures. The struggle to understand the content and the process of human social behavior is exciting to us. That it is complex, sometimes marked by false starts and dead ends, is part of the challenge. At the beginning of the book, we said that to critique is to honor, and we invited you to become involved. If we have succeeded in making that invitation meaningful and effective, we have achieved the goal we strove for in preparing this book. The form that your involvement will take is not all that important. If, after finishing this book, you remain primarily a consumer of research, perhaps you've been persuaded to be thoughtful and careful in evaluating the choice of questions and methods by others. If, instead, you become a "doer," perhaps you've been persuaded to be thoughtful and careful in choosing your own questions and methods. By the way, we regard the doers as a far-flung tribe—a tribe that includes the likes of us and also, among others, the market researchers, the surveyors of voter opinions, the volunteers sampling community support, and the citizens' rights organizers. No matter what form their "research" takes, all of them need to gather information about social behavior; the accuracy and effectiveness of their predictions and actions depend on the quality of the choices they make in gathering and interpreting the information. And they too, like the consumers of research, can benefit from the guidelines adapted from consumer practice that we offered throughout this book.

We also hope that you begin to realize that, whether you read research or you do it, you will not find or produce the perfect study. Questions are never framed flawlessly nor are methods found that fit the problem exactly. There are a number of ways of answering questions in social psychology, grouped loosely into laboratory and field experiments; observations, surveys, and interviews; and archival searches. Each approach has its staunch adherents, but no one method is inherently better suited to answer every question. As we have said many times before, it is the question that must dictate the choice of method. This is not to say that a given investigator need use different methods. But, as a consumer of research, you must ask yourself whether the method chosen fits the problem at hand. Consistent findings arising from different approaches increase one's confidence in their generality and stability. Another general question to be addressed when evaluating research concerns the degree of confounding that may have entered in. Some confounding is so serious as to suggest that the study not be bought. As indicated in the comparison of studies in each chapter, other flaws are damaging to relatively lesser extents. Finally, a critical question in the evaluation of method is the kind and amount of information the method yields. What can be learned from a given method? Will it provide the information needed to answer the question? It cannot be said often enough that the question comes first.

The methods presented in this book have been organized according to two dimensions—subject awareness and manipulation of antecedent conditions. These dimensions were selected simply to provide a means of comparing the methods; our choice does not imply that a study high or low on either or both dimensions is objectively better than one differently characterized. The question is always "Better for what?" Some experimental social psychologists would argue that low subject awareness and high manipulation of conditions constitute the best approach to all problems in social psychology. We hope that the pairing of studies using different approaches has led you to other conclusions. Some questions seem to benefit from the subject's full attention to what is sought or from the assessment of social behavior in its rich natural context. The two dimensions offered here are by no means exclusive. They facilitate some useful comparisons to which others can be added.

We also hope that after reading the book you are persuaded that no study, even with the most apt choice of methods, provides the final and definitive answer. This book has taken a comparative approach, presenting two research selections in each chapter, in order to convey some sense of the progressive nature of the field of social psychology. Each study taken alone has little meaning; each study integrated with others yields a more precise understanding of social behavior. We have tried to give a picture of the "what" of social psychology as it exists at the time of our writing. You are reading it at some later time, when some new studies have been added and new interpretations made. We hope that you, having bought some of the "how" of the field, are thereby in a better position to appreciate and evaluate current and future additions.

REFERENCES

Abelson, R. Comment on group shift to caution at the race track. *Journal of Experimental Social Psychology,* 1973, *9*(6), 517–521.

Agnew, N. McK., & Pyke, S. W. *The science game: An introduction to research in the behavioral sciences.* Englewood Cliffs, N.J.: Prentice-Hall, 1969.

Aiello, J. R., & Jones, S. E. Field study of the proxemic behavior of young school children in three subcultural groups. *Journal of Personality and Social Psychology,* 1971, *19*(3), 351–356.

Ajzen, I., & Fishbein, M. The prediction of behavior from attitudinal and normative variables. *Journal of Experimental Social Psychology,* 1970, *6*, 466–487.

Ajzen, I., & Fishbein, M. A Bayesian analysis of attribution processes. *Psychological Bulletin,* 1975, *82*, 261–277.

Alland, A., Jr. *The human imperative.* New York: Columbia University Press, 1972.

Allport, G. W. Attitudes. In C. Murchison (Ed.), *Handbook of social psychology.* Worcester, Mass.: Clark University Press, 1935.

Allport, G. W. *The nature of prejudice.* Reading, Mass.: Addison-Wesley, 1954.

Ardrey, R. *The territorial imperative.* New York: Atheneum, 1966.

Argyle, M., & Dean, J. Eye contact, distance and affiliation. *Sociometry,* 1965, *28,* 289–304.

Aronson, E. Dissonance theory: Progress and problems. In R. P. Abelson, E. Aronson, W. J. McGuire, T. M. Newcomb, M. J. Rosenberg, & P. H. Tannenbaum (Eds.), *Theories of cognitive consistency: A sourcebook.* Chicago: Rand McNally, 1968.

Aronson, E. Some antecedents of interpersonal attraction. In W. Arnold & D. Levine (Eds.), *Nebraska Symposium on Motivation* (Vol. 17). Lincoln: University of Nebraska Press, 1969. Pp. 143–173. (a)

Aronson, E. The theory of cognitive dissonance: A current perspective. In L. Berkowitz (Ed.), *Advances in experimental social psychology* (Vol. 4). New York: Academic Press, 1969. (b)

Aronson, E. *The social animal.* San Francisco: W. H. Freeman, 1972.

Aronson, E., & Carlsmith, J. M. Experimentation in social psychology. In G. Lindzey & E. Aronson (Eds.), *Handbook of social psychology* (Rev. ed.)(Vol. 2). Reading, Mass.: Addison-Wesley, 1968.

Aronson, E., & Linder, D. Gain and loss of esteem as determinants of interpersonal attractiveness. *Journal of Experimental Social Psychology,* 1965, *1,* 156–171.

Aronson, E., & Mills, J. The effect of severity of initiation on liking for a group. *Journal of Abnormal and Social Psychology,* 1959, *59*(2), 177–181.

Aronson, E., Willerman, B., & Floyd, J. The effect of a pratfall on increasing interpersonal attractiveness. *Psychonomic Science,* 1966, *4,* 227–228.

Ashmore, R. The problem of intergroup prejudice. In B. Collins, *Social psychology.* Reading, Mass.: Addison-Wesley, 1970.

Bailey, R. C., Helm, B., & Gladstone, R. The effects of success and failure in a real life setting: Performance, attribution, affect and expectancy. *The Journal of Psychology,* 1975, *89,* 137–147.

Bandura, A. *Aggression: A social learning analysis.* Englewood Cliffs, N.J.: Prentice-Hall, 1973.

Bandura, A., & McDonald, F. J. The influence of social reinforcement and the behavior of models in shaping children's moral judgments. *Journal of Abnormal and Social Psychology,* 1963, *67,* 274–281.

Bandura, A., Ross, D., & Ross, S. A. Imitation of film-mediated aggressive models. *Journal of Abnormal and Social Psychology,* 1963, *66,* 3–11.

Bandura, A., & Walters, R. H. *Adolescent aggression.* New York: Ronald Press, 1959.

Bandura, A., & Walters, R. H. *Social learning and personality development.* New York: Holt, Rinehart & Winston, 1963.

Banta, T. J., & Hetherington, M. Relations between needs of friends and fiancees. *Journal of Abnormal and Social Psychology,* 1963, *66,* 401–404.

Barefoot, J. C., Hoople, H., & McClay, D. Avoidance of an act which would violate personal space. *Psychonomic Science,* 1972, *28*(4), 205–206.

Barnlund, D. C. A comparative study of individual, majority, and group judgment. *Journal of Abnormal and Social Psychology,* 1959, *58,* 55–60.

Barocas, R., & Karoly, P. Effects of physical appearance on social responsiveness. *Psychological Reports,* 1972, *31,* 495–500.

Barocas, R., & Vance, F. L. Physical appearance and personal adjustment counseling. *Journal of Counseling Psychology,* 1974, *21*(2), 96–100.

Baron, R. A. Effects of magnitude of model's apparent pain on observer reaction time. *Psychonomic Science,* 1970, *20,* 229–231.

Baron, R. A. Exposure to an aggressive model and apparent probability of retaliation from the victim as determinants of adult aggressive behavior. *Journal of Experimental Social Psychology,* 1971, *7,* 343–355.

Baron, R. A. Reducing the influence of an aggressive model: The restraining effects of peer censure. *Journal of Experimental Social Psychology,* 1972, *8,* 266–275.

Baron, R. A., & Kepner, C. R. Attraction toward the model and model's competence as determinants of adult imitative behavior. *Journal of Personality and Social Psychology,* 1970, *14,* 335–344.

Bartlett, D. L., Drew, P. B., Fahle, E. G., & Watts, W. A. Selective exposure to a presidential campaign appeal. *Public Opinion Quarterly,* 1974, *38,* 264–270.

Bateson, N. Familiarization, group discussion, and risk taking. *Journal of Experimental Social Psychology,* 1966, *2,* 119–129.

Batson, C. D. Rational processing or rationalization?: The effect of disconfirming information on a stated religious belief. *Journal of Personality and Social Psychology,* 1975, *32,* 176–184.

Baumrind, D. Some thoughts on ethics of research: After reading Milgram's "Behavioral study of obedience." *American Psychologist,* 1964, *19,* 421–423.

Baxter, J. C. Interpersonal spacing in natural settings. *Sociometry,* 1970, *33*(4), 444–456.

Bell, B. D. Cognitive dissonance and the life satisfaction of older people. *Journal of Gerontology,* 1974, *29,* 564–571.

Bem, D. J. An experimental analysis of self persuasion. *Journal of Experimental Social Psychology,* 1965, *1,* 194–218.

Bem, D. J. Self-perception: An alternative interpretation of cognitive dissonance phenomena. *Psychological Review,* 1967, *74,* 183–200.

Berkowitz, L. *Aggression: A social psychological analysis.* New York: McGraw-Hill, 1962.

Berkowitz, L. The concept of aggressive drive: Some additional considerations. In L. Berkowitz (Ed.), *Advances in experimental social psychology* (Vol. 2). New York: Academic Press, 1965.

Berkowitz, L. Impulse, aggression and the gun. *Psychology Today,* 1968, *2*(4), 19–22.

Berkowitz, L. (Ed.). *Roots of aggression.* New York: Atherton Press, 1969.

Berkowitz, L. Reporting an experiment: A case study in leveling, sharpening, and assimilation. *Journal of Experimental Social Psychology,* 1971, *7,* 237–243.

Berkowitz, L. Social norms, feelings and other factors affecting helping and altruism. In L. Berkowitz (Ed.), *Advances in experimental social psychology* (Vol. 6). New York: Academic Press, 1972. Pp. 63–108.

Berkowitz, L., & Daniels, L. Responsibility and dependency. *Journal of Abnormal and Social Psychology,* 1963, *66,* 429–436.

Berkowitz, L., & Geen, R. G. Film violence and the cue properties of available targets. *Journal of Personality and Social Psychology,* 1966, *3,* 525–530.

Berkowitz, L., & Green, J. A. The stimulus qualities of the scapegoat. *Journal of Abnormal and Social Psychology,* 1962, *64,* 293–301.

Berkowitz, L., & LePage, A. Weapons as aggression-eliciting stimuli. *Journal of Personality and Social Psychology,* 1967, *7,* 202–207.

Berkowitz, L., & Rawlings, E. Effects of film violence: An inhibition against subsequent aggression. *Journal of Abnormal and Social Psychology,* 1963, *66,* 405–412.

Berscheid, E., & Walster, E. *Interpersonal attraction.* Reading, Mass.: Addison-Wesley, 1969.

Berscheid, E., & Walster, E. A little bit about love. In T. L. Huston (Ed.), *Foundations of interpersonal attraction.* New York: Academic Press, 1974.

Blank, A. D. Effects of group and individual conditions on choice behavior. *Journal of Personality and Social Psychology,* 1968, *8,* 294–298.

Blumenthal, H., Kahn, R., Andrews, F., & Head, K. *Justifying violence: Attitudes of American men.* Ann Arbor, Mich.: Survey Research Center, Institute for Social Research, University of Michigan, 1972.

Bogardus, E. S. A social distance scale. *Sociology and Social Research,* 1933, *17,* 265–271.

Bogel, D. *Toms, Coons, Mulattoes, Mammies and*

Bucks. New York: Bantam, 1973.

Borofsky, G. L., Stollak, G. E., & Messé, L. A. Sex differences in bystander reactions to physical assault. *Journal of Experimental Social Psychology,* 1971, *7,* 313–318.

Brehm, J. W., & Cohen, A. R. *Explorations in cognitive dissonance.* New York: Wiley, 1962.

Brehm, J. W., Gatz, M., Goethals, G., McCrommon, J., & Ward, L. *Psychological arousal and interpersonal attraction.* Unpublished manuscript, 1970. (Available from authors.)

Brown, R. *Social psychology.* New York: Free Press, 1965.

Brown, R. Development of the first language in the human species. *American Psychologist,* 1973, *28,* 97–100.

Bryan, J., & Davenport, M. *Donations to the needy: Correlates of financial contributions to the destitute.* Unpublished study, 1968. Princeton, N.J.: Educational Testing Services. Cited on p. 104 in L. Berkowitz, Social norms, feelings, and other factors affecting helping and altruism. In L. Berkowitz (Ed.), *Advances in experimental social psychology* (Vol. 6). New York: Academic Press, 1972. Pp. 63–108.

Bryan, J. H., & London, P. Altruistic behavior by children. *Psychological Bulletin,* 1970, *73,* 200–211.

Bryan, J. H., & Test, M. Models and helping: Naturalistic studies in aiding behavior. *Journal of Personality and Social Psychology,* 1967, *6,* 400–407.

Bryan, J. H., & Walbek, N. The impact of words and deeds concerning altruism upon children. *Child Development,* 1970, *41,* 747–757.

Buckhout, R. Changes in heart rate accompanying attitude change. *Journal of Personality and Social Psychology,* 1966, *4,* 695–699.

Buss, A. H. *The psychology of aggression.* New York: Wiley, 1961.

Buss, A. H. Physical aggression in relation to different frustrations. *Journal of Abnormal and Social Psychology,* 1963, *67,* 1–7.

Buss, A. H., Booker, A., & Buss, E. Firing a weapon and aggression. *Journal of Personality and Social Psychology,* 1972, *22*(3) 296–302.

Byrne, D. Interpersonal attraction and attitude similarity. *Journal of Abnormal and Social Psychology,* 1961, *62,* 713–715.

Byrne, D. *An introduction to personality: A research approach.* Englewood Cliffs, N.J.: Prentice-Hall, 1966.

Byrne, D. Attitudes and attraction. In L. Berkowitz (Ed.), *Advances in experimental social psychology* (Vol. 4). New York: Academic Press, 1969.

Byrne, D. *The attraction paradigm.* New York: Academic Press, 1971.

Byrne, D., & Clore, G. L. A reinforcement model of evaluative responses. *Personality: An International Journal,* 1970, *1,* 103–128.

Byrne, D., Ervin, C. R., & Lamberth, J. Continuity between the experimental study of attraction and real-life computer dating. *Journal of Personality and Social Psychology,* 1970, *16,* 157–165.

Byrne, D., & Griffitt, W. Similarity versus liking: A clarification. *Psychonomic Science,* 1966, *6,* 295–296.

Byrne, D., & Griffitt, W. Interpersonal attraction. *Annual Review of Psychology,* 1973, *24,* 317–336.

Byrne, D., & Nelson, D. Attraction as a linear function of proportion of positive reinforcements. *Journal of Personality and Social Psychology,* 1965, *1,* 659–663.

Calder, B. J., & Ross, M. *Attitudes and behavior.* Morristown, N.J.: General Learning Press, 1973.

Calhoun, L. G., Peirce, J. R., & Dawes, A. S. Attribution theory concepts and outpatients' perceptions of the causal locus of their psychological problems. *Journal of Community Psychology,* 1973, *1,* 37–39.

Campbell, D. T. From description to experimentation: Interpreting trends as quasi-experiments. In C. W. Harris (Ed.), *Problems in measuring change.* Madison: University of Wisconsin Press, 1963.

Campbell, D. T., Kruskal, W. H., & Wallace, W. P. Seating aggregation as an index of attitude. *Sociometry,* 1966, *29,* 1–15.

Campbell, D. T., & Stanley, J. C. Experimental and quasi-experimental designs for research on teaching. In N. L. Gage (Ed.), *Handbook of research on teaching.* Chicago: Rand McNally, 1963. (Also published separately as *Experimental and quasi-experimental designs for research.* Chicago: Rand McNally, 1966.)

Carey, J. T. Changing courtship patterns in the popular song. *American Journal of Sociology,* 1969, *74,* 720–731.

Carlsmith, J. M., Collins, B. E., & Helmreich, R. L. Studies in forced compliance: I. The effect of pressure for compliance on attitude change produced by face-to-face role playing and anonymous essay writing. *Journal of Personality and Social Psychology,* 1966, *4,* 1–13.

Carmichael, S., & Hamilton, C. V. *Black power: The politics of liberation in America.* New York: Vintage Books, 1967.

Cartwright, D. Risk taking by individuals and groups: An assessment of research employing choice dilemmas. *Journal of Personality and Social Psychology,* 1971, *20,* 361–378.

Cartwright, D. Determinants of scientific progress: The case of research on the risky shift. *American Psychologist,* 1973, *28,* 222–231.

Chaikin, A. L., & Darley, J. M., Jr. Victim or perpetrator: Defensive attribution of responsibility and the need for order and justice. *Journal of Personality and Social Psychology,* 1973, *25,* 268–275.

Chapanis, N. P., & Chapanis, A. Cognitive dissonance: Five years later. *Psychological Bulletin,* 1964, *61,* 1–22.

Cheyne, J. A., & Efran, M. G. The effect of spatial and interpersonal variables on the invasion of group controlled territories. *Sociometry,* 1972, *35,* 477–489.

Church, J., & Insko, C. A. Ethnic and sex differences in sexual values. *Psychologica—An International Journal of Psychology in the Orient,* 1965, *8,* 153–157.

Clark, C. X. Race, life style and rule flexibility: A field experiment in institutional behavior. *Organizational Behavior and Human Performance,* 1975, *13,* 433–443.

Clark, R. D. Group-induced shift toward risk: A critical appraisal. *Psychological Bulletin,* 1971, *76,* 251–270.

Clark, R. D., & Willems, E. P. Where is the risky shift? *Journal of Personality and Social Psychology,* 1969, *13,* 215–221.

Clark, R. D., & Word, L. E. Why don't bystanders help? Because of ambiguity? *Journal of Personality and Social Psychology,* 1972, *24*(3), 392–400.

Cleaver, E. *Soul on ice.* New York: McGraw-Hill, 1968.

Clement, D., & Sullivan, D. W. No risky shift effect with real groups and real risks. *Psychonomic Science,* 1970, *18*(4), 243–245.

Cline, V. B. Interpersonal perception. In B. A. Maher (Ed.), *Progress in experimental personality research* (Vol. 1). New York: Academic Press, 1964.

Cook, S. W. A comment on the ethical issues involved in West, Gunn, and Chernicky's "Ubiquitous Watergate: An attributional analysis." *Journal of Personality and Social Psychology,* 1975, *32,* 66–68.

Cox, K. Social effects of integrated advertising. *Journal of Advertising Research,* 1971, *10,* 41–44.

Cox, O. D. *Caste, class and race: A study in social dynamics.* New York: Doubleday, 1948.

Cronbach, L. J. Processes affecting scores on "understanding others" and "assumed similarity." *Psychological Bulletin,* 1955, *52,* 177–193.

Cunningham, J. D., & Kelley, H. H. Causal attributions for interpersonal events of varying magnitude. *Journal of Personality,* 1975, *43,* 74–93.

Darley, J., & Latané, B. Bystander intervention in emergencies: Diffusion of responsibility. *Journal of Personality and Social Psychology,* 1968, *8*(4), 377–383.

Darley, J., & Latané, B. Norms and normative behavior: Field studies of social interdependence. In J. Macaulay & L. Berkowitz (Eds.), *Altruism and helping behavior: Social psychological studies of some antecedents and consequences.* New York: Academic Press, 1970. Pp. 83–101.

Deaux, K. To err is humanizing. But sex makes a difference. *Representative Research in Social Psychology,* 1972, *3,* 20–28

Deaux, K. Anonymous altruism: Extending the lost letter technique. *Journal of Social Psychology,* 1974, *91,* 61–66.

DeFleur, M. L., & Westie, F. R. Verbal attitudes and overt acts: An experiment on the salience of attitudes. *American Sociological Review,* 1958, *23,* 667–673.

Delgado, J. M. R. *Physical control of the mind.* New York: Harper & Row, 1969.

DeLong, A. J. Dominance-territorial relations in a small group. *Environment and Behavior,* 1970, *2,* 170–191.

Deutsch, M., & Collins, M. E. *Interracial housing: A psychological evaluation of a social experiment.* Minneapolis: University of Minnesota Press, 1951.

Deutsch, M., & Krauss, R. M. *Theories in social psychology.* New York: Basic Books, 1965.

Dillehay, R. C. On the irrelevance of the classical negative evidence concerning the effect of attitudes on behavior. *American Psychologist,* 1973, *28,* 887–891.

Dion, D. L., Baron, R. S., & Miller, N. Why do groups make riskier decisions than individuals? In L. Berkowitz (Ed.), *Advances in experimental social psychology* (Vol. 5). New York: Academic Press, 1970.

Dion, K., Berscheid, E., & Walster, E. What is beautiful is good. *Journal of Personality and Social Psychology,* 1972, *24,* 285–290.

Dollard, J., Doob, L., Miller, N., Mowrer, O. H., & Sears, R. R. *Frustration and aggression.* New Haven, Conn.: Yale University Press, 1939.

Donnerstein, E., Donnerstein, M., & Koch, C. Racial discrimination in apartment rentals. *Journal of Social Psychology,* 1975, *96,* 37–38.

Doob, A. N., Carlsmith, J. M., Freedman, J. L., Landauer, T. K., & Tom, S. The effect of initial selling price on subsequent sales. *Journal of Personality and Social Psychology,* 1969, *11,* 345–350.

Dosey, M., & Meisels, M. Personal space and self protection. *Journal of Personality and Social*

Psychology, 1969, *11,* 93–97.

Duke, M. P., & Kiebach, C. A brief note on the validity of the comfortable interpersonal distance scale. *Journal of Social Psychology,* 1974, *94,* 297–298.

Duke, M. P., & Nowicki, S. A new measure and social learning model for interpersonal distance. *Journal of Experimental Research in Personality,* 1972, *6,* 119–132.

Dutton, D. G. Reactions of restauranteurs to blacks and whites violating restaurant dress regulations. *Canadian Journal of Behavioral Science,* 1971, *3,* 298–302.

Dutton, D. G., & Lake, R. A. Threat of own prejudice and reverse discrimination in interracial situations. *Journal of Personality and Social Psychology,* 1973, *28,* 94–100.

Edney, J. J. Property, possession and permanence: A field study in human territoriality. *Journal of Applied Social Psychology,* 1972, *2,* 275–282.

Edney, J. J. Human territoriality. *Psychological Bulletin,* 1974, *81,* 959–975.

Efran, M. G. The effect of physical appearance on the judgment of guilt, interpersonal attraction and severity of recommended punishment in a simulated jury task. *Journal of Research in Personality,* 1974, *8,* 45–54.

Efran, M. G., & Cheyne, J. A. Shared space: The cooperative control of spatial areas by two interacting individuals. *Canadian Journal of Behavioral Science,* 1973, *5,* 201–210.

Efran, M. G., & Cheyne, J. A. Affective concomitants of the invasion of shared space: Behavioral, physiological, and verbal indicators. *Journal of Personality and Social Psychology,* 1974, *29,* 219–226.

Ehrlich, D., Guttman, I., Schonbach, P., & Mills, J. Post-decision exposure to relevant information. *Journal of Abnormal and Social Psychology,* 1957, *54,* 98–102.

Ellis, A., & Harper, A. *Creative marriage.* New York: Stuart, 1961.

Elms, A. C. *Social psychology and social relevance.* Boston: Little Brown, 1972.

Eron, L. Relationship of TV viewing habits and aggressive behavior in children. *Journal of Abnormal and Social Psychology,* 1963, *67,* 193–196.

Eron, R. V., Huesman, L. R., Lefkowitz, M. M., & Walder, L. O. Does television violence cause aggression? *American Psychologist,* 1972, *27,* 253–263.

Evans, G. W., & Howard, R. B. Personal space. *Psychological Bulletin,* 1973, *80*(4), 334–344.

Fanon, F. [*Black skin, white masks*] (C. L. Markmann, trans.). New York: Grove Press, 1967.

Feather, N. T., & Simon, J. G. Reactions to male and female success and failure in sex-linked occupations: Impressions of personality, causal attributions, and perceived likelihood of different consequences. *Journal of Personality and Social Psychology,* 1975, *31,* 20–31.

Feldman-Summers, S., & Kiesler, S. B. Those who are number two try harder: The effect of sex on attributions of causality. *Journal of Personality and Social Psychology,* 1974, *30,* 846–855.

Felipe, N. J., & Sommer, R. Invasions of personal space. *Social Problems,* 1966, *14,* 206–214.

Fendrich, J. M. A study of the association among verbal attitudes, commitment, and overt behavior in different experimental situations. *Social Forces,* 1967, *45,* 347–355.

Feshbach, S., & Singer, R. D. *Television and aggression.* San Francisco: Jossey-Bass, 1971.

Festinger, L. *A theory of cognitive dissonance.* Stanford, Calif.: Stanford University Press, 1957.

Festinger, L. The psychological effects of insufficient rewards. *American Psychologist,* 1961, *11,* 1–11.

Festinger, L. *Conflict, decision and dissonance.* Stanford, Calif.: Stanford University Press, 1964.

Festinger, L., & Carlsmith, J. M. Cognitive consequences of forced compliance. *Journal of Abnormal and Social Psychology,* 1959, *58,* 203–210.

Festinger, L., Riecken, H., & Schachter, S. *When prophecy fails.* Minneapolis: University of Minnesota Press, 1956.

Festinger, L., Schachter, S., & Back, K. *Social pressures in informal groups: A study of human factors in housing.* New York: Harper, 1950.

Fishbein, M., & Ajzen, I. Attitudes and opinions. *Annual Review of Psychology,* 1972, *23,* 487–544.

Fishbein, M., & Ajzen, I. Attribution of responsibility: A theoretical note. *Journal of Experimental Social Psychology,* 1973, *9,* 148–153.

Fishbein, M., & Ajzen, I. *Belief, attitude, intention, and behavior: An introduction to theory and research.* Reading, Mass.: Addison-Wesley, 1975.

Flanders, J. P., & Thistlethwaite, D. L. Effects of familiarization and group discussion upon risk taking. *Journal of Personality and Social Psychology,* 1967, *5,* 91–97.

Forston, R. F., & Larson, C. U. The dynamics of space: An experimental study in proxemic behavior among Latin Americans and North Americans. *Journal of Communication,* 1968, *18,* 109–116.

Freedman, J. L., Levey, A. S., Buchanan, R. W., & Price, J. Crowding and human aggressiveness.

Journal of Experimental Social Psychology, 1972, *8,* 528–548.

Fromm, E. Man would as soon flee as fight. *Psychology Today,* 1973, *7,* 35–45.

Gaertner, S., & Bickman, L. Effects of race on the elicitation of helping behavior: The wrong number technique. *Journal of Personality and Social Psychology,* 1971, *20,* 218–222.

Geen, R. G., & Stonner, D. The meaning of observed violence: Effects on arousal and aggressive behavior. *Journal of Research in Personality,* 1974, *8,* 55–63.

Gerard, H. B., Conolley, E. S., & Wilhelmy, R. A. Compliance, justification and cognitive change. In L. Berkowitz (Ed.), *Advances in experimental social psychology* (Vol. 7). New York: Academic Press, 1974.

Gerard, H. B., & Mathewson, G. C. The effects of severity of initiation on liking for a group: A replication. *Journal of Experimental Social Psychology,* 1966, *2,* 278–287.

Gergen, K. J., Gergen, M. M., & Meter, K. Individual orientations to prosocial behavior. *Journal of Social Issues,* 1972, *28,*(3), 105–130.

Goffman, E. *Relations in public.* New York: Basic Books, 1971.

Goldstein, J. H., & Arms, R. L. Effects of observing athletic contests on hostility. *Sociometry,* 1971, *34,* 83–90.

Gouldner, A. The norm of reciprocity: A preliminary statement. *American Sociological Review,* 1960, *25,* 161–178.

Griffitt, W., Nelson, J., & Littlepage, G. Old age and response to agreement-disagreement. *Journal of Gerontology,* 1972, *27,* 269–274.

Hall, E. T. *The silent language.* Garden City, N.Y.: Doubleday, 1959.

Hall, E. T. *The hidden dimension.* Garden City, N.Y.: Doubleday, 1966

Hardyck, J., & Braden, M. Prophecy fails again: A report of a failure to replicate. *Journal of Abnormal and Social Psychology,* 1962, *65,* 136–141.

Harris, M. B. Mediators between frustration and aggression in a field experiment. *Journal of Experimental Social Psychology,* 1974, *10,* 561–571.

Hartnett, J. J., Bailey, K. G., & Gibson, F. W., Jr. Personal space as influenced by sex and type of movement. *Journal of Psychology,* 1970, *76,* 139–144.

Harvey, J. H., Harris, B., & Barnes, R. D. Actor-observer differences in the perceptions of responsibility and freedom. *Journal of Personality and Social Psychology,* 1975, *32,* 22–28.

Hastorf, A. H., Schneider, D. J., & Polefka, J. *Person perception.* Reading, Mass.: Addison-Wesley, 1970.

Heider, F. *The psychology of interpersonal relations.* New York: Wiley, 1958.

Hernton, C. C. *Sex and racism in America.* New York: Grove Press, 1965.

Hetherington, E. M., & McIntyre, C. W. Developmental psychology. In M. A. Rosenzweig & L. W. Porter (Eds.), *Annual Review of Psychology,* 1975, *26,* 97–136.

Hokanson, J. E. Psychophysiological evaluation of the catharsis hypothesis. In E. I. Megargee & J. E. Hokanson (Eds.), *The dynamics of aggression.* New York: Harper & Row, 1970.

Homans, G. C. Social behavior as exchange. *American Journal of Sociology,* 1956, *63,* 597–606.

Hornstein, H. A., Fisch, E., & Holmes, M. Influences of a model's feeling about his behavior and his relevance as a comparison other on observers' helping behavior. *Journal of Personality and Social Psychology,* 1968, *10,* 222–226.

Horowitz, I. A. The effect of group norms on bystander intervention. *Journal of Social Psychology,* 1971, *83,* 265–273.

Horowitz, M., Duff, D., & Stratton, L. The body buffer zone: An exploration of personal space. *Archives of General Psychiatry,* 1964, *11,* 651–656.

Huston, T. L. *Foundations of interpersonal attraction.* New York: Academic Press, 1974.

Insko, C. A. *Theories of attitude change.* New York: Appleton-Century-Crofts, 1967.

Isen, A. M. Success, failure, attention and reaction to others. *Journal of Personality and Social Psychology,* 1970, *15,* 294–301.

Isen, A. M., & Levin, P. F. The effect of feeling good on helping: Cookies and kindness. *Journal of Personality and Social Psychology,* 1972, *21,* 384–388.

Jellison, J. M., & Riskind, J. A social comparison of abilities interpretation of risk-taking behavior. *Journal of Personality and Social Psychology,* 1970, *15,* 375–390.

Johnson, D. A., Porter, R. J., & Mateljan, P. L. Racial discrimination in apartment rentals. *Journal of Applied Social Psychology,* 1971, *1*(4), 364–377.

Johnson, D. L., & Andrews, R. C. Risky shift phenomenon tested with consumer products as stimuli. *Journal of Personality and Social Psychology,* 1971, *20,* 382–385.

Jones, E. E., & Davis, K. E. From acts to dispositions: The attribution process in person perception. In L. Berkowitz (Ed.), *Advances in experimental social psychology* (Vol. 2). New York: Academic Press, 1965.

Jones, E. E., & Nisbett, R. E. *The actor and the observer: Divergent perceptions of the causes of behavior.* Morristown, N.J.: General Learning

Press, 1971.

Jones, J. M. *Prejudice and racism.* Reading, Mass.: Addison-Wesley, 1972.

Jones, S. A. A comparative proxemic analysis of dyadic interaction in selected subcultures in New York City. *Journal of Social Psychology,* 1971, *84,* 35–44.

Kahan, J. P. A subjective probability interpretation of the risky-shift. *Journal of Personality and Social Psychology,* 1975, *31,* 977–982.

Kaplan, A. *The conduct of inquiry: Methodology for behavioral science.* San Francisco: Chandler, 1964.

Katz, I. Experimental studies of Negro-white relationships. In L. Berkowitz (Ed.), *Advances in experimental social psychology* (Vol. 5). New York: Academic Press, 1970.

Katz, P. A. *Towards the elimination of racism.* Elmsford, N.Y.: Pergamon, 1975.

Kaufmann, H. *Aggression and altruism.* New York: Holt, Rinehart & Winston, 1970.

Kelley, H. H. Attribution theory in social psychology. In D. Levine (Ed.), *Nebraska Symposium on Motivation* (Vol. 15). Lincoln: University of Nebraska Press, 1967.

Kelley, H. H. *Attribution in social interaction.* Morristown, N.J.: General Learning Press, 1971.

Kelley, H. H. The processes of causal attribution. *American Psychologist,* 1973, *28,* 107–128.

Kelman, H. C. Attitude change as a function of response restriction. *Human Relations,* 1953, *6,* 186–214.

Kelman, H. C. Human use of human subjects: The phenomenon of deception in social psychological experiments. *Psychological Bulletin,* 1967, *67,* 1–11.

Kelman, H. C. Attitudes are alive and well and gainfully employed in the sphere of action. *American Psychologist,* 1974, *29,* 310–324.

Kerckhoff, A. C., & Davis, K. E. Value consensus and need complementarity in mate selection. *American Sociological Review,* 1962, *27,* 295–303.

Kiesler, C. A., Collins, B. E., & Miller, N. *Attitude change: A critical analysis of theoretical approaches.* New York: Wiley, 1969.

Kiesler, C. A., & Goldberg, G. N. Multidimensional approach to the experimental study of interpersonal attraction: Effect of a blunder on the attractiveness of a competent other. *Psychological Reports,* 1968, *22,* 693–705.

Kiesler, C. A., & Munson, P. A. Attitudes and opinions. *Annual Review of Psychology,* 1975, *26,* 415–456.

King, B., & Janis, I. Comparison of the effectiveness of improvised vs. non-improvised role-playing in producing opinion changes. *Human Relations,* 1956, *9,* 177–186.

Kleck, R. The effects of interpersonal affect on errors made when constructing a stimulus display. *Psychonomic Science,* 1967, *9,* 449–450.

Kleck, R. Effects of stigmatizing conditions on use of personal space. *Psychological Reports,* 1968, *23,* 111–118.

Knowles, E. S., & Johnsen, P. K. Intrapersonal consistency in interpersonal distance. *JSAS Catalog of Selected Documents in Psychology,* 1974, *4,* 124. (Ms. No. 768)

Knox, R. E., & Inkster, J. A. Postdecision dissonance at post time. *Journal of Personality and Social Psychology,* 1968, *8,* 319–323.

Kogan, N., & Wallach, M. A. *Risk taking: A study in cognition and personality.* New York: Holt, Rinehart & Winston, 1964.

Kogan, N., & Wallach, M. A. The risky-shift phenomenon in small decision-making groups: A test of the information-exchange hypothesis. *Journal of Experimental Social Psychology,* 1967, *3,* 75–85.

Kovel, J. *White racism: A psychohistory.* New York: Pantheon, 1970.

Kuethe, J. L. Social schemas. *Journal of Abnormal and Social Psychology,* 1962, *64,* 31–36.

Kuethe, J. L. Pervasive influence of social schemata. *Journal of Abnormal and Social Psychology,* 1964, *68*(3), 248–254.

Kusyszyn, I., & Bettridge, L. No postdecision dissonance at post time. *Proceedings of the 81st Annual Convention of the American Psychological Association,* 1973, *8,* 273–274.

Kutner, B., Wilkins, C., & Yarrow, P. R. Verbal attitudes and overt behavior involving racial prejudice. *Journal of Abnormal and Social Psychology,* 1952, *47,* 649–652.

Langer, E. J., & Abelson, R. P. The semantics of asking a favor: How to succeed in getting helping without really dying. *Journal of Personality and Social Psychology,* 1972, *24*(1), 26–32.

Lanzetta, J. T., & Hannah, T. E. Reinforcing behavior of "naive" trainers. *Journal of Personality and Social Psychology,* 1969, *11,* 243–252.

LaPiere, R. T. Attitudes vs. actions. *Social Forces,* 1934, *13,* 230–237.

Latané, B., & Dabbs, J. *Sex and helping in Columbus, Seattle, and Atlanta.* Paper presented at the meeting of the American Psychological Association, Honolulu, August 1972.

Latané, B., & Darley, J. *The unresponsive bystander: Why doesn't he help?* New York: Appleton-Century-Crofts, 1970.

Latané, B., & Rodin, J. A lady in distress: Inhibiting effects of friends and strangers on bystander intervention. *Journal of Experimental Social Psychology,* 1969, *5,* 189–202.

Laumann, E. O. Friends of urban men: An

assessment of accuracy in reporting their socio-economic attributes, mutual choice and attitude agreement. *Sociometry,* 1969, *32,* 54–69.

Leab, D. J. *From Sambo to Superspade: The black experience in motion pictures.* Boston: Houghton Mifflin, 1975.

Lerner, M. The desire for justice and reactions to victims. In J. Macaulay and L. Berkowitz (Eds.), *Altruism and helping behavior: Social psychological studies of some antecedents and consequences.* New York: Academic Press, 1970. Pp. 205–229.

Lerner, R. M., & Frank, P. Relation of race and sex to supermarket helping behavior. *Journal of Social Psychology,* 1974, *94,* 201–203.

Levinger, G. Little sand box and big quarry: Comments on Byrne's paradigmatic spade for research on interpersonal attraction. *Representative Research in Social Psychology,* 1972, *3,* 3–19.

Levinger, G., & Breedlove, J. Interpersonal attraction and agreement: A study of marriage partners. *Journal of Personality and Social Psychology,* 1966, *3,* 367–372.

Levinger, G., & Gunner, J. The interpersonal grid: I. Felt and tape technique for measurement of social behavior. *Psychonomic Science,* 1967, *8,* 173–174.

Levinger, G., & Schneider, D. J. Test of the "risk is a value" hypothesis. *Journal of Personality and Social Psychology,* 1969, *11,* 165–169.

Levinger, G., & Snoek, J. D. *Attraction in relationship: A new look at interpersonal attraction.* Morristown, N.J.: General Learning Press, 1972.

Leyens, J. P., Camino, L., Parke, R. D., & Berkowitz, L. Effects of movie violence on aggression in a field setting as a function of group dominance and cohesion. *Journal of Personality and Social Psychology,* 1975, *32,* 346–360.

Lieberson, S., & Silverman, A. R. The precipitants and underlying conditions of race riots. *American Sociological Review,* 1965, *30,* 887–898.

Likert, R. A technique for the measurement of attitudes. *Archives of Psychology,* 1932 (Whole No. 140).

Linder, D. E. *Personal space.* Morristown, N.J.: General Learning Press, 1974.

Linn, L. S. Verbal attitudes and overt behavior: A study of racial discrimination. *Social Forces,* 1965, *44,* 353–364.

Liska, A. Attitude-behavior consistency as a function of generality equivalence between attitude and behavior objects. *Journal of Psychology,* 1974, *86,* 217–228.

Little, K. B. Personal space. *Journal of Experimental Social Psychology,* 1965, *1,* 237–247.

Little, K. B. Cultural variations in social schemata. *Journal of Personality and Social Psychology,* 1968, *10*(1), 1–7.

London, P. The rescuers: Motivational hypotheses about Christians who saved Jews from the Nazis. In J. Macaulay and L. Berkowitz (Eds.), *Altruism and helping behavior: Social psychological studies of some antecedents and consequences.* New York: Academic Press, 1970. Pp. 241–250.

Lorenz, K. *On aggression.* New York: Bantam Books, 1966.

Lott, A. J., & Lott, B. E. Group cohesiveness as interpersonal attraction: A review of relationships with antecedent and consequent variables. *Psychological Bulletin,* 1965, *64*(4), 259–309.

Lott, D. F., & Sommer, R. Seating arrangements and status. *Journal of Personality and Social Psychology,* 1967, *7,* 90–95.

Lovaas, O. Effect of exposure to symbolic aggression on aggressive behavior. *Child Development,* 1961, *32,* 37–44.

Madaras, G. R., & Bem, D. J. Risk and conservatism in group decision-making. *Journal of Experimental Social Psychology,* 1968, *4,* 350–365.

Malamuth, N. M., & Feshbach, S. Risky shift in a naturalistic setting. *Journal of Personality,* 1972, *40,* 38–49.

McCauley, C., Kogan, N., & Teger, A. I. Order effects in answering risk dilemmas for self and others. *Journal of Personality and Social Psychology,* 1971, *20,* 423–424.

McCauley, C., & Stitt, C. L. Reply to Abelson's comment on "Group shift to caution at the race track." *Journal of Experimental Social Psychology,* 1973, *9,* 522–525.

McCauley, C., Stitt, C. L., Woods, K., & Lipton, D. Group shift to caution at the race track. *Journal of Experimental Social Psychology,* 1973, *9,* 80–86.

McGee, M. G., & Snyder, M. Attribution and behavior: Two field studies. *Journal of Personality and Social Psychology,* 1975, *32,* 185–190.

McGrew, J. M. How open are multiple dwelling units. *Journal of Social Psychology,* 1967, *72,* 223–226.

McGrew, P. L., & McGrew, W. C. Interpersonal spacing behavior of preschool children during group formation. *Man-Environment Systems,* 1975, *5*(1), 43–48.

McGuire, W. J. Attitudes and opinions. *Annual Review of Psychology,* 1966, *17,* 475–514.

McGuire, W. J. Some impending reorientations in social psychology: Some thoughts provoked by Kenneth Ring. *Journal of Experimental Social Psychology,* 1967, *3,* 124–139.

McGuire, W. J. The nature of attitudes and

attitude change. In G. Lindzey & E. Aronson (Eds.), *Handbook of social psychology.* Reading, Mass.: Addison-Wesley, 1968.

Medway, F. J., & Lowe, C. A. Effects of outcome valence and severity on attribution of responsibility. *Psychological Reports,* 1975, *36,* 239–246.

Mehrabian, A. Relationship of attitude to seated posture, orientation and distance. *Journal of Personality and Social Psychology,* 1968, *10,* 26–30.

Metee, D. R., & Wilkins, P. C. When similarity "hurts": Effects of perceived ability and a humorous blunder on interpersonal attractiveness. *Journal of Personality and Social Psychology,* 1972, *22,* 246–258.

Mezei, L. Perceived social pressure as an explanation of shifts in the relative influence of race and belief on prejudice across social interactions. *Journal of Personality and Social Psychology,* 1971, *19,* 69–81.

Milgram, S. Behavioral study of obedience. *Journal of Abnormal and Social Psychology,* 1963, *67,* 371–378.

Miller, D. T., & Norman, S. A. Actor-observer differences in perceptions of effective control. *Journal of Personality and Social Psychology,* 1975, *31,* 503–515.

Miller, N. E. The frustration-aggression hypothesis. *Psychological Review,* 1941, *48,* 337–342.

Morgan, W. G. Situational specificity in altruistic behavior. *Representative Research in Social Psychology,* 1973, *4,* 56–66.

Moriarty, T. Crime, commitment, and the responsive bystander: Two field experiments. *Journal of Personality and Social Psychology,* 1975, *31*(2), 370–376.

Morris, D. *The naked ape.* New York: McGraw-Hill, 1968.

Mosher, D. L., & Scodel, A. A study of the relationship between ethnocentrism in children and the ethnocentrism and authoritarian rearing practices of their mothers. *Child Development,* 1960, *31,* 369–376.

Moyer, K. E. *The physiology of hostility.* Chicago: Markham, 1971.

Murstein, B. (Ed.). *Theories of attraction and love.* New York: Springer, 1971.

Myers, D. G., & Lamm, H. The polarizing effect of group discussion. *American Scientist,* May-June 1975, *63,* 297–303.

Nelson, S. Nature/nurture revisited I: A review of the biological bases of conflict. *Journal of Conflict Resolution,* 1974, *18*(2), 285–335.

Newcomb, T. M. *Personality and social change: Attitude formation in a student community.* New York: Holt, Rinehart & Winston, 1943.

Newcomb, T. M. *The acquaintance process.* New York: Holt, Rinehart & Winston, 1961.

Nisbett, R. E., & Caputo, G. C. *Personality traits: Why other people do the things they do.* Unpublished manuscript. Yale University, 1971.

Nisbett, R. E., Caputo, G. C., Legant, P., & Marecek, J. Behavior as seen by the actor and as seen by the observer. *Journal of Personality and Social Psychology,* 1973, *27,* 154–164.

Orne, M. T. Demand characteristics and the concept of quasi-controls. In R. Rosenthal and R. L. Rosnow (Eds.), *Artifact in behavioral research.* New York: Academic Press, 1969. Pp. 143–179.

Oshikawa, S. Can cognitive dissonance explain consumer behavior? *Journal of Marketing,* 1969, *33,* 44–49.

Oshikawa, S. Dissonance reduction or artifact. *Journal of Marketing Research,* 1971, *8,* 514–517.

Page, M. M., & Scheidt, R. J. The elusive weapons effect: Demand awareness, evaluation apprehension, and slightly sophisticated subjects. *Journal of Personality and Social Psychology,* 1971, *20*(3), 304–318.

Patterson, G., Littman, R., & Bricker, W. Assertive behavior in children: A step toward a theory of aggression. *Monographs of the Society for Research in Child Development,* 1967, *32* (5, Serial No. 113).

Patterson, M. L. Compensation in nonverbal immediacy behaviors: A review. *Sociometry,* 1973, *36,* 237–252.

Pettigrew, T. F. Personality and sociocultural factors in intergroup attitudes: A cross-national comparison. *Journal of Conflict Resolution,* 1958, *2,* 29–42.

Pettigrew, T. F. Regional differences in anti-Negro prejudice. *Journal of Abnormal and Social Psychology,* 1959, *59,* 28–36.

Phares, E. J., & Wilson, K. G. Responsibility attribution: Role of outcome severity, situational ambiguity and internal-external control. *Journal of Personality,* 1972, *40,* 392–406.

Piliavin, I. M., Rodin, J., & Piliavin, J. A. Good samaritanism: An underground phenomenon? *Journal of Personality and Social Psychology,* 1969, *13,* 289–299.

Polit, D., & LaFrance, M. Sex differences in reaction to spatial invasion. *Journal of Social Psychology,* in press.

Pruitt, D. G. Choice shifts in group discussion: An introductory review. *Journal of Personality and Social Psychology,* 1971, *20,* 339–360.

Pruitt, D. G., & Teger, A. I. The risky shift in group betting. *Journal of Experimental Social Psychology,* 1969, *5,* 115–126.

Reik, T. *A psychologist looks at love.* New York:

Farrar & Rinehart, 1944.

Reingen, P. H. Risk taking by individuals and informal groups with the use of industrial product purchasing situations as stimuli. *The Journal of Psychology*, 1973, *85*, 339–345.

Ring, K. Experimental social psychology: Some sober questions about frivolous values. *Journal of Experimental Social Psychology*, 1967, *3*, 113–123.

Rokeach, M. Belief versus race as determinants of social distance. *Journal of Abnormal and Social Psychology*, 1961, *62*, 187–188.

Rokeach, M., Smith, P. W., & Evans, R. I. Two kinds of prejudice or one? In M. Rokeach (Ed.), *The open and closed mind*. New York: Basic Books, 1960.

Rosenberg, M. J. When dissonance fails: On eliminating evaluation apprehension from attitude measurement. *Journal of Personality and Social Psychology*, 1965, *1*, 28–42.

Rosenfeld, H. M. Effect of an approval-seeking induction on interpersonal proximity. *Psychological Reports*, 1965, *17*, 120–122.

Rosenthal, A. *Thirty-eight witnesses*. New York: McGraw-Hill, 1964.

Rosenthal, R. *Experimenter effects in behavioral research*. New York: Appleton-Century-Crofts, 1966.

Rosenthal, R., & Rosnow, R. L. (Eds.). *Artifact in behavioral research*. New York: Academic Press, 1969.

Ross, A. E. Effect of increased responsibility on bystander intervention: The presence of children. *Journal of Personality and Social Psychology*, 1971, *19*, 306–310.

Rotter, J. B. Generalized expectancies for internal versus external control of reinforcement. *Psychology Monographs*, 1966, *80*(1, Whole No. 609).

Rotter, J. B. An introduction to social learning theory. In J. B. Rotter, J. E. Chance, & E. J. Phares (Eds.), *Applications of a social learning theory of personality*. New York: Holt, Rinehart & Winston, 1972.

Rozelle, R. M., & Baxter, J. C. Impression formation and danger recognition in experienced police officers. *Journal of Social Psychology*, 1975, *96*, 53–63.

Rozelle, R. M., & Campbell, D. T. More plausible rival hypotheses in the cross-lagged panel correlation technique. *Psychological Bulletin*, 1969, *71*(1), 74–80.

Rubin, Z. Measurement of romantic love. *Journal of Personality and Social Psychology*, 1970, *16*, 265–273.

Rubin, Z. From liking to loving: Patterns of attraction in dating relationships. In T. L. Huston (Ed.), *Foundations of interpersonal attraction*. New York: Academic Press, 1974. (a)

Rubin, Z. Lovers and other strangers: The development of intimacy in encounters and relationships. *American Scientist*, 1974, *62*, 182–190. (b)

Rudestam, K. E., Richards, D. L., & Garrison, P. Effect of self-esteem on an unobtrusive measure of altruism. *Psychological Reports*, 1971, *29*, 847–851.

Ryan, W. *Blaming the victim*. New York: Vintage Books, 1971.

Rychlak, J. The similarity, compatibility or incompatibility of needs in interpersonal selection. *Journal of Personality and Social Psychology*, 1965, *2*, 334–340.

Schachter, S. Deviation, rejection, and communication. *Journal of Abnormal and Social Psychology*, 1951, *46*, 190–207.

Schachter, S. The interaction of cognitive and physiological determinants of emotional state. In L. Berkowitz (Ed.), *Advances in experimental social psychology* (Vol. 1). New York: Academic Press, 1964.

Schaps, E. Cost, dependency and helping. *Journal of Personality and Social Psychology*, 1972, *21*, 74–78.

Sears, D. O., & Abeles, R. Attitudes and opinions. *Annual Review of Psychology*, 1969, *20*, 253–288.

Sechrest, L. Nonreactive assessment of attitudes. In E. P. Willems & H. L. Raush (Eds.), *Naturalistic viewpoints in psychological research*. New York: Holt, Rinehart & Winston, 1969.

Semin, G. R., & Glendon, A. I. Polarization and the established group. *British Journal of Social and Clinical Psychology*, 1973, *12*, 113–121.

Severy, L. J., & Davis, K. E. Helping behavior among normal and retarded children. *Child Development*, 1971, *42*, 1017–1031.

Shaver, K. G. Defensive attribution: Effects of severity and relevance on the responsibility assigned for an accident. *Journal of Personality and Social Psychology*, 1970, *14*, 101–113.

Shaver, K. G. *An introduction to attribution processes*. Cambridge, Mass.: Winthrop, 1975.

Shaw, J. I., & Skolnick, P. Attribution of responsibility for a happy accident. *Journal of Personality and Social Psychology*, 1971, *18*, 380–383.

Sherif, M., Harvey, O. J., White, B. J., Hood, W., & Sherif, C. W. *Intergroup conflict and cooperation: The Robber's Cave experiment*. Norman, Okla.: University of Oklahoma Book Exchange, 1961.

Sigall, H., & Ostrove, N. Beautiful but dangerous: Effects of offender attractiveness and nature of the crime on juridic judgment. *Journal of Personality and Social Psychology*, 1975, *31*, 410–414.

Silverman, B. I. Consequences, racial discrimination, and the principle of belief congruence. *Journal of Personality and Social Psychology*, 1974, *29*, 497–508.

Silverman, B. I., & Cochrane, R. The relationship between verbal expressions of behavioral intention and overt behavior. *Journal of Social Psychology*, 1971, *84*, 51–56.

Silverman, I. In defense of dissonance theory: Reply to Chapanis and Chapanis. *Psychological Bulletin*, 1964, *62*, 205–209.

Sommer, R. *Personal space: The behavioral basis of design.* Englewood Cliffs, N.J.: Prentice Hall, 1969.

Sommer, R., & Becker, F. D. Territorial defense and the good neighbor. *Journal of Personality and Social Psychology*, 1969, *11*(2), 85–92.

Staub, E. A child in distress: The influence of age and number on children's attempts to help. *Journal of Personality and Social Psychology*, 1970, *14*, 130–140.

Staub, E. Helping a person in distress: The influence of implicit and explicit "rules" of conduct on children and adults. *Journal of Personality and Social Psychology*, 1971, *17*, 137–144.

Staub, E. Instigation to goodness: The role of social norms and interpersonal influence. *Journal of Social Issues,* 1972, *28*(3), 131–150.

Staub, E. Helping a distressed person. In L. Berkowitz (Ed.), *Advances in experimental social psychology* (Vol. 7). New York: Academic Press, 1974. Pp. 293–341.

Staub, E., & Sherk, L. Need for approval, children's sharing behavior and reciprocity in sharing. *Child Development*, 1970, *41*, 243–252.

Stein, D. D. The influence of belief systems on interpersonal preference: A validation study of Rokeach's theory of prejudice. *Psychological Monographs*, 1966, (*8*, Whole No. 616).

Stoner, J. A. F. *A comparison of individual and group decisions involving risk.* Unpublished master's thesis, Massachusetts Institute of Technology, 1961.

Storms, M. D. Videotape and attribution process: Reversing actors' and observers' points of view. *Journal of Personality and Social Psychology*, 1973, *27*, 165–175.

Stricker, L. J., Messick, S., & Jackson, D. N. Evaluating deception in psychological research. *Psychological Bulletin*, 1969, *71*, 343–351.

Suedfeld, P. (Ed.). *Attitude change: The competing views.* Chicago: Aldine-Atherton, 1971.

Taylor, S. E. Some frameworks to bridge cognitive and social psychology: Discussion. In J. S. Carroll & J. W. Payne (Eds.), *Cognition and social behavior.* Hillsdale, N.J.: Lawrence Erlbaum Associates, 1976. (Distributed by the Halsted Division of John Wiley & Sons.)

Taylor, S. E., & Koivumaki, J. M. The perception of self and others: Acquaintance affect and actor-observer differences. *Journal of Personality and Social Psychology*, 1976, *33*, 403–408.

Taylor, S. P., & Epstein, S. Aggression as a function of the interaction of the sex of the aggressor and the sex of the victim. *Journal of Personality*, 1967, *35*, 474–486.

Tedeschi, J. T., Smith, R. B., & Brown, R. C. A reinterpretation of research on aggression. *Psychological Bulletin*, 1974, *81*(9), 540–562.

Thibaut, J. W., & Kelley, H. A. *The social psychology of groups.* New York: Wiley & Sons, 1959.

Thurstone, L. L. *The measurement of social attitudes.* Chicago: University of Chicago Press, 1931.

Tiger, L. *Men in groups.* New York: Random House, 1969.

Toman, W. The duplication theorem of social relationships as tested in the general population. *Psychological Bulletin*, 1971, *78*, 380–390.

Triandis, H. C. A note on Rokeach's theory of prejudice. *Journal of Abnormal and Social Psychology*, 1961, *62*, 184–186.

Triandis, H. C. *Attitude and attitude change.* New York: Wiley, 1971.

Turner, C. W., & Berkowitz, L. Identification with film aggressor (covert role taking) and reactions to film violence. *Journal of Personality and Social Psychology*, 1972, *21*, 256–264.

Turner, C. W., Layton, J. F., & Simons, L. S. Naturalistic studies of aggressive behavior: Aggressive stimuli, victim visibility, and horn honking. *Journal of Personality and Social Psychology*, 1975, *31*(6), 1098–1107.

Turner, C. W., & Simons, L. S. Effects of subject sophistication and evaluation apprehension on aggressive responses to weapons. *Journal of Personality and Social Psychology*, 1974, *30*(3), 341–348.

Uranowitz, S. W. Helping and self attributions: A field experiment. *Journal of Personality and Social Psychology*, 1975, *31*, 852–854.

Vidmar, N. Group composition and the risky shift. *Journal of Experimental Social Psychology*, 1970, *6*, 153–166.

Vidmar, N., & Crinklaw, L. D. Attributing responsibility for an accident: A methodological and conceptual critique. *Canadian Journal of Behavioral Science*, 1974, *6*, 112–130.

Vinokur, A. Distribution of initial risk levels and group decisions involving risk. *Journal of Personality and Social Psychology*, 1969, *13*, 207–214.

Vinokur, A. A review and theoretical analysis of

the effects of group processes upon individual and group decisions involving risk. *Psychological Bulletin,* 1971, *76,* 231–250.

Walker, D. N., & Mosher, D. L. Altruism in college women. *Psychological Reports,* 1970, *27,* 887–894.

Walker, T. G., & Main, E. C. Choice shifts in political decision-making: Federal judges and civil liberties cases. *Journal of Applied Social Psychology,* 1973, *2,* 39–48.

Wallach, M. A., Kogan, N., & Bem, D. J. Group influences on individual risk taking. *Journal of Abnormal and Social Psychology,* 1962, *65,* 75–86.

Wallach, M. A., Kogan, N., & Bem, D. J. Diffusion of responsibility and level of risk taking in groups. *Journal of Abnormal and Social Psychology,* 1964, *68,* 263–274.

Walster, E. Attribution of responsibility for an accident. *Journal of Personality and Social Psychology,* 1966, *3,* 73–79.

Walster, E. "Second guessing" important events. *Human Relations,* 1967, *20,* 239–250.

Walster, E., Aronson, V., Abrahams, D., & Rottman, L. Importance of physical attractiveness in dating behavior. *Journal of Personality and Social Psychology,* 1966, *5,* 508–516.

Walster, E., & Berscheid, E. Adrenaline makes the heart grow fonder. *Psychology Today,* 1971, *5,* 47–62.

Walster, E., Walster, G., Piliavin, I., & Schmidt, L. "Playing hard-to-get": Understanding an elusive phenomenon. *Journal of Personality and Social Psychology,* 1973, *26*(1), 113–121.

Warner, L. G., & DeFleur, M. L. Attitude as an interactional concept: Social constraint and social distance as intervening variables between attitudes and action. *American Sociological Review,* 1969, *34,* 153–169.

Watkins, T. A., & Johnson, H. H. *The effect of the Chapanis and Chapanis criticism on cognitive dissonance research.* Paper presented at the meeting of the Midwestern Psychological Association, Cleveland, May 1972.

Watson, O. M. *Proxemic behavior: A cross-cultural study.* The Hague: Mouton, 1970.

Watson, O. M., & Graves, T. D. Quantitative research in proxemic behavior. *American Anthropologist,* 1966, *68,* 971–985.

Webb, E. J., Campbell, D. T., Schwartz, R. D., & Sechrest, L. *Unobtrusive measures: Nonreactive research in the social sciences.* Chicago: Rand McNally, 1966.

Weiner, B. New conceptions in the study of achievement motivation. In B. A. Maher (Ed.), *Progress in experimental personality research* (Vol. 5). New York: Academic Press, 1970.

Weiner, B., Frieze, I., Kukla, A., Reed, L., Rest, S., & Rosenbaum, R. M. *Perceiving the causes of success and failure.* Morristown, N.J.: General Learning Press, 1971.

Weitz, S. Attitude, voice and behavior: A repressed affect model of interracial interaction. *Journal of Personality and Social Psychology,* 1972, *24*(1), 14–21.

West, S. G., Gunn, S. P., & Chernicky, P. Ubiquitous Watergate: An attributional analysis. *Journal of Personality and Social Psychology,* 1975, *32,* 55–65.

Wheeler, L., & Wagner, C. M. *The connotation of generosity.* Paper presented at the meeting of the Eastern Psychological Association, Washington, D. C. April 1968.

White, M. J. Interpersonal distance as affected by room size, status, and sex. *Journal of Social Psychology,* 1975, *95,* 241–249.

Wicker, A. W. Attitudes versus actions: The relationship of verbal and overt behavioral responses to attitude objects. *Journal of Social Issues,* 1969, *25,* 41–78.

Willis, F. N., Jr. Initial speaking distance as a function of the speaker's relationship. *Psychonomic Science,* 1966, *5*(6), 221–222.

Winch, R. F. *The modern family.* New York: Holt, 1952.

Winch, R. F. *Mate-selection: A study of complementary needs.* New York: Harper, 1958.

Wispé, L., & Freshley, H. Race, sex and sympathetic helping behavior: The broken bag caper. *Journal of Personality and Social Psychology,* 1971, *17,* 59–64.

Wolosin, M. A., Wolosin, R. J., & Zajonc, R. B. Individual and group risk-taking in a two-choice situation. *Journal of Experimental Social Psychology,* 1968, *4,* 89–106.

Wolosin, M. A., Wolosin, R. J., & Zajonc, R. B. Group risk-taking in a two-choice situation: Replication, extension, and a model. *Journal of Experimental Social Psychology,* 1969, *5,* 127–140.

Woodmansee, J., & Cook, S. W. Dimensions of verbal racial attitudes: Their identification and measurement. *Journal of Personality and Social Psychology,* 1967, *7,* 240–250.

Yakimovich, D., & Saltz, E. Helping behavior: The cry for help. *Psychonomic Science,* 1971, *23*(6), 427–428.

Yinon, Y., Shoham, V., & Lewis, T. Risky shift in a real vs. role-played situation. *Journal of Social Psychology,* 1974, *93,* 137–138.

Zimbardo, P. G. The effect of effort and improvisation on self-persuasion produced by role playing. *Journal of Experimental Social Psychology,* 1965, *1,* 103–120.

INDEX

Acquaintance process (Newcomb), 31
Actor-observer differences (*see* Attribution)
Aggregation index, 273
Aggression, 123–155
   Aggression Machine (Buss), 130
   antisocial behavior, 134
   Berkowitz Paradigm, 130–131
   in children:
      effects of filmed aggression, 127
      effects of television, 132, 134–136
      naturalistic observation, 133
      social-learning approach, 133
   cross-species generalization, 125–126
   cues, role of, 128
      Berkowitz on, 137 ff.
      Turner et al. on, 143 ff.
   deception in research, 129–131, 153
   ethical problems in research, 129–130, 156
   explanations of, 124–128
      ethological, 124–125
      frustration-aggression, 126
      social-learning, 127–128, 133
   filmed:
      effects on adults, 129
      effects on children, 127
   identification processes in, 128–129
   instincts, 61, 124–125
   learned versus performed, 128
   models (for adults), 128
   race riots, 132–133
   reduced through sports, 125–126
   research methods, 129–136
   sex differences, 155
   weapons effect:
      Berkowitz on, 137 ff.
      reversal of, 154–156
      Turner et al. on, 143 ff.
Altruism (*see* Prosocial behavior)
Ambiguity in emergencies, 90–92
Antecedent conditions, manipulation of, 12, 298
Antisocial behavior (*see* Aggression)
Approval seeking, in interpersonal spacing, 64

Archival search:
   in aggression, 132–133
   in attraction, 30–31
   in prejudice and racism, 272–274
Arousal, in attraction, 22–23
Attitude:
   as basis for attraction, 21
   similarity of, and attraction, 25–26, 31, 32
      among friends, 31
      Byrne et al. on, 43–44
Attitude-behavior discrepancy, 266–268
      (*see also* Prejudice and racism)
Attitude change (*see* Cognitive dissonance)
Attraction, 19–55
   arousal level, 22–23
   attractiveness, 24–25, 32
      Byrne et al. on, 43–44, 46–49
   birth order, 26–27
   blunders, effects of, 25
   cognitive processes in, 21–22
   comparison level, 21
   cultural background, 30–31
   determinants of, 23–27
      competence, 25
      complementarity, 26–27
      physical attractiveness, 24–25, 32
      proximity, 23
      self-disclosure, 29
      similarity, 25–26, 32
   durability of findings, 55
   evaluation of others, 23
   explanations of, 21–22
      arousal theory, 22–23
      exchange models, 21
      labeling theory, 22–23
      reinforcement theories, 21–22
      reward theory, 21
      similarity, 21
   liking:
      and interpersonal distance, 59
      and loving, 23, 32
   love (*see also* Love Scale)
      as attitude, 33
      components of (Rubin), 23

Attraction (continued)
    and gaze, 32 ff., 37–40
    and liking, 23, 32
        Rubin's definition, 33
  proximity as a measure of, 47–48
  research methods, 27–31
  similarity in, 25–26, 32
    Byrne et al. on, 43–44
Attractiveness, physical:
  and attraction, 24–25, 32
    Byrne et al. on, 43–44, 46–49
  of victims, 92
Attribution: 189–229
  actor-observer differences, 197–203, 229
    information and processing, 193–194
    Jones and Nisbett on, 215–216
    roles, 197–198
    Storms on, 211–212
    visual orientation, 204–205
  cost-quality of research, 228–229
  environmental forces (Heider), 192–193
  flashy merchandising in, 229
  generality, 193–195
  hedonic relevance, 193
  in institutional racism, 264
  internal versus external causes, 189–190
  measurement difficulties, 228
  models of, 192–195
  as person perception, 191
  personal forces (Heider), 192–193
  research methods, 198–202
  of responsibility, 196–197
    in ambiguous situations, 90–92
  subject awareness, 199
  success and failure, 195–196
    ability, 195
    effort, 195–196
    luck, 196
    task difficulty, 196
  therapy, application to, 212–214
  videotape and the attribution process (Storms), 204–214

Belief congruence, in prejudice, 265–266
Berkowitz Paradigm, 130–131
Birth order, 26–27
Blaming the victim, 264
Blunders, in attraction process, 25
Bystander effect, 80, 120–121 (see also Prosocial behavior)

Choice-Dilemma Questionnaire (Kogan & Wallach), 159–160
Claim (Goffman), 62
Cognitive dissonance, 231–260
  criticism of the theory, 237–240
    effort expended, 237

Cognitive dissonance (continued)
    expectancy effects in studies, 241
    forced compliance, 235
    interpretation problems, 238–239, 258–259
    operational definitions, 256–257
    postdecision dissonance, 241, 243
  reduction of, 234–235
  research, 235–237
  research methods, 240–243
  theoretical explanations, 235
  theory of, 233–234
Cognitive processes:
  in ambiguous situations, 90–92
  in attraction, 21
  in prejudice, 264
  in prosocial behavior, 90–92
Comfortable Interpersonal Distance Scale (Duke & Nowicki), 67
Comparison level in attraction, 21
Compensation, in interpersonal distancing, 62
Competence, in attraction, 25
Competition (Sherif study), 263
Complementarity, in attraction, 26–27
Conflict, group, 263
Conformity, in prejudice, 264–265
Control, locus of (Rotter), 63
Cost-quality relation of research, 5–6, 85, 228–229, 293–294
Critique of research, value of, 17–18, 297–298
Cross-lag correlation, 135–136
Cross-species comparisons, 61–62, 125
  in aggression research, 125
  in interpersonal distancing, 61–62
Crowding, 58
Cultural background, in attraction, 30–31
Cultural differences:
  in interpersonal distancing, 60–61, 67 ff., 76–82
  in social schemata, 69–76
  studied with foreign students, 85

Deception:
  in aggression studies, 129–131, 153
  ethical problems, 119–120
    in aggression research, 129–131, 156
    in attribution research, 228–229
    in prosocial-behavior studies, 119–120
    West on, 223–224
  justification question, 156
  methodological problems, 119–120
Decision making, group (see Risky shift)
Demand characteristics, 9
  in aggression studies, 154
  in Baxter and Little studies, 83–84

Density, 58
Design problems:
  in attribution study, 226–227
  in dissonance study, 257–258
Diffusion of responsibility, 90
  Darley and Latané on, 100–101
  in group decisions, 161
Discrimination, 262 (*see* Prejudice and racism)
Dissonance (*see* Cognitive dissonance)
Distancing (*see* Interpersonal distancing)
Durability of research findings:
  in attraction, 55
  in dissonance, 259
  in interpersonal distancing, 85
  in prejudice and racism, 296
  in prosocial behavior, 120–121
  in risky shift, 187

Egocentric territory (Goffman), 62
Environmental forces (Heider), 192–193
Epistemology, psychological, 191
Equal interval scale, 271–272
Ethics, in social-psychological research, 129–131, 156, 228–229
  West et al. on, 223–224
Ethological approach:
  to aggression, 124–125
  to interpersonal distancing, 61–62
Evaluation apprehension, 9
  in dissonance study, 236
Experiments, 8–10
  field, 9–10
  field study, 10–11
  laboratory, 8
Experimental artifacts, 9
  expectancy effects in dissonance, 241
Experimental conditions:
  control, 8–10, 12
  standardization of, 119
External locus of control (Rotter), 63
Eye contact, 62
  in attraction, 32 ff.
  in interpersonal distancing, 62

Factor analysis:
  in Love Scale construction, 54
Factorial design, Berkowitz example, 131
Field experiment, 9–10
Field study, 10–11
Flashy merchandising, 4–5
  in aggression research, 156
  in attribution research, 229
  fun-and-games approach (Ring), 4
  in prosocial-behavior studies, 96
  in risky shift, 186

Freudian theory in prejudice, 263
Friendship (*see* Attraction)
Frustration-aggression hypothesis, 126

Gaze:
  and love, 38–40
  avoidance of, 62
Generality in attribution process, 193–195
Generalization problems:
  in attraction studies, 51 ff.
  Byrne et al. on, 42–43, 48–49
  cross-species:
    in aggression, 125–126
    in interpersonal spacing, 61–62
  in interpersonal-distancing studies, 85
  in prosocial-behavior studies, 120–121
  in risky-shift studies, 162–165
  with subjects in Love Scale, 53
Group-conflict theory:
  Sherif study on competition, 263
Group decision making (*see* Risky shift)

Hedonic relevance, attribution theory, 193
Helping behavior (*see* Prosocial behavior)

Infatuation, 22
Information processing, in attribution, 193–194
  Jones and Nisbett on, 215–216
Inhibition, of helping behavior, 94
Internal locus of control (Rotter), 63
Interpersonal attraction (*see* Attraction)
Interpersonal distancing, 57–85
  approval seeking, 64
  class variables, 65–66
  contact versus noncontact cultures, 60–61, 70
  cross-species comparisons, 61–62
  cultural influences, 60–61, 62
    Baxter on, 76 ff.
    class and race, 66, 67–68
    Hall's proxemics, 60–61
  explanations of:
    compensation, 62
    ethological view of, 61–62
    learned, 62–63
    possessiveness, 61–62, 66–67
    social-learning theory (Rotter), 62–63
    sociological approach (Goffman), 62
  group development (children), 66
  intimacy, 59, 62
  invasion, 59
    reaction of invader, 64–65
  liking and, 59
  locus of control (Rotter), 63

Interpersonal distancing (continued)
  markers, 59, 65
  operational definitions, 63–64
  proxemics (Hall), 60–61
  racial differences, 61
  research methods, 63–67
  setting, internal or external, 81
  sex differences, 59–60
    Little on, 70–72, 74, 76
  size of room, 64
  social schemata (Kuethe), 67, 85
    Little on, 69 ff.
  status, 59
  stigmatizing condition, 59
  subject awareness, 64–67
  territorial possessiveness, 66–67
Interpersonal Judgment Scale (Byrne), 27, 44–49
Intimate distance (Hall), 60
Instinct, in aggression (*see* Ethological approach)
Invasion, spatial, 59
  reaction of invader, 64–65

Labeling theory of attraction, 22
Laboratory experiment, 8
Likert scale, 271
Liking (*see* Attraction)
Locus of control (Rotter), 63
Love (*see* Attraction)
Love Scale (Rubin), 32, 34–37, 54–55

Manipulation of antecedent conditions, 12, 298
  in dissonance studies, 242–243
  in prosocial-behavior studies, 118
Markers, spatial, 59, 65
Marxist views of prejudice, 263
Measurement problems:
  in Baxter and Little studies, 84
  in prejudice research, 269–270
  in Storms and West et al. studies, 228
  in Weitz study, 293
Measures, unobtrusive, 13
Methods:
  comparison of, 12–13
  description of, 15
Multifactor Racial Attitude Inventory, 272

Naturalistic observation, 12
  attraction research, 30–31
  interpersonal-distance behavior, 65–66
  prejudice and racism, 272–274
Nonverbal communication, 32, 62

Observation, naturalistic (*see* Naturalistic observation)
Operational definitions:
  aggression, 63
  altruism, 63
  attraction, 54
  dissonance, 256–257
  interpersonal distancing, 63–65
  prosocial behavior, 63, 95

Participant observation, 242–243
Personal distance (Hall), 60
Personal forces (Heider), 192–193
Personalism, in attribution, 193
Personal space, Sommer, 58
  Goffman, 58, 62
Person perception, in attribution, 191
  accuracy of, 191
Phantom other (*see* Simulated-stranger condition)
Possessiveness, in interpersonal distancing, 61–62
Prejudice and racism, 262–296
  attribution processes in, 264
  belief congruence, 265–266
  conformity, 264–265
  definition of, 262
  discrimination:
    economic, 285–286
    in housing, 268–273, 285–292
    reverse, 275
  explanations of, 262–266
    personality and societal, 262–263
    socialization, 264
    social psychological, 264
  Freudian view of, 263
  projection, 263
  racism, institutional, 264
  research methods, 269–276
  segregation (Johnson et al.), 285–286
  stereotyping, 264, 273–274
Projection in prejudice, 263
Prosocial behavior, 87–121
  ambiguity of situation, 90–92
  bystander effect, 80, 120–121
  in children, 96–97
  cognitive processes in, 90–91
  dependency as determinant of, 95
  diffusion of responsibility, 90–92
    Darley and Latané study of, 100–106
  emergencies, 90–92
  familiarity with situation, 92–93
  group size:
    Piliavin on, 108, 113–116, 115–116
  implicit rules of, 93
  indifference/apathy, 104–105

Prosocial behavior (continued)
  modeling, 98
  mood, 93–94
  norms, 89–90
    contradictions among, 89–90
    reciprocity, 89, 97
    social responsibility, 89
  operational definitions, 95
  presence of others, 94
  race, 96
    Piliavin on, 108, 111–112, 115–116
  research methods, 94–97
  sex differences, 118
    in intervention, 91
    and race, 96
  situation specificity, 95
  thefts, 95–96
  time interval, modeling, 118
  victim characteristics, 91–92, 95–98
    Piliavin on, 108, 111–113, 115–116
Proxemics (Hall), 60–61
Proximity:
  attraction, determinant of, 23
  attraction, measure of, 47–48
  aversiveness to, 64–65
  territorial claims by, 64–65

Race and class:
  possible confound of, 274–275
  Weitz on, 281–282
Race riots, 132–133
Racism (see Prejudice and racism)
Racist, aversive versus dominative (Kovel), 269
Randomization:
  of experimental procedure, 119
  of subjects, 8, 10
Reactivity:
  questionnaires, 29
  self-report measures, 54
Reciprocity, norm of (Gouldner), 89
Referencing, in reports, 6–7
Reinforcement theories of attraction, 21–22
Replication in research, 5
Research methods, in social psychology, 8–11
Responsibility:
  attribution of (see Attribution)
  diffusion of (see Prosocial behavior)
Risky shift, 157–187
  Choice-Dilemmas Questionnaire, 159–160
  conservative shift items, 185
  design problems, 184
  durability and stability, 164–165
    of instrument, 183–184, 187
  explanations, 160–162

Risky shift (continued)
  gambling methods, 163
  interpretive problems, 184–185
  measurement problems, 183–184
  replications, 160
  research methods, 162–165
  skewed distribution, 185–186
  subject awareness problem, 164
  typical experiment, 159–160
Rules, implicit, in helping behavior, 93

Scales:
  construction, 54–55
  equal-interval type, 271–272
  interpersonal-distance behavior, 66–67
  Interpersonal Judgment Scale (Byrne), 27, 44–49
  Likert scale, 271
  Love Scale (Rubin), 35
  Multifactor Racial Attitude Inventory, 272
  summated rating scale, 271
  Thurstone scale, 271–272
  validity, 36–37, 54–55
Scapegoating, 263
Segregation, Johnson et al. on, 285–286
Self-disclosure, in attraction, 29
Self-observation in therapy:
  Storms on, 212–214
Severity of initiation, 245 (see also Cognitive dissonance)
  Aronson and Mills study on, 245–249
Sex differences:
  in aggression research, 155
  in interpersonal distancing, 59–60
    Baxter on, 76 ff.
  in Love Scale, 36–37
  and social schemata:
    Little on, 70, 71–72, 74
Significance, statistical, 258
Similarity of attitudes (see Attraction)
Simulated-stranger condition, 52
  in laboratory experiments, 28
  Byrne et al. on, 44
Simulations, 294–295
Social-class conflict and prejudice, 263
Social-desirability problem, 53
  in the attraction studies, 53
Social distance (Hall), 60
Socialization in prejudice, 264
Social-learning explanation:
  of aggression, 127
  of interpersonal distancing (Rotter), 62–63
Social norms, violation of, 132–133

Social protest as violence, 133–134
Social-responsibility norm, 89
Social schemata (Kuethe), 67
　Little on, 69 ff.
　reflecting spacing behavior, 85
Spacing behavior (*see* Interpersonal
　　distancing)
Stereotyping, in racism, 264, 273–274
Stigmatizing condition, 59
Subjects:
　awareness, 12, 64–67, 298
　cultural differences, 83–85
　random selection and assignment, 8
　representativeness of students, 51–53
　suspiciousness, 153–154
Success and failure, attribution of, 195–196
Summated rating scale, 271
Surveys and interviews:
　in attraction research, 27, 31
　in attribution research, 200–201
　in dissonance research, 243
　in interpersonal distancing research, 66–67
　in prejudice-racism research, 270–272
　in prosocial behavior research, 97
Suspicion (*see* Subjects)

Television violence:
　and aggression, 132, 134–136
Territoriality, 58
　and aggressiveness, 61
　egocentric (Goffman), 62
　fixed (Goffman), 62
　and interpersonal distancing, 61–62
　possessiveness in, 66–67
　situational (Goffman), 62
　time-territoriality relation, 66–67

Territorial claims:
　by markers, 59, 65
　by presence alone, 64–65
Therapy:
　attribution principles, Storms on, 212–214
Thurstone scale, 271–273
Time-series design, 14

Unobtrusive measures, 13

Validity:
　convergent, 5, 293
　external, 10
　internal, 10
　of scales (*see* Scales)
Variables:
　confounded:
　　in aggression studies, 154
　　in attribution studies, 226–228
　　in interpersonal distance studies, 85
　　in prejudice studies, 293–295
　control of conditions, 8–10, 12
　　in prosocial behavior studies, 118–119
　dependent and independent, 8
Victim:
　blaming of, 264
　characteristics of, 91–92, 95–98
Videotape and therapy:
　Storms on, 212–214
Violence:
　social protest as, 133–134
　television and aggression, 132

Weapons effect (*see* Aggression)
　reversal of effect, 154–156
Wrong-number technique, 274